National Parliaments and the European Union

The Constitutional Challenge for the Oireachtas and Other Member State Legislatures

National Parliaments and the European Union

The Constitutional Challenge for the Oireachtas and Other Member State Legislatures

Edited by
Dr. Gavin Barrett

CLARUS PRESS

Published in association with the Institute of European Affairs

Published by
Clarus Press Ltd,
Griffith Campus,
South Circular Road,
Dublin 8.

Typeset by
Datapage International Limited,
18 Docklands Innovation Park,
East Wall Road,
Dublin 3.

Printed by
MPG Books Ltd
Victoria Square, Bodmin, Cornwall.

ISBN
10 Digit No.
1-905536-02-X

13 Digit No.
978-1-905536-02-3

Preface

1. What This Book Is About

In each member state of the European Union, the national parliament is regarded as holding a key role in the lawmaking process. Indeed, this state of affairs is invariably regarded as one of the hallmarks of a democratic state.[1] Increasingly, however, national parliaments in Europe as elsewhere have found themselves confronted in the exercise of this role with a wide range of challenges – ranging from the general dominance of the executive branch of government to the (associated) grip in which parliaments are held by political parties, to the high degree of technical expertise required to understand properly much of modern legislation, to the (related) well-nigh unmatchable influence exerted by expert professional civil services on the conduct of government to the rise of alternative systems of accountability for the executive branch of government, to the phenomenon of globalisation, and to challenges which are cross-border both in their nature and in the solutions which they demand.

One such challenge for national parliaments – the one which gives this book its name – has been the need to find and secure an appropriate role for national legislatures in the radically-altered power structure which pertains in those policy fields in which law-making has been shifted to European Union level. With the perspective offered by virtue of the half-century which has passed since the signature of the Treaty of Rome in 1957, membership of what is now the European Union can be seen to have involved – as indeed it was intended to from the beginning by its founders[2] – a continuous process of transfer to European level by member states of legislative and decision-

[1] Of which there have been a vastly increasing number in recent years. According to one recent account, three-quarters of the way into the twentieth century, there were still only thirty democracies in the world. By 2005, however, no less than 119 of the world's 190 countries were democracies. (See more generally M. Mandelbaum, "Democracy Without America – The Spontaneous Spread of Freedom", (2007) 86 International Affairs No. 5, 119 at 120).

[2] One need look little further for evidence of this than the text of the Schuman Declaration of 9 May 1950, available online at the time of writing at http://www.robert-schuman.eu/declaration_9mai.php

making powers in a broad range of policy fields.[3] The transfer of law-making power has, however, in turn generated a number of conundrums, both for the member states and for the European Union itself. And one such challenge (and at the same time, opportunity) – as noted above, the key one for the purposes of this book – has been that of defining and establishing the relevance of the national parliaments of the member states in the new power structure which pertains in a wide variety of policy areas. This particular Gordian knot (or perhaps task of Sisyphus) is one which should arguably be of concern not merely national parliaments themselves, but member states generally, the European Union and, for that matter, anyone with an interest in democracy.

In practice, it has been a challenge which has occasioned ongoing deliberation for many years at both national and European level. *Within* member state systems, much, if not most thought has had to be given to the question of how to avoid excessive dominance of the legislative branch of national government by the executive branch – indeed how to maintain any kind of substantive role for the legislature – in those fields in which laws are enacted at European level. The backdrop to concerns here is of course provided by the phenomenon of members of national executives – *i.e.*, government ministers from twenty-seven Member States – meeting regularly to agree to European-wide legislation on any one of what is now a very broad range of issues.[4] Although the idea of each national parliament exercising control over its national executive (and more particularly over the national minister who forms the representative of the relevant state in the Council of the European Union) in relation to any given policy issue has tended to be uncontroversial in nature, great difficulty has attended attempts to give effect to it in almost every member state. Indeed, much of this book is taken up with both examination of (and reflection upon) how the attempts made to date to make national executives answerable in relation to their European-level legislative activities can and do work in practice, both in general and within selected member states (including Ireland).

---

[3] Even if that process of transfer has proved in practice to be a somewhat more intermittent one than originally intended.

[4] It is sometimes therefore thought that where legislative competence in a policy field is transferred to the European level, there is a automatic shift in power at domestic level from the legislative branch of government to the executive. There will invariably be an escape from *formal* control by the domestic legislature to some extent. Whether this represents a shift in real power is another matter, however, since in some cases (and certainly in the case of, for example, the Irish legislature) the existence of formal powers of control over the executive by the legislature in the enactment of domestic legislation tends to mask the reality of almost complete *de facto* domination of the legislature by the executive – a domination exercised *via* the mechanism of party political control.

At European level, reflection, discussion and – to a now-greater degree than before – treaty changes have had their focus on efforts to define the appropriate level (if any) of institutionalisation of the involvement of national parliaments in European-level lawmaking. Various aspects of the developments which have taken place over the years (particularly in the last two decades) are referred to in some detail in a number of chapters in this book including those by Andreas Maurer,[5] Adam Cygan,[6] Kerse,[7] David Siritzky,[8] Morten Knudsen and Yves Carl.[9] The most significant very recent developments in this regard now include the Protocol on the Role of National Parliaments in the European Union and the Protocol on the Application of the Principles of Subsidiarity and Proportionality – two measures which were originally annexed to the Constitutional Treaty [10] but which under the Lisbon Treaty are now to be annexed to the Treaty on European Union and the Treaty on the Functioning of the European Union[11] (the new title for what up to now has been the Treaty Establishing the European Community[12]).

2. How This Book Is Organised

This book is divided into three parts. Part I contains some general reflections on national parliaments and the European Union today, focusing mainly, but far from exclusively, on their success or lack of it in exercising control over national governments. The particular experience of Ireland and the Oireachtas is then looked at in Part II, with emphasis being placed on areas of increasing salience, such as security and defence policy, asylum and immigration and justice and home affairs generally. Finally, in Part III, the experience of a selection of other Member State parliaments in confronting the same challenge – namely, those of the United Kingdom, France, the Nordic States, the Netherlands and Slovenia – is examined.[13] The parliaments chosen, while

[5] See in particular pp. 49–52 and 72–100.

[6] See in particular pp. 128–137.

[7] See in particular pp. 349–351, and 367–375.

[8] See in particular pp. 445–449.

[9] See in particular pp. 457–475.

[10] See in particular regarding these Protocols the chapters contributed to this book by Andreas Maurer at pp. 85–100 thereof, Christopher Kerse at p. 351 and pp. 367–375 thereof; David Siritzky at pp. 446–449 thereof and Morten Knudsen and Yves Carl at pp. 474–483 thereof.

[11] See in this regard the texts of the two Protocols themselves. The Protocol on the Role of National Parliaments in the European Union is additionally to be annexed to the Treaty establishing the European Atomic Energy Community.

[12] See Article 2(2) of the Lisbon Treaty.

[13] The experience of some states is also examined briefly in chapters located other than in Part III of this book. Thus Andreas Maurer's chapter has observations to make on the functioning of scrutiny in Germany. (See in particular pp. 90–91 and 100–102). Adam Cygan also offers some reflections on the record of the United Kingdom's House of Commons. (See in particular pp. 137 to 141).

necessarily limited in number in a book of this size and focus, nonetheless provide the opportunity to compare the approach which has been taken within the European Union in the large state, the medium-sized and the small state, the state in which legislative scrutiny of European-level national executive action is perceived to have been relatively successful and that in which it has not, the state which is a relative newcomer to the European Union and the state which has been involved since the original Treaties of Rome were signed.

The contents of this book – which derives it origins from a conference held in 2005 – may be taken to be up-to-date to approximately Spring 2006, although some references to events after that period have been possible. Given the gestation period of the book, references in individual chapters are made to the Constitutional Treaty, rather than the Lisbon Treaty, the text of which was agreed with unprecedented dispatch by all of the now-27 member states at Lisbon on 18 October 2007 – a few days before the writing of this preface. The ongoing relevance of the reflections offered in this book has been unaffected, however, since notwithstanding some presentational alterations,[14] no substantive changes of any kind have been made by the Lisbon Treaty to any of the text of the Constitutional Treaty itself relating to national parliaments and only one substantive revision[15] and one substantive addition[16] have been made to the two Protocols which were originally annexed to the Constitutional Treaty relating to the role of national parliaments. The timing of the agreement on the Lisbon Treaty has enabled – if only just – a detailed analysis of its impact to be added to this book in the form of an introduction.

A number of acknowledgments are in order – apart from that of the obvious debt owed to all of the authors of this work. The support of the Research Director of the Institute of European Affairs, Jill Donoghue, for this project was key. I would also like to thank Jim O'Brien, the former Head of the

---

[14] The main such change being the introduction of a new general article to reflect the role of national parliaments in the form of a new Article 12 of the Treaty on European Union (to be inserted by Article 1(12) of the Lisbon Treaty). The new Article 12 adds nothing in terms of substantive content to the rights which were provided for national parliaments under the Constitutional Treaty.

[15] *Viz.*, both (a) the "six-week" period required under Article 4 of the Protocol on the Role of National Parliaments in the European Union to elapse between the time a draft legislative act is made available to national parliaments and the date when it is placed on a provisional agenda for the Council and (correspondingly) (b) the period of "six weeks" which Article 6 of the Protocol on the Application of the Principles of Subsidiarity and Proportionality specifies is to be given to national parliaments and chambers to send a reasoned opinion on subsidiarity are to be altered to periods of "eight weeks".

[16] *Viz.*, the addition of Article 7(3) of the Protocol on the Application of the Principles of Subsidiarity and Proportionality.

European Parliament Office in Dublin, Professor Brigid Laffan and David McCartney, Managing Director of Clarus Press. Others who played significant roles at various points in this project have included Professor Paul O'Connor (until very recently Dean of the School of Law of University College), Dr. Garret FitzGerald, Senator Maurice Hayes, Dick Roche TD, Ruairí Quinn TD, Dr. John Temple Lang, Geraldine Byrne Nason, Alan Dukes, Dr. Neil Maddox, the staff of the Institute of European Affairs (most particularly Patrick King and Margaret Ahearne), Della, Michael, Conor and Dr. Max Barrett, Colonel André and Hélène Roussel-Coumont and Dr. Wolfgang Heusel, Director of the Academy of European Law, Trier, as well as Sabine Weinand and Julia Teusch of that institution's library.

The financial support needed to initiate the project which has culminated in this publication came from a grant from the Irish Research Council for the Humanities and Social Sciences. Without the further support of the Communicating Europe Initiative of the Department of Foreign Affairs, and the Seed Funding Scheme of University College Dublin this book would not have come abou. Its conclusion was facilitated by the grant to the writer of a University College Dublin President's Research Fellowship and the welcome provided by the Université Robert Schuman, Strasbourg for which I thank Florence Benoit-Rohmer (President of the university), Professor Patrick Foulon and Céline Montibeller of the Collège Doctoral Européen, and Professor Eric Maulin, Director of the Institut des Hautes Études Européennes. Last but not least, thanks for emotional support are due to my three children, Marie-Hélène, Stéphane and Sébastien and to my wife Madeleine, who made sterling but unsuccessful efforts to keep their irresistibly hilarious invasions of my study in moderate check during the organising, writing and editing process.

This book is dedicated to my son Stéphane. It is published in association with the Institute of European Affairs, but does not in any way purport to represent the views of that body or indeed to present views of any person or institution other than the personal opinions of each of the authors who have been gracious enough to provide their thoughts for inclusion in it.

Gavin Barrett, 25 October 2007
Institut des Hautes Études Européennes,
Université Robert Schuman,
Strasbourg.

Contents

List of Contributors

Gavin Barrett is a senior lecturer and a President's Research Fellow at the School of Law, University College Dublin and a visiting scholar at the Institut des Hautes Études Européennes, Strasbourg.

Leonard F.M. Besselink is Jean Monnet Professor in European Constitutional Law and Professor of Constitutional Law at the Instituut voor Staats- en bestuursrecht, University of Utrecht.

Tony Brown represents the Labour Party on the Steering Committee of the National Forum on Europe, and was a founder member of the Institute of European Affairs.

Yves Carl is the permanent representative of the Luxembourg Chamber of Deputies to the European institutions and a former member of the COSAC Secretariat.

Cathryn Costello is a senior research fellow in European Community and Public Law, Worcester College, Oxford University.

Adam Cygan is a senior lecturer in law at the Centre for European Law and Integration, Faculty of Law, University of Leicester.

Danica Fink-Hafner is Professor of Political Science and Head of the Centre for Political Science Research at the Faculty of Social Sciences, University of Ljubljana.

Ronald Holzhacker is Assistant Professor of Political Science at the University of Twente, the Netherlands.

Christopher Kerse is Second Counsel to the Chairman of Committees, House of Lords and Visiting Professor at King's College London.

Morten Knudsen is the principal advisor on European Union affairs in the Danish Parliament and a former member of the COSAC Secretariat.

Andreas Maurer is Head of Unit I – EU Integration, at the Stiftung Wissenschaft und Politik, German Institute for International and Security Affairs, Berlin and a lecturer in the postgraduate programme in European Studies at the Humboldt and Free University, Berlin.

Michael McDowell has held the offices of Attorney General of Ireland, Minister for Justice, Equality and Law Reform and Tánaiste (Deputy Prime Minister) of Ireland and is a leading Senior Counsel.

Katherine Meenan is a consultant on EU affairs, a vice-chairperson of the Institute of European Affairs and was consultant to the most recent Joint Oireachtas Committee on European Affairs.

Lia O'Hegarty is a consultant on legislation and public affairs, a member of the Irish Human Rights Commission and the former Parliamentary Legal Adviser to the Houses of the Oireachtas.

Tapio Raunio is Professor of Political Science at the Department of Political Science, University of Turku.

David Siritzky is an administrator in the French *Assemblée Nationale*, where he works for the European Delegation. He lectures in European Law at the Institute of Political Studies, Paris and in Constitutional Law at the University of Panthéon-Assas (Paris II).

John Temple Lang practises law with the international firm Cleary Gottlieb Steen and Hamilton, Brussels and London LLP. He is a Professor at Trinity College, Dublin and a Senior Visiting Research Fellow at the University of Oxford.

Ben Tonra is Jean Monnet Professor of EU Foreign, Security and Defence Policy at the Geary Institute, University College Dublin.

Matti Wiberg is Professor of Political Science at the Department of Political Science, University of Turku.

Introduction

A New Improved Formula? The Treaty of Lisbon and National Parliaments

Gavin Barrett[*]

1. Background And Context

What member states would probably now agree was an unwisely-named Treaty Establishing a Constitution for Europe was formally signed by the representatives of the member states of the European Union in Rome on 29 October 2004. During the subsequent required process of ratification by all member states,[1] a majority of French and then Dutch voters opted to reject the possibility of ratification in their countries, in referendums held on 29 May 2005 and 1 June 2005 respectively. The wounds inflicted on the Constitutional Treaty on these dates were eventually to be deemed mortal in nature, notwithstanding the ultimate ratification of this Treaty in eighteen of the other member states of the European Union.[2] The terminal nature of the blows inflicted, however took a lengthy period to be unanimously accepted by the member states – not least because such acceptance presented the member states with the need either to admit the collective failure of their plans for the future of the European Union or to present – unanimously –some alternative course of action which would deliver a functioning and acceptable constitutional structure at European level. For a time, therefore, the 2005 referendums plunged Europe into an interregnum of uncertainty as to the constitutional future of the Union. This period has only now – over two years later – reached what is likely to be its end-phase, with the agreement of the 27 member states at Lisbon on the final text of the Reform Treaty,

---

[*] Senior Lecturer and President's Research Fellow, School of Law, University College Dublin, Visiting Scholar, Institut des Hautes Études Européennes, Université Robert Schuman, Strasbourg. What follows is a revised and expanded version of material which is to be published in the February 2008 edition of the European Law Review.

[1] See Article IV-447 of the Constitutional Treaty.

[2] Unlike the Treaty of Maastricht, therefore, the ratification process of which required two referendums in Denmark before that country's electorate gave its approval, and the Treaty of Nice, the ratification process of which similarly required two referendums in Ireland, the Constitutional Treaty was never resubmitted to any recalcitrant national electorate for reconsideration.

now to be known as the Treaty of Lisbon. (An element of uncertainty lingers. After its formal signature in December, the Lisbon Treaty will proceed to ratification in the member states, with the aim being to complete the ratification process before the European Parliament elections in June 2009.[3] Ireland, apparently alone of the 27 member states, will hold a referendum as part of its ratification process.[4])

Although the two year interlude which has passed since the French and Dutch referendums may not seem a particularly short period of time, the reality is that the Lisbon Treaty has had an extraordinarily brief gestation period. It is interesting to compare the process which led to the agreement of the Constitutional Treaty: the initial public announcement leading to the elucidation and negotiation of this text was constituted by the Laeken Declaration on 15 December 2001. The agreement of the final text under the Irish Presidency occurred on 18 June 2004 – over two and a half years later. In contrast, the analogous public announcement leading to the Lisbon Treaty took place on 22 June 2007 at the Brussels European Council and substantive agreement on the final text (comparable in its scope to the Constitutional Treaty) was reached at Lisbon on 18 October 2007[5] – in other words, not even four months later. The extraordinary comparative rapidity with which the text of the Lisbon Treaty emerged is of course explained by the new Treaty's being largely a repackaging of measures already agreed in the Constitutional Treaty, and that the vast bulk of its contents required neither renegotiation nor even substantial reformulation from the form the equivalent provisions had taken in the earlier Treaty.[6] Already in June, Ireland's Minister of State for European Affairs was predicting that "perhaps more than 90%" of the original Constitutional Treaty text would survive in the Lisbon Treaty.[7] And indeed, the

---

[3] See statement to this effect on the website of the Council of Ministers (available at the time of writing at http://www.consilium.europa.eu/cms3_fo/showPage.asp?id=1297&lang=en).

[4] Probably in May or June 2008. See J. Smyth, *"Summer date most likely for Ireland's referendum"* Irish Times, 20 October, 2007.

[5] The speed of the replacement of the Constitutional Treaty may be illustrated by the fact that on its own terms, the Constitutional Treaty was scheduled to enter into force on 1 November, 2006. (See Article IV-447(2) thereof). Thirteen days before this date was even reached (and after having engaged in a 'period of reflection' of over two years during which no overt action was taken) the member states had *already* agreed the contents of the Lisbon Treaty which would succeed it.

[6] Other than that necessitated by the fact of the Lisbon Treaty being cast as a document which amends the existing Treaties whereas the Constitutional Treaty was framed as a stand-alone text.

[7] Quoted from address by Minister of State for European Affairs Dick Roche TD to seventy-ninth plenary session of the National Forum On Europe, St Patrick's Hall, Dublin Castle, 5 July 2007 (available at time of writing at http://www.forumoneurope.ie/index.asp?locID=204&docID=12587cd220f6). See further in this regard, M. Hennessy, *"Substance of EU constitution still intact, says Ahern"* 25 June 2007, G. FitzGerald, *"Treaty changes are only presentational"*, Irish Times, 30 June 2007

approach underlying the Lisbon Treaty has clearly been that of producing a document which preserves in substance the overwhelming bulk of the Constitutional Treaty's content but which is stripped of the Constitution-like trappings which the earlier document possessed. Put in other words, the Lisbon Treaty consists of the substance of the Constitutional Treaty without its style. That the design of the Lisbon Treaty reflects this approach was also explicitly acknowledged in the Presidency Conclusions of the June 2007 Brussels European Council in which it was stated that

> "the constitutional concept, which consisted in repealing all existing Treaties and replacing them by a single text called 'Constitution' *(sic)*, is abandoned. The Reform Treaty will introduce into the existing Treaties, which remain in force, the innovations resulting from the 2004 IGC... "[8]

Equally clear is the unstated hope underlying the member states' agreement on the Lisbon Treaty that even if (or perhaps because) the form of the Lisbon Treaty is less simple, less structured, less elegant and indeed less inspiring a text than the Constitutional Treaty,[9] it will also prove itself less politically indigestible than the earlier Treaty did – particularly in member states where its ratification process can be expected to be a difficult one.

Insofar as concerns national parliaments in particular, the text of the Constitutional Treaty itself made a series of provisions. Every single one of these provisions have survived into the Lisbon Treaty in more or less identical form to that which they took in the Constitutional Treaty. Nine provisions are at issue here.

1) Article I-11 of the Constitutional Treaty provided that "national parliaments shall ensure compliance with" the principle of subsidiarity in accordance with the procedure set out in the Protocol on the application of

---

[8] See Annex I ("Draft IGC Mandate") to the Presidency Conclusions of the Brussels European Council 21–22 June 2007 (11177/07 CONCL 2, Brussels, 23 June 2007). (The '2004 IGC' mentioned in the text refers to the intergovernmental conference which agreed the Constitutional Treaty.) Similarly, parag. 3 of the same Annex affirmed that the Treaties as amended by the Reform Treaty would not have a constitutional character while at the same time parag. 4 signalled that the innovations resulting from the 2004 IGC would be integrated into the amended Treaties.

[9] Hence the reported observation by the Luxembourg prime minister, Jean-Claude Juncker regarding the draft Lisbon Treaty that "the Constitutional Treaty was an easily-understandable treaty. This is a simplified treaty which is very complicated." Irish Times editorial, 25 June, 2007. Similar sentiments underlay the Financial Times editorial published the same day *"Clumsy EU deal is better than none"* Financial Times, 25 June 2007.

the principles of subsidiarity and proportionality. (According to this principle, in areas which do not fall within its exclusive competence, the Union shall act only if and insofar as the objectives of the proposed action cannot be sufficiently achieved by the member states but can rather, by reason of the scale or effects of the proposed action, be better achieved at Union level.)[10]

This provision of the Constitutional Treaty is repeated practically verbatim by the new form of Article 5 of the Treaty on European Union which is to be substituted into the latter Treaty by Article 1(6) of the Lisbon Treaty.

2) Article III-259 of the Constitutional Treaty provided that national parliaments were to ensure that proposals and legislative initiatives submitted under the sections of that Treaty dealing with judicial cooperation in criminal matters and police cooperation complied with the principle of subsidiarity "in accordance with the arrangements laid down by the Protocol on the application of the principles of subsidiarity and proportionality."

This provision is repeated – effectively verbatim – in a new Article 69 of the Treaty on the Functioning of the European Union[11] to be inserted in the latter Treaty by Article 2 (64) of the Lisbon Treaty.

3) Article IV-444(3) of the Constitutional Treaty provided for a right of veto on the part of any national parliament of any initiative taken by the European Council to authorise the so-called 'simplified revision procedure' (by which was meant the European Council's authorising, in a given area or case, either that the Council act by qualified majority instead of by unanimity or that the Council act in accordance with the ordinary legislative procedure rather than in accordance with a special legislative procedure). Under Article IV-444(3), if a national parliament made known its opposition within six months of the date of its (required) notification of such an initiative, the decision could not be adopted by the European Council.

This provision is repeated – again, effectively verbatim – in a new Article 48(7) of the Treaty on European Union to be inserted in the latter Treaty by Article 2 (289) of the Treaty of Lisbon.

---

[10] Article I-11(3) of the Constitutional Treaty.

[11] Which is to be the new name for the Treaty establishing the European Community under Article 2(1) of the Treaty of Lisbon.

4) Article I-18(2) of the Constitutional Treaty imposed an obligation on the European Commission to draw national parliaments' attention to proposals to deploy the so-called 'flexibility clause' (*i.e.*, the Treaty article used for the adoption of measures where action by the Union proves necessary but insufficient Treaty powers exist to empower the Union to do so[12]).

This provision is repeated – once more, to all intents and purposes, verbatim – in a new Article 352(2) of the Treaty on the Functioning of the European Union to be inserted in the latter Treaty by Article 2(289) of the Treaty of Lisbon.

5) Article IV-444(3) of the Constitutional Treaty required that national parliaments be notified of any initiative taken by the European Council to authorise the so-called 'simplified revision procedure' (by which was meant the European Council's authorising, in a given area or case, either that the Council act by qualified majority instead of by unanimity or that the Council act in accordance with the ordinary legislative procedure rather than in accordance with a special legislative procedure).

Article IV-444(3) is repeated – again, effectively verbatim – in a new Article 48(7) of the Treaty on European Union to be inserted in the latter Treaty by Article 1(56) of the Treaty of Lisbon.[13]

6) Article IV-443 of the Constitutional Treaty, which related to the so-called ordinary amendment procedure (requiring *inter alia* a Convention and an inter-governmental conference) required that proposals for the amendment of the Constitutional Treaty be notified to national parliaments.[14]

The relevant sentence of Article IV-443 is repeated verbatim in a new Article 48(2) of the Treaty on European Union to be inserted in the latter Treaty by Article 1(56) of the Treaty of Lisbon.[15]

---

[12] The relevant article was Article I-18 under the Constitutional Treaty, and is to be Article 352 of the Treaty on the Functioning of the European Union.

[13] As already noted at point (3) above. Obviously, enjoyment of an Article IV-444(3)/ Article 48(7) right of notification by national parliaments is a condition precedent to the exercise of the veto power for national parliaments described at (3) above.

[14] Any such proposals (which could be by the government of a member state, the European Parliament or the Commission) were required by Article IV-443(1) to be submitted to the Council which was then required to submit them to the European Council.

[15] Note that other aspects of the new article differ from its defunct predecessor in the Constitutional Treaty, however, although not in a manner relevant in the present context.

7) Article I-58 of the Constitutional Treaty required national parliaments to be notified of the application of any European State which wished to become a member of the Union.[16]

The relevant sentence of Article I-58 is repeated word for word in amendments effected to Article 49 of the Treaty on European Union to be inserted in the latter Treaty by Article 1(57) of the Treaty of Lisbon.[17]

8) Article III-260 of the Constitutional Treaty provided that national parliaments should be informed of the content and result of the evaluations of the implementation by member state authorities of Union policies in the area of freedom, security and justice which were provided for in that Article.

The relevant sentence of Article III-260 is repeated verbatim in a new Article 70 of the Treaty on the Functioning of the European Union to be inserted in the latter Treaty by Article 2(64) of the Treaty of Lisbon.[18]

9) Article III-261 of the Constitutional Treaty provided that national parliaments should be kept informed of the proceedings of a standing committee which it provided should be set up within the Council in order to ensure that operational cooperation on internal security was promoted and strengthened within the Union.

This provision is repeated – effectively word for word – in a new Article 71 of the Treaty on the Functioning of the European Union to be inserted in the latter Treaty by Article 2 (64) of the Treaty of Lisbon.

It will be seen from the foregoing therefore that insofar as the existing provisions contained in the text of the Constitutional Treaty are concerned, nothing of any significance has changed: all of these provisions are carried over into the text of the Treaty on European Union or of the Treaty on the Functioning of the European Union by the Lisbon Treaty either word for word or with changes of a merely technical nature.

Looking merely at what has been *retained* from the Constitutional Treaty does not give the full picture. Also to be considered is what has been *added*

[16] Such applications were required by Article I-58(2) to be addressed in the first place to the Council.
[17] Note that other aspects of the new article differ from its defunct predecessor in the Constitutional Treaty, however, although not in a manner relevant in the present context.
[18] Note that some aspects of the new article differ from its defunct predecessor in the Constitutional Treaty, however, although not in a manner relevant in the present context.

by the Lisbon Treaty. The Presidency Conclusions of the Brussels European Council of June 2007 stated the general objective of the new Treaty that "concerning national parliaments, their role will be further enhanced compared to the provisions agreed in the 2004 IGC".[19] However, only one addition to the text salvaged from the Constitutional Treaty itself was signalled in this connection: "a new general article" to "reflect the role of national parliaments".[20] This new general article was subsequently adopted in the form of a new Article 12 of the Treaty on European Union (to be inserted by Article 1(12) of the Lisbon Treaty). It provides as follows

> "National Parliaments contribute actively to the good functioning of the Union:
> (a) through being informed by the institutions of the Union and having draft legislative acts of the Union forwarded to them in accordance with the Protocol on the role of national Parliaments in the European Union;
> (b) by seeing to it that the principle of subsidiarity is respected in accordance with the procedures provided for in the Protocol on the application of the principles of subsidiarity and proportionality;
> (c) by taking part, within the framework of the area of freedom, security and justice, in the evaluation mechanisms for the implementation of the Union policies in that area, in accordance with Article 70 of the Treaty on the Functioning of the European Union, and through being involved in the political monitoring of Europol and the evaluation of Eurojust's activities in accordance with Articles 88 and 85 of that Treaty;
> (d) by taking part in the revision procedures of the Treaties, in accordance with Article 48 of this Treaty;
> (e) by being notified of applications for accession to the Union, in accordance with Article 49 of this Treaty;
> (f) by taking part in the inter-parliamentary cooperation between national Parliaments and with the European Parliament, in accordance with the Protocol on the role of national Parliaments in the European Union."

This new provision had no counterpart in the Constitutional Treaty. However, it adds precisely nothing in terms of substantive content to the rights which were provided for national parliaments under the Constitutional Treaty. Nor does it in any way enhance or improve upon the rights for national parliaments which are otherwise provided for under in the Lisbon Treaty (either under other Treaty provisions – which have already been looked

[19] See para. 11 of Annex I ("Draft IGC Mandate") to the Presidency Conclusions of the Brussels European Council 21–22 June 2007, at p. 17 thereof, cited at n. 8 above.
[20] *Ibid.*.

at in the text above – or under the provisions of protocols – which are looked at in the text below).[21] Article 12 merely serves the function of highlighting the role which national parliaments play at European level, and thus, like so many other provisions of the Lisbon Treaty, *prima facie* involves no more than a change in presentational style from the approach of the Constitutional Treaty.

Were the foregoing all that the Lisbon Treaty involved, then notwithstanding the rhetoric of the June 2007 Brussels European Council Presidency Conclusions, the rights the Lisbon Treaty provides for national parliaments would represent no visible improvement at all on those provided for in the Constitutional Treaty. However, the intention expressed at the June 2007 Brussels Council to enhance further the role of national parliaments compared to the provisions agreed in the 2004 IGC involved further two substantive changes which must be mentioned here. Both such improvements however involved the text of Protocols to the Constitutional Treaty rather than the text of the Constitutional Treaty itself.

This should be explained. Annexed to the Constitutional Treaty were thirty-six protocols, the legal force of which was to be no less than that of Treaty articles.[22] The first two of these annexed protocols – the Protocol on the Role of National Parliaments in the European Union, and the Protocol on the Application of the Principles of Subsidiarity and Proportionality are of relevance to the topic of this book. Although aspects of both of these Protocols are discussed at varying length in various chapters which follow,[23] for the purposes of clarity it is proposed to take the time to summarise their contents briefly here and to examine the impact of the Lisbon Treaty.

2. The Protocol on the Role of National Parliaments in the European Union

The Protocol on the Role of National Parliaments in the European Union annexed to the Constitutional Treaty, was composed of ten articles under two

---

[21] Perhaps it is only fair to enter the caveat here that one can never know in advance the significance which will be accorded to a provision of one of the constitutive Treaties by the European Court of Justice – as the case-law of the Court of Justice on the citizenship provisions of the Treaty establishing the European Community amply demonstrates. See the account of this case-law in A. Arnull, A. Dashwood, M. Dougan, M. Ross, E. Spaventa and D. Wyatt, *Wyatt and Dashwood's European Union Law* (fifth edition, Thomson Sweet and Maxwell, London, 2006) at 664 to 671.

[22] Indeed, according to the Constitutional Treaty itself, the Protocols were to be regarded as forming an integral part of that Treaty (See Article IV-442 of the Constitutional Treaty).

[23] See further A. Maurer, *infra*, at 85 to 100; C. Kerse, *infra*, at 351 and 367 to 375; D. Siritzky, *infra*, at 446 to 449; and M. Knudsen and Y. Carl, *infra*, at 474 to 483.

Titles.[24] The first Title was styled "Information for National Parliaments". In it, provision was made for Commission consultation documents[25] and (broadly-defined) legislative acts[26] to be forwarded directly to national parliaments. Provision was also made for national parliaments to send a reasoned opinion on whether a draft European legislative act complied with the principle of subsidiarity (in accordance with the procedure laid down in the second Protocol examined here – the Protocol on the Application of the Principles of Subsidiarity and Proportionality).[27] It was further provided that a six-week period should elapse between a draft legislative act being made available to national parliaments in the official languages of the Union and the date when it is placed on a provisional agenda for the Council,[28] with the normal rule being that no agreement could be reached on a draft legislative act during those six weeks.[29] Further, a ten-day period was required to elapse between the placing of a draft legislative act on the provisional agenda for the Council and the adoption of a position.[30] Beyond this, the first Title of the Protocol provided for the agendas and outcomes of Council meetings being forwarded to national parliaments,[31] the forwarding of Court of Auditors reports to national parliaments, and, for national parliaments being informed of any European Council initiative to authorise the so-called 'simplified revision procedure' at least six months in advance of the European Council adopting any decision.[32]

The second Title of the Protocol on the Role of National Parliaments in the European Union, entitled "Interparliamentary Cooperation", made provision

---

[24] Title I contained the first eight, and Title II the remaining two.

[25] Article 1 of the Protocol on the Role of National Parliaments in the European Union.

[26] Article 2 of the Protocol on the Role of National Parliaments in the European Union – note that the version of the Protocol annexed to the Constitutional Treaty referred to "European legislative acts", but the word "European" was systematically extirpated from the Lisbon Treaty version of the Protocol.

[27] Article 3 of the Protocol on the Role of National Parliaments in the European Union.

[28] *I.e.*, for its adoption or for the adoption of a legislative procedure.

[29] Article 4 of the Protocol on the Role of National Parliaments in the European Union. Exceptions to the six-week period were permitted in cases of urgency, although the reasons for the urgency were required to be stated in the act or position of the Council. Exceptions to the prohibition on reaching agreement during the six-week period were also provided for "in urgent cases for which due reasons have been given".

[30] *Ibid.*. Again, an exception was provided for "in urgent cases for which due reasons have been given".

[31] Article 5 of the Protocol on the Role of National Parliaments in the European Union.

[32] Article 6 of the Protocol on the Role of National Parliaments in the European Union. The 'simplified revision procedure' is described at point 3 of the text above, on p. xx.

for the European Parliament and national parliaments together organising such cooperation.[33] It further provided that a conference of parliamentary committees for Union affairs could submit any contribution it deemed appropriate for the Commission, Parliament or Council as well as promoting the exchange of information and best practice between national parliaments and the European Parliament in addition to organising interparliamentary conferences on specific topics.[34]

Under the Lisbon Treaty, a Protocol with exactly the same title and the same numbering is now to be annexed to the Treaty on European Union, to the Treaty on the Functioning of the European Union and to the Treaty establishing the European Atomic Energy Community. With only one exception, every single provision of the Protocol on the Role of National Parliaments in the European Union has now been reproduced in effectively identical terms.[35] The sole substantive change of any kind whatsoever provided for under the new version of the Protocol (if one can call it that) is that the "six-week period" required under Article 4 of the Protocol to elapse between a draft legislative act being made available to national parliaments in the official languages of the Union and the date when it is placed on a provisional agenda for the Council is to be changed to an "eight-week period".[36] Apart from this one change, however (which addressed the source of concerns which had been expressed regarding the relevant terms of the Constitutional Treaty[37]), every provision remains as it emerged from the 2004 intergovernmental conference.

---

[33] Article 9 of the Protocol on the Role of National Parliaments in the European Union.

[34] Article 10 of the Protocol on the Role of National Parliaments in the European Union.

[35] The only changes being that references to the "Constitution" and individual provisions thereof have been replaced by references to the relevant constitutive Treaty (*i.e.*, as the case may be, the Treaty on European Union, the Treaty on the Functioning of the European Union or the Treaty establishing the European Atomic Energy Community) and the relevant provisions thereof. Further the references in the original Protocol to "European" legislative acts have been replaced by references simply to legislative acts.

[36] See now Article 4 of the Protocol. This change is exactly as was envisaged in the Brussels Presidency conclusions of June 2007, (See para. 11 of Annex I ("Draft IGC Mandate") to the Presidency Conclusions of the Brussels European Council 21–22 June 2007, at p. 17 thereof, cited at n. 8 above.)

[37] See in this regard the concerns of national parliaments raised in this regard in the COSAC Report on the Results of COSAC's Pilot Project on the Third Railway Package to Test the 'Subsidiarity Early Warning Mechanism', presented to the XXXIII COSAC, Luxembourg, 17–18 May 2005 and reproduced in G. Amato and J. Ziller, *The European Constitution* (Edward Elgar, Cheltenham, 2007) at 217 thereof.

3. The Protocol on the Application of the Principles of Subsidiarity and Proportionality

The Protocol on the Application of the Principles of Subsidiarity and Proportionality annexed to the Constitutional Treaty, was composed of ten articles.[38] The Protocol required each institution to ensure constant respect for the principle of subsidiarity and proportionality[39] and the Commission to consult widely before proposing legislative acts.[40] The Protocol also repeated the obligation imposed on a number of Community institutions and bodies by the Protocol on the Role of National Parliaments in the European Union to forward draft legislative acts to national parliaments, but added to this the further obligation to forward amended drafts as well.[41] Under the Protocol on the Application of the Principles of Subsidiarity and Proportionality, draft legislative acts were to be required to be justified with regard to the principles of subsidiarity and proportionality, to contain a detailed statement making it possible to appraise compliance with these two principles, and to take account of the need for any burden they imposed to be minimised and commensurate with the object to be achieved.[42]

The most innovative feature of the Protocol consisted of the compliance-monitoring system it created. Under this, any national parliament or chamber thereof could send, within six weeks of the date of transmission of a draft legislative act, an opinion stating why it considered that the draft in question did not comply with the principle of subsidiarity,[43] and account had to be

---

[38] In addition to a two-clause preamble noting, *inter alia,* that the High Contracting Parties were resolved to establish the conditions for the application of the principles of subsidiarity and proportionality, and to establish a system for monitoring the application of those principles.

[39] Article 1 of the Protocol on the Application of the Principles of Subsidiarity and Proportionality.

[40] Articles 2 and 3 of the Protocol on the Application of the Principles of Subsidiarity and Proportionality. An exception was provided for in cases of exceptional urgency, but in this situation the Commission was required to give reasons for its decision in its proposal. Additionally, under Article 9 of the Protocol, an annual report on the application of Article I-11 of the Constitutional Treaty (now to be Article 5 of the Treaty on European Union) on the principles of conferral, subsidiarity and proportionality was to be required of the Commission.

[41] See Article 4 of the Protocol on the Application of the Principles of Subsidiarity and Proportionality and compare Article 2 of the Protocol on the Role of National Parliaments in the European Union.

[42] Article 5 of the Protocol on the Application of the Principles of Subsidiarity and Proportionality.

[43] Article 6 of the Protocol on the Application of the Principles of Subsidiarity and Proportionality. Under the same article, the reasoned opinion was to be sent to the Presidents of the European Parliament, the Council and the Commission, and, if it had not originated with any of these, was to be forwarded to its originating institution, body or member states by the President of the Council.

taken of such reasoned opinions.[44] Further, each parliament was given two votes (allocated to the individual chambers in bicameral systems)[45] and where reasoned opinions on a draft legislative act's non-compliance with the principle of subsidiarity represented at least one third of all the votes allocated to national parliaments, the draft was required to be reviewed.[46] The effect of such a review was limited: it was specifically provided by the Protocol that the originating institution, body or member states might decide to maintain, amend or withdraw the draft. Reasons had to be given, however, for the relevant decision.[47]

The Protocol also provided that the Court of Justice should have jurisdiction in actions brought[48] or notified [49] by member states on behalf of their national parliament (or a chamber of it) for infringement of the principle of subsidiarity by a European legislative act.[50]

Under the Lisbon Treaty, a Protocol with exactly the same name and the same numbering is to be annexed to the Treaty on European Union and the Treaty on the Functioning of the European Union. With two exceptions, every provision of the original Protocol on the Application of the Principles of Subsidiarity and Proportionality has been reproduced effectively verbatim in the new version.[51]

---

[44] Article 7 of the Protocol on the Application of the Principles of Subsidiarity and Proportionality.

[45] *Ibid.*, at para. 1 thereof. (The paragraph numbering was introduced only in the Lisbon Treaty version of the Protocal, it should be noted.)

[46] *Ibid.*, at para. 2 thereof.

[47] *Ibid.*. The threshold was a quarter of votes allocated to national parliaments rather than a third in the case of a draft legislative act submitted on the basis of Article III-264 of the Constitutional Treaty on the area of freedom, security and justice (now Article 76 of the Treaty on the Functioning of the European Union on the area of freedom, security and justice).

[48] In accordance with the rules laid down in Article III-365 of the Constitutional Treaty (now to be Article 263 of the Treaty on the Functioning of the European Union).

[49] *I.e.*, in accordance with their legal order.

[50] Article 8 of the Protocol on the Application of the Principles of Subsidiarity and Proportionality. Under the same provision, the Committee of the Regions was also given the right to bring such actions – again, in accordance with the rules laid down in Article III-365 of the Constitutional Treaty (now Article 263 of the Treaty on the Functioning of the European Union) – against European legislative acts for the adoption of which the Constitutional Treaty (now the Treaty on the Functioning of the European Union) provided that it be consulted.

[51] The only changes are technical ones, or ones which are consequential on the new format of the reform of the constitutive treaties: hence references to the "Constitution" and individual provisions thereof have been replaced by references to the relevant constitutive Treaty (*i.e.*, as the case may be the Treaty on European Union, the Treaty on the Functioning of the European Union or the Treaty establishing the European Atomic Energy Community) and the relevant provisions thereof. Further the references in the original Protocol to "European" legislative acts have been replaced by references simply to legislative acts, and with the reversion to the traditional terminology, the expression "directive" is used in Article 5 instead of "European framework law".

Two substantive changes have been made, however. First (and in line with the change made to the Protocol on the Role of National Parliaments in the European Union) the period of "six weeks" which Article 6 specifies is to be given to national parliaments and chambers to send a reasoned opinion on subsidiarity is to be altered to one of "eight weeks".[52]

Secondly, and more substantially, an additional Paragraph 3, extending and seeking to reinforce the subsidiarity control mechanism,[53] has been added to Article 7. According to the new Paragraph 3, under the ordinary legislative procedure, where reasoned opinions on the non-compliance with the principle of subsidiarity of a proposal for a legislative act represent at least a simple majority of the votes allocated to national parliaments under Article 7,[54] then not alone does a review requirement similar to that already stipulated in Article 7[55] apply, but additionally, the further requirement is imposed that

> "if it chooses to maintain the proposal, the Commission will have, in a reasoned opinion, to justify why it considers that the proposal complies with the principle of subsidiarity. This reasoned opinion, as well as the reasoned opinions of the national Parliaments, will have to be submitted to the Union legislator, for consideration in the procedure:
>
> (a) before concluding the first reading, the legislator (the European Parliament and the Council) shall consider whether the legislative proposal is compatible with the principle of subsidiarity, taking particular account of the reasons expressed and shared by the majority of national Parliaments as well as the reasoned opinion of the Commission;

[52] Article 6 of the Protocol. Again, this is exactly as was envisaged in the Brussels Presidency conclusions of June 2007. (See para. 11 of Annex I ("Draft IGC Mandate") to the Presidency Conclusions of the Brussels European Council 21–22 June 2007, at p. 17 thereof, cited at n. 8 above.)

[53] See in this regard para. 11 of Annex I ("Draft IGC Mandate") to the Presidency Conclusions of the Brussels European Council 21–22 June 2007, at p. 17 thereof, cited at n. 25 above.

[54] This requirement means that unlike Article 7(2), which is activated where reasoned opinions on non-compliance with the principle of subsidiarity represent only one third of all votes allocated to national parliaments, the Article 7(3) procedure can not be used as a backdoor method for an outvoted minority in the Council of Ministers to delay legislation to which it objects, since the Article 7(3) procedure will only come into play when reasoned opinions representing a majority of votes allocated to national parliaments comes into play.

[55] More precisely, Paragraph 2 thereof. Under both Article 7(2) and 7(3), the Commission may decide to maintain, amend or withdraw the draft after the required review. There would appear to be no reason why the obligation under both Article 7(2) and Article 7(3) could be complied with *via* the same review process.

(b) if, by a majority of 55% of the members of the Council or a majority of the votes cast in the European Parliament, the legislator is of the opinion that the proposal is not compatible with the principle of subsidiarity, the legislative proposal shall not be given further consideration."

The New Article 7(3) of the Protocol on the Application of the Principles of Subsidiarity and Proportionality – An Assessment

The additional paragraph added to Article 7 of the Protocol on the Application of the Principles of Subsidiarity and Proportionality is clearly the most significant change concerning national parliaments introduced by the Lisbon Treaty. Indeed, apart from the two-week extension of the period originally proposed to be given to national parliaments to examine draft legislative texts and give a reasoned opinion on subsidiarity,[56] the extension of Article 7 is the *only* change by the Lisbon Treaty from the agreement which emerged from the 2004 intergovernmental conference concerning the role of national parliaments which can be expected to make any difference at all in practice.

It is not entirely clear if (a) the Lisbon Treaty's drafters intended to make Article 7(3) an alternative special procedure which would replace entirely the rules laid down under Article 7(2) (which, it will be recalled, apply wherever reasoned subsidiary non-compliance opinions represent at least one third of votes allocated to national parliaments) and apply wherever the ordinary legislative procedure operated and reasoned subsidiary non-compliance opinions represent at least a majority of votes allocated to national parliaments; or if (b) the obligations imposed by Article 7(3) are intended to be *cumulative* with those which apply already under Article 7(2). The evidence on this point is mixed. On the one hand, the new Article 7(3) begins with the word "furthermore"[57] which would seem to indicate that the obligations it imposes are cumulative with those set out in Article 7(2). On the other hand, the express repetition in Article 7(3) of an obligation to review a legislative proposal (an obligation which *already* applies under Article 7 wherever

[56] See Article 4 of the Protocol on the Role of National Parliaments in the European Union and Article 6 of the Protocol on the Application of the Principles of Subsidiarity and Proportionality.

[57] In the English-language version. This is translated as 'außerdem' in the German version, "en outre" in the French text and "ina theannta sin" in the Irish language version, all of which are equally authentic, and all of which versions have the same connotation in this respect as the English-language one. (See in this regard Article 40 of the Treaty on European Union to be inserted by Article 1(62) of the Lisbon Treaty and see Article 314 of the Treaty on the Functioning of the European Union to be inserted by Article 2(294) of the Lisbon Treaty).

reasoned subsidiary non-compliance opinions represent at least one third of votes allocated to national parliaments) would appear to indicate an intention on the part of the drafters of the Treaty that the requirements of Article 7(3) be alternative rather than cumulative. On this point hinges the question of whether reasons must be given by the Commission for its decision to maintain, amend or withdraw draft legislation under the ordinary legislative procedure, where a majority of national parliamentary votes assert non-compliance with the subsidiarity principle. This obligation is found in Article 7(2) but not repeated in Article 7(3). Thus if the requirements of Article 7(3) are cumulative, this obligation will apply even under the ordinary legislative procedure where reasoned subsidiary non-compliance opinions represent a majority of votes allocated to national parliaments. If, on the other hand, the requirements of Article 7(3) are alternative, the Article 7(2) obligation to give reasons has no application in those circumstances. It applies (wherever the ordinary method of legislation is involved) only where reasoned subsidiary non-compliance opinions represent at least one third but less than a majority of votes allocated to national parliaments.

Perhaps the best approach to adopt in assessing the importance of the new Article 7(3) is to examine each of the requirements which it stipulates and to ask how much added value each brings.

(i) The Requirement of a Review

The new requirement of a review can not be said *per se* to add much if anything to the subsidiarity control mechanism under Article 7 of the Protocol on the Application of the Principles of Subsidiarity and Proportionality. A review requirement already existed under the original version of Article 7; and in contrast with the new Paragraph 3, the review originally provided for is triggered by reasoned opinions representing a mere *third* of all votes allocated to national parliaments. Further, again in contrast with the new Paragraph 3, the original review obligation applies to *all* draft legislative acts – not just draft legislative acts under the ordinary legislative procedure. Further, and implicit in this last point, the original obligation affects the wide group of actors capable of producing a draft legislative act [58] – not just the Commission, as will be the case with the new Paragraph 3 procedure. Finally, unlike under the new Paragraph 3 obligation, the original 'review and reasons' obligation will apply not just to legislative proposals, but also in certain circumstances to mere recommendations, initiatives and

[58] *Viz.*, the Commission, a group of member states, the European Parliament, the Court of Justice, the European Central Bank, the European Investment bank.

requests for the adoption of a legislative act.[59] Thus (subject to the observations made below) if the new Article 7(3) requirement of a review by the Commission had been left out of the Protocol, this would of itself have made no difference.

(ii) The Requirement of a Reasoned Opinion

What of the second subparagraph of the new Article 7(3)?[60] This has two aspects. In the first place, it requires that if the Commission chooses to maintain a proposal after the review required in the first subparagraph,then that institution will have to justify in a reasoned opinion why it considers that the proposal complies with the principle of subsidiarity.

Prima facie, and subject to what is observed below, this requirement seems to be another one which adds little of substance to the subsidiarity control mechanism under the Protocol on the Application of the Principles of Subsidiarity and Proportionality. There is, after all, already a more universal obligation under Article 5 – an obligation to justify *all* draft legislative acts – including Commission legislative proposals [61] – with regard to the principles of subsidiarity and proportionality. Indeed any draft legislative act is required by Article 5 to contain a detailed statement making it possible to appraise compliance with these principles, a statement in which, *inter alia,* the "reasons for concluding that a Union objective can be better achieved at Union level shall be substantiated by qualitative and, wherever possible, quantitative indicators".[62]

---

[59] Under Article 3 of the Protocol on the Application of the Principles of Subsidiarity and Proportionality, the concept of "draft legislative acts" is to mean "proposals from the Commission, initiatives from a group of Member States, initiatives from the European Parliament, requests from the Court of Justice, recommendations from the European Central Bank and requests from the European Investment Bank for the adoption of a legislative act."

[60] This provision is quoted in the text above between n. 55 and n. 56.

[61] See definiation of 'draft legislative acts' in Article 3 of the Protocol on the Application of the Principles of Subsidiarity and Proportionality.

[62] The Article 5 justification obligation is an extensive one indeed. The full text of Article 5 is as follows.

> "Draft legislative acts shall be justified with regard to the principles of subsidiarity and proportionality. Any draft legislative act should contain a detailed statement making it possible to appraise compliance with the principles of subsidiarity and proportionality. This statement should contain some assessment of the proposal's financial impact, and, in the case of a directive, of its implications for the rules to be put in place by Member States, including, where necessary, the regional legislation. The reasons for concluding that a Union objective can be better achieved at Union level shall be substantiated by qualitative and, wherever possible, quantitative indicators. Draft legislative acts shall take account of the need for any burden, whether financial or administrative, falling upon the Union, national governments, regional or local authorities, economic operators and citizens, to be minimised and commensurate with the objective to be achieved."

The fact that the original Article 5 obligation to justify applies to *all* draft legislative acts (including in certain circumstances mere recommendations, initiatives and requests for the adoption of a legislative act[63]) – and not just draft legislative acts under the ordinary legislative procedure – makes it apply to a broader range of documents than Article 7(3). It also automatically implies that the Article 5 obligation affects the wide group of actors capable of producing a draft legislative act[64] – not merely the Commission, as with the new Article 7(3) procedure. And further, of course, Article 5 is not subject to the requirement (which is a prerequisite to Article 7(3)'s application) of the existence of reasoned non-compliance opinions which represent the majority of votes allocated to national parliaments – or to the further restriction limiting Article 7(3)'s application to where the Commission decides to maintain its proposal in the face of such a majority. All of the foregoing means that the new Article 7(3) requirement of a reasoned opinion by the Commission already seems to require nothing which is not already required by the more widely applicable original obligation which was and continues to be found in Article 5.

A further point concerning this requirement under Article 7(3) should be noted here too – this time in contradistinction to Article 7(2). This is that the new Article 7(3) will require only the provision of a reasoned opinion justifying the original legislative proposal – *not* a reasoned opinion justifying the Commission's decision to maintain the proposal. (Under Article 7(2), in contrast, it is the reasons underlying the decision to maintain the proposal which must be given – or more accurately the reasons underlying *any* Commission decision regarding a legislative draft, be it to maintain, amend or withdraw a draft[65]). As noted above, it is not however clear whether the requirements of Article 7(3) are cumulative with those in Article 7(2) – in other words, it is not clear if Article 7(2) has any application where Article 7(3) applies and *vice versa*. If Article 7(2) and Article 7(3) are mutually exclusive, then the introduction of the new Article 7(3) will mean a requirement of a reasoned opinion by the Commission which will substitute

[63] Under Article 3 of the Protocol on the Application of the Principles of Subsidiarity and Proportionality, the concept of "draft legislative acts" is to mean "proposals from the Commission, initiatives from a group of Member States, initiatives from the European Parliament, requests from the Court of Justice, recommendations from the European Central Bank and requests from the European Investment Bank for the adoption of a legislative act."

[64] *Viz.*, the Commission, a group of member states, the European Parliament, the Court of Justice, the European Central Bank and the European Investment Bank.

[65] See generally, what under the Lisbon Treaty is to become Article 7(2) of the Protocol on the Application of the Principles of Subsidiarity and Proportionality.

for more extensive obligations under Article 7(2)[66] and which[67] involves merely the taking of action which should normally already have been taken by the Commission in the discharge of its obligations under Article 5 of the Protocol.

(iii) The Requirement to Submit Reasoned Opinions to the Community Legislator

The second aspect of the new Article 7(3)'s second subparagraph is its requirement that the reasoned opinion required of the Commission under Article 7(3), as well as the reasoned opinions of the national Parliaments, will have to be submitted to the Union legislator[68] (which means in this context, the Council and the European Parliament[69]). While the specific requirement that the Commission actually submit its reasoned opinion to these bodies is new to the Lisbon Treaty, it has to be pointed out that the Commission is already obliged *in any case* by Article 4 to forward its draft legislative acts to the Union legislator – and such legislative acts are required under Article 5 to be both justified with regard to the principle of subsidiarity and to contain a detailed statement making it possible to appraise compliance with this principle.[70] The Union legislator should therefore *already* be in possession of the Commission's views as to why the latter considers that any of its proposals comply with the principle of subsidiarity.[71] As for the Article 7(3) requirement that the reasoned opinions of the national parliaments be submitted to the Union legislator, this too seems somewhat redundant, since such opinions are in any case, according to Article 6, supposed to be sent to the Presidents of the European Parliament and the Council in the first place.[72]

[66] Which, as has been seen, involve the giving of reasons for a decision to maintain, amend or withdraw draft legislation. To this extent, Article 7(3) would involve a step in the wrong direction.

[67] Unlike Article 7(2) in this regard.

[68] It is true that the words "for consideration in the procedure" are found here – but they add nothing to the obligation and are in any case merely repetitive of what is to be found in the next clause of Article 7(3), which is examined in the text below.

[69] See Article 289 of the Treaty on the Functioning of the European Union to be inserted by Article 2(236) of the Treaty of Lisbon.

[70] The Article 5 obligation extends in both regards also to the principle of proportionality.

[71] And even if the Union legislator had been sufficiently inattentive on that occasion, it seems likely that the reasons which would have been provided, in compliance with the existing Article 7 obligation, by the Commission for its decision to maintain, amend or withdraw draft legislation would have presumably have revealed its thoughts on the point, obviating any real need for the new provision in this regard in Article 7(3).

[72] As well as the President of the Commission. See also in this regard Article 3 of the Protocol on the Role of National Parliaments in the European Union.

(iv) Hearing Both Sides of the Subsidiarity Question

The foregoing considerations must lead us to ask hard questions. Is what we have seen of Article 7(3) up to this point appropriately to be dismissed as a matter of mere repackaging and presentation (however justified this might be by political necessity) rather than substance? Do the obligations which we have seen are imposed by Article 7(3) constitute the mere repetition of requirements already adequately provided for elsewhere in the Protocol on the Application of the Principles of Subsidiarity and Proportionality (and indeed to some extent be considered backsliding upon them)? Ironically, notwithstanding the distinct lack of originality or novelty about much of what we have seen so far in Article 7(3), these provisions may in fact afford the Commission with one crucial advantage which is not provided for elsewhere in the Protocol – namely an opportunity to defend its own initial justification of the proposal. In other words, the foregoing elements of Article 7(3) offer the Commission a chance, having read the reasoned opinions of the national parliaments which assert *non-compliance* with the principle of subsidiarity by a Commission proposal to restate its case for having respected the principle of subsidiarity in the light of (and contrary to) any assertions to the contrary which may have been made by the majority of national parliaments in their reasoned opinions. It may be that the Commission will have nothing to add to what should have been its own already extensive justification of its proposals with regard to the principle of subsidiarity under Article 5. But should it be that any national parliament has raised an issue which has *not* been addressed in the Commission's original justification of its proposal, the Article 7(3) Commission obligation to produce a reasoned opinion justifying its proposal ensures a chance for the Commission to counter the condemnatory assertions made by national parliaments or at least to raise contrary arguments. Seen in this way, the apparently repetitive requirements of Article 7(3) perform the valuable function of ensuring that when the question of subsidiarity is put before the Council and the European Parliament by national parliaments by virtue of the subsequent provisions of Article 7(3), these institutions are presented with *both* sides of the argument. The provisions of Article 7(3) represent a constitutional-level approach very much reminiscent of the administrative law principle *audi alteram partem*.[73]

[73] See regarding this principle in European law, Case 17/74 *Transocean Marine Paint v. Commission* [1974] ECR 1063.

(v) The Requirement to Consider the Question of Compatibility with Subsidiarity

Ultimately, however, the value which the new Article 7(3) procedure will have will largely depend on its last two subparagraphs: Article 7(3)(a) and (b), to which it is proposed to turn now.[74] Article 7(3)(a) provides that before concluding the first reading in the ordinary legislative procedure, the Union legislator – *i.e.*, the Council and the European Parliament – "shall consider" whether the legislative proposal is compatible with the principle of subsidiarity, taking particular account of the reasons expressed and shared by the majority of national parliaments as well as the reasoned opinion of the Commission. This requirement goes a certain distance beyond what has heretofore been in the Protocol on the Application of the Principles of Subsidiarity and Proportionality which although it sets out a procedure whereby national parliaments' reasoned opinions are sent to the Presidents of the European Parliament, the Council[75] requires only that these institutions[76] "take account of the reasoned opinions" without actually requiring them to consider of the correctness or otherwise of the view that the relevant legislative proposal is incompatible with the principle of subsidiarity.

(vi) The Power to Block Legislation

The real novelty of Article 7(3) is to be found, however, in Article 7(3)(b), which goes on to stipulate that if a majority of 55% of Council members *or* a majority of the votes cast in the European Parliament – either, it appears will suffice – are of the opinion that the legislative proposal is not compatible with the principle of subsidiarity, then it "shall not be given further consideration". By this means Article 7(3) inserts for the first time into the subsidiarity compliance-monitoring system the possibility of draft legislation at European Union level being banished from the legislative agenda on the grounds that its adoption would violate the subsidiarity principle.

From the procedural standpoint, it will be easier for the European Parliament to block legislation under the Article 7(3) procedure than is normally the case for that institution under the ordinary legislative procedure, since all that is

---

[74] See quotation of these provisions in the text above between n. 55 and n. 56.

[75] As well as the President of the Commission. See in this regard Article 6 of the Protocol on the Application of the Principles of Subsidiarity and Proportionality. See also Article 3 of the Protocol on the Role of National Parliaments in the European Union.

[76] As well as the Commission, and, where appropriate, a group of member states, the Court of Justice, the European Central Bank or the European Central Bank, "if the draft legislative act originates from them".

required under Article 7(3)(b) to deny the possibility of a legislative proposal being given further consideration is that a majority of the votes *cast* in the European Parliament adjudge the proposal incompatible with the principle subsidiarity.[77] (Under the ordinary legislative procedure, in contrast, the European Parliament has more difficulty in blocking legislation. It must act by an absolute majority *of its component members* in order to prevent a proposal from being adopted.[78])

In contrast, it will be made more *difficult* for the Council to block a proposal than it normally is for that institution to block legislation under the co-decision procedure. In order to block a legislative proposal on grounds of non-compliance with subsidiarity under Article 7(3), a *majority* of 55% of the members of Council have to consider that the proposal is not compatible with subsidiarity. In the current European Union of 27 states, this means that not less than 15 of them will be required to block the proposal on the grounds that it breaches subsidiarity. (Contrast the rule prevailing under the ordinary legislative procedure where, because of the compromise on qualified majority voting rules reached at the 2007 intergovernmental conference, a *minority* of member states of a minimum size varying over time from 14 to 8 to 13 member states[79] will be able to block adoption of a measure).

It is not easy to understand the reasoning underlying the choices concerning voting requirements which were made regarding Article 7(3) by the intergovernmental conference. In the normal order of matters, however, given the generally more pro-integration view of the European Parliament when compared to that of the Council, one would expect the Parliament to tend to be the less likely to the two institutions to adopt a favourable approach to

---

[77] This ease of decision works both ways, however. Thus all that is needed for a proposal to survive the European Parliament's subsidiarity assessment is to attain a simple majority of the votes cast in Parliament, not a majority of Parliament's component members.

[78] A rule which effectively involves absentee members of Parliament being counted as voting in favour of a proposal. See Article 289(1) of the Treaty on the Functioning of the European Union (as inserted by Article 2(236) of the Lisbon Treaty and Article 294 of the Treaty on the Functioning of the European Union as amended by Article 2(239) of the Lisbon Treaty.

[79] These figures are based on the membership of the Union remaining at 27. See in this regard respectively Article 3(3) and Article 3(2) of the Protocol on Transitional Provisions (to be annexed by the Lisbon Treaty to the Treaty on European Union, to the Treaty on the Functioning of the European Union and to the Treaty establishing the European Atomic Energy Community); Declaration (No. 4) on Article 16(4) of the Treaty on European Union and Article 238(2) of the Treaty on the Functioning of the European Union; Article 16(4) of the Treaty on European Union (to be inserted by Article 1(17) of the Lisbon Treaty) and Article 238(2) of the Treaty on the Functioning of the European Union (to be inserted by Article 2(191) of the Lisbon Treaty).

assertions of non-compliance with subsidiarity. The voting rules *may* be designed to avoid making it too easy to deploy the principle of subsidiarity to block legislation in the institution most likely to yield to political pressures to do exactly this – the Council of Ministers. At any rate the net effect of the rules is to make it more difficult for the Council to block a legislative proposal on this basis (at least using this procedure) than for any other reason. Overall, the net effect of the foregoing is that if even a minority of 13 out of the 27 states consider that a proposal is compatible with the principle of subsidiarity and a simple majority of the votes *cast* in the European Parliament[80] are to the same effect, then the proposal will survive the new Article 7(3) subsidiarity-compliance control procedure. (It should be noted that somewhat unusually – as is also the case with the allocation of votes to national parliaments under Article 7, however – the votes of small states count in the Council for exactly the same in this regard as those of large member states, as no population-based weighting is attached to the votes).

Will the role of national parliaments be enhanced under Article 7(3) because of the blocking provision in Article 7(3)(b)? The answer to this is that it will: under Article 7(3), national parliaments will now in effect be able to collectively initiate a procedure which *may* possibly prevent the adoption of legislation at European level. However, their role in this regard is a tightly circumscribed one. In the first place, as has been seen above, under Article 7(3) national parliaments do not get the final decision that a Commission proposal is incompatible with the principle of subsidiarity (and therefore shall not be given further consideration). Rather, the ultimate arbiters of this question under Article 7(3) become the European Parliament and the Council of Ministers. Thus in effect, national parliaments (and only should they choose to do so) are given the right to take on collectively only the role of a kind of prosecutor regarding legislative proposals which are supposedly incompatible with the principle of subsidiarity. The role of judge (or perhaps jury) in this regard is reserved to the Council and the European Parliament – the very institutions who have always *each* had the option of blocking legislation for any reason which seemed to them sufficient – including that they felt the principle of subsidiarity had been violated – a case, to some extent, of *plus ça change, plus c'est la même chose*.[81]

[80] Which of course is not as onerous a requirement as that of obtaining a majority of the full membership of the Parliament.

[81] A saying first used by the French writer Jean-Baptiste Alphonse Karr in his satirical journal *Les Guêpes* in 1849.

Far from having the right to determine the issue of subsidiarity non-compliance themselves, national parliaments will not now even have the (lesser) right even to force the issue of subsidiarity onto the European Parliament's and the Council's agenda merely by virtue of a majority of reasoned opinions alleging non-compliance with the principle. This is because in order for the Parliament and Council to be compelled under Article 7(3) to consider this issue, the *additional* factor – above and beyond such a majority vote – must be present that the Commission must choose to maintain its proposal. Should the Commission decide to withdraw it – or perhaps more significantly, should the Commission choose simply to *amend* its proposal[82] – then the Article 7(3) procedure comes to an end. No role is envisaged for the European Parliament or the European Council under Article 7(3) in this situation. (It seems that a Commission amendment of its proposal is regarded as sufficient reaction to the majority national parliamentary view).

Overall, under Article 7(3), national parliaments have been given the procedural tools to make the adoption of proposed legislation somewhat more difficult, but not necessarily to prevent it entirely. They can compel action on the part of the European Commission, and if this institution remains intransigent, then on the part of the Council and the European Parliament – but they can not determine the outcome of such action.

Overall, how significant is Article 7(3)? Any mechanism which creates the possibility of proposed European Union legislation being finally derailed is obviously of significance, and the subsidiarity control mechanism certainly acquires some extra teeth because of the addition of Article 7(3), even if those teeth have been kept warily by the Lisbon Treaty drafters from doing too much damage to the adoption of Union legislation by the careful assignment of crucial roles in the process to the Commission, the Council and the European Parliament.

Article 7(3)'s significance will obviously depend at least partly on the extent to which it is used. A number of observations can be made in this regard – all of them tending to the conclusion that the use of Article 7(3) may be somewhat limited in practice. In the first place, as has already been pointed out, Article 7(3) only applies where the *ordinary* legislative procedure applies. Where this is not the case, then for better or worse, there is no change whatever

[82] Under Article 7(3), it is provided that "the Commission may decide to maintain, amend or withdraw the proposal". It is only "if it chooses to maintain the proposal" that Article 7(3), paragraphs (a) and (b) come into play.

to the rules that applied in relation to national parliaments under the Constitutional Treaty (apart from the extension of the six-week period provided for in each of the two Protocols discussed here).

Secondly, since the deployment of Article 7(3) will require a majority of the votes allocated to national parliaments to assert non-compliance with subsidiarity on the part of a legislative proposal, no matter how often it is used, Article 7(3) will certainly come into play less often than the mechanism which was already provided for in Article 7 (which requires only a third of votes allocated in order to be deployed).

A third limiting factor stems from the political reality that the majority in national parliaments can normally be expected to support their national executive.[83] On this basis, it seems somewhat unlikely that a majority of such parliaments will find non-compliance with the principle of subsidiarity unless the executives in these countries wish them to reach such a finding. In other words, it seems possible – and even likely – that Article 7(3) will only ever come into play only when a majority of national governments want it to. Another way of saying this is that Article 7(3) will only ever come into play when proposed legislation can not be adopted anyway, because there is insufficient support for it in the Council.

On the other hand, in any situation when Article 7(3) ever does come into play, the Commission, Council and Parliament will be dealing with a situation in which votes representing a majority of those allocated to national parliaments assert that the principle of subsidiarity is breached. In political terms, a level of political pressure will have been created which will almost certainly require some institutional action in response. As has been seen, a range of possibilities other than the blockage of the legislation will exist in this situation, however: amendment or withdrawal of the proposal by the Commission, blockage of the measure by either the European Parliament or the Council, or merely the Community legislator considering the matter and deciding that the subsidiarity principle will not be violated, and therefore proceeding with the proposal.

In the light of all of the foregoing, it seems fair to predict that blockage of legislative proposals under Article 7(3) is likely to be a highly exceptional and unusual situation. A certain level of difficulty in blocking proposals is not entirely inappropriate, of course, if one wishes the adoption of legislation at

[83] At least in those states where the executive is legally answerable to parliament.

European level not to be hindered to an excessive degree. The question is whether the prospect has been rendered excessively difficult by Article 7(3).

Ultimately, it may be that one of the greatest benefits of the new Article 7(3) (and indeed of the Protocol on the Application of the Principles of Subsidiarity and Proportionality generally) will be indirect in nature. It may be (and indeed, it is to be hoped) that the consciousness on the part of national parliamentarians that there will now be a system under which the input of national parliaments may make a difference at European level may motivate and stimulate national parliaments and governments alike into better equipping and resourcing national legislatures to take seriously the role they occupy in relation to the European legislative process. The auguries in this respect look reasonably promising – as may be seen in the chapters in this book by Andreas Maurer ,[84] Morten Knudsen and Yves Carl.[85] Additionally, the Lisbon Treaty's amendment to the Protocol on the Application of the Principles of Subsidiarity and Proportionality may also create a direct means for communicating to the Community legislator a groundswell of popular opinion in the member states against the adoption of a particular legislative proposal[86] – although if this is the intention or the effect of Article 7(3), the comment may be made that it seems debatable if is desirable to force the square peg of popular opposition to individual European legislative proposals through the metaphorical round hole constituted by a procedure focusing on the highly technical legal question of whether subsidiarity has been breached or not. Ultimately, only time and experience will tell how wisely and well the member states have acted in agreeing upon Article 7(3) and in providing the structure envisaged generally by the Treaty of Lisbon for a European-level contribution by national parliaments in policy areas involving legislation at European level.

[84] See the chapter in this book by this writer at pp. 90–92 thereof

[85] See the chapter in this book by these writers at pp. 474–475 and pp. 479–483.

[86] Of the kind most recently witnessed against the original draft version of the Services Directive, subsequently adopted in heavily amended form as Directive 2006/123/EC of the European Parliament and of the Council of 12 December 2006 on Services in the Internal Market [2006] OJ L376/36.

PART I:

National Parliaments and the European Union Today - Some General Reflections

1.

Ensuring Democratic Control over National Governments in European Affairs

Tapio Raunio[1]

1. Introduction

Parliaments are regarded as central institutions in European systems of government. They elect and control the government, approve legislation, and, in many member states, as the bodies responsible for amending the constitution, hold the ultimate power in society. Yet such a constitutional perspective is arguably increasingly divorced from reality. National parliaments are usually portrayed in the academic literature as reactive institutions, casting rather modest influence on policy initiatives coming from the executive. The technicality of most legislation, strong party government, and the growing relevance of external constraints – globalisation, judicialisation through the activism of national and European courts, and delegation of policy-making authority to various public or private agencies, not least central banks – all limit the real influence of parliaments, no matter how extensive their formal powers may be.[2] However, measuring the powers of parliaments is an inherently difficult task, and hence arguments about 'the decline of parliaments' need to be treated with caution.

There is broad consensus about the impact of European integration on national parliaments. Most of the literature on the role of national parliaments in the

[1] Professor of Political Science, Department of Political Science, University of Turku. I am grateful to Peter Saramo and Matti Wiberg for their comments on an earlier version of this chapter.

[2] See P. Norton (ed.), *Parliaments and Governments in Western Europe* (Frank Cass, London, 1998); K. Strøm, W.C. Müller and T. Bergman (eds), *Delegation and Accountability in Parliamentary Democracies* (Oxford University Press, Oxford, 2003); and T. Raunio and S. Hix, "Backbenchers Learn to Fight Back: European Integration and Parliamentary Government" (2000) 4 *West European Politics* 142–168.

political system of the European Union sees them as victims of European integration.[3] Constitutionally, the issue is relatively straightforward. Powers which previously were under the jurisdiction of national legislatures have been shifted upwards to the European level (by national legislatures themselves, thereby signalling that the benefits accruing to member states from integration outweigh the losses to national parliamentary sovereignty). Amendments to the Treaties, the European Union's 'constitution', are subject to unanimous agreement between the member states. After the negotiations in intergovernmental conferences have been completed, these constitutional bargains are usually presented as 'take-or-leave-it' packages to domestic legislatures, where the only options are to accept the constitutional bargains without amendment or to reject the packages and plunge the European Union into constitutional crisis. In the Council, the increased use of qualified majority voting makes it difficult for national parliaments to force governments to make *ex ante* commitments before taking decisions at the European level, since national positions must be altered rapidly in response to the likely result of a vote. Moreover, the extensive involvement of national ministers and civil servants in drafting and implementing European Union legislation insulates or marginalises national parliaments, regardless of the Council decision rule. The resulting information deficit reduces the ability of domestic MPs to control their governments in European matters. In fact, because of the centrality of technical expertise in the European Union policy process, the true winners of European integration have arguably been bureaucrats and organised private interests at all levels of government and not directly-elected representatives – the traditional holders of legitimacy in European systems of parliamentary government.[4] Not surprisingly, the overwhelming majority of both national MPs and MEPs think that national parliamentary control of European Union legislation is weak and needs to be strengthened.[5]

While such pessimistic conclusions might actually underestimate the influence of parliaments, the challenges facing them deserve to be taken seriously. Active

---

[3] P. Norton (ed.), *National Parliaments and the European Union* (Frank Cass, London, 1996); A. Maurer and W. Wessels (eds), *National Parliaments on their Ways to Europe: Losers or Latecomers?* (Nomos, Baden-Baden, 2001); and Raunio and Hix, above, n. 2.

[4] T. Bergman and E. Damgaard (eds), *Delegation and Accountability in European Integration: The Nordic Parliamentary Democracies and the European Union* (Frank Cass, London, 2000); H. Kassim, B.G. Peters, and V. Wright (eds), *The National Coordination of EU Policy: The Domestic Level* (Oxford University Press, Oxford, 2000); and W. Wessels, A. Maurer, and J. Mittag (eds), *Fifteen into one? The European Union and its member states* (Manchester University Press, Manchester, 2003).

[5] R.S. Katz, "Representation, the Locus of Democratic Legitimation and the Role of the National Parliaments in the European Union" in R.S. Katz and B. Wessels (eds), *The European Parliament, the National Parliaments, and European Integration* (Oxford University Press, Oxford, 1999).

scrutiny by individual domestic legislatures of their governments is important in ensuring democratic input into the European Union policy process, as the principal actors in the European Union are still national governments that take decisions in the European Council and the Council. The main problem facing legislatures is how to reduce informational asymmetry in order to facilitate effective parliamentary accountability. This is where constitutional rules, both at national and European Union levels, are potentially of great significance, particularly so for those member states where the legislative branch has traditionally been weak in relation to the executive, even independently of the effects of European integration.

This chapter (which is based on literature on both executive-legislature relations and on the role of national parliaments in European integration) is an attempt to construct a model or an organisational solution that would ensure democratic control by individual national legislatures over their governments in European affairs. The first step in such an analysis is to examine the main problems facing national parliaments in modern Europe. This is done in the next section of the chapter. In the third section, ways of strengthening legislatures *vis-à-vis* their governments are suggested, with the focus being on access to information, effective use of committees, and the ability to mandate government representatives through issuing voting instructions. This section also looks at relevant recent developments in the European Union. The fourth section examines another challenge facing national parliaments, arguing that national parliaments must learn how to become involved in the open method of coordination and other new forms of governance if they want to ensure that their voice is heard in European Union decision-making. Finally, the concluding section summarises the arguments made.

2. The Main Problems Facing National Parliaments

Before identifying the main problems facing national parliaments, we must clarify what is actually meant by holding the government accountable in European Union affairs. The ability of a legislature to control the government depends on a variety of factors that include the constitutional rules and established 'ways of doing things' of the country, and party-political factors such as the composition of the governments and the cohesion of political parties.[6] As this chapter focuses on the ability of the

[6] On research explaining cross-national variation in the level of control, see T. Bergman, "National parliaments and EU Affairs Committees: notes on empirical variation and competing explanations" (1997) 3 *Journal of European Public Policy* 373–387; T. Bergman, "The European Union as the next step of delegation and accountability" (2000) 3 *European Journal of Political Research* 415–429;

parliament as an *institution* to control the government, the analysis excludes such party-political factors, and focuses exclusively on legal rules and related established practices that shape executive-legislature relations.

National parliaments have already – even were the Constitutional Treaty or a successor treaty with equivalent provisions never to enter into force[7] – quite extensive duties and rights in the European Union political system. Their main function in the European Union's policy process is to control their governments which represent the member states in the Council and the European Council. This function brings national parliaments regularly into the game, as the Council holds meetings during most weeks of the year (with approximately one hundred Council meetings per year), and the European Council meets several times every year. National parliaments are also responsible for adopting amendments to the European Union's 'constitution' according to respective national constitutional regulations. Finally, national parliaments are involved (in some member states more than others) in the implementation of European Union directives when this requires enactment of new domestic legislation. The main focus in this chapter is on the first function, that of holding the government accountable in 'normal' European Union politics.

Regardless, however, of which function of the national parliaments we are interested in, the main problem facing legislatures is informational asymmetry. It is commonly accepted that the systemic features of the European Union policy process disadvantage national parliaments. No matter how tightly national MPs control their governments in European Union matters, their input is always indirect, involving a delegation of authority to governments which represent member states in the European Union political system. In order to reduce informational asymmetry, national parliamentarians need information about (i) the preferences and negotiation

L.L. Martin, *Democratic Commitments: Legislatures and International Cooperation* (Princeton University Press, Princeton, New Jersey, 2000), 147–163; T. Raunio and M. Wiberg, "Does Support Lead to Ignorance? National Parliaments and the Legitimacy of EU Governance" (2000) 2 *Acta Politica* 146–168; A. Maurer and W. Wessels, "National Parliaments after Amsterdam: From Slow Adapters to National Players?" in Maurer and Wessels (eds.), above, n. 3; O. Rozenberg, *"The Involvement of National Parliaments in European Union Affairs. An empirical test of two variables"* ECPR Joint Sessions of Workshops, March 2002, Turin; and T. Raunio, "Holding Governments Accountable in European Affairs: Explaining Cross-National Variation" (2005, forthcoming) *Journal of Legislative Studies*.

[7] Editor's note: see in relation to the most recent developments concerning the fate of the Constitutional Treaty the introduction to this book.

strategies of their governments, and (ii) the positions of European Union institutions (*viz*., the Commission and the European Parliament) and the other member states.

The focus in this section is on three aspects of the system of parliamentary scrutiny which are important in reducing the information deficit: first, the access of national parliaments to information; secondly, the involvement of specialised committees; and thirdly, the ability to 'mandate' government representatives through issuing voting instructions. The analysis that follows is limited to the 'old' fifteen member states, for the simple reason that it is far too early at this stage to have any reliable cross-national data on scrutiny procedures in those countries that joined the Union in 2004 and 2007.[8]

(a) Access to Information

The issue of access to information has two dimensions. The first is the question of when parliaments are informed about European Union matters and when they actually start processing European issues (in other words, the issue of timing). The second is the issue of what documents parliaments have the right to receive from their governments (in other words, the issue of scope). Both timing and scope depend primarily on constitutional and legal regulations about the right of the parliament to receive information. Timing is very important, for an essential prerequisite to effective scrutiny is that legislatures receive the appropriate documents as early as possible, with MPs thus having more time to examine the proposals, which often are quite technical in nature. Moreover, as the overwhelming bulk of European Union legislation is in reality decided upon in the Council's Working Groups and in Coreper, parliaments that only get involved in the process just before the relevant Council meeting have quite marginal prospects of influencing decision-making. As regards the average time it takes for European Union documents to get from their source[9] to the office (or equivalent) of the

[8] Moreover, the analysis is largely based on data collected a few years ago and hence it does not cover more recent developments. For detailed information on national scrutiny systems and the main problems related to each national parliament, the reader should consult the relevant country-specific literature, particularly the chapters in Maurer and Wessels (eds.), above, n. 3. See also F. Laursen and S.A. Pappas (eds), *The Changing Role of Parliaments in the European Union* (EIPA, Maastricht, 1995); Norton (ed.), above, n. 3; E. Smith (ed.), *National Parliaments as Cornerstones of European Integration* (Kluwer Law International, London, 1996), M. Wiberg (ed.), *Trying To Make Democracy Work: The Nordic Parliaments and the European Union* (Gidlunds, Stockholm, 1997); and Bergman and Damgaard (eds.), above, n. 4.

[9] Which for COM documents is the Commission, and for Council documents is the Council's General Secretariat.

national parliament, ten legislatures receive the documents in approximately two weeks: Denmark (insofar as concerns merely the documents themselves, without more); Germany (when the documents are received in the minimum time normally taken); Belgium, Finland, Italy, Ireland, Luxembourg, the Netherlands, Austria and Sweden. After that there is more variation, with the remaining countries being placed in the following order in terms of the length of time taken before they receive the relevant documents. Spain, Portugal, and Germany (when the documents are received in the maximum time normally taken); France (when the documents are received in the maximum time normally taken); the United Kingdom and Denmark (insofar as concerns so-called 'factual notes'); and lastly Greece.[10]

With the partial exception of Greece, national governments in all member states routinely submit Commission legislative proposals to their parliaments. In most member states, legislatures also have the right to receive documents which concern the preparation of international agreements between the European Union and third parties, cooperation in Common Foreign and Security Policy matters and justice and home affairs issues, green and white papers, the proposal for the annual European Union budget, and Commission consultation documents. It is essential that national parliaments are kept up to date. This is because the Council and the European Parliament, particularly insofar as concerns legislation falling under the co-decision procedure, often amend initiatives to a quite significant extent. Before Council meetings the European Union Committees normally receive the agendas of the meetings together with government memoranda. The practice of supplying legislatures with explanatory memoranda, either before Council meetings or when the parliament first receives the legislative initiative, is most advanced in Austria, Denmark, Finland, Germany, Great Britain, the Netherlands, and Sweden. Such memoranda normally explain the consequences of the proposal for the country and for the European Union, and may contain the views of experts and interest groups.[11]

This brief description of the constitutional or other rules guiding national parliaments' access to information shows that there is quite significant variation between the parliaments. In general, the information rights of the national parliaments are better in the more northern member states, with the legislatures in southern European Union countries much more disadvantaged in this respect. However, even in countries where national parliaments enjoy

---

[10] Maurer and Wessels, above, n. 6 at 447.
[11] Maurer and Wessels, above, n. 6 at 439–445.

better access to information, such as Denmark and Finland, MPs regularly complain about a lack of information – particularly the kind of information that would enable them to control the government effectively. Receiving too much information is, at least in some member states, an essential part of the problem, as MPs often find it very difficult to identify the important points from the mass of documents they receive.

(b) The Role of Specialised Parliamentary Committees

The logic behind examining the involvement of specialised parliamentary committees also relates to the provision of information. Delegating European matters to specialised committees means that all MPs, and not just the small minority who are members of the European Union Committee, become routinely involved in European Union matters.[12] As a result, the parliament makes better use of its own policy expertise and is able to monitor the government's behaviour more effectively.[13] The extent to which legislatures delegate European matters downward to specialised committees varies enormously between EU member states. The system is most developed in Finland where, according to the constitution, the committees of the Eduskunta must process all bills and are therefore actively involved in scrutinising European legislation.[14] In Denmark, Germany, the Netherlands, Italy, and Sweden, specialised committees are also involved to a certain extent in the processing of European Union issues.[15] However, in the majority of parliaments, the specialised committees remain relatively marginalised as regards European issues.[16]

(c) 'Mandating' Ministers

The ability to issue voting instructions on how to vote in the Council is usually emphasised in literature on the role of national parliaments in European

[12] For example, in 1998 the average size of a European Union Committee in the 15 member states was 7.4% of all representatives. See Raunio and Hix, above, n. 2 at 156.

[13] See in particular in this regard I. Mattson and K. Strøm, "Parliamentary Committees" in H. Döring (ed.), *Parliaments and Majority Rule in Western Europe* (Campus and St Martin's Press, Frankfurt and New York, 1995).

[14] T. Raunio, *"The Parliament of Finland: A Model Case for Effective Scrutiny?"* in Maurer and Wessels (eds.) above, n. 3.

[15] Maurer and Wessels, above, n. 6 at 448–449.

[16] The same applies to plenaries. Bergman et al. concluded that in no member state legislature does the plenary get actively involved in European Union matters, with plenary involvement categorised as 'weak' in 13 countries and as 'moderate' in Finland and Italy. See T. Bergman, W.C. Müller, K. Strøm and M. Blomgren, "Democratic Delegation and Accountability: Cross-national Patterns", in Strøm *et al.* (eds.), above, n. 2 at 175.

integration. This is because of the Danish system in particular, where the European Union Committee of the Folketinget is famous for its power to constrain ministers by issuing explicit instructions on how to vote. However, this indicator is not entirely unproblematic. After all, the government depends on the support of the legislature (which can throw the government out of office) even without any constitutional powers to mandate ministers. Therefore governments can be expected to incorporate the preferences of the MPs into their negotiating positions even without any explicit mandating. This applies particularly to issues that require the approval of domestic legislatures, such as intergovernmental conferences leading to amendments of the European Union's constitutive treaties.[17] Secondly, even when the legislature does enjoy such constitutional powers, any such mandating tends to be highly selective. Finally, tight voting instructions can also be counterproductive, as decisions taken by the Council and particularly the European Council are often based on complex bargaining, involving considerable trade-offs between governments.[18] Nevertheless, the strong mandating position acts as an important pre-empting mechanism, encouraging the government to engage in a wider consultation and negotiation process with the parliament than might otherwise be the case.

In all member states there is *some* control of the government via the national parliament's European Union Committee before and/or after the Council meetings.[19] However, it must be emphasised that there is huge degree of variation in the level of control exercised by the various national parliaments. In most countries the ability to 'mandate' ministers is either completely lacking, or, where it is not, is rarely exercised. In the majority of the old 15 member states, the government merely sends information to the European Union Committee, with a minister (or a civil servant from a ministry) occasionally appearing before the committee, usually when more important matters are on the agenda. In other countries, such as Denmark and Finland, on

---

[17] T. König and S. Hug, "Ratifying Maastricht: Parliamentary Votes on International Treaties and Theoretical Solution Concepts" (2000) 1 *European Union Politics* 93–124.

[18] The Austrian case illustrates well how difficult it can be for the parliament to exercise its mandating powers. The Nationalrat has a constitutional right to issue binding mandates to Austrian ministers, but it seldom uses this right. See G. Falkner, "How Pervasive are Euro-Politics? Effects of EU Membership on a New Member State" (2000) 2 *Journal of Common Market Studies* 223–250; W.C. Müller, "Austria", in H. Kassim et al. (eds.), above, n. 4 at 201–218; and J. Pollak and P. Slominski, "Influencing EU Politics? The Case of the Austrian Parliament" (2003) 4 *Journal of Common Market Studies* 707–729.

[19] There is notable variation in the frequency of European Union Committee meetings, with most committees meeting on a weekly basis when the parliament is in session. Considering the meeting schedules of the Council and the European Council, it is reasonable to assume that the more often the European Union Committees meet, the better positioned they are to control ministers.

the other hand, ministers appear before the committee on a weekly basis and often after the Council meeting as well as before it takes place. In meetings with ministers, the European Union Committee members have the opportunity to put questions to the minister. Following this, the European Union Committee may decide if there is a majority in favour or against the government position. The European Union Committees of the Austrian Nationalrat and the Danish Folketinget have the right to issue binding voting instructions to government representatives. The mandating power of the Austrian parliament is set out in the constitution. In Denmark, the practice of mandating is so institutionalised that it is almost constitutional in character. The Dutch Tweede Kamer has similar powers in justice and home affairs matters – as does the German Bundesrat wherever a proposal requires approval pursuant to domestic law or in instances where the Länder have jurisdiction.[20]

Table 1. The main problems facing national parliaments *vis-à-vis* their governments in European Union matters.[21]

Member state	Access to information (scope + timing)	Specialised committees	Voting instructions
Austria	Strong	Weak	Moderate
Belgium	Moderate	Weak	Weak
Denmark	Strong	Moderate	Strong
Finland	Strong	Strong	Moderate
France	Moderate	Weak	Weak
Germany	Strong	Strong	Moderate
Greece	Weak	Weak	Weak
Ireland	Strong	Weak	Weak
Italy	Moderate	Weak	Weak
Luxembourg	Moderate	Weak	Weak
The Netherlands	Moderate	Moderate	Moderate
Portugal	Moderate	Moderate	Weak
Spain	Moderate	Weak	Weak
Sweden	Strong	Moderate	Moderate
The UK	Moderate	Weak	Weak

[20] Maurer and Wessels, above, n. 6 at 451–453.

[21] Sources: regarding specialised committees, see Bergman *et al.*, above, n. 2 at 175. Insofar as concerns access to information, see Maurer and Wessels, above, n. 6 and regarding voting instructions, see Bergman *et al.*, above, n. 2 at 175–176, and Maurer and Wessels, above, n. 6.

With the main problems facing national parliaments now having been examined, Table 1 compares the national parliaments in three respects: information rights, the involvement of specialised committees, and the ability to mandate ministers. The categorisations in the three columns admittedly lack precision and should be understood more as rough estimates than as exact measurements, but they nonetheless provide a decent overall picture of where national parliaments stand.[22] Concerning access to information, six out of fifteen parliaments are classified as having strong information rights. Finland and Germany are the only countries where the involvement of specialised committees was categorised as strong, with weak involvement found in nine out of fifteen countries. Turning to voting instructions, we note that only the Danish parliament has strong powers to mandate the ministers, with again nine out of fifteen countries having weak mandating powers. While it may be possible to disagree on the accuracy of the information in Table 1, one can nevertheless ascertain on the basis of the table that most parliaments are not able to exercise effective control over their governments in European affairs. There is thus a real problem that needs to be addressed. The next section suggests how this could be done.

3. Making National Parliaments Stronger in the European Union Political System

The various reform proposals aiming at strengthening the role of national parliaments in the European Union political system can be divided into two categories. The first group of proposals are suggested ways of improving the capacities of individual parliaments to hold their governments accountable at the national level. The second group of proposals, on the other hand, are arguments in favour of establishing a collective role for national parliaments through either consolidating interparliamentary cooperation or establishing a separate chamber of national MPs. As this chapter focuses on parliamentary control in the member states, the latter group of proposals will not be examined here.[23]

---

[22] For more information on the criteria behind the categorisations, see Maurer and Wessels, above, n. 6, and Bergman *et al.*, above, n. 16. Where there was contradictory information between the sources, I relied on data from the volume edited by Maurer and Wessels, as that study focused exclusively on the role of national parliaments in European integration. The different categorisations were at least partially explained by the subjective element involved in the categorisations, as both studies relied primarily on the expertise of country specialists. For example, it is quite difficult to measure the involvement of specialised committees in the handling of European Union matters.

[23] Most member states have been consistently against the establishment of a collective organ of national MPs at the European level. See T. Raunio, "Towards Tighter Scrutiny? National Legislatures in the EU Constitution" Online Paper 16/04, The Federal Trust, London, 2004.

However, developments at the European level will be incorporated into the analysis to the extent that they have an impact on parliamentary accountability at the national level.

The proposals made in this section are thus divided into two groups: those involving changes at national level, and those necessitating changes at European Union level.

(a) Developments at National Level

(i) Delegating Authority to Specialised Committees

A strong parliamentary committee system facilitates efficient control over government. Literature on committees has emphasised that committees provide MPs with the opportunity to specialise, and that such specialisation can benefit the whole parliament.[24] While there is significant cross-national variation, committees have become more influential in the majority of member states in the processing of domestic legislation. But, as the analysis in the previous section showed, most national parliaments do not really involve specialised committees in the processing of European Union matters. This means that most national MPs do not have to familiarise themselves with European Union issues unless they want to. Put simply, parliaments do not utilise the policy expertise of their memberships. Delegating authority downward to specialised committees would benefit both government and opposition parties and would bring *all* MPs into the European Union policy cycle. Legislatures should therefore institutionalise the input of specialised committees. This could be done, for example, by establishing a system where the body responsible for organising the parliament's work would automatically send the Commission initiative (or other European Union documents) both to the European Union Committee and to the relevant specialised committee. Then the specialised committee would report on the issue to the European Union Committee, with the latter then scrutinising the government position in hearings with the minister. The relevant specialised committee could obviously also organise hearings with government representatives

[24] See Mattson and Strøm, above, n. 13, and Norton (ed.), above, n. 2.

and other actors with an interest in or expertise on the issue, during the processing of the matter.[25]

(ii) Organising Hearings with Ministers before Council Meetings

Ex ante hearing of government ministers is essential for effective parliamentary scrutiny. As the discussion in the previous section indicated, finding a good balance between leaving ministers some room for manoeuvre and subjecting them to sufficient control may not always be very easy. This is probably one reason why many national parliaments have not found it wise to organise regular hearings with the ministers before the Council meetings. However, it is nonetheless essential that the minister should appear before the European Union Committee prior to the Council meeting to explain the government's position and its negotiation strategy and to get the parliament's backing for its actions. The minister should also be forced to appear before the European Union Committee after the Council meeting, especially if the Committee so decides. Only through such hearings can the national parliament keep up to date regarding what is on the European Union's agenda and the government's intended course of action. The main goal here is not to issue voting instructions or to place severe constraints on the minister. The objective is to give the MPs the chance to put questions to the minister and thereby to force the minister to study the issue at hand more thoroughly than would happen if he or she did not have to appear before the Committee. Moreover, as the final Council meeting usually just rubber-stamps decisions reached at the working group level or in the Coreper, it is essential that the European Union Committee organises hearings with ministers throughout the processing of the matter at the European level, not just before the final Council meeting.

(iii) Improving Access to Information

The information rights of several national parliaments in European Union matters have been improved in recent years. Unfortunately, however, most parliaments either still find it hard to gain access to the information they need, or else receive the information in a form which does not facilitate control of the government. There are two main ways to remedy this situation.

[25] Effective monitoring of the subsidiarity principle, as proposed by the 'early warning system' which was included in the Constitutional Treaty, is also relevant in this context as parliaments, under such a system, would have to take decisions on the division of labour. Would monitoring subsidiarity be delegated downwards to specialised committees or would it be centralised to the committee responsible for European Union matters? See F. Langdal, "Nationalla parlament och beslutsfattande på europeisk nivå" Sieps Report 2003:12, Stockholm 42; and A. Maurer and D. Kietz, "Die neuen Rechte der nationalen Parlamente: Umsetzungsprobleme und Empfehlungen" Diskussionspapier, SWP, Berlin, 2004, 6–7.

First, the government should be made to provide the parliament with any relevant information on its own account without any specific request from MPs. For example, the Finnish constitution states that

> "the Parliament has the right to receive from the Government the information it needs in the consideration of matters. The appropriate Minister shall ensure that Committees and other parliamentary organs receive without delay the necessary documents and other information in the possession of the authorities. A Committee has the right to receive information from the Government or the appropriate Ministry on a matter within its competence. The Committee may issue a statement to the Government or the Ministry on the basis of the information. A Representative has the right to information which is in the possession of authorities and which is necessary for the performance of the duties of the Representative, in so far as the information is not secret or it does not pertain to a State budget proposal under preparation.
>
> The Parliament considers those proposals for acts, agreements and other measures which are to be decided in the European Union and which otherwise, according to the Constitution, would fall within the competence of the Parliament. The Government shall, for the determination of the position of the Parliament, communicate a proposal referred to in paragraph (1) to the Parliament by a communication of the Government, without delay, after receiving notice of the proposal. The proposal is considered in the Grand Committee and ordinarily in one or more of the other Committees that issue statements to the Grand Committee. However, the Foreign Affairs Committee considers a proposal pertaining to foreign and security policy .... The Government shall provide the appropriate Committees with information on the consideration of the matter in the European Union. The Grand Committee or the Foreign Affairs Committee shall also be informed of the position of the Government on the matter."[26]

Secondly, governments should be required to explain to parliament the consequences of the issue or legislative initiative, both for the country and for European integration. While national parliaments do receive such information both from the Commission (in the text of the initiatives) and in the majority of member states, from their government (usually in the form of

[26] Sections 47 and 96 of the Finnish Constitution, the full text of which is available at www.finlex.fi/pdf/saadkaan/E9990731.PDF.

a memorandum or a summary accompanying the legislative proposal), national MPs often find it difficult to grasp the broader implications of the legislation they are scrutinising. Hence explanatory memoranda and other summaries from the government should become the norm in all member states without, however, these shorter texts replacing the full text of the initiative.

(iv) Investing Resources in Producing and Sifting Information

For several parliaments, the problem is no longer access to information, it is the amount of it. The constant stream of legislative and non-legislative documents from European Union institutions means that parliaments have to bear an additional burden. Busy agendas do not facilitate detailed scrutiny or constructive policy formulation. Moreover, in most parliaments, practically all information on European Union legislation is from their government. This increases informational asymmetry to the detriment of parliaments, as the executive branch (comprising in particular civil servants) heavily dominates the whole process of policy-making from sketching preliminary drafts of legislative proposals to actual implementation. The problem has been worsened by the fact that most European legislatures have quite limited secretarial and research staff.[27] Independent acquisition of information is important, particularly in order to learn about the consequences of the initiative and its linkages with other policy sectors. Parliaments should thus invest money in recruiting more committee and party group staff for dealing with European Union matters.

(b) Developments at European Level

The European Union is often accused of lacking transparency and openness. While such criticism is often based on incorrect information, much of European Union decision-making is still based on intergovernmental bargaining behind closed doors. Outside actors also have quite restricted access to documents and information used in reaching those decisions. Hence, any developments at the European level that reduce this secrecy should be welcomed by those interested in improving the accountability of the European Union political system. Not only would this improve the ability of the media and of citizens to follow the European Union policy process, it

[27] For information on research services in European legislatures, see W.H. Robinson, *Knowledge and Power: The Essential Connection Between Research and the Work of Legislature* (The European Centre for Parliamentary Research and Documentation, Brussels, 2002).

would also make it harder for ministers and civil servants to escape control by their respective parliaments.

The Constitutional Treaty would have gone a long way towards remedying the existing information deficit.[28] If one compares the text of the Protocol on the Role of National Parliaments in the European Union which was annexed to the Constitutional Treaty with that in the existing Protocol on the Role of National Parliaments in the European Union (which was annexed to the Treaty establishing the European Community by the Final Act of the Treaty of Amsterdam), the differences are quite significant indeed. According to the newer Protocol 'draft European legislative acts sent to the European Parliament and to the Council shall be forwarded to national Parliaments'.[29] The difference between the text of the Constitutional Treaty and the present position as established under the Amsterdam Treaty Protocol is very clear. First, under the Constitutional Treaty Protocol, all legislative proposals would have had to be sent to national parliaments, and not just 'legislation as defined by the Council in accordance with Article 151(3) of the Treaty establishing the European Community'.[30] Secondly, the legislative initiatives were to be sent directly to national parliaments, whereas under the present rules they merely have to be 'made available in good time so that the government of each Member State may ensure that its own national parliament receives them as appropriate'.[31]

National parliaments would also have gained improved access to non-legislative documents. According to the newer Protocol, all 'Commission consultation documents (green and white papers and communications) shall be forwarded directly by the Commission to national Parliaments upon publication'.[32] Here the wording was almost the same as in the Amsterdam Treaty, which stipulated that these documents were to be 'promptly forwarded' to national parliaments.[33] But, there were new documents that the national parliaments were to be entitled to

---

[28] Editor's note: see regarding the most recent developments concerning the fate of the Constitutional Treaty the introduction to this book.

[29] Protocol on the Role of National Parliaments in the European Union annexed to the Treaty establishing a Constitution for Europe, [2004] OJ C310, 16 December 2004.

[30] Protocol on the Role of National Parliaments in the European Union, annexed to the Treaty establishing the European Community by the Final Act of the Treaty of Amsterdam, [1997] OJ C340, 10 November 1997.

[31] *Ibid.*

[32] Protocol on the Role of National Parliaments in the European Union annexed to the Treaty establishing a Constitution for Europe, [2004] OJ C310, 16 December 2004.

[33] Protocol on the Role of National Parliaments in the European Union, annexed to the Treaty establishing the European Community by the Final Act of the Treaty of Amsterdam, [1997] OJ C340, 10 November 1997.

receive. These were the Commission's annual legislative programme 'as well as any other instrument of legislative planning or policy' to be forwarded 'to national Parliaments, at the same time as to the European Parliament and the Council', as well as the annual report of the Court of Auditors.[34]

Not only would national parliaments have gained much better access to documents under the Constitutional Treaty, they would also in the future have had better opportunities to follow what actually goes on in the Council. Hitherto the Council has met behind closed doors, but according to Article I-50 of the new Constitution it was to meet in public when considering and voting on a legislative proposal. In addition, the Protocol annexed to the Constitutional Treaty stated that the:

> "agendas for and the outcome of meetings of the Council, including the minutes of meetings where the Council is deliberating on draft European legislative acts, shall be forwarded directly to national Parliaments, at the same time as to Member States' governments".[35]

Should these changes ever come into effect (whether by virtue of the Constitutional Treaty or a successor treaty) national parliaments – and indeed, the media and citizens – would finally have the chance to hear and see what the ministers actually say and how they vote in the Council.[36]

---

[34] Protocol on the Role of National Parliaments in the European Union annexed to the Treaty establishing a Constitution for Europe, [2004] OJ C310, 16 December 2004. However, it must simultaneously be remembered that all the documents mentioned in this and the preceding paragraph are already available not only from the European Union's home page, but are also found in the Official Journal of the European Union which is sent *ex officio* to national parliaments.

[35] Protocol on the Role of National Parliaments in the European Union annexed to the Treaty establishing a Constitution for Europe, *ibid.* There was also a small change concerning decision-making in the Council. The Amsterdam Protocol states that six weeks shall elapse between a legislative proposal being made available in all languages to the EP and the Council and the date when it is placed on a Council agenda for decision (subject to exceptions on grounds of urgency). The newer Protocol read:

> "Save in urgent cases for which due reasons have been given, no agreement may be reached on a draft European legislative act during those six weeks. Save in urgent cases for which due reasons have been given, a ten-day period shall elapse between the placing of a draft European legislative act on the provisional agenda for the Council and the adoption of a position."

[36] The Council has since 1994 published its voting records, and since 1999 the records are available at the Council's website. But, while the final decisions are taken by the ministers in the Council, it has been estimated that even up to 90 per cent of all legislative issues are already decided by civil servants in Coreper and in the Council's working groups. As a result, actual voting in the Council is still relatively rare (see M. Mattila, "Contested decisions: Empirical analysis of voting in the European Union Council of Ministers" (2004) 1 *European Journal of Political Research* 29–50). This probably lessens the informational value (for example, through reducing the number of speeches made and the time spend on debating matters) of the Council's meetings.

However, while reforms such as those in the Constitutional Treaty would undoubtedly benefit national parliaments, both in terms of giving them better access to information and of increasing openness in the Council, more could be done at the European level to strengthen the capacity of national legislatures to hold their governments accountable. Two reforms would be particularly important: increasing the range of documents available to national parliaments, and streamlining the work of the Council and the European Council.

(i) Improving Access to Information

The basic goal should be that all European Union documents, or all official documents used in European Union decision-making, should be sent directly to national legislatures. There are still several types of document to which national parliaments do not enjoy automatic access. The obligation to send documents to national legislatures could in the future be extended to cover basically all documents used in making decisions in European Union institutions, including Common Foreign and Security Policy documents and those prepared by member states for the European Council. Moreover, further reforms that extend openness in the Council should also be welcomed. Article I-50 would have been a step in the right direction, but the logical extension of this constitutional provision would be that in the future, Council would also process non-legislative items in public. This would mean that those meetings dealing with items other than legislative issues, such as coordination of national economic and employment policies, would also be held in public.[37] In fact, were the Council to function more like a parliamentary chamber, this might also result in domestic legislatures treating European Union matters as normal politics, not having recourse to practices often used in processing foreign policy matters that emphasise national unity and secrecy.[38]

(ii) Streamlining the Work of the Council and the European Council

Politicians at national level often complain about the lack of regularity or predictability in European Union decision-making, with items appearing on the agenda of the Council and the European Council at the very last minute, or even during the meetings themselves, as part of 'pork barrel' type

---

[37] The Convention's Working Group on national parliaments had recommended in its final report that the "Council should legislate with open doors. Policy coordination as well as other activities should also be carried out with open doors as much as possible." See the European Convention, Final report of Working Group IV on the role of national parliaments, CONV 353/02, Brussels, 22 October 2002, 3–4.

[38] See H. Hegeland, "Europeiska unionen och den nya nordiska parlamentarismen" in S. Ahlbäck and A.-C. Jungar (eds.), *EU:s återverkningar på nordisk demokrati* (Uppsala Publishing House, Uppsala, forthcoming).

package-deals. This undermines effective parliamentary scrutiny at national level, as MPs have probably not had the chance to familiarise themselves with the issues and the relevant documentation. The leaders of the European Union countries took a step in the right direction in the conclusions of the Seville European Council in June 2002, adopting a set of rules guiding the formation of the agendas and the conduct of the meetings of both the Council and the European Council, but it appears that there is still room for improvement. Hence both the Council and the European Council should continue to make their work more systematic, with no urgency procedures or other short-track options.[39] Better organisation would also increase the legitimacy of the Council and the European Council and provide reassurance to voters about how the European Union institutions work.[40]

Arguably the main problem here concerns the European Council, the importance of which has increased in recent years (and would probably continue to do so were the Constitutional Treaty or a successor treaty with similar provisions to come into force). Much of the intergovernmental coordination in the European Union is carried out at the very highest political level in the European Council, particularly so in foreign policy and in fixing the European Union's long-term priorities in economic policy. The 'conclusions' of the European Council have increased rapidly in length and encompass basically all conceivable policy sectors.[41] This may not appear problematic for the national parliaments. After all, in most issues the European Council still decides by unanimity, and hence national parliaments can, at least in theory, veto any proposals they do not like. However, in reality the situation is more complicated. In order for national parliaments to exercise meaningful *ex ante* control on their governments in the European Council, the agendas of the summits would have to be available well before the European Council convenes, and the agendas should not be changed after they have been published.[42] Until now, the agendas of the European Council have often been finalised far too late and have even been changed during the

[39] See, for example, House of Commons, *Democracy and Accountability in the EU and the Role of National Parliaments*, European Scrutiny Committee, 33rd Report of Session 2001/02, 21 June 2002.

[40] See House of Lords, *A Second Parliamentary Chamber for Europe: An Unreal Solution to Some Real Problems*, Seventh Report, by the Select Committee Appointed to Consider European Union Documents and Other Matters Relating to the European Union, 27 November 2001.

[41] However, it must be emphasised that the summits are preceded by lengthy negotiations between sectoral ministers and civil servants from the member states. The European Council therefore actually 'decides' (or debates) only a minor share of the issues listed in its conclusions.

[42] The obvious exceptions could be major events, such as terrorist attacks or natural disasters, which occur after the agendas have been published and which require action from the European Council.

course of the meetings.[43] Especially in such situations, national parliaments may not want to veto *ex post facto* the decisions of the European Council, particularly as this might jeopardise the future influence of the country in European Union negotiations, and because this could embarrass the national government, both in the European context and in national media. Hence, effective parliamentary scrutiny of summits requires that the European Council works on the basis of fixed agendas that are published well in advance of the meetings.[44]

Having thus suggested in this section reforms that would strengthen parliaments *vis-à-vis* their governments, the next section examines another challenge facing national parliaments – the increasing use of the open method of coordination and other forms of intergovernmental policy coordination in the European Union's political system.

4. The Challenge Posed by Soft Law and Policy Coordination

While intergovernmental policy coordination has been a feature of the European Union's decision-making system throughout the history of integration, informal policy coordination has become much more prominent since the early 1990s. The European Employment Strategy (EES) adopted at the Essen European Council in 1994 and the coordination of national economic policies agreed in the Maastricht Treaty extended this coordination to two highly salient issue areas of domestic politics. The term 'open method

[43] The conclusions of the Seville European Council had stated that its "meetings shall be prepared by the General Affairs and External Relations Council, which shall coordinate all the preparatory work and draw up the agenda. Contributions by other configurations of the Council to the proceedings of the European Council shall be forwarded to the General Affairs and External Relations Council not later than two weeks before the European Council meeting. At a meeting held at least four weeks before the European Council, the General Affairs and External Relations Council, acting on a Presidency proposal, shall draw up an annotated draft agenda .... On the eve of the European Council meeting, the General Affairs and External Relations Council shall hold a final preparatory session and adopt the definitive agenda, to which no item may subsequently be added without the agreement of all delegations. Except for urgent and unforeseeable reasons linked, for example, to current international events, no Council or committee may meet between the final preparatory session of the General Affairs and External Relations Council and the European Council meeting." (See Presidency Conclusions, Seville European Council, 21 and 22 June 2002).

[44] The current system of the rotating Council Presidency has made the situation even worse by introducing an element of further unpredictability and discontinuity into the work of the Union. The Presidencies tend to produce a peak of activity towards the end of each six-month period (in June and in December) as there is a pressure to reach agreement before handing the Presidency over to another member state. A further problem is that, particularly in June, the European Council convenes at a time when parliaments in some countries are not in session.

of coordination' (OMC) officially became part of European Union jargon at the Lisbon European Council in 2000. OMC has four main components: (1) fixed guidelines set for the European Union, with short-, medium- and long-term goals; (2) quantitative and qualitative indicators and benchmarks; (3) European guidelines translated into national and regional policies and targets; and (4) periodic monitoring, evaluation and peer review, organised as a mutual learning process. In recent years, OMC (together with other forms of policy coordination) has been applied to a broad range of policies, including employment, social policy, environment, taxation, immigration, research, transport, working time, social protection, education, social infrastructure, regional cohesion, and social inclusion.

The increasing use of OMC and other forms of informal, non-binding, primarily intergovernmental 'soft law' instruments needs to be understood in the context of the sensitive question of dividing competencies between the European Union and its member states. European integration has reached the stage where the core areas of the welfare state, such as social policy, employment, and education are starting to be affected. In these policy areas (which are money-intensive and touch core areas of national sovereignty), it is very difficult to build the necessary consensus among national governments for transferring policy-making authority to the European level – hence the resort to intergovernmental policy coordination. The national governments want, on the one hand, to achieve highly-valued policy objectives, such as reducing unemployment and making their economies more competitive, while on the other hand, they are not willing to cede formal sovereignty to the Union. The Commission meanwhile sees these new modes of governance as a way to expand the European Union's competence in the face of resistance from the member states.[45]

The literature on OMC and other forms of soft law instruments – or 'new modes of governance' – is already quite extensive.[46] This literature has so far produced two main findings. First, it is still too early to make any definitive

---

[45] See, for example, A. Héritier, "New Modes of Governance in Europe: Policy-Making Without Legislating" in A. Héritier (ed.), *Common Goods: Reinventing European Integration Governance* (Rowman and Littlefield, Lanham, Maryland, 2002); and S. Borrás and K. Jacobsson, "The open method of co-ordination and new governance patterns in the EU" (2004) 2 *Journal of European Public Policy* 185–208.

[46] See in particular the material available at the homepage of the OMC Forum at the European Union Center of the University of Wisconsin-Madison (http://eucenter.wisc.edu/OMC) and the literature mentioned in S. Borrás and B. Greve (eds.), "The Open Method of Co-ordination: Theoretical, empirical and methodological challenges for EU studies" (2004) 2 *Journal of European Public Policy* (Special Issue).

assessments of the success of OMC. Nevertheless, while the impact of OMC varies a lot between policy areas, scholars usually point out that, unlike top-down supranational legislation, it is flexible and (supposedly) respects subsidiarity and national autonomy. The downside of this flexibility and the non-binding nature of outputs is that the European Union has few if any means to make national governments follow its recommendations.[47]

However, the more important findings in terms of national parliaments are those concerning the input of various 'stakeholders' in the process. OMC has strengthened the leadership role of the Council and the European Council, thus intruding on the Commission's right of monopoly, but on the other hand the Commission has a central role to play through its role as the institution setting objectives and issuing guidelines and recommendations to national governments.[48] The European Parliament has until now been effectively marginalised, and, more worryingly, the contribution of local and regional actors, often identified as the main stakeholders in these processes, has so far been quite disappointing. At the national level, OMC seems to be the preserve of a fairly small circle of civil servants who possess expertise on the issues. As OMC and all forms of soft law policy coordination are primarily intergovernmental in character,[49] national parliaments are thus, from a constitutional perspective, in a strong position to influence the proceedings. However, this applies only if they are willing and able to control their governments in these matters.

Significantly, the available evidence indicates that national parliaments have failed to make an impact on OMC and related processes. Examining policy coordination in employment policy, Jacobsson and her colleagues show that

---

[47] See, for example, Borrás and Greve, above, n. 46; Borrás and Jacobsson, above, n. 45; B. Eberlein and D. Kerwer, *"New Governance in the European Union: A Theoretical Perspective"* (2004) 1 *Journal of Common Market Studies* 121–142; Héritier, above, n. 45 (first citation); D. Hodson and I. Maher, "The Open Method as a New Mode of Governance: The Case of Soft Economic Policy Co-ordination" (2001) 4 *Journal of Common Market Studies* 719–746; C.M. Radaelli, "The Open Method of Coordination: A new governance architecture for the European Union?" Sieps Report 2003:1, Stockholm; S. Régent, "The Open Method of Co-ordination: A Supranational Form of Governance?" (2003) 2 *European Law Journal* 190–214; and F. Scharpf, "The European Social Model: Coping with the Challenges of Diversity" (2002) 4 *Journal of Common Market Studies* 645–670.

[48] The role of the Commission in OMC and other forms of policy coordination varies considerably between policy areas, with the Council often adopting the leading function instead of the Commission.

[49] However, in addition to the central role of the Commission and/or the Council in OMC, in several instances the non-binding policy recommendations are adopted by qualified majority voting instead of by unanimity.

National Action Plans have largely escaped parliamentary scrutiny or debates. To be sure, national parliaments have been informed about National Action Plans, but often after they have already been produced and sent off to Brussels. In some exceptional cases (*viz.*, Portugal and Ireland), national MPs did demand more information, and there were some examples of opposition parties using the European Union's recommendations to support their own claims.[50] While there are no other studies detailing the contribution of national parliaments, it is noteworthy that domestic legislatures are hardly even mentioned in other publications on OMC.

There are three main reasons why national parliaments have failed to make an impact on OMC. First, the whole process is by its very nature intergovernmental, with primarily civil servants responsible for drafting national programmes and presenting them in Brussels.[51] National MPs are informed of these preparations, but far too often this happens much too late. Secondly, national MPs may find it hard to follow OMC processes. Unlike normal European Union legislation, OMC and other forms of policy coordination often do not have any fixed deadlines ("there is no clear beginning or end") or even rules guiding the behaviour of the various actors. Given the intergovernmental or informal nature of OMC, there is also (at least in some national parliaments) procedural ambiguity about how to process these things in parliament and domestically in general.[52] For example, what are the rights of the national parliaments to receive the relevant information and documents, and how are these to be processed in the legislature. Hence it might be that national parliaments have simply not learned yet how to contribute to OMC issues, and that their contribution will become stronger over time. And thirdly, it appears that the actual impact of OMC and other forms of informal policy coordination has so far been relatively modest, if not even inconsequential, in many policy areas. As a result, national parliamentarians have not found it worthwhile to spend precious time scrutinising such processes.

---

[50] K. Jacobsson and H. Schmid, "The European Employment Strategy at the Crossroads: Contribution to the Evaluation" in D. Foden and L. Magnusson (eds.), *Five Years Experience of the Luxembourg Employment Strategy* (ETUI, Brussels, 2003); and K. Jacobsson and Å. Vifell, "New Governance Structures in Employment Policy Making? Taking Stock of the European Employment Strategy" in I. Linsenmann, C. Meyer and W. Wessels (eds.), *Economic Government of the EU: A Balance Sheet of New Modes of Policy Coordination* (Palgrave, London, 2005).

[51] Another related and highly important question, which lies beyond the scope of this chapter, is the extent to which these civil servants are subject to control by their ministers or even by their immediate superiors in the ministries. The evidence so far would largely indicate that civil servants effectively run the show, with fairly little political guidance from ministers.

[52] Jacobsson and Vifell, above, n. 50.

The challenge posed by intergovernmental policy coordination deserves to be taken very seriously, however. While the European Union is not a fully-fledged federation, its multi-level political system resembles closely the cooperative federalism characteristic of many federal states. Indeed, OMC and other forms of policy coordination are classic examples of cooperative federalism, with common objectives defined by member states together with the Commission and/or the Council, monitoring by the European Union institutions (at federal level), and implementation and choice of instruments for meeting the objectives delegated to member states. Importantly, cooperative federalism is almost exclusively intergovernmental in character, and thus it is often called executive federalism.

Regardless of how effective state parliaments are in controlling their governments, executive federalism concentrates power in the executive branch.[53] For example, in Australia cooperative federalism has resulted in a proliferation of intergovernmental committees and working groups. The ministerial meetings are characterised by low openness and transparency and reliance on informal, but still politically binding, procedures and decisions. State parliaments have often voiced complaints about being sidelined in the negotiations. Moreover, in order to make decision-making possible in the first place, decisions are increasingly taken by (qualified) majority voting which further reduces the effective sovereignty of the states.[54] Germany provides another good example. The role of the Länder in the implementation of federal laws has resulted in extensive intergovernmental cooperation, with a total of over 1,000 working groups and committees. Again, the Land parliaments have seen their role weaken due to intergovernmental cooperation.[55] Similarities with the European Union are obvious, and without the more active participation of national parliaments, the alleged deparliamentarisation caused by the European Union will be reinforced through the increased use of executive federalism in the Union.

The extended use of OMC and other forms of intergovernmental policy coordination should thus be taken seriously by national MPs. The leaders of

---

[53] R.L. Watts, *Comparing Federal Systems* (Second edition, McGill-Queen's University Press, Montreal and Kingston, 1999) 57–59.

[54] See M. Painter, *Collaborative Federalism: Economic Reform in Australia in the 1990s* (Cambridge University Press, Cambridge, 1998).

[55] See T. Börzel, "Europäisierung und innerstaatlicher Wandel: Zentralisierung und Entparlamentarisierung?" (2000) 2 *Politische Vierteljahresschrift* 225–250; and T. Börzel, *States and Regions in the European Union: Institutional Adaptation in Germany and Spain* (Cambridge University Press, Cambridge, 2002).

the European Union need to attain desired policy objectives, such as higher employment, economic growth, and indeed the combating of terrorism, but they (and also the public) are reluctant to transfer formal decision-making authority in such matters to the European level. Hence the national governments have increasingly resorted to various types of soft-law instruments for achieving their goals. But, here the European Union is facing a trade-off between output and input legitimacy. In cooperative or executive federalism, civil servants and ministers are responsible for coordinating national policies. The decision process is removed from the public sphere to intergovernmental meetings taking place behind closed doors. As a result, cooperative federalism weakens the transparency of collective decision-making and, consequently, the accountability of the representatives. Cooperative federalism by design thus emphasises output legitimacy at the expense of transparency and parliamentary accountability.

To facilitate parliamentary involvement in OMC and other non-binding forms of intergovernmental coordination, such 'soft-law' matters should be processed by national parliaments using the same procedure that is reserved for scrutinising the Commission's legislative initiatives. This would mean that ministers would be forced to explain their actions before parliamentary committees and in the plenary session (where such a requirement exists), with MPs having the chance to put questions to the ministers or other government representatives travelling to Brussels.[56] While MPs and parliamentary civil servants may object to this by saying that their desks are already full without having to process such non-binding matters, one must keep in mind that policy coordination is to an increasing extent used in questions that are highly salient for most MPs, such as employment policy, economic policy, social policy, and pension reform. Efficient scrutiny of such matters is thus significant also in terms of national legislation, as the policy choices adopted at the European level increasingly impact on and constrain member states' domestic politics. Hence parliamentarians have both an electoral incentive and a policy incentive to engage themselves in such questions.[57]

[56] G. de Búrca and J. Zeitlin, "Constitutionalising the Open Method of Coordination: What Should the Convention Propose?" (2003) CEPS Policy Brief No. 31; and Jacobsson and Schmid, above, n. 50.

[57] This way national legislators would also have the possibility to learn about developments and policy choices in other countries, hence making it possible for national parliaments to produce better laws in the future. After all, this is a key argument used in favour of OMC. See F. Duina and M. Oliver, "National Parliaments in the European Union: Are There Any Benefits to Integration?" (2005) 2 *European Law Journal* 173–195.

5. Conclusion

While most national parliaments have been rather late adapters to integration, there is no doubt that they do now exert tighter scrutiny on their governments than even a decade ago, and that this positive trend should not be reversed. The Constitutional Treaty, if it ever comes into force (or a successor treaty with equivalent or even stronger provisions), will do its share in facilitating a stronger role for national legislatures, but in the end it is up to national MPs themselves to decide to what extent they want to become involved in European Union matters.

The proposals for reform put forward in this chapter would make parliaments stronger players in European Union politics. However, despite facing similar problems, and despite parliaments learning best practices from each other (as happened in the case of the enlargement in 2004 when the parliaments of the new member states studied the scrutiny systems in the 'old' European Union countries), it is likely that parliaments will not produce a uniform response to these challenges. As literature on organisations suggests, change is often incremental and path-dependent, with institutions adapting their procedures gradually in response to changes in their environment.[58] After all, there are quite notable differences between the political systems and/or political cultures of European Union member states. Some parliaments have throughout their recent history placed more emphasis on scrutinising the government's legislative initiatives (for example, the Nordic parliaments), while in other countries the MPs understand their role quite differently.[59] Finally, comparative research indicates that the level of scrutiny depends partly on non-institutional factors, such as public opinion on integration, the type and strength of the government (the share of parliamentary seats it controls, the unity of government parties, and the resulting changes in government/opposition dynamics) and the salience of issues on the European Union's agenda.[60] While these factors speak against national parliaments adopting a similar model for scrutinising their governments in European Union issues, the reform proposals put forward in this chapter should at least facilitate tighter scrutiny at national level.

---

[58] See D.G. Dimitrakopoulos, "Incrementalism and Path Dependence: European Integration and Institutional Change in National Parliaments" (2001) 3 *Journal of Common Market Studies* 405–422.
[59] Bergman, above, n. 6 (first citation); Bergman, above, n. 6 (second citation); and Maurer and Wessels, above, n. 6 at 448–453.
[60] See Raunio, above, n. 6; R. Holzhacker, "National Parliamentary Scrutiny over EU Issues. Comparing the Goals and Methods of Governing and Opposition Parties" (2002) 4 *European Union Politics* 459–479.

2.
Shifts in Governance: National Parliaments and Their Governments' Involvement in European Union Decision-Making

Leonard F.M. Besselink[1]

The European Union has developed into a composite legal order governed by a complex system of relations which can be characterised as multilevel governance. The role of parliaments is of prime importance in the study of this multilevel system, insofar as parliamentary democracy is a hallmark of government. The interactions between the various levels of government are complex. This chapter presents some thoughts on the question of how involvement in European Union decision-making influences the constitutional relations between national governments and their respective parliaments.[2]

The chapter proceeds in three steps. First, the hypothesis is put forward that governments have been the primary actors in the process of European integration and still occupy a pivotal position which is to the detriment of parliaments. Secondly, the hypothesis is developed that European Union decision-making forces parliaments into a more 'monist' position, by which is meant the separateness of the roles of governments and parliaments is reduced. In a semi-presidential system of government as in France (or in *parlementarisme rationalisé*, as the French would prefer to say), parliament – at least in theory – has expanded its constitutional role, which means a trend towards less dualism (by which is meant less separateness in the respective roles of parliament and government). On the whole, in parliamentary systems of government too, the process of scrutiny

---

[1] Jean Monnet Professor in European Constitutional Law, Professor of Constitutional Law, Instituut voor Staats- en bestuursrecht, University of Utrecht.

[2] The purpose of this chapter is to develop a number of hypotheses. The evidence used is mainly anecdotal in nature, something which lawyers are quite comfortable with (perhaps too readily so). However, the anecdotal nature of the evidence at this stage does not invalidate the hypotheses sought to be illustrated.

of European Union decision-making by national parliaments, particularly in the field of legislative measures, also leads to a decrease in dualism. Thirdly and finally, some attention is devoted to the question of whether this makes European Union decision-making more legitimate from a parliamentary point of view.

1. The Primacy of Governments

European integration originated as a foreign affairs matter. Such matters are traditionally dominated by national executives. National parliaments play a role only in the margins. For decision-making in the European Union this is still the case: ostensibly a union of the citizens, in reality it is more a union of executives. The day-to-day process of European integration hinges crucially on the activity of the Council of the European Union and the European Council. The Council is a European institution, but its members are national government representatives, who still see the Council as theirs, not the European Union's.[3] The European Council is European in its meeting places, but national in its composition (comprising the heads of state and of government[4]), as its name testifies. In the sphere of delegated decision-making by the Commission, the infamous 'comitology' system extends the power of national executives into the executive heart of 'Brussels'. Decision-making is primarily the business of the executive branches of national governments, represented by ministers in the Council but more importantly by civil servants from all and any national ministerial departments operating in the shade of the Council and its countless committees and working parties, and perhaps equally importantly in Commission *couloirs*.

It is not a very bold assertion to state that the role of national executives in European Union affairs contributes to the primacy of the national executive over parliament. This shift towards the predominance of the executive in the national context is not caused by European integration, though it contributes greatly to it. The classic idea in most European constitutional systems of the *trias politica* was that the legislature, *i.e.,* parliament, should be supreme among the three powers, while the executive and judiciary were to be bound by, and subjected to the laws passed by the legislature. In fact, as matters have developed throughout Europe, the executive has become dominant over the parliament. In the national context, the executive stands both at the beginning of the decision-making process through its policy initiatives and as initiator of legislation, and at the end as the instance which is to execute

---

[3] Only when those representatives are back home do they refer to the European Union as 'Brussels', an alien body to which less well-received decisions are attributed.
[4] In addition to the President of the Commission.

and apply the laws which it has mostly itself initiated and which often grant it wide discretionary powers.

Large scale delegation of legislative powers to the executive, which is the rule in most European countries, has further contributed to this. The counterweight to the executive is no longer parliament, which tends to have an interest in keeping the government of the day in power and in facilitating its pursuance of its policies, rather than 'making life difficult' for it, as it is sometimes perceived. Instead of parliament, the courts have now been charged with, or have taken upon themselves, the task of protecting citizens from undue interference by public authorities with their rights and liberties. In fact, the triangle of the *trias politica*, in which the legislature used to be at the top, has been turned upside down, with the executive and courts keeping each other in balance at the top, while parliament has a more subservient role to play.

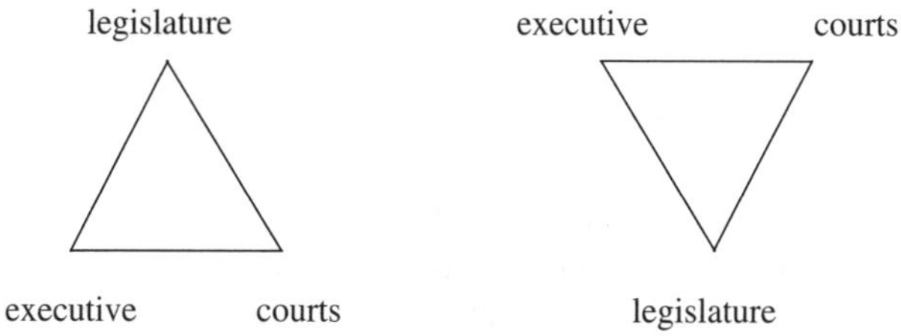

The role of policy initiation in the European Community lies with the Commission. But it is the national executives which stand foremost in the process when it comes to member state involvement. These days, within the context of parliamentary scrutiny of European Union decision-making, parliaments are also informed about policy initiatives and draft decisions. But this is as a counterweight to the national executive's role with regard to those initiatives and drafts. National parliaments by definition come second.

Decision-making in the European Union no longer involves members of national parliaments directly, as there are hardly any members of national parliaments who are also members of the European Parliament. Somewhat paradoxically, this has become the case since the European Parliament has become more important as a co-legislative organ of the European Community, with a mandate derived from its direct election. But the European Parliament has no formal powers to hold the Council or its members to account – something which would have meant, had nothing been done in this respect, that national executives were without direct political control by parliaments.

Scrutiny of European Union initiatives and draft decisions by national parliaments is designed as a step towards remedying this. It seeks to establish a measure of accountability for national executives, which otherwise act in the shade provided by the European Union institutions, away from the scrutiny to which they are in principle exposed when they act at home. But the particular multi-level context in which such scrutiny of European Union initiatives and draft decisions by national parliaments takes place has effects of its own on constitutional relations between national parliaments and their governments.

2. Political Supervision by Parliaments

The six original member states were the last to adapt their systems of parliamentary political supervision to this shift of policy-making to a location outside their traditional remit, even where it concerned the behaviour of their own representatives in the Council. It took them sometimes a quarter of century (or even longer) to introduce more or less systematic forms of parliamentary scrutiny of European Union decision-making, which the second generation of member states (the United Kingdom, Denmark, and Ireland) had put in place from early on in their membership. Still this scrutiny is understood as a form of surrogate supervision of their national representatives in the Council of the European Union and the European Council. Scrutiny of what happens in the many European Union fora which are populated with national civil servants is not, to the knowledge of the present author, brought systematically – if at all – into focus by national parliaments. What government representatives actually do and decide in 'Brussels' is still only within the reach of parliaments to a limited extent. Decisions can be delayed at most: only rarely can they formally be prevented as they could in the national context.

Yet in terms of constitutional change, member states have been prepared to face up to the consequences of organising parliamentary scrutiny. The most drastic constitutional change was undertaken in France. The semi-presidential system (*parlementarisme rationalisé*) had implied that it was not allowed for parliament to express its wishes into resolutions addressed to the government: parliament was not to interfere with governmental prerogative.[5] The process of European integration made a decisive rupture in this system of limited parliamentary government when the Treaty of Maastricht led to the introduction of Article 88-4 in the 1992 revision of the French Constitution, which explicitly gave the power to both houses of parliament to adopt resolutions concerning drafts of European legislative measures. Initially, these resolutions – which at least formally were to be addressed to the French government – could be said to concern parliament's own field of competence, that of the *lois*,[6] (although it

[5] Conseil constitutionnel, Nos. 59-2 and 3 DC, 17, 18, 24 June 1959, Recueil Conseil constitutionnel 58.
[6] See Art. 34 of the 1958 Constitution.

was quite clear that some European Community legislative measures might not be so restricted). However, Article 88-4 was extended in 1999 to cover all other European Union documents and draft decisions as well, and hence parliament's power was increased so as to cover European Union affairs where there was no equivalent parallel power in the national context. Thus, the French parliament had broader powers in European Union affairs than it had in purely national affairs. From the point of constitutional principle, the system of government was in a sense pierced so as to allow for the expansion of the parliamentary principle in a manner which the system otherwise did not accommodate. This constitutional change has brought the French parliament more or less in line with the position of other parliaments which function within a more straightforward parliamentary system. In fact, the French representatives in the Council could thus also consider themselves forced to reserve their position on a particular decision under the influence of parliament's possible objections. (This point was set out in a circular letter written by the Prime Minister in 1994).

The strictly dualist system on which the semi-presidential system (*parlementarisme rationalisé*) was based, was thus turned into one which – in European Union affairs – can hardly be distinguished from ordinary parliamentary systems of government. One possible explanation for this trend towards a more 'monist' relationship between parliament and government in European affairs may be the strengthening of a government's position in the Council. A national parliament's objections to a draft decision could after all be translated politically to a firmer position in the Council. Problems in parliament might be played as a political card in refusing to agree to any particular proposal. There is no clear picture on whether and how often this card has been played by various representatives. Although the Danish parliament has no formal powers of consent or approval of draft decisions, the alleged existence of a 'Danish situation', about which other members of the Council used to complain, suggests that the Danish government has from time to time in the past used this card. But as a matter of fact, it is not only for the French that a similar obligation now pertains.[7] There is also an obligation on the British[8] as well as on the German[9]

---

[7] Prime Minister's circular dated 19 July, 1994.

[8] This is on the basis of a Resolution of the House of Commons which was originally adopted in 1980 (House of Commons Journals 1979-1980, 819), then reconfirmed in a resolution of 24 October 1990, (see House of Commons Journals CJ, 1989-90, 646) before being reformulated in a resolution of 17 November 1998 (as to which see Hansard, 17 November 1998, cols 803–804). The relevant resolution is regularly published in an appendix to the Standing Orders of the House of Commons. Regard should also be had to the equivalent Resolution of the House of Lords of 6 December 1999, which is reproduced in the annex to the chapter in this volume by Christopher Kerse.

[9] Art. 23(3) of the *Grundgesetz*.

representative to reserve their positions in the Council until the relevant house of parliament has had a chance to pronounce on a certain proposal. The Dutch representative even needs the formal *consent* of parliament to binding decisions under the third pillar. However, in other European Union matters, there is not even a duty to reserve the Dutch position in the Council until parliament has had a chance to express itself.

3. The Role of Legislatures in Parliamentary Systems

We have seen how in France the position of the national parliament towards the government was extended in the field of political control beyond the scope of its restricted legislative power (*domaine de la loi*). It is now intended to look at the role of parliament within the ambit of its legislative role.

What has been said in this chapter about the classic triangular relationship of the *trias politica* being turned upside down, not only applies to political relationships, but also to legislation as such. In continental Europe, an important heritage of the French revolution is the idea that the representatives of the sovereign people, assembled in parliament, should hold the power to make rules which are binding on citizens. From this flowed the principle of legality, that is to say the principle that authority over citizens should be based on laws established by acts of parliament.[10] Within the *national context*, this idea has come under pressure during the twentieth century. This was very much a consequence of the growth of the welfare state. Public authorities were to provide citizens not merely with guidance in the form of prohibitions, commands, and grants of rights, but also as a provider of all kinds of public goods, from education and public health services, to a wide range of subsidies and fiscal facilities in economic, social and cultural fields, and many other services. This required the legislature to grant sufficient – in practice, large – discretionary powers to the executive in order for it to attain agreed policy objectives. This comprised the delegation of law-making powers to executive bodies. Thus the principle of legality was at least in part emptied of substance. Parliaments were sovereign in granting permission to the executive to do as it thought fit in large areas of the exercise of public powers.

[10] Clearly, this idea creates a tension between legality and the rule of law, particularly when this is articulated as majoritarian democracy versus human rights. It is here that courts step into the political triangle, where they have assumed co-equal rank with the executive at the broad top of the upside-down triangle.

Moreover, the assumption of legality developed in a purely national context, in which sovereignty was conceived in terms of highest authority and highest legislature *tout court*. It was acknowledged that international relations were a source of norms, but this was an issue dealt with by each constitutional system in its own national manner. The principle of legality – a legality seen as flowing from the national legislature (*i.e.*, parliament) – did not cater for supranational actors determining, let alone exercising, public authority within states.

As for the legislature *at European Union level*, member states are represented only in the Council and the European Council, whereas the Commission has no clear relation with the member states (except for the power to propose the candidate members of the Commission, which since the events of October 2004 has proven to be considerably more limited than it used to be).[11] The European Parliament is still stated to consist 'of representatives of the peoples of the States brought together in the Community',[12] although the very low turnout in direct elections to the European Parliament compromises the representative nature of the institution politically.

For the member states, the legislative process has acquired an extra vertical dimension, which – figuratively speaking – goes up higher than the national supreme legislature. This has further enhanced executive dominance: decisions taken at European Union level have to be implemented at national level. Even when this implementation has to take the form of legislation, national parliaments are often marginalised or bypassed. Very often, member states have arranged their own legislation in such a manner that implementation of European Community decisions through legislative measures can be done on the basis of delegated legislation, that is to say through executive decrees issued by the government or even by individual ministers. In at least some member states, this is also done in cases where in a purely national situation the relevant legislative measure would have taken the form of an act of parliament.

The most extreme form of implementation through delegated instruments is the executive measure which amends or repeals acts of parliament. Hence, a parliament's own legislation can be made undone and amended by executive

---

[11] See the series of contributions in "The Barroso Drama: Reality for the EU Constitution" (2005) 2 *European Constitutional Law Review 153–225.*

[12] Art. 189 of the European Community Treaty. Art. I-20 of the Constitutional Treaty speaks of 'representatives of the Union's citizens'.

act. Albeit authorised by an act of parliament itself, this is the ultimate setting aside of parliament. It is ironic that this most supreme form of parliamentary sovereignty – the sovereign act of abolishing one's sovereignty in certain cases – was invented by the mother of all parliaments. Other countries, or rather their executives, who are usually the ones to discover these *curiosa* when it suits them, have quickly learnt about these 'Henry VIII' clauses – without apparently understanding their origin,[13] nor the particularities of the conditions and safeguards at present provided in the British context.

(a) The Example of the Netherlands

This is for instance the case in the Netherlands, where respective governments have tried hard to push for 'Henri VIII' clauses in situations where the executive itself had proved unable to meet the time limits for implementing European Community measures via the timely introduction of implementing bills in parliament. The proposals led to resistance in the Dutch Upper House in 1998, when such a clause was proposed in a bill amending the Telecommunications Act. The objections were strictly constitutional in nature: the attribution of legislative power by the Constitution is to parliament and government acting together; hence, blanket delegation to the government – or even individual ministers – to amend, repeal or make law without an explicit basis, withdrew the constitutional powers of parliament with respect to legislation. A rather voluminous dossier developed. It was accompanied by parliamentary debates in the Upper House, a resolution of the same House expressing the view that a constitutional basis had to be created for such clauses also in exceptional circumstances, and a rather elaborate study of the matter was written at the request of the minister in charge of constitutional affairs.[14] Reports by an interdepartmental advisory committee,[15] and a very critical advisory opinion of the Council of State (*Raad van State*)[16] led to a revised view being

[13] Henry VIII's Royal Proclamations acquired the force of law through an Act of Parliament of 1539, which *de facto* and *de iure* permitted the passing of legislation, as well as its amendment or repeal, by royal proclamation.

[14] L. Besselink, H. Kummeling, R. De Lange and P. Mendelts, *De Nederlandse Grondwet en de Europese Unie* [The Constitution of the Netherlands and the European Union], (Europa Law Publishing, Groningen, 2002).

[15] *Versnelde implementatie van EG- en andere internationale besluiten*, [Accelerated Implementation of EC- and other international decisions] Advies van de Interdepartementale Commissie Europees Recht [Advisory Opinion of the Interdepartmental Committee on European Law], February 1999.

[16] Kamerstuk 26 200 VI, B.

presented in a memorandum of the government headed by Prime Minister Kok,[17] in which it was concluded that this type of clause could be resorted to only in exceptional circumstances. This convinced the Kok cabinet to drop the disputed provision in the bill amending the Telecommunications Act.

The days in power of that Prime Minister are over, however. And the matter was one for the upper house only: the lower house (in the Netherlands a chamber which has not been prone to reflection on constitutional matters) never showed the least interest in the matter.[18] The subsequent cabinet, headed by Prime Minister Balkenende, quite happily continued the introduction of very broad delegation provisions in bills, and even of provisions which are identical (or nearly identical) to the controversial provision of the Telecommunications Act. This cabinet, when faced with criticism from individual MPs who had the feeling that they were being sidestepped where the implementation of European Community decisions was concerned, usually referred to the pressure of (unmet) time limits. It never referred to the memorandum of the Kok cabinet and avoided any reference to constitutional complications.

In July 2004, the Minister for Justice published a memorandum in which he developed a framework for implementation of European Community decisions, which merits summing up. The starting point is that the States-General (the official name of the Dutch parliament) should no longer be involved, or at least should be involved to the minimum extent, in the implementation process. Where a European Community directive leaves an element of discretion, it is to be for the government to exercise. And where there is little discretion, acts of parliament should delegate the implementation to the individual ministers who are to carry out the

[17] *Kamerstukken Tweede Kamer* [Parliamentary Documents of the Lower House] 26 200 VI, nr. 65, 7. For an overview in the English language up to the year 2001, see W. Hins, "An Ambiguous Story about the Supremacy of EC Law: Report from the Netherlands" in T. Van Damme and J. Reestman, *Ambiguity in the Rule of Law: the Interface between National and International Legal Systems* (Europa Law Publishing, Groningen, 2001), at 85–94.

[18] In only one of the committees of the House did a discussion of the view of the Kok Cabinet take place. Even this discussion was a hasty and superficial one, in which members did not seem to be aware of the entire contents of the file. Members of the Upper House complained in a plenary debate about the 'horrendous' quality of the debate in the Lower House on this issue, and blamed this on the Lower House members' failure to read or inform themselves of what was happening in the Upper House. (See *Handelingen Eerste Kamer* [Minutes of the Upper House] of 10 October 2000, at 2–57). It may be noted in passing that the spokesman for the Christian Democrats in the said committee discussion was Mr Balkenende – the successor to Mr Kok as Prime Minister.

implementing regulations, thus leaving little room for the separation of powers. The view of the Minister for Justice was that it is only when 'drastic national choices' (*'ingrijpende nationale keuzes')* are to be made, that there should be a role for parliament.[19] At the same time, the view was put forward that in the preparation of European Community directives, parliament should be involved more intensely, because at that stage there would be more scope for discretionary choices.[20] In cases of necessity, one should "act as circumstances dictate", which probably means that the principles outlined for involvement do not apply, *i.e.* that parliament can be bypassed. In a final paragraph, the Minister for Justice pointed out that this memorandum closed the discussion of 'legislative technique', and that at a later stage a more profound discussion could follow concerning the European Union and its place in the [national] Constitution'. This implies that, according to the Minister for Justice, these 'legislative techniques', which involve resort to large scale executive law-making, do not touch upon constitutional issues – a remarkable view indeed.

As if this was not enough, the offensive against parliamentary involvement in implementation was continued by the Minister for Economic Affairs. This Minister introduced a Bill on the Making of and Implementation of European Community Decisions in the Fields of Energy, Post and Telecommunications in which all implementation was to be delegated to him. In exchange, promises were made with regard to parliamentary involvement in the decision-making with regard to relevant European Community directives. This move woke even the lower house from its constitutional slumber in such legislative affairs. In response to questions and criticism, the Minister replied by offering the well-known reasoning that European Community legislation requires rapid implementation and that this should not be frustrated by parliamentary procedures. The Minister's proposed scheme was that Parliament could have a say in advance as to desirable outcomes in Brussels, but not once things are decided and done at European Union level. As to the question of whether it might not be better that a basis for such an

---

[19] *Kamerstukken Eerste Kamer* [Parliamentary Documents of the Lower House], 29 200 VI, F second reprint, Letter of the Minister of Justice to the Upper House, 27 July 2004, at 2: 'To the extent that the relevant directive leaves no or little discretion to member states, delegation to the competent minister is to be preferred; in other cases delegation in principle to the government. This will make it possible to attain a situation in which the necessity to make acts of parliament is principally limited to situations in which the Constitution explicitly requires an act of parliament or in which a directive requires drastic national choices or a change in scope of existing national legislation' [author's translation].

[20] *Ibid.*, at 3.

approach be provided in the Constitution, the Minister limited himself to saying that that was not a matter for the Minister of Economic Affairs alone.[21]

(b) The Irish Case: Eliminating the Relevance of National Constitutional Principles?

All this must seem somewhat strange to an Irish public, given the approach of the Irish Constitution to the European Community and its legislation. The Irish Constitution is much stronger than the Dutch one, which, unlike its Irish counterpart, does not have a modifying role which has frequently and effectively thwarted government and parliament in relation to central policies. (This distinction between the two systems is perhaps due to the constitutional prohibition on the Dutch courts reviewing the constitutionality of acts of parliament). Also, in its relations to the outside world, the Irish Constitution is strictly dualist. Together, these factors required a strong, constitutionally entrenched form of incorporation of European Community law to be deployed, something that was done in Article 29.4.10°, which effectively sets aside anything in the Constitution that might be an obstacle to European Community and European Union decisions being effective.[22] In many ways, and somewhat paradoxically, the remaining provisions of the Constitution thus seem to be made irrelevant to the effect of European Community law in the national legal order. Interestingly, however, the *Meagher* case is proof that in fact in the field of implementation of European Union law, national constitutional principles are in the end decisive.[23] Under the ruling in this case, the constitutionality of delegating legislative power to a minister pursuant to the European Communities Act 1972 is made dependent on whether this may be said to be necessitated by the obligations of European Union membership. This in turn depends on whether the measure involved is merely giving effect to principles and policies contained in the European Community decision to be implemented. This test is the one which applies, under national constitutional law, to the delegation of legislative power under Article 15.2 of the Constitution, which also covers

---

[21] See *Kamerstukken Tweede Kamer* 29474, No. 6.

[22] Article 29.4.10° provides that: "no provision of this Constitution invalidates laws enacted, acts done or measures adopted by the State which are necessitated by the obligations of membership of the European Union or of the Communities, or prevents laws enacted, acts done or measures adopted by the European Union or by the Communities or by institutions thereof, or by bodies competent under the Treaties establishing the Communities, from having the force of law in the State".

[23] *Meagher v Minister for Agriculture* [1994] 1 IR 329.

'Henri VIII' clause-type situations, allowing ministers to amend and repeal acts of parliament. This is taken (at least in *Meagher*) to be the logical consequence of Article 29.4.10°, and of the obligations imposed by membership of the European Union.

Historically legislation is constitutionally at the heart of parliaments' functions. But we must conclude that this function is being heavily eroded to the advantage of executive law-making. This is not as such caused by European integration, but strongly promoted by the shift towards European levels which it has implied.

The view taken by Irish law of the legality of delegating implementation to ministers is made dependent on whether what is involved concerns the mere implementation of policies and principles contained in the instrument to be implemented. Whether this is really the case in concrete instances, is in the final instance not a political decision by parliament on the political meaning of whatever discretion there might or might not be, but determined by courts on the basis of a legal construction of the European decision at hand. So it leads to a shift away from parliament to the executive and the judiciary.

Compensation is looked for in the involvement of national parliaments in the stages prior to definitive decision-making at European Union level. Such involvement certainly enhances the role of national parliaments, at least in the member states where such possibilities were previously absent (predominantly the original six member states). Much of course depends on the practice. In some member states, the actual powers of scrutiny are not constitutionally, or even legally, entrenched. This concerns particularly the sanctioning of such scrutiny, *e.g.*, the obligation on representatives to reserve their position in the Council until a national parliament has had the chance to scrutinise or discuss the draft decision. This can make the prior scrutiny of European Union measures an altogether weaker instrument of parliament than legislation – even when it concerns implementing legislation which requires few choices to be made.

The input which a national parliament can have through prior scrutiny is also, of necessity, smaller and weaker than in the case of national legislation. So a true justification of the shift in the constitutional relationship between executive and parliament is rather to be sought in the fact of European Union membership as such (*i.e.*, that there is simply less national parliamentary legislative power as a consequence of European integration) than in the particular phase at which a parliament can have input in the legislative process.

It is worthwhile drawing attention to another aspect of this. When scrutiny is undertaken, this in a sense forces parliament into agreements in advance on the substance (and sometimes the negotiability) of an intended European Union decision. One effect of this is that parliament may thus limit its discretion in terms of political judgement when it comes to implementation of that decision. In a way, scrutiny brings parliament and government into a more monistic relationship: they do not stand in tension with one another, but in unison. At European level, this reinforces the articulation of coherent national positions and thus reinforces the position of member states. At national level, however, this may have a weakening effect on the position of parliaments *vis-à-vis* their governments. In turn, this weakened position may become a further justification of 'Henry VIII' clauses and the eclipse of parliamentary legislation. Hence, the constitutional principle of the primacy of parliamentary legislation at national level is eroded in the case of European Union decisions which require national legislation.

Of course, in parliamentary systems of government there may also be (more or less extensive) powers of executive law-making (or even some form of prerogative governmental powers to take decisions of general application) which governments can use without the explicit consent of parliament. This reflects a certain sphere of governmental activity which is fenced off from parliamentary interference, but is not free from a general political oversight by parliament, in that it could give rise to a loss of confidence which may threaten the functioning of government, and may force the government to resign. Here we have a practically dualist situation, with the ultimate power of censure at the background.

This contrasts with the situation of European Union decision-making and parliamentary prior scrutiny. As we concluded above, here the situation arrived at, precisely because of prior parliamentary scrutiny, is rather more monist than dualist. In this situation a power of censure is not, however, easily usable either with regard to European Union decision-making itself, or in relation to implementing decisions at national level. A minister is not easily compelled to resign because of the results of European Union decision-making. Nor would such resignations be very sensible in the context of implementing decisions at national level, when such implementing decisions are required to have a particular content anyway. In relation to European Union decision-making, such a resignation may lead to a different political point of view being expressed in the Council, but not necessarily to a different political majority in the Council. In the context of the implementation of decisions at national level, such a resignation might lead to a different political majority, but that majority would then have to attain the same result. In short, parliamentarism does not function in the manner it could in national contexts. It is rightly said that parliamentary systems – though their distinguishing character is the power to force governments or members thereof to resign – in practice *mainly* have the function of sustaining the government: in European Union affairs, one is tempted to say that in practice parliaments can *only* have that function.

4. Does a Role for National Parliaments Increase the Democratic Legitimacy of the European Union?

What has been said so far does not involve denying that national parliaments have a contribution to make to the democratic legitimacy of the European Union. First of all, scrutiny is an instrument which holds national representatives in European Union fora to account. It is an instrument of accountability even in the absence of effective parliamentary sanctions. Secondly, involvement of popular representation in European Union decision-making may increase, almost by definition, democratic legitimacy – at any rate as long as European Union decisions do not reach such levels of unpopularity and controversy that the impossibility of translating national legislative rejection into a veto (as is the case when it comes to majority voting at European level) leads to outright rejection at national level in terms of their acceptability. This situation thus marks the horizon of national parliaments' contribution to the democratic legitimacy of the European Union.[24] Here the European Parliament should ideally take over the legitimising role of the institutions of democratic representation. Its role has increased in the legislative domain of the European Community to the point where it is nearly equivalent to that of national legislatures. However, in terms of political control, its role is practically limited to the Commission. This is not a negligible role. It was seen in particular in the events of October 2004 concerning the investiture of the Barroso Commission that the Parliament can also restrain the ambitions of member state executives.[25] But it is limited. It is inconceivable that the European Parliament would hold the Council or European Council to account to the extent that it could censure

[24] A national parliament may make life more difficult for a Minister, but it will not easily force a Minister to resign over a position he has taken in the Council – if a national parliament has that power at all (The French *Assemblée*, for example, has this power *vis-à-vis* the government, but not as regards acts of the President in the Council in the composition of the Heads of State and Government or in the European Council, nor *vis-à-vis* individual ministers; the *Sénat* has no power of censure).

[25] See the series of contributions in "The Barroso Drama: Reality for the EU Constitution" (2005) 2 *European Constitutional Law Review* 153.

it or any of its members politically. The European Union will therefore never be a true parliamentary system.

5. Conclusion

Can the tide be turned, and the hypothesised monist tendencies (which in the context of European Union politics means a weakening of national parliaments) be countered, and the hypothesis falsified? There are possible ways in which parliaments could partially withdraw themselves from the solidifying tendencies indicated above, which reduce their critical role. This would actually also be how national parliaments could take advantage of the multi-layered nature of the European Union.

To do this, parliaments would have to hold their representatives to account not merely in terms of the negotiating inputs of their executives in the European Union decision-making process, or merely for their success as national representatives in the Council (or European Council). They should also hold them to account for the actual decisions taken by the Council. Ministers, when returning from Brussels to their capitals, stand in their parliaments not merely as ministers representing the national government, but also as representatives of the Council. Even if they voted against a certain decision, parliaments could hold them to account as representatives of the Council. Albeit in principle without sanction, this would create a forum of accountability for European Union decisions taken by the Council. This change in perspective would diminish the perceived necessity of homogeneity of parliament and executive, which could create the distance which is needed to retain room for criticism, a political space for deliberation and criticism which nestles the European Union in an established environment for political debate which somehow seems closer to citizens than 'Brussels' (let alone Strasbourg) seems to be.

Possibilities for such an increased critical distance were also to be found in the Protocol on the Application of the Principle of Subsidiarity and Proportionality which was annexed to the Constitutional Treaty. It is true that the mechanism devised in the Protocol, if it (or a similar mechanism in a successor treaty) ever comes into force, may foster competition between the European Parliament and national parliaments rather than legitimise the Commission or Council from the point of view of national parliaments and in democratic terms.[26] It is also true that ways already exist – at least for the

[26] Editor's note: see, concerning the most recent pre-publication developments concerning the fate of the Constitutional Treaty, the introduction to this book.

parliaments of some member states – in which views may be addressed to the institutions and actions may be brought before the Court of Justice.[27] But what is most important is the conception of national parliaments which the Protocol annexed to the Constitutional Treaty manifested. First, it made clear that national parliaments were not to address their views to their own government (and nor were their views to be transmitted by their government) but instead national parliaments were to address them directly to the European institutions.[28] Secondly, the jurisdiction of the European Court of Justice in relation to national parliaments was made explicit by Article 8 of the Protocol. A role remained for the member state, inasmuch as the first paragraph of Article 8 provided for actions for infringement of the principle of subsidiarity being brought by member states in accordance with Article III-365 of the Constitutional Treaty.[29] The very same paragraph of Article 8 immediately added, however, that the Court of Justice should also have jurisdiction in cases 'notified by [the member states] in accordance with their legal order on behalf of their national Parliament or a chamber of it'. The language was interesting, because it revealed that apart from the actions by member states under Article III-365, there was also to be a different action (although it was not called an action) which was that by a national parliament or a chamber of it. This was not an action by a member state (meaning, in effect, its government) but merely an action which was to be 'notified by' it.

The independent role envisaged for national parliaments was neatly brought out in the body of the Constitutional Treaty, by the Article I-11(3) provision that the institutions of the European Union were to apply

---

[27] Infringement on the part of one of the Community institutions of the time limits found in the existing (Amsterdam) Protocol on the Role of National Parliaments in the European Union could affect the validity of the European Community measures concerned. However, no national parliament has so far brought a complaint before the European Court of Justice because of such an infringement.

[28] See Art. 6, first paragraph, of the Protocol on the Application of the Principles of Subsidiarity and Proportionality.

[29] Art. III-365(1) provides for review by the Court of Justice of the European Union of the legality of European laws and other acts producing legal effects. Art. III-365(2) of the Constitutional Treaty provides that "or the purposes of para. 1, the Court of Justice of the European Union shall have jurisdiction in actions brought by a Member State, the European Parliament, the Council or the Commission on grounds of lack of competence, infringement of an essential procedural requirement, infringement of the Constitution or of any rule of law relating to its application, or misuse of powers".

the principle of subsidiarity, and the national parliaments to ensure their compliance with it.[30]

If provisions such as these ever come into force, either in the Constitutional Treaty or (as now seems more likely) in a successor treaty, then national parliaments will become true actors in their own right in the European Union, prised away from the grip of their governments in the particular context of European Union decision-making.

[30] Art. I-11(3), indent 2 provides that "the institutions of the Union shall apply the principle of subsidiarity as laid down in the Protocol on the application of the principles of subsidiarity and proportionality. National Parliaments shall ensure compliance with that principle in accordance with the procedure set out in that Protocol".

3.
National Parliaments in the Architecture of Europe After the Constitutional Treaty

Andreas Maurer[1]

It is conventional wisdom that, to an increasing extent, the importance of national parliaments has reduced as the political system of the European Union has evolved. By passing successive Treaty amendments and revisions, national parliaments are supposed to have accepted shifts of competences to the European level which reduce their final say over major areas of traditional legislative powers and their political control over governments.

The Convention on the Future of Europe (the body which produced the first draft of the Constitutional Treaty) brought about a debate on the optimal times and places for parliamentary involvement in European Union affairs. The major questions addressed by this chapter are those of why, and under which legal and political circumstances, political actors have argued for various forms of parliamentary participation in European Union policy-making. The paper starts with an analysis of how national parliaments participate in European Union policy-making. How have national parliaments acted in, reacted in, and adapted to a dynamic institutional and procedural set-up? How have parliamentary actors in different national and socio-political settings, and created by different national traditions, 'acclimatised' to common challenges, constraints and opportunities (for which they are mainly responsible themselves, having ratified the basic set-up of these institutional and procedural structures)?

[1] Head of Unit I – EU Integration, Stiftung Wissenschaft und Politik, German Institute for International and Security Affairs, Berlin; lecturer in the postgraduate programme in European Studies, Humboldt and Free University, Berlin. Editor's note: see, in relation to the most recent pre-publication developments concerning the fate of the Constitutional Treaty, the introduction to this book.

Given the growing prominence of the European Union system and its daily output of legally significant decisions of all kinds,[2] the extent of the participation and involvement of parliaments in it is an issue of vital importance insofar as concerns the overall importance and role of these parliaments. The way in which national parliaments are involved in European Union policy-making is a significant indicator of the fundamental choices the national systems and the European Union are making in their conduct of multi-level and multi-actor governance. It is of major importance to the legitimacy of the constitutional set-up of the European Union member states and of the Union itself. Any reform of the participation of national parliaments in European Community or European Union affairs will affect the capabilities of all political institutions at both national and European level to deal with the challenges of public policies. The form of institutional arrangements adopted will tell us something about the future shape of the European polity in the broader sense.

1. Accommodating Parliaments in a Multi-level Structure: the Analytical and Theoretical Framework

(a) The European Union's Problems with Regard to Parliamentary Democracy

The partial or complete transfer of national competences to the European Community and Union has involved an immediate loss of national parliaments' legislative powers in favour of the Council of Ministers, the European Commission and – to a lesser degree and at a later stage – in favour of the European Parliament. (Only after the introduction of the so-called co-operation procedure and the co-decision procedure did the European Parliament gain important rights in the field of European Community legislation. But even after Maastricht, Amsterdam and Nice, the transfer of national parliamentary powers to the European level did not entail a complete and direct transfer of original legislative powers to the European Parliament).

As regards policy-making at national level in European Community and European Union politics, this loss of legislative powers in the upstream process of European Union policy-making may be compensated for by an increase in the national parliaments' control function *vis-à-vis* their

[2] As indexed in the CELEX system. See further A. Maurer and W. Wessels "The EU matters: structuring self-made offers and demands" in W. Wessels, A. Maurer and J. Mittag (eds.). *Fifteen into one? The European Union and its member states* (Manchester University Press, Manchester, 2003), 43–44.

governments.[3] Since the decision by the German *Bundesrat* (the upper house of the German parliament) in 1957 to create a special European Community Affairs Committee,[4] national parliaments have established institutions and procedures to scrutinise their governments in the European Community and European Union decision-making process more effectively. Nevertheless, the degree, orientation, and depth of parliamentary involvement vary a lot. Different meanings are attributed to 'control', 'participation', and 'scrutiny', and parliamentary involvement ranges from simple *ex post facto* information rules to so-called parliamentary scrutiny reserves to mandatory procedures.[5] Although some parliaments are provided with large, indeed comprehensive quantities of European Union documents, they do not necessarily influence their governments' stance in the Council of Ministers. Clearly, the effectiveness of parliamentary impact on the formation and alteration of national views towards a given piece of European Union draft legislation does not depend solely on the quantity and type of documents provided, but also on the timing of intra-parliamentary proceedings, on institutional capacities, and on the personnel resources available to deliberate efficiently and effectively on a given document.

(b) The Constitutional Bases for Parliamentary Participation in European Union Integration

With the growth of, and increasing differentiation within the European Union system,[6] national parliaments experienced a loss in influence which could not simply be blamed on the 'Brussels bureaucracy' and could not be adequately made up for by the increase in influence of the European Parliament alone. By the end of 1980s, it became obvious that national parliaments' 'own' governments and administrations were using their links to European Union institutions with the effect, whether intended or otherwise, of reducing parliamentary powers and control. With a few exceptions like the Danish *Folketing*, national parliaments felt increasingly

[3] S. Schüttemeyer "Funktionsverluste des Bundestages durch die europäische Integration?" (1979) 2 *Zeitschrift für Parlamentsfragen* 261.

[4] The Bundesrat is the upper House of the German Parliament.

[5] See the contribution by A. Maurer and W. Wessels in A. Maurer and W. Wessels (eds.), *National Parliaments on their ways to Europe. Losers or Latecomers* (Nomos, Baden-Baden, 2001). For earlier findings, see G. Laprat, Gérard, "Parliamentary Scrutiny of Community Legislation: An Evolving Idea", in F. Laursen and S. Pappas (eds.), *The Changing Role of Parliaments in the European Union* (European Institute of Public Administration, Maastricht, 1995) at 4–10; P. Norton (ed.) "National Parliaments and the European Union" (1995) 3 *Journal of Legislative Studies* (Special Issue).

[6] As to which, see Maurer and Wessels, above, n. 5.

marginalised as 'slow adapters'.[7] The Maastricht Treaty's Declaration No. 13 on the Role of National Parliaments in the European Union generated some extra powers for national parliaments within the framework of their national constitutions.[8] Although the Declaration was of political significance only, it did contain some key indicators for measuring and comparing the participation of national parliaments in the European Union – *viz.* (a) the institutionalisation of parliamentary structures, instruments, and procedures for dealing with European Union policy-making at the national level; (b) the substantial scope of parliamentary control resulting from the extent of documents forwarded to parliaments by their governments; (c) the methods used by national parliaments with regard to the organisation of filtering documents within the parliamentary bodies; (d) the timing and management of parliamentary scrutiny; and (e) the potential and real impact of parliamentary scrutiny on the Government's room for manoeuvre within the European Union Council of Ministers.

Building on the experiences gained with the implementation of the Maastricht Treaty, the 1996/1997 intergovernmental conference which agreed the Amsterdam Treaty also agreed to the Protocol on the Role of National Parliaments in the European Union (henceforth 'PNP').[9] The PNP addressed the issues of the scope of information for parliaments, the timing of parliamentary scrutiny, and the institutional provisions for locking interparliamentary co-operation into the inter-institutional framework of the European Union. The PNP, which at present serves as the main European Union-wide legal basis for structuring national parliamentary involvement in EU affairs, provides the following:

First, national parliaments are to receive all pre-legislative Commission documents such as green and white papers or communications. These documents are to be forwarded promptly to national parliaments. However, the Protocol does not answer the question of whether it is the governments of the member states, the European Commission, or any other European institution which is to provide the parliaments with these documents. Instead, it simply stipulates that each Member State may ensure that its own parliament receives the proposals 'as appropriate'. Thus the PNP does not

---

[7] This term is explained in the text below.

[8] See the documentation reproduced by A. Krekelberg in Maurer and Wessels, above, n. 5, document no. 1.1.

[9] See the documentation reproduced by A. Krekelberg in Maurer and Wessels, above, n. 5, document No. 2. The Protocol was annexed to the Treaty on European Union and to the Treaties Establishing the European Communities.

oblige the governments to submit all legislative proposals to their parliaments. Secondly, the PNP implicitly excludes several types of documents from the general provision for the transmission of legislative proposals to national parliaments: all documents falling under the Second Pillar of Common Foreign and Security Policy (the 'CFSP'), all documents regarding entry into enhanced co-operation arrangements, all documents prepared by member states for the European Council, and all documents falling under the procedure under the Protocol integrating the Schengen acquis into the framework of the European Union.

The PNP also includes a commitment to inform parliaments about the European Union's rolling agenda. In the first place, the Commission is to ensure that any legislative proposal is 'made available in good time'. Secondly, a six-week period has to elapse between the issuing of 'a legislative proposal or a proposal for a measure to be adopted under Title VI of the Treaty on European Union' (which relates to police and judicial cooperation in criminal matters) and the date when it is put on the agenda for decision by the Council.[10] These two provisions are geared to allow governments to inform their parliaments about the proposal and leave time for discussion. However, the Protocol does not constrain governments to use the time provided by the European Union institutions for informing their parliaments. Thus, the PNP has provided a wide range of opportunities for parliaments and governments to negotiate on the content and the procedures to be applied for the implementation of the PNP.

Apart from its provisions on the improvement of unilateral parliamentary scrutiny mechanisms, the PNP also recognised the Conference of European Affairs Committees (COSAC) as a contributor to a more effective participation of national parliaments in European Community and European Union Affairs. The PNP specifies three areas in particular for deliberation within the COSAC framework. Hence COSAC:

> "may address to the European Parliament, the Council and the Commission any contribution which it deems appropriate on the legislative activities of the Union, notably in relation to the application of the principle of subsidiarity, the area of freedom, security and justice as well as questions regarding fundamental rights".[11]

---

[10] Meaning the decision either to adopt an act or to adopt a common position.

[11] The PNP specifically provides that COSAC may examine "any legislative proposal or initiative in relation to the establishment of an area of freedom, security and justice".

These provisions of the PNP lead directly to the question of whether COSAC may become the appropriate body for deliberation on these issues. The focus on the area of freedom, security and justice, and on fundamental rights policies has to be interpreted in the light of the European Union's para-constitutional development within the time-frame of the Amsterdam intergovernmental conference, and reflects the political and legal sensitivity of these issues in EU member states at the time of the negotiation of the Amsterdam Treaty. If one factors in the consultative role of the European Parliament in the relevant policy area, one can observe the introduction of a certain, ideal kind of three-level scrutiny mechanism here. On one level, the European Parliament is to monitor the European level of decision-making in the First and the Third Pillar. On a second level – provided that they organise their scrutiny mechanisms effectively – national parliaments may unilaterally monitor their governments on matters falling within these policy areas. On a third level, COSAC is enabled to deliberate upon these issues as an intermediary between the European Parliament and national parliaments.

There have been at least three shortcomings insofar as concerns the implementation of the PNP. First, the PNP did not improve the lack of parliamentary control with regard to the CFSP/European Security and Defence Policy pillar. The European Union's Foreign and Security policy was introduced as a *domaine réservé* of the Council and its administrative substructure. Democratic control of these policy fields was completely excluded. Secondly, neither the European Parliament, nor national parliaments, nor COSAC were either asked or allowed to monitor the process of transferring the 'Schengen *acquis*' into the European Community and the European Union. (Nor does the PNP allow national parliaments, the European Parliament or COSAC to participate in the new form of European Union governance, the so-called 'open method of co-ordination'). Thirdly, COSAC delegations have continued to be composed of national parliamentarians who are members of the national parliamentary committees responsible for handling European Community and European Union affairs rather than the committees on civil liberties, justice and/or home affairs. It is hardly conceivable that national parliamentarians who mainly deal with horizontal European Union issues would be those most suited to deliberate effectively on matters falling within, for example, the field of freedom, security, and justice.

(c) Diagnosis: National Parliamentary Participation Prior to the Convention

(i) Institutionalisation and Institutional Adaptation: The Creation of Committees

As regards institution-building within national parliaments for the purposes of digesting the outcome of Amsterdam, it can be seen clearly that the role of national parliaments has concentrated on 'one-level'-scrutiny and advice within a model framework of the government-legislature relationship.[12] The way in which this role has been exercised by national parliaments has depended on the constitutional and political context of the country involved. Parliaments have made some important changes to their procedures concerning the examination of EC/EU issues. Three major evolutions have occurred which are worth considering: (a) a greater specialisation of parliamentarians with regard to policy areas and functions of parliaments; (b) greater activity on the part of committees within the management of parliamentary business; and – as a result of the two aforementioned changes – (c) a higher rate of segmentation and fragmentation of parliamentary bodies and groups.

In some cases (those of Denmark, Sweden, Finland, Germany and Austria), European Union Committees perform as key interlocutors for government representatives in order to voice a more or less binding opinion on a given document. Moreover, several of these Committees (those in Denmark, Sweden, Finland and France) function as transmission belts between their parliaments and public opinion by organising hearings and by managing European Union-related internet pages. Finally, all European Union Committees of the European Union 'pre-enlargement fifteen' participate in COSAC as their main inter-parliamentary co-operation network. Thus it may be seen that there has been some convergence in organisational adaptation, *i.e.*, through the setting-up of specific bodies within parliaments which deal with the documentation arriving in from the policy processes of the European Community and the European Union.

The growing prominence of Community and Union affairs might lead one to expect that parliaments would adjust their existing resources accordingly. Thus, in institutional terms, one would expect that parliaments would alter the composition and the relative strength of their European Union Committees *vis-à-vis* other committees. However, Table 1 indicates the composition of European Union Committees has remained a rather stable share of the total membership of national parliaments

[12] See P. Norton (ed.) "National Parliaments and the European Union" (1995) 1 *Journal of Legislative Studies* (Special Issue). The two possible levels of scrutiny are the national level and the European level.

Table 1: Ratio of European Union Committee members in relation to the total strength of Parliament in percentage terms [13]

Member State	House	1987/88	1992/93	1995/96	1999/2001
Belgium	Chambre	9.43	9.43		
				15.79	13.57
	Senate		20.75		
Denmark	Folketing	9.71	9.71	9.71	9.50
Germany	Bundestag	2.5	6.45	7.44	5.9
	Bundesrat	37.77	31.88	33.33	33.33
Finland	Eduskunta	-	-	12.5	12.5
France	Assemblée	3.13	6.23	6.23	6.23
	Senate	5.60	11.24	11.24	11.24
Greece	Voulí	-	10.33	10.33	10.33
UK	Commons	2.46	2.46	2.46	2.43
	Lords	1.87	1.87	1.87	3.00
Italy	Camera	n.a.	8.1	7.94	7.62
	Senate	7.92	7.92	7.36	7.36
Ireland	Dáil				
	Senate	11.06	11.06	7.52	8.41
Luxembourg	Chambre	n.a.	18,33	18,33	18,33
Netherlands	Tweede Kamer	17.33	17.33	17.33	16.66
	Eerste Kamer	n.a.	n.a.	17.33	14.66
Austria	Nationalrat	-	-	14.75	15.85
	Bundesrat			11.48	25.0
Portugal	Assembleia	10,0	10,0	11,74	11,74
Sweden	Riksdag	-	-	4.87	4.87
Spain	Camera				
	Senate	n.a.	6.63	6.63	6.44

However, the information recorded in Table 1 does not permit one to conclude that parliaments are immune to the dynamics of European Union integration. European Union Committees can be seen as one specific

[13] The sources of information for this Table are A. Maurer, "National Parliaments in the European Architecture: From Latercomers' Adaptation towards Permanent Institutional Change?" in Maurer and Wessels, above, n. 5, at. 27–76; T. Raunio and M Wiberg, "Does Support Lead to Ignorance? National Parliaments and the Legitimacy of EU Governance" (2000) 2 *Acta Politica* 146; in addition to the internet sites of the Inter-Parliamentary Union and of national parliaments.

representation of institutional adjustment, but we should not confine our view to the development of such bodies and their membership. The creation of European Union Committees is only one specific way for parliaments to get involved through special institutional provisions.

Some national parliaments have become more active on European Union affairs. As the country studies in the volume edited by Maurer and Wessels[14] show, the EU Committee not only of the Danish *Folketing*, but also that of the French parliament, the German parliament, the Dutch Second Chamber, the Austrian *Nationalrat* and the Finnish *Eduskunta* have built upon their formal legal powers to veto governmental positions and developed their potential leverage regarding European Community and European Union affairs. They are not dependent merely on the filtered European Union information provided by their governments, but generate their own – additional – information about the European Union's daily business. Further, they are not confined merely to deliberating on incoming European Union draft legislation, but rather produce and pass resolutions, voice their opinion on given issues, and ask their governments to act in accordance with their opinions in the Council of Ministers.

(ii) The Scope of Information and the Sifting of Documentation

Information is the ultimate basis for participation in public policy-making. The scope of parliamentary participation in European Community and European Union affairs depends on the extent of the documentation forwarded to parliaments by their governments. The country reports in Maurer and Wessels explored the extent to which national parliaments receive draft proposals of European Community legislative acts and other European Union acts, *i.e.* white and green papers, recommendations, declarations, documents produced by COREPER, Council Working Groups, the European Parliament and its Committees, etc. The extent of information forwarded to national parliaments may be restricted according to national hierarchies of norms.[15] The French Constitution's concept of proposals containing provisions of a legislative nature implies that parliament has a right to receive only those draft acts, which, were they to be adopted in France, would constitute laws within the meaning of Article 34 of the French Constitution. Article 88-4 of the French Constitution leaves to the *Conseil d'État* and the Government the decision whether draft proposals constitute legislative acts.[16]

The supply of information is much more comprehensive in Denmark, Finland, Germany, the Netherlands, Austria, Sweden, and the United Kingdom. The

[14] Above, n. 5

[15] See the contribution by A. Szukala and O. Rosenberg in Maurer and Wessels, above, n. 5.

[16] See in more detail the chapter in this volume by David Siritzky.

parliaments of these states not only have access to the documentation provided by the European Commission, the Council, the European Parliament, and the other European Union institutions, but have succeeded in binding their governments to provide comprehensive explanatory information in order to facilitate the sifting of documents by MPs and committees. These focused government 'translations' of European Union information are of great political relevance, since they allow MPs not only to discuss the documents as such, but also their government's perspective on a given issue. Explanatory information has influenced national debates concerning the issue of competences (in Belgium, Germany and Austria), respect for the subsidiarity principle (in Denmark, Germany and France), the financial implications of a proposed act (in Germany, Denmark, the Netherlands, Sweden, Finland and the United Kingdom), the state of play regarding given policy issues as well as the (perceived) progress of negotiations (in Denmark, Germany, France, Sweden, and the United Kingdom).

As regards the initial phases of the European Union's policy cycle, parliaments and governments in Denmark, Germany, the United Kingdom, and the Netherlands fine-tuned the mechanisms for drafting short commentary sheets on incoming draft acts of the European Commission.

A continuing source of dissatisfaction for both the European Parliament and national parliaments was the fact that relatively new, post-Single European Act policy fields and new modes of governance[17] evade any parliamentary guidance or control.[18] Some of these fields have evolved recently, *i.e.*, foreign policy and common security, justice and home affairs, economic and monetary policy in the context of EMU, the Euro Group's policies within the framework of the Growth and Stability Pact and the so-called 'open method of co-ordination' (OMC) policies. In these areas, neither the Amsterdam nor the Nice Treaty reforms have made any progress towards inclusion of at least one level of parliamentary participation, whilst they have sanctioned particularly innovative

---

[17] As to which, see H. Wallace, "Analysing and Explaining Policies" in H. Wallace and W. Wallace (eds.), *Policy-Making in the European Union*, (fourth edition, Oxford University Press, Oxford, 2000), at 65–81; B. Kohler-Koch, "The Evolution and Transformation of European Governance" in B. Kohler-Koch and R. Eising (eds.), *The Transformation of Governance in the European Union* (Routledge, London and New York, 1999) at 14–35; W. Wessels, Wolfgang and I. Linsenmann, "EMU's Impact on National Institutions: Fusion Towards a gouvernance économique or Fragmentation?" in K. Dyson (ed.), *European States and the Euro: Europeanization, Variation, and Convergence* (Oxford University Press, Oxford, 2002).

[18] See here the European Commission's *White Paper on European Governance* (COM(2001) 428, 27 July, 2001) at 21–22.

decisions, in strictly intergovernmental form (such as those concerning the introduction of a political and military structure for common crisis reaction forces or the setting up of new intergovernmental committees in the fields of EMU and employment). New modes of governance have thus created new democratic deficits on both European and national levels. The recent tendency to replace the 'Community method' became obvious with the heads of state and governments' decisions on the European Security and Defence Policy, on the Lisbon process, and on the G-5 initiatives in the field of police cooperation, where the intergovernmental dimension in steering the Union had been strengthened, as expressed most clearly in the emphasis given to the role of the European Council. The serious limits, as regards both transparency, 'traceability', and 'monitorability', of the Council's activities, were merely touched upon in a few provisions of the Amsterdam Treaty.[19]

The scope of information in these areas has been and remains particularly low in the southern European parliaments (Greece, Spain, Portugal) and in Ireland. The parliaments of France and the United Kingdom have had to fight for the application of existing information routines in the European Community area to the intergovernmental policy areas. Comparing their relative positioning in 1991–1992 and 1997–1999, both parliaments developed from being 'weak adapters' to being 'national players'.

While conquering ground in the classic areas of European Community policy-making, national parliaments have lost influence in other 'vital' policy areas. Even after the Treaties of Amsterdam and Nice, parliamentary involvement in the Common Foreign and Security Policy and in the field of Police and Judicial Co-operation in Criminal Matters depends on the willingness of governments to keep their legislatures informed of intergovernmental events. It is not unusual for parliaments to be made aware of international agreements only at the time of their presentation to the legislature for ratification. As both areas feature co-operation that remains officially outside the European Community arena, the traditional domestic scrutiny procedures for Community legislation do not automatically apply. Information remains a vital tool for processes of scrutiny and accountability, and parliaments depend heavily on executives and/or interest groups for this key resource.

---

[19] See A. Maurer, Parlamentarische Demokratie in der Europäischen Union. Der Beitrag des Europäischen Parlaments und der nationalen Parlamente (Nomos, Baden-Baden, 2002) at 345–361.

Table 2: Evolution of Supplementary Information Practices from 1992–2003

	1992/1993		1997/1999	2003		
	Initial	**Continuous**	**Initial**	**Continuous**	**Initial**	**Continuous**
B	0	0	2	Unchanged	2	1
DK	2	3	Unchanged	Unchanged	Unchanged	Unchanged
D	2	3	Unchanged	Unchanged	Unchanged	Unchanged
E	0	1	2	Unchanged	2	1
F	1	0	3	3	3	3
GR	0	0	Unchanged	Unchanged	1	Unchanged
I	1	1	Unchanged	Unchanged	1	Unchanged
IRL	1	0	2	Unchanged	2	Unchanged
LUX	0	On demand	2	Unchanged	2	Unchanged
NL	3	2	Unchanged	Unchanged	Unchanged	Unchanged
A	n.a.	n.a.	2	2	3	3
P	0	0	Unchanged	Unchanged	1	Unchanged
S	n.a.	n.a.	2	1	3	2
SF	n.a.	n.a.	3	3	Unchanged	Unchanged
UK	3	2	Unchanged	3	Unchanged	Unchanged

Legend for the initial phases of the European Union's policy cycles ('Initial'): 0 = no supplementary information; 1 = some supplementary information (such as summaries of the draft); 2 = document summaries, agendas and minutes of Council of Ministers; 3 = substantial supplementary information like financial forecasts, analyses on constitutional implications, subsidiarity/environmental impact assessment/social affairs forecast sheets etc.

Legend for the decision-making phase of the European Union's policy cycles: ('Continuous'): 0 = no information at all; 1 = short-hand information about the envisaged dates of the decision-making process; 2 = commented information about the stance of other European Union actors in the decision-making process; 3 = complete and timely information about each stage in the decision-making process; On demand = new information on the decision-making process is available only on specific demand by an MP or by committees.

(iii) Timing and Management

Parliamentary involvement in European Union affairs is a product of efficient procedures. Parliaments are confronted with the growing diversity of inter-institutional deliberation and decision-making processes at the Brussels/Strasbourg level of the Council and the European Parliament. A closer look at the constitutive treaties of the European Community and of the European Union reveals a clear trend towards procedural ambiguity over time.[20] What is meant by this is that Treaty amendments have led to differentiation in the procedures used for decision-making with a variety of possibilities existing regarding which rules will apply. As a result, Treaty provisions do not dictate clear categorisations of rules to be applied to specific sectors. Instead, member states and supranational institutions can, in an increasing number of policy fields, select whether a given piece of secondary legislation – be it a regulation, a directive or another type of legal act – should be decided upon (a) by unanimity or by qualified majority in the Council; (b) according to the consultation, cooperation or (since Maastricht) the co-decision procedure; (c) with or without participation by the European Parliament; and (d) with or without consultation with the Economic and Social Committee, the Committee of the Regions, or similar institutions. In other words, different procedural blueprints and inter-institutional codes compete for application and raise the potential for conflict between the actors involved.[21]

From a national government's perspective, this growing variety of institutions and procedures means a mixed set of opportunity structures and '*engrenage*-like'[22] networking systems for access to, and participation in the policy-making cycle of the Community and of the Union.[23] National

[20] See Maurer and Wessels, above, n. 5.

[21] See for a detailed analysis Maurer and Wessels, above, n. 5.

[22] See C. Sasse, E. Poullet, D. Coombes and G. Deprez, *Decision-Making in the European Community* (Praeger, New York/London, 1977). See also the contribution by A. Maurer in Maurer and Wessels, above, n. 5. *Engrenage* is a term which was introduced with the so-called Monnet method. Abélès has defined *engrenage* as 'an action trap in which agents, once set in a specific course of action, find themselves obliged to take a set of further actions that point them in a direction in which they did not necessarily intend to go'. *Engrenage* thus refers to the thickening of interactions between national structures and the institutional apparatus of the European Union. See M. Abélès, *Identity and Borders: An Anthropological Approach to EU Institutions, Twenty-First Century Papers* (On-line Working Papers from the Center for 21st Century Studies, University of Wisconsin – Milwaukee, Number 4, December 2004, available at the time of writing at www.uwm.edu/Dept/21st/workingpapers/abeles.pdf), at 4.

[23] See P. van der Knaap, "Government by Committee: Legal Typology, Quantitative Assessment and Institutional Repercussions of Committees in the European Union" in R. Pedler and G. Schäfer (eds.), *Shaping European Law and Policy: The Role of Committees and Comitology in the Political Process* (EIPA, Maastricht, 1996) at 83–116. The Council itself has noted that some two thirds of its rolling agenda is dealt with by COREPER, 70% of this being agreed upon at Working Group level. See Council of the European Community, *Der Rat der EG* (Official Publications Office, Luxembourg, 1990) at 22. See also W. Wessels, Die *Öffnung des Staates* (Leske and Budrich, Opladen, 2000) at 228–229.

parliaments are thus confronted with an ever-growing realm of policy-making infrastructures, which are less open to parliamentary oversight than bodies bringing together politicians. Unlike the component units of the Council (governmental administrations and services, and the Council Secretariat), national parliaments have to employ a more limited set of resources according to the variety of institutional-procedural codes. Some member states facilitate the management of parliamentary European Union business, because the efficient sift of EC/EU draft legislation is in their own interest: Given that ministers are bound by decisions of their Parliament in Denmark, the Netherlands, Austria, Germany and Finland, the respective governments must forward the relevant documents within a certain period of time, which allows parliamentarians to examine them before the meeting of the Council of Ministers.

About half of the fifteen pre-2004 enlargement member state parliaments are able to run with their governments in EC/EU affairs effectively. Theoretically, parliaments could manage the problem of timely information by relying on the sources of documentation which are open to every citizen in the Union. Commission initiatives and European Parliament draft reports are available on the internet the day after their adoption. However, parliaments usually seek to get relevant information officially, *i.e.,* translated into their official language, stamped by their governmental service, etc. In this regard, parliaments hamper themselves (although their reasons for doing so are understandable). Because their constitutional role is that of acting on behalf of their electorates either in cooperation with, or *vis-à-vis*,a constitutionally-delimited set of institutions, their deliberations tend only to start when information is 'officialised' in the national context – in other words, when it is officially transmitted to them by the government.

(iv) The Meaning and Socio-Political Orientation of 'Scrutiny'

In dealing with European Community and European Union affairs, parliaments are confronted with an issue which they must resolve for themselves in one of two ways. This may be explained as follows. In order to facilitate the digestion of incoming draft acts of the Community or of the Union, national parliaments have created specific bodies, which are entitled to sift documents, to prepare reports, and to draft resolutions for plenary meetings. But the way in which such parliamentary committees work varies, not only by reference to the volume of documents which has to be dealt with, but also depending on the general orientation of the committees' work and on the respective focus of committee and plenary meeting. Hence, whereas European Union Committees in Denmark, Finland, Austria, and the United Kingdom House of Commons deal with incoming Community and European Union documentation as *the* committee in charge of the whole scrutiny process, other European Union Committees (those in Germany, the Netherlands, Sweden and Italy) are simply regarded as the first – sifting – institution within parliament in order to facilitate the further consideration of the relevant documents within specialised standing committees. European Union Committees in the latter countries specialise themselves on some European issues like intergovernmental conferences, enlargement and other – horizontal – themes of the European Union's long-term agenda, whereas the first group of European Union Committees-in-charge need to digest each incoming European Union dossier on behalf of their parliament. These European Union Committees need much more time to deliberate European Union issues. Necessarily, they meet more frequently than European Union Committees of the second kind.

The basic orientation of parliaments in European Union affairs also differs with regard to the nature of the scrutiny process. Hence, the parliaments of Denmark, Austria, Sweden, and France focus their European Union-related activity on the formulation and issuing of voting instructions for their respective government members of the Council of Ministers. These parliaments build on an ideal of a bipolar legislature-government scenario. Other parliaments follow a more open and consensual approach (as in the Netherlands, Germany, Finland), or a more supportive one (as in Ireland, Italy, Belgium, Luxembourg, Portugal, Spain, and Greece) *vis-à-vis* their governments. The main rationale of scrutiny in these parliaments is to ensure that interested parliamentarians can track the European Union policy cycles according to the constitutional rules.

Finally, the approach taken to the different stages in the European Union policy-making cycle also generates different time constraints for parliamentarians and their European Union Committees. If parliaments anticipate legislation at Community or European Union level, their scrutiny process starts earlier and the involved committees meet more frequently. If parliaments adopt a more reactive stand by focusing on European Union legislation which has already been adopted, their timing and management of the European Union scrutiny process is less intensive and less frequently exercised.

European Union Committees also face the problem of remaining locked in the national organisation of parliamentary business. This problem with the 'one-level-only' approach[24] manifests itself in the fact that the handling of European

---

[24] By which is meant the approach of focusing on politics solely at the national level rather than at European level as well.

Union affairs certainly does not influence the rolling agenda of national parliaments. And in contrast with government ministers, parliamentarians need to allot their capacities to pursue several agendas. Members of European Union committees do not get re-elected by focusing their campaign on their handling of European Union affairs. In addition, and partly from the same reason, parliaments' agendas remain oriented towards national debates. With few exceptions,[25] European Union committees remain 'outsiders' in their parliaments, and are perceived as 'European Union-ised Trojan horses', which challenge the competences and, more importantly, the reputation of other committees.

Table 3: Basic Orientation of Parliamentary Scrutiny in European Community and European Union Affairs [26]

(1) Parliament's Working style	(2) Nature of Scrutiny processes			(3) Consideration of phases in European Union policy cycles		
	Orientation towards supportive Scrutiny		Orientation towards formulating and/or voting instructions	Anticipative, ex-ante examination of EC/EU draft legislation		Reactive, ex-post consideration of EC/EU legislation
Main Focus on European Union Committee	Fin, Irl		Dk, A	Dk, Fin, A, UK	Irl	
		F, UK				
Strong Involvement of Specialised Standing Committees	D, Nl, Fin, I		S	D, F, NL, S		I
Focus on Plenary sessions	B, Gr, Lux, P, E			B, Lux	P, E	Gr

(v) Influence and Impact: Parliaments as 'Supportive Scrutinisers'

The impact of parliamentary scrutiny differs between those parliaments which are legally able to mandate their government's representative before a

[25] See the contributions by F. Laursen on the Danish Parliament and by T. Raunio on the Finnish Parliament in Maurer and Wessels, above, n. 5.

[26] The classification in this Table is the author's own. The sources of information relied upon are the country studies in Maurer and Wessels, above, n. 5; Maurer, above, n. 19; and Raunio and Wiberg, above, n. 13.

Council decision takes place (which is the case in Denmark, in the German *Bundesrat*, in the Netherlands *Tweede Kamer* insofar as cooperation in the Third Pillar is concerned, in the Austrian *Nationalrat*, and in Finland) and parliaments which simply do not have any means for effectively influencing their government's standpoint in the Council of Ministers (which is the case in Greece, Italy, Ireland, and Portugal). It should be noted in this context that the legal position may differ from that in practice. Whereas the Danish, Finnish, and Dutch parliamentarians make use of the possibility of formulating mandates (or of assenting to draft mandates for) for their governments, their counterparts in Germany and Austria engage in this practice less frequently. Other parliaments (*viz.*, those of France, Luxembourg, Belgium, Spain, and the United Kingdom) are able to express their views on particular proposals, but their governments decide whether to integrate those views in their position or not.

A tendency can be observed on the part of some parliaments to help their governments' position in the Council by imposing a so-called parliamentary scrutiny reserve. Scrutiny reserve mechanisms apply to all three Pillars of the Union in Denmark, Austria, France, and the United Kingdom, and, in the Netherlands, to the Third Pillar only. Parliamentary scrutiny reserves, however, are an ambiguous instrument for influencing governments. If a government is politically dependent on day-to-day support from parliament, scrutiny reserve mechanisms may well be a device which help to keep the Government 'onside' with its parliamentarians. However, Montesquieu's separation of powers is only a model. Apart from the case of Denmark, governments are not systematically controlled by their parliament. Hence, use may be made of scrutiny reserves by governments in order to provide a scapegoat for their deployment of a veto in the Council of Ministers. As one House of Commons official has observed:

> "from a tactical viewpoint, it can be useful to Ministers to be able to go into Council in the knowledge that Parliament has approved the stance they wish to take – or even to be able to say, 'Parliament would not tolerate my agreeing to this'".[27]

It is worth noting, in this context, that parliamentary scrutiny reserves take the form of requests rather than of legally binding commands. Such a request:

---

[27] E. Flood, "Interaction between the Government and Parliament in the Scrutiny of EU Decision-Making", in Finnish Parliament/COSAC Presidency (eds.), "National Parliaments and the EU: Stock-taking for the Post-Amsterdam Era" (2000) 1 *Eduskunnan Kanslian Julkaisu* 63.

> "is not a mandate. If the Government agrees, the resolution may be a trump for it in European negotiations. If it disagrees, the Government is not bound by the resolution".[28]

A scrutiny reserve mechanism also works as a sword of Damocles in parliament-government relations, remaining unused as long as the relations between a government and the government majority in parliament work well, but nonetheless strengthening the parliament's potential in worst-case-scenarios of conflict between legislature and executive (*i.e.,* where even the government's majority in parliament opposes a governmental viewpoint). However, the logic underlying a reserve mechanism is a parliament which acts as a 'supportive scrutiniser'[29] of, rather than a systematic opponent of its government.

The protagonists of a strengthened role of national parliaments in European Union affairs favour the wider use of the so-called 'Danish model' of parliamentary oversight. The Danish model consists in the decisive – although not formal – power of the European Affairs Committee of the *Folketing*. This committee gives the Government a mandate before important decisions are taken by the Council of Ministers. The Danish model can be explained:

> "by the presence of minority governments which has made it imperative to current governments to inform and to take the opinion of the committee into careful consideration".[30]

Besides this factor, the small size and the unicameral nature of the Danish parliament must be taken into consideration to understand why this model works rather well despite the complex and cumbersome European Union decision-making process which normally discourages any regular exercise of mandate control by parliaments on national governments. Finally, both the Danish party system and public opinion provide a sufficient 'critical mass' for the Government to respect the *Folketing*'s views. The Danish system of parliamentary control has made Denmark good at implementing European

---

[28] L. Dubois "The European Union: An Opportunity for the French Parliament to Recover Powers?" in E. Smith, *National Parliaments as Cornerstones of European Integration* (Kluwer Law International, The Hague and London, 1996) at 60.

[29] See the contribution by S. Hölscheidt in Maurer and Wessels, above, n. 5.

[30] N. Sidenius, B. Einersen and J. Sorensen, "The European Affairs Committee and Danish European Union Politics", in M. Wiberg (ed.), *Trying to Make Democracy Work: The Nordic Parliaments and the European Union* (Gidlunds, Stockholm, 1997) at 27.

Union legislation. And the mandate-giving part of the process ensures that post-decision political problems can usually be avoided even under minority governments. But is it possible to export this 'success story' of parliamentary oversight into other national systems? The essential framing factors – minority governments, Eurosceptical parties and the *Folketing* as a Parliament which can perform as a single actor either with or against the government – would be difficult to find in any other member state. In sum, the Danish case remains a unique archetype of a parliament in a suitable position to form its own political views about the daily issues of European Union business in an effective manner.[31]

2. An Analysis: The One-Level-Only Problem of National Parliamentarians

(a) Strong Policy-Making Parliaments vs Parliaments with Modest Policy-Making Power

One model of classifying national parliaments derives from early studies by Mezey[32] subsequently modified by Norton.[33] Both authors developed frameworks for classifying legislatures in various countries. They are based on two basic indicators: the *policy-making strength* of the legislature and the *support for the legislature*. Only the first of these is relevant in the present context.[34] Mezey defined policy-making strength as 'the constraint that the legislature is capable of placing on the policy-making activities of the executive'.[35] Mezey distinguished between three categories of parliaments:

- parliaments possessing strong policy-making power based on the power to veto policy proposals and on the possibility of making modifications or finding compromises in the course of the policy process;

[31] The parliaments of Finland, Austria and Sweden have followed the same path, although their scrutiny systems are less binding on their governments. See generally regarding the parliaments of Denmark, Sweden, Finland, and Norway, the chapter in this volume by Matti Wiberg and Tapio Raunio.

[32] See M. Mezey, *Comparative Legislatures* (Duke University Press, Durham, North Carolina, 1979) at 21–44.

[33] See P. Norton, "Parliament and Policy in Britain: The House of Commons as a Policy Influencer" (1984) 2 *Teaching Politics* 198.

[34] As this chapter is concerned only with the role parliaments play in the European decision-making process, it is not proposed to deal with Mezey's second criterion, which relates to the general profile of legislatures.

[35] M. Mezey, "Classifying Legislatures", in *Comparative Legislatures*, above, n. 32.

- parliaments with modest policy-making power characterised by the right to modify (but not to reject) policy proposals; and
- parliaments having little or no policy-making power and thus being unable either to modify or reject proposals issued by the executive.

Norton's work concentrated on the first two categories. He underlined the fact that having a right to *reject* policy proposals does not automatically entail parliament having a real, *i.e.* proactive policy-making power.[36] Accordingly, the category of parliaments possessing strong policy-making power should encompass 'policy-making' legislatures which can modify or reject policy proposals *or substitute policies of their own*, while the category of parliaments with modest policy-making power should only include 'policy-influencing' legislatures with the power to modify and to *reject* but not to *substitute* policy proposals.[37] The difference between these two categories lies in the qualification of parliaments as legislative bodies which are able to generate their own sets of proposals which may substitute for the original government position.[38]

(b) A Further Categorisation of Parliaments and Parliamentarians: Multi-Level Players, European Players, National Players, and Slow Adaptors

A further form of classification of parliaments and parliamentarians may by helpful.[39] Such actors (represented in Figure 1) have been classified elsewhere by this writer as 'multi-level players', 'European players', 'national players', and 'slow adaptors'.[40]

36 Mezey has criticised the notion of "parliaments possessing the power to reject but not to modify". For him, it is "inconceivable that a legislature could have the power to reject proposed legislation but not have the power to modify it". (See Mezey, above, n. 32, at 43, footnote 1).

37 P. Norton, "Introduction" in P. Norton (ed.), *Parliaments in Western Europe* (Frank Cass, London, 1990) at 5, and Norton, above, n. 33 at 201.

38 In the context of European legislation, the question should be whether national parliaments are able to substitute their policy for the original proposals of the government on the so-called 'common positions' of the Council of Ministers.

39 Even if the four archetypes proposed are in some ways, ideals or heuristic models.

40 These categorisations were first defined in the writer's contribution to Maurer and Wessels, above, n. 5. They bear some relation to formal provisions to be found in national constitutions and in the Treaties. However, beyond this 'legal constitution', the question of how actors use the European Union's 'opportunity structures', developing additional or even competing channels of influence to those set out in the law need to be explored.

Figure 1: Categorisations of actors in a two-level model

	Participation in the National Arena		
Participation in the Brussels / Strasbourg Arena		Strong ⇒ ⇒ ⇒ ⇒ ⇒ ⇒ ⇒ ⇒ Weak	
	Strong ⇑ ⇑ ⇑ ⇑ ⇑ ⇑ Weak	Multi-level players Dk, Fin	European players European Parliament
		S, D, B, UK, F	
		National players A, NL	Slow adapters Irl, Lux, I, E, P, Gr

'Multi-level players' (square 1) are taken as the best performing actors, since they are able to work both at European Union and at member state level. Because such actors take the logic of multi-level governance seriously, they allot both personnel and financial resources to different levels and loci of interaction (such as the Council's Working groups, COREPER *etc.*). In addition, multi-level players adapt to the evolution of the European Union with effective reorientations of policy instruments and resources. Multi-level players are able to use their access to one level of governance to increase their influence on the other level, with their investments or personnel and financial resources thus permitting the creation a virtuous circle of involvement.

'European players' (square 2) can be defined as bodies which are primarily located in and focused on the Brussels/Strasbourg arenas. Given their rather low rate of direct access to the national arenas of European Union governance, they are not as competitive as the 'multi-level players'. They adapt to the EU's system by revising and focusing their instruments *vis-à-vis* the other EU actors at this level without explicitly considering the roles of national or sub-national actors. Thus, to take the European Parliament, we must acknowledge that the potential realm of its activity is restricted: as a 'European player', the European Parliament's parliamentary groups, committees and its plenary session all meet in the Brussels/Strasbourg arena. Unlike the members of the Council, MEPs are not called to permanently reorient from one context to another. Whether they perform as 'constituency-representatives' at home, as 'co-legislators' in the conciliation committee of the co-decision procedure, or as 'international communicators' within one of the European Parliament's interparliamentary delegations, their role-attribution remains the same: They represent the aggregated interests of the peoples of the European Union.

A 'national player' (square 3) is a body with efficient and effective means to give voice to its interests within the relevant national arenas. Its endeavours are focused on the national level with the possibility of shifting or pooling the existing resources in relation to the EU level not being considered. In the European Union policy-making cycle, these actors are present during the preparation and implementation phases, but not in the crucial arenas of European Union joint decision-making. In this regard, the role of national parliamentarians seems to be similar to that of MEPs: they are elected in one context (here, the national one). Re-election is a question of success or failure at one level of policy-making (again, here, the national one). Like the European Parliament – and unlike the members of the Council's structure – their main locus of interaction and focus of attention is 'one-dimensional'.

The 'slow adapter' (square 4) has the same (*i.e.,* national) orientation as the national player. But it differs from the national player in that the (national) adaptation to new European Union contexts remains low. This actor is not capable of maintaining the *status quo ante* in relation to its prerogatives at domestic level, insofar as this national level is now linked to the European Union level. Thus, in a vicious cycle, the losers of multi-level games suffer from a continuous fall in their influence. Their low investment in resources leads to a decreasing rate of participation.

(c) Applying the Proposed Models and Categorisations

Parliaments such as the Danish *Folketing*, and those of Finland, Austria, and Sweden, which have followed a similar path to scrutiny (even if their scrutiny systems are less binding on their governments than that of Denmark), certainly meet at least Mezey's (although not Norton's) criteria for strong policy-making in European issues and, at least according to Mezey's definition, fulfil the criteria for strong policy-making in European issues and are thus 'national players'. Their performance is based in some measure on the power to veto, as well as on the possibility of modifying positions and of directing compromises in the course of the national policy process. The policy-forming strength of the parliaments of Germany and the Netherlands in Community and European Union matters is similar to that of this group. However, the consensual policy-making style and the continuing pro-European consensus among the political parties in these countries prevents parliamentarians from engaging in systematic confrontation with their governments. Thus they perform as potential or latent 'national players'. The French and the United Kingdom parliaments are both cases of modest policy-making legislatures who wish to play the role of 'national players'. Both parliaments are able to comment on incoming Community and European Union information and to voice their opinions via reports, resolutions, and so-called parliamentary scrutiny reserves.

But they are not able to change in an effective manner a proposed governmental reaction to a Community or EU proposal. The remaining parliaments in the pre-enlargement fifteen (Ireland, Belgium, Luxembourg, Italy, Spain, Portugal, and Greece) should be categorised as 'slow adapting' parliaments, which are not willing or able to affect their government's stance in European Union negotiations.

This performance highlights that the majority of MPs have not become strong multi-level players. In comparison with national governments and administrations, and with intermediary bodies such as lobbies and NGOs, parliamentarians are less competitive, especially in situations where participation in the policy-making cycle in Community and Union affairs at both levels is of a major importance. In this sense, those national parliaments which are slow adapters and reluctant multi-level players are still 'losers' in the evolution of the European Union system. The late efforts which many of them made in the 1990s have not led to a fundamental upgrade of their relative role *vis-à-vis* their governments.

The performance of the 'slow adapters' and 'reluctant multi-level players' requires explanation.[41] A good place to start is with the role normally attributed to national parliaments as major *actors*.[42] The demand for participation of 'parliament' as such presupposes that a parliament is more than an arena, but rather is an autonomous institution in its own right. However within the European Union's parliamentary democracies, most national legislatures are clearly divided into factions of majority and opposition, and the dominating cleavage between the pro-government and the anti-government groups also determines behaviour towards European Union issues.[43] Thus the parliamentary majority feels represented by the Government of the day – not by a few of their members in COSAC, or even by some of their party members in the European Parliament. Parliamentary scrutiny in this situation consists of participation and of involvement without developing a systematic anti-governmental stance. In consensual democracies, opposition parties and their parliamentary groups will follow the Government's politics as 'supportive scrutinisers' to an even greater extent.[44] This role applies both to the typical

[41] Leaving aside the paradox involved in, on the one hand, the self-inflicted losses of power experienced by parliaments and the demands for parliamentary involvement in policy-making in European matters on the other.

[42] See the contribution by A. Maurer in Maurer and Wessels, above, n. 5.

[43] See A. Lijphart, *Patterns of Democracy. Government Forms and Performance in Thirty-Six Countries* (Yale University Press, New Haven and London, 1999) pp. 62–89.

[44] See in this regard the analysis by B. Hoetjes on the Dutch system and S. Hölscheidt on the German system in Maurer and Wessels, above, n. 5.

parliamentary systems in most of the European Union countries as well as to the semi-presidential system of France. The 'classic' parliament-versus-government style of scrutiny applies only in the United Kingdom majoritarian system and the Danish parliamentary system, the hallmark of which is minority governments.

If we take seriously the 'real' way in which parliaments have evolved over the last two centuries, then it will be seen that the slow and weak adaptation of national parliaments in Community and European Union affairs is not just the product of benign neglect of governments or mismanagement of the MPs involved. It is the unavoidable consequence of fundamental trends in our parliamentary systems. This point is a different one to the one made earlier on the non-intervention of parliaments in external affairs. It is not part of a state-centric view but follows the logic of party government.

Table 4: Categorisations of real national parliamentary participation in European Union affairs

	1. Scope of Information			**2. Start of parliamentary scrutiny**		
	ECT	**TEU: CFSP and HJA**	**European Union information dependent on government's policy**	**After Commission's initiative**	**After common position of the Council decision**	**During all stages of European Union making**
D	C	C	Very low	✓	✓	✓
F	C	R	High	✓*	✓*	
I	R	R	High	✓	-	-
NL	C	R	Low	✓	✓	-
B	C	R	Low	✓*	-	-
Lux	R	R	High	✓*	-	-
GB	C	R	Low	✓*	✓*	✓*
Dk	C	C	Very low	✓	✓	✓
Irl	R	R	High	-	✓*	-
E	R	R	Very high	✓	-	-
P	R	R	Very high	✓	-	-
Gr	R	R	Very high	-	-	-
A	C	C	Very low	✓	✓	✓
S	C	C	Very low	✓	✓	✓
Fin	C	C	Very low	✓	✓	✓

	3. Frequency of Committee meetings	4. Organisation and Management of intraparliamentary European Union proceedings	5. Impact of Scrutiny on government's room of manoeuvre Low	Veto or Delaying	Very high: Co-Participation
D	High	Reactive	-	✓	✓
F	High	Proactive	-	✓	-
I	Low	Reactive	✓	-	-
NL	High	Reactive	-	✓	-
B	Low	Reactive	✓	-	-
LUX	Low	Reactive	✓	-	-
GB	High	Reactive	-	✓	-
DK	High	Reactive	-	-	✓
IRL	Low	Reactive	✓	-	-
E	Low	Reactive	✓	-	-
P	Low	Reactive	✓	-	-
GR	Low	Reactive	✓	-	-
A	High	Proactive	-	✓	✓
S	High	Proactive	-	✓	✓
SF	High	Proactive	-	✓	✓

Legend: C = Comprehensive; R = Restricted; • =Applies; •*=Parliament reports frequent failure on part of government to transmit documents in timely manner.

The matter may be looked at from another direction, however (and in the light of the post-Nice and Convention debates on the future of the Union). Given the increased importance of Community and European Union affairs, stronger participation and direct participation on the part of national parliaments at European Union level would affect the basic way national governments and parliaments functioned in general. Stronger – more direct and less delegated – involvement of parliaments would thus erode traditional patterns of policy-making in our polities, for better or for worse.

The more a national system belongs to the category of system which involves close unity between a majority party and government, the less the extent to which its parliament is directly and independently engaged either on the European Union or on the national level. The fact that many parliaments may be categorised as 'slow adapters' or 'weak performers' is something which depends on the roles which national systems implicitly attribute to their parliaments.

On the other hand, the evolution of parliaments which are 'multi-level players' seems to depend to a greater extent on government-parliament relationships. Hence, both parliaments which can be described as 'slow adapters' and parliaments which can be termed 'national players' invest time and personnel in the various inter-parliamentary cooperation regimes which are offered and managed by the European Parliament. The difference here is the formality of the regimes being invested in. The French parliament could be classified as *the* protagonist of cooperation mechanisms being more institutionalised. The reason for this is to be found in the French political system and the rather weak role accorded to parliament in both national and European policy-making. 'Playing the multi-level game', from a French parliamentary perspective, compensates for links which are missing in the national system. A second fundamental reason for becoming an efficient multi-level player is based on the European Union's own dynamics. Institutional and procedural differentiation, and the continuous trend towards the institutional amalgamation of public policy instruments and actors[45] at the European, national, and sub-national levels of governance push each actor to generate effective and efficient means for participation and influence. Unless national parliaments turn into efficient multi-level players, they remain structurally handicapped from becoming competitive.

3. National Parliaments and the Convention on the Future of Europe

The role of national parliaments in European integration was one which became a central issue for the Convention on the Future of Europe, the body which produced the initial draft of the Constitutional Treaty. Previously, the 2000 Nice intergovernmental conference, in its Declaration on the Future of the Union,[46] had stated that this was one of the four topics to be placed at the centre of a rather vast and ambiguous debate, which was destined to result in

[45] On the concept of the amalgamation of public policy instruments see K. Deutsch *et al.*, *Political Community and the North Atlantic Area; International Organization in the Light of Historical Experience* (Greenwood Press, New York, 1957); L. Lindberg and S. Scheingold (eds.), *Regional Integration: Theory and Research* (Harvard University Press, Cambridge, Mass., 1971); L. Lindberg and S. Scheingold, *Europe's Would-Be Polity: Patterns of Change in the European Community* (Prentice-Hall, Englewood Cliffs, N.J., 1970); W. Wessels, "Comitology: fusion in action. Politico-administrative trends in the EU system" (1998) 5 *Journal of European Public Policy* 209; and W. Wessels, "An Ever Closer Fusion? A Dynamic Macropolitical View on Integration Processes" (1997) 35 *Journal of Common Market Studies* 267.

[46] This was Declaration No. 23 adopted by the intergovernmental conference. See the documentation by A. Krekelberg in Maurer and Wessels (above, n. 5), document no. 3.

a new intergovernmental conference to be convened in 2004. The Declaration by the intergovernmental conference could be read in different ways, and reflected a set of views which were not clearly defined by the Heads of State and Government among themselves, and which diverged as regards the institutional architecture and overall development of the larger Union which was about to come into being. The Declaration raised the general questions of how democratic the integration process was, and of whether the European Union could be democratised by modified institutional and/or para-constitutional rules.

(a) Ways of Improving National Scrutiny Systems

Initially, the debate about how to strengthen national parliaments concentrated on how to involve them more directly at the European levels of decision-making. Nevertheless, since scrutiny of their own government continues to represent one of their most important 'European functions' of national parliamentarians, it is important to analyse what kind of improvements could have been made at national level – irrespective of the Convention's outcome. To encourage parliaments to analyse and improve their systems, 'best practice' studies had been proposed within such self-regulating fora of national parliaments as COSAC. In contrast to this kind of informal recalibration process, the idea put forward in speeches in Spring 2000 by Fischer, Blair, and Chirac was that of according national parliaments certain rights in the European Treaties. It remained open whether this would be done by extending the scope of existing rights included in the PNP or by inserting into certain Treaty articles provision for specific functions, roles, and powers being accorded to national parliaments.[47]

(i) The Informal Way: Best Practice

Comparison of the different national systems was already facilitated within COSAC and – to a much lower extent – within the Conference of Speakers of European Parliamentary Assemblies. The proceedings in the Convention on the Future of Europe on the issue of national parliaments induced a fresh wave of analysis of the different systems. In particular, the Working Group on National Parliaments (Working Group IV) acted as an open forum for inter-parliamentary exchange about the pros and cons of national parliamentary scrutiny. Many contributions to Working Group IV explained national characteristics of modes of parliamentary participation and the

[47] See House of Commons European Scrutiny Committee, European Scrutiny in the Commons – Thirtieth Scrutiny Report (available at www.parliament.the-stationery-office.co.uk).

scrutiny systems. Some even made specific proposals for improving their own national procedures or explained several mechanisms that could be of use to other parliaments.[48] In particular, the national parliaments which are the weaker national players, as well as the candidate states, may have profited from these comparisons. Yet the extent to which best practice studies[49] will stimulate changes, and should therefore be institutionalised (for example in 'a forum of best practices' which could be part of COSAC[50]), is questionable Arguably the effects of such comparisons are very limited. Copying the European affairs scrutiny system of another parliament may not mean copying the effect it has. There are too many other factors (such as the political system, the political culture and – most importantly – the orientation of parliamentary participation in European Union affairs[51]) which determine how the system works in practice. In the Convention, proposals to institutionalise best practice systems were seen to be helpful, but many members argued that it might not necessarily help to bring about real success in terms of improving effectiveness, given that there were too many relevant country-specific factors that would have to be taken into account. As it is very unlikely that a weak national player can develop into a strong European player by learning from another (for example, from the Danish parliament), the effects produced by copying best practice are likely to remain weak.

(ii) Minimum Rights for National Parliaments: Extending the Scope of the Amsterdam Protocol

More success could have been obtained in a more formal way, *viz.* by granting further rights to national parliaments, as had been done in the Amsterdam Protocol on the Role of National Parliaments in the European Union. Proposals to reformulate the PNP provisions as obligations binding the governments and the European institutions were made by several

---

[48] Prionsias de Rossa MEP described the changes which at that time had been recently agreed between Irish political parties to the Irish scrutiny mechanism and which were later incorporated in the the European Union (Scrutiny) Act 2002. According to him, the drafting of the changes which had been agreed had been "greatly facilitated by the exchange of information on best practice with many other parliaments". (P. de Rossa, *Role of National Parliaments*, WD 010 - WG IV, Brussels, 15 July 2002). See also the contribution of Hans Van Baalen (Member of the Dutch Parliament), *On Time It Is Too Late* (WD 011 - WG IV, Brussels, 15 July 2002). Kimmo Kiljunen (a representative of the Finnish Parliament), recommended the use of reserves in the Council to other parliaments. See K. Kiljunen *Securing the Influence of National Parliaments – Use of Reserves in the Council* (WD 016 - WG IV, Brussels, 22 July 2002).

[49] Which were proposed by G. Stuart in *Mandate of the Working Group on National Parliaments* (CONV 74/02 Brussels, 30 May, 2002).

[50] A proposal made by de Rossa, above, n. 48.

[51] See regarding these, Table 3 above.

members of the Convention. The idea was that by extending, in an amended PNP, the breadth of information to be provided, parliaments could be provided with a better, *i.e.*, European Union-regulated position *vis-à-vis* their governments. A different and less formal approach was suggested by the House of Commons – that of adopting a 'Charter for National Parliaments', which would include the:

> "broad principles and objectives to guide national parliaments in relation to their role in the European Union and to which national parliaments would subscribe".[52]

The Charter proposed would have been a binding instrument for national parliaments but not for European institutions or governments. However, most members in Working Group IV reacted rather negatively to this proposal, highlighting the problems of binding national parliaments via treaty changes that would require constitutional changes in the Member states.[53]

New Treaty articles that would specifically define the role of national parliaments might have been an effective way to raise the awareness of the 'European functions' of MPs. But even a simple reform of the PNP might have spurred constitutional changes. A further relatively simple change was proposed by Working Group IV chairman, Mendez de Vigo, who asked that the Commission and not the member states' governments be defined as responsible for forwarding legislative proposals directly to national parliaments.[54] According to an earlier COSAC resolution, proposals could be forwarded 'as soon as they are adopted by the college of Commissioners' –

---

[52] This Charter was to include "a pledge by national parliaments to promote the openness and transparency of decision-making in the European Union; a pledge by national parliaments to review their own procedures with a view to increasing the opportunities for holding their own government ministers to account in relation to EU decision-making, and a pledge by national parliaments to review their own procedures with a view to promoting the engagement of the citizen in the European Union". See House of Commons European Scrutiny Committee, above, n. 47.

[53] This question was also raised in the first meeting of Working Group IV. The need to respect national constitutional requirements was also stressed there – as it is in the existing (Amsterdam) Protocol on the Role of National Parliaments in the European Union. (See European Convention Secretariat to Working Group IV *National Parliaments* (Summary of the meeting held on 26 June 2002, CONV 128/02 , WG IV, Brussels, 1 July 2002) at 3 thereof.)

[54] The Chairman of Working Group I also enclosed this proposal on his list of points to be examined. See I. Mendez de Vigo (Chairman of Working Group I), *Initial Proposals for Conclusion*, Working Group I on the Principle of Subsidiarity, WG I- WD 09,CONV 210/02, Brussels, 29 July 2002 , See also de Rossa, above, n. 48.

preferably 'by electronic means'.[55] For its part, the Commission indicated it:

> "would have no difficulty in sending proposals directly (to national parliaments) if Member States are content that this is consistent with each country's constitutional relationship between governments and national parliaments".[56]

The idea indirectly limited the scope of information forwarded to national parliaments, since Commission proposals apply to First Pillar matters only. Interestingly, no member of Working Group IV raised the question about the self-restriction of national parliaments in this specific regard.

There were doubts as to whether a majority of member states and parliaments would support changes to the PNP that could interfere to some extent in the 'constitutional organisation and practice of each Member State'.[57] As the House of Commons put it:

> "parliaments, as sovereign bodies, will want to decide how best to exercise their own scrutiny role according to their own traditions and norms".[58]

Most proposals that were made in the Convention were thus limited in effect to possibilities for involving national parliaments directly at European level, either by establishing new mechanisms or even by establishing a new institution comprised of national parliamentarians.

(b) When and How Should National Parliaments be Involved at European Level?

Other proposals for new roles and new bodies comprised of national parliamentarians had been made throughout the debate on the future of

---

[55] Adopted at the XXIIIrd COSAC, Versailles, October 2000 (see www.cosac.org/en/meetings/previous/23/).

[56] See European Commission, *Implementation by the Commission of the Amsterdam Protocol on the Role of National Parliaments in the European Union*, Paper from the Commission to Working Group IV (WD 009 - WG IV, Brussels, 12 July 2002, p. 4).

[57] To use the wording of the preamble to the Amsterdam Protocol on the Role of National Parliaments in the European Union.

[58] See House of Commons European Scrutiny Committee, above, n. 47.

Europe and prior to the negotiations of the Nice Treaty.[59] By drawing attention to the subject, these different visions also helped the issue to be included in the priority list of the Nice agenda, as well as on the agenda of the Convention. Such proposals for a '*second chamber*' comprised of national parliamentarians either in the European Parliament or independent of it, or for a (permanent) '*congress*,' or a '*subsidiarity committee*' were not new.[60] For the first time, however, they were part of a European Union-wide debate. It seemed questionable, however, whether the Convention's focus should be on the question of what manner and by which institutions national parliaments might best be involved (*e.g.*, *via* a congress, a committee, or a chamber). The question of where and when to involve national parliaments at the different levels and during the different stages of the European Union policy process seemed more essential. The Convention thus examined *at what stages* national parliaments could participate in this project. The following possibilities were discussed: involvement in the making of primary law by the Convention or intergovernmental conferences; participation in the legislative process; and participation in the appointment procedures, if these were remodelled.

(i) Involvement in the Making of Primary Law: the Convention as a Model

As the constitutional character of the European treaties has become more and more apparent and 'their modifying impact on the normative reality of the national constitutions ... undeniable, a more direct involvement of citizens and their democratic representatives in the process [of Treaty revisions] needs to be organised'.[61] Until the Convention on the Future of Europe commenced, national parliaments had only been indirectly involved in the making of primary law. The institutionalisation of the Convention would alter the modus of Treaty revision fundamentally and this would be – as most observers acknowledged – a step in the right direction.[62] The advantages of institutionalising the Convention consist of the deliberative nature of parts of its proceedings (namely, the early phases of joint problem definition, as well

[59] As for example in certain speeches by the German Foreign Minister Joschka Fischer (as to which see n. 95 below, the British Prime Minister Tony Blair (as to which see n. 96 below) and the French Prime Minister Lionel Jospin (as to which see n. 100 below).

[60] See K. Pöhle, "Das Demokratiedefizit der Europäischen Union und die nationalen Parlamente. Bietet COSAC einen Ausweg?" in (1998) 1 *Zeitschrift für Parlamentsfragen* 82, at p. 85.

[61] See I. Pernice, *The Role of National Parliaments in the European Union* (WHI-Paper 5/01, Juli 2001, Walter Hallstein-Institut) at p. 4.

[62] Committee on Constitutional Affairs, European Parliament, *Report on Relations Between the European Parliament and the National Parliaments in European Integration* (23 January 2002, Rapporteur: Giorgio Napalitano).

as the debates within the working groups) and the public debates it gives rise to prior to an intergovernmental conference. However, a Convention produces only limited side-effects for national parliaments, because the additional method of Treaty revision which it constitutes applies only temporarily and thus can be combined with other new mechanisms for involving national parliaments only during a rather short time-frame. The Convention on the Future of Europe had no formal powers and only prepared the ground for the intergovernmental conference. During the Convention, national parliamentarians (or at least the few representatives of each parliament) were directly involved at the European level and learned of the different points of view of other MPs, MEPs, and government representatives. They gained – and actively contributed to – 'first-hand experience of European Union affairs'.[63]

(ii) Direct Involvement in the Legislative Process: a Role in Policing Compliance with the Subsidiarity Principle?

National parliaments implement a large amount of European legislation without having a real, *i.e.*, *ex ante* say in the decision-making processes. In addition, most European Union directives contain such precise provisions that national parliaments only get to rubber-stamp what has already been decided in Brussels.[64] Given the large differences in effectiveness of the national scrutiny procedures, many members of the Convention proposed to involve national parliaments directly and at an earlier stage in the legislative process at European Union level. The arguments put forward concentrated on two issues: first, guaranteeing an equal standard of participation for national parliaments; and secondly, granting national parliaments a role in policing compliance with the principle of subsidiarity. On the other hand, the *Conventionnels* did not raise the Maastricht-Amsterdam-Nice parliamentary deficits insofar as concerns (a) the Common Foreign and Security Policy, or European Security and Defence Policy; (b) enhanced cooperation; or (c) the (intergovernmental) open method of co-ordination. Accordingly, within the Convention, the issue of subsidiarity became increasingly regarded as *the* political question to be addressed to national parliaments.[65] Proposals were made which identified different stages for national parliaments to be involved in the legislative process – in co-shaping the broad political agenda

---

[63] A. Duff, *Role of National Parliaments* (Paper for Working Group IV, Working Document 4, Brussels, 5 July, 2002) at 5.

[64] See Praesidium of the European Convention, *The Role of National Parliaments in the European Architecture* (Brussels, 29 May 2002, CONV 67/02, p. 5).

[65] Mendez de Vigo, above, n. 54.

(*i.e.*, the pre-legislative phase) and in participating in the legislative and in the post-legislative phase.

(iii) A New Role in Shaping the Broad Political Agenda?

With regard to giving national parliaments a role in the long-term monitoring (or, to use the German term, *Vorfeldbeobachtung*), Working Group IV of the Convention discussed the involvement of parliaments directly in the preparation of the Commission's annual work and legislative programme.[66] Inviting national parliaments to put forward their demands and opinions on pre-legislative material means activating a parliamentary scrutiny mechanism at the earliest possible stage. At present, national parliaments receive the legislative programme from the European Parliament (which is the institution that is jointly responsible for the Programme together with the Commission).[67] This way, national parliaments are able to plan when and what to scrutinise or implement, since the legislative programme:

> "establishes the priorities in the legislative field and fixes a timetable for the submission by the Commission of all the proposals and documents contained in the programme and for their examination by Parliament and the Council".[68]

National parliaments may question their ministers:

> "to ascertain what their governments think of the Legislative Programme as proposed, and to find out the priorities their ministers have set".[69]

It might, however, be advantageous if there were European, rather than national debates. This could be achieved in cooperation with the Commission and the European Parliament. British and Irish members of the Convention on the Future of Europe thus proposed the organisation of regular hearings of

---

[66] See A. Maurer, *Beyond Unilateral Scrutiny: The Scope of Options* (Paper for Working Group I (Subsidiarity),Working Document 7, Brussels, 16 July 2002). See also Secretariat of the European Convention, Working Group IV on National Parliaments, *Summary of the Meeting Held on 18 July 2002* (CONV 204/02, Brussels, 16 July 2002) and Secretariat of the European Convention, Working Groups on Subsidiarity and National Parliaments, *"Summary of the Joint Meeting on Monday 22 July, 2002"* (CONV 210/02, Brussels, 30 July 2002).

[67] Laprat, above, n. 5, at 14.

[68] Information on the Commission's Programme of Work and Legislative Initiatives and Rule 57 of Parliament's Rules of Procedure on the Homepage of the European Parliament, at wwwdb.europarl.eu.int/dors/oeil/en/inter21.htm.

[69] Laprat, above, n. 5, at 12

Commissioners within national parliaments after they have received the programme.[70] The presence of Commissioners in national parliaments would ensure that all deputies could participate (and not merely a minority as is the case with COSAC or joint parliamentary meetings). Nevertheless, these hearings could also take place together with those in the European Parliament.[71] These hearings could be followed by debates taking place simultaneously in all parliaments.[72] Real improvement of the parliamentary influence would involve parliaments being able make their voice heard. This could at first be done individually[73] and then collectively – for example by using mechanisms which have already been established (such as COSAC meetings, but also specialised national parliamentary committee meetings). Concerns expressed by national parliaments could first be presented to the European Parliament, which would take them into account in the legislative process.[74] Furthermore, reports could also be sent to the Commission and also, in particular, to the General Affairs Council, which prepares decisions on the following year's programme.[75] Further, this kind of anticipatory scrutiny should not only be restricted to the annual legislative programme of the Commission but also apply to the programmes of the Council and the European Council. Thus the multi-annual programme of the European Council and the annual operating programme of Council Activities proposed by the Seville European Council[76] might also be scrutinised by national parliaments.[77]

[70] The European Scrutiny Committee of the House of Commons proposed that parliament request "a 'Queen's Speech' type briefing from the Commission on its annual legislative programme (similar to the broad economic guidelines and the financial framework)." See European Scrutiny Committee of the House of Commons, above, n. 47.

[71] This had already been proposed by the European Parliament. See European Parliament, Committee on Constitutional Affairs *Working Document on the Commission's Annual Legislative Programme (Rule 57 of the Rules of Procedures)* (Rapporteur: C. Malmström, PE 304.282, 31 August, 2001).

[72] Duff, above, n. 63.

[73] "National parliaments or national parliamentary committees could then publish a consultation document on the forthcoming legislative programme, request submissions from interest groups, civil society, etc and then feed this back to the Commission". See European Scrutiny Committee of the House of Commons, above, n. 47.

[74] See Maurer, above, n. 46, at 15.

[75] Duff, above, n. 63.

[76] From December 2003 onwards, the European Council started to adopt a Multi-Annual Strategic Programme for the three years to come. In addition, according to the Presidency Conclusions of the European Council held at Seville on 21 and 22 June, 2002, an "annual operating programme of Council activities shall be submitted to the General Affairs Council in December each year. This programme shall be proposed jointly by the next two Presidencies in line and shall have regard, inter alia, to relevant points arising from the dialogue on the political priorities for the year, conducted at the Commission's initiative. The final version of the annual programme shall be drawn up on the basis of the General Affairs Council's discussions."

[77] De Rossa, above, n. 48.

Only some of these ideas found their way into the final version of the Constitutional Treaty. However, it was not the intergovernmental conference, but the Convention itself which cut back the proposals on the pre-legislative involvement of national parliaments. Thus the report by Working Group IV of the Convention on the role of national parliaments suggested that the Commission should transmit the annual policy strategy and the annual legislative and work programme to national parliaments, that interparliamentary conferences on specific issues could be convened as the need arose, and that 'European weeks' should be organised each year to create a common window for European Union-wide debates on European issues in every member state. In the final version of the Convention's draft Consititutional Treaty, however, (and later in the Constitutional Treaty itself), these proposals were reduced to Article 1 of the Protocol on the Role of National Parliaments in the European Union, according to which the Commission was required to forward the annual legislative programme as well as any other instrument of legislative planning or policy to national parliaments, at the same time as to the European Parliament and the Council.

(iv) A New Warning Mechanism in the Legislative Phase?

Apart from improving the level of involvement of national parliaments in the pre-legislative phase by means of scrutiny of the annual strategies and legislative programmes of the European institutions, the vast majority of the Convention's members, its Praesidium as well as the Convention President, Valéry Giscard d'Estaing, all sought to strengthen national parliaments' role within the legislative phase. Currently, national parliaments can make their positions known to their national governments and the European Parliament, but do not have a real say in the legislative process at the European level. At the Convention, proposals were made ranging from general vetoes on legislative proposals,[78] to calls for a new 'political body',[79] to simple mechanisms assuring that national parliaments are at least consulted.

If the discussions in Working Groups IV and I of the Convention are analysed, it can be seen that a majority of the proposals made called for an 'early warning mechanism' for national parliaments to prevent breaches of the principle of subsidiarity, and to ensure that concerns by national parliaments were taken more fully into account by European Union

---

[78] A proposal by Jens-Peter Bonde, MEP, See European Scrutiny Committee of the House of Commons, above, n. 47.

[79] See for example P. Glotz, D. Hübner, R. McSharry and P. Moscovici, *Division of Competencies* (CONV 88/02, CONTRIB 46, Brussels, 14 June 2002) at 4.

legislators.[80] A mechanism was proposed not only in order to enable parliaments to react to Commission documents but also to allow national parliamentarians to interfere at later stages of the legislative process, since Commission proposals can be significantly altered by the European Parliament and the Council.[81] With regard to the co-decision procedure, Andrew Duff MEP sought the introduction of a 'complaint procedure' which would have been triggered by a significant majority of national parliaments. By issuing 'a reasoned amendment', this majority would have been able to ask for a third reading within the Conciliation Committee. If the Council and the European Parliament wanted to retain their original positions, they would have had to achieve a higher threshold (a 'super QMV' in the Council and an absolute majority in the European Parliament) during the voting procedure. Duff recommended that national parliaments should be allowed four weeks to register such complaints and to submit a reasoned amendment.[82]

(v) Parliamentary Participation in Procedures of Appointment

By legitimising the decisions made by their national governments, national parliaments also have a role to play in controlling the governments' European appointment policies.[83] Despite the changes brought about at Maastricht and Amsterdam, which strengthened the role of the European Parliament,[84] and of the President of the Commission (in selecting the Commissioners), national governments still play a central role in the nomination procedures.[85] This is also true of nominations to leading positions at other European institutions (for example the European Court of Justice, the Court of First Instance, the European Central Bank, the Court of Auditors, and others).[86] Given that there are hardly any legal provisions at national level which provide for parliamentary participation in these appointment procedures,[87] it seemed to be essential for the Convention to examine possible new ways of involving

[80] See Secretariat of the European Convention, Working Groups on Subsidiarity and National Parliaments, above, n. 47. See also I. Mendez de Vigo, above, n. 54.

[81] K. Kiljunen *Oversight of Subsidiarity* (WD 007 - WG IV, Brussels, 5 July 2002). Kiljunen was a Finnish Parliament representative at the Convention.

[82] Duff, above, n. 63.

[83] Duff, above, n. 63.

[84] Under Article 214(2) of the EC Treaty, the European Parliament has to give its consent to the nomination of the President and of the College of Commissioners.

[85] Pernice, above, n. 61, at 8.

[86] *Ibid.*

[87] *Ibid.*

national parliaments – at national[88] or even at European level. With regard to the latter possibility, proposals had been made to involve national parliaments in the election or nomination of a 'President of the Union',[89] the idea being that further executive powers could then be assigned either to the Commission or to the Council. French, Spanish, and British proposals called for the nomination of a President of the Council[90] as opposed to proposals for electing the President of the Commission.[91] In both cases national parliaments could have been involved. Andrew Duff called for the President of the Commission to be elected by some form of assembly comprised of European and national parliamentarians.[92] Suggestions along these lines were also made by the President of the Commission at the time of the Convention on the Future of Europe, Romano Prodi.[93] Different ideas were put forward by the President of the Convention, who wanted to see national parliaments equipped with fewer powers in this regard. According to him, there could be some role for national parliaments in 'confirming' the nominations of the heads of state or government.[94]

---

[88] Even in the absence of revolutionary decisions, such as that to elect the President of the Union or the Commission, there would still be possibilities for involving national parliaments in national nomination procedures by giving them at least a direct say on who is nominated by each government as a candidate for such a position. (See Pernice, above, n. 61, at 16).

[89] Barrau envisaged a Congress that would elect a "President of the Union" on the basis of a list drawn by the Heads of State and Government. Normally this term refers to a President of the Council, although Barrau is not very clear on this. See A. Barrau (of the Assemblée nationale française), *National Parliaments* (Contribution to the Convention, CONV 84/02, CONTRIB 40, Brussels, 31 May 2002).

[90] The idea of an appointed EU Council President was put forward by Mr Chirac in a speech in Strasbourg on 7 March, 2000 and was also supported by the British Prime Minister Blair and the then Spanish premier Aznar. The idea of a Council president was also favoured by Valéry Giscard D'Estaing, President of the Convention on the Future of Europe. See G. Parker, "France and UK call for new force at top of EU", *Financial Times*, 15 May, 2002.

[91] This would have been in line with the view of the European Commission, the European Parliament and others who were in favour of ascribing executive power to the Commission and developing a true bicameral system (consisting of Council and European Parliament).

[92] Using the term "congress", Andrew Duff spoke in favour of the German pattern for the election of the Federal President – a "Bundesversammlung" (literally, "federal assembly") composed of the whole European Parliament and an equal number of national parliamentarians meeting to elect the new President of the Commission every five years in July immediately following the elections to the European Parliament. (See Duff, above, n. 63, at 5).

[93] G. Parker, "Prodi changes his mind on electing European president", *Financial Times*, 29 July, 2002.

[94] Describing his idea of a congress, however, Giscard d'Estaing mentioned only the possibility that national parliaments might play some role in some nomination procedures – and was not very clear on this. (See V. Giscard, d'Estaing *"La dernière chance de l'Europe unie"*, an article published on 22 July, 2002 in *Le Monde* and on 23 July in the *Süddeutsche Zeitung* (Nr. 168,)).

(vi) New Institutions or Reforms of Existing Mechanisms?

The most radical proposals regarding new forms of involvement had been those involving the creation of a 'second chamber' or 'third chamber', the former meaning a chamber within the European Parliament,[95] and the latter meaning a new, independent chamber.[96] The first proposal implied that the present European Parliament would become the lower chamber, with the upper chamber being comprised of representatives of the national parliaments, either with the same number of representatives per state, or with the number of representatives varying accordingly to the population of the state. The idea risked: '[duplicating] national representation at the European level unless the Council was substituted by such a second chamber'.[97] Unless the Council was prepared to subject itself to such a revolutionary reform, the danger would arise that the functions of the institutions would overlap. This might not necessarily be the case with a third chamber, which would not have legislative competences, but perhaps some role in the second and the third pillar.[98] Nevertheless, these proposals would have rendered the institutional system more complex rather than more transparent.[99] Other proposals referred to a 'permanent conference' or a 'congress'[100] or a 'parliamentary subsidiarity committee'.[101] These were presented as more flexible arrangements than the idea of a second or third chamber. Regular meetings could take place on an *ad hoc* basis.[102]

These ideas largely ignored already-extant mechanisms such as COSAC, however. For, independently of whatever precise role that one might attribute to some new body, there were various possibilities for reforming COSAC. If

---

[95] This idea was put forward, for example, by Vaclav Havel in March 1999 in the French Senate. See French Senate, *Une deuxième chambre européenne* (Report 381 (2001–2002) by D. Hoeffel, (available at www.senat.fr/rap/r00-381/r00-381_mono.html) and also by Joschka Fischer in *Vom Staatenverbund zur Föderation - Gedanken über die Finalität der europäischen Integration*, Speech at Humboldt University, 12 May, 2000.

[96] See for example the speech made by Tony Blair in Warsaw on 6 October, 2000 (available at www.number-10.gov.uk/output/Page3384.asp).

[97] Pernice, above, n. 61, at 13.

[98] See in this regard the proposals made by Tony Blair in his speech, above, n. 76.

[99] See F. Pflüger (Member of the German *Bundestag* and *Bundestag* Chairperson for European Affairs, *"Europa wohne Bürger? Mehr Parlament wagen?"* (Europa-Fokus Niedersachsen, Ausgabe 2001/3/ August 2001, available at www.eiz-niedersachsen.de/europafokus/pdf/ef-2001-3.pdf).

[100] Speech made by then French Prime Minister Lionel Jospin on 28 May, 2001 in Paris, Maison de la Radio, (reported on in Europa-Fokus Niedersachsen, Ausgabe 2001/3/ August 2001, available at www.eiz-niedersachsen.de/europafokus/pdf/ef-2001-3.pdf).

[101] Pernice, above, n. 61, at 15.

[102] Kiljunen above, n. 81.

'heavy mechanisms' were to be avoided[103] because of their potential negative consequences for the European institutions and the decision-making process, a reformed COSAC seemed to be a more appropriate solution. Although it might imply that COSAC change its name and composition,[104] COSAC could easily play a role in safeguarding subsidiarity, in some appointment procedures, in debating both the legislative programme of the Commission and the multi-annual programme of the European Council, and it could even play a role in the Common Foreign and Security Policy.[105] There could be also 'non-routine joint conferences of MPs and MEPs' which would discuss particularly problematic dossiers (such as enlargement or the reform of the Common Agricultural Policy), bringing together specialists rather than the European Union generalists of national parliaments' EC/EU Affairs Committees.[106]

4. The Result of the Convention and of the Subsequent Intergovernmental Conference

The Constitutional Treaty, if it ever comes into force, or any successor treaty which maintains its provisions in this regard,[107] will provide national parliaments with a new set of powers for participating in European Union decision-making.

Thus, under Article I-18(2), the attention of national parliaments was to be drawn to any Commission initiative with regard to the so-called flexibility clause, under Article I-18(2).

They were to be notified of any initiative taken by the European Council to authorise the Council to act by qualified majority where the Treaty provides the Council should act by unanimity, or to allow the adoption of legislation by the ordinary legislative procedure rather than by a special legislative

[103] Mendez de Vigo, above, n. 54.

[104] See the Danish proposal for developing COSAC into a "Forum of the Parliaments" in Proposals for Enhancing the Role of the National Parliaments in European Politics and for the Reform of COSAC into the Forum of Parliaments – Draft Contribution for the COSAC meeting in Copenhagen, 16–18 October, 2002 (European Affairs Committee of the Danish Parliament/the Danish COSAC Chairmanship, Christiansborg, 11 July 2002).

[105] See also proposals for a "Parliamentary Conference on ESDP" by the Committee on Constitutional Affairs, of the European Parliament, above, n. 62, at 22. See also reference made to the Chevalier/Mahoux-Report by K. De Gucht, *Another Role for National Parliaments in the EU*, (CONTRIB 63, CONV 183/02, Brussels, 11 July 2002).

[106] Duff, above, n. 63.

[107] Editor's note: see, concerning the most recent pre-publication developments concerning the fate of the Constitutional Treaty, the introduction to this book.

procedure, under Article IV-144. In addition, Article IV-444(3) provided each national parliament with a right to veto any such transfer from unanimity to qualified majority voting in Council or from the special to the ordinary legislative procedure.

They were to be notified of the application of any European State wishing to become a member of the European Union, under Article I-58(2).

Under Article III-259, they were to ensure that proposals and legislative initiatives submitted concerning the creation of an area of freedom, security, and justice, and relating to judicial cooperation in criminal matters and police cooperation comply with the principle of subsidiarity. Further, they were to be informed of the content and results of the evaluations of Union policies in the field of freedom security and justice provided for in Article III-260.

Under Article III-261, they were to be kept informed of the proceedings of the Standing Committee to be set up within the Council to ensure that operational cooperation in internal security is promoted and strengthened within the European Union.

They were to be notified of proposals submitted to the Council of Ministers for the amendment of the Constitutional Treaty, under Article IV-443(1).

The most important reform proposed by the Convention (and retained by the subsequent intergovernmental conference) was the new mechanism of direct parliamentary participation in the application of the subsidiarity principle. Under the Constitutional Treaty's Article I-11 and the annexed Protocol on the Application of the Principles of Subsidiarity and Proportionality, the Commission was to send its legislative drafts directly to all national parliaments for a 'preliminary reading'. Parliaments were to have six weeks from the proposal's transmission to draft their position on whether the proposal complied with the subsidiarity principle or not. All positions were to be weighted and counted: unicameral parliaments were to have two votes, in bicameral parliaments, each chamber had one vote. If one third (one quarter for proceedings under Article III-264 concerning draft legislative acts on judicial cooperation in criminal matters and police cooperation) of all chambers drew up negative positions, the Commission had to review its proposal and subsequently withdraw, amend, or maintain it. This first round was to take place exclusively between the Commission and the chambers of national parliaments. It was only after that 'reading' that the Commission submits the possibly revised proposal to the ordinary legislative process. Finally, the possibility was open to those parliaments which had adopted a negative position of taking legal action against the Commission at the European Court of Justice on the grounds of an infringement of the subsidiarity principle. During the Court proceedings, parliaments were to be represented by their governments which were to act on their behalf.

Assuming these (or similar) provisions ever come into force, what will be the procedural and institutional consequences for national parliaments? Two possibilities can be envisaged. First, it is conceivable that parliaments would submit explicitly positive positions to the Commission. In this way, a parliament could on the one hand support its government's position *vis-à-vis* third parties, and, on the other, it could clarify its own point of view at this early stage and set limits on its own government's negotiations in the Council of Ministers. It is also likely that such positive positions would send signals to the European Parliament, as the positions of its major political groups in Brussels or Strasbourg became clear.

Secondly, however, it is also likely that strong governments would use the mechanism to back up their position in Brussels by simply advising parliaments to submit negative positions. The instrumentalisation of parliaments, something which occurs at present in France and in the United Kingdom, could become a general rule. Thus the effective use of the mechanism would depend not only on institutional arrangements but on the self-perception of parliaments regarding their scrutiny role *vis-à-vis* the executive and the European Union institutions. Strongly-scrutinising parliaments (insofar as European Union business is concerned) would behave differently from those which tend to support their government in international and European affairs. Fulfilling any desire on the part of national parliaments to use the opportunity to engage in direct, active participation and scrutiny would necessitate a certain structural re-organisation, because of the crucial variables of cost and time. Effective scrutiny within the short period of six weeks would require a centralised, comprehensive, efficient parliamentary organisation able to collect, filter and digest information independently of governmental expertise.

In most parliaments, the European Union Committees would remain (or else become) the central bodies responsible for receiving, collecting, selecting, and forwarding all European Union documents to specialised parliamentary committees. Ideally (assuming the existence of a strong filtering and processing function on the part of the European Union Committees in relation to other parliamentary committees), the European Union Committees would be in overall charge in dealing with the Commission's proposals. The policy-focused standing committees would have consultative status only and be asked to give their opinion on the relevant draft. The procedure would be different if the European Union Committees and the special committees remained of equal status. In this case, it is more likely that at an earlier stage an independent body (*e.g.* the parliamentary praesidium, a parliamentary unit, etc.) would coordinate the forwarding of documents to the committees in charge and those with consultative status. One or more rapporteurs of the respective committees would then draw up a 'subsidiarity monitoring report' and as a result of this, add a proposal for the parliamentary position on the Commission's draft. If the special committees or the European Union Committees were not charged with acting on parliament's behalf, the position would then be forwarded to the plenary in the form of a resolution proposal. After a formal decision, the position would be passed on to the European Union Commission.

Article 5 of the Constitutional Treaty's Protocol on the Application of the Principles of Subsidiarity and Proportionality would have obliged the Commission to provide precise justification for its proposals with regard to the principles of subsidiarity and proportionality. For several years now, the Commission has already added a subsidiarity statement (*fiche de subsidiarité*) to its proposals. Under Article 5, any draft European legislative act was to contain a detailed statement making it possible to appraise compliance with the principles of subsidiarity and proportionality. Article 5 mentioned explicitly that the statement should contain some assessment of the proposal's financial impact and, in the case of a framework law, of its implications for the rules to be put in place by the member states, including regional legislation. If the Commission arrived at the conclusion that an objective would be met most efficiently at European Union level, it had to be able to give qualitative and, wherever possible, quantitative evidence. And, according to Article 5, draft European legislative acts should:

> "take account of the need for any burden, whether financial or administrative, falling upon the union, national governments, regional or local authorities, economic operators and citizens, to be minimised and commensurate with the objective to be achieved".

It was to be expected that the Commission would rely upon parliaments to produce any necessary data. Thus parliaments would have to think of a procedure for replying to such requests within the framework of the 'early warning system'. They would have to generate their own information (or make use of governmental expertise) by the time of the planning stage was reached in respect of a proposal of the Commission. Otherwise parliaments might at a later stage end up being pressed for time and

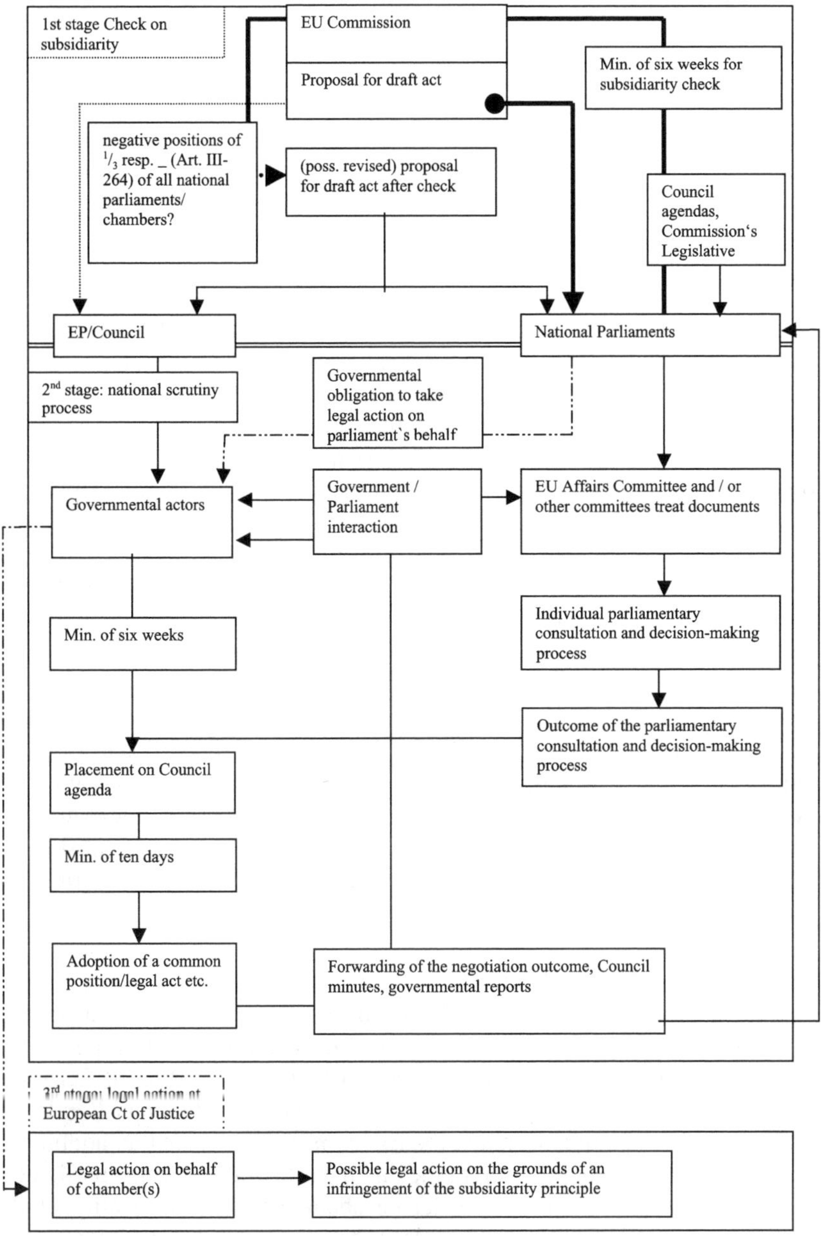

Graph 1: The participation of national parliaments in European Union policy-making as proposed by the Constitutional Treaty.

completely dependent on governmental expertise – thereby lessening their influence.

A European Parliament-like rapporteur-system could serve to prevent an instrumentalisation of the mechanism by governments trying to impose their political objectives via a parliamentary majority. The system could allow MPs in the position of being a committee's rapporteur (and an expert in the respective field of knowledge) to distinguish themselves by taking a stand, possibly even against the governmental position.

If an early warning system of the kind laid down in the Protocol on the Application of the Principles of Subsidiarity and Proportionality is ever implemented, the still widespread claims of a decrease in parliaments' influence due to the European integration process will cease to bear close examination. The immediate possibility of objection by parliaments – outside formal governmental influence and with the direct supply of information – before the actual legislative process begins will strengthen parliaments' autonomy *vis-à-vis* their governments. The right to give their opinion directly *ex ante* and to take legal action if overruled *ex post facto* could – if taken seriously – lead to an emancipation of parliaments *vis-à-vis* their governments.

The European Parliament would not be likely to simply ignore the new actors – either national parliaments or the strengthened European Council. However, whether an emancipation of national parliaments *vis-à-vis* their governments would lead to stronger cooperation between the European Parliament and national parliaments would depend more on a shift of orientation on the part of national parliamentarians than on any reorganisation of the European Parliament.

(a) Possible Consequences

Several national parliaments in the European Union used the ratification process of the Treaty Establishing a Constitution for Europe as an opportunity for increasing the efficiency of their participation in European Union politics. On 12 May, 2005, the day on which the German *Bundestag* ratified the Constitutional Treaty, the *Bundestag* also debated an additional, supplementary law aimed at strengthening the role of the German parliament in European Union affairs. The debate about the constitutionality of the European Arrest Warrant made it clear that there is a habitual malaise at national level concerning the making of European Union policy. National parliaments still lack basic ability and willingness to participate in and scrutinise decisions made by their governments in the Council of Ministers.

How else can one explain the fact that the German Government, with the tacit consent of the *Bundestag*, agreed to a European Union Framework Decision, which was then implemented into national law by the parliament without any real difficulty and that it was only then, when the law was to be applied, that its compatibility with the German *Grundgesetz* (Basic Law) was called into question? The ongoing debate should have started much earlier, specifically before and during the negotiations for the framework decision in the European Union institutions, because at those stages of the decision-making process, national parliaments can still exercise influence via their governments with respect to the content of decisions.

(b) A New Round of Parliamentary Adjustments

In many parliaments the then-pending ratification of the Constitutional Treaty initiated a new wave of proposed reforms. First, the rights and duties of national parliaments under the Constitutional Treaty had to be anticipated. This involved above all the implementation of the new procedure for subsidiarity control by national parliaments. Secondly, the Constitutional Treaty – as a further step towards the deepening of European integration – gave those parliaments which had until now utilised their scrutiny and participation mechanisms rather inadequately, a fresh reason to examine or (where this was appropriate) to change their existing practices of parliamentary participation in, and scrutiny of national involvement in European Union politics. As early as February 2005, France amended its constitution on the basis of two comprehensive reports of its National Assembly.[108] The British House of Commons[109] and the Finnish parliament[110] also presented extensive assessments of their previous work and their initial proposals for reform. Several parliaments of the new member states have already ratified the Constitutional Treaty and introduced new parliamentary practices for the scrutiny of European Union politics that, at least formally, are very efficient.

---

[108] Rapport No. 2024 déposé par la Délégation pour l'Union européenne sur la révision constitutionnelle préalable à la ratification du traité établissant une Constitution pour l'Europe (rapporteur : P. Lequiller, Assemblée nationale, 12 January, 2005); Rapport No. 2033 de la commission des lois sur le projet de loi modifiant le titre XV de la Constitution (rapporteur : M. Pascal Clément, Assemblée nationale, 24 January, 2005).

[109] See House of Commons European Scrutiny Committee, *Aspects of the European Constitutional Treaty* (Fourteenth Report, 23 March 2005).

[110] See Report of the Committee to assess EU scrutiny procedures, Eduskunta, *Improving EU Scrutiny* (2005) 4 *Eduskunnan Kanslian Julkaisu*.

(c) Subsidiarity Control

Under the Constitutional Treaty (or under whatever treaty succeeds it, should the substance of its provisions be maintained), the new rights for national parliaments would be conferred for the first time directly by primary European Union law. Therefore their implementation should take place in a similar manner in most of the member states. Under the Constitutional Treaty, national parliaments were to examine European Union draft legislation to see if it conformed with the principle of subsidiarity.[111] Whether parliaments would be able to make use of their new rights during the examination of subsidiarity would depend entirely on the detailed provisions of rules of procedure, portfolio arrangements or agreements between the government and parliament. Several parliaments of the new member states anticipated the introduction of the 'subsidiarity check' as long ago as 2004 and adjusted their intra-parliamentary procedures accordingly. In the parliaments of the Baltic states, for example, the subsidiarity check has been built into the existing regular scrutiny process for European Union affairs.[112] In these states, the European Union committees are responsible for the central coordination of the subsidiarity review. The governments as well as standing committees include an assessment of the question of subsidiarity in their positions on European Union draft legislation which they submit to the European Union committees. If on the basis of this review, the European Union committees determine that a piece of draft legislation does not comply with the subsidiarity principle, the matter is submitted to the vote of the plenary assembly. Many of the older member states are also installing a subsidiarity control mechanism into the existing scrutiny procedures, pursuant to which the final decision on whether legislation complies with the principle of subsidiarity is to be left to the vote of a plenary session of the applicable chamber(s) of parliament.

---

[111] See Article I-11(3) of the Constitutional Treaty and the annexed Protocol on the Application of the Principles of Subsidiarity and Proportionality.

[112] On European Union scrutiny procedures in the Baltic States see A. Maurer and D. Kietz "Die nationalen Parlamente im Rahmen des EU-Verfassungsvertrages" (2005) 1 *Forum Parlament* 19. On the Visegrad parliaments, see D. Zajc, "A Reconsideration of the Role of the ECE Parliaments in the Process of Europeanisation", in M. Szabó (ed.), *The Challenge of Europeanisation in the Region: East Central Europe* (Hungarian Political Science Association, Budapest, 1996); O. Adamcová, "Chamber of Deputies of the Parliament of the Czech Republic and European Affairs", (2004) 1 *Forum Parlament* 2; J. Kysela, *On the Current Role of Second Chambers in the Process of European Integration* (Senate of the Czech Republic, Prague, 2003); G. Sanford, "Parliamentary Control and the Constitutional Definition of Foreign Policy Making in Democratic Poland" (1999) *Europe-Asia Studies* 51,5; J. Dieringer and A. Stuchlík, "Die Europäisierung der Parlamentsarbeit in Ungarn und der Tschechischen Republik" (2003) *Südosteuropa*, 7–9.

In practice, however, the subsidiarity review mechanism would be likely to be of limited use. The Finnish parliament has correctly pointed out that procedures already exist at European level in order to check compliance with the requirement of subsidiarity. Thus in the process of drafting legislation, the European Commission asserts in all of its proposals that it has complied with the principle of subsidiarity. An inter-institutional agreement also obliges the Council of Ministers and the European Parliament to examine whether a proposal complies with the principle of subsidiarity. And indeed, nothing prevents national parliaments even now from carrying out a subsidiarity check within the scope of the customary scrutiny of the content of the European Union politics of their governments and – whenever there is doubt on the point – making their governments vote against the legislative plan. Thus, the new procedure plays at most a complementary role. With regard to the intra-parliamentary implementation of the subsidiarity examination, it should be recalled that it is each national parliament as a whole and not a minority of its members which is to be allowed to exercise the right to sue in the European Court of Justice. Otherwise, even the filing of a groundless suit before the Court with no chance of success could be effectively instrumentalised in the media by Eurosceptical parties.

In spite of these limitations, the proposed new procedure could make a contribution to the strengthening of national parliaments in the European Union institutional set-up if it were used in a well thought-out manner. Before the actual process of legislating begins at European level, parliamentarians would be able to check directly whether their governments had complied with the division of competences between the European Union and its member states (as laid down by European Union treaties which national parliaments have themselves ratified). The issuing of reasoned opinions commenting on the issue of compliance with the principle of subsidiarity would be capable of having a disciplining effect on the European Union Commission during the drafting of legislation. Whether the Commission would ultimately make changes to draft legislation would clearly depend on how many parliaments expressed reservations. In this regard, parliaments would have to think seriously about how they could share their findings, following their own subsidiarity checks, in order to coordinate reservations submitted to the European Union Commission.

A majority of parliaments believe that a parliament's taking a case to the European Court of Justice after the passing of a draft law would be a worst-case scenario. The Court itself does not believe that this method would be used very frequently. The main effect of the creation of the possibility of a lawsuit would be to cause the Commission (as well as the Council and the

European Parliament) to think matters through seriously before electing to go against the will of national parliaments and regulate matters at European Union level. Nevertheless, if some parliaments did bring cases to the European Court of Justice, this could have the positive side effect that the Court, by means of its jurisprudence, would contribute to the legal clarification of the rather vague concept of subsidiarity.

In reality, the proposed subsidiarity review mechanism, if it ever came into force, would be intertwined with the established procedures for scrutinising European Union affairs, some of which have existed for forty years. As a result, all twenty-five parliaments would be compelled to take a critical look at their roles in the process of adoption of European Union legislation. Against this background, many parliaments are about to examine their general participation and scrutiny mechanisms and arrange them more efficiently.

(d) Comprehensive and Timely Scrutiny of European Union Politics

The Constitutional Treaty – or any substantively similar successor treaty – would, if ratified, deepen European integration in additional policy areas and would require parliaments to adapt their work flows accordingly. In the centre of the ongoing debates is the call for parliaments (a) to better anticipate issues; (b) to screen more efficiently European Union documents for relevant information; (c) to adjust to the deepening of integration in the field of justice and home affairs; and (d) to improve their communication policies.

(i) Strengthening Pre-Legislative Work

The majority of decisions in the Council of Ministers are made at a low – *i.e.,* working – level within this institution (for example, in Working Groups or in the Committee of Permanent Representatives). Thus, if members of national parliaments want to influence the decisions made by their governments in these working-level Council bodies, they must issue their reasoned opinions on draft legislation as early as possible. In practice, this means that parliaments have to be able to deliver a written opinion shortly after the submission of draft legislation by the Commission. In order to meet this short deadline, a parliament will already need to have taken a detailed look at the facts before the draft legislation was submitted. Since only a few of the mass of European Union decisions affect vital national interests, appropriate screening of the documents is required as well.

It is possible to screen documents effectively and to anticipate potential issues, as has been demonstrated, for example, by the Baltic parliaments. The

Lithuanian parliament has developed an efficient screening system in order to protect themselves from being flooded with European Union documents.[113] All of its standing committees deliberate on the Commission's annual legislative programme, and then sub-divide the programme's legislative proposals into 'very relevant', 'relevant', and 'not very relevant' initiatives. This list of initiatives is then submitted to the European Union and the Foreign Affairs Committees of the Lithuanian parliament. Once draft legislation is proposed by the Commission, the Lithuanian parliament deals with it with greater or lesser intensity, depending on the relevance assigned to it. In this way, this parliament knows well in advance which drafts it will have to deal with in the course of the year. The annual legislative programme is accessible on the internet, and includes extensive explanations and statistics. This system could hardly be better for preparing parliament to deal with future legislation.

Subsidiarity control could also be simplified if preparations for it began before the official submission of a proposal, *e.g.*, if government ministries began dealing with draft legislation well before it was officially submitted by the Commission. The ministries could be obliged to provide the parliamentary committees with relevant information in advance of the submission of the legislation. In Finland, the government sends its information on planned legislation to parliament at the point in time when the European Union Commission is still conducting informal consultations with its designated groups of experts, which takes place before the official submission of draft legislation. In addition, parliaments should acquire independent non-governmentally sourced information to supplement their official sources of information.

In addition to the Commission's annual legislative programme, there are other documents which enable the comprehensive tracking of European Union affairs: the Commission publishes a working programme for the upcoming five years as well as Green Books on subject areas in which legislation is planned for subsequent years. These documents are excellent tools for 'predicting' the direction of future proposals of the Commission. In addition, the Commission consults with representatives of civil society and holds discussions on planned legislation in the pre-legislative phase. (The example of the European Union chemicals guideline, REACH, has made

[113] See D. Kietz, "The German Parliament and European Politics, Making Better Use of Existing Powers and Opportunities Arising from the European Constitutional Treaty" (SWP Comments, No. 20/2005, May 2005).

clear to all parliamentary actors the extent to which non-governmental and non-parliamentary institutions can participate in informal European Union procedures). These procedures effectively announce European Union legislative initiatives well in advance of the formal legislative process. In addition, the Council has recently begun writing triennial, annual and semi-annual strategy and working programmes. Although these programmes do not go into specific items of planned legislation in detail, they do describe the planned focal points for Council legislation. Moreover, they give insight into the 'soft law' procedures that take place outside of the community sphere, in the context of the coordination of labour, social, and economic policies. These processes should be followed more attentively by national parliaments, especially given that the European Parliament is not involved in them.

(ii) Waiting Until the Last Minute

After the formal submission of draft legislation by the Commission, national governments forward the text, the government's position as well as (depending on the country) supplementary information to their parliaments. The earlier this occurs, the greater the chance of parliament exercising influence. Instead of viewing the proposal of the Commission as the earliest point in time when parliament can commence its review of draft legislation, the arrival of the proposal should be considered the *latest point in time* to deal with it. The governments of the Baltic states direct all documents to the European Union committees at a very early point. In Lithuania, in the case of 'very relevant' or 'relevant' submissions, the government's position has to have reached the European Union committee within fifteen days of the receipt by the government of the draft legislation (accompanied by supplemental information!). The parliamentary committees thus still have the opportunity to deal with the text before the beginning of consultations within the Council working groups. The completion and further development of the positions of the government and the parliament then proceed in parallel with the negotiations in the European Union institutions, and they can be followed openly by everyone involved via a special electronic information system.

(iii) A New Challenge: The Direct Transmission of Information

Several individual provisions of the Constitutional Treaty, as well as the Protocol on the Role of National Parliaments in the European Union which was annexed to it, contemplated the direct transmission of a multitude of European Union documents by European Union institutions to national parliaments. Up until now, European Union documents have been received by governments and then forwarded to their parliaments – selectively, and sometimes with significant delays. The proposed new rules were designed to make sure that all national parliaments could exercise their scrutiny rights fully and in a timely manner. All parliaments would receive, among other items, consultation documents, legislative programmes, and draft legislative acts. Insofar as the last of these is concerned, the forwarding obligation was however limited to legislative acts as defined in Article I-34 of the Constitutional Treaty, specifically European laws and European framework laws. Thus, parliaments would have to continue to rely on the goodwill of their governments, if, for example, they wanted to examine documents relating to the Common Foreign and Security Policy or the open method of coordination. Moreover, the European Parliament would only be involved to a limited extent, if at all, in these fields. The national parliaments would therefore have had to be aware of their special obligation to scrutinise their governments' conduct in the Council of Ministers.

Many parliaments, however, think that they would be overwhelmed by the direct transmission of documents by the European Union institutions. They fear that they would be flooded with European Union documents and thus hindered in the performance of their oversight function. The careful screening of documents would be required in this case. Parliaments should already, without reservation, be insisting on the right to determine for themselves which documents they would like to receive. This requires using more personnel to identify documents of interest. However, given the fact that at least 50 per cent of national legislation has its origins in European Union legislation and that the legislative competence of the Union applies to almost all areas of domestic policy – including some very sensitive areas – it should be obvious that personnel and technical resources should be concentrated in this field. A refusal by a parliament, on the basis of tight personnel resources, to treat European Union politics with the appropriate level of importance would be equivalent to its not fulfilling its democratic obligations.

Assuming that European Union politics are *de facto* domestic politics, they require a correspondingly high amount of work. The three Baltic parliaments, for example, have provided their European Union committees with a relatively high number of representatives and staff. In the Lithuanian parliament, for example, the European Union Committee, which has 25 members and nine staff workers, is by far the largest committee. Moreover, each standing committee has at its disposal at least one advisor specialising in European Union affairs. All three countries have, moreover, sent one to two employees to the European Parliament Directorate for Relations with National Parliaments, in order to make their parliaments aware of developments that affect national interests as soon as possible. The high degree of respect accorded to European Union affairs can also be seen in the staffing of the European Union Committees with high-ranking politicians.

The European Scrutiny Committee of the British House of Commons is composed of sixteen MPs, who are supported by a staff of sixteen.[114] Its main task is, above all, to sift through the approximately 1,000 legislative and non-legislative documents emanating from the three Pillars of the Union which are sent to parliament by the government. This parliament attaches particular importance to being well supplied with information in order to be able to judge in a relatively independent manner the relevance of these documents. In 2004, 559 documents were classified as legally or politically relevant, and 53 documents were recommended for further handling by other committees after in-depth examination.

(iv) The Particular Case of Justice and Home Affairs

The extent of access to documents and the right to issue opinions in the framework of the Second and Third Pillars (which deal with, respectively foreign and security policy, and police and criminal justice cooperation) vary widely in the different national parliaments. In this context, one may focus on the most dynamic field, cooperation in justice and home affairs, which has become increasingly important since the Treaty of Amsterdam. By now, such cooperation spans the First and Third Pillars and takes in traditionally key areas of national sovereignty such as police, judicial systems, and immigration and asylum policy. Should the Constitutional Treaty (or a successor treaty with similar provisions) ever be ratified, qualified majority decisions by the Council and the co-decision procedure would, to a large extent, become the rule in this field. Moreover (provided, again, that the blueprint of the Constitutional Treaty were adhered to), the pillar structure of the European Union would be done away with and all the features of justice and home affairs be integrated into one Treaty Title. As a result, scrutiny by the European Parliament and the European Court of Justice would be strengthened. Initiatives in this sector would also automatically fall under the control of those national parliaments which have at present still not been authorised to issue opinions to their national governments in this policy field. All national parliaments, however, would have to pay closer attention to the deeper integration of this highly sensitive field and use their scrutiny rights to the fullest. Integration in the field of the civil and criminal law, in

[114] See further in relation to this body the chapter in this volume by Adam Cygan.

particular, runs the risk of conflicting with member states' constitutional laws, as has been demonstrated by the case of the European Arrest Warrant.

Given that cooperation in justice and home affairs impinges on highly sensitive elements of the constitutions of European states, additional specific scrutiny rights for national parliaments were written into the Constitutional Treaty in relation to this policy field. Accordingly, under the Constitutional Treaty, national parliaments were to be involved in the evaluations of Europol[115] and Eurojust,[116] and the evaluation of the implementation of the area of freedom, security, and justice,[117] and were also to be informed about the operational coordination between the national ministries in this field.[118] Should the Treaty (or a successor treaty with equivalent provisions) ever enter into force, European Union laws would specify exactly how parliaments would participate in these evaluations, and it is submitted that parliaments should take this opportunity, should it arise, to work closely with their governments to shape these laws. It may be added that the French parliament did at one point consider the replacement of non-binding resolutions with binding negotiating mandates for the government in this policy field. This option was ultimately rejected by it, however, because the (pro-government) majority in parliament felt it undesirable to place too many obstacles in the path of the government.

(e) Communication Policy and Europeanisation

At present, many European Union citizens are either Eurosceptical or apathetic about European integration. This is illustrated by the difficulties which were encountered in the attempt to secure ratification of the Constitutional Treaty in some of the founding member states of the European Community. One of the causes for this ambivalent mood is surely the fact that parliaments are not fulfilling their communication role *vis-à-vis* their populations to the extent which is necessary. Unfortunately, there was only a rather brief discussion of this deplorable state of affairs at the time of the last European Parliament elections. However, it is not only the citizens, but also parliamentarians themselves who are inadequately informed about European issues. In most parliaments, in the fifty years since the creation of the European Union, there has only ever been a small circle of well-informed specialists in European matters gathered together in the European Union and the Foreign Affairs

[115] Art. I-42 and Art. III-276 of the Constitutional Treaty.

[116] Art. III-273 of the Constitutional Treaty.

[117] Art. I-42 and Art. III-260 of the Constitutional Treaty.

[118] Art. III-261 of the Constitutional Treaty.

Committees. The majority of parliamentarians in standing committees are not even aware of the various ways in which they can influence the European Union legislative process. It is time for these parliamentarians to see themselves as part of the European Union legislative process. The legislative process on the national level is still too often perceived as independent from the European Union legislative process or even in conflict with it.

In order to remedy the situation, in various countries the following measures, among others, have been implemented or discussed: In France, Great Britain and Finland, it is aimed to hold regular plenary debates to discuss the most important European Union topics. Although, for the most part, such debates have been legally permissible for some time, they have seldom been held. Since 2003, monthly question-and-answer sessions with the government dedicated exclusively to European Union matters have been held during a plenary sitting of the French National Assembly and broadcast on television. The French parliament has experimented with 'Europe days', during which, for example, the European Commission's annual Legislative Programme can be discussed by the entire parliament.[119]

All parliaments want to strengthen their cooperation with European Union politicians. The Baltic states have continued the pre-accession practice of having the Prime Minister deliver an annual report on European Union affairs. In Lithuania, the entire parliament discusses the annual Legislative Programme of the Commission. Finland and France have expanded the European-Union-related web pages of their parliaments and given them a prominent place on their homepages. In France, the establishment of an internet forum is planned with the purpose of serving as a platform for consulting with civil society on European Union draft legislation.

(f) The 'Fitness' for Europe of the German *Bundestag*[120]

The *Bundestag* (the lower House of the German parliament) is one of those parliamentary chambers in Europe which has formally been endowed with

[119] The holding of such days has not been made into a general requirement, however.

[120] See A. Maurer and P. Becker, *Die Europafähigkeit der nationalen Parlamente. Herausforderungen des EU-Verfassungsvertrages für den deutschen Parlamentarismus*, SWP-Studie, No. S23/2004; D. Kietz, above, n. 100; and the contributions of experts to the hearing of the German *Bundestag* on the Ratification Law for the Constitutional Treaty, *Öffentliche Anhörung zum Entwurf eines Gesetzes zu dem Vertrag vom 29 Oktober 2004 über eine Verfassung für Europa sowie über weitere Gesetzentwürfe und Anträge zur Stärkung der Rolle des Deutschen Bundestages in Angelegenheiten der Europäischen Union*, (*Deutscher Bundestag*) (held on 16 March, 2005. The minutes of this hearing are available at the time of writing at www.bundestag.de/parlament/gremien15/a20/oeffentlichesitzungen/a20-prot_66.pdf).

far-reaching possibilities for participating in European Union affairs. However, it has not even come close to exhausting these possibilities. Formally, the Bundestag has for long had comprehensive information rights with respect to all three Pillars of the Union. The European Union Committee can issue opinions on draft legislation which the German government has to take into account in negotiations in the Council of Ministers. However, the European Union Committee rarely issues such opinions. If the *Bundestag* wants to diminish the power of the charge frequently levelled against it that it is not 'fit' for Europe, it must get to know the full details of its existing rights and make use of them more effectively. All too often, standing (parliamentary) committees do not discuss the content of European Union draft legislation with the government. A common reason for the lack of such discussions is the parliamentarians' inadequate knowledge: (a) of the possible effects of the European legislation; (b) of the European political process; and (c) of their own ability to exercise influence in this process.

The *Bundestag*, like all other national parliaments of European Union member states, is competing for information, participation and effective access to the inner workings of European Union institutions. The fact that some of the 'young' East European parliaments have already overtaken the German parliament in this competition should be alarming. European Union legislation now affects all aspects of citizens' daily lives, without their being fully aware of the full extent of its regulatory scope. The inadequate tracking and scrutiny of European Union decisions by the German parliament and media, as in the cases of the European Arrest Warrant and the Anti-Discrimination Directive, has had a negative effect on citizens' views both of the European Union and of the German parliament. More information, more frequent substantive discussions arranged in a timely manner, the involvement of civil society and the 'translation' of complicated issues into comprehensible form could stimulate the interest of both citizens and decision-makers in European Union-related topics.

As with the national legislative process, the government must engage in a continuous negotiation process regarding its European policy with both the opposition and, more importantly, its own factions in the *Bundestag*. Such a process requires the active participation of the *Bundestag*, whose focus should be on an anticipatory and continuous scrutiny of the government's European Union policy. A good model is the Finnish parliament's practice of regularly issuing opinions setting guidelines for the government in negotiations in the Council of Ministers. The Finnish model of day-to-day parliamentary involvement in European Union affairs has for long been favourably regarded as efficient and practical. It would be a good idea if the *Bundestag*, in reassessing its own future participation rules for European politics, closely examined the Finnish model and – if possible – drew inspiration from it.

5. Conclusions

National parliaments have provided the formal frame of legitimacy in which European integration could take place. Because of the transfer of powers to European level, their legislative role has been significantly undermined. However, given that national parliaments themselves have ratified each successive Treaty revision, they can scarcely be seen as 'losers' of the integration process. The self-inflicted deprivation by national parliaments of their original legislative powers in favour of the upstream process of European Community and European Union policy-making is capable, in any case, of being compensated for in some measure by an increase in national parliaments' powers of control over their governments.[121] National parliaments have not 'failed' to adapt to the changed domestic and European environment – but the process of adaptation has been rather slow and reactive, rather than anticipative and proactive. This is true of their responses both at European and at national level. By now, several forms of cooperation at the European Union level have been established, helping national parliaments to obtain direct information on developments at supranational level. Cooperation with other parliaments and in particular the European Parliament has become an integral part of their day-to-day affairs. National parliaments are participants in the European Union's multi-level game. However, they do not yet speak with a forceful collective voice. Nor do they use the collective fora in which they participate as means to establish or to mirror some kind of a 'European public'. Resolutions passed by interparliamentary conferences do not yet have any effect on the European institutions (apart perhaps from the European Parliament) or on the European decision-making process, or indeed on national parliaments themselves.

The role national parliaments play in the European Union thus consists mainly of their 'one-level' activities. Initially, the institutional responses to the challenges of European integration were similar in all parliaments. The procedures which have been established, however, have subsequently been shaped by country-specific factors and these factors have also affected the way in which the established mechanisms work. This is why some parliaments are better scrutinisers of their governments than others, and why the role of national parliaments in the European Union (in terms of participating and having an impact) differs.

[121] See S. Schüttemeyer, above, n. 3.

This analysis does not mean that national parliaments do not exercise essential 'European functions'. All national parliaments engage in some form of action *vis-à-vis* the European Union. Their European role consists in legitimising the primary and secondary law of the Union by deliberating on and ratifying Treaty amendments, or by giving assent to acts which might have implications for national constitutions. This may be only a small impact, because in doing this, national parliaments decide upon matters that have been decided already (in Brussels). The modest possibilities they have to be involved at an earlier stage stem in the main from effective participation in the national policy formulation process.

National parliaments are important European actors when it comes to the process of implementation of European Union law. This task is a vital and necessary one insofar as concerns communicating the multi-level nature of the European Union and the number of actors involved in it. National parliaments have to continue to hold their governments accountable. This is why reforms of national procedures and mechanisms are more important than focusing on additional rights at the European level. To a limited extent, progress may be made here by means of best practice mechanisms. Benchmarking also be of some help but its effects in spurring real changes may be limited. Further consideration should be given to the already extant rights of national parliaments under the Protocol on the Role of National Parliaments in the European Union agreed at Amsterdam and the Constitutional Treaty's own Protocol on the Role of National Parliaments in the European Union (or the equivalent provisions, should these be agreed upon, in a successor treaty).

Better forms of involvement at European Union level will continue to exist in relation to tasks which are exercised on a temporary basis, such as participation in Conventions or a role in possible new appointment procedures. However, the existing structures which constitute the means by which national parliaments might become multi-level actors could also be reformed. In particular, COSAC and joint meetings of specialised committees provide a good basis for reforms below the level of Treaty amendments. National parliaments should offer proof of their future added value in exercising their powers with regard to the early warning mechanism: at the pre-legislative stage this could be through scrutiny of the legislative programme of the Commission and the (multi-)annual strategies of the Council and the European Council. This task would also help parliaments to plan and time their actions and reactions at national level, and to Europeanise their institutions beyond the core of the European Union affairs committees.

4.

Ensuring Democratic Scrutiny of European Union Affairs – Prior to Treaty Amendments

John Temple Lang[1]

1. Introduction

In the wake the failure of the French and Dutch referendums on the Constitutional Treaty, one focus of attention has of necessity had to be methods of securing democratic scrutiny without Treaty amendments. Even now, much could be done in this way without waiting until the electorates in all European Union member states are willing to proceed with Treaty reform.[2]

2. The 'Democratic Deficit'

What is called the democratic deficit in the European Union arises in two ways. 'First Pillar' measures under the European Community Treaty are proposed by the Commission, approved or at least discussed by the European Parliament, adopted by the Council, and after adoption are subject, if necessary, to judicial review by the Community Courts. This is the 'Community method'. Apart from cases where the Parliament discusses but need not necessarily agree, the 'democratic deficit' arises primarily because the Council is composed of representatives of national executives, not legislatures, and because the Council discusses and votes in secret, so that it is not clear what each national representative has said and done.

The second way in which the democratic deficit arises is where the Community method does not apply. Measures do not need to be proposed by the Commission or discussed by the Parliament, and there is no judicial

---

[1] Cleary Gottlieb Steen and Hamilton, Brussels and London LLP; Professor, Trinity College, Dublin; Senior Visiting Research Fellow, University of Oxford.

[2] Editor's note: see the introduction to this book in relation to the most recent developments in this regard prior to publication.

review by the Community Courts. This situation arises in the whole area of Common Foreign and Security Policy (the 'Second Pillar') and in much of the area now called Police and Judicial Cooperation (the so-called 'Third Pillar'). In this situation, the democratic deficit is more obvious and more serious, because proposals are not necessarily publicly known before they are discussed by the Council, there need be no discussion in the European Parliament, and the Council, as usual, negotiates and votes in secret.

In both situations, part of the cure for the democratic deficit lies in the hands of national parliaments. Unless Council debates are public, only national parliaments can insist on finding out what Ministers intend to do, and what they did, in the Council. Thus only national parliaments can usefully criticise a Minister if what he or she did was unauthorised or unwise.

In the second situation, the *only* democratic control is that provided by the national parliaments. This is particularly important because none of the safeguards provided by the Community method apply. Matters not subject to the Community method are at least as important, and in many cases more important, than First Pillar matters.

3. Prerequisites for Democratic Control to be Effective

There are several prerequisites for effective democratic control by national parliaments, in both situations. One is adequate information, available in time to allow it to be used. A second is adequate staff to go through the large amount of information which can be obtained, identify the issues which need discussion by legislators, and suggest the considerations to be taken into account. These are prerequisites in all European Union member states, and they are fulfilled to very differing extents.

These prerequisites are particularly important where the Community method does not apply, because there is no procedure which ensures that a proposal is made known publicly, as Commission proposals are, or that any explanation for the proposal will be given publicly while it is being discussed. Second and Third Pillar measures are often controversial and sensitive, and those who propose such measures are not always keen that they should be openly and fully discussed. This means that a committee of a legislature cannot rely entirely on the national civil servants of the member state in question. Civil servants generally have a tendency to minimise the controversial aspects of any proposal, and this tendency is probably greater when the proposal has been made by their opposite numbers in other ministries than when it has been made by the Commission.

At the conference which ultimately gave rise to this book,[3] there was fairly general agreement that the Oireachtas committees concerned with European Union matters need more resources. There are, in essence, two ways in which these could be satisfactorily provided. First, the committees themselves could be given funds to spend on getting information and advice, on primarily legal aspects. Secondly, the Departments most concerned, Foreign Affairs and Justice, could give contracts to a body such as the Institute of European Affairs, to provide independent advice and information directly to the committees (which should be published). Merely making more civil servants available to the committees, while helpful, would not be enough.

However, no national parliament need rely entirely on its own resources in this respect. Parliamentary committees in different member states increasingly exchange information and call one another's attention to controversial aspects or important implications of measures being considered by the Council. This is particularly important to ensure that parliamentary scrutiny does not come too late to be effective; even the Danish European Affairs Committee apparently sometimes fails to meet deadlines. It is also particularly important where the Community method does not apply, and where in consequence measures such as the highly important European Arrest Warrant can be rushed through the Council with too little time for consideration. It is important also because small member states inevitably will not have enough legislators with the time and the expertise to consider all aspects of every measure which they might need to consider. Smaller member states could benefit greatly from cooperation with committees of larger states, whether informal or though the Conference of Community and European Affairs Committees of Parliaments of the European Union (COSAC).

The number of measures which require scrutiny has increased enormously as a result of the development of the Second and Third Pillars. This would mean greatly increased work for national parliaments' committees even if it was not thought necessary, as it should be, to give priority to matters not discussed by the European Parliament. Staff resources and arrangements which might have been sufficient for First Pillar matters which were initiated

[3] This conference was entitled *Ireland, Europe and the Challenge of Democracy – Ensuring Democratic Control over Government Affairs in the European Union* and was held on 20 May 2005 in Dublin under the auspices of the Faculty of Law of University College Dublin and the Institute of European Affairs.

by the Commission and discussed by the European Parliament are clearly inadequate for measures not subject to either safeguard, and not subject to judicial review in the Community Courts.

A particularly important area for national parliamentary scrutiny is the miscellaneous group of matters dealt with by 'comitology', that is, by committees of national civil servants meeting in Brussels to consider Commission proposals on what may be, but not always, technical issues.[4] These matters are not usually dealt with by ministers, and may not even be brought specifically to the attention of ministers. On these matters in particular, parliamentary committees must be able to question civil servants as well as ministers, and must be able to do so, when necessary, before the relevant meeting of the committee in question (since decisions are often taken at a single meeting). Holding Council meetings in public would not solve this problem, because the effective decisions are often taken by the committees.

4. The Special Problem of Democratic Scrutiny of the Open Method of Coordination of National Policies

An important conclusion which was repeatedly referred to in the discussion is that scrutiny by national parliamentary committees is needed for subjects dealt with by the open method of coordination, the non-legal, non-legislative, method of discussion and voluntary cooperation. This technique was initiated in Lisbon in 2000 and was thought appropriate for broad long-term policies on, *e.g.*, employment, pensions, and immigration, which do not need and may not be suitable for specific measures at European Union level. Since these matters are obviously important in the long term, and since they do not necessarily give rise to identifiable or specific national measures, at least in the short term, some discussion, even by a whole national parliament and not merely a committee, is obviously needed from time to time. Again, this is particularly necessary because matters dealt with under the open method of coordination are not subject to Commission proposals or to discussion by the European Parliament. Matters dealt with under the open method of coordination are particularly difficult to make subject to effective scrutiny by national parliaments because they are not only intergovernmental, but vague, long-term, and amorphous as well. Again, a prerequisite for effective scrutiny is adequate information and resources for national parliamentary committees, and close cooperation between national

[4] See Council Decision 1999/468 of 28 June 1999 laying down the procedures for the exercise of implementing powers conferred on the Commission (the "Comitology" Decision) [1990] OJ L184/23, 17 July, 1999.

parliaments. This will need a deliberate effort: many governments would be reluctant to admit, *e.g.*, that current pension levels cannot be maintained in the future without greater individual contributions, or that unemployment cannot be reduced without freer markets, or that immigration must continue to maintain an adequate supply of labour. It is most important to ensure public discussion of questions which governments least want to discuss.

The purpose of effective parliamentary consideration of European Union measures is to ensure that important implications are seen and discussed in time, that ministers and civil servants know what legislators think of particular proposals, and that they are accountable afterwards for what they said and how they voted. If Council debates were open to the public, in legislative discussions, and not closed like diplomatic negotiations, legislators would still need to be able to find out how a minister intends to vote and why, and to make him or her accountable afterwards. Because Council debates are secret, it has been possible, in all member states, for ministers to blame 'Brussels' for unpopular measures for which they themselves voted and to which they knew they could not object. Accountability does not primarily mean blaming ministers for not being more successful negotiators: it means attributing responsibility honestly, explaining European Union measures openly, and on occasion describing the negotiation process which led to them.

5. The Need for Explanation

Ireland's National Forum on Europe under the excellent chairmanship of Maurice Hayes has done much to explain the European Union to the Irish people, a task which should have been carried out by successive ministers (not primarily by member of Oireachtas committees) and serious journalists. The unsatisfactory debates leading up to European Union referendums in Ireland and elsewhere show that public understanding of the European Union, though much greater in Ireland than in England, is still inadequate. It is now increasingly widely understood that several member states, perhaps most of them, need something like the National Forum. In the medium term, a forum would be unnecessary if Oireachtas committees were able to discuss European Union measures thoroughly – provided that their discussions were adequately reported in national newspapers and other media.

'Men more frequently require to be reminded than informed'.[5] Even the reasons for the Community method are forgotten by or unknown to many

[5] A saying attributed to Samuel Johnson.

politicians who should understand them. Among those reasons are the need for proposals for European Community measures to be made by the Commission so as to safeguard, as far as possible, the interests of minorities who may be outvoted, and the need for democratic discussion of all such measures.[6] The Community method is designed to make majority voting acceptable, but this depends also on democratic control of voting in Council. Where the Community method unfortunately does not apply, scrutiny by national parliamentary committees provides the only safeguard, not only for legitimate interests, but for ensuring some degree of public comprehension and acceptance.

It is sometimes said that part of the 'democratic deficit' is due to the fact that the Commission is not elected. This comment misunderstands the role of the Commission, which has no power to adopt new measures or policies (but rather only to propose them), and disregards the need for the Commissioners to be as independent as possible from national interests and from the majority in the European Parliament. These requirements mean that it would be wholly inappropriate that Commissioners should be elected, either by national bodies or voters, or by the European Parliament.

6. Suggestions for Improvements in Democratic Scrutiny And Control

Several of the chapters in this book describe the difficulties which exist for national parliaments in attempting to exercise more democratic control.

[6] J. Temple Lang and E. Gallagher, *The Role of the Commission and Majority Voting* (Institute of European Affairs, Dublin, Occasional Paper No. 7, 1995); J. Temple Lang and E. Gallagher, "What Sort of European Commission Does the European Union Need?" (2002) 1 *Europarättslig Tidskrift* 81; J. Temple Lang, "How Much do the Smaller Member States Need the European Commission?" (2002) 39 *CML Rev.* 315; J. Temple Lang, "Institutional Changes in the European Union to Prepare for Enlargement: Which Role for the Commission?" (2000) 2 *ERA-Forum* 2, at 2–9; J. Temple Lang, "Community Constitutional Law" in B. Laffan (ed.) *Constitution-building in the European Union* (Institute of European Affairs, Dublin, 1996), at 124 and 217; J. Temple Lang, "The Commission: The Key to the Constitutional Treaty for Europe" (2003) 26 *Fordham International Law Journal* 1598, J. Temple Lang, "The Main Issues after the Convention on the Constitutional Treaty for Europe" (2004) 27 *Fordham International Law Journal* 544. See also F. Lamoureux, "La Constitution 'Pénélope' une Refondation Pour en Finir Avec les Replâtrages" (2003) *Revue du Droit de l'Union Européenne* (January), at 13 (correctly describing the 'Community method' but omitting any reference to the sole right of initiative in describing the role of the Commission): A. Mattera, "Les Zones d'Ombre du Projet de Constitution Dans l'Architecture Institutionnelle de l'Union est la Composition de la Commission" (2003) *Revue du Droit de l'Union Européenne* (January), at 5–12 (assessing the Convention's proposals on the Commission as a 'solution fâcheuse pour grands et petits').

Some of these difficulties are not due to, or confined to the special features of European Union affairs. In his chapter, however, Professor Raunio makes a number of suggestions for improving the capacity of individual parliaments to exercise their powers. Specialised committees, with adequate resources, are obviously essential. Hearings with ministers before and after important Council meetings (although not before meetings which the minister certifies are unimportant) are clearly necessary, and should be held as often as possible. Ministers might be more willing to do this if they were sure that the legislators would repeat their explanations to wider audiences.

Perhaps because he comes from a country with the great Nordic tradition of open government, Professor Raunio arguably lays insufficient emphasis on the need for better freedom-of-information measures both at Community level and at national level in other member states. Both the Commission and the Irish civil service have interpreted the measures applying to them restrictively and sometimes obstructively. The Irish attitude is not, of course, confined to European Union affairs, but it is particularly serious in that context, since national policy issues as well as private rights are likely to be involved. Beyond Professor Raunio's suggestions, there are several other more ambitious changes which would be worthwhile in themselves, and which would significantly increase the scope for democratic scrutiny of European Union affairs.

The first and most important of these changes would be for the discussions in the Council of Ministers, and the European Council,[7] to be held in public, with the media present. This change was envisaged by the Constitutional Treaty, so it already has the agreement of all the authorities of the 25 member states. But it does not require a Treaty amendment, or even a change in European Union legislation. It could be done overnight. It would clearly be valuable in itself for the public to know what is said and done during Council meetings, just as it is valuable for the public to be able to know what is said in any legislative chamber. But the change is suggested here because it would, at a stroke, enable national parliaments to know what was really going on in the Council, to see what their ministers say and how they vote, and to understand whatever the difficulties might be of achieving agreement. There should be a published verbatim report of Council proceedings, just as there is a verbatim report of the proceedings of the European Parliament.

---

[7] Editor's note: under Art 4 of the Treaty on European Union, the European Council brings together the heads of state or government of the member states and the President of the Commission.

A second, more ambitious change, also inspired by the Constitutional Treaty, would be for the Houses of the Oireachtas to resolve that they could instruct the Government, if necessary, to bring proceedings in the Court of Justice to challenge the validity of European Union measures, as being contrary to the principles of subsidiarity and proportionality. Again, no Treaty amendment or national legislation would be needed to enable the Dáil and Seanad to adopt such resolutions, or to act on them if and when the occasion arose. Unlike the previous suggestion, this could be done at any time without the cooperation of any other member state. It would encourage the Oireachtas to understand that it could exercise control over European Union developments, and would encourage Oireachtas committees to feel that if they had strong views, effect could be given to them.

This suggestion goes further than did the Constitutional Treaty, because it applies the possibility of challenge on the grounds of proportionality as well as subsidiarity. As the possibility already exists of a national parliament instructing its government to challenge a European Community measure in the Court of Justice, on *any* ground, this creates no legal difficulty. Indeed, proportionality and subsidiarity issues are closely linked.[8] However, it is worth mentioning that European Community regulations could also be challenged on the ground that they are too vague to be compatible with the principle of legal certainty. Since European Community legislation is sometimes badly drafted because it includes inadequately-considered language suggested in the Council or the European Parliament, this is a useful possibility.

A third change could be made without legislation at either national or European Union level, but would require the assent of the Commission (which however could hardly be refused). Individual members of the Commission could be invited to come to Dublin regularly to discuss their current proposals and policies. It is now clear that the Commissioners should be doing much more to explain their proposals and to discuss them in public in national capitals (and indeed in provincial centres) in all member states. This would not necessarily need to be done always by Commissioners. Some Directors-General spend a surprisingly large proportion of their time at conferences explaining the policies for which they are responsible. It would be more worthwhile for them to discuss policies with legislators, and it

[8] S. Weatherill, "Better Competence Monitoring" (2005) 30 *European Law Review* 23. The Constitutional Treaty proposed to give one third of national parliaments a right to block a proposal on subsidiarity grounds. Giving effect to this right would require a treaty amendment.

would be helpful to both parties for this to be done regularly, as a matter of routine, and not only when some particularly controversial or difficult problem arises. This would also enable Commission representatives to sound out national political opinion, and would provide legislators with another source of information on Commission activities and thinking.

Another practice which could easily be adopted is for Members of the European Parliament (and not only Irish MEPs) to visit the Oireachtas Committees for discussions. Again this would be more effective if it was done routinely, and not merely *ad hoc* when a controversy has arisen. There is at present too little communication between even Irish MEPs and Members of the Oireachtas.

Professor Raunio rightly calls attention to the clauses of the Protocol on the Role of National Parliaments in the European Union (which was annexed to the Constitutional Treaty) which would have required draft European legislative acts sent to the Council and Parliament to be sent simultaneously to national parliaments.[9] This is something which could be done immediately, without any Treaty changes. It could be done with all European Union documents, not only those mentioned in the Constitution. It is particularly important that documents *not* prepared by the Commission should be brought to the attention of national parliaments in this way.

Another practical suggestion is prompted by the practice of the CDU/CSU in Germany, which from time to time publishes foreign policy discussions and statements which have contributed greatly to informing German public opinion, *e.g.,* in 1994 on Germany's special interest in the need for enlargement of the European Community. Such documents do *not* need to be produced by political parties in office, and might be franker if they came from parties which were not. They may be more widely read, and more lastingly available, than the deliberations of parliamentary committees. They do not necessarily need to embody the results of intensive investigation or research, as long as they are carefully considered. For example, an objective statement of the arguments for and against further enlargement of the European Union, and in particular the accession of Turkey to the European Union (in spite of the fact that the possibility of Turkey's accession was confirmed at the Nice Summit in 2000 and again at the Summit in December 2004), would now be a useful corrective to the unwise and alarmist expressions of concern made by some politicians since the referendums in

[9] See in this regard Art. 2 of the Protocol on the Role of National Parliaments in the European Union.

France and the Netherlands. Legislators should not improvise reactions, without consideration, to developments or proposals: they should assess them within the framework of previously discussed policy and policy considerations. The 'No' votes in France and the Netherlands have made it more necessary, not less, to explain and confirm the policy of the European Union towards Turkey and on enlargement in general. When policies have not been fully explained, the important reasons for them are not always understood or remembered.

7. Democratic Discussion of Long-Term Strategic Issues

It is important that all these contacts and activities should be concerned at least as much with long-term strategic issues as with current short-term matters. Governments everywhere tend to be concerned primarily with immediate or short-term issues. Genuine long-term leadership by politicians is rare, in Ireland and at present also elsewhere in Europe. Public opinion should be enabled to give careful consideration to long-term issues of European Union policy, on the basis of objective discussion of different points of view.

For example, there are several profoundly important issues which are now, or should be, under discussion in the European Union: the reform of the Community budget and of the Common Agricultural Policy, the economic policies of States which influence the euro, liberalisation of services, enlargement, and the future accession of Turkey. This is not the place to discuss these issues, though they have always been at least as important as the Constitutional Treaty. But they all need to be discussed and considered carefully, objectively and from a long-term viewpoint. It would be quite wrong for decisions on these important issues to be taken without discussion in the Oireachtas.

There is a special reason in Ireland (and in some other member states) why informed discussion, in public and by legislators, of long-term strategic or policy issues is particularly important. All the issues just mentioned are capable of influencing the result of a referendum in Ireland or elsewhere. Ireland has already had six referendums on European issues, and may have more. It is therefore extremely important, indeed vital, that there should be thorough, informed, calm, objective discussion of these issues to inform public opinion and as far as possible to avoid voting which is primarily or exclusively influenced by ignorance, resentment, prejudice, or short-term political considerations, or by a wish to maintain an unsustainable *status quo*. Even the National Forum for Europe, while it is still active (or its equivalent in other countries, now being rightly recognised as necessary in many member states), cannot fairly be expected, and certainly should not be relied on, to provide all the public discussion needed on such long-term questions of European Union policy.

All of these activities and objectives for Oireachtas committees are relevant to the question of how to provide better-informed and more effective democratic control in Ireland as elsewhere. In this context, another important point should be made. Some people claim that it is improper for the same question to be put to the people in a referendum more than once. Several comments are appropriate. First, it sometimes becomes clear during a referendum campaign that public opinion on some of the issues considered or felt to be relevant is inadequately or indeed incorrectly informed. Where that is so, it is no doubt often due to failure by politicians to inform and lead. But whatever it is due to, the fact must be recognised. If it is recognised only during the referendum campaign, it may be too late to inform public opinion, particularly in countries where the public has no great confidence in politicians, and perhaps particularly little in the politicians in office. So intelligent long-term discussion of issues likely to influence referendums is essential in every member state in which referendums are likely or even possible. Even in member states in which no referendum will be held, it is important in a democratic society for the people to understand and approve, or at least accept, the main directions of national and European policy.

The second comment is prompted by Switzerland, the European country which has by far both the most and the longest experience with referendums. Whether due to ignorance or prejudice, those who claim that it is wrong to suggest a second referendum on any issue are clearly and absolutely contradicted by the Swiss practice. In Switzerland, it is universally accepted that, on any issue, the result in a first referendum may not be a well-considered one, because the issue was not 'ripe' or mature, or public opinion not sufficiently considered. That is no doubt the appropriate practice in a very conservative country where many important issues are put to referendums. But Switzerland is not the only country in Europe with conservative voters: French voters are extremely conservative on the subject of subsidies for farmers, (and indeed for other people). In most countries, sacred cows cannot be relied on to disappear in a single referendum. Indeed one referendum campaign may be necessary to get public opinion to give enough attention to an issue for a well-considered result to be obtained in a second referendum.

8. Conclusions

It will be seen that none of the suggestions made here are, or should be, controversial. They are all so clearly desirable, and have already been so clearly accepted in principle, that there should be no objection on the grounds that undesirable features of the Constitutional Treaty are being introduced by the back door.

Promoting more democratic scrutiny is concerned with long-term policy objectives as well as short-term issues, and the means to ensure it should be carefully designed with both in mind. Legislators should ensure that all of the most important long-term strategic issues for the European Union are carefully considered well before it becomes necessary for parliaments or peoples to decide on them. Effective scrutiny must be well-informed scrutiny, and it is simply not possible, even for legislators and certainly not for peoples, to become well-informed overnight about large, complex long-term policy or strategic issues with which they are not familiar. It has been said that 'people tend to choose problems their own size', and wise statesmanship will concentrate on the most important issues in the long term, especially if they are also difficult ones. Governments in France and the Netherlands have now had salutary lessons in the dangers of failing to ensure that national and European Union policies are fully explained and discussed. French voters who voted against change, in favour of subsidies, or against foreigners or freer trade, may well have been wrong, but their prejudices arose because so little had been done by French politicians to explain and discuss any of these issues.

It is particularly important to ensure careful public discussion of issues where changes, of some kind, are necessary, and where the short-term interests of voters are likely to be against them. Protectionism is addictive, and subsidies, especially when paid for by foreigners, even more so. Politicians who occasionally are compelled to provide leadership must prepare the ground on issues on which the exercise of leadership, however reluctant or unusual, will be necessary. Only an active system of democratic discussion and scrutiny can prepare public opinion on major issues, and only a prepared public opinion can enable or allow politicians to take sound decisions. Where, as in most member states, governments are not providing leadership, and in particular where even politicians elected to office are distrusted, it is all the more necessary for legislators to ensure that there is frank and honest public discussion of important issues.

Democratic scrutiny is particularly important when official action, whether of the Irish authorities or the European Union institutions, may be unpopular, or may involve disadvantages as well as benefits. Whatever the best decisions may be in such circumstances, public discussion is essential. Peoples are better-educated and informed than they used to be, and in referendums they are asked to take very great responsibilities, both for themselves and, increasingly, for other peoples. Democratic scrutiny is not only concerned with the wisdom or desirability of particular measures. It must also be concerned with the most important directions of policy. It is not concerned only, and should not be concerned primarily, with short-term measures taken on the initiative of governments, but it should also be concerned with desirable actions *not* taken or necessary policies *not* adopted.

Public discussion of strategic policy issues facing Europe is particularly necessary in Ireland for several reasons. Ireland is a small country, whose foreign policy is preoccupied with Northern Ireland and our position within the European Union, rather than the policies which the European Union as a whole should adopt. Important national decisions are increasingly taken in referendums. As in France and the Netherlands, there is a risk that voters will try to vote against change or against short-term inconvenience. As in France, there is little political leadership. As in France, there is a reluctance to accept the inevitable, in particular the ongoing and inevitable reform of the Common Agricultural Policy.

Even an enlarged Council – in which 27 member states are represented – is, and will no doubt continue to be, simultaneously one chamber of a bicameral legislature and a forum for intermittent diplomatic negotiations. It follows that democratic control of the Council, whether by national parliaments or, as far as the Treaty provides, by the European Parliament, has special characteristics. But there is no reason why this control must be ineffective, and no reason why the existing degree of control by the Oireachtas and other member state parliaments cannot be substantially improved. The most important single step for this purpose would be a Council decision to hold all legislative debates in public. Any closed meetings, *e.g.*, on international economic negotiations, should be rare and fully justified. That would have many benefits and would also facilitate democratic control.

The changes suggested here which do not need the agreement of other member states, if they were first made by a few states, would almost certainly be widely copied, as a result of peer pressure and cooperation within COSAC.

It will be seen that most of the steps needed to provide more democratic control over European Union affairs could be taken without Treaty amendment and would be desirable in themselves for other reasons, in particular because they would reduce the present insufficient public awareness of European Union activities. This would reduce the scope for misrepresentation and prejudice, and would also end one of the legitimate criticisms of the European Union – the secrecy of Council deliberations.

Ending that would automatically make it easier to explain the European Union to European voters, in particular in referendums. By making the European Union easier to understand, it would make it more acceptable, and so lessen the need for referendums, as well as facilitating public discussion of the really important challenges facing the European Union in the next few years. These challenges will not be postponed or avoided by putting reform of the kind which was proposed in the Constitutional Treaty aside, although such reform might make it easier to tackle them. And even if the 'democratic deficit' is solved on the lines suggested here, the European Union will not be sure of the approval of electorates until these challenges, and in particular the economic challenges, have been dealt with.

5.
Some Reflections from the United Kingdom on the Role of National Parliaments in the European Union

Adam Cygan[1]

1. The Debate Surrounding National Parliaments

In this chapter, the manner in which national parliaments have contributed to the process of European Union integration is examined. It is acknowledged that national parliaments have lost legislative competence. However, it is contended that their democratic traditions, practices and principles are important features which the European Union must encompass if further integration is to be acceptable to the European Union citizen. The chapter involves an examination in particular of how national parliaments' review of executive activity in Council has ensured that the democratic deficit, which is regularly mentioned as an effect of European Union integration, has been restricted at national level.

A defining feature of European Union integration has been the constitutionalisation of the Union[2] and the creation of what the European Court of Justice has referred to as a 'new legal order'.[3] With the Europeanisation of policy,[4] the centre of gravity for legislative action has shifted from the national arena to European Union level. One consequence of this has been the peripheral role which national parliaments have held

---

[1] Senior Lecturer in Law, Centre for European Law and Integration, Faculty of Law, University of Leicester. Like most of the other chapters in this book, this chapter was originally presented as a paper at the conference *Ireland, Europe and the Challenge of Democracy – Ensuring Democratic Control over Government Affairs in the European Union* held on 20 May, 2005 under the auspices of the Faculty of Law, University College Dublin and the Institute of European Affairs. I would like to thank participants at that conference for their comments on earlier draft of this paper. The usual disclaimer applies.

[2] M. Poiares Maduro, *We the Court* (Hart Publishing, Oxford, 1998).

[3] Case 25/62 *Van Gend en Loos* v *Nederlanse Administratie der Belastingen* [1963] ECR 1.

[4] See Poiares Maduro, cited above at n. 2, pp. 68–78.

throughout the integration process, particularly with regard to decision-making.[5] European Union decision-making is dominated by the Union's institutions and seeks to balance the supranational (Commission), the intergovernmental (Council), and the multi-national (European Parliament). The present Treaty framework does not assign a role to national parliaments within the European Union decision-making process, as formal ratification of legislative acts is not necessary.[6]

The question of participation in European Union decision-making must be distinguished from that of the scrutiny of European Union legislative proposals carried out by national parliaments, however. The objective of this scrutiny is to provide domestic accountability of individual ministers for actions in Council. There is also the formal task of the implementation of European Community directives, which is often assigned to domestic legislatures, although it tends to leave little scope for discretion. Indeed, a failure by a national parliament in the timely and proper implementation of directives constitutes a violation of Community law, the consequence of which may be the payment of damages by the offending State.[7]

Despite their tangential role in European Union decision-making, national parliaments remain the primary legislative bodies within the member states and provide the principal form of political representation for European Union citizens. National parliaments are an embodiment of political sovereignty; they are directly elected and have the function of controlling the executive. Furthermore, national parliaments are an expression of cultural identity, and their composition broadly reflects the socio-cultural values of each member state. The constitutional theory that national parliaments are sovereign decision-making institutions is increasingly divorced from reality, however. National parliaments are now regularly portrayed as reactive institutions, exercising rather modest influence on policy initiatives coming from the executive.[8] To take the case of the United Kingdom, single parties,

[5] A. Maurer, "National Parliaments in the European Union Architecture: From Latecomers Adaptation Towards Permanent Institutional Change" in A. Maurer and W. Wessels (eds.), *National Parliaments on their Ways to Europe: Losers or Latecomers*? (Nomos, Baden-Baden, 2001).

[6] The impact which the Constitutional Treaty would have had on national parliaments and their scrutiny function is discussed below.

[7] Joined Cases C-6/90 and C-9/90 *Francovich v Italian State* [1991] ECR I-535. This judgment established the principle of Stale liability for failure by a member state to implement a directive within the transitional period allowed.

[8] See Maurer, cited above, n. 5, and T. Raunio and S. Hix, "Backbenchers Learn to Fight Back: European Integration and Parliamentary Government" (2000) 23 *West European Politics* 142 at 145.

with large majorities, have dominated Parliament here since the 1980s. This has allowed governments to push through often unpopular reforms, with the legislature having only limited ability to influence and hold the executive to account. The reorganisation of government and administration in the United Kingdom, through changes such as devolution and the extended use of agencies, has further altered the relationship between the executive and Parliament.[9] Within member states of the European Union generally, administrative changes have been effected which have extended the powers of non-governmental agencies. Raunio and Hix have argued that these developments demonstrate that European integration is not *per se* responsible for the decline of influence by national parliaments, and that:

> "notwithstanding the transfer of constitutional, executive and legislature powers to the European level, the overall impact of European integration on parliamentary government in the domestic area has actually been rather modest".[10]

Taking account of the foregoing, together with what Maduro has referred to as the Europeanisation of law and policy within the member states, it may be argued that national parliaments are fighting a rearguard action to maintain their influence. For by now, most government policy is influenced or directed by European Union objectives.[11] Furthermore the development of soft law and the open method of coordination has made additional inroads on domestic competence and through a process of 'creeping competences',[12] has brought additional policy areas within the scope of the European Union. Scrutiny of policies introduced via the Open Method causes problems for national parliaments, as their procedures are geared towards the evaluation

---

[9] P. Norton (ed.) *Parliaments and Governments in Western Europe*. (Frank Cass, London, 1996).

[10] See Raunio and Hix, cited above, 8 at 143.

[11] To address the specific point of Raunio and Hix, while there undoubtedly is a domestic political and legislative agenda, this cannot be considered in isolation from that of the European Union. (It may be noted that even legislative proposals dealing with domestic issues are capable, in certain circumstances of infringing the general principles of European Union law).

[12] D. Hodson and I. Maher, "The Open Method as a New Mode of Governance: The Case of Economic Policy Coordination" (2001) 39 *Journal of Common Market Studies* 719. For the application of the open method of coordination to European Union social policy, see E. Szyszczak, "The New Paradigm for Social Policy: a Virtuous Circle?" (2001) 38 *Common Market Law Review* 1125. For its application to asylum and immigration policy, see B. Bogusz, "Modes of Governance for a European Union Immigration Policy – What Role for the Open Method of Coordination" in B. Bogusz, R. Cholewinski, A. Cygan and E. Szyszczak (eds.), *Irregular Migration and Human Rights: Theoretical, European and International Perspectives*, (Kluwer Law International, The Hague, 2004).

of hard law. The open method, formalised at the Lisbon European Council in 2000, encourages a process of social learning between member states to seek shared solutions to common problems. The defining feature of the open method is that it does not follow the traditional Community method of decision-making that leads to hard legislative acts.

The Open Method has strengthened the leadership role of the European Council which takes the lead in policy coordination, with the Commission adopting a strategic role by setting objectives and issuing guidelines and recommendations to national governments.[13] At present, the European Parliament is on the periphery of this process. At the national level, the Open Method falls within the activities of civil servants who possess expertise on the issues, and in this sense shares many of the features of the comitology process. As the Open Method is primarily intergovernmental in character, national parliaments are constitutionally in a strong position to influence the proceedings. The difficulty lies in finding the parliamentary time to conduct the necessary scrutiny. Furthermore, reviewing often abstract guidelines or targets which are set by the Commission is not a priority for national parliaments within a busy parliamentary timetable.

National parliaments have not been rendered completely irrelevant even at European level, however, even bearing in mind the effects of increasing constitutionalisation here. On the contrary, national parliaments have a key role within the European Union, not least because it is from their membership that the executive of most member states is composed and it is therefore national parliaments which ultimately provide most of the members of the Council. Furthermore, the Laeken Declaration,[14] the Convention on the Future of Europe (which provided the first draft of the Constitutional Treaty) and the Constitutional Treaty have all recognised that national parliaments are integral to a European Union constitutional settlement.

National parliaments have through their democratic traditions contributed to improving the legitimacy of European Union law and laid the foundations for the ongoing process of parliamentarisation of the European Union. This process has gradually brought the norms of domestic parliamentary

[13] The role of the Commission in the Open Method varies considerably between policy areas, with the Council often adopting the leading function instead of the Commission.

[14] Laeken European Council December 15 2001. Available at*www.europa.eu.int/futurum/documents/offtext/doc151201_en.htm.*

procedure and activity into the decision-making process of the European Union. For example co-decision, which seeks a legislative compromise between the European Parliament and the Council, is based upon a process of negotiation and discussion. It can be argued that this process of conciliation has its roots in the best traditions of coalition government which is a feature in many member states. Though parliamentarisation has not led to a veto for national legislatures, the process has led to acknowledgment of the significance of their democratic credentials. The Constitutional Treaty sought to place upon national parliaments an increased role in securing democratic legitimacy for the European Union. The issue that this raises is the extent to which, if at all, national parliaments wish to take on this role and whether they have the procedures which can deliver it

2. The Heterogeneity of Scrutiny within National Parliaments

Scrutiny of European Union legislative proposals is the single most important task for national parliaments insofar as concerns their European activities. While the procedure may be different within each parliament, the objective is the same – that of securing executive accountability in the process of European Union decision-making. There are two key issues for national parliaments in scrutinising European Union legislative proposals. These are the prompt provision of the necessary documentation, and the question of time – with the overriding objective of the scrutiny process being to influence the minister *prior* to the Council adopting its definitive common position.[15]

National parliaments have developed their own scrutiny mechanisms to oversee the European Union policy of their respective governments. The procedural differences that exist with regard to the practice of scrutiny in the member states account, at least in part, for the variations between national parliaments as regards the frequency and vigour of scrutiny carried out. Within this context, the call for national parliaments to help bridge the democracy gap contains one inherent flaw – namely the fact that their procedures are not uniform, a factor which ultimately prevents standardised scrutiny within all national parliaments. The Council has acquired a role which is greater than that derived from its composition of ministerial representatives from 27 member states. Consequently, as a legislative institution, this raises question of accountability and legitimacy.

[15] *Democracy and Accountability in the EU and the Role of National Parliaments: Vol I* (2001–02, HC 152-xxxiii-I), 22 at para. 33.

Accordingly, is Council decision-making collectively legitimised through the individual domestic accountability of its component parts or does national scrutiny merely fulfil national priorities?

Even if an aggregate democratic legitimacy were possible, this still leaves the already identified problem that national parliaments are not a homogeneous grouping. Each member states has developed its own parliamentary traditions and significant differences exist in the electoral process. This will lead to either coalition or single party governments which can dominate a parliament to differing degrees. France, for example, has a semi-presidential system, whereas the United Kingdom parliamentary system remains fixed upon a process of executive accountability to Parliament. This United Kingdom tradition is carried through in the scrutiny of European Union affairs, even though the process of European Union decision-making is not readily compatible with a process of national parliamentary scrutiny. In federal member states such as Belgium, the sub-national entities enjoy considerable rights of participation in the formulation of European Union policy. (Despite this prominence in several member states, sub-national parliaments rarely attract attention in the present institutional context. Though ministers drawn from sub-national institutions are permitted under Article 205 of the EC Treaty to represent the member state at Council meetings, such ministers represent the entire member state and not just the region from which they are drawn). In Denmark, the mandating of ministers is a key principle of parliamentary activity. While this secures ministerial accountability, it is doubtful that it would be possible for the Council to function were all member states to adopt this method of scrutiny. Finally, the recent enlargement process has brought member states into the European Union in which parliamentary democracy remains a relatively new concept.

The form and degree of European scrutiny in a national parliament is primarily a matter of domestic history, political culture, attitudes of political parties and institutional balance of power.[16] In practical terms, the committees in all member states differ in activity and productivity, a phenomenon which is closely related to the procedures under which they operate and interact with the government and the rest of their parliament. All committees participate in COSAC, the Conference of Community and European Affairs Committees of Parliaments of the European Union, but

[16] See Conclusions of Working Group IV of the Convention on the Future of Europe, the function of which was to examine the role of national parliaments in the EU. A record of its proceedings is available at http://european-convention.eu.int/doc_register.asp?lang=EN&Content=WGIV.

Norton has argued that the very term 'European Affairs Committees' is misleading as its use can 'convey an impression of uniformity that does not exist'.[17]

There are two basic models for those parliaments attempting to carry out serious scrutiny. The first variety is the document-based model, as adopted by the United Kingdom parliament. The second type is referred to as a 'mandating' model, pioneered by the Danish parliament and followed, with modifications, by certain other parliaments.[18] The former supposedly concentrates on the early stage of legislation, when a Commission draft legislative proposal is first adopted, while the latter tends to focus on the conclusion of negotiations in the Council. There are, however, degrees of overlap between the two methods. For example, the House of Commons will attempt to scrutinise a proposal when significant amendments are made in the European Parliament and the Council towards the end of the co-decision process. Similarly, a House of Commons resolution recommending documents for further debate by the European Scrutiny Committee could be regarded as a rudimentary and general form of mandate. The views of the Select Committee will be thereby made known to the government who will have to demonstrate good reasons for ignoring them.

The Danish parliament has comprehensive arrangements to obtain draft legislation and other European Union documents when they are produced, together with government explanatory memoranda. Since 1996, it has held hearings and produced opinions on some Commission Green and White Papers. This mirrors in large part the European Scrutiny Committee in the House of Commons which, since its 1999 amendment to the Standing Orders, is not exclusively focused on legislative documents. This committee will, when necessary, question ministers before or after Council meetings. Yet it remains questionable whether either type of committee has the time or necessary resources to cover both documents and Council agendas systematically.

The Danish model of mandating operates almost entirely through the *Folketing's* European Affairs Committee. In the week prior to the Council meeting, the responsible minister presents the government's desired mandate

---

[17] See Norton, above, n. 9 at 188.

[18] This model is followed to lesser degrees by other Nordic parliaments. See generally regarding the scrutiny mechanisms in the Nordic states, the chapter in this volume by Tapio Raunio and Matti Wiberg.

to the committee, running through the Council agenda, and explaining the government's proposed negotiating position. This will provide both the history and substance of the items to be discussed and the likely attitudes of other member states. The mandate sought by the government is therefore an oral one, formulated by the minister. Following the minister's presentation of the mandate, there are questions and a debate during which the minister can make modifications to the mandate. Finally, the chairman of the committee seeks to establish, without a formal vote, whether there is a majority against the proposed mandate.

Each party representative at the meeting carries a voting weight reflecting his or her party's strength in the *Folketing*. Voting does not depend on individual MPs attending the meeting. It is very rare for there to be a majority against a mandate. Such a majority has the consequence that the minister may not support legislation at the Council meeting. More often, amendments are made to the mandate originally proposed by the minister. The mandate is politically binding on the government, and there is an ongoing debate in Denmark as to whether it is also legally binding. Following Council meetings ministers publish reports on their outcome, allowing the committee to check whether the mandate was observed. If the committee desires clarification, it can take written or oral evidence from the minister.

Member states which joined the European Union from 2004 on had the benefit of having been able to consider the scrutiny mechanisms already in place in the fifteen pre-enlargement member states. It is still too early, however, to accurately evaluate the practice in such new member states, apart from their experience in overseeing the accession negotiation process. Categorisation of such national parliaments into groups of stronger and weaker players is less straightforward than it may seem, primarily because there has been no uniformity in post-communist political development or parliamentary procedure.[19] To take some examples, Estonia, Latvia and Slovenia may have the potential to maintain a relatively strong scrutiny system, given the stable parliamentary and governmental systems in these countries. However, none of these has chosen to follow the Nordic model based on the mandate. Instead, they have chosen to follow a more document-based process. Different considerations apply in other countries which joined

[19] A. Fraga, "Wanting more power ... a struggle for what? Comments on the report by Mr. Tapio Raunio 'Parliamentary Scrutiny of EU Decision-Making: Comparing National Systems'" in *National Parliaments and the EU – Stock-Taking for the Post-Amsterdam Era* (October 1999, COSAC seminar paper submitted by Finnish Eduskunta), Eduskunnan Kanslian Julkaisu 1/2000.

in the last enlargement, such as Poland and the Czech Republic, since these have different political structures, with weak coalition government having characterised the period since 1989. In yet other new member states, there is a dominant executive or president. No new member state can be classified as openly Eurosceptical, but there are established anti-European Union parties within parliaments, which participate in European Union Affairs Committees. The common feature of the new Central European member states is that they experienced an interruption of parliamentary democracy during decades of authoritarian rule.[20] Although the new member states have been able to profit from their late accession,[21] other factors have been capable of outweighing that advantage, such as small size and the limited resources available to parliaments.

From this brief overview it is evident that there is a lack of a common approach within the member states as regards their electoral process, their parliamentary practice and the status of their European Affairs Committees. These factors influence both the process of scrutiny in national parliaments and the extent to which national parliaments participate in European Union affairs. The level of participation and the priority given to it within the parliamentary timetable will impact upon the extent to which citizens are aware of European Union affairs. Yet the lack of a formal collective procedural framework to European Union affairs amongst national parliaments should not necessarily be considered as being an obstacle to effective ministerial scrutiny. Basic scrutiny objectives are contained within the Amsterdam Protocol on the Role of National Parliaments,[22] and at the very minimum provide national parliaments with a statement of their obligations. This common ground and norms of the Protocol facilitates for national parliaments the individual task of ministerial accountability through application of their own procedures. By its very any nature, any form of collective scrutiny, beyond the expectations of the Protocol on the Application of the Principles of Subsidiarity and Proportionality which was annexed to the Constitutional Treaty,[23] would require, in order for it to function, either the creation of some new supranational institution or specific guidance (perhaps in the form of a Council decision) as to what are the principles and expectations of scrutiny.[24]

---

[20] This was also the case in Portugal, Spain and Greece prior to European Union accession.

[21] T. Bergman, "National Parliaments and European Union Affairs Committees: Notes on Empirical Variation and Competing Explanations" (1997) *4 Journal of European Public Policy* 373–387.

[22] As to which, see text below.

[23] Examined in the text below.

[24] It may be noted that neither such development seems desirable to this writer.

Under existing arrangements, scrutiny of executive action in European Union affairs is contributing to improved accountability and democracy in the European Union. While it is not the primary objective of domestic scrutiny to provide a comprehensive system of accountability of European Union institutions, or even to bridge the democracy gap to the European Union citizen, the scrutiny activities of national parliaments do contribute to a more general objective of parliamentarisation of the European Union.

3. The Position of National Parliaments since Maastricht

There is a degree of irony in the fact that agreement was reached on giving national parliaments an increased prominence only on the agreement of the Constitutional Treaty.[25] Cynics could argue that national governments woke up very late to the idea that domestic legislative chambers have a distinct role to play in an enlarged European Union. The Constitutional Treaty recognised the unease expressed from within member states during the Convention that the process of European Union integration lacked democratic credibility. Accordingly, that Treaty sought to encompass the principles of parliamentary representative and participatory democracy in Articles I-46 and I-47. These provisions were a tacit admission that the European Union must work harder to make these principles the norm. Together with Article I-11 and the revised Protocol relating to national parliaments, the Constitutional Treaty moved the process of parliamentarisation of the European Union forward and brought together more closely national and supra-national institutions in the pursuit of this objective.

Placing national parliaments at the centre of this democratic reform had two aspects. First, it imported directly into the Constitutional Treaty the democratic principles upon which national parliaments function. Secondly, the Treaty makers were seeking to assign national parliaments a role in bridging the democracy gap that exists between citizens and European Union institutions. This latter objective was to be achieved primarily by utilising the representative features of national parliaments.

(a) Developments in Parliamentary Scrutiny – From Maastricht to Amsterdam to the Constitutional Treaty

Since the coming into force of the Treaty of Maastricht, three further treaties have been agreed, and two of these – the Treaty of Amsterdam, and that of

---

[25] Editor's note: see, as regards the most recent pre-publication developments concerning the Constitutional Treaty, the introduction to this book.

Nice – have entered into force. All of these Treaties have sought to increase the competences of the European Union and brought more decision-making within the co-decision procedure. The position of national parliaments has also been addressed and it is proposed to examine the main provisions of relevance here.

At Maastricht, two Declarations were agreed relating to national parliaments. Declaration 13 stated that 'it is important to encourage greater involvement of national Parliaments in the activities of the European Union'. This objective was to be achieved mainly through improved access to information, the provision of adequate and timely information being crucial for national parliaments when scrutinising Council activities. The related point which this Declaration recognised was that when participating in European Union affairs national parliaments are dependent upon the provision of information from third parties. Furthermore, Declaration 13 stated that:

> "governments of Member States will ensure, *inter alia*, that national Parliaments receive Commission proposals for legislation in good time for information or possible examination".

The member states recognised at Maastricht that there was a need for parliamentarisation of European Union activity. Central to achieving this was closer cooperation between national parliaments and the European Parliament. In particular, this required that the democratic credentials of national parliaments be emphasised, as well as the importance of these qualities to further European Union integration. From this it can be seen that re-engaging with the European Union citizen through the proxy assistance of national parliaments – a core objective of the Constitutional Treaty – has its roots in the Maastricht Treaty. Declaration 14 tried to breath life into the 'Assizes', the joint conference of the European Parliament and national parliaments which had convened only once in Rome in November 1990.[26]

---

[26] The Assizes were originally proposed by the French President Francois Mitterrand who wished to see national parliaments take a more proactive role in European affairs. The actual title of the Assizes held in Rome was the Conference of the Parliaments of the European Community. 173 of the delegates were from national parliaments and 85 represented the European Parliament. The proceedings were largely dominated by the European Parliament delegation. The delegates sat in party groups, not according to national affiliation, and the final declaration broadly reflected the European Parliament's programme for revising the Treaty and pursuing an agenda of democratisation. See C. Bengtson, "National Parliaments in European decision-making: A real prospect or wishful thinking?" The Federal Trust Online Paper 29/03, London, September 2003.

The Assizes were to 'meet as necessary' and to 'be consulted on the main features of the European Union',[27] and were partly intended to import parliamentary norms and principles into the process of European Union integration.

Secondly, the Maastricht Treaty introduced the principle of subsidiarity. The purpose of this principle is to ensure that in those areas where the European Union had acquired exclusive competence it would act:

> "only in so far as the objectives of the proposed action cannot be sufficiently achieved by the Member States and can therefore by reason of proposed action be better achieved by the Community".[28]

Subsidiarity, as expressed in what is now Article 5 of the Treaty Establishing the European Community, is largely a political concept. Its aim is to ensure decision-making at the lowest possible level of governance. Given this objective, the principle is one whose application is ripe for *ex ante* review by national parliaments. Agreement on the Edinburgh Guidelines[29] on the application of the subsidiarity principle constituted a recognition that the subsidiarity provisions of the Maastricht Treaty were too vague.

Compared to Declaration 13, the Protocol on the Role of National Parliaments in the European Union, which came into being at the time of the agreement on the Amsterdam Treaty, provided a clearer and more formal status for national parliaments. The Amsterdam Treaty also incorporated the Edinburgh subsidiarity guidelines into a Protocol on the Application of the Principles of Subsidiarity and Proportionality.[30] While both of these Protocols had greater legal force than the Maastricht Declarations, there remained an absence of a process through which national parliaments could enforce these provisions. Thus in terms of the enforcement of subsidiarity, national parliaments were not granted the legal capacity to challenge, *ex post facto*, the adoption of a legislative measure which they considered to offend the principle, and have been reliant upon national governments to pursue any breaches identified.

The Constitutional Treaty addressed the issue of enforcement and included a mechanism through which subsidiarity would be enforced, and

---

[27] Declaration 14, Treaty on European Union, [2002] OJ C325, 24 December 2002.

[28] See now Art 5 of the Treaty Establishing the European Community.

[29] Agreed by the member states at the Edinburgh European Council. See Annex 1 to Part A EC Bulletin 12-1992, 14.

[30] See paras. 4 and 5 of the Amsterdam Protocol.

simultaneously sought to strengthen the role of national parliaments. Working Group IV of the Convention on the Future of Europe which produced the first draft of the Constitutional Treaty identified monitoring and enforcement of subsidiarity as one of three crucial issues issue facing national parliaments.[31] Working Group IV stated in its Final Report that:

> "in particular, national parliaments have a central responsibility to advise, scrutinise and hold to account their own government ministers for their performance in Council, especially when considering whether legislation is best adopted at national or European level." [32]

Under Article I-11 of the Constitutional Treaty and the accompanying Protocol on the Application of Subsidiarity and Proportionality, national parliaments would have gained the power to send any legislative proposal back for review. This would have been possible, broadly speaking, if one third of them agreed that the proposal infringed the principle of subsidiarity.[33] The importance of any such development would be twofold. First, it would be very difficult to ignore the strongly held views of one third of national parliaments. In practice, any proposal meeting such opposition would be very unlikely to prosper, not least because, if one third of national parliaments were against any proposal, their governments would be too. Consequently it would be hard to put together the qualified majority needed to pass the law in question. Secondly, it would give national parliaments a direct say in the European Union's law-making procedures for the first time. Under existing Treaty arrangements, there is no obligation either on member states or on the Commission even to inform national parliaments about draft European Union laws. Under the new mechanism, all national parliaments must be notified independently, and given six weeks to respond.

(b) Present Arrangements: the Operation of the Amsterdam Protocol on National Parliaments

The objective of the Amsterdam Protocol is to provide specific time periods which are aimed at all actors involved in the legislative process, which, if followed, will provide national parliaments with adequate time to scrutinise legislative proposals. The Protocol provides that

[31] The other two issues were, first, the improved scrutiny of the executive, and secondly, the role and function of multilateral networks or mechanisms involving national parliaments at the European level.

[32] See p. 10 of the Final Report of Working Group IV.

[33] Or one quarter, in the case of a draft European legislative act submitted on the basis of Article III-264 of the Constitutional Treaty on the area of freedom, security and justice.

> "a six-week period shall elapse between a legislative proposal or a proposal for a measure to be adopted under Title VI of the Treaty on European Union being made available in all languages to the European Parliament and the Council by the Commission and the date when it is placed on the on a Council agenda for decision … *subject to exceptions on grounds of urgency*, the reasons for which shall be stated in the act or common position".[34]

There are a number of identifiable defects with the Protocol which undermine the ability of national parliaments to effectively influence the minister. First, the Protocol covers only 'legislative' proposals and would not automatically cover other documents which may nonetheless have a significant legal and political impact. It also leaves the Council to decide which acts are of a legislative nature.[35]

Secondly, the Protocol does not give any additional period beyond the six weeks referred to in order to allow for the scrutiny of a proposal which has been substantially revised by the European Parliament during the second reading in the co-decision procedure. Thirdly, the 'urgency' exceptions are vague and open to abuse because they only have to be justified *ex post*, by which time it will be too late for a national parliament to raise objections to the measure which has already been given approval. It is then open to a member state or to a European Union institution to challenge the measure before the Court. National parliaments would not appear to have the necessary *locus standi* before the Court of Justice to initiate such a challenge themselves.

Thus in the absence of any commitment in the Protocol, national parliaments do not automatically get to review an amended proposal. This has been criticised by the House of Commons.[36] The revised measure could raise very specific questions of legal or political importance which the original measure did not. Consequently, while the co-decision procedure addresses the democratic deficit at European Union level by enhancing the role of the European Parliament, a democratic deficit in terms of ministerial accountability to parliament is created at the national level. At this point the scrutiny of the original common position has become obsolete.

---

[34] Emphasis added.

[35] See Art 2 of the Protocol.

[36] See *Democracy and Accountability in the EU and the Role of National Parliaments: Vol I*, above, n. 15, at 22, para. 35.

In discussions on the reform of the Amsterdam Protocol at the Convention on the Future of Europe, Working Group IV recommended that:

> "parliamentary scrutiny reserves should be given a clearer status in the Council's rules of procedure. Such reserves should furthermore have a specified time limit, so as not to unnecessarily block the decision procedure".[37]

However, there would have been problems with the inclusion of a specified time limit since the opportunity for scrutiny by national parliaments varies, depending on how promptly each government provides an explanatory memorandum which forms the basis of the scrutiny. The overriding problem is that amongst national parliaments there is no consistent approach as to how scrutiny reserves should be used, as different member states have different political and legal priorities.[38]

In practice, national scrutiny reserves do take account of the political realities which govern decision-making in the Council, and tend to recognise that efficient decision-making is important. To take the example of the United Kingdom scrutiny reserve, this allows a minister to agree to a proposal in Council prior to the completion of scrutiny when this is in the United Kingdom's national interest. The reserve, which was first introduced in 1990, has also consistently included a clause allowing for decisions to be taken exceptionally on grounds of urgency.[39] Under the United Kingdom provisions, the minister may breach the reserve but must provide *ex post* justification of the decision to the national parliamentary chamber. In these circumstances, the House of Commons would expect a clear explanation of how the measure benefited the United Kingdom, and that any further delay would fundamentally undermine the interests of the United Kingdom.

Problems with effective scrutiny arise for national parliaments in three circumstances: first, when the minister votes in Council, prior to the completion of scrutiny by the appropriate committee. Secondly, difficulty arises when the European Parliament proposes amendments to a proposed measure. The third form of difficulty occurs when the Conciliation

---

[37] CONV 353/02 at para. 20.

[38] Of the pre-2004 enlargement member states of the European Union, the United Kingdom, Denmark, Sweden and the Netherlands were the most frequent users of a scrutiny reserve, whereas Greece, Portugal, and Spain applied a reserve infrequently.

[39] *Ibid.*

Committee agrees on a joint text which is substantially different from the Council's common position.

In the Convention on the Future of Europe, Working Group IV considered the latter two issues very closely. The Commons European Scrutiny Committee, in its evidence to Working Group IV, noted that the first six weeks – referred to in the Amsterdam Protocol – were arguably the least important part of the legislative timetable.[40] However, the final version of the revised Protocol on the role of national Parliaments in the European Union which was annexed to the Constitutional Treaty maintained the requirement that a six-week period elapse (although this period now started only with a draft European legislative act being made available to national Parliaments in the official languages of the Union) by the date when a draft legislative act was placed on a provisional agenda of the Council for adoption. COSAC proposed that there should be – in addition to what is contained in the Amsterdam Protocol – a requirement that a minimum of fifteen days elapse between the final reading of the proposal by the Committee of Permanent Representatives (Coreper) and the Council formally taking a decision on it,[41] in order to allow for scrutiny of any amendments proposed by the European Parliament or arising out of the Conciliation Committee. The final version of the Protocol annexed to the Constitutional Treaty provided that a ten-day period should elapse between the placing of a draft European legislative act on the provisional agenda for the Council and the adoption of a position.[42]

(c) The Constitutional Treaty and National Parliaments

Over the years, in contrast with the idea of increasing the formal presence for national parliaments in the institutional architecture of the European Union as part of a process of parliamentarisation, the Treaties have opted for democratisation through the granting of additional powers to the European Parliament.

Working Group IV in the Convention of the Future of Europe concluded, however, that national parliaments have a distinct role to play within the European Union and that enhancing their involvement would help to strengthen the democratic legitimacy of the Union and have the effect of bringing the European Union closer to its citizens. Anchoring ownership of

---

[40] *Democracy and Accountability in the EU and the Role of National Parliaments: Vol I*, above, n. 15, at 24 at para. 38.

[41] See *http://european-convention.eu.int/docs/wd4/3464.pdf.*

[42] Para. 4 of the Protocol on the Role of National Parliaments in the European Union. An exception was made for urgent cases for which due reasons had been given.

the European Union in the member states was considered of major importance to achieve these goals. Since the Maastricht Treaty, the European Union's commitment to improved democracy, more transparency and a recognition of the role of the individual have been paramount objectives. It is no coincidence that the Maastricht Treaty simultaneously recognised the importance of national parliaments and introduced the concept of citizenship of the European Union. Taken together, these developments are part of the long-standing objective of re-engaging with the citizen and demonstrating that integration is a relevant concept to them. What better way of disseminating this message to citizens than through their national parliaments?

Working Group IV underlined that the relationship between elected legislatures at all levels of governance should not be based upon legislative competition. The process of parliamentarisation of the European Union involves institutions at *all* levels of governance learning from each other and working together to secure executive accountability. Each legislature has a distinct role but all, in theory at least, share the common burden of bringing the European Union closer to citizens and improving the democratic legitimacy of the Union.

When the European Union consisted of fewer member states, and when the influence and contribution of national parliaments could therefore have been greater, national parliaments were on the margins of European integration. Furthermore, their potential for democratising the European Union was largely ignored. The adoption of the Constitutional Treaty's provisions was intended to send out the message of a more democratic, accountable, and transparent European Union. However, in the adoption of legislation at European Union level, the formal role of national parliaments was to be confined to monitoring the application of the subsidiarity principle.[43] Issues which arose from the changes proposed in the Constitutional Treaty included whether *ex ante* monitoring of subsidiarity would guarantee national parliaments a pivotal place in the decision-making process.[44] Also, would the emphasis placed on putting national parliaments at the centre of political decision-making improve the quality and legitimacy of legislation in the eyes

---

[43] See Art I-11 of the Constitutional Treaty and the annexed Protocol on the Application of the Principles of Subsidiarity and Proportionality. Art I-11(3) provides that national parliaments are to ensure compliance with [the principle of subsidiarity] in accordance with the procedure set out in the Protocol.

[44] On this issue generally see S. Weatherill "Better Competence Monitoring" (2005) 30 *European Law Review* 23.

of European Union citizens? And if this is the intention, could it be achieved in the absence of a collective institution which would represent national parliaments at European Union level and through which they could adopt a coordinated approach towards subsidiarity and European Union affairs generally?

The relevant changes introduced by the Constitutional Treaty appeared, at first sight, to reinforce the idea that national parliaments should perform an individual rather than a collective scrutiny role. For although the monitoring of subsidiarity was to require collective action to attain the necessary one-third majority required by the Treaty to block a measure, the Treaty was silent on how in practice this would be achieved. Using COSAC[45] as a forum to provide this might have provided the basis for a solution, although COSAC includes representatives from the European Parliament, an institution which is likely to have a different view of whether a measure conforms with the subsidiarity principle to that of national parliaments.

The primary criticism to be made of Article I-11's provisions on subsidiarity review was that they could only function if national parliaments cooperated in order to obtain the necessary one-third threshold. This might have proven difficult in the light of the maximum six-week period available. In this time period, national parliaments would be mostly concerned with completing their domestic scrutiny of the measure within the confines of a hectic parliamentary timetable. Furthermore, to galvanise the opposition of one-third of national parliaments, a 'leader' would be required to coordinate opposition and ensure consistency.

Working Group IV of the Convention on the Future of Europe did also consider more radical proposals such as the creation of a specific forum through which national parliaments could express a clearer collective voice. Suggestions for reforms ranged from the creation of a Chamber of national parliamentarians next to the European Parliament,[46] or an Assizes-type Congress of Parliaments.[47] The European Union Committee in the House of

[45] The full English title of this body is the Conference of Community and European Affairs Committees of Parliaments of the European Union. The abbreviation comes from the French title of the forum, "Conférence des organes spécialisés dans les affaires communautaires et européennes des parlements de l'Union européenne". See further in relation to COSAC, the chapter in this volume by Morten Knudsen and Yves Carl.

[46] See House of Lords Select Committee on the European Union, *A Second Parliamentary Chamber for the EU: an Unreal Solution to some Real Problems* (2001-2HL 48).

[47] A. Barrau, *National Parliaments* (2002) (CONV 84/02, Contribution 40).

Lords had earlier considered whether either type of forum could form a second legislative chamber in the European Union, and more generally whether there was any need for such an institution.[48] The House of Lords concluded that even if such a second chamber could function, it doubted whether there was any appetite among national parliaments to transfer the scrutiny function to such an institution.

This writer's view would be that the disadvantages of such a step would have far outweighed the benefits, and reinforce the view that scrutiny of Council decision-making must be executed by national parliaments through their own procedures. The introduction of any second chamber at European Union level, and thus an additional actor, would have only compounded the lack of transparency within the European Union legislative process and added to delays.[49] Furthermore, it is inconceivable that national parliaments would surrender the scrutiny function completely and not wish to participate in some form of review. Finally, the detrimental effect on efficiency would have weighed against an additional input from such a second chamber. In any system of parliamentary democracy it is highly likely that the views of a parliamentary majority will coincide with the views of the government which is represented in the Council. If there is a divergence of view between the parliamentary majority and the government, such conflicts are better resolved domestically within the domestic parliamentary forum. This strengthens the argument that national parliaments' involvement in European Union affairs reflects domestic priorities rather than the pursuit of a wider collective agenda. That is not say that national parliaments do not share concerns in relation to European Union decision-making. Giving effect to the principle of ministerial accountability is an aspect of every national parliament's European Union activities, but it is the everyday practice in relation to the execution of this scrutiny where the differences remain.

4. Conducting Effective Scrutiny – The Example of the House Of Commons

National parliamentary review of European Union affairs is very much a task that is carried out according to domestic parliamentary traditions. That is not to suggest that national parliaments cannot learn from each other and

[48] See House of Lords Select Committee on the European Union, above, n. 46.

[49] E. Caspar *National Parliaments* (2002) (CONV 81/02, Contribution 37); K. Kimmo, M. Vanhanen, E. Helle, R. Korhonen, *Contribution from members of the Convention representing the Finnish Parliament on the role of National Parliaments in the European Union* structure (2002) CONV 82/02, Contribution 38.

cooperate, it is merely an acknowledgement that when conducting scrutiny national parliaments do not form a collective unit. If the parliamentary oversight mechanisms for European scrutiny are compared, it is evident that significant differences exist in terms of procedural and institutional set-ups. Some national parliaments are bicameral, with the powers of the upper chambers varying. While all parliaments have established European Affairs Committees, or have assigned the oversight function to an existing committee, the role, competence and composition of these committees differs. Some committees permit MEPs to sit as members while others, such as the House of Commons committee, are confined to national Members of Parliament. The participation in the scrutiny procedures of parliamentary actors, whether these be European Affairs Committees, specialist standing committees or the plenary, also varies. The purpose of this section is to consider how the House of Commons, as the primary legislative chamber in the United Kingdom, carries out scrutiny and what contribution this has made to the parliamentarisation of European Union affairs in the United Kingdom.[50]

The system of scrutiny in the House of Commons has, for over thirty years, remained firmly based on the examination of documents. The Standing Orders of what is today called the European Scrutiny Committee have evolved since 1973.[51] Today, its broader remit now permits review of, not only legislative proposals, but also other documents[52] such as Green and White Papers.[53] The Standing Orders require the Committee to consider whether a document raises questions of 'legal and political importance'.[54] To aid in this assessment, the lead government department provides an Explanatory Memorandum which serves the primary function of assessing the likely impact of the proposal and the government's attitude towards it. Until the Select Committee has completed this scrutiny task, the scrutiny reserve restricts the ability of the Minister to give agreement, or otherwise,

[50] The contribution made by the House of Lords Select Committee on the European Union to scrutiny in the United Kingdom Parliament is considered elsewhere in this volume by Christopher Kerse.

[51] Although the first significant amendment to the terms of reference only occurred in 1999. See House of Commons Debates of 17 November 1998 at col. 779.

[52] In practice this covers any document which is lodged within Parliament, of which there are approximately 1,100 per year, all of which are considered by the Committee.

[53] This change in the terms of reference brings the Commons Committee in line with that of the Lords, although there remain significant differences as to how each Committee handles any given document.

[54] Standing Order 143.

in Council to the legislative proposal. Following the 1999 amendment to the Standing Orders, the Committee has developed a role which is more proactive than before. In addition to fulfilling the Standing Orders by monitoring each document for its legal or political importance, there are three further roles which the Scrutiny Committee performs on behalf of the House. First, it acts as an information and access point for the House of Commons, providing information on European legislative proposals in comprehensible form, and highlighting the politically and legally sensitive initiatives (an important task, given the large number of initiatives). Secondly, the Committee monitors the activities of the government in Council. Finally, the Committee keeps the legal, procedural and institutional developments in the European Union under review.

Despite changes to its Standing Orders, the Committee is still not required to express a formal view on the merits of the legislative proposal, though it is evident from Committee reports that, when appropriate, it will express concern or approval of a document. Unless the Committee recommends a document for debate, this will mean that it has cleared the scrutiny hurdle, which in practical terms means that the scrutiny reserve is lifted.[55]

If the Select Committee recommends that a document be debated further, this debate will take place within one of the European Standing Committees and only rarely on the floor of the House itself.[56] The European Standing Committees[57] did not come in to existence until 1991, with debate of documents up until then taking place exclusively on the floor of the House of Commons. These debates were characterised as being held late at night and with a turnout of the 'usual participants'. Generally, this would include those MPs who were either pro- or anti-European Union and who would be inclined to rehearse the same arguments on each occasion, rather than actually debate the document at hand. To improve the quality of debate, the Procedure Committee recommended that five European Standing Committees be established which would take the debate away from the floor of the House of Commons and enable a degree of specialist knowledge to

---

55 House of Commons Scrutiny Reserve Resolution of 17 November, 1998.

56 Although debates can take place on the floor of the House, the Scrutiny Committee can not compel the government to provide parliamentary time for this.

57 The number of Standing Committees in existence has not remained constant since 1991 and has at any given time reflected both thematic priorities in the European Union and the fact that finding members to staff these Standing Committees has been difficult. For a detailed history of the European Standing Committees see A. Cygan, *The United Kingdom Parliament and European Legislation* (Kluwer Law International, The Hague, 1998) at Chap. 4.

develop on the part of MPs who are interested in European affairs.[58] From this perspective, the establishment of the Standing Committees has been a positive development and added to the quality of the scrutiny which takes place.[59] The focus of the debate is now centred on the substance of the document before the Standing Committee, as the rules of procedure permit only a maximum of two and a half hours for debate to be concluded.[60]

The scrutiny system in its present form undoubtedly possesses a number of strengths and has contributed to improved decision-making. Firstly, the House of Commons reviews every document to ascertain its legal and political importance to existing law and policy of the United Kingdom. This includes benchmarking the provision against the subsidiarity principle. Secondly, it has placed ministerial accountability at the centre of Common's European activities. Each document deposited requires written evidence from the appropriate minister who can be questioned further if the Committee recommends that a document should require formal debate. Thirdly, the Committee can, if necessary, complete the scrutiny and report in a matter of days to ensure that the minister is made aware of the Commons' position. Finally, the scrutiny reserve, the cornerstone of the scrutiny process, ensures that ministers are conscious of the importance of work of the Committee, especially when they are attending the Council of Ministers. The scrutiny reserve remains the most important weapon in the Select Committee's armoury because when applied it can prevent a minister from giving final consent to the common position in Council if domestic scrutiny has not been completed.[61] Where a reserve is ignored, the minister must explain the 'special reasons' for doing so, which involves the minister coming immediately before the House and explaining how the measure is of benefit to the United Kingdom. Taken as a complete package, these practices create an atmosphere of accountability for government when engaging in European Union affairs which the minister is conscious of when attending the Council.

---

[58] See *Fourth Report from the House of Commons Select Committee on Procedure – The Scrutiny of European Legislation* (1988-89 HC 622- I) at para. 65.

[59] The full procedure for debate in Standing Committee can be found in Standing Order No.16.

[60] The debate concludes with the Standing Committee passing a motion which will require the final approval of the Commons Chamber. For more detail on the mechanics of the scrutiny process see Cygan, above, n. 57.

[61] The Minister may however proceed if the European Scrutiny Committee has waived the reserve on grounds of urgency or national interest protection, or if the matter at hand is "confidential, routine or trivial or is substantially the same as a proposal on which scrutiny has been completed". (See Art 4 of the House of Commons Scrutiny Reserve Resolution of 17 November 1998.)

The fundamental issues facing the House of Commons when executing its scrutiny function remain the same today as they were thirty years ago. The European Scrutiny Committee has observed on numerous occasions[62] that there still are weaknesses with the current arrangements, most notably the lack of a clear status in Council for the scrutiny reserve. The House of Commons has been at the forefront of highlighting to the Council the importance of the reserve and why it should be given a clearer status in the Council's rules of procedure. The primary issue relating to the United Kingdom scrutiny reserve is that it is an internal parliamentary mechanism which requires the cooperation and goodwill of the government to operate effectively. The Committee has highlighted that to ensure effective accountability of the executive it must receive not only all the relevant documentation, but also that this is available in advance of the Council meeting to enable scrutiny to be concluded.[63] The Scrutiny Committee has consistently stated that the overriding objective of the scrutiny process is to influence the minister *prior* to the Council adopting its definitive common position. In the absence of effective provisions at European Union level it must fall back on insisting that the obligations within the scrutiny reserve are consistently applied. But enforcing the scrutiny reserve is part of a wider problem faced within many national parliaments of enforcing executive accountability more generally. This more general absence of political accountability on the part of national executives to national parliaments is, in part, the answer why executive accountability in the particular sphere of European Union affairs remains unsatisfactory.[64]

Though scrutiny of European Union affairs by the House of Commons remains primarily a domestic issue, the wider impact of this activity should not be underestimated. The developed and efficient procedures of the Commons, together with those in the House of Lords, provide a comprehensive and complementary package of parliamentary review of European Union affairs in the United Kingdom. Several national parliaments from the states which acceded to the Union in 2004 have considered the United Kingdom experience of practice and procedure with regards to European Union affairs. Bergman identifies later accession as being a factor

[62] See for example the evidence presented by the Select Committee on European Legislation to the Select Committee on Procedure (1988-89 HC 622-I at paras 43–74).

[63] See *Democracy and Accountability in the EU and the Role of National Parliaments: Vol I*, above, n. 15, at 22 at para. 33.

[64] See Select Committee on the Modernisation of the House of Commons, *The Scrutiny of European Business* (2004-05 HC 465-I) at paras 5–9.

that positively influences the strength of parliamentary oversight[65]: newer member states may profit from the older member states' experience. Finland, which acceded to the European Union in 1995, is often praised for adopting a scrutiny mechanism which, although not exactly following the Danish principle of mandating ministers, still outperforms most other national parliaments.[66]

The European Union has since the Amsterdam Treaty encouraged member states to exchange information and best practice with regard to policy implementation, administration, and governance through the open method of coordination. This process of peer learning should also encompass national parliaments and their accountability mechanisms. National parliaments should pursue closer cooperation where they have shared interests, without necessarily providing a prescriptive single methodology towards scrutiny. In the absence of such cooperation, it is difficult to see how the substantive aims of Article I-11 of the Constitutional Treaty can be met.

Finally, and as part of the process of parliamentarisation it is important not to forget the need for a positive relationship between national parliaments and the European Parliament. The quality and depth of the scrutiny carried out by national parliaments may provide guidance to Committees within the European Parliament Committees in their dealings with the Council. Though national parliaments and the European Parliament have different perspectives and operate different procedures, they do share the common objective of promoting accountability of the institutions. While they remain 'competitor' institutions within the co-decision procedure and in which national parliaments are eager to scrutinise the input of the European Parliament, they both desire workable and relevant legislation which will be acceptable and beneficial to the citizen.

---

65 *Ibid.*

66 Bergman, above, n. 21.

PART II:

Ireland, the Oireachtas and the European Union

6.
Oireachtas Control over Government Activity at European Union Level: Reflections on the Historical Context and the Legal Framework

Gavin Barrett[1]

1. Introduction

The signing of the Treaty Establishing the European Economic Community in 1957 and Ireland's entry into the EEC, as it then was, in 1973 can in retrospect be seen as the laying of two foundation stones for the construction of the present era of unprecedented economic and political success for this country. One might have been forgiven for failing to see the magnitude of what had been achieved by Ireland's accession in the years that immediately followed the taking of this step. Before the fruits of membership could be harvested, the crippling effects of oil crises, followed by inflation, economic recession and large-scale unemployment had first to be worked through by Ireland. This was above and beyond any of the normal economic adjustments and institutional reforms which might have been expected to be required by and to accompany membership.

Within a number of years of Ireland's joining the Community, the realisation became ever clearer that at European level too, a succession of adjustments to the institutional machinery of EEC would be needed, were the Community itself ever to fulfil its potential. In the first place, institutional reforms were required, most importantly the gradual dismantling of the understanding that decision-making could be carried out in the Community only when unanimous agreement existed (a decision forced on its unwilling fellow member states by de Gaulle's France through the so-called Luxembourg Accord of 1966). The initial step towards more widespread majority voting at Community level – effected by the Single European Act in 1987 – succeeded in facilitating the establishment on a much firmer basis of the Common Market (rechristened the Single European Market at this time). A

[1] Senior Lecturer and President's Research Fellow, School of Law, University College Dublin, Visiting Scholar, Institut des Hautes Études Européennes, Strasbourg.

succession of further institutional reforms brought about by the Treaties of Maastricht (1992), Amsterdam (1997) and Nice (2001) paved the way for subsequent enlargements and the gradual evolution of an exclusively economically-focused European Economic Community of only six members in 1957 to the present European Union of twenty-seven member states, with much broader political aims and objectives.[2] The process of change at European level has rarely been an easy one – as the political convulsions over the Treaty Establishing a Constitution for Europe have most recently shown.

As regards the initial adjustments and adaptations required of Ireland and its fellow member states by virtue of the process of integration, it would be inaccurate to regard these as now complete, however. The need for adjustment has in several respects been an ongoing one. This is not merely because the constantly changing and evolving nature of integration requires a correspondingly evolving response (although this is certainly true). It is also because some of the original challenges stemming from Ireland's adherence to the European Union have arguably not yet been adequately met. This chapter focuses on one area where the need for adjustment may be described as ongoing and has certainly been a source of controversy in relatively recent times. This is the field of Oireachtas involvement in controlling governmental activity in European Union matters. The role of the Oireachtas in European affairs may be viewed in many respects as that of an intermediary, transmitting, on the one hand, the views of the electorate to the institutions of executive governance and, on the other, informing the electorate of what legislative and other business is being conducted at European Union level. Overlapping with these functions is the task of exercising some form of democratic control on the executive concerning its activities at European level.

In this regard it will be recalled that the activities of the Irish executive at European Union level are exercised *via* the participation of government ministers in the Council of Ministers. Of the three 'political' institutions at Community level, the European Commission, the European Parliament and the Council, it is clearly the Council which is at present most in need of control by national parliaments. The European Parliament, after all, is subject to the discipline of being answerable to voters in direct elections. As for the Commission, its institutional role requires a measure of political

[2] This is not to forget the European Atomic Energy Community and the now-expired European Coal and Steel Community Treaty, although from an early point the key Community has always been the European Economic Community (known since 1993 as the European Community).

independence.[3] It is any case controlled both by its need for member state cooperation in order to achieve its objectives, and – to an increasing and arguably not always wholly desirable extent [4] – by the European Parliament. (One example of such control in action was seen in the forced collective resignation in 1999 of the Santer Commission). The Council of Ministers, in contrast, is subject to no comparable collective control as a body. Its individual members are subject only to whatever control is imposed on them by their national political structures. The question of how well the Oireachtas exercises influence over the Irish Government in European matters, and more specifically, over Irish ministers in the Council is one which the rest of this chapter concerns itself. In brief, although (as we shall see) the position may well have improved significantly in recent years, much remains to be done, at least if the view is taken that a situation of almost complete executive dominance is not appropriate. The present reality is still accurately encapsulated by paraphrasing Tonra's summary (found in that writer's chapter in this book) of the position of the Oireachtas:[5]

> "it must be acknowledged…that the Oireachtas has not had a strong record…Despite formal constitutional provisions which indicate otherwise, the political reality is that the Oireachtas is effectively the servant of the executive rather than its master. The combination of powerful party whips, a tradition of comparatively strong majority-holding governments (single and multi-party), an electoral system which is seen to reward assiduous constituency work over legislative activity and, overall, a comparatively weak committee structure, has traditionally undermined the Oireachtas' capacity to hold the executive to account." [6]

In short then, there appears to a policy area where domestic institutional arrangements may leave room for further adjustment – but herein lies something of a rub. For the question of what the nature of such adjustments should be is one the answer to which depends on one's views on what the

[3] See more generally, E. Gallagher and J. Temple Lang, "What Sort of European Commission Does the EU Need?" *Challenge Europe*, Issue 7, 14 February 2002, (available at http://www.cpc.eu/en/ce.asp?TYP=CE&LV=177&see=y&t=42&PG=CE/EN/detail&l=3&AI=166) and the chapter by John Temple Lang in this book.

[4] See in this regard, J.-P. Jacqué, "The Principle Of Institutional Balance" (2004) 41 *Common Market Law Review* 383.

[5] It is only fair to note that Tonra is speaking in the context of foreign policy, where challenges are particularly pronounced. His observations also apply with considerable force outside that particular context, however.

[6] B. Tonra, "Democratic Oversight over the Irish Government in the Field of the Common Foreign and Security Policy" in this volume, 243 at 244.

relative roles of Government and Oireachtas should be, and whether European affairs are to be a special category in which the normal rules governing relationship between legislature and executive in Ireland do not apply.

2. An Unhappy Context? The Relationship Between the Legislature and the Executive in Ireland

> "It might well be that for all the supra-national and non-parliamentary bodies that influence governance, the biggest democratic deficit may be sitting at our own doorstep."
>
> Barry Andrews, TD [7]

In discussing the relationship between the legislature and the executive in Ireland in relation to European affairs, it is appropriate to put this relationship in its broader context of the traditional relationship between these two branches of Irish government generally. This context is relatively little-known, and part of the reason for this lies with the wording of the Irish Constitution. Every student of Irish constitutional law is introduced at some point to Article 28 of the 1937 Constitution which – after establishing that the executive power of the State shall (subject to the provisions of the Constitution) be exercised by or on the authority of the Government [8] – purportedly establishes the ground rules of the relationship between the political branches by providing that "the Government shall be responsible to Dáil Éireann".[9]

In fact, however, everyday reality is very different to the impression created by these words, which, even at the time they were written, were misleading, and constituted little more than a genuflection which it was felt obligatory to make in the direction of a constitutional theory already well out of date in 1937. Chubb has observed, regarding the gap here between words and fact, that

> "the explanation for this apparent, albeit mild political schizophrenia is not difficult to discern. A constitution is a legal document expressing mainly legal relationships. It is usually written in conventional, even traditional, language, embodying the concepts of accepted political and constitutional theory, in this case of nineteenth-century British liberalism. The politicians subscribed to these ideas in much the same way as many people subscribe to their religion, their behaviour from Monday to Saturday often reflecting a bending to the pressures and exigencies of everyday life."[10]

---

[7] B. Andrews, "Who Runs This Country? Certainly Not Dáil Éireann" *Irish Times*, 19 July 2003.

[8] Article 28.2 of the Constitution.

[9] Article 28. 4.1°.

[10] B. Chubb, *Cabinet Government in Ireland* (Institute of Public Administration, Dublin, 1974), 8.

Nineteenth Century Liberalism – and the Twentieth Century Westminster Model

Part and parcel of the nineteenth-century liberal concept of government to which implicit reference was (and continues to be) made in the 1937 Irish constitution is the principle of the supremacy of parliament – the idea that parliament holds the ultimate power to make laws and control the action of government, and the administration.[11] A later refinement was that the people hold ultimate power, but that nonetheless this power, between elections, is delegated to parliament.[12] The essential idea here is the attractive one of a chain of command reaching downwards from the people to the parliament onwards to the government and the administration. Such ideas have exercised a powerful hold on the imagination right up to the present time and are reflected to some degree in the manner in which both the 1922 and 1937 Constitutions were worded. By the beginning of the twentieth century, however, it was clear that this was no longer an accurate description of the Westminster model of government. By then, matters had moved on to a form familiar to this day in both Britain and Ireland: governments being produced as the direct consequence of general elections (the results of which are registered by the composition of parliament) and subsequently ruling the country with the assistance of a professional civil service; such governments being led by a prime minister (or Taoiseach, in Ireland) who is the leader of the party (or coalition of parties) that has won the general election; maintenance of such governments in power in both houses by parliamentarians who are party loyalists; some degree of collective and individual answerability of ministers to (and hence influence by) parliament, but in practice, because of party loyalty and discipline, as well as the notion of collective cabinet responsibility, little likelihood of dismissal of the government by parliament in the normal run of events[13]; government proposals publicly discussed in parliament, but almost invariably passed

---

[11] Other – sometimes contradictory ideas – which found currency in nineteenth century British political theory and which are also reflected in the Irish constitution are the separation of powers (seen *e.g.*, in the classification by Article 6 of the Constitution of the powers of government as legislative, executive and judicial) and the principle of the sovereignty of the people (seen *e.g.*, in the Preamble of the 1937 Bunreacht with its reference to "We, the people of Éire", as well as *e.g.*, in Article 6.1 of the Bunreacht, with its assertion that "all powers of government, legislative, executive and judicial, derive, under God, from the people, whose right it is to designate the rulers of the State and, in final appeal, to decide all questions of national policy, according to the requirements of the common good.").

[12] See Chubb, above, n. 10, at 9-12. See more generally A. Birch, *The British System of Government* (10th edition, Routledge, London, 1998).

[13] The Dáil has dismissed two governments in its history – in 1982, the coalition led by Garret FitzGerald, and in 1992, the coalition led by Albert Reynolds.

with concessions made only in relation to details; and political parties outside parliament helping to mobilise the electorate at election time and forming the forum in which political leadership could be attained.[14]

In contrast to the nineteenth century liberal understanding, with its idea of parliaments controlling governments, what has been called the early twentieth-century Westminster approach involves a far lesser role for parliament. Indeed the so-called 'efficient secret' of the Westminster system has been the effective fusion of the executive and the legislature under the control of the former. Insofar as the respective legislative roles of the two branches are concerned,

> "the *government* operates at the critical stage in the public decision-making process, namely the point at which the needs, desires, ideas and demands of the community, and their reactions to suggestions from politicians, are precisely formulated into proposals for legislation and governmental action. Once formulated, these proposals are very likely to go through. At the next succeeding stage, [parliament] will give them the status of law and thus formally legitimise them, but it will probably not make a positive contribution of major importance to their content. Thus it has been rightly said that parliaments in systems such as this are not so much law-making as law-declaring bodies." [15]

Further increasing the centrality of the executive's role in any political system using the early twentieth-century Westminster approach is that the government sits at the confluence of streams of advice and opinion not only from parliament (which in this regard is only one voice of many) but also from interest groups, political parties and, crucially, highly expert civil servants. And of course, the head of government will also be a party leader and leader of the majority in parliament as well. Such, then, were the features of the parliament-executive relationship inherited by the new Irish State in 1922.

The 1922 Constitution

The drafters of the Irish Free State Constitution of 1922, the first constitution of the new, internationally recognised state which emerged after the war of independence, began their task by replicating the structures of early twentieth century British government, even while they used the language of

[14] See more generally, Chubb, above, n. 10, at 12 to 16.
[15] Chubb, above, n. 10, at 16. Emphasis added.

nineteeth-century liberalism. If this had been all they had done, this might have been a straightforward recipe for continued executive dominance. But the drafters of the 1922 document harboured genuine intentions to rein in the executive. Thus they grafted onto the British-style structures a number of institutions which deviated from the original model and were serious attempts, if not to substitute, then at least to moderate, the power of the new state's executive. Thus, for example, provision was made for referendums – to be held on the written demand of two-fifths of the members of Dáil Eireann or of a majority of the members of Seanad Eireann – which would effectively out-vote the government.[16] So too was provision for the initiation by a minimum number of voters of proposals for laws or constitutional amendments.[17] The governing 'Executive Council' – stipulated, like its modern counterpart, to be responsible to Dáil Eireann – was constitutionally limited to the small number of between five and seven ministers appointed on the nomination of its President (the equivalent of the present-day Taoiseach) [18] – and here again the legislature could flex its muscles, in that the Constitution provided that the number of ministers could be raised to twelve by the addition of further so-called extern ministers "nominated by Dáil Eireann on the recommendation of a Committee of Dáil Eireann chosen by a method to be determined by Dáil Eireann, so as to be impartially representative of Dáil Eireann."[19] Each such minister was individually "responsible to Dáil Eireann alone for the administration of the Department or Departments of which he is the head" and no such Minister could be removed from office during his term otherwise than by the Dáil itself, in strictly regulated circumstances designed to avoid executive dominance.[20] This was not all. The President was to be appointed on the nomination of the Dáil, and all other Ministers appointed with its assent, with the retirement from office of all required if the President ceased to retain the support of a majority in the Dáil. Nor could the Oireachtas be dissolved on the advice of an Executive Council which had ceased to retain the support of a majority in Dáil Eireann.[21] Above and beyond all these constitutional provisions, it is

[16] Article 47 of the 1922 Constitution.

[17] Article 48 of the 1922 Constitution.

[18] Article 51 of the 1922 Constitution.

[19] Article 55 of the 1922 Constitution. The term 'extern minister' was not found in the text of the Constitution but came into later popular usage. See Chubb, above, n. 10, at 16.

[20] *Viz.*, "for stated reasons, and after the proposal to remove him has been submitted to a Committee, chosen by a method to be determined by Dáil Eireann, so as to be impartially representative of Dáil Eireann, and the Committee has reported thereon." (See generally Article 56 of the 1922 Constitution).

[21] Article 53 of the 1922 Constitution.

interesting to note the expressed intentions of some of the founders of this state that Westminster-style party discipline ought not to prevail but, instead, that the Oireachtas be a "deliberative assembly in the fullest sense of the word" in which each legislative proposal would be "analysed only on its merits" and there would be "the maximum of individual liberty for the deputies in the Dáil".[22]

These careful plans notwithstanding, political power was not successfully redistributed between the two branches of government. The political conditions needed to enable the constitutionally-intended rebalancing of power between executive and legislature simply never obtained. Even from the beginning, the degree of political support for them never seemed entirely assured: it is noteworthy that even the above-described system of rebalancing had involved a considerable climbdown on the originally more radical proposals of the 1922 Constitution's drafters (who had, for example, envisaged an Executive Council limited to only four members).[23] In any case, whatever hopes of success such plans to rein in the executive might otherwise have had, the death knell for the idea of a powerful legislature in the Irish State certainly rang with the emergence of two major post-Civil War political party blocs vying fiercely with each other for national political control. This kind of intense party loyalty facilitated executive control. Rigid adherence to party lines meant that discretions constitutionally conferred on the Oireachtas could in effect be exercised by the government (whose members, after all, controlled the dominant political party). In political reality, executive hegemony over the legislative branch was therefore established, a situation that has pertained in Ireland right up to the present day. In consequence, ever since, decision-making has come to be taken at that level and in private, rather than in the deliberative assembly that the founders of the State had originally hoped for. The Oireachtas failed to become the place where the decisions were made.

Contrary to the original intentions of the drafters of the 1922 Constitution, therefore, a more-or-less textbook Westminster-style approach to government prevailed. Institutional rules were quickly amended so as to more accurately reflect this political reality. (Thus, for example, external ministers were effectively done away with by a combination of constitutional amendment and political practice in 1927). As Chubb pointed out, "the 'un-

[22] Kevin O'Higgins, Minister for Home Affairs, speaking in the Dáil on 12 October, 1922. (Dáil Debates cc. 1558-60). Quoted in Chubb, above, n. 10, at 23.
[23] Chubb, above, n. 10, 22 to 24.

British' institutions were shed within five years, and cabinet government in the British style was firmly established."[24] The failure of early attempts to ensure that dominance of parliament would not be as absolute in the new state as it had been as Westminster should not, however, be seen as the consequence of the taking advantage of party loyalties by a cynical executive. As has already been noted, sufficient scepticism had already existed as to the workability of plans to share power between the legislature and the executive as to require such plans to have been considerably diluted already by the time the 1922 Constitution was adopted. And it is noteworthy too that post-1922, the Oireachtas majority dutifully toed the party line in taking the constitutional, legislative and political steps needed to consolidate executive power – motivated at each such step, one assumes, not only by party discipline, but also by awareness of the unpalatable reality that empowerment of the Oireachtas could involve empowerment of the Opposition – and apparently preferring the emasculation of parliament as preferable to handing some of the levers of political control to ex-Civil War opponents, led by Eamon de Valera.

The 1937 Constitution

Although in terms of its constitutional significance, the coming into force of the 1937 *Bunreacht* under de Valera's Fianna Fáil was obviously an event of seminal importance, it essentially involved more of the same, from the point of view of executive-legislature relations – the continuation of the twentieth century Westminster model of government, with a patina of wording included here and there in the Constitution capable of misleading the careless or unwary into thinking that classical liberal theory, with its attendant notion of parliament as the dominant branch of government, prevailed. Indeed, perhaps ironically, if anything, the 1937 Constitution entrenched the Westminster model of executive-legislature relations even more firmly than had previously been the case. Symptomatic of this was that, unlike in 1922, no provision was made in the new Constitution for the provision for 'extern ministers'. Further, the role accorded to the new office of Taoiseach was, as Chubb put it, such "as to elevate the Taoiseach formally and in practice to the position of a strong British prime minister".[25] One example of the enhanced prime-ministerial role was that the Taoiseach was given the power to bring about the termination the appointment of any member of the Government.[26]

[24] Chubb, above, n. 10, 21. One could quibble with the time-scale. The possibility of voter-initiated constitutional amendments was removed in 1928, when the government saw that it might be used to achieve a result it did not approve of.

[25] Chubb, above, n. 10, at 16, 33.

[26] Article 13.3 of the 1937 Bunreacht.

Another was that the Taoiseach, rather than the cabinet as a whole, was given the power to bring about the dissolution of the Dáil.[27]

Post-1937[28]

It is a testament to the enduring nature of the early-twentieth century Westminster model on the Irish political scene that seventy years after the adoption of the present Constitution, a fundamental rebalancing of the powers of executive and legislature has never occurred. Certainly until very recently, even basic improvements in the workings of parliament have tended to take place at a snail's pace. Parliamentary reforms in Ireland have mostly tended to come about many years, even decades after they were first proposed, although recent years have certainly seen an increased rate of change.

Fianna Fáil governments, which held power initially for an uninterrupted period of sixteen years from 1932 to 1948, tended – like their first predecessor governments – to have little interest in sharing power with the Opposition, and the party system hardened decisively into a 'Fianna Fáil against the rest' mould which was to endure for over fifty years. It was perhaps in consequence of this generalised approach that, as MacCarthaigh has observed,

> "notwithstanding two three-year periods in government between 1948 and 1957, the main opposition parties failed to give Dáil Éireann the means to hold future governments ... successfully to account. Indeed, it appears that the inter-party coalitions were so eager to keep Fianna Fáil out of government that they engaged in the very thing they criticised it for – closed and unaccountable government."[29]

It might have been thought that the second sixteen-year period of uninterrupted Fianna Fáil governments would have given the Opposition adequate time to reflect upon the fact that the long-term disadvantages of a wholly adversarial political system are likely to outweigh its short-term gains. Indeed, when the long period of rule by Fianna Fáil came to an end

---

[27] Article 13.2 of the 1937 Bunreacht. Contrast Article 53 of the 1922 Constitution. In neither the 1922 nor the 1937 Constitution was such power uncircumscribed, depending as it did on retention of the support of a Dáil majority.

[28] See generally here, M. MacCarthaigh, *Accountability in Irish Parliamentary Politics* (Institute of Public Administration, Dublin, 2005) at 70–93.

[29] M. MacCarthaigh, above, n. 28, at 71.

under the 1973 Fine Gael-Labour Coalition led by Liam Cosgrave, five *ad hoc* Dáil committees were established to consider important legislation. However, this proved to be something of a false dawn. These committees failed to present any real challenge to the government, in part because of their weak powers and temporary nature. The same government made a further contribution to Oireachtas reform by implementing the vast bulk of the reforms which had already been recommended by the Fianna Fáil-appointed 1971–2 Sub-Committee on Reform of Dáil Procedure. Ironically, however, many of these reforms had nothing to do with – and indeed some militated against – a reduction the adversarial nature of the political system.

The return to power of Fianna Fáil with a massive majority in 1977 finally saw Fine Gael moving to align its position with the more long-standing calls of the much smaller (and therefore even more parliamentarily disadvantaged) Labour Party for reform. However, it was only in 1983, under the second Fine Gael-Labour Coalition of Garret FitzGerald that a comprehensive select committee system was introduced facilitating non-adversarial discussion of various cross-departmental issues. This was to prove a short-lived reform. A Fianna Fáil government led by Charles Haughey came to power in 1987, and with its leader's advocacy of the merits of single-party government, these select committees were not re-established.

MacCarthaigh has argued that the failure of Fianna Fáil to secure an overall majority in the snap election subsequently called by Charles Haughey in 1989 should be seen as a 'critical juncture' in the development of parliamentary accountability in Ireland, on a par in this regard with the adoption of the 1922 and 1937 Constitutions. This is because it marked the point of origin of what is likely to be a permanent shift to Coalition governments in this country – a change which, he argues, by introducing other 'veto players' (in the shape of coalition partners) in the process of government will inevitably move Ireland closer to consensual government.[30]

If Ireland is indeed moving in this direction, however, progress along this road has been slow in the intervening period. Certainly, there has been some movement. The Fianna Fáil-Labour Party coalition of 1992 saw the introduction of a system of joint committees. Some of these committees (such as the Joint Committee on Foreign Affairs) were departmentally aligned. Some of them (such as that on women's rights) were not. This overall committee system was maintained in place by the Rainbow Coalition of 1994–1997, and

[30] M. MacCarthaigh, above, n. 28, at 84–87.

indeed by the two Fianna Fáil-Progressive Democrat administrations which ruled the country after this – although a certain dimunition in momentum was perceptible, with a reduction in the number and the size of joint committees since 1997. In the period of existence of the twenty-ninth Dáil (dissolved at the end of April 2007) there were thirteen such committees.[31]

To say that the committee system introduced in 1992 continues to exist is not to say that it is effective. Some useful work has certainly been done by such committees, but, for various reasons which will be returned to presently, the committee system has failed to develop as it could have. The effect of this, combined with the powerlessness of the Seanad, has meant that no kind of fundamental rebalancing of the powers of executive and legislature has ever occurred in Ireland. In sum, this country still operates a version of the early twentieth century Westminster model, only lightly modified by recent reforms. Such is the context in which Oireachtas intervention in European affairs operates. It is a political system in which, as Chubb has put it, the Oireachtas has only a comparatively modest role as a policy-maker, and one which it does not perform well.[32]

3. Controlling the Government's Actions in Europe – the Role of Oireachtas Committees[33]

In the light of the foregoing discussion, it can scarcely come as a surprise to learn that the Oireachtas had no serious role in controlling or monitoring the actions of the Government in European matters prior to the entry of Ireland into the EEC. This is a situation which stood in marked contrast with the pre-entry situation in many other European countries – such as Denmark (which joined at the same time as Ireland and whose legislature had been involving itself in European matters since as far back as 1961), and later, Finland, Sweden and Slovenia.[34] The historically subservient role of the Oireachtas

[31] See, for details of these, http://www.oireachtas.ie/ViewDoc.asp?fn=/documents/committees 29thdail/JointCommittees.htm&CatID=12&m=c. Note that the successor committees have yet to be established at the time this book is going to press.

[32] Chubb, above, n. 10, at 65.

[33] See generally B. Laffan, "National Parliaments and Domestic Core Executives", paper delivered at the conference *Ireland, Europe and the Challenge of Democracy – Ensuring Democratic Control over Government in European Union Affairs,* held at Europe House, Dublin, Friday, 20 May 2005.

[34] Contrast the positions in *e.g.,* Slovenia and Denmark, Finland and Sweden, detailed in, respectively D. Fink-Hafner, "Ensuring Democratic Control over National Government in European Affairs – the Slovenian Experience" and T. Raunio and M. Wiberg, "Too Little, Too Late? Comparing the Engagement of Nordic Parliaments in European Union Matters", both of which are chapters in this volume, to be found at 393 and 379 respectively.

was probably the dominant factor here. The relatively uncontroversial nature of the objective of Irish membership of the Community – reflected in the massive 83 per cent vote in favour of entry in the 1972 referendum on this topic – has been argued to have been a possible further contributory factor (were any needed) for such torpor, by ensuring that there would be no pressure on the government to set up any such parliamentary body.[35] On Irish entry to the Community, however, a role was finally created for the Oireachtas, in that provision was made for the creation of a Joint Oireachtas Committee on the Secondary Legislation of the European Communities. As its name would suggest, this Committee, which came into being in July, 1973, under the newly-elected Fine Gael-Labour coalition, drew its membership from both the Dáil and the Seanad with political parties being represented in proportion to the number of their representatives in each House. The existence of the Committee represented very slight progress in redressing the balance between executive and the legislature (although in the context of membership of the Community which could be expected, given its institutional make-up, to reinforce the prerorogatives of the executive). Thus it permitted the development of some expertise in European matters among that small body of parliamentarians who made up its members, with future President – then Senator – Mary Robinson playing a significant role in its activities.[36]

The Committee was to see its terms of reference gradually expanded over time.[37] But overall (as its name would suggest) it was confined to a relatively minor role in the Irish democratic process, and was crippled by a range of further problems including (but not confined to) an unrealistically large workload, delays in the production of its reports, a general lack of regard for its output and a lack of resources, including research support.[38] Even what little advantage it had in terms of its intellectual resources and institutional memory was affected by the fact its membership endured only as long as the relevant parliamentary term. There was certainly never any prospect of such a Committee exercising any serious control or influence over the government. In 1993 – ironically, at a time when the involvement of the

[35] Laffan, above, n. 33. See for a study of referendums in the Irish political system see R. Sinnott, "Cleavages, Parties and Referendums: Relationships Between Representative and Direct Democracy in the Republic of Ireland" (2002) 41 *European Journal of Political Research* 811.

[36] See more generally M. Robinson, "Irish Parliamentary Scrutiny of EC Legislation" (1979) 16 *Common Market Law Review* 9.

[37] *Ibid.*. See also D. Walsh, "Irish Parliamentary Scruting of EU Measures on the Free Movement of Persons: Going Through the Motions?" (2005) 40 Irish Jurist 261 at 263.

[38] See for example in this last regard the revealing report to be found in the *Irish Independent* of 19 July 1974.

Labour Party in the Reynolds-led Fianna Fáil-Labour coalition resulted in an increase in the role or Oireachtas Committees – an end was put to the existence of the Joint Oireachtas Committee on Secondary Legislation when it was subsumed into the Foreign Affairs Committee. As might have been expected, this effort to deal with European affairs in the Oireachtas as a form of sub-category of foreign affairs generally was not a success, and was to be a short-lived venture. Under the 'Rainbow Coalition' led by John Bruton, a Joint Committee on European Affairs was established in 1995. In keeping with the evolving more favourable attitude of parties other than Fianna Fáil to committees,[39] the new Committee was given a wider remit than the earlier Joint Committee on Secondary Legislation. Notwithstanding this reform, however (and the retention of this new Committee under the Ahern-led Fianna Fáil-Progressive Democrat governments from 1997 onwards[40]), the reality of the conduct of Ireland's relations with the European Union was that they remained utterly executive-dominated.

The shock defeat of the government side in the first Nice referendum campaign in June 2001 was to result in changes. The consequences of these events has been as good an illustration as any of the enduring truth of Monnet's dictum that "people only accept change when they are faced with necessity, and only recognise necessity when a crisis is upon them".[41] In this case, the necessity which made itself evident was that of the political necessity to redress at least to some degree the almost complete imbalance of power in Ireland between legislature and executive in European matters before another constitutional referendum necessary to permit ratification of the Nice Treaty could be held. In one way, it was ironic that the ratification of the Treaty of Nice provided the flashpoint for the emergence of this issue, since the actual content of the Treaty of Nice had little if anything to do with it. Nonetheless, the ratification process of the Nice Treaty provided an opportunity for the issue to be raised, which it was – most prominently in a May 2001 article in the *Irish Times* by a former Attorney General, John Rogers, in which he announced his personal preparedness to vote against enabling ratification of the Treaty of Nice in the then forthcoming referendum.[42] Those of Rogers' arguments which were based on the

[39] See M. MacCarthaigh, above, n. 28, at 72 to 93.

[40] The most recent Joint Oireachtas Committee on European Affairs at the time of writing was established in the wake of the May 2002 general election, following Orders of Dáil Éireann on 27 June 2002 and of Seanad Éireann on 17 October 2002.

[41] J. Monnet, *Memoirs* (Collins, London, 1978).

[42] J. Rogers, "Voters Should not be Blackmailed into Voting Yes to Avoid Giving Offence" *Irish Times*, 19 May 2001.

substantive text of the Nice Treaty arguably took insufficient account both of political realities and of the institutional needs of enlargement, and were in any event to produce no substantive reaction in terms of amendments: the Treaty would later be ratified with the relevant provisions still in place. But Rogers' objections to the fact that the State had "not sought to adjust its domestic institutions and constitutional arrangements" and that "the Oireachtas has been entirely sidelined in the context of legislation emerging from the institutions of the Community" were a different matter. These words struck an undeniable chord (although, puzzlingly, the fact that the Oireachtas had also been confined to an extremely limited role in the context of *domestic* legislation for the previous six decades seemed to escape the attention of almost all contributors to this debate). At any rate, after the defeat of the initial Nice referendum in June 2001, the Government felt compelled to defuse the issue of the limited role of the Oireachtas in European affairs before putting a constitutional referendum before the electorate again in October 2002.

A revised system of scrutiny and oversight was thus introduced by the Fianna Fáil-Progressive Democrat Government in the Summer of 2002. This was done at first informally, and then, at least in part, given a legislative basis with the enactment of the European Union (Scrutiny) Act, 2002. Because, at the time of its enactment, the Government was faced with the prospect of a further referendum on the Treaty of Nice, it strove for a large measure of consensus in relation to this measure. The compromise forged as a result has endured to the present.

The reformed system of Oireachtas scrutiny in European affairs introduced at this time has two aspects to it.[43] In the first place, there is a system of review of European Union-level legislative proposals, whereby, as summarised by O'Hegarty in her own chapter in this volume (in which the new system is analysed in further detail):

> "the Government forwards to the European Union Committee all legislative proposals (across all three Pillars of the Union), together with information notes outlining the purpose, significance and implications of the texts presented. The Sub-Committee [44] then conducts a preliminary survey of the various proposals, with a view to prioritising them.

[43] See generally in relation to these the chapters in this book by Katherine Meenan and Lia O'Hegarty.

[44] This refers to the Sub-Committee on European Scrutiny appointed by the Oireachtas Joint Committee on European Affairs.

> Prioritisation means making a 'judgment-call' about which proposals are most significant in terms of policy, in order to ensure that adequate time and attention can be devoted to these. Proposals which have been identified for further scrutiny are then referred to the relevant sectoral committees to be considered in greater detail."[45]

This obviously represented a significant change in practice. The new system is also, however, a carefully restricted one. The effect of a recommendation made either by the European Union Committee or by any other Committee is limited indeed. Thus the relevant Government Minister is obliged merely to "have regard to any recommendations made to him or her from time to time … in relation to a proposed measure".[46] He or she is thus not bound by any veto or even by a scrutiny reserve. Furthermore, even this limited obligation placed on Government ministers is subject to exceptions. It does not apply "where there is insufficient time for the carrying out of the procedures aforesaid and the performance of the functions of the Houses of the Oireachtas"[47] or "to a proposed measure which, in the opinion of the Minister, is confidential".[48]

The second aspect of Oireachtas oversight of the executive since 2002 is one that derives from practice rather than law, and to this day remains unsupported by legislative provision, the Government having to declined to make provision in this regard in the 2002 Act. It consists of the arrangement that Government Ministers, or Ministers of State make themselves available, (in particular before meetings of the Council of Ministers and the European Council) for discussions with the European Union Committee or the relevant sectoral committee, as appropriate. (The Government which left office in 2007 is understood to have suggested that the norm should be for a Minister

---

[45] O'Hegarty, above, n. 43 at 281–282. Note in this regard s. 2(1) of the European Union (Scrutiny) Act, 2002, whereby

> "as soon as practicable after a proposed measure is presented by the Commission of the European Communities or initiated by a Member State, as the case may be, the Minister shall cause a copy of the text concerned to be laid before each House of the Oireachtas together with a statement of the Minister outlining the content, purpose and likely implications for Ireland of the proposed measure and including such other information as he or she considers appropriate."

[46] S. 2(2) of the 2002 Act, which refers to recommendations "by either or both Houses of the Oireachtas or by a committee of either or both such Houses". The reference to recommendations by either or both Houses of the Oireachtas has in practice been largely superfluous to date since reference onwards by a Committee of issues referred to them for full Oireachtas debates, although a theoretical possibility, do not normally occur. (See O'Hegarty, above, n. 43 at 286.) Note also the possibility of Ministers or officials being invited to appear before a committee. (*Ibid.*)

[47] S. 2(3) of the 2002 Act.

[48] S. 3(1) of the 2002 Act.

to be requested to appear before the relevant sectoral committee in the week before the relevant meeting of the Council of Ministers.[49])

One aspect of this latter practice is that prior to each meeting of the Council of Ministers when it meets as the General Affairs and External Relations Council, the Joint Oireachtas Committee on European Affairs is given an opportunity to meet either with the Minister for Foreign Affairs or the Minister of State for European Affairs to discuss the Council's agenda. In 2006, the Joint Committee on European Affairs held only six meetings in advance of General Affairs and External Relations Council meetings, a frequency which constituted a light legislative control indeed bearing in mind that there were no less than thirteen such Council meetings at European level in 2006.[50]

A final element of the post-2002 scrutiny or overview process which merits mention is the fact that s. 2(5) of the European Union (Scrutiny) Act, 2002 requires that every Government Minister make a report to each House of the Oireachtas not less than twice yearly in relation to measures, proposed measures and other developments concerning the European Communities and the European Union in relation to which he or she performs functions.

Although the creation of such scrutiny mechanisms has been an improvement on the previous situation, their effectiveness in securing executive accountability remains open to doubt. With the second method of scrutiny mentioned above, as with the first, the relevant Irish Minister is not bound in any way by the position taken by the Oireachtas, and the benefit of these processes has been questioned. One Minister in the last Government (the Fianna Fáil-Progressive Democrat coalition which left office in mid-2007) was prepared to assert to this writer that he had never heard a useful contribution made at any committee meeting involving the deployment of the second method of scrutiny. Meenan, on the other hand, has been able to

---

49 O'Hegarty, above, n. 43, at 288.

50 See Paragraph 4.1, Sub-Committee on European Scrutiny of the Joint Oireachtas Committee on European Affairs, *Fourth Annual Report on the Operation of the European Union (Scrutiny) Act 2002:1 January 2006 to 31 December 2006* (March 2007). Details of the Joint Oireachtas Committee's meetings can be seen at http://debates.oireachtas.ie/CommitteeMenu.aspx?Dail=29&Cid=EU Regarding the frequency of the Council meetings see the Council's own website at http://www.consilium.europa.eu/cms3_applications/Applications/newsRoom/loadbook.ASP?target=2006&infoTarget=&MAX=1&BID=71&LANG=1&cmsId=349.

Note that the number of Council meetings is much higher if one is not prepared to deem each (separate) meeting of the General Affairs and External Relations Councils as the one event for present purposes.

cite a small number of examples of where meetings of the Joint Oireachtas Committee on European Affairs clearly have had an impact on Government policy (and indeed European policy generally, when Ireland has happened to have held the Presidency of the Council of Ministers at the relevant time).[51] In addition, it does *seem* likely that, as the same writer has observed, "specific, well-informed views, expressed in a consensual, cross-party setting" will tend to have an impact on ministerial positions.[52] On the other hand, given the lack of research capacity on the part of Oireachtas committees, it is not clear how often well-informed views are capable of being made available to Ministers in such meetings. And in any case, the extent to which Ministers actually appear before Oireachtas Committees has clearly varied considerably. Thus, for example, O'Hegarty could point out first, that by 2006 all hearings of the Committee on Communications, Marine and Natural Resources (a Committee chosen by that writer as a representative example) had involved detailed questioning of officials, but "*never* of a Minister" and secondly, that there had also been very little scrutiny of ministerial performance in the Council of Ministers.[53]

4. Analysing the Performance of the Oireachtas

Various methods of classifying national parliaments have been put forward which can be used to gauge the relative strength of the Oireachtas in European affairs (*i.e.*, compared to other national parliaments).[54] Thus, for example, Mezey has distinguished between (a) parliaments strong enough to veto policy proposals, modify them or compromise over them, (b) parliaments having the more modest right to modify, but not reject, policy proposals, and finally (c) parliaments which can neither modify nor reject proposals put forward by the executive.[55] Norton, in contrast, is prepared to classify none of the foregoing as parliaments with strong policy-making power. For Norton, a parliament is strong only if it can generate its own proposals which it can substitute for the original government proposal.[56] Whether one accepts Mezey's or Norton's definition of what is to deemed to be strength in a legislature, however, it is clear that the Oireachtas, notwithstanding recent reforms, cannot be defined as a strong legislative body, when judged by such

---

[51] See K. Meenan, above, n. 43, at 318

[52] *Ibid.*.

[53] O'Hegarty, above, n. 43, at 290. Emphasis added.

[54] See for a good summary here, A. Maurer, "National Parliaments in the Architecture of Europe in the Light of the Constitutional Treaty" in this volume, 47 at 65.

[55] M. Mezey, *Comparative Legislatures* (Duke University Press, Durham, North Carolina, 1979).

[56] P. Norton, "Parliament and Policy in Britain: the House of Commons as a Policy Influencer" (1984) 13 *Teaching Politics* 198 (cited in Maurer, above, n. 54 at n. 33).

criteria. Indeed, insofar as concerns European affairs, one writer, Maurer, has classified the Oireachtas as a parliament which is a 'slow adaptor' to the reality of European integration, with a relatively weak involvement in policy-making at both national and European levels. Thus according to Maurer, even insofar as concerns *national-level* policy-making in European matters Ireland's parliament is comparatively weakly involved – especially when compared to member states such as Austria and the Netherlands. As for the participation of the Oireachtas in European – (*i.e.,* Brussels-) level policy-making, this is also weak, compared in particular to that of the parliaments of *e.g.,* Finland or Denmark. Maurer's classification exercise was carried out before the 2002 reforms were put into effect, but those reforms do not in any case appear to have been far-reaching enough to justify a reclassification of Ireland's performance according to his typology.

Why has the performance of the Oireachtas been so weak? An inherited tradition of strong executives and weak legislatures, which has been examined above, is clearly one historical reason. What may perhaps be regarded as a corollary of this – the extremely weak committee structure in both Houses of the Oireachtas also merits mention beyond that already made above. When it comes to analysing any system of scrutiny which has at its core the operation of an Oireachtas committee, there is a need to understand the context in which such committees operate.

This context is that there is frequently little if any electoral incentive for TDs to participate actively in any such committees. One Government minister, who had some years earlier lost his seat in the Dáil before eventually being re-elected and gaining ministerial office, observed to this writer that he had on entering the Dáil for the first time been warned by an older and more experienced politician on the opposing side of the political divide that one could 'talk oneself out of' the lower House. The accuracy of this warning had subsequently been made clear when a period of very dedicated committee work on the part of the future minister was followed by the loss of his Dáil seat, almost ending his political career and leaving him to appreciate ruefully the dangers which attend the payment of more attention to Oireachtas committee work than the servicing the (non-legislative) needs of consituents.

Political near-death experiences of this nature illustrate the reality that TDs who wish to retain their Dáil seats ignore at their peril the general lack of media interest or, for that matter, public interest, in the work of Oireachtas committees. For now, constituency work – in other words attempting to assist constituents in dealing with the administration – is considerably more valuable in securing their re-election. The consequences are somewhat inevitable: in such circumstances, it is simply not possible for the work of

Oireachtas committees to be the top priority of their members. Necessarily, the work of such committees suffers as a result. They frequently do not use all their powers. Nor are they competitive in securing resources: hence, a large part of the increased resources made available to members of the Oireachtas in recent years in the wake of the enactment of the Oireachtas Commission Act 2003 has been used – with the agreement of all of the political parties – to provide assistance which enables TDs to carry out their constituency role, rather than to support their functions as legislators.[57]

As if such impediments to the effectiveness of Oireachtas committees as mechanisms of accountability were not enough, the usefulness of such committees is also severely restricted as a result of a rivalry between political parties. This ensures that membership of such committees is determined primarily by party allegiance (and within political parties, as a form of patronage) rather than expertise in a particular subject area. Party loyalty will also ensure that a Minister can in general rely on approximately half of any Oireachtas Committee having little political incentive to show the work the Minister has done in a poor light through strong criticism. Eight members of the seventeen-member Joint Oireachtas Committee on European Affairs in place until mid-2007 belonged to Government parties. Meenan notes, in her own chapter in this volume, that this Committee has traditionally operated on a bipartisan basis and seeks never to call votes,[58] a description which might seem to contradict the image presented of a committee handicapped by political considerations from demanding accountability. However, such bipartisanship only seems possible because virtually the *entire* Committee – rather than merely those of its members who belong to government parties – sees its role as one broadly supportive of the Irish Minister in Europe, as opposed to a role whereby the legislature impose real accountability on the executive. As Meenan puts it "the *modus operandi* of the Joint Committee is consensual rather than confrontational."[59] In the context of European affairs, however, a bipartisan and broadly pro-European stance (in the last Oireachtas, on the part of all but one member of the Committee on European Affairs) has come, perhaps paradoxically, at the price of reducing its impact as a mechanism of executive accountability. The situation in the Joint Committee is to be contrasted with the far more challenging reception that can await Government ministers in the legislatures of other similar-sized EU member states. Hence, the recent alleged failure by the Danish foreign

[57] The question of resources is considered further in the text below.
[58] K. Meenan, above, n. 43, at 312.
[59] *Ibid.*, at 315.

minister to brief the Danish parliament in relation to the application to an Iranian opposition group of EU legislation targeted at terrorist organisations led to an Opposition MP drafting a formal rebuke for the Minister to be voted on by the relevant parliamentary committee.[60] As of yet, collective willingness to adopt such a confrontational approach has failed to evolve in the Oireachtas.[61]

5. Lessons to be Learned from Home and Abroad?

It is not easy to imagine a significant rebalancing of the relationship of the Oireachtas and the government in European affairs in the absence of such a rebalancing taking place in relation to other policy areas. Nevertheless, from time to time, suggestions are made as to how legislative scrutiny of the executive can more effectively be carried out by parliaments of European Union member states in the specific field of European affairs. Among the ideas which have been put forward as methods for enhancing the effectiveness of national parliamentary scrutiny have been (a) the need for adequate resources to be provided to enable legislatures to carry out this role; (b) the need for such scrutiny to involve a real process of dialogue between legislatures and executives; (c) the need for intervention on the part of national legislatures at an early point in the European Union policy-making process; (d) the need for legislatures to consult with individuals and bodies outside the legislature itself; (e) the need for national legislatures to co-ordinate their schedule with that of the Council of Ministers; (f) the need for legislatures proactively to seek information themselves rather than merely rely on whatever information is given to them by the executive; and (g) the need for legislatures to vary their approach to scrutiny depending on the policy field or integration method at issue.[62] It is worth considering how well the Oireachtas rates by reference to such suggestions.

(a) The need for resources

The funding made available to the Oireachtas and its members has increased considerably in recent years. However, in considering whether the need has

---

60 See A. Rettman "Iran mujahidin to challenge EU terror list" *EU Observer*, 10 May 2005.

61 For a critical examination of some of the reasons for the more powerful position of the legislatures *vis-à-vis* executives in Nordic countries, see T. Raunio and M. Wiberg, above, n. 34.

62 See in relation to some of these suggestions, D. Jones, *UK Parliamentary Scrutiny of EU Legislation* (CBI and the Foreign Policy Centre, London, 2005, available at http://fpc.org.uk/fsblob/432.pdf) at pp. 7 to 10. See also the 'Copenhagen Parliamentary Guidelines', adopted at the Twenty-Eighth Conference of Committees for European and Community Affairs of the European Union Parliaments (COSAC) [2003] or C154/1, which describe themselves as "guidelines for relations between governments and parliaments on Community issues (instructive minimum standards)".

been met for adequate resources to be provided to enable the legislature to carry out its largely committee-based task of scrutiny of the executive in European policy-making, it is instructive to mention that the latest published estimates of the Houses of the Oireachtas Commission foresee total expenditure in 2007, on the expenses of *all* Oireachtas Committees, as less than one and a half million euro – an amount similar to that spent in 2006 – out of a total anticipated budget of over 122 million euro for the Oireachtas as a whole.[63] To put this figure in context, this is slightly over half the estimated cost in 2007 of 'televising of proceedings of Dáil Éireann and Seanad Éireann and other services' and is *less* than the anticipated expenditure in respect of catering and bar staff employed by the Joint House Services Committee. It is scarcely any wonder, given such a small, and clearly inadequate level of investment in the committee system generally,[64] that the system of scrutiny of European policy-making – heavily centred as it is on committee work – is also under-resourced. The most recent annual report on the operation of the European Union (Scrutiny) Act 2002 observes that "one of the most serious concerns the [Sub-Committee on European Scrutiny] has had during the development of Oireachtas scrutiny is the level of resources which have been available" and noted that "concerns remain at the level of administrative support available to support this process."[65] Indeed the very last words of the report consist of the observation that "adequate resources are required to facilitate the [Sub-Committee] in particular to take full advantage of technological advances. The ever increasing recognition of the role of national parliaments and the requirement to engage citizens in European affairs requires this."[66]

(b) The need for scrutiny to involve a real process of dialogue between the legislature and the executive

It has already been noted that the system of legislative scrutiny introduced in Ireland in 2002 suffers from the limitation that no provision is made for Government ministers to be bound by any veto or even by a scrutiny reserve.

---

[63] See Houses of the Oireachtas Commission, *Statement of Estimates of the Amount of Moneys Required in Respect of Ongoing Expenditure for the Period Beginning on 1 January 2007 and Ending on 31 December 2007* (PRN A6/1673, October 2006) (published in accordance with section 13 of the Houses of the Oireachtas Commission Act 2003 and available at http://www.oireachtas.ie/documents/commission/Estimates2007.doc).

[64] Meenan has described the entire Oireachtas committee system as "woefully short of resources" (K. Meenan, above, n. 43 at 319).

[65] Sub-Committee on European Scrutiny of the Joint Oireachtas Committee on European Affairs, *Fourth Annual Report on the Operation of the European Union (Scrutiny) Act 2002:1 January 2006 to 31 December 2006* (March 2007) at p. 73 thereof.

[66] *Ibid.*.

The holding of the executive to account by the Oireachtas is further hobbled by another factor – the failure to make the process of legislative scrutiny involve in any meaningful sense a dialogue between the legislature and executive. In no Committee does there appear to have been any meaningful practice of following up issues once these have been initially raised or discussed in a particular Committee meeting. A good example of the lack of feedback may be seen in the case of the Joint Oireachtas Committee on European Affairs, which is briefed only *before* meetings of the General Affairs and External Relations Council, and not after.[67] This is not untypical. Having expressed their views to Government ministers, Oireachtas Committees have generally, to date, remained starved of information as to the outcome, if any, of their own contribution to the European policy-making process.[68] This seems a critical lacuna in the system of legislative overview of the executive by Oireachtas committees,[69] and one which appears at odds with the basic principle enshrined in the Copenhagen Parliamentary Guidelines that "the national parliament shall have an opportunity to follow up on its government's decisions in the Community system."[69a]

(c) The need for national legislatures to time their interventions at an early stage in the European-Union policy-making process

The need for national legislatures to time their intervention at as early a point as possible in the European Union policy-making process, in order to

[67] Or, more accurately, Council*s*.

[68] See O'Hegarty, above, n. 43, at 295–296.

[69] Interestingly, the Joint Oireachtas Committee on European Affairs now engages in some limited dialogue with the European Commission, which has made internal administrative arrangements to deal with observations received from national parliaments. The last annual report of this Committee observes that it

> "views the Commission's decision to consider and respond to comments from national parliaments as an important signal in the increasing cooperation between the Commission and national parliaments in EU policy making. The Committee has for some time engaged directly with the European Commission by sending contributions to Commission Proposals, White Papers and Green Papers. The new Commission initiative, which provides an official channel of communication between national parliaments and the Commission, will reinforce this exchange and cooperation."

(See Joint Oireachtas Committee on European Affairs, *Annual Report 2006 (*January, 2007) (available online at http://www.oireachtas.ie/documents/committees29thdail/europeanaffairsreports/Annual_Report_2006.doc) at pp. 15-16).

[69a] Cited above at n. 62, at p. 1 thereof. Note also the recommendation in guideline 4 of the Copenhagen Guidelines that "the Government must forward minutes of Council meetings within a short time frame after the meetings."

maximise any prospect of influencing the eventual outcome of the European policy-making process, is one that is frequently stressed.[70] This need is not being met in the Irish context. This is not necessarily entirely the fault of the executive: even after proposed measures have been referred to the Oireachtas by the government for scrutiny, a time-lag of several months has tended to occur between this referral and the actual scrutiny by the relevant Oireachtas sectoral committee.[71] Influence, in any case, is sometimes more usefully exercised before an individual European legislative proposal is published by the Commission: in other words, when work programmes or Commission green or white papers are published. In this respect, although O'Hegarty has noted that the Sub-Committee on European Scrutiny has "routinely" examined green and white papers (and to this may be added the observation that the Joint Oireachtas Committee on European Affairs has itself – albeit infrequently – made contributions in respect of Commission green and white papers[72]), sectoral Oireachtas committees do not seem typically to involve themselves in scrutiny of Commission work programmes or other preparatory documents.[73] It is true that the Work Programme of the Joint Oireachtas Committee on European Affairs is at least informed by the Work Programmes of the European Commission for the calendar year and of the Presidency of the Council at least for the first half of the calendar year. But the effect even of this is moderated by the need to take into account various other factors such as the Joint Committee's own priorities and its work in progress, including the ongoing work of the Scrutiny Sub-Committee.[74]

(d) The need for legislatures to consult with individuals and bodies outside the legislature itself

The need for legislatures to consult with individuals and bodies outside the legislature itself is sometimes mentioned as a *desideratum* when it comes to matters European.[75] Such meetings with non-members of the legislature may seek to serve a number of functions. In the first place, they may involve an effort by the legislature to better inform itself about initiatives at European

[70] See in this regard *e.g.*, T. Raunio, *"Ensuring Democratic Control over National Governments in European Affairs"* in this volume, 3 at 7.

[71] O'Hegarty, above, n. 43, at 290.

[72] See in this regard *e.g.*, the Joint Oireachtas Committee on European Affairs, *Annual Report 2006*, above, n. 69, at para. 9.1 thereof.

[73] O'Hegarty, above, n. 43, at 290 and 295.

[74] See Joint Oireachtas Committee on European Affairs, *Joint Oireachtas Committee on European Affairs Work Programme 2007* (February, 2007) available at http://www.oireachtas.ie/documents/committees29thdail/work%20programme/EA2007.doc)

[75] See *e.g.*, D. Jones, above, n. 62 at p. 8.

level and about relevant policy considerations.[76] Meetings may also involve an attempt to keep government ministers and other players in the European policy-making process (such as European Commissioners or members of the European Parliament) better informed of the national parliamentary perspective. Thirdly, they may involve an effort to stimulate awareness on the part of interest groups within the Irish electorate (such as farmers, trade unions or employers) of legislative or executive action proposed or being taken at European Union level.

The degree of involvement of parliamentary outsiders obviously varies from one Oireachtas Committee to another. The Committee on Communications, Marine and Natural Resources, for example, has invited interest groups to meetings (such as non-governmental organisations when discussing the internet, and fisheries groups in discussing marine issues).[77] As for the Joint Committee on European Affairs itself, in recent times, it appears to have made considerable efforts to involve Oireachtas 'outsiders', both as invitees before and as participants in the Joint Committee. Insofar as involving them as *participants* is concerned, according to the relevant Orders of Reference,[78] certain persons who are not appointed to the Committee from the membership of the Dáil or Seanad may attend meetings of the Joint Committee and take part in proceedings (although without having a right to vote or to move motions and amendments) *viz.,* (i) members of the European Parliament elected from constituencies in Ireland (including Northern Ireland); (ii) members of the Irish delegation to the Parliamentary Assembly of the Council of Europe; and (iii) at the invitation of the Joint Committee, other – *i.e.,* non-Irish – members of the European Parliament.

Examples of bringing in outsiders as *invitees* may be seen in the list of persons invited before of the Joint Committee on European Affairs in the first three months of 2007. In this period, the Committee engaged in a discussions with an admirably catholic (although perhaps somewhat eclectic) selection of interlocutors consisting of the Commissioner for Fisheries and Maritime

---

[76] According to its own website (http://euaffairs.ie/), the Joint Oireachtas Committee on European Affairs receives oral presentations from individuals and bodies "in order to hear their views and perspectives on issues under consideration."

[77] O'Hegarty, above, n. 43, at 290.

[78] These are to be found in Appendix I to Joint Oireachtas Committee on European Affairs, *Annual Report 2006,* above, n. 69. See in this regard the Orders of Reference made by Dáil Éireann on 16 October 2002 at paragraph 2(c) thereof, and the Orders of Reference made by Seanad Éireann on 17 October 2002 at paragraph 1(c) thereof.

Affairs, the Foreign Minister of Armenia and the Speaker of Slovakian Parliament.[79] Looking at the entire period covered by its 2006 Annual Report,[80] the Joint Committee's own Annual Report records having met during this time with three Irish government ministers, two Irish junior ministers,[81] the Ukrainian foreign minister,[82] six representatives of European Union institutions,[83] three ambassadors to Ireland,[84] three delegations sent from parliaments of European countries,[85] a representative of one intergovernmental organisation[86] and of one non-governmental organisation,[87] seven Irish government department officials,[88] four statutory bodies or agencies,[89] representatives of the Irish Farmers Association plus one academic from Trinity College. In addition the Joint Committee held what it referred to as 'informal private meetings' with five other officials or public representatives from other European countries.[90] Committee members have also engaged in a considerable amount of travel – in the course of 2006, Committee members engaged in a total of 29 individual trips abroad (of, at times, varying seeming degrees of usefulness) to Austria, Finland, Estonia, Belgium, Lithuania, Latvia, Bulgaria, Romania, Monaco, Italy, Russia and France.[91]

While one cannot dispute that a considerable level of activity has been involved in the organisation or attendance of many of the above such

---

[79] These met with the Committee on 6 March, 28 February and 7 February 2007 respectively. See the Joint Committee's website at http://debates.oireachtas.ie/CommitteeMenu.aspx?Dail=29&Cid=EU

[80] See Paragraph 8 of Joint Oireachtas Committee on European Affairs, *Annual Report 2006,* above, n. 69.

[81] By its own account, in the period under report the Select Committee on European Affairs met with the Minister of State for Foreign Affairs on only two occasions, which seems a surprisingly small number of meetings.

[82] *Viz.,* that of the Ukraine.

[83] Ranging from the President of the European Parliament to a Head of Unit within a Directorate-General of the Commission.

[84] *Viz.,* those from Finland, Romania and Bulgaria.

[85] *Viz.,* those of France, Poland and Iceland.

[86] *Viz.,* former Commissioner Peter Sutherland in his capacity as Special Representative of the UN Secretary-General for Migration.

[87] The Immigrant Council of Ireland.

[88] Although it may be noted that four of these were from the same department, that of Transport.

[89] The Ombudsman, a representative of FÁS, the Equality Authority, the Marine Institute)

[90] *Viz.* the Deputy Foreign Minister of Moldava, the Bulgarian Minister for Labour, the Cypriot Ambassador to Ireland, the German Minister for State for Europe and a member of the French National Assembly.

[91] See the Joint Oireachtas Committee on European Affairs, *Annual Report 2006,* above, n. 69, at para. 10 thereof.

meetings, it does seem legitimate to query how systematically linked such work was with the objectives of providing some input into the legislative or policy-making process at European level or with controlling government activity in this regard, and further how effective such activities have been. In other words, the Joint Committee on European Affairs may well have succeeded in better informing itself about European affairs through such meetings, but whether it has achieved any more than that seems open to question. The usefulness of the Oireachtas as an entity for transmitting information 'upwards' to policy-making players is severely restricted by the lack of provision made for Government ministers to be bound by any veto or scrutiny reserve by Oireachtas committees and more generally, by the failure to make the process of legislative scrutiny generate a meaningful sense a dialogue between the legislature and executive. The usefulness of the Oireachtas as an entity for transmitting information 'downwards' seems to have been hobbled by the very limited ability which the Oireachtas has had to date in attracting the attention of either the electorate or the media in the work it does. Although, according to its most recent annual report, "the Joint Committee on European Affairs has given high priority in its work programme to raising national awareness of European issues and to reconnecting the people with the European Union and its institutions",[92] it would be difficult to view the Joint Committee as having been a major success in this respect. Such work arguably continues to be better done by the National Forum on Europe, a body which it is noticeable that the government has felt the need to maintain in existence for several years.[93]

(e) The need for national legislatures to co-ordinate their schedules with that of the Council of Ministers

In order to maximise the influence of the Oireachtas on the executive when Government ministers participate in Council meetings, there is an obvious need to for the Oireachtas to coordinate its schedule with that of the Council of Ministers. At least some effort has been made in this regard since the new system of overview was introduced in 2002, in that Government departments now forward draft and revised agendas for Council meetings to the secretariat of the Sub-Committee on European Scrutiny which then notifies

[92] See the Joint Oireachtas Committee on European Affairs, *Annual Report 2006*, above, n. 69 at para. 7.1 thereof.

[93] See generally, T. Brown, *"Ireland's National Forum on Europe: Helping to Make Up for the Democratic Deficit?"* in this volume at 323. To gain an idea of the Forum's activities, see the Forum's website at http://www.forumoneurope.ie/.

all other Oireachtas committees. In addition (as already noted in the text above), the last government is reported to have suggested that the norm be that a Minister be requested by the relevant Oireachtas committee to appear before it in the week prior to the relevant Council meeting.[94] (In practice, it may be noted, such appearances have indeed become the norm for some individual Government ministers but certainly not all of them.[95])

Much, however, clearly remains to be done. Thus, for example, the meetings of the Joint Oireachtas Committee on European Affairs, although reasonably frequent and regular during the parliamentary calendar, tend to take place *only* during that time. This is notwithstanding the fact that the European-level activities of the government it supervises are not so temporally restricted.

(f) The need for legislatures to seek information proactively themselves rather than rely on whatever information is given to them by the executive

The need for legislatures to seek out information proactively themselves rather than to have it provided to them by the executive has been suggested as desirable if effective scrutiny in the field of European affairs is to be assured. This need, if it is one, is not met in Ireland. In practice, what happens in Ireland is that information comes *via* government departments. Hence, it is the Department of Foreign Affairs which is responsible for forwarding all European Union documents to the relevant Government department which then forwards the documents along with an information note to the Sub-Committee on European Scrutiny.[96] This is in line with the approach of the European Union (Scrutiny) Act, 2002, according to s. 2(1) of which, as soon as practicable after a proposed measure is presented (*i.e.,* at European Union level) by the Commission or initiated by a member state, the relevant Minister shall cause a copy of the text concerned to be laid before each House of the Oireachtas "together with a statement of the Minister outlining the content, purpose and likely implications for Ireland of the proposed measure and including such other information as he or she considers appropriate." In practice, the information note also states the anticipated negotiation period and the expected implementation date of the measure.[97]

---

[94] O'Hegarty, above, n. 43, at 288.

[95] See the discussion in the text above concerning the Committee on Communications, Marine and Natural Resources.

[96] See Para. 4.2 of the Sub-Committee on European Scrutiny of the Joint Oireachtas Committee on European Affairs, *Fourth Annual Report on the Operation of the European Union (Scrutiny) Act 2002:1 January 2006 to 31 December 2006* (March 2007).

[97] *Ibid.*.

In this process, the Department of Foreign Affairs acts as a liaison point between the Oireachtas and the Government departments, ensuring that the Sub-Committee on European Scrutiny is provided with information notes on all proposals falling within the terms of the European Union (Scrutiny) Act, 2002 and on all documents that the Sub-Committee has requested to be examined. There is no suggestion of any bad faith on the part of anyone involved in any of this work. Nonetheless it does seem to involve somewhat peculiar institutional logic to compel a legislature seeking to hold to account a Government minister to depend on that minister's department for virtually all of the information it needs to carry out this task. At the very least, it would appear desirable that additional sources of information be available to Oireachtas committees in this situation, so that a legitimately critical approach may be taken in consideration by the Oireachtas of the executive's performance of its tasks. At present, however, the Sub-Committee on European Scrutiny appears to engage in its work on the basis only of "detailed examination of the material presented [*i.e.,* in the above-described manner] and the conclusions of additional enquiries made by [its] Policy Advisor in relation to these matters."[98] Improvement here is clearly desirable, either or both at the level of the Sub-Committee on European Scrutiny, or on the part of the various sectoral committees who carry out the actual scrutiny and need to acquire and deploy the appropriate information resources to ensure accountability.

Two recent improvements in this regard are worthy of note. The first is that in 2006, national parliaments gained the ability to exchange directly EU-related information via IPEX the Interparliamentary EU Information Exchange – a website set up as the result of a series of decisions taken by the Conference of the Speakers of EU Parliaments in 2000, 2003 and 2004.[99] Not only can the Oireachtas now benefit from information uploaded by other parliaments on to this site, but since September 2006, the Sub-Committee on EU Scrutiny itself has commenced uploading information in relation to Irish scrutiny of EU legislation onto the IPEX database.[100] Another effect of this initiative is of course that badly-lacking "public visibility, accountability, appreciation and understanding of what the Houses and their Members do on a day to day basis is maintained and improved."[101]

98 *Ibid.*.

99 The IPEX website address is http://www.ipex.eu/ipex/cms/pid/

100 Paragraph 8.3 of the Sub-Committee on European Scrutiny of the Joint Oireachtas Committee on European Affairs, *Fourth Annual Report on the Operation of the European Union (Scrutiny) Act 2002:1 January 2006 to 31 December 2006* (March 2007).

101 *Ibid.*.

A second initiative, which may lead to some long-term improvement, is that since September 2006, the European Commission has transmitted proposals for EU legislation and also discussion documents relating to legislation directly to national parliaments at the same time as these are sent to the Council and the European Parliament. Interestingly, the Sub-Committee on European Scrutiny asserted in its 2006 report that the Joint Oireachtas Committee on European Affairs had for some time engaged directly with the European Commission by sending contributions to Commission proposals, white papers and green papers. The Sub-Committee expressed the hope that the new Commission initiative, "which provides an official channel of communication between national parliaments and the Commission, will reinforce this exchange and cooperation."[102] The Commission initiative furnishes Irish parliamentarians with a further alternative source of information to the national administration in relation to such proposals, although clearly much remains to be done in this respect.

(g) The need for the legislature to vary its approach depending on the policy field or integration method being scrutinised

Finally, it would seem barely more than a truism to observe that in order to maximise the influence of legislative scrutiny of executive action in the European policymaking field, appropriate account must be taken of – and appropriate adjustment made for – the kind of European action which is being scrutinised. Significant European Union activity now occurs in a wide range of fora (ranging from the Council of Ministers (including CoRePer) to the Commission to the Parliament to a multitude of technical committees to institutions such as the European Central Bank) and in relation to an extremely broad range of policy areas (ranging, for example, from justice and home affairs to foreign and security policy to internal market rules) subject to a broad range of procedural rules (ranging from the co-decision procedure to comitology to social dialogue to the open method of co-ordination). It seems clear that a differentiated approach needs to be taken to controlling the activities of the executive in such a context. There is little, if any, evidence that any such approach has yet been taken by the Oireachtas. Indeed, discussions with this writer revealed limited awareness – even within the membership of the last Joint Committee on European Affairs itself – of what the highly significant (although admittedly arcane) open method of co-ordination has involved at European level.

---

[102] Para. 8.4, *ibid.*.

6. The Future – Grounds for Optimism or Pessimism?

Insofar as concerns the relationship between the legislature and the executive in Ireland in relation to European affairs, there has been considerable reform, largely stemming from the time of debate over the Treaty of Nice. Notwithstanding this, however, any realistic assessment of the role of the Oireachtas in European matters must conclude that it is not much different to its role in every other area of policymaking – that is to say, the Oireachtas occupies a relatively weak and indeed subservient role in its relations with the executive.

There are historical and – at least in some respects – logically plausible explanations for this state of affairs. From the historical point of view, as has been seen in the text above, we continue to live with an executive-legislature relationship, the main features of which were established (with the support of the members of the Oireachtas themselves) in the period just after independence was achieved and which has been continued largely unaltered in being since then by successive administrations of every political variety. From a logical point of view, the maintenance of a situation in which the executive branch of government plays the leading role is far from indefensible. A considerable portion of the growth in power of the modern executive state stems from the need for all states to cope with the complexity of modern life, necessitating the creation of a large, expert and multi-dimensional civil service. In the particular case of European policy matters, this complexity has manifested itself in the shape of the adoption at European level of a flood of necessary but highly technical legislation relating to everything from the Common Agricultural Policy to the establishment and regulation of various aspects of the Single European Market.[103] There are efficiency considerations which must be borne in mind when structuring the relationship between each national executive and legislature in such circumstances (indeed, one is likely to be told *sotto voce* by Danish officials that the much stronger Danish system of parliamentary control of the executive is not without considerable drawbacks in terms of the amount of flexibility it leaves to representatives of the Danish government to respond to sometimes rapidly changing circumstances in discussions within the Council of Ministers). In addition, there may be some unavoidable structural reasons explaining at least some of the relative weakness of the Oireachtas *vis-à-vis* the government. Thus, for example, in

[103] The manner in which the European Union has become the global pace-setter for technical regulation of various kinds is the subject of T. Buck, "Standard bearer: how the European Union exports its laws", *Financial Times*, 10 July 2007.

judging the failure of the Oireachtas to establish a committee system capable of holding the executive properly to account, we need to take into account arguments such as that of Meenan, who has argued that because of the limited size of parliament in a country as small as Ireland, it will never be possible to develop the kind of committee system that exists in the United Kingdom.[104] There is thus perhaps an element of advisability in being cautious about what one wishes for in arguing for a radically altered delineation of competences between the executive and the legislature.

Clearly, however, not every aspect of the lack of balance in the relationship between the Oireachtas and the government is inevitable. Ongoing policy choices are being made in this respect (and not by a disinterested party but rather by the institution of government which benefits the most from present arrangements *viz.,* the executive). There are signs that the choices which have been made have been less than ideal. Opposition criticisms of the government attitude to the Oireachtas are of course far from infrequent,[105] even if the temptation may exist to dismiss them as made for political reasons. However, in the very recent past, even government backbenchers have been occasionally prepared to express publicly their concern at their relative inability to influence policy.[106] Indeed by June 2006, such frustrations were felt sufficiently strongly to result in sixteen Fianna Fáil deputies – then, as now, members of the dominant party in the ruling coalition – signing a letter inviting other backbench TDs in this party to a meeting outside normal party structures, although it was ultimately decided to abandon the planned meeting when the government agreed to consider setting up a new party committee through which backbencher voices could be heard.[107] Further evidence, albeit of a different kind, that all may not be not well as regards the balance prevailing in this State between legislature and executive was provided by a national survey commissioned by the Houses of the Oireachtas Commission in 2006 which produced the finding that sixty per cent of respondents did not regard the work of the national parliament as important.[108] This survey was deemed by the Houses of the Oireachtas Commission to show clearly the need

---

104 Meenan, above, 316.

105 See the reported comments of the leader of the largest Opposition party (Fine Gael), Enda Kenny TD, reported in S. Collins, *"Government defeats proposal to shorten Dáil's summer recess", Irish Times*, 6 July 2006.

106 See *e.g.,* B. Andrews, above, n. 7.

107 See M. Brennock, "Backbenchers want to influence policy and have voices heard", *Irish Times*, 24 June 2006.

108 See Houses of the Oireachtas Commission, *Annual Report 2006* (available online at http://www.oireachtas.ie/documents/commission/reports/2006_Annual_Report.pdf) at p. 15 thereof.

to promote the work of parliament and its members, which seems a reasonable conclusion.[109] But arguably changes of substance in the role of the Oireachtas, not merely improvements in presentation, are also needed. There seems little point in trying to communicate the significance of the Oireachtas to the population at large if the reality is that it is for most of the time a largely impotent institution.

The focus of this chapter is on the Oireachtas role in controlling the executive in the European policy-making field. In the last section above a list of *desiderata* has been set out, which, if met, might improve the performance of the Oireachtas in this regard. Beyond changes of the nature suggested in the section above, however, changes that would succeed in shifting the balance of power between the Oireachtas and the executive in a real sense in European affairs would require much more radical reform in the Houses of the Oireachtas. Thus, for example, it may be noted that in its control of the government's policy-making in European matters, the present role of the Oireachtas is an undeniably, and perhaps, given electoral needs of its members, unavoidably, part-time affair, something which considerably reduces its effectiveness. In all of 2006 (which was not an election year), the Joint Oireachtas Committee on European Affairs succeeded in meeting on only thirty occasions. In its 2007 Work Programme, the Committee expressed the intention to meet weekly in 2007. However, general election years (of which 2007 was one) involve Oireachtas committee debates occurring on a radically less frequent basis. Thus, six months into 2007 (which was an election year) the Joint Committee had succeeded in holding debates on a total of only six occasions.[110] This number of debates was not expected be increased until a period of over nine to ten months in total had expired, since by virtue of the lengthy summer adjournment, Oireachtas committees are not expected to be established until October or even November, 2007.[111] All general elections,

[109] See in this regard the Houses of the Oireachtas Commission, *Annual Report 2006,* above, n. 108, the Oireachtas Commission, *Strategic Plan 2007–2009* (available online at http://www.oireachtas.ie/documents/commission/strategic_plan/2007-2009-English.pdf) and M. Donohoe, "Dáil, Seanad plan to blow dust off image" *Irish Times*, 18 June 2007.

[110] Details of such meetings are provided on the Committee's own website at http://debates.oireachtas.ie/CommitteeMenu.aspx?Dail=29&Cid=EU
and at Annex 3 of Joint Oireachtas Committee on European Affairs, *Annual Report 2006,* above, n. 69. According to the *Annual Report 2006*, the Dáil Select Committee met on two occasions in all in 2006 and the Sub-Committee on European Scrutiny met on sixteen occasions in this year. (*ibid.,* at p. 5).

[111] It may be argued that 2007 itself was exceptional even among election years in having involved an election followed relatively quickly by the summer recess, but similar serious delays in establishing committees also occurred on the occasion of both of the two previous most recent elections in 1997 and 2002 – a point acknowledged by the Government Chief Whip in July 2007. (See M. Donohue, "Just seven days of Oireachtas business in four months for TDs", *Irish Times*, 3 July 2007.)

even if not followed (as on this and on the two previous occasions) by the summer recess, involve breaks of some months in the already light and essentially part-time control of the executive which Oireachtas a committees normally provide.[112] Yet it must be recalled that the business of neither the Government nor the European Union comes to a halt during such times.

Apart from the essentially part-time nature of Oireachtas control, and the sometimes major gaps in continuity which occur in its exercise, an intertwined difficulty in having the Oireachtas play an effective role is that the clientelistic nature of Irish politics results in the necessity for politicians to spend far more time servicing the advocacy needs of their electorate than engaging in legislative work. It is difficult to envisage any change occurring in this situation without the reform of the Irish electoral system – and it is not clear that even this particular reform would be enough to reduce adequately the relative emphasis placed on constituency work rather than legislative activity on the part of members of the Dáil.[113]

By way of conclusion, it may be said that those reforms which have been introduced in the relationship between the legislature and the executive in the field of European policy-making have undoubtedly been welcome. However, a truly significant shift in power from executive to legislature in relation to the activities of the Irish State in the European policy-making activities remains elusive. This is not, it must be emphasised, a phenomenon confined to the European policy-making field. It stretches across all areas of policy and law-making in Ireland. Real change in the present scenario is likely to require broad-ranging fundamental reforms, including of the Oireachtas itself, and affecting its role in all policy fields, not just that of European law and policy. Whether such reforms will ever come about, however, remains to be seen.

---

[112] See M. Donohue, "Just seven days of Oireachtas business in four months for TDs", *Irish Times*, 3 July 2007, in which it was reported that in the first four months of the thirtieth Dáil (which was elected in late May 2007 and sat for the first time in mid-June), TDs will have engaged in parliamentary business on only seven days. See also S. Collins, "Government defeats proposal to shorten Dáil's summer recess", *Irish Times*, 6 July 2007 and M. O'Regan, "Call for shorter adjournment of House rejected", *Irish Times*, 6 July 2007.

[113] See for some reflections regarding the electoral system, M. Laver "TDs Have Not Thought Out Results of Changing PR System" *Irish Times*, 2 July 1998, G. FitzGerald, "People Entitled to Have Voting System Choice Put Before Them" *Irish Times*, 26 February 2000. The latter article is by a former Taoiseach.

7.
Democratic Control over Governmental Action in European Matters: the Example of Justice and Home Affairs

Michael McDowell[1]

1. Introduction

Cooperation among the member states of the European Union in justice and home affairs has evolved, from modest beginnings, over a considerable period. Democratic control over that cooperation has also developed from equally modest beginnings. This chapter will seek to trace the development of that democratic control by reference to the evolution of the cooperation in justice and home affairs from its conception (largely outside the framework of the Treaties) to the comprehensive new framework which the Treaty Establishing a Constitution for Europe was intended to create.

2. The Evolution of Cooperation in Justice and Home Affairs

(a) The Situation Prior to Maastricht

Cooperation in justice and home affairs among the member states of the European Union predated the formal Treaty arrangements created by the Treaty of Maastricht.[2] It has been ongoing since 1975 when TREVI[3] was

[1] Michael McDowell has held the offices of Attorney General of Ireland, Minister for Justice, Equality and Law Reform and Tánaiste (Deputy Prime Minister) of Ireland and is a leading Senior Counsel.

[2] Already, in its original 1957 form, the Treaty Establishing the European Economic Community (also known as the Treaty of Rome) included as one of its objectives the free movement of workers within the Community, but it approached free movement primarily from an economic perspective. Art. 220 of the Treaty, however (under which member states agreed to enter into negotiations with each other with a view to securing for the benefit of their nationals the simplification of formalities governing the reciprocal recognition and enforcement of judgments of courts and tribunals awards) did lay the basis for the development of intergovernmental cooperation in the civil law field.

[3] TREVI was an acronym for Terrorisme, radicalisme, extrémisme et violence internationale (terrorism, radicalism, extremism and international violence).

established as a forum for police cooperation in response, in the first instance, to terrorist activity in the member states. Cooperation was gradually widened to include other forms of crime and later migration matters. Meetings at ministerial level also became a feature of this developing intergovernmental cooperation.

The Single European Act, which entered into force on 1 July 1987, represented the first significant modification of the Treaty of Rome, with the goal being established of the creation of an internal market in which the free movement of persons was ensured.[4] This was to act as a key spur to the further development of cooperation in justice and home affairs.[5] A 'Political Declaration' on the free movement of persons linked to the Single European Act committed member states to cooperation as regards thc cntry, movement, and residence of third-country nationals as well as combating terrorism, drug trafficking and other forms of crime.[6] At the same time, a second General Declaration, however, made clear that member states reserved to themselves the right to take such measures as they considered necessary to control immigration and combat crime.[7]

The establishment of the Ad Hoc Immigration Group can be traced to the Single European Act, as can the association of the European Commission with aspects of the developing intergovernmental cooperation. Significant differences in approach were, however, also to emerge as to how that area without internal frontiers in which the free movement of persons was ensured should be developed. This was in turn to lead to the negotiation of the Schengen Agreement on the gradual abolition of checks at internal borders by a group of five member states also outside the framework of the Treaties in 1985.[8]

---

[4] In a new Art. 8a in what was then the EEC Treaty, inserted by Art. 13 of the Single European Act.

[5] The new Art. 8a provided that "the Community shall adopt measures with the aim of progressively establishing the internal market over a period expiring on 31 December 1992 .... The internal market shall comprise an area without internal frontiers in which the free movement of goods, persons, services and capital is ensured in accordance with the provisions of this Treaty".

[6] Political Declaration by the governments of the Member States on the free movement of persons annexed to the Final Act of the Conference of the Representatives of the Governments of the Member States convened at Luxembourg on 9 September 1985.

[7] General Declaration on Arts 13 to 19 of the Single European Act annexed to the Final Act of the Conference of the Representatives of the Governments of the Member States convened at Luxembourg on 9 September 1985.

[8] *Viz.*, Belgium, France, Germany, Luxembourg, and the Netherlands. The Schengen Agreement was given effect to by the Schengen Convention of 1990 and subsequently integrated into the framework of the Treaties with the entry into force of the Treaty of Amsterdam.

(b) The Treaty of Maastricht (1992)

The Treaty on European Union, also known as the Treaty of Maastricht,[9] established the European Union and brought cooperation in justice and home affairs within the new structures of the Union and expanded and strengthened that cooperation. Three 'Pillars', representing three distinct approaches to European integration, made up the new European Union. The First Pillar consisted of the three pre-existing European Communities[10] – and was characterised by traditional Community decision-making methods. The Second Pillar consisted of provisions on a Common Foreign and Security Policy,[11] and the Third Pillar covered cooperation in justice and home affairs.[12] The Second and Third Pillars were based on the more traditional forms of intergovernmental cooperation which had developed outside the framework of the European Communities.

The Treaty of Maastricht made the development of 'close cooperation on justice and home affairs' one of the objectives of the new European Union,[13] with provision being made in Title VI of this Treaty that member states would regard as 'matters of common interest' for the purposes of achieving the objectives of the Union (and, in particular the free movement of persons), asylum policy; rules governing the crossing by persons of external borders; immigration policy and policy regarding nationals of third countries; the combating of drug addiction; the combating of international fraud; judicial cooperation on civil matters; judicial cooperation in criminal matters; customs cooperation; and police cooperation in certain areas (*e.g.*, preventing and combating terrorism, unlawful drug trafficking, other forms of serious international crime, *etc.*).[14]

The institutional arrangements for the purpose of the development of cooperation in justice and home affairs continued to emphasise the intergovernmental nature of that cooperation. The right of initiative was not the exclusive prerogative of the Commission but rather one which the member states shared with the Commission in some (but not all) areas.[15] Joint positions,

---

[9] This Treaty entered into force on 1 November 1993.

[10] *Viz.*, the European Economic Community (now rechristened the European Community by the Treaty on European Union), the European Coal and Steel Community and the European Atomic Energy Community.

[11] Provided for in Title V of the Treaty on European Union.

[12] The relevant provisions were contained in Title VI of the Treaty on European Union.

[13] Art. B of the Treaty on European Union (in its original form).

[14] Art. K.1 of the Treaty on European Union (in its original form).

[15] Under Art. K.3(2), member states retained an exclusive right of initiative for the purposes of judicial cooperation in criminal matters, customs cooperation, and police cooperation.

joint actions, and conventions were used in place of traditional Community instruments, and unanimity remained the primary decision-making mechanism in the Council.[16] Similarly, while the European Parliament did acquire a new role in this area, this role was, as we shall see, limited.[17]

(c) The Treaty of Amsterdam (1997)

The Treaty of Amsterdam[18] further changed the nature of justice and home affairs cooperation by making the development of the Union as 'an area of freedom, security and justice' one of the five key objectives of the Union.[19] The Treaty saw cooperation in justice and home affairs matters divided between the Treaty Establishing the European Community and the Treaty on European Union. The areas of free movement, visas, asylum, immigration, and judicial cooperation in civil matters, as well as certain other pre-existing arrangements under the Schengen Convention were integrated into the First Pillar Community framework by way of a new Title IV of the EC Treaty. The remaining areas of justice and home affairs cooperation – police cooperation, customs cooperation, and judicial cooperation in criminal matters – were left subject to strengthened Third Pillar arrangements under Title VI of the Treaty on European Union.

Under the new Title IV of the EC Treaty, Community instruments and Community decision-making arrangements would now apply to cooperation in asylum, immigration, *etc.* Certain pre-existing features of cooperation under the previous Title VI arrangements, however, were retained for a transitional five-year period. These included recourse to decision-making by

[16] Art. K.3(2) and K.4(3).

[17] See Art. K.6 of the Treaty on European Union (in its original form). Under the Treaty of Maastricht, provision was made for one exception to the Title VI arrangements in justice and home affairs cooperation. The question of third countries whose nationals were required to be in possession of a visa when crossing the external borders of member states was made subject to Community law and the Community method of decision-making (under Art. 100c of the EC Treaty as inserted by Art. G (23) of the Treaty on European Union (in its original form)). Provision was also made in Title VI of the Treaty on European Union for a 'passerelle' whereby other aspects of justice and home affairs cooperation could be made subject to Art. 100c procedures (Art. K.9 of the Treaty on European Union (in its original form)) but recourse was never had to this possibility.

[18] This Treaty entered into force on 1 May 1999.

[19] Hence the provision of Art. 2 of the Treaty on European Union as inserted and renumbered by the Treaty of Amsterdam that: "the Union shall set itself the following [objective] … to maintain and develop the Union as an area of freedom, security and justice, in which the free movement of persons is assured in conjunction with appropriate measures with respect to external border controls, asylum, immigration and the prevention and combating of crime".

unanimity for most purposes and the retention of the member states' right of initiative.

The Treaty of Amsterdam also strengthened the arrangements for cooperation in the area of police, customs, and judicial cooperation in criminal matters under Title VI of the Treaty on European Union. The Commission acquired a right of initiative which was shared with member states. New legal instruments, including framework decisions and council decisions, became available for the purpose of developing cooperation in this area. Decision-making for most purposes remained by way of unanimity.[20]

More generally, the Treaty of Amsterdam mandated the development of cooperation in justice and home affairs by defining in more precise terms than had previously been the case the objectives which were to be pursued. Under Title IV, these included, for example,[21] the adoption within a period of five years of minimum standards for the reception of asylum seekers, for the qualification of nationals of third countries as refugees, and for the procedures for the grant and withdrawal of refugee status. These objectives also included a more general mandate for the development of judicial cooperation in criminal matters, and a strengthened Europol in the context of Title VI.[22]

The Second Protocol agreed at Amsterdam[23] made provision for the incorporation into the Treaty framework of the Schengen arrangements and *acquis*. Special arrangements were made for Ireland, the United Kingdom, and Denmark, however, both as regards the Schengen *acquis*[24] and as regards cooperation under Title IV of the EC Treaty. Under the Second Protocol agreed at Amsterdam, Ireland and the United Kingdom are not parties to the Schengen agreements but may participate in all or part of the relevant arrangements.[25] Similarly – but under separate Protocols – Ireland, the United Kingdom, and Denmark are not automatically bound by the

[20] Art. 34 Treaty on European Union, Consolidated Treaties.

[21] See Art. 63 of the EC Treaty.

[22] See Art. 29 of the Treaty on European Union as amended at Amsterdam.

[23] The Protocol integrating the Schengen *acquis* into the framework of the European Union (annexed by the High Contracting Parties at Amsterdam to the Treaty on European Union and to the Treaty Establishing the European Community).

[24] Note that all European Union member states other than the United Kingdom and Ireland are full participants in the Schengen system, as are Iceland and Norway.

[25] See the Protocol integrating the Schengen acquis into the framework of the European Union, agreed at Amsterdam.

provisions of Title IV.[26] Under special arrangements set out in these Protocols, Ireland may, however, opt in to measures in this area. These special arrangements would have implications for the role of the Oireachtas, as shall be seen in the text below.

(d) The Treaty of Nice (2001)

The Treaty of Nice[27] made a number of further technical changes in the justice and home affairs area, including the immediate extension of qualified majority voting and co-decision to judicial cooperation in civil law matters (with the exception of aspects relating to family law), and the further reinforcement of transitional measures enabling the extension of qualified majority voting to other aspects of Title IV of the EC Treaty.[28] Other changes included provision for the establishment of Eurojust[29] and the further development of provisions for enhanced cooperation.[30]

3. Developing the role of the European Parliament

(a) Prior to Maastricht

The role of the European Parliament in exercising democratic oversight and control in the area of justice and home affairs cooperation has evolved over time, with the institutional framework. The nature of this role has been influenced both by developments in relation to the European Parliament (which evolved from the European Assembly and whose members have been directly elected since 1979) and by factors unique to the justice and home affairs area.

Although the European Parliament saw its role significantly strengthened by the Single European Act by virtue of the introduction of the 'cooperation procedure' between the Council and the European Parliament in relation to certain kinds of measures, it had no formal role in exercising oversight over the developing cooperation in justice and home affairs matters as long as that cooperation took place outside the framework of the treaties.

---

[26] See respectively, the Protocol on the position of the United Kingdom and Ireland, and the Protocol on the position of Denmark.

[27] This Treaty entered into force on 1 February 2003.

[28] See Art. 2(4) of the Treaty of Nice and Art. 67 of the EC Treaty.

[29] See Art. 1(8) of the Treaty of Nice and Art. 31 of the Treaty on European Union.

[30] Thus building on the provisions for closer cooperation first agreed at Amsterdam. See Arts. 40, 40a and 40b of the Treaty on European Union as substituted by Art. 1(9) of the Treaty of Nice.

(b) The Treaty of Maastricht

The Treaty of Maastricht made provision for a role for the European Parliament in relation to the developing cooperation in justice and home affairs for the first time. providing that:

> "The Presidency and the Commission shall regularly inform the European Parliament of discussions in the areas covered by this Title.
>
> The Presidency shall consult the European Parliament on the principal aspects of policies in the areas referred to in this Title and shall ensure that the views of the European Parliament are duly taken into account.
>
> The European Parliament may ask questions of the Council or make recommendations to it. Each year, it shall hold a debate on the progress made in implementation of the areas referred to in this Title".[31]

More generally, the Treaty of Maastricht saw the replacement of the co-operation procedure by the 'co-decision' procedure which gave the European Parliament the role of co-legislator with the Council for the purpose of Community measures in certain areas. This meant that, in the areas to which it applied, the European Parliament, by an absolute majority, could accept, amend, or reject Council legislative proposals. These arrangements did not, however, apply in relation to those visa aspects of justice and home affairs cooperation covered by the EC Treaty, in respect of which the obligation on the Council was to consult the European Parliament.

Title VI continued to reflect the essentially intergovernmental nature of cooperation in justice and home affairs matters. That is why the roles of both the Commission and Parliament in this area were more limited than those which applied for the purposes of the Community Treaties. The European Parliament had nevertheless acquired a role in the future development of cooperation in justice and home affairs even if, at this stage, its rights extended only to being informed of discussions in the areas covered by Title VI, being consulted on the principal aspects of activities rather than individual legislative measures, and being able to ask questions and make recommendations. The Treaty of Maastricht was in that sense a significant milestone in the development of democratic oversight at European Union level.

---

[31] Art. K.6 of Title VI of the Treaty on European Union (in its original form).

(c) The Treaty of Amsterdam

The Treaty of Amsterdam brought further enhancements to the role of the European Parliament in relation to justice and home affairs matters. This was the result both of the integration of asylum and immigration matters into the Community framework in Title IV of the EC Treaty and of the strengthened role for the European Parliament under Title VI of the Treaty on European Union.[32] It was also the result of the strengthening, more generally, of co-decision procedures within the Community framework.

Under Title VI of the Treaty on European Union, (now directed largely at police, customs and judicial cooperation in criminal matters) the Council was obliged to consult the European Parliament before it adopted framework decisions, decisions, or conventions.[33] The European Parliament, for its part, was required to deliver its opinion within a specified time limit which could be fixed by the Council but which could not be less than three months. In the absence of any opinion being delivered within the specified time limit, the Council was entitled to adopt the measure.[34] The requirement on the Presidency and the Commission to inform regularly the European Parliament of discussion in the areas covered by Title VI[35] and the right of the European Parliament to ask questions and make recommendations, both of which were first set down in the Treaty of Maastricht, were also preserved.[36] There was also a requirement to consult the European Parliament in relation to any proposal to have recourse to the 'passerelle' allowing the transfer of measures from Title VI of the Treaty on European Union to Title IV of the EC Treaty.[37]

The position of the European Parliament was also strengthened in relation to legislative measures under Title IV of the EC Treaty (*i.e.*, in the area of visas, asylum, immigration, and other policies related to free movement of persons). There was now a requirement – similar to that just mentioned in the context of Title VI of the Treaty on European Union – to consult the European Parliament in relation to Community legislative instruments before their adoption.[38] The position of the European Parliament under Title IV of

---

[32] Which now dealt largely with police and judicial cooperation in criminal matters.
[33] Art. 39(1) of the Treaty on European Union.
[34] Art. 39(1) of the Treaty on European Union.
[35] Art. 39(2) of the Treaty on European Union.
[36] Art. 39(3) of the Treaty on European Union.
[37] Art. 42 of the Treaty on European Union.
[38] Art. 67 of the EC Treaty as inserted by Art. 2(15) of the Treaty of Amsterdam.

the EC Treaty did not equate therefore with its role under traditional First Pillar arrangements. This was because transitional arrangements provided, as a general rule, that the Council would continue to act on the basis of unanimity on a proposal from the Commission or on the initiative of a member state.[39] The transitional arrangements, however, also foresaw further enhancements in the Parliament's role after a period of five years. Those transitional arrangements were subsequently built on by the Nice Treaty and are dealt with further below in that context.

The Amsterdam Treaty, more generally, expanded the scope of, and simplified the operation of, the co-decision procedure.[40] The agreement of both the Council and European Parliament became necessary for the adoption of legislation under this procedure. The Treaty also contained provisions strengthening the role of national parliaments.[41]

The primary significance of the Amsterdam Treaty, therefore, lay first in the requirement to consult the European Parliament in relation to individual legislative measures adopted in the framework of the Third Pillar, rather than in relation to the principal aspects of policies (as had been the case since the Treaty of Maastricht had come into force), and secondly in the prospect it opened up in the First Pillar for the extension of the co-decision procedure to aspects of immigration, asylum, etc. in due course.

(d) The Treaty of Nice

The Treaty of Nice strengthened the role of the European Parliament in relation to a number of areas of First Pillar justice and home affairs cooperation and reinforced the dynamic introduced by the Treaty of Amsterdam allowing for the development of the European Parliament's role in relation to certain areas of such cooperation. The significance of the Nice Treaty lay in the extension of co-decision procedures (under which the European Parliament becomes in effect the co-legislator with Council) to aspects of justice and home affairs cooperation for the first time, together with its firm commitments to further such extension.

Insofar as concerns measures in the field of judicial cooperation in civil matters having cross-border implications, provision was made for qualified

[39] Further, the role of the European Parliament was limited to consultation even in respect of those visa measures which, under the Amsterdam Treaty, were made immediately subject to qualified majority voting.

[40] See now Art. 251 of the EC Treaty as amended by Art. 2(44) of the Treaty of Amsterdam.

[41] Protocol No. 9 on the Role of National Parliaments in the European Union.

majority voting and co-decision arrangements applying here immediately after the entry into force of the Treaty of Nice.[42] Provision was also made for qualified majority voting and co-decision applying to the adoption of certain measures in the area of asylum automatically – after Community legislation had been adopted defining the common rules and basic principles which applied.[43] And a (non-binding) Declaration adopted at Nice committed the Council to the further extension of co-decision, with 1 May 2004 as the target date for the purpose of measures directed to certain aspects of immigration policy. Other areas were to follow as quickly as possible thereafter.[44]

The Treaty of Nice made no changes in relation to the role of the European Parliament for the purposes of Title VI of the Treaty on European Union.

(e) Developments Since the Coming into Force of the Treaty of Nice

The transitional arrangements provided for in the Treaties of Amsterdam and Nice have resulted in a further strengthening of the role of the European Parliament in the intervening period. Certain visa matters became automatically subject to co-decision procedures from 1 January 2004. More importantly, under a 2004 Council Decision,[45] co-decision arrangements

[42] See Art. 67(5) of the EC Treaty as inserted by Art. 2(4) of the Treaty of Nice. Any aspects of measures relating to family law were excluded, however. Note in this regard that the Treaty of Nice entered into force on 1 February 2003).

[43] See Art. 67(5) of the EC Treaty as inserted by Art. 2(4) of the Treaty of Nice.

[44] Declaration on Art. 67 of the Treaty Establishing the European Community. The provisions to which qualified majority voting and co-decision were to be extended with effect from 1 May 2004 were measures setting out the conditions under which third country nationals shall have freedom to travel within member states for period no more than three months in duration (provided for by Art. 62(3) of the EC Treaty) and measures on illegal immigration and illegal residence, including repatriation (under Art. 63(3)(b) of the EC Treaty). Measures relating to the standards and procedures to be followed by member states in carrying out checks on the external borders of member states were to be made subject to qualified majority voting and co-decision from the date on which agreement was reached on the scope of the measures. Finally the Declaration provided that the Council would endeavour to apply the co-decision procedure to the remaining areas covered by Title IV from 1 May 2004 or as soon as possible thereafter. Note also the – legally binding – Protocol on Art. 67 agreed at Nice in which provision was made for the extension of qualified majority voting in order to adopt measures under Art. 66 of the EC Treaty (which relates to cooperation between departments of national administrations in areas covered by Title IV of the EC Treaty) – subject, however, only to a requirement to *consult* the European Parliament.

[45] Council Decision providing for certain areas covered by Title IV of Part Three of the Treaty establishing the European Community to be governed by the procedure referred to in Art. 251 of that Treaty (15226/04, JAI 499, ASIM 49, Brussels 15 December 2004). In accordance with the Protocol annexed to the Treaty of Amsterdam, both Ireland and the United Kingdom notified the Council of their intention to take part in the adoption and application of the Decision.

were extended to the majority of other areas dealt with by Title IV from 1 January 2005. The areas concerned include measures concerning internal and external borders, immigration policy concerning illegal immigration and residence, and measures promoting a balance of effort in receiving refugees. The only area of Title IV now excluded from the scope of the co-decision provisions are those dealing with aspects of immigration policy other than illegal immigration.

Democratic control at the level of the Union through the European Parliament has clearly therefore developed quite significantly in the period since the Treaty of Maastricht. Parliament, instead of being simply consulted on the principal aspects of the polices being pursued by Council in the Title IV area, is now co-legislator for many purposes and must be consulted on all individual legislative measures in the remaining areas. The European Parliament has likewise acquired the right to be consulted in respect of all legislative measures (*i.e.,* framework decisions, decisions, and conventions) in the Title VI area dealing with police and judicial cooperation in criminal matters.

The significance of the role and opinion of the European Parliament becomes very obvious when one attends the Justice and Home Affairs Council, which is now one of the busiest Council formations. The opinions of the European Parliament are taken very seriously by ministers, especially in those areas where the Parliament has the power of co-decision. The importance of the European Parliament is also reflected in the increased attention devoted to it by the member states holding the Presidency of the European Union.

During Ireland's Presidency of the European Union from January to June, 2004, a great deal of attention was devoted to liaising with the European Parliament. I appeared before the LIBE Committee[46] in January 2004, and before the plenary session of the European Parliament in February 2004. Other ministers appeared even more frequently. I found parliamentarians to be very well informed, with cohesive and well-developed opinions backed up by excellent research and support facilities. It would be an unwise minister and a foolish Presidency which treated the European Parliament with anything less than the respect it deserves. Indeed, any Presidency that did so could very quickly find itself in serious difficulties. The European Parliament has thus become a key player in the development of cooperation at Union level.

---

[46] LIBE is the 'Libertés civiles, justice et affaires intérieures' Committee of the European Parliament or, in English, the Civil Liberties, Justice and Home Affairs Committee.

4. Oireachtas Scrutiny

The gradual acquisition of democratic oversight by the European Parliament in the European Union area has been mirrored to a considerable degree at a national level in Ireland. Cooperation outside the framework of the Treaties was not originally subject to scrutiny under the first generation of arrangements for scrutiny of European Community business (which consisted primarily of the Joint Committee on Secondary Legislation of the Communities).

After the coming into force of the Treaty of Maastricht, developments in relation to justice and home affairs cooperation were reported to the Oireachtas twice yearly.[47] Commitments entered into in that framework could also give rise to a need for legislation and be subject to scrutiny by the Oireachtas in that way. The Europol Act 1997, for example, gave effect to the Europol Convention which was agreed under Title VI of the Treaty of Maastricht.

More generally, the establishment in May 1993 of the Joint Committee on Foreign Affairs, with broad powers to scrutinise European Union matters, brought a new dimension to Oireachtas scrutiny, as did the subsequent establishment of a separate Joint Committee on European Affairs in March 1995 which took over the function of scrutinising European Union matters.

The establishment of Oireachtas committees of this nature, with broad powers within their area of competence, to scrutinise the activities of the government and the European Union, has been widely welcomed within the Oireachtas. Together with subsequent developments such as the eighteenth amendment to the Constitution and the adoption of the European Union (Scrutiny) Act 2002, which are discussed below, it can now be reasonably asserted that Oireachtas Committees have both the powers and the remit to permit them to scrutinise European Union matters in considerable depth and detail.

(a) The Eighteenth Amendment of the Constitution

The Oireachtas acquired greater direct oversight of justice and home affairs cooperation as a result of the Treaty of Amsterdam and the resulting eighteenth amendment of the Constitution. As has already been seen, under the Amsterdam accord, provision was made for special arrangements to

---

[47] The six-monthly reports on developments in the European Communities made to each House of the Oireachtas in accordance with s. 5 of the European Communities Act 1972 were extended to include a section about justice and home affairs matters.

apply to Ireland, the United Kingdom, and Denmark for the purposes both of cooperation under Title IV of the EC Treaty and for the purposes of the Protocol incorporating the Schengen *acquis* into the Treaty framework. The effect of these special arrangements was that Ireland was not bound by the relevant provisions but that it could opt into individual measures under Title IV and the Schengen arrangements.

The eighteenth amendment of the Constitution, approved by referendum in 1998, amended Article 29.4.6 of the Constitution to make provision for these (and other) new possibilities created by the Treaty of Amsterdam. It did so by providing that the state could exercise the relevant options or discretions "subject to the prior approval of both Houses of the Oireachtas".[48] The effect of the eighteenth amendment is therefore that prior Oireachtas approval must be obtained before Ireland can agree to participate in any Title IV measure, the Schengen *acquis*, or other enhanced cooperation arrangements, or agree to framework decisions under Title VI and other Council decisions under that Title which impact on the legislative role of the Oireachtas.

The provisions contained in the eighteenth amendment of the Constitution are essential to the operation of a proper system of scrutiny, as they impose an obligation for prior Oireachtas approval in regard to key areas of justice and home affairs. Taken in tandem with the adoption of the European Union (Scrutiny) Act 2002,[49] it can be unambiguously stated that the structures now in place are sufficient to enable the Oireachtas to properly scrutinise the activities of the executive in the area of justice and home affairs. The actual operation of the relevant provisions is discussed below.

(b) The European Union (Scrutiny) Act 2002

The defeat of the first Nice Treaty referendum opened up a debate on the relationship between the Oireachtas and European Union law-making and the relationship between European Union legislation and the Constitution. Speaking to the Institute of European Affairs at that time, I made the point that

> "in the context of the European Union, a regulation or directive is effectively irreversible once made. Insofar as it delimits and curtails the

[48] The full text of Art. 29.4.6 now reads: "The State may exercise the options or discretions provided by or under Articles 1.11, 2.5 and 2.15 of the Treaty referred to in subsection 5° of this section and the second and fourth Protocols set out in the said Treaty but any such exercise shall be subject to the prior approval of both Houses of the Oireachtas".

[49] This is discussed in the text below. See also the chapter in this book by Lia O'Hegarty.

> terms of constitutional rights and guarantees, such a measure has the status of sovereign legislation. It is remarkable, therefore, that present legislative practice has imposed no prior obligation of consultation in routine legislative matters and an obligation to seek at least the consent of the Oireachtas where such a measure would inevitably control or delimit Constitutional guarantees .... In short, it seems to me that there is a strong case, in terms of democracy, constitutionalism, and autonomy for a far-reaching reform of the interaction of the Oireachtas with European policy and legislation affairs ... a full blooded and committed reform in this area would require not merely that the Oireachtas be given greatly increased resources; it would also demand that a core of consciousness, adequately resourced, be created at the centre of Government to ensure that the collective responsibility of the Cabinet and its procedures, have full effect in relation to these European matters".[50]

I was not alone in that view. Improved procedures were introduced by way of the European Union (Scrutiny) Act 2002.[51] This Act laid down new procedures to be followed by ministers in relation to the scrutiny of European Union measures by the Houses of the Oireachtas. The scrutiny arrangements require the relevant Minister to lay a copy of proposed measures[52] before each house of the Oireachtas together with a statement outlining:

> "the content, purpose and likely implications for Ireland of the proposed measure and including such other information as he or she considers appropriate".[53]

Ministers are required to have regard to any recommendations made by either or both Houses of the Oireachtas in respect of such proposed measures.[54] Every minister of government is also required to make a report to each house of the Oireachtas not less than twice yearly in relation to measures, proposed measures, and other developments in relation to the

---

[50] Address by this writer (at the time, Attorney General of Ireland) to the Institute of European Affairs, 18 June 2001.

[51] See in more regard concerning the 2002 Act, the chapters in this volume by Lia O'Hegarty and by Katherine Meenan.

[52] Regulations, directives, measures requiring approval in accordance with the terms of Art. 29.4.6 as well as proposed Joint Actions and Common Positions under Arts 14 and 15 of the Treaty on European Union.

[53] S. 2(1) of the 2002 Act.

[54] S. 2(2) of the 2002 Act.

European Communities and the European Union in relation to which he or she performs functions.[55]

It is a matter for the Sub-Committee on European Scrutiny of the Joint Committee on European Affairs, on receipt of the proposed measure and accompanying information note, to decide what scrutiny arrangements will apply to particular measures. They can refer measures to relevant sectoral committees, such as the Joint Committee on Justice, Equality, Defence and Women's Rights in the case of justice and home affairs measures. Such referrals are quite commonplace and the relevant committee can make their own decision as to how they wish to proceed.

The position of the Oireachtas in terms of the operation of its committees was further strengthened by the enactment of the Oireachtas Commission Act 2003. In terms of structure and the provision of independent resources for the Oireachtas and legislation, the necessary pieces are now in place to allow for the development of detailed scrutiny by the Oireachtas of European Union measures.

(c) The Operation of the Eighteenth Amendment to the Constitution and of the European Union (Scrutiny) Act 2002 in the Field of Justice and Home Affairs

From the time these scrutiny arrangements commenced in July 2002, up until May, 2005, the Department of Justice, Equality and Law Reform submitted 82 information notes to the Oireachtas.[56] Between January 2003 and 1 June 2005, the Department sought and obtained Oireachtas approval, as required by Article 29.4.6 of the Constitution, to exercise Ireland's Title IV opt-in in respect of 12 measures.[57] As part of the overall scrutiny process, in the period from the commencement of the Oireachtas scrutiny arrangements in July

[55] S. 2(5) of the 2002 Act.

[56] Five information notes were submitted to the Houses of the Oireachtas from July to December 2002. Thirty were submitted in 2003, 31 in 2004, and 16 between January and May 2005.

[57] The Title IV measures placed before the Houses of the Oireachtas have been (i) Council Directive on minimum standards for giving temporary protection in the event of a mass influx of displaced persons and on measures promoting a balance of effort between members states in receiving such persons and bearing the consequences thereof (placed before the Oireachtas on 5 February, 2003); (ii) the proposal for a Council regulation on procedures for amending the SIRENE Manual (placed before the Oireachtas on 1 July 2003); (iii) the proposal for a regulation of the European Parliament and Council on the law applicable to non-contractual obligations (Rome II) (placed before the Oireachtas on 14 October 2003); (iv) an Italian initiative with a view to adopting a Council Decision on the organisation of joint flights for removal from the territory of two or more member states of third-country nationals who are subjects of individual removal orders (placed before the Oireachtas

2002 to 11 November 2005, officials from the Department also briefed Oireachtas sectoral committees on individual proposals on twelve occasions in relation to a total of sixteen proposals or green papers. These briefings related to proposals in the areas of Title IV of the EC Treaty (as well as other non-Title IV First Pillar measures) and Title VI of the Treaty on European Union. Briefings were provided by ministers on nine occasions to relevant Oireachtas Committees, both prior to and after Justice and Home Affairs Council meetings. In relation to measures in the Title VI area, the Department sought and obtained Oireachtas approval to participate in the adoption of eight such measures between January 2003 and May 2005.[58]

---

on 11 November 2003); (v) an Italian initiative with a view to adopting a Council Directive on assistance in cases of transit through the territory of one or more member states in the context of removal orders by member states against third-country nationals (placed before the Oireachtas on 11 November 2003); (vi) the proposal for a Council Regulation laying down a uniform format for visas for third-country nationals (placed before the Oireachtas on 17 December 2003); (vii) the proposal for a Council Regulation laying down a uniform format for residence permits for third-country nationals (placed before the Oireachtas on 17 December 2003); (viii) the proposal for a Council Decision establishing the European Refugee Fund for the period 2005–2010 (placed before the Oireachtas on 4 May 2004); (ix) the proposal for a Regulation of the European Parliament and the Council creating a European Order for Payment Procedure (placed before the Oireachtas on 26 May 2004); (x) the proposal for a Council Directive on a specific procedure for admitting third-country nationals for purposes of scientific research (placed before the Oireachtas on 29 June 2004); (xi) the proposal for a Council Decision providing for certain areas covered by Title IV of Part Three of the Treaty establishing the European Community to be governed by the procedure referred to in Article 251 of that Treaty (placed before the Oireachtas on 1 December 2004); and (xii) the proposal for a Regulation of the European Parliament and of the Council establishing a European Small Claims Procedure (placed before the Oireachtas on 1 June 2005). Note that the dates in brackets indicate when the matter was considered by the relevant Oireachtas committee (*i.e.* the date on which approval was sought) and not the date on which permission was formally granted by the Oireachtas.

[58] The measures concerned were (i) the proposal for a Council Framework Decision on combating corruption in the private sector (19 February 2003); (ii) the proposal for a Council Framework Decision on the execution in the European Union of orders freezing property or evidence (19 February 2003); (iii) the proposal for a Council Decision determining which provisions of the 1995 Convention on simplified extradition procedure between the Member States of the European Union and of the 1996 Convention relating to extradition between the Member States of the European Union constitute developments of the Schengen *acquis* in accordance with the Agreement concerning the Republic of Iceland's and the Kingdom of Norway's association with the implementation, application, and development of the Schengen *acquis* (19 February 2003); (iv) the proposal for a Council Framework Decision on mutual recognition of financial penalties (26 November 2003); (v) the proposal for a Framework Decision on Confiscation of crime-related proceeds, instrumentalities, and property (26 November 2003); (vi) the proposal for a Council Framework Decision laying down minimum provisions on the constituent elements of criminal acts and penalties in the field of illicit drug trafficking (26 May 2004); (vii) the proposal for a Council Framework Decision on the application of the principal of mutual recognition to confiscation orders (26 May 2004); and (viii) the proposal for a Council Framework Decision on attacks against information systems (26 May 2004).

Five six-monthly reports were also submitted to the Oireachtas between 1 January 2003 and July 2005.[59] Each report provided an overview of proposals submitted by this Department to the Oireachtas under the Oireachtas scrutiny arrangements, as well as an overview of significant developments in European Union policy in the area of Justice and Home Affairs.

The Oireachtas obtains a further opportunity to exercise oversight where primary legislation is required to transpose the relevant provisions of European Union law into domestic law. Acts adopted in recent years which have given effect to measures adopted in the context of justice and home affairs cooperation at European Union level have included the Extradition (European Union Conventions) Act 2001, the European Arrest Warrant Act 2003, the Criminal Justice (Joint Investigation Teams) Act 2004 and the Criminal Justice (Terrorist Offences) Act 2005.

There is no doubt that effective scrutiny of European Union matters is both time-consuming and resource-intensive but this is a price well worth paying. On 5 September 2002, in the second stage debate in the Dáil on the Twenty-Sixth Amendment of the Constitution Bill 2002 (the purpose of which was to allow the State to ratify the Nice Treaty), I stated that:

> "as a member of Government, I know just how tempting it can be to conduct our European business behind closed doors and far from the critical gaze and comment of third parties. Increased Oireachtas scrutiny of EU policy and legislation will undoubtedly complicate the day-to-day life of the Executive, but that is no justification for our continuing democratic deficit. On the contrary, the apparent cost in terms of time and resources is not really a cost at all in democratic terms. Ireland, in my view, would pay a far higher price in the long term if we failed to address and overcome the absence of overt domestic democratic scrutiny of our European agenda".[60]

This remains my view. However, the establishment of an effective system of scrutiny will make many demands on all concerned. Change in this area is

---

[59] Covering, respectively, the periods January–June 2003, July–December 2003, January–June 2004, July–December 2004, and January–June 2005. Note that the first of these report also included an overview of proposals submitted to the Oireachtas prior to 1 January 2003. The dates in bracket indicate the date that the matter was considered by the relevant Oireachtas committee (*i.e.,* the date approval was sought) and not the date on which permission was formally granted by the Oireachtas.
[60] Dáil Debates, vol. 554, cols. 128–129 (5 September 2002).

usually incremental in nature as it proceeds more from experience than from *a priori* analysis. During the same debate in the Dáil, I observed in this regard that

> "the challenge of the democratic deficit is not only one for the executive: the Houses of the Oireachtas and the Members of these Houses must rise to the challenge as well. If proposals for EU policy and law are to receive timely and effective scrutiny, Deputies and Senators will have to put in long hours of work in Committee .... New methods of prioritising scrutiny arrangements on EU matters will be needed. New expertise and new openness to external advice and assistance will also be required in both Houses. In short, remedying the democratic deficit which exists will require large change and commitment from every side in this House and in Seanad Éireann".[61]

I was certainly not alone in expressing such views. Similar sentiments were also expressed by members of the government and other members of the Oireachtas. I still hold these views and I believe that more work needs to be done in this area. In order to properly undertake the scrutiny function, Oireachtas committees require an appropriate level of resources, commitment from the committee members concerned, commitment from the executive and, of course, the oxygen of publicity.

In terms of resources, the Oireachtas Commission Act 2003 which was signed into law on 14 July 2003 is a key piece of legislation. The functions of the Commission are set out in the legislation and include providing for the running of the houses of the Oireachtas and the administration and management of the Office of the Houses of the Oireachtas. This includes the oversight of expenditure, the exercise of staff functions (*via* the Secretary General), and the production of strategic plans, annual reports, estimates, and information. These arrangement are similar to those in a number of other parliaments in the European Union and elsewhere, and should facilitate the Oireachtas in its consideration of the appropriate level of resources to be allocated to committees so that they can properly discharge the scrutiny function.

The establishment of an Oireachtas Commission should also facilitate, over time, a more detailed consideration of the demands which an effective system of committee scrutiny is likely to make on members of the

[61] Dáil Debates, vol. 554, col. 129 (5 September 2002).

Oireachtas. The Oireachtas itself is best placed to determine how members might be assisted, resourced or facilitated in order to meet the demands of a vibrant committee system.

Effective scrutiny also requires a certain level of publicity so that the public can be properly informed. In a modern democratic society, this cannot occur in an effective fashion without the active participation of the media, in the broadest sense. From experience, I know that media coverage of Oireachtas committee business in particular leaves a great deal to be desired. While there may be legitimate reasons for this, these reasons need to be examined in detail and the necessary steps taken, in conjunction with relevant media bodies, to ensure more complete coverage across the range of media of Oireachtas business, especially of the committee system. I doubt that this will be an easy undertaking but it is absolutely essential if our democracy is to thrive and an effective scrutiny function further developed. The appropriate forum for such a debate to commence is the Oireachtas itself.

I believe that, with the establishment of the Oireachtas Commission, all the necessary ingredients are in place both to commence, structure, and progress such a debate. The committees have both the necessary powers and the remit to effectively scrutinise European Union matters. For my part, I, as minister, have always emphasised my willingness to appear before Oireachtas committees, especially the Joint Committee on Justice, Equality, Defence and Women's Rights as regards justice and home affairs measures. However, notwithstanding the dedication of the many members of the Oireachtas who assiduously participate in the committee system, I believe, as indicated above, that more remains to be done in this area if a truly comprehensive and robust system of scrutiny is to develop.

5. The Treaty Establishing a Constitution for Europe

Should the Constitutional Treaty – or, as now seems more likely, a successor treaty with equivalent provisions – ever enter into force,[62] a number of important changes will be effected in relation to the manner in which cooperation in the justice and home affairs area is organised. The

[62] Following the referendum results in France and the Netherlands, the European Council initiated a process of reflection and debate in all member states. The decision was taken at this point not to set a date for a referendum in Ireland until the picture became clearer at the European level, although Ireland remained deeply committed at this time to the Constitutional Treaty as a measure representing the best available response to the challenges facing the enlarged Union. (Editor's note: see the introduction to this book in relation to the most recent pre-publication developments concerning the Constitutional Treaty.)

Constitutional Treaty maintained the creation of an area of freedom, security, and justice as one of the key objectives of the Union,[63] with Part III, Title III, Chapter IV of the Constitutional Treaty (under the rubric 'Area of Freedom, Security and Justice') dealing with all aspects of that cooperation. Key features of the Constitutional Treaty in this regard included: (a) the objectives of freedom, security, and justice being restated and updated; (b) the creation of unified decision-making arrangements with recourse to a single set of legislative instruments; (c) the ordinary legislative procedure[64] applying, subject to limited exceptions; (d) the special arrangements for Ireland, the United Kingdom, and Denmark being retained; and (e) a strengthened role for the European Parliament and member state parliaments.

It is the proposed strengthened role of the European Parliament and member state parliaments in the decision-making process on which this writer wishes to focus for the purpose of this chapter. That strengthened role derived in part from aspects of the Constitutional Treaty which had general application but also from aspects of the Constitutional Treaty which were specific to the area of freedom, security, and justice.

That strengthened role of the European Parliament was, in part, a natural consequence of the extension of the ordinary legislative procedure[65] to new areas of freedom, security, and justice cooperation. This included all remaining areas of immigration and asylum policy[66] as well as most aspects of judicial cooperation in criminal matters[67] and police cooperation.[68] Judicial cooperation in civil matters remained subject to the ordinary legislative procedure under the Constitutional Treaty for all purposes with the exception of family law.[69] Thus were the Constitutional Treaty (or a

---

[63] Art. I-3(2) and I-42 of the Constitutional Treaty. This was in keeping with the process begun by the Treaty of Maastricht and further developed in large measure by the Treaty of Amsterdam.

[64] The 'ordinary legislative procedure' was a new term used by the Constitutional Treaty for the procedure it laid down whereby the Parliament and Council jointly exercised legislative functions. The procedure was to be governed by Art. III-396 of the Constitutional Treaty and was to take the place of the existing co-decision procedure, which was governed by Art. 251 of the EC Treaty.

[65] See previous footnote

[66] Arts III-265 to III-268 of the Constitutional Treaty.

[67] Arts III-270 to III-274 of the Constitutional Treaty. The ordinary legislative procedure was to apply for all purposes other than in relation to decisions under Arts III-270 and III-271 extending the scope of those provisions, and as regards the possible establishment of a European Public Prosecutor's Office from Eurojust under Art. III-274 of the Constitutional Treaty. These decisions were to remain subject to a requirement of unanimity in the Council.

[68] Arts III-275 to III-277 of the Constitutional Treaty. The exceptions in the case of police cooperation related to operational police cooperation measures under Arts III-275 and III-277.

[69] Art. III-269 of the Constitutional Treaty.

successor treaty with equivalent provisions) to enter into force, the European Parliament would become co-legislator for the purpose of the great majority of measures to be adopted concerning the 'Area of Freedom, Security and Justice'.

The European Parliament would also continue to be consulted in matters in which unanimity was required at the level of the Council. In addition, the consent of the European Parliament would be required where the Constitutional Treaty allowed additional areas of cooperation, over and above those already set out, to be identified.[70] The consent of the European Parliament would also be required before a European law could make provision for the possible establishment of a European Public Prosecutor's Office.[71]

In addition, specific provision was also made in the context of proposed European laws governing Eurojust and Europol for those laws to determine arrangements for involving the European Parliament and national parliaments in the evaluation and scrutiny of Eurojust's and Europol's activities.[72] New arrangements for the purpose of evaluating implementation by member state authorities of Union policies under Chapter IV were provided for – as was a requirement to inform the European and national parliaments of the content and results of those evaluations.[73] Likewise provision was made for the establishment of a committee with the purpose of ensuring that operational cooperation on internal security was promoted and strengthened. The European Parliament and national parliaments were to be kept informed of the proceedings of this committee.[74]

Chapter IV made special reference and provision for the role of national parliaments in the justice and home affairs area in the context of ensuring compliance with the principle of subsidiarity. Thus Article III-259 provided that:

> "national Parliaments shall ensure that the proposals and legislative initiatives submitted under sections 4 and 5 of this Chapter[75] comply with

---

[70] Arts III-270(2) and III-271(1) of the Constitutional Treaty.

[71] Art. III-274 of the Constitutional Treaty.

[72] Arts III-273 and III-276 of the Constitutional Treaty.

[73] Art. III-260 of the Constitutional Treaty.

[74] Art. III-261 of the Constitutional Treaty.

[75] Note that sections 4 and 5 of Chapter IV govern, respectively, judicial cooperation in criminal matters and police cooperation.

the principle of subsidiarity, in accordance with arrangements laid down by the Protocol on the application of the principles of subsidiarity and proportionality."

The key provisions for this purpose in the Protocol referred to (which was annexed to the Constitutional Treaty)[76] were Articles 6 and 7. Article 6 allowed national parliaments to issue a reasoned opinion where they believed a draft legislative instrument did not comply with the principle of subsidiarity.[77] Article 7 required the relevant Union institution to take account of any such reasoned opinion and required them to review a draft legislative proposal where reasoned opinions had been received which represent a third of the votes allocated to the national parliaments of member states in the normal way. However, the threshold for the purpose of legislative measures concerning police and judicial cooperation in criminal matters was a quarter – not a third – of the votes allocated to national parliaments.[78]

The strengthened role of member state parliaments under the Constitutional Treaty was also in part a function of the strengthened arrangements for consultation which would have applied by virtue of the revised Protocol on the role of National Parliaments.[79] That strengthened role was also the result of the other specific references to national parliaments in the context of the justice and home affairs cooperation which have already been referred to (such as their role – together with the European Parliament – in relation to

---

[76] Protocol No. 2 on the Application of the Principles of Subsidiarity and Proportionality.

[77] Art. 6 provided that "any national Parliament or any chamber of a national Parliament may, within six weeks from the date of transmission of a draft European legislative act, send to the Presidents of the European Parliament, the Council and the Commission a reasoned opinion stating why it considers that the draft in question does not comply with the principle of subsidiarity. It will be for each national Parliament or each chamber of a national Parliament to consult, where appropriate, regional parliaments with legislative powers".

[78] Art. III-264 of the Constitutional Treaty and Art. 7 of the Protocol on the Application of the Principles of Subsidiarity and Proportionality.

[79] Protocol No. 1 on the Role of National Parliaments in the European Union. The Protocol made provision for the provision of information to national Parliaments. Art. 2 required copies of all legislative proposals and Commission consultation documents to be sent to the parliaments in the member states at the same time as they are being submitted to the Council and the European Parliament. Legislative measures could not be placed on a Council agenda until at least six weeks had elapsed following their transmission except in urgent cases. Art. 3 made provision for the making of reasoned opinions in accordance with Art. 6 of the Subsidiarity Protocol. The Protocol also required other information, including Council agendas, to be made available to national parliaments as well as making provision for inter-parliamentary cooperation.

Eurojust, in relation to Europol, and in relation to the envisaged standing committee within the Council the purpose of which would have been to ensure that operational cooperation on internal security was promoted and strengthened within the Union).[80]

The changes which the Constitutional Treaty would have made would therefore have had the potential to significantly strengthen the oversight role which both the European Parliament and member state parliaments can play for the purpose of the further development of cooperation in the justice and home affairs domain.

The Twenty-Eighth Amendment of the Constitution Bill 2005

The Constitutional Treaty – or any successor constitutive treaty which might be agreed – would require ratification by all member states in accordance with their own constitutional requirements, were it ever to enter into force. Insofar as concerns the Constitutional Treaty, the Irish government published the Twenty-Eighth Amendment to the Constitution Bill 2005 on 28 May 2005.[81] This provided for the necessary amendment to Article 29 of the Constitution to be put to the people by referendum to enable the State to ratify the Constitutional Treaty. The proposed amendment to the Constitution would have preserved key elements of the existing constitutional arrangements regarding the role of the Oireachtas in the area of cooperation in justice and home affairs and built on them.

The proposed new subsection 6 of Article 29, in particular, would have continued the requirement of prior Oireachtas approval for the exercise by the State of the options and discretions which are provided in the Constitutional Treaty in relation to participation in enhanced cooperation,[82] the Schengen arrangements,[83] and measures in the area of asylum, immigration, civil law, and certain aspects of police cooperation.[84]

---

[80] Art. III-261 of the Constitutional Treaty. Art. III-261 made provision for entitlement on the part of both the European Parliament and of national parliaments to be kept informed of the proceedings of this committee.

[81] Bill No. 15 of 2005.

[82] See in this regard Arts I-44, III-270(4) and III-271(4) of the Constitutional Treaty in the context of justice and home affairs cooperation.

[83] As to which see Protocol (No. 17) on the Schengen *Acquis* Integrated into the Framework of the European Union, which was annexed to the Constitutional Treaty.

[84] Protocol (No. 19) on the Position of the United Kingdom and Ireland on Policies in Respect of Border Controls, Asylum and Immigration, Judicial Cooperation in Civil Matters and on Police Cooperation, which was annexed to the Constitutional Treaty.

It would have introduced a similar requirement for prior Oireachtas approval before the state could agree European decisions which would have the effect of changing voting arrangements for the purpose of judicial cooperation in the family law aspects of civil law cooperation,[85] extending the scope of judicial cooperation in criminal matters,[86] or measures relating to the establishment of a European Public Prosecutor's Office.[87]

The proposed amendment to the Constitution would therefore not only have preserved the existing Oireachtas scrutiny arrangements in relation to justice and home affairs matters but would have strengthened those arrangements.

6. Conclusion

This chapter has sought to outline, in a general way, the manner in which democratic oversight and control over governmental action in the justice and home affairs area has evolved over time. The evolution of democratic control has mirrored the development of cooperation on the justice and home affairs area through the mechanism of successive treaties. We have seen how cooperation in justice and home affairs has developed by reference to the various treaties which have represented the key staging posts in the development of the European Community and the European Union.

Some of these treaties have been of more importance than others but all have been of significance in their own right. This is because every stage has helped to create and develop the crucial ingredient of trust, which was essential to development at each subsequent stage. Moreover, each phase has, in turn, given rise to its own dynamic. The gradual accumulation of experience by member states, initially through the method of intergovernmental cooperation but increasingly through the Community method, has been instrumental in building the trust necessary to both widen and deepen cooperation in the justice and home affairs area within the framework of the treaties. Moreover, as the legal basis for cooperation in this area shifted increasingly to the treaties, the need and demand for formal democratic oversight and control also increased.

A striking aspect of the development of both cooperation in this area and the means of democratic control is how quickly they have evolved within the framework of the treaties in a relatively short space of time. One of the most important benefits of intergovernmental cooperation in this area is that it

[85] See here Art. III-269(3) of the Constitutional Treaty.
[86] As to which see Arts III-270(2)(d) and III-271(1).
[87] See regarding these, Arts III-274(1) and III-274 (4).

gradually established the framework within which mutual trust developed to the extent that member states increasingly recognised both the desirability and the benefits of establishing more durable arrangements within the legal framework of what are now the European Community and the European Union. The existence and scope of these arrangements has also driven demands for greater democratic accountability.

Democratic control both at the level of the Union itself and at member state level remains vitally important. It can be argued that the need for such control is greater in relation to justice and home affairs than in other policy areas, given that measures in the justice and home affairs area have the potential to impact on constitutional rights and guarantees and hence, are more likely to raise significant policy and political issues.

The Constitutional Treaty – or any successor treaty which contained equivalent provisions – would clearly have the potential to enhance democratic control, both at the level of the Union and at the national level. New possibilities were created in the Constitutional Treaty with a view to ensuring that the principle of subsidiarity would be properly observed by the Union institutions. There is, however, a danger that we will do no more than pay lip service to that principle unless we are prepared to submit legislative proposals to rigorous scrutiny. However, ensuring that the potential which the Constitutional Treaty (or an equivalent successor treaty) creates for greater democratic control is achieved will, as indicated above, require greater commitment on the part of all actors concerned including the government and Oireachtas here in Ireland and the Union institutions at European level.

Although the relevant provisions of the Constitutional Treaty, which had much to offer in this area, have not been adopted, it is the case that, at national level, the necessary framework is now in place to facilitate the detailed scrutiny by the Oireachtas of European Union affairs. The extent to which this opportunity is seized depends on numerous factors, many of which, since the establishment of the Oireachtas Commission, now fall within the competence of the Oireachtas itself. However, other key actors, such as the executive and the media, must also play their part if we are to succeed in taking advantage of the opportunities which now exist in this area. I have long believed, as I have indicated in the Oireachtas and elsewhere, in the absolute necessity for democratic accountability of the activities of the executive in European Union affairs through the mechanism of effective scrutiny by the Oireachtas. With the necessary legal and institutional framework in place, I believe that the initiative now lies with the Oireachtas to take the necessary steps to develop the undoubted potential of the system of Oireachtas scrutiny.

8.
European Community Asylum and Immigration Policy-Making – Integrating a Role for the Oireachtas?

Cathryn Costello[1]

1. Introduction

This chapter is concerned with European Community policy-making in immigration and asylum matters and examines the role (actual and potential) of the Oireachtas in this context.

One account of European integration posits national governments as its main architects, having designed it to enable themselves to escape domestic political accountability mechanisms. National parliaments in this account are thus the 'losers' of European integration.[2] However, this view risks idealising national democracies, by exaggerating the powers national parliaments exercise on the domestic scene. Moreover, it ignores the opportunities the European Union provides for national parliaments.[3] The current focus on national parliaments in European Union affairs should not be conceived of as re-investing traditional legislative powers in national parliaments or reasserting lost accountability mechanisms, but rather creating a *new* deliberative role. In the Irish case in particular, there can be no doubt that the Oireachtas is and always has been a particularly weak check on executive power, and its actual (as opposed to

---

[1] Senior Research Fellow in European Community and Public Law, Worcester College, Oxford University.

[2] For example, Schmidt refers to the 'deparliamentarisation' of the member states (V.A. Schmidt, "European 'Federalism' and its Encroachments on National Institutions" (1999) *Publius* 19. See more generally A. Maurer and W. Wessels (eds.), *National Parliaments on their Way to Europe* (Nomos, Baden-Baden, 2001)).

[3] T. Raunio, "Two Steps Forward, One Step Back? National Legislatures in the Draft EU Constitution", Paper presented at the Federal Trust Conference, *Towards a European Constitution* (London, 1–2 July 2004); T. Raunio and S. Hix, "Backbenchers Learn to Fight Back: European Integration and Parliamentary Government" (2000) *West European Politics* 142; F. Duina, "National Parliaments in the European Union: Are There Any Benefits to Integration?" (2005) *European Law Journal* 173.

formal) legislative role is marginal.[4] Moreover, the Oireachtas is not only politically weak, it also lacks the institutional capacity to take on robust European scrutiny. This has long been recognised,[5] yet until relatively recently, attempts to enhance Oireachtas scrutiny of European Union decision-making have been ineffective. Three particular features of European Union immigration and asylum policy-making make the development of a more robust new role more pressing and indeed more likely.

First, immigration and asylum has been the subject of intense European Community legislative activity since the Treaty of Amsterdam came into force in 1999. In the subsequent seven years (the period under consideration in this chapter), a range of European Community legislative measures have been adopted. This represents an opportunity for national parliaments, as they tend to be more adept at scrutinising formal European Community law-making than informal activity. However, such informal activity is also a feature of European Union governance, as a range of administrative interactions lead to informal policy coordination and operational cooperation in the immigration and asylum fields. These informal processes tend to escape not only national, but also European parliamentary scrutiny, due to their very nature.

Secondly, immigration and asylum are highly salient policy areas, such that we can reasonably expect national politicians to take an interest in them. One does not need to be a liberal intergovernmentalist to accept Moravcsik's explanation of low domestic interest in traditional European Community policy areas as attributable to the low voter salience of those issues.[6] Immigration and asylum, however, in contrast to, say, internal market regulation, capture voter and political interest like few other issues of European Community competence. Thus, national parliamentarians have an electoral and policy incentive to engage with these issues.

Thirdly, Ireland participates selectively in European Community law-making on immigration and asylum. Opting in requires approval by both Houses of the Oireachtas. Thus, the Oireachtas has greater formal powers here than in any other area of European Community activity. This chapter considers whether those formal legal powers have resulted in an actual increase in accountability and scrutiny of executive action at the national level.

---

[4] M. Gallagher, "Parliament" in J. Coakley and M. Gallagher (eds.), *Politics in the Republic of Ireland*, Fourth edition, (PSAI Press and Routledge, Dublin and London, 2005) 126.

[5] See, for example, M. Robinson, "The Role of the Irish Parliament" (1974) 22 *Administration* 3.

[6] A. Moravcsik, "In Defence of the Democratic Deficit: Reassessing Legitimacy in the European Union" (2002) *Journal of Common Market Studies* 603.

In this chapter, the manner in which the Oireachtas has exploited the opportunity offered (or perhaps risen to the challenge) which is posed by the confluence of these three features is examined. Part 2 sets out the key institutional and legal features of Title IV of the Treaty Establishing the European Community (henceforth the EC Treaty), which deals with visas, asylum, immigration, and other policies related to free movement of persons. Part 3 outlines the legal mechanisms relating to Ireland's selective participation under Title IV of the EC Treaty. Part 4 then provides an overview of the manner in which those powers have been exercised, examining formal asylum and immigration law-making. Part 5 then outlines current trends in these areas, which pose further challenges for national parliamentary scrutiny. In light of the previous discussion, conclusions are drawn on the operation of the mechanisms to date, and challenges ahead are identified.

2. Title IV of the EC Treaty – Community Competence in Asylum and Immigration

The Treaty of Rome of 1957 instigated a process aimed at the creation of an advanced form of economic integration, a common market in which cross-border exchange of the factors of production – not merely products (*i.e.*, goods and services) but also labour and capital – would be liberalised. The original economic rationale underlying the common and internal market could have, and arguably should have embraced migration of at least those so-called 'third-country nationals' resident within the territory of a member state. In other words, given the status of their labour as a factor of production, the rules governing the movement of such workers should also have been liberalised. However, it became clear at an early point that such an interpretation was not acceptable to most member states, and that the issue of the movement of third-country nationals was – subject to one exception – originally viewed as escaping the Community context.[7]

[7] The exception related to the free movement of services, where the original Treaty provided for the extension of the freedom to non-nationals. (See now Art. 49(2) of the EC Treaty, which provides that "the Council may, acting by a qualified majority on a proposal from the Commission, extend the provisions of the Chapter to nationals of a third country who provide services and who are established within the Community.") However, this is not to suggest that existing European Community rules do not affect the position of third-country nationals. In fact there is a disparate set of rights which third-country nationals derive from Community law. For a discussion of these rights, see H. Staples, *The Legal Status of Third Country Nationals in the EU* (Kluwer Law International, The Hague, 1999); M. Hedemann-Robinson, "An Overview of Recent Legal Developments at Community Level in Relation to Third Country Nationals Resident Within the European Union, with Particular Reference to the Case Law of the European Court of Justice" (2001) *Common Market Law Review* 325.

At the time of the Single European Act, much debate surrounded the question of whether a core internal market provision (now Article 14 of the EC Treaty) would entail the abolition of internal border controls for third-country nationals.[8] Several member states strongly objected to any such interpretation, in particular the United Kingdom.[9] Due to these conflicts, those member states in favour of the abolition of border controls (*viz.*, Belgium, the Netherlands, Luxembourg, France, and Germany) set up the Schengen system in 1985, which dissipated the pressure to abolish internal border controls under what is now Article 14 of the EC Treaty. The Schengen system operated outside the constitutional constraints of the Community. It was however envisaged that the Schengen system would operate as a 'laboratory' or 'engine' to push border politics back onto the Community agenda.[10] The Schengen *acquis* evolved into a complex legal and institution apparatus, comprising the Schengen Agreement,[11] the Schengen Implementing Convention,[12] various Accession Protocols,[13] and many

---

[8] Art. 14 provides, *inter alia,* that the internal market shall comprise an area without internal frontiers in which the free movement of goods, persons, services and capital is ensured in accordance with the provisions of this Treaty. As it happens, the European Court of Justice subsequently adopted a more restrictive interpretation of Art. 14 of the EC Treaty. See Case C-378/97, *Wijsenbeek* [1999] ECR I-6207.

[9] See the General Declaration (No. 6) on Arts 13 to 19 of the Single European Act which was annexed to the Final Act of the Single European Act at the insistence of the United Kingdom. This stated that "nothing in these provisions shall affect the right of Member States to take such measures as they consider necessary for the purpose of controlling immigration from third countries, and to combat terrorism, crime, the traffic in drugs and illicit trading in works of art and antiques". Note also the similarly-annexed Political Declaration by the Governments of the Member States (No. 13) on the free movement of persons, which stated: "In order to promote the free movement of persons, the Member States shall cooperate, without prejudice to the powers of the Community, in particular as regards the entry, movement and residence of nationals of third countries. They shall also cooperate in the combating of terrorism, crime, the traffic in drugs and illicit trading in works of art and antiques". At the time of writing, both such Declarations may be found at www.eu.int/eur-lex/en/treaties/selected/livre4_c.html.

[10] A. Wiener, "The Embedded Acquis Communautaire. Transmission Belt and Prism of New Governance" (1998) *European Law Journal* 294.

[11] This was signed on 14 June 1985. The agreement aimed to create a framework to abolish border controls on goods and persons between participating states.

[12] Although the Convention Implementing the Schengen Agreement was signed on 19 June 1990, it did not enter into force until 26 March 1995. It sets out detailed provisions on the abolition of border controls, the application of common external border controls, police cooperation, and measures on responsibility for processing asylum claims.

[13] The original Schengen Agreement of 1985 was signed by Belgium, France, Germany, Luxembourg, and the Netherlands. Over the next seven years, all of the other European Union member states joined, with the exception of the United Kingdom and Ireland, who, post-Amsterdam, participate selectively.

decisions and declarations adopted by the Schengen Executive Committee, as well as acts of bodies on which the Executive Committee conferred implementing powers.[14]

The Treaty on European Union created a new area of intergovernmental activity in the Third Pillar, which included asylum and immigration. Under the Treaty on European Union, the Third Pillar was characterised by a cumbersome five-tier intergovernmental process. Various non-binding measures were adopted under this system, which were criticised for their dilution of international human rights standards.[15] The only significant binding measure, insofar as concerns either immigration or asylum law, was the Dublin Convention,[16] dealing with the allocation of responsibility for processing asylum claims, and introducing a notion of burden-sharing into European Union asylum policy. Although, in some instances, these measures were poorly implemented at national level,[17] a policy convergence emerged through the construction of common terms such as 'safe third country' and 'safe country of origin' in asylum law,[18] and the generalisation of certain policy instruments, such as carrier sanctions. At the implementation level, a range of interactions were evident including operational cooperation between border police, liaison officers, data exchange, and technological cooperation in a variety of areas. Thus, the area has been characterised by 'intensive transgovernmentalism'[19] to use Wallace's terminology. Officials

---

[14] See Council Decision 1999/435 of 20 May 1999 concerning the definition of the Schengen acquis for the purpose of determining, in conformity with the relevant provisions of the Treaty establishing the European Community and the Treaty on European Union, the legal basis for each of the provisions or decisions which constitute the acquis [1999] OJ L176/1.

[15] The measures included the London Resolution on a harmonised approach to questions concerning host third countries, 30 November 1992; London Resolution on manifestly unfounded applications for asylum, 30 November 1992; London Conclusions on countries where there is generally no serious risk of persecution, 30 November 1992; Council Resolution on minimum guarantees for asylum procedures 20 June 1995; Council Resolution on burden-sharing with regard to the admission and residence of displaced persons on a temporary basis, 25 September 1995; Joint Position of 4 March 1996 defined by the Council on the basis of Art. K.3 of the Treaty on European Union on the harmonised application of the definition of the term 'refugee' in Art. 1 of the Geneva Convention.

[16] Convention determining the state responsible for examining applications for asylum lodged in of other the Member States of the European Communities [1997] OJ C254/1.

[17] S. Peers, *Mind the Gap! Ineffective Member State Implementation of European Union Asylum Measures* (ILPA, London, 1998).

[18] See C. Costello, "The Asylum Procedures Directive and the Proliferation of Safe Country Practices: Deterrence, Deflection and the Dismantling of International Protection?" (2005) *European Journal of Migration and Law* 35.

[19] H. Wallace & W. Wallace (eds.), *Policymaking in the European Union* (fourth edition, Oxford University Press, Oxford, 2000), at 28.

from national interior ministries created an institutional framework marred by lack of coherence, consistency, democratic scrutiny, and legal accountability.[20] The process of Europeanisation allowed these officials to overcome their domestic legal and political constraints,[21] contributing to a particular security-dominated view of migration and asylum issues. While at national level one expects the views of justice ministers and officials to be tempered both by cross-cabinet deliberations, and by other concerns such as human rights and foreign policy articulated by other players, the European Union processes are characterised by a dense network of like-minded officials, with a strong cross-border agenda-setting and implementation role.

The Treaty of Amsterdam marked the communitarisation of immigration and asylum policy[22] and the integration of the Schengen acquis[23] into the Treaty on European Union and the Treaty Establishing the European Community. The Council was required to adopt asylum and immigration measures in a range of fields by May 2004.[24] Nonetheless, the pre-Amsterdam era of intensive transgovernmentalism has had lasting effects, despite these significant legal and institutional changes. Title IV's institutional features set it apart from normal Community mechanisms. Judicial control by the European Court of Justice is restricted.[25] For a

[20] T. Kostakopoulou, "The 'Protective Union': Change and Continuity in Migration Law and Policy in Post-Amsterdam Europe" (2000) *Journal of Common Market Studies* 497, at 498.

[21] V. Guiraudon, "European Integration and Migration Policy: Vertical Policy-making as Venue Shopping" (2000) *Journal of Common Market Studies* 251. See also E. Thielemann, "Explaining Stability and Change in European Asylum Policy" (Paper presented at the American Political Science Association Annual Meeting, San Francisco, 30 August – 2 September 2001).

[22] 'Communitarisation' refers to the fact that asylum (together with visa, immigration and civil judicial cooperation) issues were brought under the European Community Treaty, in the form of the new Title IV of the EC Treaty. These issues went from being 'Union' to 'Community' competences.

[23] See J. de Zwaan, "Opting Out and Opting In: Problems and Practical Arrangements under the Schengen Agreement" (1998) 1 *Cambridge Yearbook of European Legal Studies* 107.

[24] The five-year deadline applies to agreeing minimum standards on the following areas of asylum policy: determining the member state responsible for examining an asylum claim; reception conditions of asylum seekers; the qualification of third-country nationals as refugees and beneficiaries of subsidiary protection; procedures for granting and withdrawing refugee status; and, standards for giving temporary protection (Art. 63 of the EC Treaty). For immigration policy, the five-year deadline only applies to measures for the abolition of border controls within the European Union (Art. 62(1) of the EC Treaty) and some measures on external borders, including visas for up to three months (Art. 62(2) of the EC Treaty).

[25] Although inter-institutional litigation is common under Title IV, the preliminary reference procedure – the main avenue for individuals to hold member states to their Community law bargains, test the validity of Community legislative measures *and* prompt uniform interpretations of European Community law – is significantly restricted. Under Art. 68 of the EC Treaty, only national courts and tribunals 'against whose decisions there is no judicial remedy under national law' are empowered to

transitional period of five years after the coming into force of the Treaty of Amsterdam, not merely the European Commission, but also member states, could make proposals. After the transitional period, the Commission's right of initiative became exclusive (but it is still obliged to examine any request made by a member state that it submit a proposal to the Council).[26] For the same transitional period of five years, unanimity was required in the Council for the adoption of legislative measures, with the European Parliament merely having the right to be consulted.[27] Indeed, it was not until December 2004 that the Council exercised its option to subject most of Title IV to qualified majority voting and co-decision with the Parliament.[28]

In the context of the continued dominance by the Council of law-making in this area, a number of Council working groups, with both information-sharing and policy-elaboration functions, have emerged. These include the High Level Working Group on Asylum and Migration,[29] the Asylum Working Party,[30] the Working Party on Migration and Expulsions, the Strategic Committee for Immigration, Frontiers and Asylum (SCIFA),[31] and many

---

refer and indeed are obliged to refer if they consider that a decision on the question is necessary to enable them to give judgment. As a result, two preliminary references in the immigration field have to date been deemed inadmissible. Case C-51/03, *Georgescu* [2004] ECR I-3203; Case C-45/03, *Dem'Yanenko* [2004] OJ C106/16. See generally, S. Peers, "Who's Judging the Watchmen? The Judicial System of the 'Area of Freedom, Security and Justice'" (1998) 18 *Yearbook of European Law* 337.

26 Art. 67 of the EC Treaty.

27 During this transitional period the only measures which could be adopted by qualified majority vote were those concerning the list of countries whose nationals had to be in possession of visas when crossing external borders and those whose nationals were exempt from that requirement, and concerning a uniform format for visas. (Art. 62(2)(b)(i) and (iii) of the EC Treaty). Note that the Treaty of Amsterdam entered into force on 1 May 1999.

28 Council Decision 2004/927 of the Council providing for certain areas covered by Title IV of Part Three of the Treaty establishing the European Community to be governed by the procedure referred to in Art. 251 of that Treaty [2004] OJ L396/45. Ireland opted in to this measure on 7 December 2004. See S. Peers "Transforming Decision Making on EC Immigration and Asylum Law" (2005) *European Law Review* 285.

29 In December, 1998, the High Level Working Group on Asylum and Migration was established to produce Action Plans on the root causes of migration. It comprises high level officials from ministries of justice and home affairs and foreign affairs as well as Commission and Council Officials.

30 The Working Party gathers officials from the ministries responsible for asylum in order to discuss proposals in the asylum field.

31 This committee's role is to draw up strategic guidelines for matters relating to immigration, external borders, and the right to asylum.

others.[32] As well as a lawmaking process with a strongly intergovernmental bent, administrative cooperation and information exchange in this field is dense and highly institutionalised.

The Schengen Information System (SIS) became operational in March 1995. This extensive database is housed in Strasbourg. The SIS database is backed up by bureaux in each state which provide on request more detailed information/intelligence. It is supplemented by the little-known SIRENE[33] database which permits the exchange of additional information, such as fingerprints and photographs, to that held on the SIS, as well as facilitating the 'free standing' exchange of police information. Current proposals would extend the range of information held in the system considerably beyond the immigration field.[34] The operation of the SIS has been subject to much criticism, particularly as it may be difficult to challenge non-admission and deportation decisions based on information contained therein.[35] In March 1999, the United Kingdom applied to take part in some aspects of Schengen, including the Schengen Information System (SIS). The Council granted the request in 2000.[36] Ireland followed suit, and was admitted on 28 February 2002.[37] The Commission had issued opinions on the two applications, stressing that the partial participation of the two member states should not have the effect of reducing the consistency of the *acquis* as a whole.

---

[32] For an overview, see C. Costello, "Administrative Governance and the Europeanisation of Asylum and Immigration Policy" in H. Hofmann and A. Türk (eds.), *EU Administrative Governance* (Elgar Publishing, London, 2006).

[33] This stands for 'Supplementary Information Requests at the National Entry'.

[34] Initiative of the Kingdom of Spain with a view to adopting [a Justice and Home Affairs Council Decision] concerning the introduction of some new functions for the Schengen Information System, in particular in the fight against terrorism [2002] OJ C160/7.

[35] See, for example, the report by the United Kingdom human rights group JUSTICE, The Schengen Information System: a human rights audit, available at www.justice.org.uk. This report is discussed by M. Colvin, "The Schengen Information System: a human rights audit" (2001) *European Human Rights Law Review* 271. For discussion focusing on judicial control in one member state, see E. Guild, "Adjudicating Schengen: National Judicial Control in France" (1999) *European Journal for Migration and Law* 419.

[36] Council Decision 2000/365 of 29 May 2000 concerning the request of the United Kingdom of Great Britain and Northern Ireland to take part in some of the provisions of the Schengen *acquis* [2000] OJ L131/43.

[37] Council Decision 2002/192 of 28 February 2002 concerning Ireland's request to take part in some of the provisions of the Schengen *acquis* [2002] OJ L64/20.

3. Ireland and Title IV of the Treaty Establishing the European Community

(a) The Amsterdam Protocols

Ireland, the United Kingdom, and Denmark have opted out of both the Schengen Integration Protocol and Title IV of the Treaty Establishing the European Community. The opt-out of the United Kingdom and Ireland has its origins in a particular British conception of border politics and general reluctance in the United Kingdom in relation to participation in European policies.[38] The argument often propounded is that the British conception of internal security depends on strict border control, with internal liberty thereby guaranteed. In contrast, the 'continental system' depends less on border control and more on internal checks, exemplified by the use of national identity cards which citizens must carry at all times. While the contrast is no doubt overstated, it does influence the construction of national interests in this area. Ireland's opt-out is in turn attributed to the need to maintain the Common Travel Area between the United Kingdom and Ireland.[39]

Accordingly, in deciding whether to take part in measures in the immigration area, one of the principal considerations is the consequences of the measure for the common travel area.[40] This is reflected in Ireland's 'Declaration on Article 3 of the Protocol on the Position of the United Kingdom and Ireland', which was annexed to the Final Act of the Amsterdam intergovernmental conference, and in which Ireland undertook to exercise its right to opt into Title IV measures 'to the maximum extent compatible with the maintenance of its Common Travel Area with the United Kingdom'. The Protocol to the Treaty of Amsterdam on the position of Ireland and the United Kingdom provides that each state has three months from the date of the presentation of the proposal or initiative to the Council to notify the President of the Council in writing of its wish to participate in the adoption of the measure.[41] Ireland can also opt to participate after a measure has been adopted.[42] As will be seen

[38] See generally A. Wiener, "Forging Flexibility – The British 'No' to Schengen" (1999) *European Journal of Migration and Law* 441.
[39] For a general discussion, see B. Ryan, "The common travel area between Britain and Ireland" (2001) *Modern Law Review* 855.
[40] A further protocol to the Treaty of Amsterdam, the Protocol on the Application of Certain Aspects of Art. 7a of the Treaty Establishing the European Community to the United Kingdom and to Ireland, preserves the Common Travel Area.
[41] Art. 3 of the Protocol on the Position of the United Kingdom and Ireland.
[42] Art. 4 of the Protocol on the Position of the United Kingdom and Ireland.

below, this deadline has proved problematic in Ireland. In the light of the content of the Declaration, comparisons are drawn throughout the chapter between the opt-ins by Ireland and the United Kingdom. As will be seen, Ireland has not adhered to the Declaration.

The respective mechanisms for opting into measures under Title IV of the EC Treaty, on the one hand, and Schengen measures, on the other, differ. The United Kingdom and Ireland may opt in to measures under Title IV of the EC Treaty as of right. In contrast, their opting into measures that form part of the Schengen *acquis* must be approved by the Council unanimously, in accordance with Article 4 of the Schengen Protocol.[43] However, where measures build on the Schengen *acquis*, Article 5 of the Protocol appears to allow Ireland and the United Kingdom to participate without such approval.[44] However, this does not seem to be the Council's interpretation at present. At the time of writing, two disputes concerning the interaction between Articles 4 and 5 are before the European Court of Justice,[45] both concerning the Council's refusal to allow the United Kingdom to participate in Schengen-building measures, namely the European Border Guard[46] and the Passports Regulation.[47] The Council argues that participation in Schengen-building measures under Article 5 is only permissible if the United Kingdom (or Ireland) has, pursuant to Article 4 of the Protocol, already sought and

[43] Art. 4 of the Protocol Integrating the Schengen Acquis into the Framework of the European Union provides: "Ireland and the United Kingdom of Great Britain and Northern Ireland, which are not bound by the Schengen acquis, may at any time request to take part in some or all of the provisions of this acquis. The Council shall decide on the request with the unanimity of its members referred to in Article 1 and of the representative of the Government of the State concerned".

[44] Art. 5 of the Protocol Integrating the Schengen Acquis into the Framework of the European Union provides, insofar as relevant, as follows:

> "1. Proposals and initiatives to build upon the Schengen acquis shall be subject to the relevant provisions of the Treaties. In this context, where either Ireland or the United Kingdom or both have not notified the President of the Council in writing within a reasonable period that they wish to take part, the authorisation referred to in Article [11] of the Treaty establishing the European Community or Article [40] of the Treaty on European Union shall be deemed to have been granted to the Members States referred to in Article 1 and to Ireland or the United Kingdom where either of them wishes to take part in the areas of cooperation in question ...".

[45] Case C-77/05, *United Kingdom v Council ('Border Agency Regulation')* [2005] OJ C82/25 (pending); Case C-137/05, *United Kingdom v Council ('Passports Regulation')* [2005] OJ C 132/16 (pending).

[46] Council Regulation 2007/2004 of 26 October 2004 establishing a European Agency for the Management of Operational Cooperation at the External Borders of the Member States of the European Union [2004] OJ L349/1.

[47] Council Regulation 2252/2004 of 13 December 2004 on standards for security measures and biometrics in passports and travel documents issued by Member States [2004] OJ L385/1.

obtained the approval of the other member states for participating in those parts of the *acquis* on which the subsequent regulations are based. The United Kingdom disputes this interpretation, and argues that Articles 4 and 5 are to be read separately. Ireland has intervened in support of the United Kingdom position.[48]

(b) The Amsterdam Amendment to the Irish Constitution

The Irish Constitution was amended to facilitate Ireland's accession to the (then) European Economic Community. While the Supreme Court has given a broad interpretation of what was 'necessitated' by the obligations of Community law, a different approach was needed to allow Ireland's selective participation under Title IV of the EC Treaty, and the other areas in which the Amsterdam Treaty allowed optional participation. Accordingly, Article 29.4.6° provides that:

> "the State may exercise the options or discretions provided by or under Articles 1.11 [relating to police and judicial cooperation in criminal matters], 2.5 [a general provision allowing a group of member states to develop closer cooperation] and 2.15 [which inserted Title IV— concerning visas, asylum and immigration—into the EC Treaty] of the [Amsterdam] Treaty and the second and fourth Protocols [which relate respectively to opting into measures building on Schengen and to opting-in under Title IV of the EC Treaty] set out in the said Treaty but any such exercise shall be subject to the prior approval of both Houses of the Oireachtas".

The scope of 'options and discretions' has yet to be judicially explored. In the context of Title IV of the EC Treaty, however, it encompasses all measures, as Ireland participates selectively in this area as a whole. Similarly, as regards closer cooperation generally, participation is by its nature optional.

Insofar as concerns the revised Third Pillar of the European Union on police and judicial cooperation in criminal matters, it would be possible to read the reference to 'options and discretions' in an analogous manner, which would mean that it would apply where Ireland has a choice as to whether to participate or opt in, in which case it would refer principally to the exercise

[48] See the Order of the President of Court of Justice, 17 August 2005 concerning interventions. At the time of writing, this Order may be read on the Court's website. Other interveners in this case are the Commission, Spain, the Slovak Republic, and Poland.

of the option whether to grant the Court of Justice jurisdiction in this field under Article 35 of the Treaty on European Union. However, a different practice has evolved, whereby all framework decisions under the Third Pillar are treated as requiring parliamentary approval. This was explained by the Minister for Justice, Equality and Law Reform in the following terms:

> "by virtue of the fact that important constitutional issues arose in respect of one of the draft framework decisions now before the House, the Government has decided, having taken the advice of the Attorney General that, while it has not been the norm to refer proposals for Council framework decisions to the Houses of the Oireachtas, the better course would be to bring all proposals for framework decisions before the Houses".[49]

As O'Hegarty notes in her chapter in this book, the options referred to by Article 29.4.6° are assumed to include in the main measures under Title IV of the Treaty Establishing the European Community (which, as has been seen, concerns visas, asylum, immigration, and other policies related to the free movement of persons and for which there is a specific opt-in mechanism) as well as framework decisions under Title VI of the Treaty on European Union (which contains provisions on police and judicial cooperation in criminal matters).

This broader interpretation of 'options and discretions' is welcome, in that it increases the parliamentary role. In addition, it brings symmetry between Title IV of the EC Treaty and Title VI of the Treaty on European Union. Given the security-based approach to migration policy prevalent at European Union level, there are strong interlinkages between the two policy areas. By requiring parliamentary approval for participation in both areas, what would otherwise be the anomalous outcome of having greater parliamentary control over the executive's action in relation to non-criminal aspects of migration control policy is avoided. However, it is question-begging in that there is no particular rationale for having enhanced parliamentary participation in respect of police and judicial cooperation in criminal matters. The rationale for the enhanced parliamentary role over Title IV of the EC Treaty is that Ireland has formally opted out of this area. In contrast, it is a full participant under Title VI of the Treaty on European Union on police and judicial cooperation in criminal matters. If framework decisions made in this policy area warrant such additional domestic consideration, why not decisions in other areas sensitive areas in which the European Union or European Community legislates?

[49] Dáil debate on the European Arrest Warrant on 12 December 2001. (See Dáil Debates, vol. 546, cols. 887–888.)

(c) The Amsterdam Constitutional Amendment and European Scrutiny

The constitutional amendment which facilitated Irish ratification of the Treaty of Amsterdam provides for a potentially highly significant role for the Oireachtas. Without explicit parliamentary approval, participation in measures under Title IV of the EC Treaty is unconstitutional. However, due to the three-month deadline for opting in, the Oireachtas may have insufficient time to consider the proposal properly. Moreover, the role of the Oireachtas is to assent to participation in the negotiations on the proposal, rather than holding the minister to account for the stance he or she takes in those negotiations.

The challenge for the Oireachtas is to transform the reactive approval requirement into a proactive role. Irish parliamentarians were from the outset aware of the potential of their veto to develop into a scrutiny reserve.[50] Under the terms of the Amsterdam Protocol on the Position of the United Kingdom and Ireland, the opt-in would appear to be a once-and-for-all, all-or-nothing matter. However, it may be that under the Irish Constitution, some leeway exists for conditions to be imposed on an opt-in – conditions which could bind ministers domestically as to how they negotiate in the Council. Thus procedural conditions could be imposed, such as a requirement to regularly inform the relevant sectoral committee of the Oireachtas of developments. This could even be taken to the extent of requiring a second formal approval of Ireland's participation when the final text emerged. Thus, the opt-in could be effective under the Protocol, and yet conditional at the domestic constitutional level. In this way, a particularly strong scrutiny reserve could emerge.

In practice, if the Oireachtas does not approve an opt-in to negotiations, it may be presented with the option of approving an opt-in to the agreed measure. Formally, Ireland would not have been involved in the negotiations on the resultant measure, although it appears in practice that the United Kingdom and Ireland do still participate in Council meetings. A senior official of the Department of Justice, Equality and Law Reform has explained that:

> "the non-exercise of our option [to opt in] does not prevent our participation in discussions on the proposals in the relevant Council Working Parties – and we are fully engaged in those discussions – as we have a right to participate by virtue of our Council membership."[51]

[50] See further the chapter by Lia O'Hegarty in this volume in relation to the legal advice offered by her on the Amsterdam Protocol and on Art. 29.4.6° of the Constitution.

[51] D. Costello, "Ireland and the Development of the Common European Asylum Policy" (paper presented at the Irish Centre for European Law Conference on Refugee Law, 2 March, 2002) at 8.

In such a context, the role of the Oireachtas is likely to be reduced to a rubber stamp, unless appropriate use is made of the normal scrutiny mechanisms as regards Title IV of the EC Treaty proposals, even when Ireland has not formally opted in to a measure.

The period under consideration, between 1999 and 2005, coincides with the initial rejection by the Irish electorate of the Nice Treaty by referendum, and the consequent formal enhancement of parliamentary scrutiny mechanisms in Ireland.[52] The procedures for Oireachtas oversight of the European Union are now partly set out in the European Union (Scrutiny) Act 2002.[53] The government must now set before the European Affairs Committee's Sub-Committee on European Scrutiny all European Union proposals as well as information notes which set forth their content, aims, and national implications. This includes proposals 'requiring the prior approval of both Houses of the Oireachtas pursuant to Article 29.4.6 of the Constitution.[54] The Sub-Committee's role is to sift proposals and decide which to refer to relevant Oireachtas sectoral committees for further consideration. The second aspect of parliamentary scrutiny is set out in Oireachtas agreed procedures concerning preparations for European Union Council meetings and European Council summits.[55] Ministers are now required, at the request of an appropriate committee, to come before the committee to discuss in detail the agenda for that Council meeting and the Irish position on those issues. The minister is not obliged to take the advice of the committee.

Whether the Oireachtas exploits its role to the full depends on the interactions between the Joint Committee on European Affairs, the Sub-committee on European Scrutiny and relevant sectoral committees, in particular, the Joint Committee on Justice, Equality and Law Reform. In particular, it remains to be seen whether synergies between the opt-in powers and general scrutiny powers will emerge.

4. Parliamentary Control and Scrutiny of Selective Participation

This Part sets out Ireland's selective participation in Title IV measures to date, in order to examine the use to which these parliamentary powers have been put.

---

[52] See generally, C. Costello, "Ireland's Nice Referenda" (2005) *European Constitutional Law Review* 357.

[53] See in more detail in this regard the chapters in this volume by Lia O'Hegarty and Katherine Meenan.

[54] See the definition of 'measure' in s. 1(1)(d) of the European Union (Scrutiny) Act 2002.

[55] These agreed procedures are constituted by understandings, rather than formal written agreements, but they have been outlined in the Dáil. See Dáil Debates, vol. 554, col. 575 (9 October 2002).

(a) Asylum Law

(i) Opting In

The first of the asylum measures into which Ireland opted was the Eurodac Regulation, which provides for the fingerprinting of asylum seekers. The opt-in motions were approved in October 1999, with some debate taking place in the Dáil.[56] It has subsequently opted into all asylum measures under Title IV of the EC Treaty, with the exception of the Reception Conditions Directive, which is discussed below. Thus, the Oireachtas approved participation in the European Refugee Fund in April 2000.[57] The motions in both houses of the Oireachtas to opt in to the Dublin II Regulation were then passed in October 2001.[58] On this occasion, the decision to exercise the option provided for in the Amsterdam Protocol on the Position of the United Kingdom and Ireland was taken with little debate. However, one TD had already raised concerns about the approach which had been taken to the opt-ins, when the matter had been referred to the Joint Committee on Justice, Equality, Defence and Women's Rights just two days previously.[59] Ireland opted into the Refugee Definition Directive in February 2002.[60]

---

[56] See Dáil Debates, vol. 509, cols 290–314 (13 October 1999) and Seanad Debates, vol. 160, col. 705–730 (13 October 1999).

[57] Council Decision 2000/596 of 28 September 2000 establishing a European Refugee Fund, [2000] OJ L252/12). See Dáil Debates, vol. 517, col. 1251 (11 April 2000) and Seanad Debates, vol. 162, col. 1640 (12 April 2000).

[58] See Dáil Debates, vol. 543, cols 18–19 (25 October 2001) and Seanad Debates, vol. 168, cols 393–394 (18 October 2001).

[59] On that occasion, Brendan Howlin TD had stated that

> "clarity is necessary on the reporting mechanism. I want to raise the referral to the joint committee of [the subject matter of the motion], which is an alternative arrangement to the Dublin Convention. While I have no difficulty with it being debated by the committee, I want to alert the Government to the fact that every proposal under this heading comes at the last minute with a telephone call to Opposition spokespersons saying there is not time and it will have to be referred without debate. The cavalier attitude of the Department of Justice, Equality and Law Reform to very important issues should not be tolerated by the House. Even the Government gets late notice. This protocol has been with the Department of Justice, Equality and Law Reform for three months and did not go to Cabinet until 9 October. In future we will not agree to simply referring these matters to committees at the last minute, with late briefings and inadequate preparation."

(Dáil Debates, vol. 542, cols 1150–1151 (23 October 2001)).

[60] Council Directive 2004/83 of 29 April 2004 on minimum standards for the qualification and status of third country nationals or stateless persons as refugees or as persons who otherwise need international protection and the content of the protection granted [2004] OJ L304/12. See Dáil Debates, vol. 547, cols 1121–1122 (5 February 2002) and Seanad Debates, vol. 169, cols 202–203 (13 February 2002).

It will be seen from the foregoing that in most instances, Oireachtas approval was sought as the three-month deadline for opting-in to negotiations on the relevant measure was close to expiry. In contrast, Ireland opted into the Temporary Protection Directive[61] long after it had been agreed at European Union level, in February, 2003.

(ii) The Asylum Procedures Directive

The Asylum Procedures Directive has proved the most difficult and controversial of the European Community asylum measures, and so it is proposed to focus on this measure.[62]

The Commission first proposed a directive on asylum procedures in 2000,[63] but due to lack of political agreement, issued a revised proposal in 2002.[64] Throughout the drafting process, standards were lowered, guarantees reduced, and exceptions expanded. It is no exaggeration to say that under the directive, exceptional procedures will become the norm. As a result, in March 2004 an alliance of non-governmental organisations called for the withdrawal of the draft directive, noting

> "with deep regret that the most contentious provisions are all intended to deny asylum seekers access to asylum procedures and to facilitate their transfer to countries outside the European Union".[65]

---

[61] Council Directive 2001/55 on minimum standards for giving temporary protection in the event of a mass influx of displaced persons and on measures promoting a balance of efforts between member states in receiving such persons and bearing the consequences thereof [2001] OJ L212/12. See Dáil Debates, vol. 561, cols 1274–1275 (19 February 2003) and Seanad Debates, vol. 171, col. 847 (25 February 2003).

[62] Council Directive 2005/85 of 1 December 2005 on minimum standards on procedures in Member States for granting and withdrawing refugee status [2005] OJ L326/13. For critique, see C. Costello, *ILPA Analysis and Critique of Council Directive on minimum standards on procedures in Member States for granting and withdrawing refugee status (30 April, 2004)* (ILPA, London, July, 2004), available at the time of writing at www.ilpa.org.uk. See also C. Costello, above, n. 18.

[63] Proposal for a Council Directive on minimum standards on procedures in Member States for granting and withdrawing refugee status 24 October 2000 [2001] OJ C62 E/231.

[64] Amended Proposal for a Council Directive on minimum standards on procedures in Member States for granting and withdrawing refugee status, 18 June 2002 [2002] OJ C291 E/143.

[65] ECRE, ILGA Europe, Amnesty International, Pax Christi International, Quaker Council for European Affairs, Human Rights Watch, CARITAS-Europe, Médecins Sans Frontières, Churches' Commission for Migrants, Save the Children in Europe, *Call for withdrawal of the Asylum Procedures Directive* (22 March, 2004). Concerns were reiterated by ECRE, Amnesty International, and Human Rights Watch Press Release, "Refugee and Human Rights Organisations across Europe Express their Concern at the Expected Agreement on Asylum Measures on breach of International Law" (28 April, 2004).

In addition, the United Nations High Commissioner for Refugees, Ruud Lubbers, made an unprecedented intervention concerning the draft directive,

> "warning that several provisions ... would fall short of accepted international legal standards ... [and] could lead to an erosion of the global asylum system, jeopardising the lives of future refugees".[66]

The day after political agreement was reached on the directive, the High Commissioner reiterated his concerns, in particular in relation to the directive's provisions regarding safe third countries and its provisions concerning non-suspensory appeals, which would allow member states to deport asylum seekers whilst their appeals were pending. He noted in particular that the directive would allow:

> "a number of ... restrictive and highly controversial practices that are currently only contained in one or two member states national legislation but could, as of 1 May, 2004, be inserted in the legislation of all 25 European Union Member States".[67]

Ireland opted into the negotiations in 2001. Although the first Commission proposal had been withdrawn and a new proposal issued in 2002, it appears that no separate opt-in was deemed necessary. The manner of the first opt-in itself left much to be desired. Thus on 6 February 2001, TDs expressed concern in the Dáil that the proposal had not been brought to the Oireachtas sooner. Although the Taoiseach disputed the fact that there had been a delay, the formal proposal had been issued in October 2000, and clearly it could have been put before the Oireachtas before it was, at which time the expiry in mid-February of the three-month period allowed for opting into negotiations loomed.[68]

---

66 UNHCR Press Release, "Lubbers calls for EU asylum laws not to contravene international law" (29 March 2004).

67 UNHCR Press Release, "UNHCR regrets missed opportunity to adopt high EU asylum standards" (30 April 2004).

68 Hence the following exchange in the Dáil between Nora Owen TD and the Taoiseach, Bertie Ahern TD:

> "Mrs. Owen: I understand the Minister for Justice, Equality and Law Reform should have brought this motion to the House three months ago but failed to do so. Hence, the Government is now trying to rush it through the House. We have reluctantly agreed to it being taken today, but it is a disgrace that other Members of this House who are not on the committee on Justice, Equality, Defence and Women's Rights will not have an opportunity to prosecute the Government on its disastrous policy with regard to asylum seekers and refugees and that only speakers from the three main parties will be able to speak. I would

One TD expressed concern that the House

> "act for once as a real parliament in matters of European competence. We are all bamboozled sometimes by the complexity of legal instruments coming from the European Union … I am not satisfied and neither should Members be with a situation where a Community instrument is almost finalised in negotiations between talented and able public servants acting on instructions from a Government or Department and where we are presented with net issues to which we say 'yea' or 'nay'. Even then, they are presented late or at the last minute and we are told there is very little time for debate.
>
> Wc had a discussion on EURODAC not on thc basis of whcthcr wc wanted to be part of the process to see what a common system of asylum treatment should be within the European Union, rather on the basis of what was agreed and whether we accepted it in the knowledge that a Government majority existed to force it through anyway. Things are done differently in other national parliaments of the European Union. I say this in the hope that the Minister listens in a fair and open way".[69]

A decision was taken to refer the matter to the Joint Committee for Justice, Equality and Law Reform for further consideration. The matter first came before the Seanad on 7 February 2001, and the then Minister of State at the Department of Justice, Equality and Law Reform, Mary Hanafin TD, provided an explanation for the urgency of the opt-in measure, ascribing the delay which had occurred in bringing the matter before the Oireachtas to the late communication of the measure to the relevant government department, the need for interdepartmental consultation on the measure, and the

---

like an explanation from the Taoiseach on why it is being rushed in at this stage, forcing the House to agree reluctantly to put it through. Could we have an explanation of what happened in regard to this proposal which should have been passed about three months ago?
The Taoiseach: Normally a motion such as this would be referred to a committee without debate. Time has been allocated so that Members can make their points, after which it can be debated at the committee. I am not aware of any delay. However, the point can be made during the debate.
Mrs. Owen: There has been a delay. Our information is that the Minister for Justice, Equality and Law Reform neglected it and hence must now put it through by 12 February. That is not the way to do business. I will rise again on the next matter. We are reluctantly agreeing to [the motion] in its current format, but it is not something we on this side of the House will give in to on every occasion"

(Dáil Debates, vol. 529, cols 1271–1273 (6 February 2001)).

[69] Brendan Howlin TD (Dáil Debates, vol. 529, cols 1292–1293 (6 February 2001)).

Oireachtas recess from which the houses had just returned.[70] She then provided an overview of the proposal, and a general debate about refugee protection issues ensued. The Seanad also resolved to refer the matter to the Joint Committee. The Joint Committee having considered the matter on 8 February 2001, the Dáil approved the opt-in motion without debate on 13 February.[71] The matter came to the Seanad once more on 14 February, and that house passed the motion to opt in to the negotiations on the Asylum Procedures Directive.[72] One senator did express concern that the issue came back to that house a mere week after it had been referred to the committee,[73] but no explanation for this having occurred appears on the record.

Ireland, which at this time held the Presidency of the Council of Ministers, was instrumental in achieving final agreement on the text.[74] In his general

---

[70] The minister of state stated: "It is important for me to clarify why the matter is only now coming before the House for consideration. Although this proposal was actually sent formally to the Council by the Commission at the end of October last year the final text as communicated to the Council only became available to the Department in mid-November. Prior to considering whether the State should exercise its option under Title IV, the necessary interdepartmental consultations had to take place and then Government approval had to be sought for the exercise of the option. Although copies of the proposal for a directive were laid before both Houses on 9 January, 2001, due to the intervening Christmas recess, which took up nearly half of the 12 weeks 'opt-in' period, it is only now, on the return of both Houses, that the necessary motions can be considered. The consequences of the presentation of this proposal by the European Commission to Council is that if the State wishes to opt into discussions from the beginning, we have until 14 February, 2001 to inform the President of the Council of our intentions. Failure to opt in at this time does not prevent us from participating in Council discussions. However, we would not be able to opt in until such time as the negotiations have been concluded and the measures adopted, and our ability to influence the outcome of the discussions would be correspondingly limited. The United Kingdom has recently conveyed its decision to the Council to exercise its option in respect of the Council directive. This initiative is the first major proposal in a series of measures which are aimed at creating a common European asylum system" (Seanad Debates, vol. 165, cols 22–23 (7 February 2001)).

[71] The motion (moved by the Minister of State at the Department of the Taoiseach, Séamus Brennan TD) was "that Dáil Éireann approves the exercise by the State of the option, provided by Article 3 of the fourth Protocol set out in the Treaty of Amsterdam, to notify the President of the Council that it wishes to take part in the adoption and application of the following proposed measure, namely a proposal for a Council Directive on minimum standards on procedures in member states for granting and withdrawing refugee status a copy of which proposed measure was laid before Dáil Éireann on 9 January, 2001".

[72] The motion provided "that Seanad Éireann approves the exercise by the State of the option, provided by Article 3 of the fourth Protocol set out in the Treaty of Amsterdam, to notify the President of the Council that it wishes to take part in the adoption and application of the following proposed measure, namely a proposal for a Council Directive on minimum standards on procedures in member states for granting and withdrawing refugee status a copy of which proposed measure was laid before Seanad Éireann on 9 January, 2001".

[73] See the contribution by Senator Brendan Ryan, Seanad Debates, vol. 165, col. 217 (14 February 2001).

[74] D. Ackers, "The Negotiations of the Asylum Procedures Directive" (2005) *European Journal of Migration and Law* 1 at 25–26.

presentation to the Joint Committee on Justice, Equality, Defence and Women's Rights, the Minister for Justice, Equality and Law Reform mentioned the agreement reached on the Procedures Directive, which together with the Qualifications Directive, represented a:

> "significant milestone in the development of a common European Union asylum policy. They represent, together with the Council regulation replacing the Dublin Convention and the asylum reception directive, the final two cornerstones of that policy. Their adoption also means that the time limits set by the Amsterdam treaty for this purpose have been met."[75]

No member of the Joint Committee raised any concerns about the controversial content of the Directive at that presentation. Indeed, although the relevant minister makes regular presentations to that committee, the discussion in committee tends to focus on domestic, if not parochial, aspects of asylum policy.

Clearly, the opt-in was dealt with in a perfunctory matter, despite the reservations expressed by members of the Dáil and Seanad. No consideration seems to have been given to a conditional opt-in, in other words a scrutiny reserve. A second problem stemmed from the tortuous negotiations on the measure. Ireland opted into deliberations on one measure, but that original proposal was withdrawn. Arguably, a second opt-in was required for the second proposal.

Aside from any legal requirement to opt in again, in order for a scrutiny process to be meaningful, it must be based on an accurate up-to-date text. In the United Kingdom, as Kerse outlines in his chapter in this volume, when in the course of legislation a new text is produced, such as an amended Commission proposal (as was the case here), a new document is thereby generated and the scrutiny process begins again. Thus, in the United Kingdom, the Asylum Procedures Directive was subject to multiple examinations as the text developed (or rather deteriorated.) The European Union Committee published its first report in 2000, based on the first Commission Proposal.[76] Subsequent versions of the directive and of particular articles were furnished to the committee for scrutiny. Each was subjected to examination by the relevant sub-committee. In addition, there

[75] Presentation by the Minister for Justice, Equality and Law Reform (Michael McDowell TD) to the Joint Committee on Justice, Equality, Defence and Women's Rights (vol. 65 of the Proceedings of the Joint Committee (19 May 2004).)

[76] *Minimum Standards in Asylum Procedures* (Eleventh Report, 2000–2001, HL Paper 59).

was correspondence with the government and two further meetings took place between the sub-committee and the minister and her officials.[77]

(iii) Staying Out – the Directive on Reception Conditions

In the asylum field, Ireland has opted into all measures with the notable exception of the Directive on Reception Conditions.[78] The decision not to opt into this directive was attributed by a senior official to the fact that it was not possible to opt into deliberations within three months, as 'a major part of the period was during the recess of the Houses of the Oireachtas'.[79] Ireland's non-participation in the directive was the subject of a question in the Dáil on 6 February 2003.[80] On that occasion, the Minister for Justice, Equality and Law Reform reported that 'the modalities in relation to the exercise of the State's Fourth Protocol option[81] in respect of this directive are under consideration at the present time'. A recent publication explains the decision to stay out in the following terms:

> "many of the key provisions of this Directive, although the responsibility of a number of Government Departments and agencies, are already covered by national procedures. The Government state that national standards exceed those provided for in the Directive and that the exercise of the option in respect of this Directive is under consideration at the present time".[82]

Ireland's failure to opt into the Directive on Reception Conditions contrasts with the facts that the United Kingdom has opted in, and that it seems inconsistent with Ireland's Amsterdam Declaration. Insofar as the role of the

---

77 See Evidence by Caroline Flint MP on Asylum Procedures (First Report, 2003–2004 Session, HL Paper 8) and Further Evidence by Caroline Flint MP on Asylum Procedures (Eighteenth Report, 2003–2004 Session, HL Paper 106).

78 Council Directive 2003/9 of 27 January 2003 laying down minimum standards for the reception of asylum seekers [2003] OJ L31/18.

79 D. Costello, *Ireland and the Development of the Common European Asylum Policy* (paper presented at the Irish Centre for European Law Conference on Refugee Law, Dublin, 2 March, 2002) at 8.

80 Aengus Ó Snodaigh TD asked the Minister for Justice, Equality and Law Reform if the Government planned to opt in to the Directive and if he would make a statement on the matter (Dáil Debates, vol. 560, col. 1489 (6 February 2003)).

81 *I.e.,* Ireland's option to opt into a measure under the Amsterdam Protocol on the Position of the United Kingdom and Ireland.

82 E. Quinn & G. Hughes, *Policy Analysis Report on Asylum and Migration: Ireland 2003 to Mid-2004* (ESRI/European Migration Network, 2005), at 20.

Oireachtas is concerned, there is a need to monitor policy areas in relation to which Ireland does not exercise its opt-in, a topic which will be discussed further in the next section.

(b) Immigration Law

Immigration policy as defined in Title IV of the EC Treaty is far from comprehensive in scope.[83] The Treaty provides for measures being adopted within five years for the abolition of border controls within the European Union[84] and for some measures on external borders, including visas for periods of up to three months, to be adopted within the same time-frame.[85] The five-year period does not apply to other areas of immigration law, which is defined in terms of the conditions of entry and long-term residence, including family reunification[86] and measures on illegal immigration, including repatriation.[87]

While the Council has adopted Directives on Family Reunification[88] and Student Immigration,[89] in other respects, common rules on immigration admissions have not emerged. The Commission proposal for a general Directive on the Conditions of Entry and Residence of Third Country Nationals for the Purpose of Paid Employment or Self-Employment[90] was withdrawn in the face of opposition in the Council. Ireland had opted into this measure,[91] although not into the first two. A recent policy initiative from the Commission, the January 2005 Green Paper on a EU Approach to Managing Economic Migration,[92] is highly tentative. Instead, Title IV measures have continued to develop elaborate immigration control systems, without common rules on who may enter the European Union legally.

---

[83] See, for example, J. Monar, "Justice and Home Affairs in the Treaty of Amsterdam: Reform at the Price of Fragmentation" (1998) *European Law Review* 320.

[84] Art. 62(1) of the EC Treaty.

[85] Art. 62(2) of the EC Treaty.

[86] Art. 63(2)(3)(a) of the EC Treaty.

[87] Art. 63(2)(3)(b) of the EC Treaty.

[88] Council Directive 2003/86 of 22 September 2003 on the right of family reunification [2003] OJ L251/12.

[89] Council Directive 2004/114 of 13 December 2004 on the conditions of admission of third-country nationals for the purposes of studies, pupil exchange, unremunerated training or voluntary service [2004] OJ L375/12.

[90] COM (2001) 386 final, 11 July 2001.

[91] 12 December 2001.

[92] COM (2004) 811.

Ireland participates selectively in this already imbalanced European Union immigration policy, tending to opt into immigration control measures,[93] rather than immigrants' rights measures.[94]

Neither Ireland nor the United Kingdom has opted into the Directive on the Status of Long-Term Resident Third Country Nationals.[95] This directive is one of the few cases of positive mutual recognition, in a system characterised by the prevalence of 'negative mutual recognition', whereby refusals of entry and status have consequences beyond the member state concerned.[96] In the United Kingdom, detailed scrutiny of *whether* to opt in took place,[97] and the decision not to do so was explained. The United Kingdom objection focuses not on the rights the directive grants to long-term residents in their country of residence, but the grant of the right to move to other European Union member states. Thus, the Home Office explains that:

> "whilst the proposed Directive contains many provisions which are entirely consistent with [its] policy on participation in EU immigration measures, giving third country nationals an enforceable right to enter the United Kingdom, without any checks and safeguards, is not".[98]

However, this reasoning is not entirely persuasive when the measure is viewed in context. Currently, so-called third-country nationals do acquire

---

[93] For example, Council Decision 2004/573 on the organisation of joint flights for removals from the territory of two or more Member States, of third-country nationals who are subjects of individual removal orders, [2004] OJ L261/28; Council Directive 2001/40 on the mutual recognition of decision concerning expulsion of third country nationals, [2001] OJ L149/34. Ireland opted in on 27 February 2002. This directive is complemented by Council Decision of 23 February, 2004 setting out the criteria and practical arrangements for the compensation of the financial imbalances resulting from the application of Directive 2001/40 on the mutual recognition of decisions on the expulsion of third-country nationals, [2004] OJ L60/55. Ireland does not seem to have opted into this measure yet.

[94] See J. Handoll, "Ireland" in I. Higgins and K. Hailbronner (eds.) *Migration and Asylum Law and Policy in the European Union* (Cambridge University Press, Cambridge, 2004), at 179

[95] Directive 2003/109 of 25 November 2003 on the legal status of long-term resident third country nationals, [2004] OJ L16/44. See S. Peers, "Implementing equality? The Directive on long-term resident third-country nationals" (2004) *European Law Review* 437; T. Kostakopolou, "'Integrating' Non-EU Migrants in the European Union: Ambivalent Legacies and Mutating Paradigms" (2002) *Columbia Journal of European Law* 187.

[96] This is a feature of the 'Dublin II' system, the mutual recognition of expulsion decisions, and the Schengen Information System.

[97] House of Lords European Union Committee, *The Legal Status of Long Term Resident Third Country Nationals* (Fifth Report, 2001–2002 Session).

[98] Letter from Lord Rooker to Lord Brabazon of Tara of 7 August 2001 (Appendix 4 to the House of Lords Report, *ibid.*).

rights to move to other European Union countries automatically on naturalisation. In the absence of common rules on naturalisation, the directive introduces a status akin to denizenship, an intermediate status between alienage and citizenship. Both Ireland and the United Kingdom have relatively open naturalisation policies, so third-country national immigrants to both countries can, if they opt for naturalisation, acquire full European Union citizenship rights to enter other European Union countries. However, third-country national immigrants to other European Union countries do not find it so easy to obtain naturalisation. Nor will their newly acquired denizenship status allow them to enter the United Kingdom or Ireland. Once again, the failure by Ireland to opt in to a measure will thus create an imbalance, with immigrants to Ireland gaining rights to move to other European Union countries through naturalisation much more easily than immigrants to other European Union countries will gain such rights to enter Ireland. Whatever the merits of staying out, the Directive on the Status of Long-Term Resident Third Country Nationals warrants proper open scrutiny in the Irish context. This has been lacking to date.

In its 2004 Progress Report, the Department of Justice, Equality and Law Reform cites as one of its achievements the adoption at European Union level of the Council Directive on the Residence Permit Issued to Victims of Trafficking.[99] The directive allows member states to grant victims of trafficking who cooperate in the prosecution of traffickers a temporary residence permit. Victims are to be afforded a month-long reflection period in order to decide whether to cooperate, to be followed by a determination by the national authorities of eligibility for the temporary permit. However, Ireland and the United Kingdom have not opted into this measure. In the United Kingdom, the Home Office has attributed the failure to opt in to the need to allow the Immigration Service to deport illegal immigrants. It views the 30-day reflection period as potentially applicable to 'the majority of illegal entrants' and hence likely to disrupt that Service.[100] However dubious

---

[99] Council Directive 2004/81 of 29 April 2004 on the residence permit issued to third-country nationals who are victims of trafficking in human beings or to third country nationals who have been the subject of an action to facilitate illegal immigration, who co-operate with the competent authorities, [2004] OJ L261/19. See Department of Justice, Equality and Law Reform, *Progress Report* (November 2004) available at www.justice.ie/80256E010039C5AF/vWeb/flJUSQ69FFQB-en/$File/ProgressRpt.pdf.

[100] Letter from the Home Office Minister to the chairman of the House of Lords European Union Committee, (WA 149, HL Hansard, 27 June, 2002), cited in V. Mitselegas, "A Common EU Immigration and Asylum Policy: National and Institutional Constraints" in P. Shah (ed.), *The Challenge of Asylum to Legal Systems* (Cavendish, London, 2005), at 135.

this 'logic of abuse' assumption, there is at least an explanation for the failure to opt in. In Ireland, opting out has not appeared to warrant any parliamentary concern.

The main exception to Ireland's general approach of staying out of primary immigration measures relates to the Directive on the Admission of Third Country Nationals for Scientific Research,[101] to which Ireland has opted in, while the United Kingdom has not.[102] On 29 June 2004, opting in was approved by the joint committee. In the committee proceedings, several members praised the utility of the scrutiny measures, and a degree of political learning was evident in the debate.

Ryan's critique of the United Kingdom's participation in immigration control measures is equally applicable to Ireland. He argues that Community immigration control measures are 'essentially commitments as among states between which border controls have been abolished'.[103] In other words, common border controls are justified in Schengenland as a flanking measure to internal free movement.[104] However, Ireland and the United Kingdom have not abolished controls on intra-Community migration and travel. As such, when they participate in common European Community control measures, they add an additional layer of control, with no concomitant internal free movement. This issue has been repeatedly raised in the context of United Kingdom parliamentary scrutiny of Title IV of the EC Treaty. In its most recent report, the House of Lords European Union Committee wrote:

> "we again urge the Government to participate fully in EU immigration and asylum policy. We believe that it would be to the advantage of the United Kingdom to do so. It is damaging to be seen as only partially engaged in this important area of policy. The United Kingdom's recent exclusion from measures in which it would be in its interests to participate underlines the increasing difficulty of maintaining its present position and

---

[101] COM(2004) 178 of 16 March 2004. Now adopted as Council Directive 2005/71 of 12 October 2005 on a specific procedure for admitting third-country nationals for the purposes of scientific research, [2005] OJ L289/15.

[102] Again, this has been the subject of an exchange of correspondence between the chairman of the relevant subcommittee of the House of Lords Committee and the relevant minister. House of Lords Select Committee on the European Union, *Correspondence with Ministers* (Fourth Report, 2005–2006 Session, HL) See "Admission of Researchers" (7815/04).

[103] B. Ryan, "The United Kingdom" in Higgins and Hailbronner, above, n. 94, at 453.

[104] House of Lords European Union Committee, *Fighting Illegal Immigration: Should Carriers Carry the Burden?* (Fifth Report, 2003–2004 Session); House of Lords European Union Committee, *A Common EU Policy on Illegal Immigration* (Thirty-Seventh Report, 2001–2002 Session).

bears out, we regret to say, the warnings that we have given to this effect in the past".[105]

Thus we see that in the United Kingdom, parliament has as an independent voice, which serves to articulate a different view of how and why the United Kingdom should engage with European Community immigration policy. Such a voice has yet to emerge from the Oireachtas.

5. The Future: Current Trends and the Impact of the Constitutional Treaty

At present, four key trends are emerging in the immigration and asylum fields which will impact on the developing role of national parliaments. These are: (1) operational cooperation, (2) informal policy coordination, (3) domestic implementation, and (4) externalisation. Each of these poses particular challenges for national parliaments, above and beyond the scrutiny of normal European Community legislative processes. The ratification of the draft Constitutional Treaty appears to have been dealt a mortal blow by the French and Dutch referendum defeats.[106] Nonetheless, the contents of the Constitutional Treaty relating to immigration and asylum will have continued resonance, particularly as they may be put in place by way of a successor treaty, ordinary European Community legislation, or even through inter-institutional practice and agreements. As such, they warrant consideration here, and may assist in meeting the emergent challenges.

(a) Operational Cooperation

The first trend is towards operational cooperation, rather than common rule-setting. The Hague Programme[107] is predominantly operational, rather than legislative. The five years of frenetic post-Amsterdam legislative activity appear to have exhausted officialdom. In contrast, in this field, operational cooperation has preceded and indeed overtaken any common rule-setting in a range of areas. During its Presidency of the European Union, the Irish government also emphasised operational cooperation over common rule-

[105] House of Lords European Union Committee, *Economic Migration to the EU* (Fourteenth Report, 2005–2006 Session).

[106] Editor's note: see the introduction to this book in relation to the most recent pre-publication developments concerning the Constitutional Treaty.

[107] *The Hague Programme: Strengthening Freedom, Security and Justice in the European Union* (extract from Presidency Conclusions of the Brussels European Council, 4–5 November 2004).

setting, for example in the area of deportation policy.[108] The Borders Agency and Visa Information System exemplify this trend. Specific accountability mechanisms are required in order to deal with such entities, and the Constitutional Treaty, regardless of its fate, may provide some inspiration in this regard.

This point is particularly apparent in relation to border controls, and more particularly the European Borders Agency[109] (the full title of which is the European Agency for the Management of Operational Cooperation at the External Borders of the Member States of the European Union). This commenced operations on 1 May 2005 in Warsaw. The United Kingdom and Ireland remain excluded from participation. This is because the other member states characterised the measure as based on the Schengen *acquis* requiring their unanimous agreement before the United Kingdom could participate. As previously mentioned, the United Kingdom is currently challenging its exclusion, with Ireland intervening in support.[110] Nonetheless, the agency has already been the subject of parliamentary scrutiny in the United Kingdom, with the House of Lords Report raising serious concerns.[111]

Insofar as its tasks are concerned, the agency coordinates and develops the operational cooperation between member states in the field of control and surveillance of the external borders, carries out risk assessments, monitors the implementation of a joint training plan, follows up on the development of research relevant for the control and surveillance of the external borders, supports cooperation between experts in emergency situations, and coordinates operational cooperation between member states in the field of removal of third-country nationals illegally residing in the member states.

---

[108] Irish Presidency of the European Union, *European Union return policy – enhancing practical cooperation*, (Documents prepared for the informal meeting of the Justice and Home Affairs Ministers Dublin, Ireland, 22–23 January 2004, available at www.statewatch.org/news/2004/jan/European-Returns-policy.pdf.

[109] In November 2003, the Commission proposed a Regulation on the European Border Agency, which was agreed in April 2004 in the form of Council Regulation (EC) No. 2007/2004 of 26 October 2004 establishing a European Agency for the Management of Operational Cooperation at the External Borders of the Member States of the European Union, [2004] OJ L349/1.

[110] Case C-77/05, *United Kingdom v Council ('Border Agency Regulation')*, [2005] OJ C/82/25 (pending); Case C-137/05, *United Kingdom v Council ('Passports Regulation')*, [2005] OJ C132/16 (pending).

[111] House of Lords European Union Committee, *Proposals for a European Border Guard*, (Twenty-Ninth Report, 2002–2003 Session).

These general tasks reflect the ongoing contestedness and ambiguity surrounding the role and competence of the agency. Its objective of establishing an 'efficient, high and uniform level of control' requires criteria to determine whose movements must be controlled. Otherwise, this question remains inherently ambiguous.

The competence of the member states to control their borders remains. In addition, Article 2(2) attempts to preserve national competences in this field. Member states may continue to cooperate with other member states or third countries, 'where such cooperation complements the action of the Agency'. Nonetheless, they must refrain from activity that would jeopardise the functioning of the agency or the attainment of its objectives. Although few provisions have been made to ensure the accountability and scrutiny of the agency, there is nonetheless already talk of increasing its powers. The Hague Programme foresees that this review of the agency's tasks 'should include the feasibility of the creation of a European system of border guards'.[112]

Again, in the Irish context, there has been no domestic parliamentary consideration of the Border Guard. While those measures in which Ireland does not initially participate may not seem to warrant scrutiny as they are being negotiated, it must be remembered that opting in after their finalisation will often occur. In this situation, the role of the Oireachtas will become a purely formal one – that of rubber stamping Ireland's participation in a measure agreed without its involvement. Genuine scrutiny must entail examination with all measures as they are developed at European Community level, lest the role of the Oireachtas become more apparent than real.

(b) The Visa Information System

In June 2002, the Council adopted Conclusions on the Development of a Visa Information System:

> "an extremely capacious and powerful database containing personal and biometric data relating to all third-country nationals who ask for a visa to enter the European Union, regardless of the outcome of the visa application".[113]

---

[112] See the Hague Programme, above, n. 107, at p. 16.

[113] F. Pastore, "Visas, Borders, Immigration: Formation, Structure, and Current Evolution of the EU Entry Control System" in N. Walker (ed.), *Europe's Area of Freedom, Security and Justice* (Oxford University Press, Oxford, 2004), at 118.

Thus, it should include over 20 million records annually, to be held for ten years. It is to share a common technical platform with the second version of the Schengen Information System (SIS II). The Council Conclusions of 19 February 2004 identify a range of aims for the system, ranging from the implementation of visa policy to fighting terrorism, readmissions and the implementation of the Dublin II Regulation. The decision to establish the system was made by the Council on 8 June 2004.[114]

However, considerable legal changes are required in order to make the Visa Information System operational. Thus, in December 2004, the Commission proposed a formal regulation.[115] At the time of writing, the Council appeared likely to adopt the Visa Information System regulation by qualified majority vote, in co-decision with the European Parliament, within a matter of months. However, in the light of the Council's decision of June 2004 and other important decisions taken by the Council in the form of informal conclusions, without going through formal legislative channels,[116] the Council may well have rendered the creation of the Visa Information System a *fait accompli*. The proposed regulation does not clarify the permissible uses of Visa Information System data, as is apparent from the decision to allow law enforcement officers access to this information.[117] In effect, through a mixture of informal conclusions and the instigation of operational changes, the European Parliament's role has been marginalised. A battle looms on this issue. Parliament's rapporteur has made it clear that the European Parliament will insist on its full legislative involvement,[118] and has stated that:

> "the European Parliament is being placed in an impossible position by being asked to decide by co-decision on the substance of the VIS proposal

---

114 Council Decision 512/2004 establishing the Visa Information System (VIS) [2004] OJ L213/5.

115 Commission Proposal of 28 December 2004 for a Regulation of the European Parliament and of the Council concerning the Visa Information System (VIS) and the exchange of data between Member States on short-stay visas (COM(2004) 835 final).

116 For example, the decision to allow national law enforcement authorities to have access to the Visa Information System. See Council Conclusions, 7 March, 2005, Council Doc. 6811/05. This is highlighted in *Comments of Standing Committee of experts in international immigration, refugee and criminal law on the draft proposal for a Regulation concerning the Visa Information System (VIS)* (Utrecht, April, 2005), at p. 3, available at www.statewatch.org/news/2005 /may/meijers-vis-report.pdf.

117 *Ibid.*

118 Baroness Sarah Ledford MEP who has stated her intention to "make use of the equal legislative power between Parliament and Council to exercise full and detailed scrutiny over the VIS proposal, including the need for, amount of, and access to sensitive data such as fingerprints. Governments cannot just decide to hijack the system as a national policing tool, with no data protection rules at EU level". (See www.sarahludfordmep.org.uk/news/465.html).

without having before it the whole series of other intended measures necessary to effective operation of VIS".[119]

In 2004, the Oireachtas Subcommittee on European Scrutiny referred the Visa Information System proposal to the Joint Committee on Justice, Equality, Defence and Women's Rights 'for information'. At the time of writing, no substantive examination of the measure has yet to take place, nor has any formal opt-in decision been made. The United Kingdom and Ireland do not participate in the common visa policy. The United Kingdom did apply to participate in the Visa Information System, but this was regarded as a Schengen-building measure and so participation was excluded.[120] This matter is likely to be revisited when the European Court of Justice gives its ruling in the Border Agency and Passports Regulation cases.[121]

(c) Informal Policy Convergence

To date, the European Community has not adopted common immigration rules, except in limited areas. Thus, an attempt has been made to bring about convergence in national primary immigration law through the softer coordinative mechanism of the open method of coordination.[122] While to date this attempt does not appear to have been particularly successful,[123] it may well become the focus of attention as hard law-making becomes more challenging in an European Union of 25 member states. Moreover, even without applying the open method of coordination as such, common approaches may emerge through the operational cooperation outlined above, which may develop informally into common rules over time. Such a move away from formal European Community legislation poses particular challenges for national parliaments.

---

[119] Committee of Civil Liberties, Justice and Home Affairs *Working Document on the Proposal of 28 December, 2004 for a Regulation of the European Parliament and of the Council concerning the Visa Information System (VIS) and the exchange of data between Member States on short-stay visas* (15 March, 2005) at p. 2.

[120] Mitsilegas, above, n. 100, at n. 71.

[121] Above, n. 45.

[122] This is the term given to the informal policy coordination process applicable in some European Community policy areas, such as economic policy and the European employment strategy.

[123] Commission Communication of 11 July 2001 on an open method of coordination for the Community immigration policy (COM (2001) 387 final). A. Caviedes, "The Open Method of Co-Ordination in Immigration Policy: a Tool for Prying Open Fortress Europe?" (2004) *Journal of European Public Policy* 289.

Raunio has identified the main reasons national parliaments have failed to engage in the open method of coordination processes, reasons which are equally, if not even more applicable to other forms of informal policy coordination. The reasons include first, the fact that national civil servants, the main actors, inform national parliaments too late for consideration to be meaningful. Secondly, with the open method of coordination and non-legislative processes, there is often no clear beginning or end to the process, with the result that national parliaments are unable to keep track of it, or to time a decisive intervention. Thirdly, the procedural ambiguities of these processes make a national parliamentary role all the more difficult to carve out.[124] Thus, Raunio's view, the move towards the:

> "extended use of [the open method of coordination] and other forms of intergovernmental policy coordination at least partially cancel out the positive constitutional developments [for national parliaments proposed in the Constitutional Treaty.]"[125]

His proposed solution is to have national parliaments apply the same procedures as those reserved for scrutinising the Commission's legislative initiatives.[126]

(d) Domestic Implementation

The third key trend consists of the domestic implementation and institutionalisation of legislative measures adopted under Title IV of the EC Treaty. In Ireland, transposition by way of executive rather than legislative action is generally constitutionally permissible.[127] However, notwithstanding this constitutional licence, it is to be hoped that such measures will be implemented by way of legislative action. Particularly in the asylum field, where the directives themselves contain broad facilitative provisions which could be construed as permitting fundamental rights violations, careful

---

124 T. Raunio, "Much Ado About Nothing? National Legislatures in the EU Constitutional Treaty" (2005) 9 *European Integration online Papers (EIoP)* No. 9, at p. 9. (See http://ideas.repec.org/a/erp/eiopxx/p0135.html.)

125 Raunio, *ibid.*, at p. 11.

126 *Ibid.*, citing G. de Búrca & J. Zeitling, "Constitutionalising the Open Method of Coordination: What Should the Convention Propose?" (2003) *CEPS Policy Brief* No. 31; K. Jacobsson and H. Schmid, "The European Employment Strategy at the Crossroads: Contribution to the Evaluation" in D. Foden and L. Magnusson (eds.), *Five Years Experience of the Luxembourg Employment Strategy* (ETUI, Brussels, 2003).

127 *Meagher v Minister for Agriculture and Food* [1994] 1 IR 329; *Maher v Minister for Agriculture and Food* [2001] 2 IR 139.

implementation is the only way to prevent judicial challenges.[128] This may provide an opportunity to re-assert some modicum of domestic accountability. However, it can be no substitute for influencing the process at the European Union level. We should not expect national implementation to cure all the defects in European Community measures.

(e) Externalisation

The fourth trend is toward greater externalisation of asylum and migration control. This means that accountability mechanisms should also develop which may break the hold of interior ministries on these issues. It may prove difficult to engage other ministries and councils in immigration and asylum issues, but as funding spent on these projects continues to increase, this may well change. Thus the new AENEAS programme is devoted specifically to European Union cooperation on financial and technical assistance to third countries in the area of migration and asylum, with a very sizeable budget of €120 million.[129] There are moves at European Union level to cooperate on migration control matters with states with dubious human rights records such as Libya. These developments may well arouse interest beyond the corridors of the Department of Justice, Equality and Law Reform. One could expect a growing interest in the Department of Foreign Affairs in European Union immigration and asylum matters. However, whether this will translate into a greater role for the Joint Oireachtas Committee on Foreign Affairs remains to be seen. As Tonra points out in his chapter in this book, foreign policy is not traditionally subject to significant parliamentary control.

(f) The Constitutional Treaty

The Constitutional Treaty would have provided an enhanced role for national parliaments by imposing an obligation under European Union law on the Commission to communicate proposals to them,[130] and by the creation of the subsidiarity early warning mechanism.[131] Both of these mechanisms could be

[128] As regards the Asylum Procedures Directive, see Costello, above, n. 62. On the Refugee Definition Directive, see G. Gilbert, "Is Europe Living Up to Its Obligations to Refugees?" (2004) *European Journal of International Law* 963, at 979–980.

[129] Parliament and Council Regulation 491/2004 of 10 March 2004 establishing a programme for financial and technical assistance to third countries in areas of migration and asylum [2004] OJ L80/1.

[130] See the Protocol on the Role of National Parliaments in the European Union annexed to the Treaty establishing a Constitution for Europe.

[131] As to which, see the Protocol on the Application of the Principles of Subsidiarity and Proportionality annexed to the Treaty establishing a Constitution for Europe.

put into effect without Treaty amendment, however, and it appears that tentative steps in that direction have been taken. In February 2005, the Commission indicated that it would increase its direct communication with national parliaments, and in particular, communicate its proposals directly to them.[132] At its meeting in London in October, 2005, COSAC decided that national parliaments which were willing to take on subsidiarity scrutiny would do so. Notwithstanding the absence of any legal obligation on European Union institutions to heed national parliaments' views on subsidiarity, COSAC took the view that national parliaments should take on this role.[133] It is understood that at the time of writing all but the Italian parliament intend to undertake this scrutiny.[134]

The Constitutional Treaty would also have brought about significant changes as regards the area of freedom, security, and justice.[135] The Constitutional Treaty would have applied the 'ordinary legislative procedure' (that is, qualified majority vote in the Council combined with co-decision with the European Parliament) to policy-making in the immigration and asylum fields, as well as to the criminal law aspects of the area of freedom, security, and justice. The impact on immigration and asylum policy-making would not have been as dramatic, in the light of the decision adopted in December 2004

---

[132] Commission Press Release, "The European Commission strengthens its relations with national parliaments – a greater voice for parliaments is a greater voice to Europe's citizens" (17 February 2005).

[133] See *COSAC Contribution Addressed to the EU Institutions* (Thirty-Fourth COSAC meeting, London 9–11 October 2005), para. 4 of which (entitled "Subsidiarity and proportionality") states that

> "those national parliaments which wish to participate shall conduct a subsidiarity and proportionality check on a forthcoming EU legislative proposal or proposals, developing their existing scrutiny role as recognised in the Protocol on the Role of National Parliaments attached to the Treaty of Amsterdam, allowing them to test their systems for reaching decisions on subsidiarity and proportionality, enabling an assessment of the justifications presented by the Commission and stressing to the Commission national parliaments' role in relation to subsidiarity and proportionality".

[134] See M. Beunderman, "National Parliaments to show the Commission the Yellow Card". (See European Observer, http://euobserver.com/18/2036.)

[135] See N. Walker, "Freedom, Security and Justice" in B. de Witte (ed.), *Ten Reflections on the Constitutional Treaty for Europe* (Robert Schuman Centre, Florence, 2003), 163. On the impact of these changes on national parliaments, see COSAC Secretariat, *Third Bi-Annual Report: Developments in European Union Procedures and Practice Relevant to Parliamentary Scrutiny* (Thirty-Third COSAC meeting, Luxembourg, 17–18 May 2005). Chapter 5 of the report is entitled "The Role of National Parliaments in the Area of Freedom, Security and Justice under the Constitutional Treaty".

to shift to qualified majority voting for decisions under Title IV of the EC Treaty.[136] Moreover, even under the Constitutional Treaty, the Irish and British opt-outs would have remained.

Some specific roles for national parliaments were foreseen. On one view, these were an encouraging development in that they established direct lines of information between European Union bodies and national parliaments. However, they tended to require reporting to national parliaments, without any necessary increase in the powers of national parliaments to act on the information provided.[137] Thus Article III-260 provided for the creation of a mutual evaluation mechanism of measures relating to the area of freedom, security and justice. Under this mechanism, member states, in collaboration with the Commission, could conduct evaluations of the implementation of Union policies, in particular in order to facilitate full application of the principle of mutual recognition. Under Article III-261, a standing committee would have been set up within the Council "in order to ensure that operational cooperation on internal security is promoted and strengthened within the Union". There was an explicit requirement under the same Article that national parliaments be informed of its proceedings. Crucially, the Constitutional Treaty would also have granted national parliaments, together with the European Parliament, a role in monitoring the activities of Europol[138] and Eurojust.[139]

Arguably this did not go far enough. In its report on Europol,[140] the House of Lords European Union Committee recommended the establishment of a joint committee of members of national parliaments and the European Parliament in order to scrutinise the work of Europol. Similarly, as regards Eurojust, the current absence of accountability mechanisms has also been criticised, and the establishment of a similar such joint committee proposed.[141] The House of Lords Report on the European

---

[136] Council Decision 2004/927, above, n. 28.

[137] Hence, see the negative appraisal by Statewatch, *The EU Constitution and Justice and Home Affairs: the Accountability Gap* (Statewatch, London, 2003) available at www.statewatch.org/news/ 2003/aug/ constitution-jha.pdf.

[138] Art. III-276 of the Constitutional Treaty.

[139] Art. III-273 of the Constitutional Treaty.

[140] House of Lords Select Committee on the European Union, *Europol's Role in Fighting Crime* (Fifth Report of 2002–2003 Session, HL 23).

[141] House of Select Committee on the European Union, *Judicial Cooperation in the European Union: the Role of Eurojust* (Twenty-Third Report of 2003–2004 Session, HL 138).

Border Guard also emphasises the need for specific accountability mechanisms.[142] In particular, it recommended that "any EU body responsible for border controls should have a clear legal basis and be subject to detailed accountability and data protection safeguards".[143] In addition, it was suggested that joint operations should be subject to clear legal rules.[144]

6. Conclusions

The opt-in mechanism under the Amsterdam Protocol on the Position of the United Kingdom and Ireland has yet to develop into a robust scrutiny mechanism. At the time of writing, the result of the United Kingdom's challenge to its exclusion from the Borders Agency and Passports Regulations case is awaited. It will clarify the location of the dividing line between the Protocol Integrating the Schengen Acquis into the Framework of the European Union and the Amsterdam Protocol on the Position of the United Kingdom and Ireland, with considerable implications for the extent of Ireland's selective participation. The three-month time limit for opting in, together with the government's tendency to act at the last minute, has thwarted the development of the requirement for Oireachtas approval into a robust scrutiny reserve. However, there is still room for political practice and constitutional conventions to develop around the opt-in, so as to create a conditional approval mechanism. Ministerial accountability would thereby be enhanced. A further important development, lacking in the initial period, would be synergy between the opt-in mechanism and the general scrutiny system. An encouraging recent development in this regard has been the referral of proposals by the Sub-Committee on European Scrutiny to the Joint Committee on Justice, Equality, Defence and Women's Rights, in advance of any decision on

[142] House of Lords Select Committee on the European Union, *Proposals for a European Border Guard* (Twenty-Ninth Report of 2002–2003 Session, HL 133).

[143] *Ibid.*, para. 84.

[144] *Ibid.*, para. 87. The Visa Information System has not been subject to a formal report by the House of Lords European Union Committee. However, the chairman of that committee has corresponded with the relevant minister in relation to the system (see House of Lords Select Committee on the European Union, Correspondence with Ministers (Fourth Report of 2005–2006 Session, HL), letter No. 208) explaining that its decision to refrain from full scrutiny of the Visa Information System report was due to the United Kingdom's position of remaining out, but that it would keep the matter under review.

opting in. This occurred, for example, on 1 July 2004, in relation to the ARGO programme,[145] and the Borders Code.[146]

At present, however, the relevant minister and departmental officials are relied upon to inform Oireachtas committees of the contents of a proposal and to make the case for opting in. Moreover, even in the Joint Committees on European Affairs and on Justice, Equality, Defence and Women's Rights, discussion has tended to focus on domestic or local aspects of policy. This is a manifestation of the typical informational asymmetry between government and parliaments in European Union matters. Some simple measures could be put in place to redress the balance and enhance the quality of information and debate. First, other bodies and individuals with interest and expertise in the field should be invited to testify more regularly, particularly on programmatic documents, such as the Hague Programme; on individual measures of major importance, such as the Long-Term Residents Directive; and on matters which are sensitive from a human rights perspective, such as the Asylum Procedures Directive. Such a deliberative process might also increase media interest in committee proceedings, and thereby increase parliamentarians' incentive to take an active role. Secondly, the Oireachtas should exploit the new willingness of the Commission to communicate directly with national parliaments, both through ongoing communication and by inviting Commission officials to testify. Thirdly, an attempt should be made to link in with debates in other national parliaments, in particular in the United Kingdom, given the similar position of the United Kingdom and Ireland insofar as concerns the Amsterdam Protocol on the Position of the United Kingdom and Ireland.

---

[145] The ARGO Programme is a new programme for administrative cooperation in the fields of external borders, visas, asylum and immigration since the Odysseus programme has come to an end (given that its budget was exhausted in 2001). This programme covers the period from 1 January, 2002 to 31 December, 2006. The programme's objectives are to promote cooperation between national administrations responsible for implementing Community rules and to ensure that proper account is taken of the Community dimension in their actions; to promote the uniform application of Community law; to increase the transparency and overall effectiveness of the actions taken by the national authorities. Council Decision 2002/463 adopting an action programme for administrative cooperation in the fields of external borders, visa, asylum, and immigration (ARGO programme). The proposal is the revision of the original programme, COM (2004) 384 Proposal for a Council Decision amending Decision No. 2002/463 adopting an action programme for administrative cooperation in the fields of external borders, visas, asylum and immigration (ARGO programme). This decision was adopted: Council Decision 2004/867, [2004] OJ L371/48.

[146] COM (2004) 391, Proposal for a Council Regulation establishing a Community Code on the rules governing the movement of persons across borders.

To date, where Ireland has not opted into negotiations on proposals under Title IV of the EC Treaty, little parliamentary scrutiny has taken place. This is problematic, for it is not merely decisions to opt in that warrant scrutiny. So too do decisions not to opt in, and for several reasons. First, European Community law-making tends to be programmatic, so that measures form policy packages. Staying out may be a bad policy choice. This may well be the case as regards the Receptions Conditions Directive (if Ireland decides to opt in after this measure has been adopted by the Council, the role of the Oireachtas role will be reduced to that of a mere rubber stamp). Secondly, selective participation may result in substantive imbalance in domestic policy, as is arguably the case when Ireland participates in immigration control measures, but not immigrants' rights ones. Thirdly, not opting in may create tensions with other European Union member states, as Ireland may be perceived as a free-rider. Arguably such tensions have fuelled the dispute in relation to participation in the European Borders Agency. Fourthly, scrutiny of the decision not to opt in may focus political attention on important policy issues, which otherwise may not find space on the domestic agenda. The Directive on the Residence Permit for Victims of Trafficking may be one such measure. Finally, scrutiny is required to assess whether Ireland is keeping to its Amsterdam Declaration to participate 'to the maximum extent compatible with the maintenance of its Common Travel Area with the United Kingdom'. It may well be that there are good reasons for Ireland not to opt in to particular measures, but such a decision warrants Oireachtas scrutiny just as much as does an opt-in.

The current opt-in and scrutiny mechanisms are reactive, and depend largely on the issue of formal proposals. The development of a more proactive role, which is capable of scrutinising the multifarious forms of European policy-making and operational activity requires considerable resources. Where European bodies emerge, like the Borders Agency and the Visa Information System, particular accountability mechanisms must be developed to provide not only information to national parliaments, but also genuine accountability. Engaging with European Community policy processes requires greater upstream scrutiny, particularly in light of the trend towards greater operational cooperation and informal policy coordination. Systems emerge gradually, and even the European Parliament can at times find itself side-lined, as the looming battle over the Visa Information System demonstrates. Rather than act in a solely reactive manner, the Oireachtas needs to take on a proactive role, a considerable challenge for an already weak and under-resourced parliament. Committees must undertake scrutiny of general policy documents, such as the Hague Programme, as well as individual legislative measures. Greater downstream scrutiny is also required. The contrast between the approach to the Asylum Procedures Directive in Ireland and the United Kingdom exemplifies the challenge of keeping abreast with the pace of legislative drafting in the Council.

The Oireachtas has to date provided a particularly weak check on executive power in the policy area which forms the subject of this chapter, with no significant legislative role. In addition, it has lacked the institutional capacity to take on robust European scrutiny. In the light of the pace of change at the European Union and domestic constitutional level during the period under review, it is unsurprising that the developments in control and scrutiny by the Oireachtas have been incremental and fitful. However, there can be no doubt but that the period examined is one of considerable institutional learning, as the time devoted to European Union asylum and immigration issues on both the floor of the houses and in Oireachtas committees has increased greatly. This is in itself a considerable improvement.

9.
Democratic Oversight over the Irish Government in the Field of the Common Foreign and Security Policy

Ben Tonra[1]

> "I am convinced that the new arrangements, when compared with the practice in other member States, if properly implemented, have the potential to place us at the top of the European league table in terms of parliamentary oversight of EU activities"
>
> (Irish Foreign Minister Brian Cowen, 17 July 2002).

1. Introduction

Parliaments have traditionally had some difficulty in maintaining effective democratic oversight over foreign policy. While they often have very specific entrenched constitutional rights in terms of declarations of war or the ratification of international treaties,[2] parliaments usually face political and administrative restrictions when monitoring day-to-day foreign policy. This is due, first, to the fact that foreign policy rarely results in formal legislation. Secondly, it is usually seen as being an area which is the special prerogative of the executive. Thirdly, it is often seen as impinging on national security and national interests in such a way that, it is argued, the normal rules of party politics should not apply. Fourthly, it is generally agreed that the arts of diplomacy are best practised outside the glare of direct public scrutiny.

For all of these reasons, parliaments find themselves struggling for influence over foreign policy. It is precisely because it is so important, however, that

---

[1] Jean Monnet Professor of EU Foreign, Security and Defence Policy, Geary Institute, University College Dublin. This chapter is, in part, based upon research conducted for a monograph by the author entitled *Global Citizen and European Republic – Irish Foreign Policy in Transition* published in 2007 by Manchester University Press.

[2] See, for example, Art. 28.3 of Bunreacht na hÉireann.

there is an ongoing need to ensure that foreign policy, outside the framework of treaty ratification, commands democratic support and is held to the highest standards of accountability.

It must be acknowledged at this point that the Oireachtas has not had a strong record in this regard. Despite formal constitutional provisions which indicate otherwise, the political reality is that the Oireachtas is effectively the servant of the executive rather than its master.[3] The combination of powerful party whips, a tradition of comparatively strong majority-holding governments (single and multi-party), an electoral system which is seen to reward assiduous constituency work over legislative activity and, overall, a comparatively weak committee structure, has traditionally undermined the capacity of the Oireachtas to hold the executive to account. Moreover, the distance which traditionally exists between foreign policy and effective parliamentary oversight has exacerbated the scale of the problem facing the Oireachtas in its oversight of Irish foreign policy.[4] Indeed, in 1990 one former Minister for Foreign Affairs described the Oireachtas as being among "the least developed legislature(s) in the European Community" and noted that it was unique in Europe in having no parliamentary committee to consider foreign affairs.[5]

The Joint Oireachtas Committee on Secondary Legislation of the European Communities, established in 1973, was the first parliamentary foray into what might – at a stretch – be seen as foreign policy. However, despite periodic attempts, it was not until 1993 that a Joint Committee on Foreign Affairs was finally established. This committee was composed of the respective Dáil and Seanad select committees. Special provision was also made for Members of the European Parliament (MEPs) and parliamentarians from the Assembly of the Council of Europe to attend and speak, albeit without voting rights.

2. The Joint Oireachtas Committee on Foreign Affairs

The Joint Committee on Foreign Affairs quickly established its own precedents and working methods. The committee's strengths flowed from its ability to set its own agenda, to review policy in greater detail than was

---

[3] M. Gallagher, "Parliament" in J. Coakley and M. Gallagher (eds.), *Politics in the Republic of Ireland*, Fourth edition, (PSAI Press and Routledge, Dublin and London, 2005), at 126.

[4] P. Keatinge, *The Formulation of Irish Foreign Policy* (Dublin, Institute of Public Administration, 1973).

[5] Peter Barry, TD, Dáil Debates, vol. 396, col. 1638 (6 March 1990).

possible in either the Dáil or the Seanad, and the fact that the Committee – in general – operated in a non-partisan way. According to members however,[6] the committee suffered from weaknesses rooted in its limited resources, its consequent dependence upon the executive, the broad and shallow nature of its agenda, and its failure successfully to engage with the public through the media.

In 2001, the Committee was composed of twenty Oireachtas members (fourteen from the Dáil and six from the Seanad). It had no substantial secretariat, no independent research staff and, until the appointment in 2000 of a parliamentary law officer, it had to rely upon the government's own Attorney General for any legal advice. The senior staff that worked with the Committee were often on a temporary secondment from the Department of Foreign Affairs. The committee could offer staff no long-term job security or career path, (its life span being limited to the five-year maximum of the Dáil itself). The situation is not very different today. In 2005, the Committee has seventeen Oireachtas members (eleven from the Dáil and six from the Seanad) with a small secretariat and policy staff that remains – according to its chairperson – insufficient for the committee to conduct its work and make its full contribution.[7]

Today, the Foreign Affairs Committee is a comparatively active committee, meeting weekly either in full plenary session or in the format of one of two of its sub-committees (*viz.*, the Sub-Committee on Development Cooperation and the Sub-Committee on Human Rights). The Committee also has a busy programme of more informal activities; private meetings with visiting foreign delegations, study visits abroad, and attending international conferences.

As acknowledged in its own annual report,[8] the Committee's agenda is essentially driven by outside events – crises, conflicts and wars. The Committee will regularly invite analysts and/or advocates to offer their expertise or perspective on particular issues and will engage in frequently robust exchanges of views both among themselves and with invited experts. Regrettably, as detailed and substantive as such discussions may be, they

[6] This information was obtained from interviews conducted by the writer with nine members of the Committee during 2001 and 2002.
[7] Annual Report of the Joint Committee on Foreign Affairs, 2003–2004, available at www.oireachtas.ie/viewpda.asp?fn=/documents/Committees29thDail/CommitteeReports2005/document5.doc.
[8] *Ibid.*

rarely engage the domestic media and so are unlikely to attract much attention. While the Committee's agenda is necessarily broad and perhaps excessively reactive, a number of themes may be identified in its work. These include countries and regions in conflict and crisis, breaches of human rights, humanitarian disasters and development cooperation, and issues pertaining to the European Union, the United Nations, and Northern Ireland. As indicated by the Committee's sub-committee structure, development and human rights issues predominate. The Committee has recently published several substantive reports on Ethiopia,[9] Uganda,[10] and on the Millennium Development Goals.[11]

The Foreign Affairs Committee also involves itself in a wide range of European issues. Through its reviews of international issues, the Committee will frequently find itself reflecting upon how, why and to what end the European Union is contributing to international peace and security. This frequently brings up the role of Common Foreign and Security Policy mechanisms. The committee has also identified a number of European issues for attention in its work programmes. In 2003, for example, the committee sought to consider a range of what it termed thematic European issues, such as the external relations of the European Union and the European Security and Defence Policy, the Convention on the Future of Europe, relations with European Union candidate states, relations with the western Balkans, and relations between Cyprus and Turkey. In addition, the Committee set itself the task of considering those European Union legislative proposals referred to it by the Joint Committee on European Affairs[12] as well as the agenda of General Affairs and External Relations Council meetings and those of the European Council – and this all while "bearing in mind the need to avoid overlap with the Joint Committee on European Affairs".[13]

3. The Joint Oireachtas Committee on European Affairs

The Foreign Affairs Committee was originally given the work of the earlier Joint Oireachtas Committee on the Secondary Legislation of the European

---

[9] *Project Ethiopia*, Joint Committee on Foreign Affairs, July 2003, available at www.irlgov.ie/oireachtas/Committees-29th-D%C3%A1il/jcfa-debates/ProjectEthiopia.pdf.

[10] *Project Uganda*, Report of the Joint Committee on Foreign Affairs, July 2004, available at www.oireachtas.ie/viewpda.asp?fn=/documents/Committees29thDail/jcfa/Project_Uganda.pdf.

[11] *Honouring our Commitments to the Developing World*, Report of the Joint Committee on Foreign Affairs, January 2005, available at www.oireachtas.ie/viewpda.asp?fn=/documents/Committees29th Dail/foreignAffairReports/jcfa-0105Developing_World.pdf.

[12] As to which, see the text below.

[13] Oireachtas Committee on Foreign Affairs' Work Programme 2002/2003, p. 5, available at www.irlgov.ie/oireachtas/Committees-29th-D%C3%A1il/ForeignAffairsReports/FAwp2002.doc.

Communities. By 1995, however, it was judged that this division of labour was unsatisfactory and a separate Joint Committee on European Affairs was established.[14] The remit of this latter committee was also extended beyond European Union legislative scrutiny to include any matter arising from Irish membership of the European Union. In addition, this committee was given the mandate to represent the Oireachtas in meetings and activities of the inter-parliamentary Conference of European Affairs Committees (COSAC) within the European Union.

The scrutiny of the Committee as originally constituted was somewhat less than systematic.[15] In its annual report laid before the Dáil in February 2001, the chairperson of the European Affairs Committee noted that such was the volume of European Union legislation and the paucity of Committee resources, that consultants had been employed to sift through European Union legislation and draw to the Committee's attention matters which might be germane for consideration.[16] Even so, consideration of that Committee's report was nearly one year overdue. While the Committee was busy with a range of pertinent debates and the production of significant reports on such issues as European Union enlargement[17] and economic and monetary union,[18] there remained only a cursory system of national parliamentary oversight of European Union legislation. Even that was problematic, for as one former member of that committee put it, the process 'was one of the most turgid, tedious experiences I have ever had'.[19] Nor was he enamoured of its relevance, observing that

> "for the three or four meetings we had, we were confronted with tomes of draft regulations, statutory instruments and so on, usually inches thick, which some unfortunate civil servant had been asked to go through to try to identify some of the major issues that might arise. It is fair to say that nobody on the Committee felt it was a worthwhile process. Certainly

---

[14] See in more detail regarding this committee, the chapters in this volume by Lia O'Hegarty, Katherine Meenan and Gavin Barrett.

[15] Chairman's Report, National Forum on Europe: the second phase of work of the National Forum on Europe, February to March 2002, p. 31, available at www.forumoneurope.ie/index.asp?locID=256&docID=596.

[16] Dáil Debates, vol. 530, col. 1029 (15 February 2001).

[17] *The Enlargement of the European Union*, Report of the Oireachtas Joint Committee on European Affairs, 1 May 2002.

[18] *Report of the Joint Committee on European Affairs on Economic and Monetary Union*, Report of the Oireachtas Joint Committee on European Affairs, 20 April 2000.

[19] Mr Michael McDowell, TD, Dáil Debates, vol. 539, col. 80 (22 June 2001).

none of the unfortunate civil servants who were charged with doing most of the work involved thought it was worthwhile and, other than providing a fig leaf in terms of accountability, it was a worthless process and one we should not repeat".[20]

This contrasted sharply with the practice of other states where, whether informally (as in Austria, Finland, Spain, and Sweden) or more formally (as in Denmark, France, and Germany),[21] parliament could exercise significant oversight of a minister going into a Council meeting. The Oireachtas was clearly at the lower end of such a spectrum – with no formal parliamentary scrutiny reserve and only the most rudimentary structures even for the purposes of exercising a review and referral function.

Of course, in Common Foreign and Security Policy matters and European Security and Defence Policy matters, the position was even worse, since decisions in these areas did not usually lead to the traditional European legislative proposals for instruments such as directives and regulations. Instead, they produced proposals for joint actions in a variety of forms; from simple political declarations, to diplomatic *démarches*, to the use of sanctions or inducements, up to the use of military force for peacekeeping purposes.[22] A further complicating factor was that both the European Affairs Committee and the Foreign Affairs Committee exercised a nominal jurisdiction over these matters with no clear division of labour between them.

As a result, many Dáil deputies interviewed by this writer felt that their committee work on foreign policy was rarely if ever a factor in Irish foreign policy formulation. They believed that at best such efforts were treated "with respect and politeness".[23] For some, the fault was seen to rest at least in part with the committees themselves, which flitted from one issue to the next with little in the way of original research and no concrete follow-up. Most other members, however, felt that the media, both print and broadcast, paid the Oireachtas as a whole very little attention, and parliamentary committees even less.

---

[20] *Ibid.*.

[21] See in more detail in this regard, the chapter in this volume by Andreas Maurer.

[22] These were defined by the Western European Union's 1992 Petersberg Declaration and incorporated into Art. 17 of the Treaty of European Union by the EU's Amsterdam Summit. They are: humanitarian and rescue tasks, peacekeeping tasks and tasks of combat forces in crisis management, including peacemaking.

[23] Quoted from interviews conducted by the writer during 2001 and 2002 with members of the Committee.

More traditional mechanisms of parliamentary oversight over the Common Foreign and Security Policy reflected many of the same weaknesses evident in the work of the committees. The use made of parliamentary questions in the Dáil for example, highlighted the fact that members' interests tended to be driven by media interest and that of non-governmental organisations rather than any sustained effort to drive foreign policy in any particular direction. Moreover, with a handful of exceptions, comparatively few deputies made any connection between national foreign policy and the Common Foreign and Security Policy.[24]

In sum, while by the end of 2004, the scope for parliamentary scrutiny over foreign policy had grown with the development of a rudimentary committee structure, there was no evidence that members of the Oireachtas had succeeded in penetrating either the national or the European Union foreign policy process. Certainly, the potential of the parliamentary committees had not yet been fully exploited.

4. Post-Nice Reforms

The weakness of the Oireachtas in scrutinising Irish ministers and European Union policy became a significant issue during the 2001 Nice Treaty debate. While the failures of the Oireachtas to exercise effective national parliamentary scrutiny could only be ascribed to the Oireachtas itself, the issue became bound up in a wider and more general critique of the Union's own democratic deficit. Thus, with the defeat in June 2001 of the referendum to amend the Constitution to permit ratification of the Nice Treaty, effective legislative oversight became a focus of high-level political concern.

In a major speech in the aftermath of the Nice Treaty defeat, the then Attorney General noted that not only was parliamentary oversight necessary to secure greater public confidence – it was, in itself, a necessary corrective to poor democratic practice. He insisted:

> "that an Irish Minister should be technically at large free to negotiate a regulation or directive which as a matter of European and Irish law the Oireachtas is absolutely bound to accept is a striking proposition".[25]

---

[24] The above observations are based on a comprehensive review by the writer of all parliamentary questions posed to the Taoiseach, the Minister for Foreign Affairs, and the Minster for Defence in the period 2004–2005.

[25] Address by Attorney General Michael McDowell to the Institute of European Affairs, 18 June, 2001.

He added that

> "it is remarkable, therefore, that present legislative practice has imposed no prior obligation of consultation in routine legislative matters and an obligation to seek at least the consent of the Oireachtas where such a measure would inevitably control or delimit Constitutional guarantees".[26]

The Labour Party moved quickly. Labour leader Ruairi Quinn, on 21 June 2001 proposed a Private Members' Bill – the European Union Bill 2001 – which would have codified a system of strict parliamentary oversight over European Union legislation and, most significantly, would also have defined the terms under which Ireland might contribute military forces through the Common Foreign and Security Policy for the European Rapid Reaction Force. In introducing this draft legislation, Deputy Quinn noted that:

> "much of the problem of accountability, and thereby the legitimacy of the European Union, lies within our domestic law and not within the inadequacies of the European Union".[27]

Nonetheless, his view was that addressing this issue was a step which would strengthen Irish democracy as well as make a contribution to the subsequent ratification of the Nice Treaty – as indeed subsequently proved to be the case.

The Labour Party Bill provided a set of procedures whereby legislative measures proposed by the Council of Ministers – in any of the three pillars of the European Union – would have to be set before the Oireachtas for formal consultation and consideration. Critically, the Bill provided that neither ministers nor officials could commit themselves to support measures in the Council or its sub-committees without the prior consideration of the appropriate Oireachtas committee. Committees would be provided with appropriate briefing material from the responsible Department and be free to conduct their own enquiries into the substance of the matter – either by written or oral evidence. Any subsequent parliamentary decision to reject a proposed measure would be binding upon the government.

The Bill also contained measures unique to handling Common Foreign and Security Policy matters. Thus it provided that the Bill's requirements as to minimum periods of advance notice of, and minimum periods for

---

[26] *Ibid.*.

[27] Dáil Debates, vol. 539, col. 72 (26 June 2001).

consideration of, any proposed measures could be set aside where a Common Foreign and Security Policy issue was time-sensitive or where a measure's confidential nature precluded advance notice. In such circumstances the government would simply have had to lay before both houses a statement of the agreed joint action, the reasons for action, and the grounds of urgency.

In addition, the Bill set out to amend the Defence Acts so as to provide for the participation of Irish defence forces in the European Rapid Reaction Force. Other than in very exceptional circumstances, existing legislation required Dáil approval for the dispatch of any armed contingent of the defence forces of more than twelve personnel as part of an "international United Nations force" authorised by the Security Council or the General Assembly.[28] Legislation provided for no other contingency under which armed personnel of the defence forces might be sent out of the State – nor did it allow for the training of defence force units overseas. The Labour Bill proposed to amend this situation by providing that military units could be despatched for service or training outside the State under the command of either the European Rapid Reaction Force or the United Nations, but only where both the United Nations and the Dáil sanctioned such service.

In his response to the Bill, the then Minister for Foreign Affairs, Mr Brian Cowen TD, noted that the Oireachtas had substantial – but as yet unexercised – oversight powers, but he agreed that there was considerable scope for improvement, not least in view of the sheer scale of European Union legislative proposals but also in view of their technical complexity. He argued, however, that the Bill did not distinguish between different decision-making procedures where implementation deadlines differed considerably. He also argued that the Bill did not refer to other measures falling short of legislation but which deserved appropriate consideration, such as Council statements, declarations, and resolutions. He also noted that both speed and flexibility was sometimes necessary to successful negotiations and that too strict a supervisory regime might tie the hands of ministers to such an extent that the national interest in such fast-moving negotiations might suffer as a result. In sum, the Minister sought to amend the Bill in such a way as would maximise its supervisory scope while maintaining the greatest possible latitude for ministers. In the Minister's own words the objective was:

> "an optimal level of accountability which ensures effective parliamentary oversight, while at the same time enabling Ministers and their

[28] See s. 2 of the Defence (Amendment) (No. 2) Act 1960.

representatives to operate within the Council with the degree of responsiveness and flexibility necessary to ensure the interests of the country are fully protected in any fast moving negotiating process".[29]

Regarding section 5 of the Bill, which dealt specifically with the Common Foreign and Security Policy, the Minister expressed himself to in be "full listening mode". Noting that he had answered more than 300 parliamentary questions in the last twelve months on Ireland's approach to European Union foreign policy questions and participated in a range of debates with both the European Affairs Committee and the Foreign Affairs Committee, he insisted that he was open to any proposal that would increase public knowledge of the Common Foreign and Security Policy. He also welcomed the Labour Party's approach to thc European Rapid Reaction Force and their efforts to reconcile Irish participation therein with requirements for a United Nations mandate.

Following the May 2002 general election, the government – which had been returned to power – swiftly introduced its own procedural changes in July. These were described as being 'two-pronged' and designed to address both stages of the European legislative process. They provided both for departmental reports on proposals for legislation being laid before the Oireachtas and for a regular system of pre-Council briefing of committees. The former gave the Oireachtas the opportunity to flag issues of concern and to contribute – if even at arms length – in the early development of European Union legislation. For their part, the pre-Council briefings, which had occurred on a more ad hoc basis previously, were now formalised so that – at least in theory – committees might contribute to the thinking of the relevant minister(s) if not – as under the Danish model – direct his or her position in the Council. The government also indicated that it would place some of these changes on an appropriate legislative footing, based upon the Labour-sponsored legislation which remained at the Committee Stage in the Dáil.[30] According to the then government Chief Whip,[31] Mr Seamus Brennan TD,

"the Dáil itself is now undergoing a historic reform of the working of its own systems ... at key times there is a requirement to take a fundamental look at how the system works and I think that key time in Europe has now

[29] Brian Cowen TD, Minister for Foreign Affairs, Dáil Debates, vol. 539, col. 88 (26 June 2001).
[30] Brian Cowen TD, Minister for Foreign Affairs, Dáil Debates, vol. 554, col. 11 (4 September 2002).
[31] This post carried responsibility for, *inter alia,* parliamentary reform.

arrived .... At the heart of these Dáil reform measures is the question of scrutinising EU legislation".[32]

When the European Union (Scrutiny) Bill 2002 finally emerged from Committee Stage in October 2002, it bore only a familial resemblance to the legislation that had initially been placed before the previous Dáil. Working together, the Government and the Labour Party had proposed a series of substantive amendments to the Bill in Committee, essentially rewriting it.[33]

In the new section 1, the Bill extended the remit of the original proposal in that it now encompassed joint actions and common positions arising from the Common Foreign and Security Policy in the Second Pillar as well as regulations and directives in the First Pillar and the Third Pillar's framework decisions and conventions. The Bill provided for a 28-day period between a committee's receipt of a Departmental information note on the content and significance of a European Union proposal to a decision by that committee as to whether it wished formally to scrutinise that proposal prior to its adoption by the Council of Ministers.

In section 2, the Bill provided that subsequent to parliamentary scrutiny, "Ministers will have regard to any recommendations made by the Oireachtas". This significantly weakened the more binding provision in the original Labour proposal. This section also provided for cases of urgency, where there was insufficient time to abide by the 28-day requirement – a situation of particular concern as regards Common Foreign and Security Policy issues. In such exceptional circumstances, the minister would be obliged to notify the Oireachtas afterwards with an accompanying statement outlining the proposal's implications for Ireland and the circumstances necessitating its adoption. This section also provided for six-monthly ministerial reports to be submitted before the Oireachtas in relation to measures, proposed measures, and other European Union developments germane to the relevant minister's department (or departments).

Section 3 of the Bill provided for what the Bill termed 'those exceptional occasions' – again, particularly likely to concern Common Foreign and

---

[32] Statement made in the National Forum on Europe on 14 March, 2002, cited in Chairman's Report, National Forum On Europe, *The Second Phase of Work of the National Forum on Europe – February To March 2002* (Stationery Office, Dublin, 2002), available at www.forumoneurope.ie/getFile.asp?FC_ID=25&docID=596.

[33] The Bill in this new form, which is described in the text which follows, was subsequently adopted as the European Union (Scrutiny) Act 2002.

Security Policy measures – when it might be necessary to guarantee confidentiality. In the debate on the Bill, the example which was offered by the Minister of what might constitute such an exceptional occasion was a decision to impose political or economic sanctions. It proposed that where this procedure was invoked, the minister concerned might report to the Oireachtas – subject, again, to any need for ongoing confidentiality. According to the Minister for Foreign Affairs, Mr Brian Cowen TD, this provision was particularly necessary in relation to Common Foreign and Security Policy matters where the publication of information "… in advance could jeopardise the successful implementation of the sanctions".[34] He went on to assure the Dáil that "of course, to the extent possible, information on any such measure would be brought to the attention of the Oireachtas as soon as possible".[35]

5. The Parliamentary Framework for Scrutiny of the Common Foreign and Security Policy – A Summary

Significant parts of the new procedures for Oireachtas oversight of the European Union were placed on a statutory footing with the final passage – on 23 October 2002 – of the European Union (Scrutiny) Act 2002. As a result, there are now two aspects to parliamentary scrutiny of European Union business.

(a) Scrutiny of Legislative and Other Proposals Emanating from the European Union

As a matter of law, the Government must now set before the European Affairs Committee's Sub-Committee on European Scrutiny all European Union legislative proposals, as well as information notes which set forth their content, aims, and national implications. The Sub-Committee then systematically examines these and decides which require further detailed scrutiny by the relevant Oireachtas sectoral committee and which either require no such further scrutiny, or simply need to be noted for information.

When the sectoral committees in turn receive such a request from the Sub-Committee, they are free to determine whether or not they wish to conduct a formal review process – which might entail hearings of oral or written testimony from various experts and interested parties.

[34] Statement made by the Minister to the Dáil on 9 October 2002 and which is reproduced at www.gov.ie/debates-02/9Oct/Sect7.htm.
[35] *Ibid.*.

(b) Scrutiny of Meetings of the Council of Ministers

The second track of parliamentary scrutiny is based not on legislation, but on agreed procedures of the Houses of the Oireachtas and relates to preparations for meetings of the Council of Ministers and summits of the European Council.[36] Prior to each, the relevant attending minister will now, at the request of an appropriate committee, come before the members of that committee to discuss in detail the agenda for that Council meeting and the Irish position *vis-à-vis* those agenda items. No obligation exists for the minister to take the advice of the committee.

Thus the final package of post-Nice reforms included (a) the European Union (Scrutiny) Act 2002, providing for formal scrutiny of a wide range of European Union legislation and other measures – including Common Foreign and Security Policy joint actions and common positions; (b) a more formal system of ministerial briefings before Oireachtas committees so as to brief them on European Union developments on a regular basis; and (c) the provision of information notes on all Commission white and green papers.[37]

(c) Parliamentary Oversight and the Common Foreign and Security Policy

In practice, exercising democratic accountability over the Common Foreign and Security Policy is problematic. In the first instance, there is an inevitable tension between those arguing for democratic accountability to be exercised at European Union level and those who insist that it can only be effectively conducted at national level. Secondly, the lines of demarcation and political control between the First Pillar Community institutions and the new foreign policy structures which were first proposed in the Constitutional Treaty (the European Union Foreign Minister, the External Action Service, the European Defence Agency, etc.) would be unclear.[38] While, for example, the European Union Foreign Minister proposed in the Constitutional Treaty was to be accountable to the Council of Ministers for his or her Common Foreign and

[36] These agreed procedures are constituted by understandings, rather than formal written agreements, but they have been outlined in the Dáil. (See Dáil Debates, vol. 554, col. 575 (9 October, 2002)).

[37] *Progress Report on the Implementation of an Agreed Programme for Government between Fianna Fáil and the Progressive Democrats. June 2002–June 2003.*

[38] Editor's note: see the introduction to this book in relation to the most recent pre-publication developments concerning the Constitutional Treaty. Note that one change envisaged in the Lisbon Treaty is the substitution of the title 'High Representative of the Union for Foreign Affairs and Security Policy' for that of 'Union Minister for Foreign Affairs'. As with many other changes effected by the Lisbon Treaty, however, this is a change of presentational style from the provisions of the Constitutional Treaty rather than one of substance.

Security Policy and European Security and Defence Policy functions, how could a national foreign minister be held accountable for the actions of any such European Union Foreign Minister? Or, indeed, should the national foreign minister be held accountable in respect of such actions?

This issue is especially acute *vis-à-vis* the European Rapid Reaction Force and its constituent proposed 'battlegroups'. With the transfer of the Western European Union's operational activities to the European Union in 2000, the Western European Union's Parliamentary Assembly (which has Irish members delegated from the Oireachtas) acts *de facto* as an inter-parliamentary forum with a treaty-based watching brief over the European Security and Defence Policy. Even though the link between the Dáil and these policies, insofar as exercised through the WEU Parliamentary Assembly, is tenuous, the Assembly is the only forum that members of the Oireachtas have for interacting with national parliamentary colleagues across Europe to oversee the Union's development of strictly intergovernmental civil and military crisis-management capabilities. The challenge for national parliamentarians in all member states is to devise ways by which this collectively-constructed European Security and Defence Policy can be effectively held to democratic account by 25 or more national parliaments.

There would therefore appear to be at least five challenges in ensuring appropriate democratic accountability in the Common Foreign and Security Policy. First there is the organic challenge. The nature of foreign and security policy is such[39] – that it is traditionally not amenable to the same kind of parliamentary scrutiny procedures as other areas of public policy.

Secondly, there is the bureaucratic challenge to democratic accountability – the existing and proposed division of political and administrative responsibilities for European Union foreign policy (including the Common Foreign and Security Policy and the European Security and Defence Policy) does not lend itself to clear lines of political responsibility and accountability. Parliamentary oversight is therefore divided between European and national levels, and is again divided between individual national parliaments and inter-parliamentary bodies, such as the Western European Union Assembly.

---

[39] See the introduction to this chapter where the peculiar nature of foreign policy as compared to other areas of public policy and the consequent difficulties in exercising democratic oversight have been mentioned.

The third challenge to ensuring appropriate democratic accountability may be termed the 'popular' challenge. A significant danger exists that the connection between European Union citizens and the key tools by which those citizens' values and interests are pursued overseas is lost. On whose behalf will the 'battlegroups' of the European Rapid Reaction Force be acting – that of Europe's citizens or of its national governments?

The fourth challenge is the international one. In employing the mechanisms of the Common Foreign and Security Policy and the European Security and Defence Policy overseas, will the Union act unilaterally or multilaterally? Will the Union place its use of military capacity or other punitive sanctions within the exclusive framework of multilateral institutions?

The fifth challenge is parliamentary in nature, and consists of the lack of standing and/or of resources on the part of national parliaments which are necessary to effective supervision.

Legally, both now and under the Constitutional Treaty (or any successor treaty which might be adopted should it contain equivalent provisions in this field) – the Common Foreign and Security Policy and the European Security and Defence Policy are essentially controlled by the national governments – each of which wields an effective veto over the conduct of any common foreign, security, and defence policy. Traditionally, where national governments retained veto powers over European Union decision-making, the assumption was that national parliaments might exercise effective democratic oversight – or at least oversight which is 'effective' in the relative terms of national parliamentary culture and constitutional tradition. As has been implied above, the spectrum of control exercised was quite wide. However, in the case of the Common Foreign and Security Policy and the European Security and Defence Policy, such oversight has not proved capable of being exercised – despite the very best efforts of (in at least some cases) well-resourced, motivated, and determined national parliaments.

In effect, the vesting of political responsibility amongst national ministers acting collectively – as opposed to within shared European Union political institutions – has netted national governments additional executive power *vis-à-vis* their own national parliaments. Even if there is effective coordination and cooperation between a national parliament and its executive on an opening position going into Common Foreign and Security Policy or European Security and Defence Policy negotiations, there is no way that parliament can exercise scrutiny over the often intricate and inevitably secret diplomatic interplay that results, leaving parliaments faced – essentially – with a *fait accompli*. Moreover, this is not a theoretical danger. We have recently seen significant politico-military decisions being taken at the level of the Council of the European Union without effective parliamentary oversight being exercised at either national, inter-parliamentary, or European Parliament level. Such decisions have included European Union-commanded military intervention operations in Congo and Macedonia.

Even where – for reasons of political tradition and/or constitutional requirement – there is close coordination between a national government and parliament, there is no *collective* parliamentary oversight being exercised. This is because any national government can only be held to account for its own political decisions and the actions (or inaction) of its own military forces. This opens the very real possibility that in a case of negligent or illegal acts on the part of a national military force within a European Union-led operation which adversely impacted upon the mission as a whole and other national forces – there might, in fact be no effective forum of democratic accountability and/or responsibility.

(d) The European Parliament

For its part, the European Parliament has only the most limited capacity to secure information on, and to review the conduct either of the Common Foreign and Security Policy or of the European Security and Defence Policy. While Parliament's limited budgetary powers give it some access to information, all of the key institutions and offices (the European Union Foreign Minister, the External Action Service, the European Defence Agency, *etc.*) lie outside its purview. Parliament has only the capacity to inform, advise, and question. It has no right to initiate or to impact policy or its implementation – and member state governments have worked very hard to ensure that this remains the case.[40]

Even the European Parliament's right to consultation is limited to only the most basic aspects of the Common Foreign and Security Policy – and it is the Council Presidency that decides on the nature and kind of information that is to be provided. While the Commission President and the College of Commissioners are accountable to Parliament, their impact on the Common Foreign and Security Policy and the European Security and Defence Policy is very limited. The Commission participates neither in the formulation of common positions[41] nor in the adoption of joint actions.[42]

---

[40] As, for example, with the creation of 'Athena', a funding mechanism for military operations.

[41] Under Art. 12 of the Treaty on European Union.

[42] Under Art. 13 of the Treaty on European Union.

Should the Constitutional Treaty – or, as is now more likely, a successor treaty with equivalent provisions – ever enter into force, it would do very little to address this situation. The Constitutional Treaty maintained the Parliament's right to question the Presidency and specified that the nominated Special Representatives[43] must brief the Parliament on their own activities. However, Parliament would have been unable to sack the proposed European Union Foreign Minister, even though he would have been a member of the College of Commissioners – for in the event of the Commission resigning or being sacked *en masse*, the European Union Foreign Minister would have remained on, appointed by and responsible to the Council.

(e) National Parliaments

What the Constitutional Treaty did provide for, however, was marginally improved information flows to national parliaments. It required, for example, that Council minutes and agendas be distributed to national parliaments at the same time as they were sent to national governments.[44] Similarly, it required that the Commission distribute legislative and policy details to parliaments when its sends these to the Council and European Parliament,[45] and the elapse of a six-week period was required before such proposals could be discussed by the Council, in order to allow national parliaments to exercise their own scrutiny functions.[46]

The absence of a dialogue between national parliaments and the Union's executive bodies is a significant weakness – undercutting the potential for real democratic accountability. In the only visible innovation by the Constitutional Treaty in this area, the annexed Protocol on the Role of National Parliaments in the European Union provided for the holding of *ad hoc* inter-parliamentary conferences. The Common Foreign and Security Policy/European Security and Defence Policy was specified as an area for attention – but such conferences would have had no decision-making role,

---

[43] It should be noted that already, under Art. 18 of the Treaty on European Union, the Council may, whenever it deems it necessary, appoint a special representative with a mandate in relation to particular policy issues. The function of special representatives is to represent the Union in specified regions and/or countries, usually with the specific task of contributing to EU efforts directed towards regional peace and stability. The power of the Council to appoint special representatives is continued under Art. III-302 of the Constitutional Treaty.

[44] Art. 5 of the Protocol on the Role of National Parliaments in the European Union.

[45] Art. 1 of the Protocol on the Role of National Parliaments in the European Union.

[46] Art. 4 of the Protocol on the Role of National Parliaments in the European Union.

and their opinions and findings would not bind national parliaments or prejudge their positions.[47]

What might also have been provided for were the steps that were proposed by Philippe Morrillon MEP on behalf of the European Parliament's Foreign Affairs, Human Rights, Common Security and Defence Policy Committee.[48] He suggested a specific division of labour between national parliaments and the European Parliament, which would have provided, on the one hand, for the former's responsibility for procurement, expenditure, and the essential decision to participate in a joint European Union military action and, on the other, for the European Parliament to have responsibility for the democratic authorisation of the specific operational mandate of that military force as well as the ultimate conduct and costs of that operation. He also argued that the European Parliament should have responsibility for the democratic oversight of the common defence policy. At the time of writing, however, (and this will remain the case even if the Constitutional Treaty or some successor treaty with equivalent provisions comes into force), the Union continues to operate its Common Foreign and Security Policy and the European Security and Defence Policy on the basis of temporary coalitions of the willing.

It must be borne in mind that national parliaments retain significant responsibilities which will impinge on the capacity of the Union to develop an effective and coherent common foreign, security and defence policy. In most member states, parliaments have final responsibility for deploying troops overseas, for defence procurement decisions and for approving defence budgets. They need to be brought into the European policy loop in a meaningful way if the Union's policy is to be effective and if it is to be grounded in democratic legitimacy.

As noted in the text above, provision was made in the Protocol on the Role of National Parliaments in the European Union which was annexed to the Constitutional Treaty for the European Parliament and the national parliaments to formulate *ad hoc* structures to foster inter-parliamentary cooperation, and in particular in the area of Common Foreign and Security

[47] Art. 10 of the Protocol on the Role of National Parliaments in the European Union.
[48] European Parliament, Foreign Affairs, Human Rights, Common Security and Defence Policy Committee, *Report on the New European Security and Defence Architecture – Priorities and Deficiencies* (EP, Brussels. Provisional 2002/2165 (INI) (27 March 2003)).

Policy and European Security and Defence Policy.[49] According to one former President of the Western European Union Assembly, such inclusive cooperation must provide for meaningful consultation, structures for substantive research and debate, an obligation on the Council to inform and reply to such a body, and channels for informal and confidential dialogue.[50]

6. THE OIREACHTAS AND PARLIAMENTARY OVERSIGHT OF THE COMMON FOREIGN AND SECURITY POLICY

Based upon all of the above – and bearing in mind the acknowledged limitations to parliamentary oversight of foreign policy in general, what has been the track record of Irish parliamentary oversight of the Common Foreign and Security Policy and the European Security and Defence Policy under the revised scrutiny procedures?

(a) The Dáil and the Seanad

From the introduction of new scrutiny procedures and legislation in 2002 to the end of March 2005, there were 76 ministerial replies to questions in the Dáil concerning the substantive nature and development either of the Union's Common Foreign and Security Policy or of the European Security and Defence Policy.[51] In the main, questions or statements by opposition parliamentarians have been critical in tone, and have come from a comparatively small number of deputies. They have queried statements, policy developments, and/or institutional changes that are implicitly or explicitly claimed to undermine or otherwise throw into question Irish foreign policy independence or Ireland's policy of military neutrality. In reply, government members – primarily the Ministers for Foreign Affairs and for Defence, but also including the Taoiseach from time to time – have insisted that these developments are entirely consistent with Irish policy and that no changes to any aspect of that policy are foreseen.

In the period 2002–2005, particular attention was given to changes which had been proposed by the Convention on the Future of Europe and, following the

[49] Art. 10 of the Protocol on the Role of National Parliaments in the European Union.

[50] Speaking notes for Armand De Decker, President of the Assembly of the Western European Union, ISIS-Europe conference on "Tackling the 'Double Democratic Deficit' and Improving the Accountability of ESDP", Brussels, 29 April 2004, as to which see www.dcaf.ch/news/Democratic_Deficit/DeDecker_englishversion.pdf.

[51] This figure does not include any debates which may have occurred in which these topics may have been discussed.

subsequent intergovernmental Conference, included in the resulting Constitutional Treaty. Ministers were called on to explain the implications for Irish foreign and security policy of the proposed European Union Minister for Foreign Affairs, the European External Action Service, the European Defence Agency, proposals for 'solidarity' and 'mutual assistance', and clauses and proposals for 'structured cooperation' in the field of defence. In all instances – and repeatedly, ministers insisted that these proposals would not bear adversely upon the conduct of, or the principles underpinning Irish foreign policy. In that context, ministers repeatedly drew attention to the acknowledgments of Irish neutrality contained in the 2002 Seville Declaration, in the Treaties themselves, and to the constitutional and legislative provisions underpinning Ireland's position on the European Security and Defence Policy and on the Common Foreign and Security Policy.

A second category of questions and statements by TDs[52] sought further clarification of common positions adopted by the European Union and how they impinged on particular crises, or else requested comment where such a common European Union position was absent. In the period under review, the greatest focus was on the Union's inability to construct a common position on the Iraqi crisis and on the subsequent invasion of that country. Other main areas where the role of the Common Foreign and Security Policy was discussed included the Middle East peace process, international efforts to combat terrorism, the defence of human rights in a number of countries, and the ongoing situation in the western Balkans.

A third main category of queries related to the European Security and Defence Policy and later proposals for the establishment of European Union 'battlegroups' as the components of the Union's European Rapid Reaction Force. Most queries were again critical, either requesting various assurances as regards Irish participation therein, or making the case that participation would compromise the principles of Irish foreign and security policy. Only a small minority of these questions or statements advocated participation – although in their replies to all such questions, ministers insisted that Irish participation would be governed by existing requirements for a United Nations mandate and that such participation was wholly consistent with, and indeed necessitated by Ireland's long tradition of peacekeeping.

In sum, the overall picture created is of an active and engaged attempt, albeit on the part of perhaps less than one dozen deputies, to hold the executive to

[52] Teachtaí Dála – members of the Dáil, the lower house of the Irish Parliament.

account on Common Foreign and Security Policy and European Security and Defence Policy issues. In the main, these debates and questions are framed negatively, by which is meant that the Common Foreign and Security Policy and the European Security and Defence Policy are seen as posing some form of threat. A minority of contributions to the debate advocate a more active Irish role and engagement with the Common Foreign and Security Policy and the European Security and Defence Policy or seek greater coherence from the Union and effectiveness in the pursuit of these policies. By and large, however, questions and debates are essentially reactive – demanding from government ministers their reaction or their position *vis-à-vis* developments elsewhere. There is, therefore, no sense in these engagements of any involvement in policy development at either a national or European level.

(b) The Foreign Affairs Committee

In the twenty-ninth Dáil from December 2002 to April 2005, the Foreign Affairs Committee met on a total of 87 occasions. Of these meetings, seventeen were meetings of the Sub-Committee on Human Rights, fourteen were meetings of the Sub-Committee on Development Cooperation, five were meetings of the Dáil's Select Committee, and 51 were meetings of the full Joint Committee.

The nature of the Committee's business was overwhelmingly in the format of expert presentations (frequently from officials of the Department of Foreign Affairs) with a subsequent discussion and/or meeting with a visiting delegation. In total, such meetings represented approximately 80 per cent of the Committee's time. These meeting were substantive, detailed, and ranged across a variety of issues. A number of topics, however, predominated in the committee's work. Thematically, those were development issues – broadly defined, human rights and responses to international crises and sovereignty disputes. Geographically in this period, the Committee was overwhelmingly preoccupied with Africa and the Middle East – with some attention also being given to particular disputes in South-East Asia and the western Balkans. In most if not all of these discussions, the role and policy of the European Union – including the Common Foreign and Security Policy – was a significant feature, with members reflecting on its impact (or lack of same), on Ireland's role therein, or ways in which that policy might be amended or pressed forward. In general terms the critique of European Union policy – and in particular the Common Foreign and Security Policy – was that it did not live up to the expectations placed upon it and that it suffered from a number of structural weaknesses.

For the Foreign Affairs Committee, the overlap of their jurisdiction with that of the European Affairs Committee concerning European Union and Common Foreign and Security Policy questions is a significant issue. There would appear to be two schools of thought among members. The first is that the remit of the Foreign Affairs Committee – including security and defence-related matters – is so broad that it is not possible to exclude European Union issues and that therefore it must take a holistic approach to its responsibilities. For others, however, the European Affairs Committee is seen as the appropriate forum in which to focus on the Union's foreign, security, and defence policies – thus allowing the Foreign Affairs Committee to concentrate more effectively on international issues. Any duplication of efforts, it is also argued, serves only to undermine the effectiveness of the Oireachtas in holding the government to account.[53]

Only the Dáil Select Committee on Foreign Affairs may deal with proposed domestic legislation, international treaties, and other agreements. It is also the forum within which the Department of Foreign Affairs' annual budget is debated. In that context, in the twenty-ninth Dáil up to April 2005, the committee dealt with six such international agreements, four of which originated with the European Union.[54] In all cases, after a brief ministerial presentation and debate, messages were forwarded to the Dáil that the Select Committee had successfully completed its consideration of these agreements.

Over the lifetime of the Foreign Affairs Committee (up to the time of writing), a mere fourteen measures had been notified to it by the European Affairs Committee's Sub-Committee on European Scrutiny.[55] In all cases, the

[53] Joint Committee on Foreign Affairs, Debates, 11 December 2002, as to which see www.irlgov.ie/committees-29/c-foreignaffairs/20021211-J/Page1.htm#1.

[54] These were the Euro-Mediterranean Association Agreements with Egypt, Algeria, and Lebanon, the Union's Association Agreement with the Republic of Chile and European Union Political Dialogue and Co-operation Agreements with Central American states and the Andean Community of Nations.

[55] Examples of these have been the Commission Decision setting out the arrangements for Community comparative trials and tests on propagating and planting material of fruit plants under Council Directive 92/34 (COM (2002) 745); the Council Decision of 22 September 2003 appointing an alternate member of the Committee of the Regions (COM 2003/684); and Commission Decision 2004/451 of 29 April 2004 on the clearance of the accounts of Member States' expenditure financed by the European Agricultural Guidance and Guarantee Fund (EAGGF), Guarantee Section, for the 2003 financial year (COM (2004) 451). The references for the remaining measures notified are COM (2004) 456; COM (2004) 465; COM (2004) 466; COM (2004) 520; COM (2004) 521; COM (2004) 558; COM (2004) 567; COM (2004) 510; COM (2004) 511; COM (2004) 522; and COM (2004) 502.

Sub-Committee recommended that no further scrutiny of these proposals was necessary and the Foreign Affairs Committee concurred in all cases without debate. Thus far, neither of the two Sub-Committees of the Foreign Affairs Committee have had any matter referred to them from the European Affairs Committee.

(c) The European Affairs Committee

In the twenty-ninth Dáil from July 2002 to April 2005, the European Affairs Committee met on a total of 129 occasions. Of these meetings, forty were those of the Sub-Committeee on European Scrutiny, seven were meetings of the Dáil's Select Committee – which sat prior to the Seanad's nomination of members to the full Joint Committee. There were no subsequent meetings of the Select Committee following the first meeting of the Joint Committee on 11 November 2002. At the time of writing, therefore, there had been a total of 82 meetings of the Joint Committee since its establishment.

Meetings of the Joint Committee are similarly dominated by presentations and subsequent discussion and debate. There are meetings on close to a monthly basis with either the Minister for Foreign Affairs or the Minister of State with responsibility for European Affairs, in advance of each General Affairs and External Relations Council (GAERC). As might be expected – based closely as these meetings are upon the actual agenda of the GAERC – a significant part of the discussion at these meetings is dominated by Common Foreign and Security Policy and associated foreign, security, and defence policy issues. These range across the gamut from European Union institutional changes related to the Common Foreign and Security Policy and the European Security and Defence Policy, to specific policy developments and the Union's implementation of the relevant policy around the world. An exceptionally wide of range of issues is covered in these two-to-three hour sessions – with a particular and ongoing focus on human rights, European Union constitutional and institutional changes impacting upon the Common Foreign and Security Policy and the European Security and Defence Policy, and current crises (such as in Iraq, the Middle East, or the Balkans). These meetings also tend to be even more focused on current events than those of the Foreign Affairs Committee. This is related to the obvious fact that the GAERC itself must be seen to be responsive to the current international situation.

In general, it is officials of the Department of Foreign Affairs who prepare these meetings, and they supply the briefing material to the committee members. Members then hear an often-detailed presentation from the minister and subsequently engage in what is regularly a robust exchange of views. At these meetings the minister is usually accompanied by senior departmental officials who may themselves be invited to make an intervention but whose usual role is to support the minister during the discussion. Ministers are in no way bound by the Committee's deliberations on the Council agenda – but frequently aver to their determination to take account of the members' views in pursuing policy within the GAERC. At the first of these new-style briefings in July 2002, the Minister of Foreign Affairs also noted the potential of duplication in these briefings with the Foreign Affairs Committee and suggested that it might be possible to schedule joint meetings, but this suggestion appears not to have been taken up by either committee.

Apart from such briefings, the committee's deliberations were divided among meetings with visiting delegations – particularly from existing and prospective European Union member states – and discussions of broader European Union developments. In the period under review, the topics of such discussions have included the Constitutional Treaty, the Lisbon Agenda, and other specific policy areas such as taxation, the European Union budget, and Turkish membership of the Union.

Insofar as concerns the Common Foreign and Security Policy and broader foreign, security, and defence policy issues, a significant overlap does appear to exist between the work of the European Affairs Committee and that of the Foreign Affairs Committee. In the period between 2002 and 2005, for example, the European Affairs Committee dedicated time to debates on human rights in Zimbabwe, Russia, and Nigeria, and a presentation by the United Nations High Commission for Refugees. The committee also decided, in 2003, to establish an Advisory Group to examine the role of the European Union in its relations with developing countries. This Group subsequently prepared a 2004 report that looked at issues such as international trade, the AIDS/HIV crisis, debt burdens, and food shortages in the developing world. The report was forwarded to government as the committee's contribution to the Irish European Union Presidency. All of the above discussions and activities were legitimate and germane to the committee's terms of reference, but it does underscore an ongoing issue of a modest overlap in responsibilities and perhaps even competition between the two committees.

Over the lifetime to date of the European Affairs Committee, just three measures have been notified to it by the Sub-Committee on European Scrutiny and none of these have related to the Common Foreign and Security Policy.

(d) The Sub-Committee on European Scrutiny

In his first report as Chairperson of the Dáil's Sub-Committee on European Scrutiny in October 2002, Deputy Gay Mitchell noted that only now were proposals for European Union legislation being examined 'in a structured and comprehensive manner' and that this was the direct result of the initial rejection of the Nice Treaty.[56] However, in his view, the function of the new supervisory system was to

> "give the Oireachtas a clear voice in the European Union legislative process, and in so doing to redress the 'democratic deficit' in relation to European Union business".

Two years later, in his annual report to the Oireachtas covering the period October 2002 to December 2003, Deputy Mitchell could conclude that the new measures had

> "operated very successfully to date and can be seen as confirming the commitment of Departments to keep the Oireachtas informed on developments in relation to European Union legislative proposals. In this way members of the Sub-Committee and of the Oireachtas as a whole are in a better position to engage with this process".[57]

As regards the Common Foreign and Security Policy, however, further developments had to be put in place. The sub-committee's report notes that as a result of their experience of the scrutiny process as originally designed, the sub-committee itself had decided that additional arrangements were necessary in order to address Common Foreign and Security Policy decisions and proposed measures which were of a highly confidential nature.[58] In the main, these decisions and measures pertained to the imposition or removal of sanctions against states, specified groups of people or even – in some cases – individuals. This resulted in a new procedure whereby highly sensitive Common Foreign and Security Policy matters could be notified to the

---

[56] Houses of the Oireachtas, Sub-Committee on European Scrutiny, First Report, *Report of the meeting of 10th October 2002* (31 October 2002), available at www.oireachtas.ie/viewdoc.asp?DocID=389&&CatID=74.

[57] Joint Committee on European Affairs' Sub-Committee on European Scrutiny, *First Annual Report on the Operation of the European Union Scrutiny Act 2002*, 10 October 2002 to 31 December 2003, Houses of the Oireachtas (October, 2004), available at www.oireachtas.ie/viewdoc.asp?DocID=3231&CatID=74.

[58] *Ibid.*.

chairperson and he would be formally briefed by the Department of Foreign Affairs. Once agreed and in place, such measures could then usually come before the full sub-committee in the normal way and be formally noted. A Protocol to this end was drawn up between the sub-committee and the Department of Foreign Affairs.

A major ongoing concern of the Sub-Committee – as with the European Affairs Committee and Foreign Affairs Committee – is the issue of resources. It is, to say the least, problematic that deputies rely upon executive agencies (*i.e.,* Government departments) to provide them with the background briefing material by which those deputies are meant to hold the executive to account. There is no suggestion here of any errors – either of commission or omission – on the part of Departmental officials, simply the pointing out of the fact that deputies can hardly be deemed to be appropriately prepared to engage with a minister when they are in large part relying upon briefing material supplied by the same officials sitting beside the minister to advise him on his replies to the deputies. Moreover, due to time constraints and due to the precise formulation of Council agendas being left to a late point in time, briefing material appears to be frequently delivered either on the morning of ministerial presentations or just shortly before this.

The Chairman of the National Forum on Europe, Senator Maurice Hayes, has already complained that in his view the European Affairs Committee's Sub Committee on European Scrutiny is 'seriously under-resourced' and has insisted – with cross-party support from within the National Forum – that this sub-committee could not do its job properly unless it got adequate research and administrative back-up.[59] One of the most serious concerns which members of the sub-committee have expressed has related to the level of staffing resources provided. In his 2004 report, the chairman reported that the committee had experienced a substantial increase in the numbers of proposals in need of analysis but that of the six staff assigned, only four were then in post, with two having been redeployed and not yet replaced. The Sub-Committee's own report observed that:

> "the Sub-Committee notes that, in comparison to similar committees of parliaments of the EU, the resources available to (the Sub-Committee) are unacceptably low and expresses its concern that this fact severely restricts

[59] Quote ascribed to chairman in National Forum Press Release dated 28 November 2002. See www.forumoneurope.ie/index.asp?locID=190&docID=296.

> the Committee's capacity to continue to carry out its mandate as envisaged by the Oireachtas on its establishment in July 2002".[60]

In part response to this situation – paralleled in other Oireachtas committees – the Government established the Oireachtas Commission in January 2004 so as to allow the Houses of the Oireachtas – within a framework budget – to determine their own strategic priorities and allocate resources in the best interests of the parliament – that function having previously rested with the Minister for Finance. Regrettably, while the design is good, the fabric may be short. The Commission's three-year budget of 295 million euro would be, according to the Commission itself, "sufficient to maintain existing levels of service over the next three years and make some additional resources available" but these additional resources do not allow the Oireachtas to put in place the kinds of support services to members and committees that exist in comparable parliamentary assemblies elsewhere in Europe and the wider developed world.[61]

7. Conclusions

A range of conclusions may be drawn from the analysis above. There is no doubt that in maintaining effective parliamentary scrutiny over the Union's Common Foreign and Security Policy and its European Security and Defence Policy, the Oireachtas faces four cumulative sets of challenges. First, there are those arising from the problematic nature of parliamentary supervision of foreign and security policy in general. Secondly, there are those arising from the comparative weakness of the Oireachtas *vis-à-vis* other parliaments in exercising effective parliamentary control over the executive. Thirdly, there are the challenges arising from the unique nature of European Union foreign, security and defence policy – which encompasses both supranational and intergovernmental decision making frameworks. Fourthly, there are those arising from the fact that in the construction of the Common Foreign and Security Policy and the European Security and Defence Policy, the exercise of executive power is further distanced from effective parliamentary control and supervision.

---

60 Joint Committee on European Affairs' Sub-Committee on European Scrutiny, *First Annual Report on the Operation of the European Union Scrutiny Act 2002, 10 October 2002 to 31 December 2003* (Houses of the Oireachtas, October 2004), to be found at www.oireachtas.ie/viewdoc.asp?DocID=3231&CatID=74.

61 Statement taken from the Houses of the Oireachtas Commission website. See www.oireachtas.ie/ViewDoc.asp?fn=/documents/Commission/default.htm&CatID=46&m=h

It is unlikely that anything substantive is capable of being done to address the first of these challenges. The very nature of foreign, security and defence policy is such that it is widely regarded as being distinct from the general run of public policy. At the same time, members of the Oireachtas might consider structures and procedures that have been put in place in other parliaments so as to exercise more effective parliamentary oversight in this policy area. For example, closed or confidential committee meetings are used to good effect in a number of parliaments, so that sensitive information can be shared between the executive and members of the legislature. While this form of activity is not open to public scrutiny, it may at least have the effect of better informing key legislators on the background to and necessity of policy decisions and thus raise the level of debate and legislative engagement in the policy process. One move in this direction is the confidential briefing of the Chairperson of the European Scrutiny Sub-Committee – why might this not be extended to the members of the Sub-Committee as a whole? Against this, of course, is the danger of creating a 'golden cage' which serves only to co-opt parliamentarians into the inner policy sanctum – serving further to marginalise other legislators and the general public.

Significant progress has been made in addressing the comparative weakness of the Oireachtas in its parliamentary scrutiny function *vis-à-vis* the European Union generally. Since July 2002, many of the necessary structural underpinnings have been put in place either on a procedural or statutory basis. Thus, the bones of an effective system exist. However, the flesh – in terms of financial resources, staffing, etc. – is still lacking. It would be inappropriate for the Oireachtas to model itself upon federal-style legislatures with extensive, expensive, and complex committee structures. Nonetheless, and at a minimum, the Oireachtas needs to be able to offer its members the basic range of research and administrative supports necessary to a modern parliament. Moreover, it would be appropriate if those staffing these structures were employed by the Oireachtas on either a full-time permanent or at least long-term contractual basis. This would ensure that members and committees benefited from some institutional memory and that staff were not looking over their shoulder while on short-term secondment. Consideration might also be given to the Oireachtas making more of its committees standing structures, which would survive from one Oireachtas to the next, so that such committees' reconstitution with each Dáil would not be at the whim of the government but rather would be automatically provided for within the Standing Orders of the Houses of the Oireachtas.

There is no indication that members of the Oireachtas are in any way unwilling to engage with ministers and officials on issues related to European foreign and security policy. However, there is also little doubt that the numbers of those interested in foreign policy are comparatively small and that most of these members would be – and would probably characterise themselves as being – sceptical critics of Irish foreign policy within the European Union. This arises, at least in part, because the existing structures provide no means by which members might see themselves as contributors to, and thereby owners of, the foreign and security policy that results. There is no comparative advantage to members of the Oireachtas – beyond party loyalty or loyalty to the government – to attempt to engage with the foreign policy process at national or European Union level, since there are no levers by which they can exercise any substantive influence, and, indeed, be seen to do so.

It is clear that the Union's foreign, security, and defence policy does not 'fit' easily into any parliamentary supervisory structure. This is reflected in the policy overlap that exists between the European Affairs and Foreign Affairs Committees. Thus far, that overlap has been managed effectively, with only minor instances of duplication. However, in a situation where time and resources are as limited as they are, a more formal and agreed division of labour between the two committees would be in order. This might entail thematic or geographic divisions or, perhaps, more use being made of joint meetings or the creation of joint sub-committees or working groups, or a combination of such approaches. The Foreign Affairs Committee, for example, might exercise supervision over the conduct of the Common Foreign and Security Policy and the European Security and Defence Policy while the European Affairs Committee scrutinised the institutional and constitutional structures underpinning the exercise of that policy.

Finally, and perhaps most problematically, how can the Oireachtas exercise effective oversight of a policy that is formally intergovernmental and yet is conducted by a composite executive which – collectively – answers to no democratic assembly? This is perhaps the most difficult issue of all, and it is one which is well beyond the capacity of the Oireachtas to address. Three basic options are open. The first is to decide that the Common Foreign and Security Policy and European Security and Defence Policy is exercised by and on behalf of the European Union and that as such, it must over time become an integral policy of that Union on the same basis as, and subject to same democratic checks and balances. This 'federalisation' of the Common Foreign and Security Policy and European Security and Defence Policy would then imply that the European Parliament should be the forum in which democratic accountability is exercised. The second is to determine that the Union's foreign, security, and defence policy will remain one of differentiated governance, and for the national parliaments and the European Parliament to agree some *modus operandi* which would ensure that all aspects of that policy are democratically accountable. The third option is to decide that the Common Foreign and Security Policy and European Security and Defence Policy should and will remain wholly intergovernmental and essentially distinct from the rest of the Union's external relations. In this last case, it would be incumbent on the national parliaments to work together either multilaterally (through, for example, COSAC) or through some delegation of responsibility (through, for example, the Western European Union's Parliamentary Assembly) to that democratic end.

Certainly in the case of the Common Foreign and Security Policy it is not yet the case that Ireland rests at the 'top of the European league table in terms of parliamentary oversight of EU activities'. Significant progress has been made domestically but much could yet be done to strengthen the underpinnings of that scrutiny function and to involve parliamentarians more meaningfully in the national, and thereby the European foreign and security policy process. At the same time, and by its very nature, the Common Foreign and Security Policy and the European Security and Defence Policy pose particular challenges to effective parliamentary oversight – challenges that no single parliament can address. These questions urgently require a robust and meaningful answer from national parliaments acting together and in concert with their colleagues in the European Parliament. Without such mobilisation, the Common Foreign and Security Policy and the European Security and Defence Policy will remain a 'place apart' in terms of the Union's own democratic deficit.

10.
Parliamentary Scrutiny of European Affairs in Ireland – The European Affairs Committee, the Scrutiny Committee, and the European Union (Scrutiny) Act 2002

Lia O'Hegarty[1]

1. Introduction

The roles of national parliaments and their European affairs committees in relation to European affairs have been well categorised by Bradley.[2] Drawing on his schema, the functions which such committees are expected to perform could be listed as (a) discussion and/or ratification, in accordance with national constitutional law, of reforms effected by treaty of European Union institutions and competences[3]; (b) the supervision of government ministers in the Council of Ministers, as well as supervision of the European Union legislative process generally; (c) the implementation of European Union primary legislation (insofar as discretion is left to the Member States in this regard); and (d) the carrying out of inter-parliamentary cooperation[4] (which is not an end in itself, but rather an aspect of the exercise of the previous functions).

---

[1] Consultant in legislation and public affairs, member of the Irish Human Rights Commission and formerly Parliamentary Legal Adviser to the Houses of the Oireachtas. The author wishes to thank Siobhán Malone, Clerk to the Joint Oireachtas Committee on European Affairs, for her assistance.

[2] K. St. C. Bradley, "The Role of National Parliaments in EU Affairs", paper delivered at the Second Annual Congress of the Irish Centre for European Law (2001). See also A. Maurer, "National Parliaments in the European Architecture: From Latecomers' Adaptation towards Permanent Institutional Change"' in A. Maurer & W. Wessels (eds.) *National Parliaments on their Way to Europe: Losers or Latecomers*? (Nomos, Baden-Baden, 2001).

[3] Decisions on certain key European Union matters such as the nature of the European Union institutions and the accession of new Member States require ratification by individual Member States in accordance with their own constitutional requirements. In Ireland, as in some other countries, some of these decisions require a referendum, which is a very special kind of "legislation" involving not only parliament but also citizens directly. Because parliament has a role, *a fortiori* the Committee on European Affairs has a role in such matters – for example, in debating whether a referendum is required in the first place and, if it goes ahead, in debating and passing the domestic legislation to be submitted for referendum.

[4] Including links with the European Parliament.

The focus of this chapter is on describing and assessing how the Irish parliament and its committees perform the second of these roles *viz.*, the supervision of Irish Government Ministers in the Council of Ministers and supervision of the European Union legislative process generally.

Constitutional Background

The purpose of parliamentary scrutiny of European Union affairs is made very clear in Ireland by the terms of the Constitution itself.[5] Article 15.2.1° of the Constitution provides that "the sole and exclusive power of making laws for the State is hereby vested in the Oireachtas: no other legislative authority has power to make laws for the State." In contrast, Article 28.2 provides that "the executive power of the State shall, subject to the provisions of this Constitution, be exercised by or on the authority of the Government."[6] This should be read in conjunction with Article 28.4.1°, which provides that "the Government shall be responsible to Dáil Éireann."

A number of points must be noted about Article 28.4.1°. In the first place, there is a considerable disjunction between theory and reality here. Both in plenary session and in committees, parliament (or more specifically the lower house of the Irish parliament, the Dáil) does rely on this principle on a regular basis in calling Government ministers to account. In practice, however, it is difficult for parliament really to call the Government to account. The fact that the Government usually has a majority in parliament, the comparative strength of resources and information available to the Government, and the very strong party whip system in Ireland are just some of the reasons for this. In addition, in latter years the growth of the administrative (or 'fourth') branch of government and the increased resort to social partnership (involving prior consultation with lobby groups before a proposal is formally initiated by the executive), not to mention membership of the European Union itself, have increased the dichotomy further, for better or for worse.

---

[5] As regards the purpose of parliamentary scrutiny in *e.g.*, the United Kingdom, see the clear role envisaged for this by the House of Lords Select Committee on the European Union, *Review of Scrutiny of European Legislation* (First Report of 2002/2003 Session).

[6] Article 29.4.1° further provides that "the executive power of the State in or in connection with its external relations shall in accordance with Article 28 of this Constitution be exercised by or on the authority of the Government."

The relationship between the above provisions and Article 29.4.10° must now be addressed. This provision states that

> "no provision of the Constitution invalidates law enacted, acts done or measures adopted by the State which are *necessitated* by the obligations of membership of the European Union or of the Communities, or prevents laws enacted, acts done or measures adopted by the European Union or by the Communities, or by institutions thereof, or by bodies competent under the Treaties establishing the Communities, from having the force of law in the State."[7]

It is not proposed here to recount herein the detailed case-law of the Irish courts on the meaning of the word "necessitated" in this constitutional provision, a topic which would merit a separate paper. For present purposes, the key point is that, once the State becomes bound under European Union Law to adopt particular measures (whether legislative or otherwise), such measures cannot be struck down as unconstitutional by reference to other articles of the Constitution. However, the argument can be made that this does not mean that the spirit, or indeed the letter, of the Constitution is rendered nugatory in respect of the Government's actual participation in European Union decision-making (whether legislative or otherwise).[8]

In terms of the spirit of the Constitution, an argument can be made that parliament should have *some* role in the creation of European Union legislation. This argument proceeds from a reassessment of the Government's role in European Union lawmaking. While traditionally this function would be categorised in domestic law as strictly executive, the traditional categorisation – and indeed the case-law pertaining to it – comes under strain in the context of the realities of the European Union and the changed nature of the State itself.[9] This tension was articulated by the then Attorney General of Ireland, Michael McDowell, some years ago. Citing Article 15.2 of the Constitution, he asked

> "should Irish Ministers have a constitutionally free hand to participate in Council meetings whose decisions can effectively abrogate the terms of the Constitution itself in adopting directives and making regulations? An

---

[7] Emphasis added.

[8] *Cf.* however the important supplementary argument which may be made on the basis of Article 29.4.1° of the Constitution and which is explained below at n. 30.

[9] See House of Lords Report, noted at n. 5 above, at para.12 thereof, where the argument is made in terms of the legislative function of Parliament.

> Irish Minister is, in Irish law, the creature of the Constitution … as a matter of Irish law an Irish Minister need not necessarily be a legal or constitutional plenipotentiary on the part of the Irish State or people … Such discretion as they enjoy, as a matter of Irish law, results either from an express or implied constitutional authority."[10]

The argument goes a step further. If one is disinclined to argue in terms of the spirit of the Constitution, the text may be turned to. It is not necessary for the purposes of this argument to question at all the classical formulation of the State's role in European Union matters as purely executive. For, even accepting the classification of participation in European Union affairs as solely an executive (not a legislative) function, the fact remains that Article 28.4 renders the Government responsiblc to the Dáil. (This is coupled with the constitutional convention of individual ministerial responsibility.) To quote McDowell again:

> "negotiation and conclusion of the State's external agreements and liabilities is classically seen as part of the 'executive power of the State'. But it is by no means clear, I think, as a matter of Irish constitutional theory, that the Government or any individual Minister, has the unlimited and unfettered right to oblige the State to make laws even to the point of abrogating established constitutional rights."[11]

The implication is that, although Article 29.4.10° provides an *ex post facto* immunity for necessitated measures, the Government and/or its Ministers are at the very least answerable – both during and after European Union negotiations – to the Dáil for their conduct of such negotiations. Furthermore, the Government is answerable for the actions of officials, for example at COREPER or in comitology committees, because officials are acting explicitly or implicitly on the authority of the Government.[12]

Two other provisions of the Irish Constitution which deserve mention at this point are Article 29.4.6° and Article 29.4.8° which stipulate that the prior approval of Parliament is required for certain "options or discretions"

---

[10] M. McDowell, "Ireland and Europe's Future Integration" [2001] *Bar Review* 480 at 483 (text of speech delivered in June 2001 to the Lawyer's Group of the Irish Institute of European Affairs).

[11] *Ibid.*.

[12] According to this reasoning, one might question whether the Seanad has a role in this matter and correspondingly, whether the Committee on European Affairs should be a Dáil committee rather than a joint committee, given that Article 28.4.1° of the Constitution provides that "the Government shall be responsible to Dáil Éireann". Such an approach might be overly purist, however, as there seems nothing inappropriate in Seanad representation on the Committee.

provided under the Amsterdam and Nice Treaties respectively. Thus, in this unique context, parliament can indeed fetter the discretion of the executive in European Union affairs.

Article 29.4.6° of the Constitution provides that "the State may exercise the options or discretions provided by or under Articles 1.11, 2.5 and 2.15 of the [Amsterdam Treaty] and the second and fourth Protocols set out in the said Treaty but any such exercise shall be subject to the *prior approval* of both Houses of the Oireachtas."[13] The options referred to appear to include in the main measures under Title IV of the Treaty Establishing the European Community (which concerns visas, asylum, immigration and other policies related to the free movement of persons and for which there is a specific opt-in mechanism) as well as framework decisions under Title VI of the Treaty on European Union (which contains provisions on police and judicial cooperation in criminal matters).

Article 29.4.8° provides that "the State may exercise the options or discretions provided by or under Articles 1.6, 1.9, 1.11, 1.12, 1.13 and 2.1 of the [Nice Treaty] but any such exercise shall be subject to the *prior approval* of both Houses of the Oireachtas."[14] The options referred to here all relate to enhanced cooperation procedures, under which a group of member states can make use of European Union institutions for the purposes of effecting deeper integration in any of a number of fields.

The mechanism for opting into Title IV measures was queried by the Joint Committee on European Affairs in early 2002. Some members of the Committee voiced concern that there was insufficient scope for parliamentary consideration of a particular proposed regulation in the Title IV area, particularly if it stood a chance of gaining future constitutional immunity.[15] Apart from the time pressure involved, there was also the question as to whether the proposed regulation ought more appropriately to have been referred to the relevant sectoral committee (*viz.*, the Committee on Justice, Equality, Defence and Women's Rights), which had more expertise to question the Minister. Members also queried whether an Irish minister, if opting into such a regulation during the course of negotiations (*i.e.*, prior to adoption), would have authority to agree the measure subject to a

[13] Emphasis added.

[14] Emphasis added.

[15] See transcript of meeting of Joint Committee on European Affairs on 20 February 2002 (transcript at Office of Editor of Debates, Houses of the Oireachtas).

parliamentary scrutiny reserve, as is the practice among some delegates from other countries. The parliamentary legal adviser advised that[16]

> "this provision is extremely clear; the meaning of 'prior approval' is not open to doubt. ... The result is that, until Oireachtas approval is given, a Minister has no power to give formal or final indication of Ireland's decision to exercise an option. This is so regardless of whether the Council of Ministers or other authority mistakenly equates provisional approval with final approval.
>
> ... when (and if) the final Council Regulation is promulgated by the European Union, it would be immune from domestic constitutional challenge. The reason for this is that the Regulation would become directly effective in Ireland and Ireland would have no discretion as to its scope or application. It might be queried how a measure to which Ireland has voluntarily 'opted-in' could be deemed to be a 'necessitated' measure. The answer is that, once (and if) Ireland opts into this measure pursuant to the Fourth Protocol, thereafter Ireland becomes bound by the Treaties in respect of that particular measure."[17]

The Committee's deliberations raised the fundamental question of how genuine "prior approval" must be for the purposes of Article 29.4. If a motion were passed by parliament only moments after a document had been received by the members, would this suffice? It would seem that this question can be answered differently depending on whether regard is paid to the letter or the spirit of the Constitution. The former seems to require purely formal approval whereas the latter arguably presupposes some element of scrutiny to give real substance to this requirement.

---

[16] See transcript of meeting of Joint Committee on European Affairs on 27 March 2002 (transcript at Office of Editor of Debates, Houses of the Oireachtas).

[17] The advice continued

> "different considerations apply, however, to other EU measures. ... Where such measures leave a degree of discretion of choice to Member States, then within that zone of choice the 'necessity' threshold would not be met. In such a case, the national implementing measure ultimately chosen to give effect to the decision, directive, etc. would be open to domestic constitutional scrutiny *in so far* as it was not necessitated."

(Note: such a constitutional challenge could be either in relation to the form of the measure (in other words, the argument made that primary legislation should have been used to comply with Article 15.2.1°) or the substance of the measure (in other words, the argument made that a constitutional right was breached thereby)).

The European Union Committee and the Scrutiny Sub-Committee

Traditionally, the committee system in the Houses of the Oireachtas has been very under-resourced but it has been strengthened in recent years. Sectoral committees are now in existence 'tracking' or 'marking' each Government Department. The Dáil and Seanad appoint two parallel sets of sectoral committees, and each pair in turn is merged to form a 'joint committee'.

The Oireachtas Joint Committee on European Affairs is the result of a merger of the Dáil Committee on European Affairs and the parallel Seanad Committee. It has been in existence since the mid-1990s. More recently the Joint Committee has appointed a Sub-Committee on European Scrutiny (hereinafter 'the Sub-Committee').

The Joint Committee on European Affairs is composed of seventeen members, of whom eleven are TDs and six are Senators. There is a Government majority on the Committee. However, it is chaired by an Opposition member. (It may be noted in passing that such 'Opposition chairs' are comparatively rare. Traditionally, however, they have been a feature of the Public Accounts Committee and more recently of the European Union Committee). As for the Sub-Committee on European Scrutiny, there are currently seven members of this, of whom five are TDs and two Senators. Again, there is a Government majority. The staff of the Joint Committee as a whole includes a clerk and a policy advisor for the European Union Committee and a clerk and a policy advisor for the Sub-Committee.[18]

2. The New Scrutiny Arrangements And The European Union (Scrutiny) Act, 2002

> "Regulations and directives can no longer be the exclusive concern of MEPs, Ministers and technocrats. They are the direct and unavoidable concern of TDs and Senators."
>
> Michael McDowell[19]

[18] Note that a substantive extract from the Orders of Reference of the European Union Committee (as passed by resolutions of both Houses of the Oireachtas) is set out in the Appendix to this chapter. Editor's note: readers should note that all references in this chapter are to the Joint Committee as it existed until the May 2007 Dáil elections, which preceded the publication of this book by a matter of weeks. This Joint Committee has not in any case been replaced by a successor committee at the time of writing.

[19] See above at n. 10, p. 484. At the time these words were written, Mr. McDowell was Attorney General of Ireland.

The 2002 Act

The Amsterdam Protocol on the Role of National Parliaments set out an indicative timescale for the consideration of Commission legislative proposals, in order to facilitate the consideration of these proposals by national parliaments.[20]

Until comparatively recently, the Amsterdam Protocol meant little in Ireland, as no proper means existed for giving effect to it. While it was open to the European Union Committee to take up any European Union matters it saw fit, this potential was not accompanied by a structured relationship with the Government.

However, since Summer 2002, new arrangements have gradually been put in place for scrutiny of the Government's participation in the European Union. First, the Government announced the initiation of a new system, on an informal basis, to enable proper parliamentary scrutiny in European Union matters. Then in October 2002, the new scrutiny arrangements -- or rather a significant aspect of them – were placed on a legislative footing with the enactment of the European Union (Scrutiny) Act, 2002 (hereinafter 'the Act').[21]

---

[20] The Protocol does not actually mandate national parliamentary participation in European Union decision-making. The question of whether that should happen is left as a matter for Member States themselves to decide. However, the spirit of the Protocol is one of encouragement of such participation and, at a basic level, the Protocol at least facilitates it to a greater degree than before, by obliging the Council to observe minimum waiting periods before the adoption of legislative proposals. Previously, a Declaration on national parliaments had been attached to the Treaty on European Union at Maastricht in 1992, recognising the importance of involvement on the part of national parliaments and emphasising the need for access to information in good time for scrutiny purposes. Subsequent to the coming into force of the Treaty of Amsterdam, the Declaration on the Future of the Union made at the time of the agreement on the Treaty of Nice emphasised the need to examine the role of national parliaments in the European Union.

[21] The parliamentary background to the Act is that, originally, the European Union Bill 2001 was introduced in the Dáil by the leader of the Labour Party, as a Private Member's Bill. During the Dáil debate the Minister for Foreign Affairs welcomed the Bill as an important contribution but underlined the need to ensure that any new procedures were workable in the domestic context *and* in accordance with Ireland's obligations at European Union level. New scrutiny arrangements were introduced in July 2002 (albeit not put on a legislative footing). These required Ministers to forward draft legislation (*i.e.*, draft Directives, draft Regulations and draft proposals under the Third Pillar) together with an explanatory memorandum to the Joint Committee on European Affairs. After the summer recess, the Government then proceeded to put scrutiny arrangements on a legislative basis. To this end, it took the shell of the European Union Bill 2001 as it then stood and ensured that it was significantly amended in parliament to reflect the Government's view of what an appropriate scrutiny mechanism was.

Before embarking on a consideration of this piece of legislation, one might ask why the Government chose to legislate in this area at all. One answer is that, at a political level, the Government wanted to demonstrate – not just to Parliament but to the entire Irish citizenry – that it was taking the scrutiny issue seriously and that it would fulfil its promises in this area. Given that the second referendum on the Nice Treaty was looming, and that one of the (many) themes discussed at the National Forum on Europe was the democratic deficit, there was a perceived onus on the Government at this time to demonstrate a solid commitment to addressing such issues. The (first) referendum to enable Ireland to sign up to the Nice Treaty had been rejected by the Irish people in July 2001. If the Government had put a second referendum to the people without making concrete and visible changes to address the concerns of the first 'no' vote, it would have found it very hard to battle allegations of cynicism and hypocrisy.

The issue of the political need, rather than the legal necessity for legislation has been addressed here. This has been quite deliberate, in that it was not *legally* necessary to put the scrutiny arrangements on a statutory footing. Indeed, one may wonder whether there is any difference in effect between the statutory system we now have and, on the other hand, what we would have had if the Government had unilaterally decided to support the scrutiny system. For example, it seems doubtful that the failure of a Minister to observe the requirements of the 2002 Act would be deemed a breach of statutory duty with significant legal consequences. It also seems doubtful that decisions made under the Act would be subjected to more than cursory judicial review.

If much of the legislation creates no legal effects, the question arises as to what its purpose is. Is it appropriate to enact legislation in order to emphasise genuine political intent in so far as that legislation is not, in any meaningful sense, enforceable at law? The emergence of purely aspirational legislation on the statute book (of which this Act is just one example) is a cause for some concern in its own right – although having been noted, it will not be addressed further in this chapter.

To date there are two broad strands to European Union scrutiny in the Oireachtas, the first of which is based on the Act and the other of which is not. These two strands will now be considered in turn.

Strand One of Scrutiny – Scrutiny of European Union Legislative Proposals

The first strand of scrutiny operates as follows. The Government forwards to the Joint Committee on European Affairs all legislative proposals (across all three Pillars of the Union), together with information notes outlining the purpose, significance and implications of the texts presented. The Sub-Committee then conducts a preliminary survey of the various proposals, with a view to prioritising them. Prioritisation means making a judgment-call about which proposals are most significant in terms of policy, in order to ensure that adequate time and attention can be devoted to these. Proposals, which have been identified for further scrutiny, are then referred to the relevant sectoral committees to be considered in greater detail. This comprehensive scrutiny by sectoral committees is very much an evolving area, and it is examined further below.

The Statutory Framework

The Act copperfastens the above mechanism by providing that

> "as soon as practicable after a proposed measure is presented by the Commission of the European Communities or initiated by a Member State, as the case may be, the Minister shall cause a copy of the text concerned to be laid before each House of the Oireachtas together with a statement of the Minister outlining the content, purpose and likely implications for Ireland of the proposed measure and including such other information as he or she considers appropriate."[22]

For convenience this will be designated the 'first ground rule'.

The term "measure" is in turn defined by the Act to mean (a) a regulation or directive adopted under the Treaty establishing the European Community; (b) a joint action adopted under Article 14 of the Treaty on European Union; (c) a common position adopted under Article 15 of the Treaty on European Union; or (d) any other measure requiring the prior approval of both Houses of the Oireachtas pursuant to Article 29.4.6° or Article 29.4.8° of the Constitution.[23]

The Act thus provides that, as a general rule, draft legislation or legislative proposals and accompanying information notes must be laid before the Houses of the Oireachtas. This provision is designed to supplement rather than to supplant the sending of all such material directly to the Joint Oireachtas

[22] S. 2(1) of the European Union (Scrutiny) Act, 2002.

[23] See s. 1 of the Act, as amended by s. 2 of the European Community (Amendment) Act, 2002. The Joint Committee on European Affairs is not confined to considering the proposed measures specified in the Act however. (See the Committee's Orders of Reference as reproduced in Annex I to this chapter.)

Committee on European Affairs. That latter practice, begun before enactment of the Act, continues. However, the laying of documents before the Oireachtas gives greater transparency to the process as a whole, because the documents are brought to the attention of all members of the Oireachtas (*e.g.*, via citations on the Houses' Order Papers).

It will be noted, insofar as concerns the first ground rule, that the time by which the documents are to be furnished to the Houses is simply "as soon as practicable" after a proposed measure is presented by the Commission or initiated by a Member State. In practice, the maximum period tends to be four weeks, in accordance with guidelines drawn up by the Department of Foreign Affairs. Aside from this qualification relating to the time within which documents must be furnished to the Houses, the first ground rule is subject to two specific and important exceptions, which are explored below.

First, however, another question must be addressed – *viz.*, the effect (if any) of any recommendations emanating from the Joint Committee on European Affairs or another sectoral committee, or indeed the Houses of the Oireachtas in full. Here again, both the political effect and the legal effect must be considered, but on this occasion they appear to coincide. The Act provides that "the Minister shall *have regard* to any recommendations made to him or her from time to time by either or both Houses of the Oireachtas or by a committee of either or both Houses in relation to a proposed measure." For the purposes of this chapter, this will be designated the 'second ground rule'. The effect of this second ground rule is that the Minister must give consideration to such recommendations emanating from parliament. Although this requirement is expressed as a legal rule, it is probably best understood as a political reality – *viz.*, that the Minister must take account of and recognise the parliamentary recommendations in some sense. The parliamentary recommendations do not actually bind the Minister, however. In other words, there is no kind of legal veto at issue here.

There are two express exceptions, each applying to *both* ground rules. The first exception is that neither ground rule shall apply "if, in the opinion of the Minister, there is insufficient time for the carrying out of the procedures aforesaid and the performance of the functions of the Houses of the Oireachtas in relation to the text aforesaid".[24]

However, in circumstances where a Minister invokes this exception to avoid the general obligation to deposit documents with the Houses, the Minister is

[24] S. 2(3) of the 2002 Act.

then bound by the Act to lay before the Houses of the Oireachtas a copy of the resultant measure, if any, which has been adopted by a European Community institution.

The second exception is that neither ground rule shall apply to a proposed measure "which, in the opinion of the Minister, is confidential".[25] However, where this exception is invoked by the Minister, he or she may nevertheless make a report in relation to the proposed measure as he or she deems appropriate in the circumstances. Such a report may be made to a parliamentary committee, or indeed to either or both Houses of the Oireachtas.[26]

It will be noted that both the exceptions mentioned above are triggered by the subjective opinion of the Minister (as to timing and as to confidentiality respectively), rather than some objectively applicable legal test.

In the original Private Member's Bill, there was a provision which would have prevented the Government from agreeing a measure if the Oireachtas had rejected it in advance (or had not completed scrutiny of it). This provision was, not surprisingly, opposed by the Government – presumably on the basis of a view that it would have placed an unconstitutional fetter on the freedom of the executive. Its rejection clearly indicates that, in terms of its characterisation as between the various typologies of national scrutiny mechanisms, the Irish version is not a veto mechanism. The question then arises as to whether we have, or could attempt to have, anything that might be described as a scrutiny reserve mechanism. The answer to this is that, while there is no such system in place at present, it is possible that such a system may be introduced on an administrative (rather than a statutory) basis.[27] For example, it would be open to the Government to adopt an informal practice whereby Government ministers could indicate at European Union level that a particular matter was subject to ongoing parliamentary consideration, while taking account of any provisional views which may have emanated from the Oireachtas.

Practice to Date

Having outlined the essential elements of the first strand of the scrutiny process, we must now consider its day-to-day workings. This is a matter

[25] S. 3(1) of the 2002 Act.
[26] S. 3(2) of the 2002 Act.
[27] The objection to doing so on a statutory basis is articulated below at n. 30 both in the text and in that footnote.

which is not addressed in any legislation. But what has emerged to date is a form of unwritten and eminently sensible practice in an area which is a relatively novel one in the Irish context. It is a practice, moreover, which is still evolving.

Proposals are sent by the Government Department with primary responsibility for the proposal to the Scrutiny Secretariat. Which Department this ought to be is usually obvious. Where there is an overlap, the Department of Foreign Affairs may assist in clarifying the division of labour, although the Department of the Taoiseach will ultimately decide which Government Department has lead responsibility.

Each Government Department must forward the proposals within its remit to the Sub-Committee, generally within four weeks, together with an Information Note in each case. In practice, Departmental information notes include as a general rule (a) the title, date and number of the document; (b) an assessment of the significance of the proposal (*e.g.,* that it is of 'major significance', 'minor significance', 'some significance' or that it is 'merely technical'); (c) the European Union institutions involved (including, *e.g.,* the specification of which Directorate General is involved in the case of the Commission); (d) the Government Department with lead responsibility;[28] (e) the legal basis of the proposal; (f) the voting method; (g) the implications for Ireland (by which is meant the substantive policy implications); (h) the consequences for national legislation (*i.e.,* whether a change to primary and/or secondary legislation would be necessitated by the proposal if implemented); and (i) the anticipated negotiating period and proposed implementation date.

The baton is taken up in the first instance by the Sub-Committee on European Scrutiny. As mentioned above, the Sub-Committee conducts a preliminary survey of the various proposals, with a view to prioritising them. The Sub-Committee is assisted in all of this by a policy advisor. The policy advisor sifts the proposals in advance and makes recommendations to the Sub-Committee. Obviously, the policy advisor is not bound in any way by the Department's prioritisation and evaluation but in practice the Department's work will greatly ease and rationalise the workload of the policy advisor and in turn that of the Committee. The policy advisor then meets the Sub-Committee in private to discuss suitable approaches to the documentation.

[28] Typically, the note will also indicate whether other Departments are involved and whether other state bodies have a potential future role.

The Sub-Committee makes a decision in respect of each document or batch of documents. This decision will be (a) to refer the proposal onwards to an appropriate sectoral committee for scrutiny; (b) to refer the proposal onwards to an appropriate sectoral committee for the purposes of information only; (c) to seek further information from the Government (in which case, further consideration can be deferred if appropriate); (d) to exempt the document from any further scrutiny; (e) to note a proposal (typically, where a document has arrived too late for scrutiny and the Sub-Committee notes the exceptional circumstances involved); or (f) on rare occasions, where a proposal is of very significant national importance, to refer the proposal to the Houses of the Oireachtas.

The triggers for further scrutiny are varied. They range from domestic financial or regulatory implications to doubts about the basis in European Union law for the measures. The Scrutiny Sub-Committee tends to meet fortnightly. Documents and accompanying briefings by the policy advisors are circulated to members three days prior to the meeting.[29] On average, about fifteen legislative measures are considered per meeting.

Where proposals are referred to a sectoral committee, that committee may proceed as it wishes, *e.g.*, by holding public hearings and/or inviting Ministers and officials to appear before it and/or requesting written briefings. It may even request a full Oireachtas debate, although insofar as this writer is aware, this has never occurred to date. Obviously, the possibilities for action here will depend on a number of factors, including the detail of the specific proposal and the relative weight of the sectoral committee's existing agenda. In this regard, it is worth noting that the Orders of Reference of each sectoral committee have been amended to include the power to consider and report to the Dáil on such proposals for European Union legislation as may be referred to the relevant committee from time to time by the Joint Committee on European Affairs. Ultimately, the Scrutiny Secretariat will inform Government Departments and the Department of Foreign Affairs of the scrutiny outcome from each sectoral committee.

There is one further aspect of this process worth mentioning at this juncture. In the earlier days, as well as forwarding specific documents to specific committees for detailed scrutiny, the Scrutiny Sub-Committee in practice

---

[29] Thus they are circulated on Monday in preparation for meetings on Thursdays.

used to refer *all* documents to *all* committees, together with notification of decisions taken at its fortnightly meetings. The purpose of this exercise was to ensure that all committees were as fully briefed as possible and that, if a particular committee or member thereof wished to explore further any document which was broadly within their remit, they could do so, notwithstanding that the Sub-Committee itself had not specifically recommended that course of action. However, this practice has been (sensibly) discontinued because of the unwieldy amount of work involved and because the Chairs of the sectoral committees were happy to accept the delineations proposed by the (Scrutiny) Sub-Committee.

Current practice is that each sectoral committee continues to be supplied with a *list* (but not actual copies) of all proposals considered at each Sub-Committee meeting, along with a note of the Sub-Committee's decision in each case. Any sectoral committee may elect to scrutinise any document not specifically referred to it but which falls within its remit. However, in the case of proposals specifically referred to it for scrutiny, it has no choice but to scrutinise – although, as indicated, the degree of scrutiny undertaken may range from a perfunctory consideration to a major inquiry.

Strand Two of Scrutiny – Scrutiny of Ministerial Action at Council Level

The second main strand of scrutiny work involves briefings by Government ministers in advance of meetings of the Council of Ministers and the European Council. This strand, unlike the previous one, does not have a statutory basis. The Government considered that it should initiate and support such an arrangement in practice but that it would not be appropriate for legislation, and informally indicated that ministers (or on occasion ministers of state) would be available at all times, and particularly in advance of meetings of the Council of Ministers, to discuss the Council Agenda with the Oireachtas Joint Committee on European Affairs and/or the relevant sectoral committee.

The Joint Committee on European Affairs deals with meetings of the General Affairs and External Relations Council. For this reason, the Minister (or, on occasion, the Minister of State) for Foreign Affairs has come before the Joint Committee numerous times in the last year, in advance of such meetings. There is clearly an overlap here with the area of interest of the Oireachtas Joint Committee on Foreign Affairs.

As regards Council meetings generally, both the Joint Committee on European Affairs and the sectoral committees have a scrutiny role.

Departments have adopted the practice of forwarding draft agendas and revised agendas for Council meetings, as they become available, to the Sub-Committee Secretariat, which notifies all other committees. It has been suggested by the Government that a minister might typically be requested by an Oireachtas committee to appear before it in the week prior to the relevant Council meeting. The Government has also suggested informally that if two committees (*e.g.*, the Joint Committee on European Affairs and a particular sectoral committee) both wish to be briefed by a Minister, this work should be coordinated so far as practicable and that if necessary a single briefing should take place at a joint meeting of the two committees.

The practicalities of this strand of scrutiny have been somewhat complicated with the rationalisation of the number of Council formations following the Seville European Council – as a result of which there are more Ministers (and *a fortiori* more sectoral committees) than there are Councils – but the necessary division of labour is gradually being worked out.

The argument can be made, with this type of scrutiny (*i.e.*, the second strand of scrutiny under consideration), as indeed it can with the first type, that the Oireachtas can not tie the hands of the Government in respect of positions taken in the Council. Indeed the approach taken in the Act rests on the implicit view that such a fetter could not be introduced by way of legislation, even if it were desired to do so.[30]

Apart from the two strands of scrutiny just examined, there is one further aspect of scrutiny which deserves brief mention at this point. The Act places a duty on every Government minister to report to the Houses of the Oireachtas at least twice yearly in relation to measures, proposed measures and other European Community and European Union developments in respect of which that Minister performs functions.[31] In practice, this procedure has failed to produce much useful debate. The reports have failed to generate a great deal of interest among members of the Dáil, and generally speaking, Government ministers, for their part, do not appear to have found the procedure to have generated much in the way of useful ideas or discussion.

---

[30] A view based on Article 29. 4.1° of the Constitution (quoted at n. 6 above), according to which it is not permissible for parliament to fetter the executive function of the Government in international affairs. *Cf.* however, the view expressed by McDowell, outlined in the text above at n. 10 *et seq.*.

[31] Note the observations in relation to this procedure in the text below preceding n. 47.

3. The Operation of Scrutiny Arrangements to Date: An Evaluation

Some Observations Regarding the Practice of Scrutiny

The Overall Picture

The Oireachtas scrutiny system can be described in summary as document-based and reactive. Overall, it has to be said that there is less engagement with the second strand of scrutiny than there is with the first.[32]

Outside the framework of the Act, arrangements have now been put in place for scrutiny of most Council decisions (which do not, as a rule, fall within the 2002 Act's definition of what constitutes a "measure")[33] as well as Common Foreign and Security Policy measures of a confidential nature (the latter are notified in confidence to the Chairman of the Sub-Committee in advance and are not circulated to the Sub-Committee proper until after the Council decision is made). The Sub-Committee also routinely examines green and white papers. It is of course always open to the Committee to elect to scrutinise matters outside the terms of the Act or indeed the agreed guidelines; the Orders of Reference envisage that it may examine a wide range of material.[34]

Case-Study: Committee on Communications, Marine & Natural Resources

The scrutiny work carried out to date by the Joint Oireachtas Committee on Communications, Marine and Natural Resources can be used as a case-study. The patterns and practices of this Committee are representative of the handful of sectoral committees which currently carry out the bulk of scrutiny (due to the subject areas covered). Some committees have had very little involvement in scrutiny to date (*e.g.*, the Committee on Education). This is likely to change slightly, however, as in future one can expect more soft law in various sectors such as education, and, in turn, more scrutiny of such soft

32 There are notable exceptions to this – *e.g.*, in the justice and home affairs area.

33 This practice emerged as a result of the Sub-Committee's Twentieth Report (2003), which concerned embryo research in the European Union, and in which it expressed grave dissatisfaction about the omission of proposed Council decisions from the scrutiny process.

34 Thus, for example, the Committee has scrutinised Common Agricultural Policy proposals in the context of Agenda 2000 (an action programme launched in 1999, the main objectives of which were to strengthen Community policies and to give the European Union a new financial framework for the period 2000–06 with a view to enlargement. On another occasion, a (non-legislative) communication regarding the sugar industry was scrutinised.

law. In addition, recently, there has been a realisation across sectoral committees that the Act should not be regarded as curtailing scrutiny of any proposals which do not come within its scope and, furthermore, that some proposals merit scrutiny while they are still at an inchoate stage before matters of fine detail are worked out.

Relatively speaking, the output from the Committee on Communications, Marine and Natural Resources is very high. The combined portfolio of the Committee means it is likely to encounter a fairly wide range of European Union proposals, both in terms of content and form. In terms of the subject matter with which it deals, there is an overlap with the Committee on the Environment and Local Government.

The following observations of a neutral nature can be made from the data. First, the Committee has to date scrutinised almost exclusively proposed regulations and directives. Secondly, the Committee has – with some exceptions – almost always supported the Department's stance (whether in favour of or against the proposal).

Positive observations which can be made are first, that the quality of briefings from Departmental officials is very high. Secondly, the Department appears to be very effective in Council-level negotiations. Thirdly, a practice has developed recently of inviting interest groups to Committee hearings, whose views appear to be relatively influential on the Committee (*e.g.*, fisheries groups, or in the case of a discussion of the internet, a wide range of non-governmental organisations in this area).

On a negative note, the following observations can be made. First, there is a considerable time-lag (amounting to several months) between referral of a measure for scrutiny and actual scrutiny (although it is true that this does not appear to have caused particular problems to date). Secondly, there is a tendency for there to be only a single hearing on each measure (although occasionally there may be more than one). Thirdly, all hearings have involved detailed questioning of officials, but never of a minister. Fourthly, there has been no scrutiny of Commission work programmes or other preparatory documents. Fifthly, there has been very little scrutiny of ministerial performance at Council level. Sixthly and finally, there is a failure in the information loop – common to all committees – in that there is no practice of following up issues (either by the Committee or the Department). Thus vital feedback to the Committee, both on specific measures as well as on the outcome (if any) of its own scrutiny, is absent.

4. Evaluation of the Practice of Scrutiny

Objectives and Performance Indicators

The focus of this chapter is not on whether there is any merit in scrutiny by national parliaments of European Union affairs. Instead, scrutiny is assumed to be a worthwhile enterprise, and the topic investigated is whether the current scrutiny system in the Oireachtas meets it assumed objectives.

The main objective of scrutiny at present is making the executive accountable in respect of European Union affairs. The House of Lords European Union Select Committee has defined scrutiny as "a process of examination and analysis of the proposals and actions of those responsible for government, with a view to ensuing that they are accountable to Parliament for their actions".[35] Similarly, Working Group IV (of the Convention on the Future of Europe (the body which produced the first draft of the Constitutional Treaty) stated that "national parliaments have a central responsibility to advise, scrutinise and hold to account their own government ministers for their performance in Council, especially when considering whether legislation is best adopted at national or European level". The core issue of accountability has already been explored in an earlier part of this chapter.

There are of course other objectives which can not be ignored:

> "national Parliaments can exercise their powers and influence *directly* only upon their own Ministers as national representatives (rather than delegates) in the Council of Ministers. Making this process effective must be the main aim of a scrutiny system. However, the *informal* influence of an effective national system may be far-reaching. For example, it can highlight concerns about legislative proposals and pinpoint flaws in them. It can provide an additional source of analysis and opinion for MEPs and for the wide range of lobby groups which seek to influence the European Parliament. It can encourage the meeting of deadlines and the better organisation of business by the institutions. ... and through the use of scrutiny reserves and otherwise it can concentrate the Council's collective mind upon the need for openness and the orderly transaction of business – not only for the benefit of national parliaments themselves but, more importantly, for the citizens they represent."[36]

---

[35] House of Lords Select Committee on the European Union, above at n. 5, at 9.

[36] *The European Scrutiny System in the House of Commons – A Short Guide* (revised edition, May 2001), at 3.

The greater flow of information on European Union matters between government and parliament is also important. As MacCárthaigh has observed,

> "the unidimensional parliament-executive dichotomy often used when discussing the role of [national parliaments] in the European Union can be misleading, and is at odds with the reality of European parliamentarism, which involves a web of interactions between government and opposition parties, front benchers and backbenchers."[37]

Even the dissemination of information downwards to the citizen is an aspect of scrutiny; it can be regarded as a kind of 'democratic indicator' within the 'multi-layered' model. During the earlier days of the scrutiny system, the Sub-Committee met with its policy advisors in private and also made its decisions in private. Information as to the outcome of such meetings was then made public. As soon as the Sub-Committee found its feet, it shifted to the more transparent practice of holding its meetings in public – although its preparatory meetings with the policy advisor have continued to take place in private. At the first public session of the Sub-Committee,[38] the Chairman stated that

> "the public sessions ... are an opportunity for the Irish electorate to see at first-hand a part of the process by which European Union legislation is advanced ... The opening-up to the public of the important scrutiny role of the Sub-Committee is a major step in putting more light onto European Union legislative proposals that can directly impact on us all."

Aside from these internal databases, a real effort is being made to provide user-friendly information to the public at large via the internet. In particular, the agendas for Sub-Committee meetings (published on Mondays) and reports of meetings now appear in this fashion. The latter now include the Departmental advice note on each legislative proposal at issue – a practice which is set to continue.

The Sub-Committee and sectoral committees are increasingly involving external interest groups in the process. Clearly, such an expanded process has

---

[37] M. MacCárthaigh "Conceptualising the Role of National Parliaments in the EU System of Governance" (Paper presented at the conference *Internationalisation of Parliaments – Role of National Parliaments in the EU* organised by the International Political Science Association Research Committee of Legislative Specialists and the Slovene Association of Political Science, Llubljana, Slovenia, 7–9 April 2005), at 14.

[38] This took place on 16 January 2003.

the potential to benefit both the committees itself and civil society generally. The chairman of the Sub-Committee has stated that

> "it is our view that the widest possible audience should feed into the scrutiny process and benefit from that process. The Committee will, in the near future, look at how best to achieve the desired level of public awareness and participation."

Any sectoral committee may invite witnesses to assist them, and indeed interest groups may approach committees to express their concern about specific proposals (although the question of who, if anyone, should be invited in to give an oral presentation is entirely at the discretion of the committee).

Returning, however, to the key object of scrutiny, *viz.*, accountability, various questions arise. How can accountability be measured? What is the meaning of output in this context? Is it a report? Is it a change in Government policy? Is it the flow of information to the Committee throughout the decision-making process? Is it parliament's ability to demonstrate influence in European Union policy-making?

Even if it were possible to define useful performance indicators, it is too early to rate the Oireachtas scrutiny system at this stage. Instead, one can inquire whether some typical success factors for successful scrutiny are present in the Oireachtas system.

Critical Success Factors

According to the Convention on Europe's Working Group on National Parliaments, the basic factors determining the effectiveness of parliamentary scrutiny are: (a) the timeliness, scope and quality of information provided; (b) the possibility for parliament to formulate a position on the European Union measure; (c) the occurrence of regular contacts and hearings with Ministers before and after Council meetings; (d) the active involvement of sectoral committees in scrutiny; (e) the occurrence of regular contacts between national parliamentarians and MEPs; and (f) the availability of support staff (including Brussels liaison staff).[39]

Maurer has emphasised the importance in particular of the scope of documentation received, the timeliness of the receipt of documentation and

[39] *Final Report of Working Group IV on the Role of National Parliaments* (CONV 353/02, 22 October 2002) at 4–5.

the impact of scrutiny by parliament on the government's room for manoeuvre.[40] Bergman has added to the foregoing variables those of the political culture of the member state (*i.e.,* whether it is in favour of or opposed to European integration), the classification of European Union affairs as a question of foreign policy or a matter of national oversight, the prevalence of minority governments, and, finally, whether European Union scrutiny is an issue in the domestic struggle for power.[41]

Key themes, therefore, are the timeliness and scope of scrutiny. There is first the question of the timeliness and scope of information and documentation furnished to the Oireachtas. Secondly, there is the question of the timeliness and scope of the scrutiny carried out in the Oireachtas. These questions overlap and will be addressed together.

There have been some difficulties with the timeliness of information emanating from Departments. In its First Report, the Sub-Committee, while indicating general satisfaction with this aspect of arrangements, expressed concern about the number of proposals adopted prior to scrutiny.[42] A number of measures concerned the imposition, removal or reduction of anti-dumping duties. Many of these measures were adopted rapidly, and prior to scrutiny. The Department of Enterprise, Trade and Employment subsequently agreed to inform the Committee at the earliest stage in the process. It suggested that this could be achieved in future by way of a brief note outlining the implications of the proposal. If and when the Commission decided to present a formal proposal, the Department would then forward the standard information note.

More importantly, the typical time-line of committee scrutiny needs to be questioned. The adoption of legislation is not a momentary event – it is a long process which involves both a pre- and post-legislative phase.[43] The possibilities for earlier – and more proactive – scrutiny of legislative and other proposals by the Oireachtas need to be considered:

---

[40] Maurer, above, n. 2.

[41] T. Bergman, "National Parliaments and EU Affairs Committees: Notes on Empirical Variation and Competing Explanations" (1997) 4 *Journal of European Public Policy* 373.

[42] Joint Committee on European Affairs: Sub-Committee on European Scrutiny, *First Annual Report on the Operation of the European Union (Scrutiny) Act 2002* (OIR J-EU 2004.27) at 6.

[43] B. Dahl, "European cooperation – a challenge for national parliaments" (address at European Law Conference of the Swedish Presidency, Stockholm, 11 June 2001).

> "While [national parliaments] are developing their capacity to make their views known on European Union legislation as it makes its way through the principal European institutions, questions remain concerning the ability of [national parliaments] to shape that legislation in its formative stages. While [national parliaments] will receive the Commission's proposed annual legislative programme,[44] it remains the case that they have little agenda-setting influence over the Commission, its consultative and expert committees. Nor indeed do they hold much sway over the increasing agenda-setting role of the European Council. …"[45]

Ideally, there should be more scrutiny of Commission annual work programmes, short-term agendas, green and white papers, reports and communications. Consideration of Council and European Council agendas should be important also – although this becomes possible only if they are agreed and published well in advance at European Union level. A wide range of action plans at Council and Commission level merit prior and subsequent scrutiny; for example, the Hague Programme (adopted in 2004 by the European Council) is now a core agenda in the field of justice and home affairs. Furthermore, scrutiny of Second and Third Pillar Documents (such as draft common positions) should commence earlier. Also, much more rigorous follow-through of subsequent drafts is needed.

There is a need to call ministers before sectoral committees more frequently, both before and after Council meetings, to seek explanations. Furthermore, there should be scrutiny of Council Working Group processes and COREPER meetings – as it may be too late to influence a proposal in any way once it formally goes before the Council.

It is one thing to adopt an elaborate system of scrutiny of European Union proposals in their initial form. But the question of what information loop exists in respect of the subsequent progress of these proposals as they make their way through successive drafts and negotiations also needs to be addressed.[46] There are two distinct issues of concern here. The first is that during the course of scrutiny, the Oireachtas will not typically be informed of developments in respect of a measure unless and until a revised measure is formulated. It will not typically be made aware of, for example, a committee report at European Union level or a list of amendments

---

[44] *I.e.,* in the event of the Constitutional Treaty being ratified.

[45] MacCárthaigh, above n. 37, at 22.

[46] *Cf.* C. Kerse, "Parliamentary Scrutiny of the Third Pillar" (2000) 6 *European Public Law* 81. See especially pp. 95–96 and 100 regarding scrutiny of successive draft documents.

recommended by the European Parliament. Of course, this kind of information is more easily accessible nowadays from the European Union institutions themselves. Nevertheless the onus should not be on the Oireachtas proactively to seek such information. An essential trigger in the scrutiny process is therefore absent, namely the ongoing flow of information about proposals as they work their way through the legislative process. A second issue of concern is that even once a proposal is adopted and *ex ante* scrutiny is therefore no longer possible, there will be a dearth of information about the outcome of the legislative process and the national contribution to it. Yet *ex post facto* scrutiny is important too. Because such information is not filtering through the system, the necessary trigger is not in place for a committee to enquire, for example, as to whether a Government representative adhered to the same mandate throughout negotiations, or whether he or she succeeded in achieving the chosen aim in the negotiations, or whether he or she pursued concerns which the committee had raised. The fact that this information does not enter the loop does nothing for the scrutiny process – not to mention the morale of committee members.

The above concerns are addressed to a degree by the biannual ministerial reports to the Oireachtas, as required by the Act. Regrettably, however, according to the Act such reports are confined to developments within a six-month period in relation to proposals which have been referred to the Oireachtas during that same period. An entire range of information, namely the subsequent progress of such measures outside that period, is not reported.

Related to the above issue is the confidentiality of some aspects of the legislative process.[47] A major change since the Laeken Summit of December 2001 has been the increased transparency of Council meetings – although there is still a distance to go in this regard. At Council level the legislative process, at any rate, has become more transparent in recent years. Of course, the appropriateness of revealing a national negotiating position in advance must be balanced against the merits of scrutiny.[48] However, there is scope for confidentiality in the scrutiny system also: for example, a committee could at least commence work in private, involving a prior oral briefing by a Government representative, and later switch to public mode when a text is published.

[47] It is worth noting that successive legislative drafts attracted a 'confidential' status in earlier years.

[48] At various points a value judgment must be made between addressing the democratic deficit via scrutiny and the efficiency of the decision-making process; see A. Cygan, *The United Kingdom Parliament and European Union Legislation* (Kluwer Law International, The Hague, 1998) at 226.

Title IV matters tend to be noted by the Sub-Committee and forwarded to the Committee on Justice, Equality, Defence and Women's Rights – most frequently 'for information', but in many cases expressly 'for scrutiny' – in advance of any decision to seek Oireachtas approval to 'opt in'. Not all such measures are considered by the Committee on Justice, Equality, Defence and Women's Rights, however. For example, the Environment Committee considered a motion to opt in to the European Council Framework Decision on the protection of the environment through criminal law.[49]

The Committee on Justice, Equality, Defence and Women's Rights tends not to scrutinise Title IV measures in advance of an opt-in motion being proffered in the Houses.[50] To say this is in no way to criticise that particular Committee. If anything, it is a symptom of its enormous workload, which is discharged in an admirable fashion, given the scarce resources made available to it. However, the fact remains that scrutiny on foot of an opt-in motion is invariably carried out in a single hearing under considerable time-constraints. It is unfortunate that the Committee repeatedly finds itself undertaking this element of scrutiny on an urgent basis, in circumstances where the measure will have been received by the Committee much earlier but will not have been earmarked due to other priorities on the agenda.

Comitology is another area deserving of greater attention.[51] It was explored by the Oireachtas Joint Committee on European Affairs and the Sub-Committee on European Scrutiny as a direct result of attempted scrutiny by various sectoral committees of decisions regarding genetically modified foods.[52] Decisions arrived at through the comitology process should not be regarded as matters for experts and as entirely immune from political scrutiny.

---

[49] This was done on 17 December 2002 pursuant to Article 29.4.6° of the Constitution, which provides, insofar as relevant, that the State may exercise the options or discretions provided by or under Articles 1.11 of the Treaty of Amsterdam but that any such exercise shall be subject to the prior approval of both Houses of the Oireachtas. (See now Council Framework Decision 2003/80/JHA of 27 January 2003 on the protection of the environment through criminal law, (OJ L 029, 5 February 2003)).

[50] This is the case regardless of whether the motion is brought before or after the relevant measure is adopted at European Union level.

[51] The House of Lords Select Committee on the European Union, above, n. 5, at 22, recommended that the Government keep the Committee informed of significant European Union proposals within the comitology framework.

[52] See official transcripts of discussions in EU Committee with K. Meenan, 16 June 2004 (OIR J-EU 2004.43) and 9 September 2004 (OIR J-EU 2004.48).

It is to be hoped that the above suggestions will be considered with a view to improving the overall timeliness and scope of Oireachtas scrutiny. Such improvement will be difficult, however, above all because the institutional practice of the Oireachtas is not geared toward scrutiny of initiatives involving abstract vague targets and timeframes. Indeed, attempts to carry out this kind of scrutiny to date have been dogged by misunderstandings. However, all concerned appear to recognise that the current arrangements must be kept under constant review, allowing for evolution over time – both in response to practical logistics and, of course, in response to changes at European Union level. There is certainly a strong effort to continually improve the scrutiny process, rather than to regard the Act as having drawn a line in the sand which obviated the need for further improvement.[53]

5. Other Relevant Work of the Oireachtas Joint Committee on European Affairs

Other aspects of the work of the Oireachtas Joint Committee on European Affairs include participation in the Conference of European Affairs Committees (COSAC). The Amsterdam Protocol on the role of national parliaments provides that COSAC may

> "address to the European Parliament, the Council and the Commission any contribution which it deems appropriate on the legislative activities of the Union, notably in relation to the application of the principle of subsidiarity, the area of freedom, security and justice as well as questions regarding fundamental rights"[54]

and, further, that it "may make any contribution it deems appropriate for the attention of the institutions of the European Union".[55]

COSAC recently adopted guidelines for relations between governments and parliaments on Community issues.[56] MacCárthaigh has observed that "COSAC has consolidated its presence within the Union's institutional infrastructure to the point where it may be considered the representative body for national parliaments at European Union level."[57] However, he adds,

[53] This situation casts further doubts on the wisdom of having legislated in this area.
[54] Para. 6 of the Protocol.
[55] Para. 4 of the Protocol.
[56] The 'Copenhagen Parliamentary Guidelines' (text adopted at the 28th COSAC Conference, Brussels, 27 January 2003).
[57] Above, n. 37, at 6.

correctly, that the influence of national parliaments in the European Union does not begin and end with COSAC. There will always be limits to collective action between national parliaments and one should not make the mistake of thinking that there is now a new collective institution for national parliaments.

The Oireachtas has recently appointed a civil servant as a designated liaison officer to be based in Brussels. As a result, a significant further improvement in the information flow between the European Union and the Oireachtas is to be expected. There are of course also European Union aspects to the European Conference of Speakers and the Conference of Parliamentary Secretaries General.

Possible New Developments

Subsidiarity Monitoring

Monitoring for compliance with the principle of subsidiarity is – or should be – regarded as already part of the role of the Joint Committee on European Affairs and other associated committees. However, if the Constitutional Treaty (or any subsequent treaty containing similar provisions) is ever ratified,[58] a formal role will be conferred on the Oireachtas which will require greater focus and coordination.

At the Nice intergovernmental conference, the role of national parliaments in the European architecture was singled out as one of the key topics to be addressed in the envisaged deeper and wider debate about the future of the European Union, and indeed the issue was subsequently addressed at the Convention on the Future of Europe. A Protocol was annexed to the Constitutional Treaty on the role of national parliaments and in addition to a Protocol on the application of the principles of subsidiarity and proportionality. The former Protocol envisaged that European Union institutions would supply national parliaments directly with documentation, thereby curbing dependence on national governments. It also envisaged the occasional sending of reasoned opinions by national parliaments to European Union institutions on issues of subsidiarity. In this way national parliaments would be given a ‘yellow card’ prerogative, which would have come into play if one third of the total votes allocated to national parliaments were in favour of the assertion that the principle of subsidiarty had been breached. [59]

---

[58] Editor’s note: see now in this regard the observations in the introduction to this book.

[59] Or one quarter of such votes where the policy field concerned is that of justice and home affairs.

In such case, the Commission would have had to review its proposal, although it would have then remained free to "maintain, amend or withdraw" it.

The envisaged timeframe was tight – the six-week window initially established by Amsterdam was to apply here. The House of Lords European Union Select Committee described this as "regrettably short",[60] and the House of Commons European Scrutiny Committee stated that

> "the six-week period allowed by the treaty for making reasoned objections is challenging, but we will often have identified well in advance forthcoming proposals we might object to on grounds of subsidiarity."[61]

"Subsidiarity' is a well-known phrase in European affairs, but its precise meaning is far from clear.[62] The essential idea is that decisions should be taken at the lowest practical level (*i.e.*, as close to the individual as possible). Subsidiarity is opposed to centralism and the unnecessary downward exercise of power. It was introduced into Community law as a general rule by the Treaty on European Union at Maastricht. The Preamble to the Treaty on European Union stated that decisions were to be taken "as closely as possible to the citizen in accordance with the principle of subsidiarity".[63] Furthermore, Article 2 of this Treaty stated *inter alia* that the objectives of the Union were to be achieved while respecting the principle of subsidiarity as defined in Article 5 of the Treaty Establishing the European Community. Article 5 of the EC Treaty provides the following definition:

> "*in areas which do not fall within its exclusive competence*, the Community shall take action, in accordance with the principle of subsidiarity, only if and in so far as the objectives of the proposed action cannot be sufficiently achieved by the Member States and can therefore, by reason of the scale or effects of the proposed action, be better achieved by the Community."[64]

---

[60] *Strengthening national parliamentary scrutiny of the EU – the Constitution's subsidiarity early warning mechanism* (Fourteenth Report of 2004–2005 Session) at 7.

[61] Sixth Report (2004–2005 Session) at 11. The Report recites (also at 11) instances of unsatisfactory replies from the relevant European Commissioner regarding concerns in relation to subsidiarity, and cautions that the Commission will need to do better in future.

[62] See however para. 5 of the Protocol on the application of the principles of subsidiarity and proportionality annexed to the Treaty on European Union and to the Treaty establishing the European Community at Amsterdam. See also Article 5 of the Treaty Establishing the European Community, referred to in the text below.

[63] See also Article 1 of the Treaty on European Union.

[64] Emphasis added.

Article 5 also provides that "any action by the Community shall not go beyond what is necessary to achieve the objectives of this Treaty." This is an invocation of the principle of proportionality, a somewhat separate, but inter-related, principle.

It will be noted from the definition quoted above that subsidiarity applies only in areas outside the exclusive competence of the European Community. Pending the potential ratification of the Constitutional Treaty, however (or any other treaty with similar clarificatory provisions),[65] it will remain far from clear which areas fall within or outside this exclusive competence.[66] Another complication is the suggestion (not accepted by this writer) that whenever the European Community exercises implied powers in an area, that area may thenceforth be regarded as falling within the exclusive competence of the Community. If that were the case, subsidiarity would be applicable only when the Community legislated for the first time in an area.[67]

Some further guidance as to the meaning of subsidiarity is available from the Amsterdam Protocol on the application of the principles of subsidiarity and proportionality. This purports to explain the conditions for the application of the principle in practice. It requires that the reasons why a Community objective can be better achieved by the Community than by the Member States be substantiated.[68]

---

[65] See now in this regard the observations in the introduction to this volume.

[66] See in this regard, Article I-13 of the Constitutional Treaty. As regards the existing position, de Búrca and de Witte have stated:

> "the exact division of powers and competences at EU level has, to date, been left to be determined rather fluidly ... In particular, the Court of Justice has conspicuously never attempted to delineate a complete doctrine of the division of powers between the EC and the Member States ... there is currently a total lack of coherence in the allocation of powers between the EU and its Member States".

Those authors take a narrow view of what constitute exclusive European Union powers, noting that the debate to date has been entirely inconclusive. They do not even accept that the regulation of the internal market is necessarily an exclusive European Union power. Shared powers and complementary powers are the norm (the latter mainly with regard to the newer policy fields added by Maastricht). See G. de Búrca and B. de Witte, "The Delimitation of Powers between the EU and its Member States" in A. Arnull and D. Wincott (eds.), *Accountability and Legitimacy in the European Union* (Oxford University Press, 2003)).

[67] This suggestion is articulated, although not necessarily approved of, by Hartley: see T.C. Hartley, *The Foundations of European Community Law* (Oxford University Press, 2003, fifth edition).

[68] The Protocol emphasises, *inter alia,* that Community action should be as simple as possible. The Community should legislate only to the extent necessary. Other things being equal, directives should be preferred to regulations and framework directives preferred to detailed measures (the former in each case leaving more scope for national decision). Care should be taken to respect well-established national arrangements and national legal systems. It will be noted that this latter aspect of the

The Protocol provides the following guidelines as indicators that the proposed action cannot be sufficiently achieved by Member States in the framework of their constitutional systems, and can therefore be better achieved by action on the part of the Community. First, the fact that the issue in question has transnational aspects which cannot be satisfactorily regulated by Member States; secondly, that actions by Member States alone or lack of Community action would conflict with the requirements of the Treaty or otherwise significantly damage Member States' interests; thirdly, that action at Community level would produce clear benefits by reason of its scale or effects compared with action at the level of the Member States. As Steiner, Woods and Twigg-Flesner have argued, "these criteria do no more than restate the problem; indeed they may even add to the difficulties because it is not even clear whether these criteria arc cumulative or alternative.[69]

There is a dilemma at the heart of this: a real difficulty arises when subsidiarity, which is essentially a political maxim, is sought to be applied as a legal test. The problem is that it is difficult to find, as a matter of law, that the principle has been breached. If one looks at any random example of European Union legislation, one will find some explanation in the preamble for why Community action is necessary or appropriate. On its own terms, the logic of such explanations will normally be impeccable. But equally, in most cases one can also construct a perfectly logical argument against Community action. On the other hand, subsidiarity must be given legal force if it is to be meaningful at all.

Weiler suggests that, given the open-textured nature of the provision on subsidiarity, the appropriate criteria for judicial review would be "reasonableness". In other words, the Court should not simply substitute its view, but decide whether, in the circumstances, the Commission or Council has given a reasonable account of the measure in terms of subsidiarity. In most cases, he surmises, the answer will be positive. Toth likewise points to the inherent difficulty in making subsidiarity justiciable – it involves complex political and economic judgments.[70] Emiliou suggests that because

Protocol deals with the form of the legal instrument (*i.e.*, whether a directive is preferable to a regulation), as opposed to its substance (*i.e.*, whether the policy sought to be achieved is justifiable in the first place). There is a tendency sometimes to reduce subsidiarity to the formal element, when that should not be the case.

[69] J. Steiner, L.Woods & C.Twigg-Flesner, *Textbook on EC Law* (Oxford University Press, 2006, ninth edition) at 51.

[70] A.G. Toth, "The Principle of Subsidiarity in the Maastricht Treaty", (1992) 29 *Common Market Law Review* 1079 at 1102.

of the subjective character of the principle, if the European Court of Justice gets involved at all, it should limit its review to manifest or grave disregard of the principle.[71]

Despite the strong criticisms which can be leveled at the law (as it has evolved to date) on subsidiarity, this is not a reason to dismiss the concept. Indeed, to the contrary, at the heart of the concept is a very important political maxim that must be given force. The vagueness in this area should not be a reason for reluctance by national parliaments to exercise their powers in this area if the draft European Union Constitution (or a subsequent treaty with similar provisions) is ratified. Instead, should this happen, parliaments should exercise those powers vigilantly. They should not hesitate to analyse, and where appropriate oppose, measures which they believe infringe the principle of subsidiarity. It is hoped that through this process new life will be breathed into the principle. If it is seen to have real political force, it can be expected that the Court in turn will take its role in this regard more seriously. Otherwise there is a real danger that the concept will be used as an empty formula by European institutions, equivalent in value to the emperor's new clothes.

A COSAC meeting on 17–18 May 2005 revealed the outcome of a exercise by national parliaments simulating the application to the Third Railway Package of the Protocol on the application of the principles of subsidiarity and proportionality annexed to the Constitutional Treaty. The test was conducted over a six-week period. It proved to be an important learning experience for the European Union Committee and Sub-Committee. It focused members' attention on the principle of subsidiarity and its rather vague nature. It also highlighted potential future difficulties in applying the concept in Ireland, especially where a measure appears to infringe subsidiarity in relation to one member state but not all of them.

6. Conclusions

According to The Final Report of the Convention's Working Group on National Parliaments,[72] the carrying out of effective scrutiny is the primary

---

[71] N. Emilou, "Subsidiarity: An Effective Barrier against 'the Enterprises of Ambition'?" (1992) 17 *European Law Review* 383, at 405.
[72] Above, at n. 39.

role of national parliaments in European matters. On the other hand, the Report concludes that it would not be appropriate to be overly prescriptive about national approaches to scrutiny. Each country must adopt – and adapt – a model from within its own constitutional structure.[73]

The position in Ireland can be summarised by saying that the power of parliamentary committees regarding European Union affairs is of a political rather than a legal nature, but that such political power is quite considerable – and is indisputably greater than before. Furthermore, it is some source of comfort that, in the space of two years year, the Irish parliament has gone from having practically no scrutiny system for European Union affairs to having developed a quite sophisticated one. It is worth reiterating that the rapid change in this area was greatly facilitated by the fact that, after decades of ignoring the issue, both the governmental and parliamentary players took sudden a leap of faith and genuinely cooperated with one another in setting up a system that works very well from the perspective of *both* institutions. The broadly simultaneous establishment of two complementary administrative processes and the investing of resources in a proper interface was a vital component of this complex process.

Nevertheless, as outlined in this chapter, many improvements could be made to current scrutiny procedures. Moreover, while catching up on that front, parliament will also need to adapt to other new roles which may arise. There must be greater recognition that national policy- and law-making is suffused with European Union policy and law. As the mechanisms of Government itself change, so too should the methods for interacting with it. MacCárthaigh has offered the following advice:

> "there is no perfect position for [national parliaments] in the European Union institutional infrastructure, and rather than seeking one, [national parliaments] might best be served by concentrating their efforts [on] making sure their voice is heard at as early a stage as possible in the process of European Union governance."[74]

Finally, one must turn to the age-old question of resources. Before the inauguration of the present scrutiny system, McDowell cautioned that

> "[a] full-blooded and committed reform in this area would require not merely that the Oireachtas be given greatly increased resources; it would

[73] See also A. Benz, "Path-Dependent Institutions and Strategic Veto Players: National Parliaments and the European Union" (2004) 27 *West European Politics* 897.

[74] Above, n. 37, at 23.

> also demand that a core of consciousness, adequately resourced, be created at the center of Government to ensure that the collective responsibility of the Cabinet and its procedures, have full effect in relation to these European matters."[75]

This momentum needs to be maintained. The Sub-Committee itself has cautioned that the "question of resources to support scrutiny across all committees has become an important question which can no longer be avoided."[76] In terms of its performance to date in the parliamentary scrutiny of European Union affairs, Ireland would perhaps be described in Maurer's typology as a slow adaptor on the way towards being a multi-level player. It is to be hoped that it continues on this journey.

APPENDIX

Paragraph 1 of the Orders of Reference of Joint Committee on European Affairs

(a) [... The functions of the Joint Committee are] to –

- (i) scrutinise, in the context of European Union issues and measures to be taken by the Council of Ministers of the European Union –
  - (I) any proposals under the Community treaties for legislation by the Council or the Council acting jointly with the European Parliament,
  - (II) any document which is published for submission to the European Council, the Council or the European Central Bank,
  - (III) any proposal for a common strategy, a joint action or a common position under Title V of the Treaty on European Union which is prepared for submission to the Council or to the European Council,
  - (IV) any proposal for a common position, framework decision, decision or a convention under Title VI on Treaty on European Union which is prepared for submission to the Council,
  - (V) any document (not falling within (II), (III), or (IV) above) which is published by one Union institution for or with a view to submission to another Union institution and which does not related exclusively to the consideration of any proposal for legislation, and

---

[75] Above, n. 10, at 483.

[76] Joint Committee on European Affairs: Sub-Committee on European Scrutiny, above, n. 42, at ii.

(VI) any other document relating to European Union matters deposited in both Houses of the Oireachtas by a Member of the Government or Minister of State,

as it may select;

(ii) consider such matters arising from Ireland's membership of the European Communities and its adherence to the Treaty on European Union, as it may select;

(iii) consider such –

(I) acts of the institutions of the European Communities,

(II) regulations under the European Communities Acts, 1972 to 1998,

(III) other instruments made under statute and necessitated by the obligations of membership of the European Communities,

as it may select;

(IV) consider such other matters as may be referred to it from time to time by both Houses of the Oireachtas;

and

(V) represent both Houses of the Oireachtas at the Conference of European Affairs Committees (COSAC);

and ...[to] report thereon to both Houses of the Oireachtas.

(b) The Joint Committee shall have:

(i) the powers defined in Standing Order 81(1) to (9) inclusive;

(ii) the power to refer a proposal for European Union legislation which has been considered by it (and which has been concluded to be of sufficient national importance to require further scrutiny) to a Joint Committee on which has been conferred the power defined in Standing Order 81(4) to consider such proposals;

and

(iii) the power to request the presence of Members of the Government (or Ministers of State nominated in their stead) (or, in the case of the European Council, the Taoiseach or Minister for Foreign Affairs) to attend before the Joint Committee and provide, in private session if so desired by the Member of the Government or Minister of State, oral briefings in advance of Council meetings to enable the Joint Committee to make known its views.

(c) The following persons may attend meetings of the Joint Committee and of its sub-Committees and may take part in proceedings without having a right to vote or to move motions and amendments –

(i) Members of the European Parliament elected from constituencies in Ireland (including Northern Ireland);

(ii) Members of the Irish delegation to the Parliamentary Assembly of the Council of Europe;

and

(iii) at the invitation of the Joint Committee or of a sub-Committee, as appropriate, other Members of the European Parliament.

The quorum of the Joint Committee shall be five, of whom at least one shall be a Member of Dáil Éireann and one a Member of Seanad Éireann.

11.
What is the Role of a Committee on European Affairs?

Katherine Meenan[1]

This chapter is intended to review the role and responsibilities of the Joint Oireachtas Committee on European Affairs in its most recent manifestation, to analyse the functioning and work of the Joint Committee, and to consider the different elements of the relationship between a small parliamentary democracy and the European Union.[2] It does not however deal with the role or work of the Sub-Committee on European Scrutiny, as this is a topic considered elsewhere in the present volume.[3]

For the purposes of this chapter, it is sought to distinguish between 'scrutiny' and 'oversight'. 'Scrutiny' may be defined for the purposes of this chapter, and very specifically in an Irish context, as dealing with a position quite a long way down the legislative pipeline. It is where parliament (or its committees) deal with what the relevant Irish legislation terms 'measures', in other words, documents which already encapsulate the proposals of the European Union institutions, and which can be accepted, amended, or rejected. Scrutiny in this sense is an absolutely essential part of the legislative process, and is particularly important to ensure the transparency of the European legislative process to the citizen. It is not policy-oriented, not strategic, and is reactive rather than proactive. 'Oversight' on the other hand, is used in this chapter to describe an ongoing review of the strategic

[1] Consultant to Joint Oireachtas Committee on European Affairs. Editor's note: readers should note that this chapter was completed before the most recent Dáil elections, which took place in May, 2007 – shortly before this book went to press. At the time of writing of this note, no successor Joint Oireachtas Committee on European Affairs has been established to replace the Joint Committee discussed in this chapter. Nor is any expected to sit until November, 2007.
[2] Here, as elsewhere in this paper, the term 'European Union' is to be regarded as encompassing the European Communities which form part of it.
[3] See the chapter in this book by Lia O'Hegarty.

issues facing the European Union and the tracking of the input which an Irish representative in the Council of Ministers is making to the policies and actions of the Union.

It will be argued that to focus on the scrutiny of legislative and other proposals, as the innovative features of the Constitutional Treaty tempted us to do, runs the risk of diverting attention from the role which national parliaments can play throughout the whole matrix of relationships of the member states with the European Union and with each other.[4]

1. Irish Parliamentary Scrutiny[5]

Interest in the parliamentary review of European affairs was stimulated by the particular historical circumstances of the rejection of the Nice Treaty by the Irish electorate in referendum in 2001. It is still difficult to determine exactly what the causes of this rejection were, but it is clear that a factor was general uncertainty among many voters about the future of the European project, allied to a real concern about inadequate information and a perceived lack of understanding of the particular implications of the Treaty changes.[6] This was combined with complacency on the part of the political establishment and a failure to take seriously the concerns of voters about the increasing impact of the European Union on their lives.

In particular there was a failure on the part of the political system, including all pro-European political parties, to get involved in the referendum campaign and an assumption that the electorate could be relied upon to turn out and to vote the right way. In fact, the electorate believed that it did not have adequate information to make such a choice, and rather than vote against, refused to vote at all. As a response to this perceived lack of information among the electorate, and in order to deal to deal with concerns over lack of transparency and understanding of European affairs, the political system began to make changes in the way European business was handled within parliament.[7] This was part of an attempt to regain ground and to

---

[4] Editor's note: see the introduction to this book in relation to the most recent developments concerning the Constitutional Treaty.

[5] For an introduction to this topic, see L. O'Hegarty "The Role of the European Committee in the National Parliaments after Accession – The Example of Ireland" (Paper delivered at the TAIEX Seminar on Parliaments and Accession to the EU, Prague, 8–9 September 2003).

[6] See in this regard R. Sinnott, "Attitudes and Behaviour of the Irish Electorate in the Referendum on the Treaty of Nice", at www.ucd.ie/dempart/workingpapers/nice1.pdf).

[7] B. Laffan and A. Langan, "Securing a 'Yes': from Nice I to Nice II" (Notre Europe Policy Paper No. 13), at www.notre-europe.asso.fr/IMG/pdf/Policypaper13.pdf).

justify the holding of a second referendum, by proving that enough had changed to make a second vote worthwhile.

Because of the historical circumstances of that time, as described in O'Hegarty,[8] the legal bases on which scrutiny and oversight (using the distinction which is proposed above) are carried out varies. 'Scrutiny' is provided for by legislation, *viz.*, by the European Union (Scrutiny) Act 2002. This work, which consists of receiving all legislative proposals, including in the area of justice and home affairs, sifting, reviewing and, if appropriate, redirecting them to the relevant sectoral committee, is done by the Scrutiny Sub-Committee of the Joint Committee on European Affairs. Thus the work of the Sub-Committee has a basis in legislation,[9] while the work of the Joint Committee on European Affairs is based on resolutions of each House. On the surface, reliance on legislation in this manner does not appear to have been particularly necessary, but presumably matters were arranged in this way so as to reassure the public that intensified scrutiny procedures would be certain to continue in future legislative periods. The committee system of the Houses of the Oireachtas developed considerably in the post-2002 legislative period as it did in the previous one (*i.e.*, from 1997 to 2002). The start of each legislative period involves a whole series of deals being made between parties regarding the setting up of committees and the allocation of chairs and members. Although no reference to the point was made in the debates on the legislation, it seems likely that there was a recognition that 'horse-trading' would be involved in the establishment of the committees – and that recourse was had to legislation in order to provide reassurance that the commitment to a proper scrutiny system was not something which could be modified or diminished in the future. The introduction of a system of parliamentary scrutiny with a legislative base guaranteed that scrutiny would be taken as seriously in the future as it was being taken in the phase leading up to a re-run of the referendum on Nice.[10]

2. The Orders of Reference of the Joint Committee on European Affairs

The work of the Joint Committee on European Affairs is governed by Orders of Reference. The Orders of Reference of the Joint Committee on European

[8] O'Hegarty, above, n. 5.

[9] Although note however that the Sub-Committee itself is not explicitly mentioned in the legislation.

[10] See J. Shaw, "The Constitutional Treaty and the Question of Ratification: Unscrambling the Consequences and Identifying the Paradoxes", *European Policy Brief* No. 10 (Federal Trust, London, 2005).

Affairs[11] stipulate the functions of the Joint Committee on European Affairs to scrutinise, to consider, and to represent. More specifically, it must scrutinise such legislative proposals at European level (whether in the Community Pillar or in the common foreign and security policy, and police and criminal justice cooperation fields) as it may select. It must also scrutinise such documents as it may select which are published by one European Union institution for submission to another. This is in addition to such other documents which it may select relating to European Union matters as are deposited by a member of the Government or a Minister of State. The Committee must consider such matters arising from Ireland's membership of the Union or Communities, acts of the Community institutions, ministerial regulations and other statutory instruments necessitated because of Ireland's membership of the Communities as it may select, in addition to such other matters as may be referred to it by either house of the Oireachtas. In addition, it must also represent both houses of the Oireachtas at the Conference of Community and European Affairs Committees of Parliaments of the European Union (COSAC) and report thereon to both houses of the Oireachtas.

What this means in practice is that the Joint Committee on European Affairs sets its own agenda and defines its own priorities. It may deal with any matter relating in any way to Ireland's membership of the European Union, and it may also review any national legislation which is the result of the transposition of European law into domestic law.

3. The Composition and Nature of the Joint Committee on European Affairs

The Joint Committee on European Affairs is made up of seventeen members. Eleven of these are members of the Dáil (or lower house) and six are senators. There are eight representatives of the two Government parties. There are two independents or non-aligned members. The Joint Committee is one of only two committees (the other being the Public Accounts Committee) which is chaired by the opposition. It has traditionally operated on a bipartisan basis and would seek never to be in a position to call a vote.

Members of the European Parliament, including those from Northern Ireland, and members of the Irish delegation to the Parliamentary Assembly

[11] Made by the Dáil on 16 October 2002. The equivalent order was made by the Seanad on 23 October 2002. The Orders of Reference of the Joint Committee on European Affairs are set out in full in Annex I to the chapter in this book by Lia O'Hegarty.

of the Council of Europe may attend and take part, although they may not vote or move motions or amendments. Interestingly, the Joint Committee on European Affairs is entitled invite other members, *i.e.,* non-Irish members of the European Parliament to attend.

Because most of the parties represented in the Oireachtas are supportive of Ireland's membership of the European Union, the consensus from which the Joint Committee on European Affairs operates is, on the whole, favourable to the principle of continued Irish membership and committed participation in most areas of European Union activity. The only representative of a Euro-sceptical party is the single Sinn Féin member.

In addition to a default position which is favourable to the European Union, there is also a considerable level of expertise on European Union affairs. The first chairperson appointed in this session was Deputy Gay Mitchell, a former junior minister in the Department of Foreign Affairs and member of the reflection group which led to the Treaty of Amsterdam, who left the Committee on his election to the European Parliament. Deputy Ruairi Quinn is a former Finance Minister who chaired the Council of Ministers, which drafted the Stability and Growth Pact. Deputy Seamus Kirk is a former Minister of State at the Department of Agriculture and Food. Given the level of expertise of the Committee, added to the attendance of members of the European Parliament, debates can be particularly well-informed.

The agenda and the longer-term work programme are set by the chair, with the advice of the clerk of the Committee, and in consultation with the Committee. Most of its deliberations are in public. It would normally meet once a week when the Dáil is sitting, although there is no absolutely rigid pattern. It also meets when the Dáil is not sitting, in September or early October.

The Joint Committee on European Affairs has the power to request the presence of members of the Government (including the Taoiseach, if the matter being addressed relates to the European Council) to come before it.

4. The Work of the Joint Committee on European Affairs

The question arises of how the Joint Committee establishes its agenda. The most significant work of the Committee is in the regular briefing, which takes place before and after each General Affairs and External Relations Council. A rhythm is established by the work of this Council. As part of the establishment of the Joint Committee on European Affairs, an undertaking was given that there would be regular briefings. As part of that understanding, the Committee seeks to adjust its schedule of work to facilitate the minister concerned. There is a wide-ranging debate with the Minister for Foreign Affairs (or more frequently, the Minister for State for European Affairs) before each meeting of the General Affairs and External Relations Council. The full agenda, with supporting documentation, is made available to members, as is a report on all decisions taken at previous Council meetings. The minister present will make a presentation on the issues for discussion and this is followed by a comprehensive and lively debate. These meetings are held in public, and the gallery is normally full of representatives of the embassies of the 24 other member states in Dublin. The number and rank of European diplomats who attend must in itself be a statement of the transparency of the process and of the quality of the information which is available. However, coverage by journalists is infrequent.

Delegations and visiting groups, including those from other parliaments, may drive the agenda to a certain extent (The number of visits from other parliaments in the context of the Irish Presidency was almost overwhelming). Some topics – such as the issue of Turkish accession to the European Union – effectively present themselves as topics because they are items of public interest. In the case of that issue, the timetable was set by the wider timetable of the European Union itself and a need for the Committee to have its own work finished and ready for presentation to the Minister of State for European Affairs in good time before the European Council which was to decide on the opening of accession negotiations with Turkey.

During the period of the Convention on the Future of Europe, the Oireachtas representatives to the Convention reported to the Joint Committee on European Affairs on a regular basis. Equally, during the intergovernmental conference which ultimately agreed the Constitutional Treaty, government representatives briefed the Committee.

From 2003 to 2004, the Joint Committee on European Affairs undertook a series of hearings on the Lisbon Process and published a report on the issues raised for Ireland.[12] The report of the committee was published before the Spring European Council of March 2004, held under the Irish Presidency. Following that European Council, the Taoiseach, as President in office of the European Council, appeared before the Joint Committee on European Affairs

---

[12] *Report on the Lisbon Strategy* (Joint Committee on European Affairs, 2004). This report is available at www.oireachtas.ie. The Lisbon process derives its name from the agreement at the March 2000 Lisbon European Council meeting to make the European Union the most competitive and dynamic knowledge-driven economy by 2010.

to discuss its report. This meeting took place in public session, and – as normal – proceeded by way of discussion and the exchange of views, rather than on the basis of a motion.

More recently, Margaret Wallström, the Commission Vice-President and Institutional Relations and Communication Strategy Commissioner appeared before the Joint Committee on European Affairs as part of the Commission's new communications programme. She has made it known that she intends to visit each of the national parliaments on a regular basis.

5. The Nature of Parliamentary Oversight

The Joint Committee on European Affairs has never sought to mandate a minister or to direct how a minister should vote in a given situation. The particular conditions which would enable this to happen are not present in the Irish parliamentary system.[13] First, for it to happen, the Government would have to be in a minority, not just on the Committee, but in the Dáil as well. In other words, the Government would have to be in the position of not being able to impose its policies. Secondly, the *modus operandi* of the Joint Committee is consensual rather than confrontational, and the position of the Committee is favourable to European integration. There is also a common awareness on the part of members of the Committee that Ireland, as a small member state, does not determine the agenda of the European Union, but rather operates 'at the margins', attempting to mitigate the negative aspects of any proposal and to enhance the positive. Thus if an issue were to arise which was of major concern to members of the Committee, the response in the Committee would be to seek to work with the executive to find a solution. Thirdly, the value of such a mandating system has been greatly reduced by the widespread introduction of qualified majority voting in the Council of Ministers, because even the most binding instructions to a minister may not be of importance if the minister can easily be outvoted in the Council.

The operation of the Joint Committee on European Affairs demonstrates the extent to which each parliamentary system responds to its own agenda, whether political or constitutional. While the role of the committees within the Oireachtas has developed dramatically even during the life-time of the current Oireachtas, their function and importance is still relatively minor compared to many other European parliaments.

---

[13] As to these conditions, see A. Maurer "National Parliaments in the European Architecture: Elements for Establishing a Best Practice Mechanism" (Paper submitted to Working Group IV of the Convention on the Future of Europe on 10 July 2002). See also the chapter in this volume by Andreas Maurer.

In the case of the Oireachtas (a 'talking parliament' in political science terms, as opposed to a Continental-style 'working parliament'), work is traditionally centred on the floor of the House, where legislation is passed as a framework, with implementation being left to secondary legislation. The direct ancestor of the Irish system is, of course, the United Kingdom system but the different scale and different voting systems mean that the operation of committees in the two parliaments is hardly comparable. For instance, in the Irish system, because of an acutely proportional voting system, Government majorities of four or five are regarded by the parliamentary whips as very comfortable, whereas in the House of Commons a majority of one hundred would represent a poor electoral showing. Equally, because of the actual size of the parliament, it will never be possible to develop the kind of committee system which exists in Westminster, because it would not be possible to provide enough members to make it function.

If a national parliament does not bind the ministers in the Council of Ministers, what then is the function of its oversight mechanisms? In a report on the operation of the comitology system,[14] the Joint Committee on European Affairs considered what its contribution might be. The Committee believed that the value of its work lay in its effect on policy orientation, in the enhancement of transparency, in the provision of information, and in being a bridge between the legislative processes of the European Union and citizens. While Oireachtas committees cannot, and do not seek to bind ministers in their votes in the Council of Ministers, this does not mean that committees have no influence on the executive. The open debate on policy issues, and the opportunity for members of the Oireachtas to make their views known, particularly in the relatively consensual forum of the Joint Committee on European Affairs, must have an influence on the actions of ministers in the Council.

Given the complexity of day-to-day European business, it is unrealistic to expect that the work of the Joint Committee on European Affairs will be followed by the general public. But, in particular with developments in the use of the internet, there is an element of reassurance for the citizen that, if he or she really wants to, the work of the Committee can be followed in detail. The full debates of the Committee are available on the internet within approximately one week of a meeting. Although it is perhaps more of a theoretical possibility than something which is done in practice, the

[14] Joint Committee on European Affairs *Comitology and Parliamentary Scrutiny* (unpublished report, 2004).

parliamentary oversight of the workings of Ireland's relationship with the European Union is capable of being studied. Transparency and access to information are two sides of the same coin. The fact that the policy debates of the Joint Committee on European Affairs on European Affairs take place in public, (whether one is speaking of real or of virtual public space), is a reassurance to the citizen that the process may be understood and that it is possible to follow the range of legislative proposals. The fact of debate and discussion in the Committee is a bridge to the citizen. Through their member of the Oireachtas, a citizen can have access to the information and an input into the debate.

6. The Influence Exerted by the Joint Committee on European Affairs

The question arises as to whether a Committee on European Affairs operating in such a fashion can have a real impact on the European Union. Certainly in the context of a national presidency of the Council of Ministers and the European Council, this possibility exists. Some examples of this may be given.

The first example consists of the decision which was taken by the Joint Committee on European Affairs to establish an advisory group to examine the role of the European Union in its relations with developing countries. The group, which was chaired by a prominent trade unionist with a background in development aid, and which included a number of high-level individuals, looked at issues such as the AIDS/HIV crisis, debt burdens and food shortages in the developing world, and also at international trade arrangements. The report was presented to the Committee who referred it to the Government with a recommendation that its findings be incorporated as part of the programme for the Irish presidency of the European Union in 2004. This report subsequently formed the basis of the approach of the Irish presidency to these issues.

Another example of the Joint Committee on European Affairs having exercised influence was seen when the Committee organised a number of hearings and wrote a report on the Lisbon process, and subsequently invited the Taoiseach (Prime Minister), directly after the European Council of Spring 2004, to express his views on the developments in this process.[15] The Committee's preparatory work was carried out in public and involved

[15] Joint Committee on European Affairs meeting of 28 April, 2004 (transcript available at http://debates.oireachtas.ie/DDebate.aspx?F=EUJ20040428.xml&Node=8#N8).

national and European experts. Although the report of the Committee was published just before the Spring European Council, the information available to the Committee and the nature of the debates which had taken place informed the work of those officials of the Irish presidency who helped prepare the Council.

These examples relate to a presidency situation, when a national parliament has the most direct relationship with the ministers who actually define Council agendas and chair Council meetings. However, it seems likely that, whether in or outside a presidency situation, specific, well informed views, expressed in a consensual, cross-party setting will always have a direct impact on a ministerial position. The systematic nature of the relationship is the main guarantee in this regard. It is perfectly possible for the executive to ignore the views of a parliamentary committee on an occasional basis – but when there is a meeting every month and when each decision of the Council of Ministers is subsequently reported back to the committee in public session, a minister knows that he or she can not go on ignoring the views of the committee

7. The Resources Available to the Joint Oireachtas Committee on European Affairs

The resources available to the Joint Oireachtas Committee on European Affairs are limited. Given that a certain amount of travel and overseas representation is required, which in itself is resource-intensive, it is remarkable that the Committee achieves the amount it does. The parliamentary system most similar to the Irish one is that of the United Kingdom, and wistful comparisons are often made with the House of Lords Select Committee on the European Union. When comparisons are made of the resources made available to the two committees, it is clear that the Oireachtas is very far behind.

A comparison of the output of the two committees shows that the House of Lords is more inclined to review issues, rather than make the more incisive recommendations typical of the Oireachtas Joint Committee on European Affairs. This may represent a more cautious approach to the European Union generally on the part of the House of Lords Select Committee, and the effects of that Committee's being a more politically-divided body. Judging by their output, however, the aspirations of the two committees are also different.

It should also be borne in mind that the absorption capacity of the House of Lords Committee and the Oireachtas Committee varies. It is understandable that members of both houses of the Oireachtas should feel overwhelmed by the volume of material waiting to be dealt with. Clearly the entire committee system is woefully short of resources, particularly in the more specialised skills. There is a constant fear that in the carrying-out of its tasks by the Joint Oireachtas Committee, something important will be missed or its importance underestimated. (Thus for example, whoever would have thought that the Habitats Directive – the effects of which gave rise to a great deal of political controversy in Ireland – would bring so much in its wake?) While it is essential that the secretariats and the support to members be enlarged considerably, staff can not exercise the mandate of duly-elected members of parliament. Ultimately, oversight is the responsibility of parliamentarians rather than staff. And while one goal of the Joint Oireachtas Committee should certainly be to do more, another – more important – one should be to do it better.

8. Scrutiny Versus Oversight

Because the brief of the Joint Committee on European Affairs is broad, and because the technical work of scrutiny is delegated to the Scrutiny Sub-Committee, the Joint Committee on European Affairs is not dependent on the flow of documentation – and is therefore in a better position than would otherwise be the case to review, on its own initiative, policy proposals on the foreign and security affairs agenda or in the justice and home affairs field. Whereas the Scrutiny Sub-Committee is reactive, the role of the European Affairs Joint Committee on European Affairs is to be proactive.

The Committee on the Modernisation of the House of Commons has distinguished between what it calls 'Council driven' and 'document driven' committees.[16] This is a valuable distinction, but even having both kinds of committee in place would probably not go far enough to meet the needs of oversight. To say this is not to underestimate in any sense the particular democratic value of the proper scrutiny of draft legislation. But the European Union is moving increasingly to a more complex, policy-driven rather than legislation-driven form of action. Thus, the European Commission, in its report on governance, has identified the need for a wider choice and more flexible policy tools within, and in addition to, traditional legislation.[17]

[16] See House of Commons Select Committee on Modernisation of the House of Commons, *Scrutiny of European Business*, Second Report of 2004/2005 Session, (Stationery Office, London, 2005).
[17] *Report from the Commission on European Governance* (Office for Official Publications of the European Communities, Luxembourg, 2003) (available at http://europa.eu.int/comm/governance/docs/comm_rapport_en.pdf).

When what is now the European Community was a strictly economic entity, it might have been possible to argue that all governance could be undertaken by legislation – whether in the form of regulation, decision, or directive. This is clearly no longer the case. The European Union now has a foreign policy, a social policy, and a home affairs policy. These are not governed by legislation, but by a much more complex set of arrangements, and the oversight of these arrangements is an important part of the parliamentary process.[18]

The open method of coordination, which 'involves concerted action by the Member States outside the competences attributed to the Union by the treaties'[19] is an increasingly important way of doing business. It was given legal recognition for the first time in the Constitutional Treaty. Hence, for example, according to Article III-210,

> "European laws or framework laws may establish measures designed to encourage cooperation between Member States through initiatives aimed at improving knowledge, developing exchanges of information and best practices, promoting innovative approaches and evaluating experiences, excluding any harmonisation of the laws and regulations of the Member States ...".[20]

Should Article III-210 (or an equivalent provision in a successor treaty) ever come into force, the deployment of the open method in the social policy field would have a basis in legislation which would appear on the agenda of a scrutiny committee. On the other hand, the work carried out under this legislation (such as the establishment of benchmarking and policy objectives) would have to pass through other committees.

It is not wished to enter into a discussion of the effectiveness or otherwise of the open method of coordination here (although it is probably true to say that the Lisbon process – the most important current example of the open method of coordination – has not been one which has impressed with its efficacy or

---

[18] It should be noted that 'scrutiny' in the sense in which this is defined at the beginning of this paper is not a subset of oversight. These are different activities with different objectives.

[19] Final report of Working Group IX on Simplification (European Convention CONV 424/02).

[20] Para. 2(a) of Art. III-210. Interestingly, the need to give a base in the Constitutional Treaty to the open method of coordination was hotly disputed in the Convention on the Future of Europe. The decision of the Convention was not to include it in the text, but reference to it was subsequently added to the text of the Constitutional Treaty by the intergovernmental conference (without its being given a name).

speed). But the point may be made that as the European Union develops and as it becomes more complex, as its geographic reach widens, and as greater economic extremes come to exist within it, it becomes progressively less likely that legislation alone will be able to deal with the complex and varied landscape which faces the decision-maker. Hence, processes such as the achievement of the Lisbon Agenda will have to be dealt with in some other way. Within the Oireachtas Committee system there are of course sectoral committees, but they are almost certainly not qualified to review an overarching policy area such as the Lisbon process in the way in which a European Affairs Committee is. It is the function of the sectoral committees of the Oireachtas to be sectoral in their approach. This creates all the more need for the Joint Committee on European Affairs to be able to retain the strategic overview. A broader approach is necessary adequately to understand and track a process such as Lisbon. The same holds good for other policy areas, such as world trade talks. The management of the work of the committee requires a long-term approach, based on a rolling work programme. There will certainly be matters of immediate concern which will be dictated by public pressure. The drafting of the agenda of the Joint Committee will need to be flexible enough to deal with these. But the European Union operates across a number of broad fronts, such as the economic, foreign relations, and internal security fields. The Joint Committee needs to be on top of these and to ensure that the searchlight of parliamentary investigation is shone in some of these areas. Concentration on the legislative output of the European Union system might mean that the work could be at the expense of the opportunity to review policy as well as law.

Can such a system work? While the Joint Committee on European Affairs is still finding its feet, the way in which it operates almost certainly contributes to its efficacy. Ministers come to meetings of the Committee knowing that they will not be subject to ambush by the Opposition. Consensual politics is a *modus operandi* which is not without its own risks. It is very easy for all sides to become bound up in this cosy arrangement. But if the objective remains the seeking of information, rather than the apportioning of praise or blame, and if this is done in the open, a consensual approach must contribute to the better surveillance of what is happening and more awareness of what should be happening.

9. The Protocol on National Parliaments and the Protocol on Subsidiarity and Proportionality Annexed to the Constitutional Treaty: A Concluding Reflection

The Protocol on the Role of National Parliaments in the European Union and the Protocol on the Application of the Principles of Subsidiarity and

Proportionality, which were annexed to the Constitutional Treaty (or any equivalent provisions which may succeed them) would present a challenge to the Joint Committee on European Affairs, were they ever to enter into force. The Constitutional Treaty proposed that legislation emanating from the European institutions would have to be communicated to each of the national parliaments, and within six weeks each parliament would be entitled to send a reasoned opinion to the Parliament, Council, or Commission if it considered that the proposal did not comply with the principle of subsidiarity.[21] The function of parliament in the envisaged process was clear, even if it raised huge questions as to how matters would be managed within each national parliamentary system and how national parliaments would communicate with each other.[22] It would be unfortunate, however, if, in the justified enthusiasm for the enhanced role of national parliaments which the draft Constitutional Treaty provided for (and which seems likely to be maintained in any successor treaty) all attention was paid to the scrutiny of draft proposals for legislation and there was not an equal allocation of resources – of time, as well as other more practical supports – to the oversight role.

[21] As is explained in more detail elsewhere in this volume, parliaments are allocated two 'votes', one for each chamber where relevant or two for a chamber in a unicameral system. If reasoned opinions represent at least one third of the votes allocated to national parliaments, then the proposal must be reviewed by which ever institution submitted the draft legislative act. In the case of proposals made relating to justice and home affairs (more specifically, proposals made on the basis of Art. III-264 of the Constitutional Treaty), the threshold is to be a quarter of the votes allocated. Foreign and security policy is not part of this process, because policy is determined on the basis of 'decisions' rather than draft legislative acts.

[22] See K. Meenan, *What the Constitutional Treaty Means: National Parliaments* (Institute of European Affairs, Dublin, 2005).

12.
Ireland's National Forum on Europe: Helping to Make Up for the Democratic Deficit?

Tony Brown[1]

1. Introduction

Thursday, 30 June 2005 saw the historic Round Room of Dublin's Mansion House – the setting of the first Dáil in 1919 – crowded with a mixture of politicians, 'social partners', civil society representatives, and media personnel. They had gathered for the fifty-seventh plenary session of the National Forum on Europe. Among the political personalities present were the Taoiseach, the Tánaiste, the Ministers for Foreign Affairs, Finance, and European Affairs and the leaders of the Fine Gael, Labour, Green, and Socialist Parties, a number of Ireland's MEPs, and a senior representative of the Social Democratic and Labour Party from Northern Ireland. The principal speaker was the President of the European Commission, José Manuel Barroso, who addressed the implications of the French and Dutch rejections of the Constitutional Treaty and outlined his hopes for an inclusive, wide-ranging debate on the future of the European Union. His address was followed by eighteen contributions from all sides of the Irish debate on Europe as well as from the business, trade union, farming, and community sectors. These interventions provoked a spirited response from President Barroso, whose strong assertion of the historical importance of the European project and rejection of xenophobic nationalism drew spontaneous applause at the session and favourable media comment afterwards.

This was, perhaps, a special occasion in the programme of the Forum. (The previous event had taken place six weeks earlier in the Donegal Gaeltacht where an audience of just thirty had debated the pros and cons of the

---

[1] The author, a founder member of the Institute of European Affairs, represents the Labour Party on the Steering Committee of the National Forum on Europe. This chapter is a revised and updated version of a 'European Essay' first published by the Federal Trust, London, in October, 2004.

Constitutional Treaty in Irish with representatives of Fianna Fáil, Fine Gael, and Sinn Féin). It nevertheless reflected the national standing which has been achieved by the Forum since its establishment following the debacle of the first Nice Treaty referendum in 2001.

2. Background: The Nice Referendums

The 2001 referendum on the Nice Treaty in Ireland was the only consultation of a national electorate on that agreement. On 7 June 2001, Irish voters rejected the proposed amendment to the Irish Constitution which would have enabled Ireland to ratify the Treaty of Nice. The vote was 54 per cent to 46 per cent against the amendment with an extremely low turn out of 35 per cent. This was a major reversal for the then coalition Government and for the main Opposition parties, as well as for key groups in civil society which had advocated a positive vote. Ireland's longstanding reputation as a truly *communautaire* member state was shattered, and the basis laid for apprehensions concerning an 'Irish problem' in respect of the ratification of the Constitutional Treaty, or any successor treaty.

Following the referendum, an opinion poll was carried out on behalf of the Dublin office of the European Commission. The key issue was the level of abstention, the main reasons for which were summed up in the following manner by Professor Richard Sinnott, designer of the research:

> "...it appears ... that more than two-thirds of people had an inadequate understanding of what the Treaty was all about. One third didn't know what it was all about at all. When you do a detailed analysis of the data you find that people's own understanding of what was going on – or rather their lack of understanding and lack of information – was a major cause of abstention ... the basic message that we would want to convey ... is that a lot more persuasion and a lot more information, basically a lot more debate and argument needs to go on so that people arrive at an understanding of European issues and of the Treaty that they themselves have confidence in." [2]

This message struck a responsive chord since the low quality of public debate in Ireland on European issues had long been recognised but not

---

[2] Presentation by R. Sinnott to the National Forum on Europe on opinion research carried out following the first Referendum on the Treaty of Nice. Dublin, 31 January 2002. (The quotation in the text above appears in the Forum Report of Proceedings of 9, March 2002). See further R. Sinnott, *Attitudes and Behaviour of the Irish Electorate in the Referendum on the Treaty of Nice* (Irish Marketing Surveys and EOS Gallup, Dublin, 2001).

adequately addressed. Political leaders in favour of the general direction of European integration had relied upon two closely-related factors in urging support for referendums on the Single European Act in 1987, the Maastricht Treaty in 1992, and the Amsterdam Treaty in 1998. First, membership of the European Community and the European Union had brought unquestioned economic and social benefits to Ireland – in agriculture, in trade, in inward investment, and in substantial transfers of resources through the Structural Funds. Indeed, viewed in retrospect, the Maastricht and Amsterdam referendum campaigns were largely exercises in saying 'yes please!' to European funding for Ireland's physical and training infrastructure. Secondly, the concrete benefits of membership were coupled with the evident political advantages for a small, island nation in taking a place at Europe's top table – in effect breaking once and for all time the historic relationship of depending on Britain, and bringing about a new relationship of formal equality within the European structures.

Together, these positive factors had led to a public attitude accurately defined as a 'permissive consensus' which, in the earlier referendums, had produced an approximate two-to-one majority in favour of ratification of each of the three treaty amendments.

The first Nice campaign saw a distinct change. While the number of 'no' votes was almost exactly the same as in the Amsterdam poll only three years earlier, many of those who had previously been certain 'yes' voters failed to show up on polling day. It was perceptively remarked that:

> "we got away with it to some extent in the Amsterdam referendum … but there was still a problem with knowledge and understanding … if you come back a couple of years later with another treaty … then you are likely actually to generate an increased sense among the public of lack of confidence in their own ability to handle the issues".[3]

A notable campaign slogan had suggested 'if you don't know, vote no!'

3. The Idea of a Forum

Prior to the first Nice referendum, the Labour Party had proposed the establishment of a representative forum to facilitate the 'deeper and wider debate on the future of the European Union' called for in the Nice Declaration on the Future of Europe. That debate had started with a speech

---

[3] R. Sinnott, *ibid.*.

by the German Foreign Minister, Joschka Fischer, at Berlin's Humboldt University in May 2000, in which he had discussed the theme 'From Confederation to Federation' and which had led to a series of responses from across the political spectrum in the member states and the candidate countries of Eastern Europe.

Labour's forum proposal, and its closely-related proposals for the strengthening of the scrutiny powers of the Oireachtas Joint Committee on European Affairs, were initially dismissed by the Government as irrelevant opposition headline-seeking. It was speedily rediscovered when the shock referendum result concentrated minds in all parties on the need for what the Taoiseach called 'a full and considered debate on European issues'.[4]

As he departed to explain the dismal outcome of the referendum to his colleagues at the Gothenburg European Council in June 2001, Bertie Ahern announced the creation of a National Forum on Europe the purpose of which was: (a) to facilitate a broad discussion of issues relevant to Ireland's membership of an enlarging Union; and (b) to consider the range of topics arising in the context of the debate on the future of Europe.[5]

At Gothenburg, the European Union leaders insisted that the ratification process for the Nice Treaty would continue despite the Irish result, but agreed that they were willing to help the Irish Government find a way forward. Minds began to focus on the precedent of the Danish rejection of the Maastricht Treaty in 1992 and its eventual acceptance in a second referendum. It became clear that Ireland and the European Union were faced with a problem requiring a solution in Ireland, which could only be delivered by a second reference of the Nice text to the people. This reality formed the backdrop to the political reaction in Dublin to the announcement that a forum would be established.

The coalition government parties – Fianna Fáil and Progressive Democrats – were now fully supportive of the Forum and saw a second referendum as essential to both Irish and European interests. The question of the timing of a new poll became the critical issue of government strategy.

The Labour Party, while somewhat cynical about the theft of its idea, welcomed the decision to establish a forum but insisted that it could succeed

[4] Statement by the Taoiseach on the National Forum on Europe, 8 September 2001.
[5] Government Statement on the National Forum on Europe, August 2001.

only if it were properly structured and resourced. It would be counter-productive to focus on the possibility of a second referendum. A broader debate would help to clarify many of the issues that were the focus of public concern.

The smaller parties – Sinn Féin, Greens, and Socialists – which had been on the 'no' side responded positively with the proviso that any forum must be balanced in its terms of reference and composition. According to them, the referendum result meant that the Nice Treaty was dead. The National Forum must address the main issues in the debate on the Union's future.

Then the main opposition party, Fine Gael, announced that it would not participate. The Forum, it argued, would be little more than a long drawn-out talking shop. Urgently needed discussion of issues related to the future of Europe should take place in parliament rather than in a detached, unaccountable body. The government, and the other parties, were engaging in a mere exercise in kicking the issue to touch, avoiding decisions and disguising serious policy differences.

Negotiations commenced on the composition and terms of reference of the Forum with an initial effort to meet the Fine Gael objections. This proved impossible but, over the summer period, the government and the other parties reached a general agreement on the practical arrangements and on a starting date. The Taoiseach wrote to the then Fine Gael leader, Michael Noonan, arguing that the National Forum was:

> "intended to complement, rather than substitute for, debate on European issues within the Oireachtas. The overall aim is to provide a focus for a wider and deeper public debate on European issues than has been the case heretofore".[6]

4. Arrangements for Establishment of the Forum

It was agreed that the inaugural meeting of the National Forum on Europe would take place on 18 October 2001 in Dublin Castle where the Forum Secretariat was provided with offices and conference facilities. The location of plenary meetings was to be the ornate St Patrick's Hall, at various times the scene of formal occasions under the British regime, of the inauguration of eight Irish Presidents, and of meetings of the European Union Council. Provision was made for holding meetings of the Forum at locations outside Dublin.

[6] Letter from the Taoiseach to the leader of the Fine Gael party, 1 August 2001.

Following consultations involving the political party leaders, an independent chairman was chosen in the person of Senator Maurice Hayes, a non-party member of the Irish Senate. Maurice Hayes had a distinguished career background in the Northern Ireland public service, as Permanent Secretary of the Department of Health and Social Services, as the first Ombudsman, and as a member of the Patten Commission on Policing. His appointment to the Irish Senate – in 1997 and again in 2002 – was in line with recent precedent whereby the Taoiseach nominates a leading figure from Northern Ireland to the upper house.

The Terms of Reference of the Forum were designed to locate its work in the framework of Ireland's experience of membership and its evolving relationship with the Union, including the context of enlargement. The agreed text was as follows:

> "the National Forum on Europe will provide the basis for an inclusive and broadly-based debate on Ireland's participation in the European Union, and on the overall functioning and future development of the Union. In this regard, and in the context of the issues raised by the debate on the Treaty of Nice, the Forum will examine Ireland's experience of and evolving relationship with the Union, and consider the implications for the Union, and for Ireland as a member, of the extensive enlargement now in prospect.
>
> Against this background of significant expansion in the membership of the Union, and with a view to contributing to the wider review now under way among all member states, the Forum will also consider the range of issues which arise in relation to the Future of Europe debate which is intended to culminate in a further Intergovernmental Conference in 2004. These issues will include the topics identified by the Heads of State or Government at the European Council in Nice in December 2000.
>
> In the first phase, to conclude within about three months, the Forum will focus on the implications of, and the preparations for, the proposed enlargement of the European Union. It will also consider the organisation and structure for the debate on the Future of Europe, which are to be decided at the Laeken European Council in December 2001.
>
> The Forum may, as it so decides, present a report or reports." [7]

[7] Terms of Reference of the National Forum on Europe (first circulated by the Department of the Taoiseach in August 2001).

5. Composition of the Forum

The agreed composition of the Forum limited membership to members of the Oireachtas (parliament) and those nominated by parties represented in the Oireachtas. Each of the seven parties with parliamentary representation was allocated seats – for delegates and alternates – on the basis of the outcome of the 1997 general election. Despite its initial refusal to participate, Fine Gael was allocated seats, which were eventually to be taken up following the 2002 general election and a subsequent change in party leadership. There was provision for representation of the independent members in the two houses. Rights of participation were given to MEPs from both the Republic and Northern Ireland.

The agreed allocation of seats in the Forum was that, in addition to there being a chairman, Fianna Fáil would have ten delegates and seven alternate members, Fine Gael would have seven delegates and five alternate members, the Labour Party five delegates and three alternate members, the Progressive Democrats three delegates and two alternate members, the Green Party two delegates and two alternate members; Sinn Féin one delegate and one alternate member, the Socialist Party one delegate and one alternate member, the independent members of the Dáil two delegates and two alternate members, and the independent members of the Senate two delegates and two alternate members. A further category of substitutes was created, mainly to cover absences due to parliamentary duties.

The formal membership of the Forum is 59, currently comprising the chairman, 26 members of the Dáil, nine senators and three MEPs, with the others including local government representatives and party policy experts. While there have been changes in personnel over the life of the Forum, the membership has been of a consistently high political status. On the eve of the 2007 general election, on the government side, membership of the Forum included the Taoiseach, Bertie Ahern, the Tánaiste, Mary Harney, the Minister for Foreign Affairs, Dermot Ahern and four other ministers. The Opposition party representatives included the leaders of Fine Gael, the Labour Party, and the Green Party, the chairperson of Sinn Féin, and as many as twelve former ministers, most of whom had served in the 1994–1997 Coalition and in the 1996 Irish Presidency of the European Union Council.

6. The Special Observer Pillar

A major issue in the negotiations leading to the establishment of the Forum had been the need to ensure that it would be as inclusive as possible and not be a closed system, replicating party political divisions and distanced from the concerns and insights of the broader community. To this end it was agreed to constitute a Special Observer Pillar with rights of participation.

Membership of the Observer Pillar conferred certain privileges: namely, the right to intervene in plenary discussions, under the authority of the chairman; access to all documents put before the plenary sessions of the Forum; circulation of agendas and associated papers; in addition to systematic consultation with the chairman and access to the secretariat.

Invitations were initially addressed to a number of organisations, including the social partners, groups active in the Nice referendum campaign or European affairs generally, registered political parties not represented in the Oireachtas, and political parties from Northern Ireland. It was indicated that membership of the Observer Pillar was not restricted and provision was made for applications from other organisations which wished to be included. Participation in the Special Observer Pillar has expanded to involve some forty large and small bodies.[8]

7. Organisation of the Forum

The practical management of the work of the Forum has been based on two permanent structures: the Forum Steering Committee and the Secretariat. The Forum Steering Committee includes the chairman and one representative from each of the seven parties and from independent deputies and independent senators. In the early days of the Forum, it met weekly to develop a balanced agenda, make decisions on speakers and venues, and establish public relations and information programmes. As the work has evolved, with patterns established, the Committee meets less frequently but remains the focus for all key decisions.

The first meeting of the Steering Committee was a somewhat tense affair. This small group included personalities who had confronted each other during the Nice referendum campaign and who held strong views on both sides of the argument. Those from the larger parties – all on the 'yes' side – were still somewhat shell-shocked. Those from the smaller ones were, at the same time, relishing their victory but deeply suspicious of the likely move to hold a second referendum. Questions of balance arose in respect of both subject matter and invited speakers. A great deal depended on the personality and independence of the chairman and on the skills of the secretariat. Neither disappointed. Senator Maurice Hayes imposed himself from the first moment and succeeded

[8] These are listed in the Annex at the end of this chapter.

in winning the confidence of all participants. His personal integrity and his willingness to listen were evident. His judgement and timing were remarkable while his refusal to put up with either intemperate exchanges or boring repetition of policies and prejudices created a focused working climate. In particular, the Steering Committee rapidly established working methods which were accepted by all participants as open and inclusive. The necessary degree of consensus emerged on all key operational issues.

By the chairman's side, the Forum's Secretary General and the small secretariat quickly established their authority and skill. The first Secretary General, Walter Kirwan, came to the Forum with a reputation gained in managing previous consultative bodies on Northern Ireland issues and in successful Irish Presidencies of the European Union Council. He established a team of seconded civil servants and specifically recruited experts in the fields of public relations and media. Since his retirement, the standards established by him have been maintained and built upon by his successors.[9] The high level of integrity and balance in all aspects of the work of the secretariat has been critical to the evolution of the Forum and to its standing.

Perhaps the most remarkable success of the two structures has been the production to date of four progress reports. At an early stage, the Steering Committee reached a consensus that a report could not be produced by drafting in committee. Each of the reports has been drafted by the chairman, on his own authority, but with time-limited consultation of the individual members of the Steering Committee to ensure that no major errors have crept in and that no important sensitivity has been overlooked. The fourth report, published in July 2004, reviewed the work of the Forum related to the outcome of the European Convention, the draft Constitutional Treaty and the intergovernmental conference, and summarised the content of the various plenary sessions, the full transcripts of which are posted on the Forum website.[10]

8. Work of the Forum – The First Phase

The Forum commenced its work at a formal Launch Session on 18 October 2001 which was addressed by the Taoiseach, party leaders and other senior

---

[9] On his retirement, Walter Kirwan was succeeded by his deputy, a senior Foreign Affairs officer, Geraldine Byrne Nason, who fully maintained the standards he had established and saw the organisation move into a new phase of activity and outreach. On her departure (to a posting in the Brussels Permanent Representation), she was succeeded by Ann Barrington, who had served in senior positions in both the Department of Foreign Affairs and the Department of the Taoiseach.

[10] The address of which is www.forumoneurope.ie.

representatives. The Taoiseach set out his vision of the Forum's role in the following terms:

> "I want our national debate to be as wide-ranging as possible and I believe that the Forum will be structured and organised to achieve that goal. I also hope that we can be as calm and as rational as possible. Let us look clearly at the facts. Let us try to distinguish between the real and the imaginary, the possible and the impossible, the likely and the unlikely. Let us all be prepared to see our assumptions and beliefs subjected to rigorous scrutiny. Let us accept that nobody has a monopoly on wisdom, on sincerity, on patriotism. Whether as political representatives or as leaders in civic society, we have a duty to conduct the debate in ways that will inform and enlighten the people we serve".[11]

A warning note was introduced by the Green Party leader, Trevor Sargent, who indicated that his party wished:

> "to ensure that this Forum is not used in order to facilitate the Government in taking the very anti-democratic decision of not accepting the will of the people and forcing another vote, Nice Mark Two, some time next year. At any rate, we are fully confident that any such re-run would lose by even a bigger margin".[12]

At the outset the Forum concentrated its attention on key aspects of the issue of European Union enlargement which had been at the heart of the first Nice referendum debate. The first seven plenary sessions addressed topics such as the enlargement process, the perspective of candidate countries, enlargement and trade and investment, environmental and social aspects of enlargement, and the links between enlargement and agriculture. From these initial exchanges it emerged that there was broad support for the enlargement project. As was noted in the first report of the Forum Chairman, "all participating parties and groups have indicated that they support enlargement – no voice opposed the process has been raised."[13] Nonetheless, there was agreement on the challenges arising from the sheer scale of the proposed expansion which implied that not only the (then) twelve candidates but the member states themselves had much to do to prepare for enlargement.

---

[11] Remarks made by the Taoiseach to the inaugural meeting of the Forum.

[12] Remarks made by the leader of the Green Party at the inaugural meeting of the Forum.

[13] Chairman's Report on the First Phase of Work of the National Forum on Europe October 2001 to January 2002, (February 2002).

During these early meetings, a set of concerns emerged around four clusters of issues linked to the future of the European Union: balances between member states; legitimacy, accountability and transparency; concerns about sovereignty and sensitive policy areas; and governance of the Union.

The working method of the Forum plenary sessions was quickly established by the chairman. Keynote speakers are invited to address the meeting. Then the chairman brings in as many members as possible, for brief comments and questions, and reverts to the speakers for responses. In a second round, members of the Special Observer Pillar get their chance to intervene. The speakers have the last word. The order in which the contributors are called is a matter for the chairman who seeks to ensure balance. On a number of occasions – for example, when the Forum addressed issues of specific concern to the social partners or to non-governmental organisations concerned with development issues – priority has been given to interventions by the relevant members of the Pillar.

In the winter period of 2001–2002, the Forum moved out of Dublin Castle and a series of what were called 'listening sessions' took place in six regional centres and in Dublin suburban locations. The growing acceptance that the government was moving towards a decision to hold a second Nice referendum gave relevance – and some political edge – to these meetings which were well attended and widely covered in local media – radio and newspapers – which are increasingly important in the Irish political scene.

In early 2002 the Forum widened its focus and held a series of plenary sessions on the Institutions of the European Union, on the Common Foreign and Security Policy and the European Security and Defence Policy, on social policy and on culture. Plenary sessions were held in Cork and Galway, attracting the attendance and participation of local political figures and interest groups. Specific local issues were aired, for example the Galway meeting was picketed by West of Ireland turf-cutters whose livelihood was seen to be under threat from the over-zealous application of the Habitats Directive.

A call for submissions from interested groups and individuals resulted in a number of plenary sessions in January and February 2002, devoted entirely to presentations drawn from among more than eighty such inputs. Several individuals made thoughtful contributions on specific issues on either side of the Nice debate. Many of the submissions were posted on the Forum website, which was also developed to provide for interactive exchange of ideas and opinions.

A feature of the work of the Forum from the beginning has been the involvement of prominent visiting speakers from existing and candidate states and from different political backgrounds. The first two plenary sessions heard presentations from John Palmer of the European Policy Centre in Brussels and from the former Prime Minister of Malta, Karmenu Mifsud Bonnici, who called for the dissolution of the European Union! The then President of the European Parliament, Pat Cox, and Commissioners Chris Patten and Margot Wallström made contributions to the debate. Other guests came from Slovenia, the Czech Republic, Austria, Denmark, the UK, and Belgium, whose European Affairs Minister, Annemie Neyts, ended her presentation with a memorable plea to Irish voters based on the closing word of Joyce's *Ulysses* – 'yes, yes, yes ...'.

9. The Second Phase

As the inevitability and timing of the second referendum became clear – and as the Convention on the Future of Europe – which would lead ultimately to the Constitutional Treaty – began its work in Brussels in February 2002, the Forum faced a challenging task. It was decided that the Forum would track the debate in the Convention and that opportunities would be provided to the public to debate key issues arising in the Nice debate in a neutral setting.

The run-up to the second referendum commenced with a plenary session of the Forum on 21 March 2002 addressed by Commissioner David Byrne and Polish Foreign Minister, Wlodzimierz Cimoszewicz. The coverage of the Convention began on 18 June 2002 with formal presentations by the three Irish members of the Convention: former European Commissioner, Ray MacSharry, for the government; and former Taoiseach, John Bruton, and Labour Party President and MEP, Proinsias de Rossa, representing the Oireachtas. There then commenced a programme of plenary and regional meetings dealing with both themes. Between June and early October 2002, the three plenary sessions addressed the issues of civil society in a new European Union, the costs and benefits of European Union accession, and the foreign policy options of smaller European Union states.

Ten regional meetings took place which dealt with subjects such as Ireland's experience in the European Union; the costs and benefits of enlargement, the place of small countries in the expanding Union, the importance of democratic accountability, and the future role of national parliaments and politicians. In each case, two keynote speakers put forward views from the opposite sides of the Nice debate before the meeting was opened to the audience for questions and opinions. In addition, four national conferences were organised to address issues of concern to specific groups identified in opinion research as most likely to abstain from voting in any referendum, namely, industrial workers, young people, women, and the farming community. While these meetings presented an opportunity for cooperation with relevant interest groups,[14] they did not excite much media interest or coverage.

Visiting speakers made a notable contribution to these meetings, including Slovenian President, Milan Kucan; Finnish Prime Minister, Paavo Lipponen; Professor Danuta Hübner from Poland;[15] Czech MP and Convention member, Jan Zahradil; leading Estonian Eurosceptic, Uno Silberg; and Professor Larry Siedentop of Oxford University, author of the widely quoted book, *Democracy in Europe*.

It emerged that 2002 would see two important political contests in Ireland. A general election was scheduled for mid-June and a second referendum on the Nice Treaty for 19 October. The Steering Committee decided that the Forum would close down for the three-week period of formal electioneering in May and June and in October. The general election saw the re-election of the Fianna Fáil–Progressive Democrat coalition, the first time that an Irish government had been re-elected since the 1960s.

10. The Second Nice Referendum

The second campaign was very different from that in 2001. The 'yes' side was determined to set the agenda and to take the relevant issues to the people. Three main themes were identified and highlighted: the imperative of enabling enlargement to proceed on schedule; acknowledgment of the many benefits of European Union membership to Ireland; and recognition of the damage to Ireland's goodwill and influence – and potentially to inward investment – which could follow a second 'no'.

The result of the referendum was a decisive 'yes'. With a turnout of 48.5 per cent, the necessary amendments to the Constitution were approved by 63 per cent to 37 per cent. Of great significance was the fact that the referendum was carried in all 42 parliamentary constituencies. This was a genuinely national result, reflecting the fact that the central issue of enlargement had dominated the campaign. Richard Sinnott once again published his assessment of the outcome, on the basis of a new opinion poll:

> "the second Irish referendum on the Nice Treaty saw a marked improvement in communication and a substantial increase in people's

[14] Such as trade unions, farm organisations, the National Womens' Council, and the National Youth Council, among others.
[15] Now European Commissioner for Regional Policy.

> sense that they could understand the issues at stake. The improvements in communications were concentrated in the mass media...and in interpersonal discussion of the issues.
>
> The Government's White Paper or summary of the White Paper and the activities of the Referendum Commission also played a role in this improved communication process. All of this was accompanied by a 25 percentage point increase in the proportion of people who felt they understood at least some of the issues involved in the Nice Treaty".[16]

Of particular significance was the indication that the National Forum had played an important role in increasing turnout. Awareness of the Forum rose from about ten per cent after the first campaign to almost sixty per cent after the second. As many as 25 per cent of the electorate stated that they found the Forum to be useful as a source of information in the period leading to the second poll.

11. The Third Phase

The eventual ratification of the Nice Treaty saw the Forum move into a further phase of its work, devoted to the work and outcome of the Convention and, later, of the subsequent intergovernmental conference. The fact that Ireland took over the European Union Presidency in January 2004 was an added and important ingredient which was taken into account as the Steering Committee planned its work programme from November 2002.

Starting with a plenary session on 14 November 2002, addressed by Dr Kirsty Hughes of the Centre for European Policy Studies, Brussels,[17] there were 29 meetings on Convention and intergovernmental conference matters. These included 21 plenary sessions and eight regional meetings. Three plenary sessions were addressed by the Taoiseach, two of these in his capacity as President of the European Council, and ten by senior ministers. The Taoiseach delivered a memorable address to the Forum on 1 July 2004, on the day immediately after the end of the Irish Presidency of the Council. He was able to report on the successful outcome of the intergovernmental conference and the adoption by the Heads of State and Government of the text of the Constitutional Treaty.

[16] R. Sinnott, *Attitudes and Behaviour of the Irish Electorate in the Second Referendum on the Treaty of Nice. Dublin* (Millward Brown Irish Marketing Surveys and EOS Gallup Europe, Dublin, 2003).
[17] Dr Hughes became, in effect, the Forum's rapporteur on the Convention.

Visiting speakers were again present at many sessions, including Convention Vice-President, Giuliano Amato, and Convention members from the United Kingdom, the Netherlands, and Romania. Professor Maria Joao Rodriguez from Portugal spoke on the Lisbon Agenda, of which she may be seen as the principal author. High Representative Javier Solana and Commissioner Chris Patten addressed aspects of the Common Foreign and Security Policy and the European Security and Defence Policy.

Following the Summer break in 2004, with a new European Parliament and a new European Commission in place, the Forum recommenced its activities as the ratification of the Constitutional Treaty moved to the top of the European Union agenda. In the absence of a firm date for a referendum in Ireland, the Forum saw its task as providing opportunities for serious discussion of the key elements of the Treaty text while giving time to consideration of other issues of concern to Ireland and the European Union at a time of rapid change and international tension.

The 2004–2005 programme began in October with the visit of the then UN Secretary General, Kofi Annan, who addressed an overflow meeting in Dublin Castle on European Union-UN Co-operation in Crisis Management. Consideration of the Constitutional Treaty commenced in November with a session entitled 'Why an EU Constitution and Why Now?' with an expert overview from Dr Kirsty Hughes. This was followed by sessions devoted to specific elements of the treaty: institutions of the Union; economic and social governance; security and defence; freedom, security and justice; and economic implications. On the broader front, sessions were held on enlargement, communicating Europe, and the initial membership experience of the new European Union member states. To recognise the position of Cork as European Capital of Culture 2005, the Forum held a plenary session in the 'southern capital' to discuss cultural diversity in the enlarged Europe. The series ended on 30 June 2005 with the visit of Commission President Barroso whose presentation inevitably concentrated on the fallout from the referendum results in France and the Netherlands,

The Forum, in conjunction with the National Youth Council of Ireland, held a successful Youth Conference on 9 April 2005, at which 120 young people from schools, youth groups, and political party organisations, debated the Constitutional Treaty in working groups and in plenary session with senior party representatives. A report of the opinions and conclusions was presented by a delegation to the Forum Submissions Day on 13 April 2005, at which twelve submissions, from among twenty or more received in reply to advertisements, were orally presented and debated and then posted on a website.

As before, this phase of the Forum's work was marked by the participation of many visitors from other European Union member states and from further abroad. Apart from the UN Secretary General and the President of the Commission, these included Commissioner Margot Wallström; John Monks, Secretary General of the European Trade Union Confederation; Richard Corbett, joint rapporteur of the European Parliament opinion on the Constitutional Treaty; and William Keegan, associate editor of *The Observer*. A plenary session in Galway which formed part of that city's 'Europe Week' in May 2005 – organised by Minister for European Affairs, Noel Treacy TD – was attended by the European Affairs Ministers of the 10 new member states and Bulgaria.

12. The Forum and the Public

The National Forum has to date published four reports prepared by its chairman. The verbatim proceedings of all plenary sessions are available either in printed form or through the extensive Forum website which also contains the various submissions and expert reports made available to members and observers. It also prepared a reader-friendly summary of the draft Constitutional Treaty together with a glossary of terms in frequent use. A revised text, summarising the final text from the intergovernmental conference was published in 2004.

A video and DVD were prepared to explain the work of the Convention. Presented by one of Ireland's most popular young television personalities, this was targeted in particular at the 'transition year' in secondary schools (in other words, 15–16-year-olds) but was well received when screened at regional meetings. It was used as the basis for successful essay and debating competitions for transition year students. A second video and DVD were prepared to explain the work of the Forum itself and to provide details of meetings, submissions, etc. This was made available at the time of an Irish Presidency initiative: the informal ministerial conference on communicating Europe held outside Dublin in April 2004, at which ministers from the member states and from some of the western Balkan states discussed strategies for informing and engaging European Union citizens. The chairman and members of the Steering Committee made presentations on the work of the Forum which evoked much interest. The third in the series of videos and DVDs, also produced in 2004, was devoted to a factual presentation of the Constitutional Treaty.[18]

---

[18] Note the favourable comment on this production by E. Blain in the *Sunday Independent*, 15 December 2004.

Attention has been devoted from the outset to the tasks of publicity and media relations. Specialist media relations officers have been employed to build a strong media profile at national and local levels. Continuing effort is required to ensure that the activities of the Forum are accorded due attention by busy national news desks. At local level, it has proved possible to meet the constant demand of local papers and radio stations for news items and for people to interview. Advance publicity of regional meetings is by way of local radio and newspaper advertisements together with interview opportunities for speakers and, very often, the Forum Chairman. Working with Independent Network News, the Forum has syndicated news pieces on plenary discussions for local radio.

13. Some Relevant Facts

To date, the National Forum has held more than a hundred meetings – consisting of 57 plenary sessions, 36 regional meetings, four national conferences, and four report launches. Apart from Dublin Castle, plenary sessions have been held in three other Dublin venues, as well as in Cork and Galway. Regional meetings have taken place in almost forty locations outside central Dublin, in most of the state's 26 counties. There have been visiting speakers from 24 countries (including 22 member states or candidate states); 26 formal presentations by government ministers and ten by Opposition party leaders.

The work of the Forum has involved a modest cost. To date, total expenditure has been in the region of five million, covering staffing, office costs, expenses of delegations, research, communications, and catering. The staff of the Forum has averaged ten, who in the main have been civil servants seconded from the Department of the Taoiseach and the Department of Foreign Affairs, with two specialists on communications and media relations.

14. Assessment

Speaking at the plenary session on 23 October 2003, the Taoiseach summed up his views on the Forum's work:

> "this Forum has proved itself a major success. Since it was established two years ago, you have provided a cross-party and cross-community space for debate on the key issues on the European Union agenda. You have examined enlargement, the Treaty of Nice, the future of Europe and the full range of European issues that impact so vitally on all of us in this country. You have handled the debate on these issues in a lucid and transparent manner .... Not only has the Forum spoken to the public in clear language, it has brought its activities to the people in a tangible way. You have travelled the length and breadth of Ireland giving everyone a chance to have their say on Europe ....

> The Forum then has made Europe accessible for Irish people. Indeed, you can claim with some justification that this is the most extensive and sustained process of public outreach and debate that exists in any of the 25 members and accession countries of the European Union".

As these comments suggest, a positive assessment can be made of the work of the Forum over the past four years. The Forum has provided a new start for debate in Ireland on European Union matters. It has offered a possibility of moving beyond the simplistic emphasis on structural funding, details of agricultural policy, and largely anecdotal descriptions of European Union regulation in practice. The initial discussion of enlargement – and the consensus it demonstrated – was critically important in the eventual ratification of the Nice Treaty. The identification, in the chairman's first report, of a number of areas of concern provided a focus for debate which had been missing in other settings. The successive phases of the work have reflected the dynamics of a period of movement and change in European affairs.

The cross-party nature of the Forum has been of particular importance in raising the level of parliamentary debate on European Union matters. The chairman has commented that

> "if public representatives are not well informed, citizens will never be. It was clear from before the Forum began that politicians, not just citizens, would have to be connected to the European debate".[19]

With parallel reforms over the past three years in the remit and working methods of the Oireachtas scrutiny committees, the positive influence of the Forum's debates and reports has been obvious to those who follow their deliberations.

The links achieved between the Forum and the activities of the Convention, the intergovernmental conference, and the Irish Presidency led to a number of stimulating sessions. The Irish Convention members brought the reality of the debates in Brussels into the mainstream of Irish political and public discourse. The full scale encounters with senior ministers on issues such as the Charter of Fundamental Rights and the Common Commercial Policy, involving not only party representatives but members of the Observer Pillar, provided opportunities to go well beyond the 'one-liners' of media interviews and the formalities of much parliamentary debate.

[19] National Forum on Europe, Report to the European Union Ministerial Conference on Communicating Europe held at Druid's Glen, Co. Wicklow, 7–8 April 2004.

The open debate with ministers was paralleled by the importance of the Forum's many visitors from across the geographical and political spectrum of the Union. From the early visit of Jens Peter Bonde, with his capacity to challenge his Europhile listeners with his mixture of focused argument and charm, to the more recent *tours de force* by Javier Solana and José Manuel Barroso, with exactly the same personal traits, visitors have made a critical input. The role played by Ireland at the heart of the Union was demonstrated by the authoritative contributions of Commissioner David Byrne and European Parliament President, Pat Cox, during their terms of office and by the Secretary General of the European Commission, David O'Sullivan.

The Forum has achieved a remarkable degree of inclusiveness. The disproportionate representation of the smaller parties has been critical, given their role in the successful 'no' campaign in 2001. The broad range of interests brought together in the Special Observer Pillar and the openness of the Forum to increase the number of observer groups has provided a more than useful platform for input from interested and informed sources. And there is strong evidence that involvement in the Forum has stimulated debate on, and serious analysis of key European issues in the member organisations of the Pillar.

A notable example of the value of this interaction arose from the plenary session on 23 October 2003, when the representative of the European Anti-Poverty Network made a direct request to the Taoiseach to seek an amendment to Article III-2 of the Draft Treaty which would highlight the fight against social exclusion. The Taoiseach requested draft wording, which was provided on the spot. The wording was tabled at the intergovernmental conference and included in the final text of the Constitutional Treaty.

The early stages of the Forum succeeded in bringing together the many protagonists of the Nice campaign – and of earlier confrontations on European themes – in relatively civilised personal interaction. The innovation of providing a buffet lunch in the Picture Gallery of Dublin Castle, with a few glasses of good wine, after each plenary proved particularly useful. On many occasions, groups from all sides carried on their discussions over coffee well into the afternoon.[20]

---

[20] The lunches were discontinued after the second phase of work, as the catering budget fell victim to the characteristic long-term vision of the Department of Finance. However, the diplomatic skills of the chairman achieved a return to lunches and wine when the Forum returned to work in the Autumn of 2004.

The national outreach achieved by the Forum has been a unique feature. In January 2002, for example, as the prospect of a second Nice referendum stimulated public interest in European affairs, the Forum held eight meetings in suburban Dublin and six regional centres in each of the four provinces. Hundreds turned up to listen, question, and express opinions. For many, these meetings provided the first opportunity to seek and obtain answers to both simple and complex questions. It could no longer be argued that no one was prepared to explain or answer. These meetings were organised to maximise local contacts. In addition to the public sessions, visits were arranged – to schools and local radio stations – and, where appropriate, seminars were scheduled with college students in relevant areas of study.

The growing interest in the specific programmes for secondary schools across the country has been encouraging, and it has been impressive to observe the facility with which students cope with the complexities, and indeed the opacity, of European Union policies and institutions. The debating finals have been organised as major occasions, with the Taoiseach attending on the most recent occasion to present prizes and speak to the young people about Ireland's place in Europe.

These are positive achievements which have firmly anchored the National Forum on Europe in the Irish political system. For those who have worked in the Forum since its inception, perhaps its greatest success has been in driving home the message that Irish membership of the European Union is not a matter for the Minister for Foreign Affairs and his diplomats, but is central to our economic and social life and critical for its future and, thus, a necessary element of political discourse at all levels.

There is one issue which does give rise to real concern in any assessment of the overall impact of the Forum. It must be admitted that media coverage of the Forum has been patchy, with some reasonable and insightful feature writing in a number of newspapers and some good radio and television discussions, but with important moments ignored or treated superficially. The hunger of many editors for 'hard' stories based on division and confrontation has proved a barrier to coverage of serious debate. It is frustrating to hear serious journalists commenting on the quality of debate at Forum sessions but admitting that it would be pointless to submit anything to the news desk beyond a reference to a sharp exchange between speakers, often on a peripheral point of disagreement.

Another difficulty is the short-term horizon of much media activity. On his arrival at the April 2004 plenary to report on the Spring European Council, the Taoiseach was surrounded by reporters demanding a quotable comment, not on the Madrid bombings or the Lisbon Agenda, but on the breaking story that a leading member of an opposition party had transgressed the new smoking ban in the parliament bar.

In this connection, the Forum, in a 2004 report, concluded that

> "the issue of how Europe communicates with its citizens has come to a head in Ireland in advance of most other European Union states because of its obligation to hold referenda on treaty changes. The National Forum on Europe has been a key element in Ireland's strategy for raising awareness and connecting the Union with Irish citizens.
>
> Recent Eurobarometer and other surveys confirm that the issue that came to the fore in Ireland remains a serious challenge for and throughout the European Union. A Union that did not engage its citizens would lack legitimacy. This challenge calls for a strong and multi-faceted response … it is also essential to bring to the citizens the message of a Union that adds value, in ways that catch their imagination and respond to their hearts and emotions. Ireland's National Forum on Europe is one response to this challenge." [21]

15. Conclusions

The Forum, under the leadership of an outstanding chairman, has established itself as an indispensable element of the national political scene, and its future seems assured as the country faces yet another referendum on Europe. It enjoys the commitment and high-level participation of the political parties and of the many civil society bodies within the Special Observer Pillar. The Forum gets a positive rating for its work from national and local media – on the international front there has been praise too[22] – but would probably prefer a little less praise and a little more in-depth coverage.

The next phase will see the Forum playing a central role in ensuring that period of reflection and engagement called for following the rebuffs to the Constitutional Treaty in France and the Netherlands (and indeed the period following this) will be focused and well-resourced in terms of opportunities for participation and relevant expert input. The Taoiseach, speaking in the Dáil on 21 June 2005 commented that in respect of the period of reflection,

[21] National Forum on Europe, above, n. 19.

[22] See text below at n. 24.

> "the National Forum on Europe has already done much to promote debate and the Government will continue to support it. It will obviously play a key role in facilitating the broad debate envisaged by the European Council".[23]

It will also seek to open up key aspects of the future evolution of the European Union. Issues which are likely to be dealt with by the Forum in the near future at the time of writing of this chapter are the latest phase of enlargement, including the future of the western Balkans, the future of the European social model, human rights, European Union foreign policy (including the Union's relations with its 'new neighbourhood' and issues of world development), and the creation of a European area of freedom, security, and justice.

The work of the Forum and its growing contacts with European political and civil society circles have generated considerable interest in the other European Union member states. Thus for example, the *Financial Times* commented in 2005 that

> "the top priority for the [June 2005] summit should be the urgent need to have an open democratic debate in every Member State – on the lines of Ireland's National Forum on Europe – on the way forward".[24]

During the period of the Irish Presidency in the first half of 2004, the Forum Steering Committee welcomed delegations from Germany and the Netherlands to discuss the structures, working methods, and practical experience of the Forum, while the chairman has been invited to visit several capitals over the past three years to speak about the Forum as a model, most recently addressing the Constitutional Affairs Committee of the European Parliament in Brussels.

Insofar as the Forum may be seen as a model, the question arises of its applicability in other countries. It is never easy to transfer such an initiative from one country to another, having regard to issues such as geography, scale, and political structures and culture. However, certain elements of the Irish experience may be relevant to any discussion of local possibilities. Four essential ingredients may be identified.

---

[23] Dáil Debates, vol. 604, col. 664 (21 June 2005).

[24] *Financial Times,* Editorial, 3 June 2005.

First, finding a chairman who can combine independence and authority is critical. Further, the structure must be characterised by political inclusiveness. The Fine Gael party's decision to stay away from the early phases of the Forum's work was a real setback while the inclusion, in the Observer Pillar, of registered parties not represented in parliament has ensured that strongly held minority views are given an airing. A third positive factor has been the opening of the structure to the representatives of social partners and civil society which has taken the debate beyond the confines of party politics. Finally, the Forum's outreach to the regions has been widely acknowledged as answering a real need.

Facing into yet another crucial phase in Europe's evolution, the National Forum has important tasks to perform. Contributing to the period of reflection and seeking to give it focus and credibility with the public will be important. So too will be the continuing need to provide a genuinely neutral space for discussion and debate which can contribute to the overall health of the democratic process.

ANNEX

Membership of the Special Observer Pillar of the National Forum on Europe

Economic Organisations

Irish Congress of Trade Unions; Irish Business and Employers Confederation; Small Firms Association; Chambers of Commerce; Civil and Public Service Union; Construction Industry Federation; in addition to five farm and rural organisations.

Political Parties not represented in the Oireachtas

Communist Party; Workers Party; Christian Solidarity Party; Christian Democrats.

Northern Ireland Parties

Social Democratic and Labour Party (SDLP); Alliance Party; Northern Ireland Womens' Coalition.

Religious Bodies

Roman Catholic Bishops Conference; Church of Ireland; Presbyterian Church; Jewish Representative Council; Islamic Cultural Centre; Religious Society of Friends (Quakers).

National Organisations

National Womens Council; National Youth Council; Irish Delegation to the Committee of the Regions; Irish Countrywomens' Association.

Social and Development Non-Governmental Organisations

Action from Ireland (AFRI); Conference of Religious in Ireland: Comhlámh (Union of Development Workers); Dóchas (Umbrella Body of Development Organisations); European Anti-Poverty Network; The Wheel (a community development coordinating body); Community Workers' Co-operative.

European Issues Organisations

European Movement; Institute of European Affairs; National Platform; Peace and Neutrality Alliance; Association of Former EU Officials.

Nice Referendum Campaigns

Ireland for Europe; No to Nice Campaign.

PART III:

Other Member State Parliaments and the European Union

13.
Parliamentary Scrutiny in the United Kingdom Parliament and the Changing Role of National Parliaments in European Union Affairs

Christopher Kerse[1]

1. Introduction

The purpose of this chapter is to explain how the system of parliamentary scrutiny of European legislation works in the United Kingdom, in particular in the House of Lords, and to describe the experience to date and assess the importance and impact of parliamentary scrutiny in the United Kingdom. In addition, a few personal comments are offered on the Protocol concerning the role of national parliaments in the European Union and the Protocol on Subsidiarity which were annexed to the Constitutional Treaty. In so doing, it is hoped to inform any discussion of the role of national parliaments under the Constitutional Treaty – or indeed any successor treaty in which the provisions of the Constitutional Treaty on this topic are substantially retained[2] – and, more generally, in prosecuting issues of subsidiarity.

2. Background – The Context and History of the Relevant Provisions of the Constitutional Treaty

While it is not intended to cover ground examined in more detail elsewhere in this book, it may be helpful to sketch briefly the context and history of the relevant provisions of the Constitutional Treaty. In recent years the involvement of national parliaments has been encouraged as a means of increasing the democratic legitimacy, the authority and the general acceptability of measures taken at European level. Involving national parliaments has gone hand in hand with the notions of subsidiarity, decentralisation, openness, and bringing Europe

---

[1] Second Counsel to the Chairman of Committees, House of Lords; Visiting Professor, King's College London. This chapter, which expresses the personal views of the writer, is based on a paper originally given at the Second Annual Congress of the Irish Centre for European Law, Dublin, May, 2001.

[2] Editor's note: see the introduction to this book in relation to the most recent pre-publication developments concerning the Constitutional Treaty.

closer to the people. The role of national parliaments in enhancing legitimacy (helping to make good the so-called democratic deficit) in relation to legislation emanating from the European Union, whether it be Community law, in the form of regulations, directives, or decisions, or obligations arising from the intergovernmental pillars of the Union[3] was acknowledged in a declaration to the Maastricht Treaty of 1992.[4] The formal position was strengthened by the Amsterdam Treaty of 1997, to which was annexed a specific protocol on the role of national parliaments, requiring copies of all proposals to be sent to national parliament and for six weeks to elapse before any decision could be taken at Union level.

The Declaration on the Future of the Union which was attached to the Treaty of Nice in February 2000 required the 2004 intergovernmental conference to address the issues of the delimitation of powers between the European Union and Member States, the simplification of the Treaties, the status of the Charter of Fundamental Rights, and the role of national parliaments. The Declaration directed attention to 'the role of national parliaments in the European architecture'. It also called for a deep and wide debate on the future of the European Union involving the people of Europe. That debate began very quickly. Various ideas were discussed, some quite radical and controversial.[5]

The Laeken Declaration of December 2001 on the Future of European Union mandated the Convention on the Future of Europe (which was established to pave the way to the 2004 intergovernmental conference) to consider, *inter alia*,

---

[3] These now consist of the Common Foreign and Security Policy, and Police and Judicial Cooperation in Criminal Matters.

[4] Declaration (No. 13) on the Role of National Parliaments in the European Union provided that "the Conference considers that it is important to encourage greater involvement of national parliaments in the activities of the European Union.
To this end, the exchange of information between national parliaments and the European Parliament should be stepped up. In this context, the governments of the Member States will ensure, *inter alia*, that national parliaments receive Commission proposals for legislation in good time for information or possible examination.
Similarly, the Conference considers that it is important for contact between the national parliaments and the European Parliament to be stepped up, in particular through the granting of appropriate reciprocal facilities and regular meetings between members of parliament interested in the same issues".

[5] For example, the creation of a second chamber of the European Parliament, the members of which would be national parliamentarians. For a discussion of some of the issues, see the Report of the European Union Select Committee, *A Second Parliamentary Chamber for Europe: An Unreal Solution to Some Real Problems* (Seventh Report, 2001–02, HL Paper 48). See also the chapter in this volume by Andreas Maurer.

how there could be more democracy, transparency, and efficiency in the European Union.[6] The Convention included a particular Working Group (Working Group IV) on the role of national parliaments.[7] The Constitutional Treaty which resulted from the Convention and the subsequent intergovernmental conference would have taken matters a significant step further. Two protocols were annexed to the Constitutional Treaty: Protocol No. 1 on the Role of National Parliaments in the European Union, and, very importantly, Protocol No. 2 on the Application of the Principles of Subsidiarity and Proportionality.[8] In addition, Article I-11(3) of the Constitutional Treaty required national parliaments to ensure compliance on the part of European legislative acts with the principle of subsidiarity in accordance with Protocol No 2. Protocol No. 2 on the Application of the Principles of Subsidiarity and Proportionality provided that if a sufficient number of parliaments raised objections regarding the compatibility of a legislative proposal with the principle of subsidiarity, the proposal had to be reviewed. The Constitutional Treaty also envisaged challenges against adopted measures being brought on behalf of national parliaments in the Court of Justice on the grounds of subsidiarity. The changes envisaged in these provisions focused the attention of national parliaments on how they might give effect to the Protocol on subsidiarity. Notwithstanding the 'no' votes in France and the Netherlands, the question of how national parliaments can police subsidiarity subsequently remained actively under discussion, as will be described below.

3. The Importance of Scrutiny by National Parliaments

Membership of the European Community involves a substantial shift of law-making power from national parliaments to the institutions of the Community, principally (at least historically) to the Council of Ministers, but also to the Commission and increasingly, with the development and expansion of the co-decision procedure, to the European Parliament (under the Constitutional Treaty, co-decision was intended to become the 'ordinary legislative procedure', applicable to most legislative acts). From the outset,

6 The Declaration stated, *inter alia,* that

> "a second question, which also relates to democratic legitimacy, involves the role of national parliaments. Should they be represented in a new institution, alongside the Council and the European Parliament? Should they have a role in areas of European action in which the European Parliament has no competence? Should they focus on the division of competence between Union and Member States, for example through preliminary checking of compliance with the principle of subsidiarity?"

7 The report of Working Group IV and the debate in the Convention plenary session on the Working Group's recommendations can be found in *Preparatory Working Documents for the European Convention* (European Communities, 2004).

8 The contents of both of these protocols are examined in some detail in the text below.

a number of member states' parliaments have sought to monitor and exercise a measure of control over their governments' agreement in the Council to decision-taking and law-making at European level. Initially, at least in the case of the United Kingdom, the reason for domestic parliamentary scrutiny of Community legislative action was to try to compensate in some measure for the loss of, or shift of, state power in farour of Community institutions. From the time of the Treaty of Maastricht and the creation of the European Union, as the fields of activity and responsibility at European level have enlarged, so parliamentary scrutiny has had to develop and adapt, in particular to European Union matters not falling under the EC Treaty. Nonetheless, keeping Parliament informed and requiring ministers to be accountable has remained at the core of the United Kingdom regime.

4. The Variety of National Scrutiny Procedures

Parliamentary scrutiny of proposed European Union legislation is a well-established fact in many member states, including the United Kingdom. The extent to which national parliaments monitor the legislative processes of the European Union, and their governments' participation in it vary from member state to member state. The precise methodology differs and reflects the constitutional, cultural and political situations in the different member states. In some member states, scrutiny is written into the national constitution and governments may not act in the Council without prior and specific authority from the national parliament (or one of its committees). In the United Kingdom, the process is essentially a political rather than a legal or formal constitutional one. Both houses of parliament are given the opportunity, on the basis of documents and information provided by Her Majesty's Government, to examine and give their views on proposals for Community legislation and other important documents, and to debate them where appropriate. The Government undertakes, subject to limited exceptions, not to agree to any proposal until each house has completed scrutiny.

5. A Brief History of Parliamentary Scrutiny in the United Kingdom

The history and work of both the European Scrutiny Committee (in the House of Commons) and the Select Committee on the European Union (in the House of Lords) can be traced back to the mid-1970s.[9] They predate references to

[9] In December 1972, both Houses appointed Select Committees to consider what procedures should be established in order to scrutinise legislative proposals and other documents emanating from the Communities. In the Commons, the Committee was chaired by Sir John Foster. The Committee laid down the basis for scrutiny in the Commons as described below. Lord Maybray-King chaired the Lords Committee. The principal recommendation of the latter Committee's report (1972–73, HL 194),

national parliaments in the Treaties. What is noteworthy is that the current systems in both houses still remain largely consistent with those 1973 Reports. Procedures have inevitably been adapted in the light of experience and events and mandates have been enlarged, but no fundamental change has taken place. That said, three important recent developments should be noted.

First, the process of parliamentary scrutiny has been the subject of very detailed and critical review in both Houses.[10] Procedures have been adapted in the light of experience and events and mandates have been enlarged (to include the Second and Third Pillars). In the House of Lords, a number of reforms were effected following the Select Committee's review and Report in 2002.[11] The reform process is continuing. Secondly, the United Kingdom National Parliament Office has been established in Brussels. It is an important point of contact between the two Houses and the Union's institutions, especially the European Parliament. The Office provides a valuable source of information for the two scrutiny committees. Thirdly, the Modernisation Committee of the House of Commons has recently proposed the establishment of a Joint Committee of the two Houses be established to consider matters related to the European Union (the Parliamentary European Committee).[12] This proposal is considered further at the end of this chapter. A number of the Modernisation Committee's other recommendations concerning the scrutiny process are set out in the description of the work of the Commons' European Scrutiny Committee immediately below.

---

presented in July 1973, was to set up a sessional select committee. The Select Committee on the European Communities was set up on 10 April, 1974. It was reappointed at the beginning of each parliamentary session until it was superseded, in December 1999, by the Select Committee on the European Union.

[10] In 1998, the scrutiny of European legislation in the Commons came under review by the Select Committee on Modernisation of the House of Commons. Reports on the scrutiny process in the Commons were prepared in 1996 and 1997, by the Select Committee on European Legislation (Twenty-Seventh Report, 1995–96) and the Select Committee on Procedure (Third Report, 1996–97) respectively. The upshot of the review was a redrawing of the terms of reference of the Commons Committee, most significantly by extending its remit to Second and Third Pillar matters. Its Scrutiny Reserve Resolution (the effect of which is explained in the text below at n. 20) has also been amended to include references to texts requiring a decision of the Council of Ministers under the Second and Third Pillars. The committee was also renamed the European Scrutiny Committee. Shortly after those changes in the Commons, the terms of reference of the Lords Scrutiny Committee were revised and the House adopted its own Scrutiny Reserve Resolution, the text of which is reproduced in the annex to this chapter. This was done essentially to bring the terms of reference into line with those of the Commons Committee, to reflect the extension of the Scrutiny Reserve to Second and Third Pillar matters, and to make clear, by adoption of its own resolution, the operation of the Scrutiny Reserve in the context of procedures in the House of Lords. The Lords Committee was renamed the European Union Committee.

[11] *Review of Scrutiny of European Legislation* (First Report, 2002–03, HL Paper 15).

[12] Select Committee on Modernisation of the House of Commons, *Scrutiny of European Business*, (Second Report, 2004–05, HC 465).

6. Parliamentary Scrutiny in the United Kingdom – The Westminster Scrutiny Committees and their Procedures

The work of the two Select Committees, the European Scrutiny Committee in the House of Commons and the Select Committee on the European Union in the Lords ('the Scrutiny Committees') has as its foundation two essential common features: first, the deposit of European Union documents and explanatory memoranda, and secondly, the use of the scrutiny reserve resolution.

(a) European Union Documents

The two Committees scrutinise 'European Union documents'[13] This term is given a broad meaning and covers proposals for Community legislation and a large variety of other documents issuing under the Treaties. They include Commission annual work programmes, green and white papers, reports and communications, reports of the Court of Auditors and, importantly, Second and Third Pillar documents (draft common strategies, joint actions or common positions in the former case, and draft common positions, framework decisions, decisions, or conventions in the latter case).[14] When in the course of legislation a new text is produced, such as an amended Commission proposal or a Council common position, a new document is thereby generated and the scrutiny process begins again.[15]

---

[13] This term is defined in House of Commons Standing Order No. 143. The definition is reproduced, in identical terms, in the motion appointing the House of Lords Committee, which is renewed at the start of each parliamentary session.

[14] Second and Third Pillar documents were brought within the terms of reference of the Commons Committee as a result of the 1998 recommendations of the Modernisation Committee, mentioned at n. 12 above. This followed reports on the scrutiny process in the Commons prepared in 1996 and 1997, by the Select Committee on European Legislation (Twenty-Seventh Report, 1995–96) and the Select Committee on Procedure (Third Report, 1996–97) respectively. The Lords Committee has historically had wider terms of reference, which enabled it to examine Second and Third Pillar instruments prior to the amendment of the definition in the Commons Standing Order of the documents to be deposited.

[15] A practical example of this can be seen in the scrutiny of the draft Directive on minimum standards on procedures in Member States for granting and withdrawing refugee status. The publication and debate of the European Union Committee's Report, *Minimum Standards in Asylum Procedures* (Eleventh Report, 2000–01, HL Paper 59) was not the end of the story by any means. Subsequent versions of the Directive and of particular articles were furnished to the Committees for scrutiny. Each was subjected to a rigorous critical examination by Sub-Committee E (Law and Institutions). There was correspondence with the Government and two further meetings between the Sub-Committee and the minister and her officials in which the committee raised questions and sought further clarification of a number of issues, not least on draft articles affecting the rights of the individual and the level of standards being proposed. See *Evidence by Caroline Flint MP on Asylum Procedures* (First Report, Session 2003–04, HL Paper 8) and *Further Evidence by Caroline Flint MP on Asylum Procedures* (Eighteenth Report, Session 2003–04, HL Paper 106). The proposal subsequently remained a controversial one. (See "Parliament Weighs Legal Challenge to Asylum Law", *European Voice*, 31 March–6 April 2005).

European Union documents are deposited in Parliament by the Foreign and Commonwealth Office within two working days of their receipt in London. Within ten days of deposit, the lead department is expected to provide an Explanatory Memorandum signed by a minister. It is the minister's evidence to Parliament and is a public document. In the case of a legislative proposal, it should include (a) a description of the subject matter; (b) details of the legal base and legislative procedure proposed for the measure and any reservations or comments the minister may have about them; (c) an assessment as to whether the proposed legislation accords with the principles of subsidiarity and proportionality; (d) a statement of the impact on United Kingdom law; (e) a statement of the Government's policy towards the document; (f) a statement of the financial implications of the proposal; and (g) the likely timetable for the Council's consideration of it.

The requirement to provide an Explanatory Memorandum is an important and valuable feature of the system. It enables the two scrutiny committees to assess the documents quickly and it establishes at the outset the accountability of ministers to Parliament and its committees for their conduct with regard to them.

The fact that the system is essentially document-based has recently been the subject of criticism. It is said that by the time a proposal formally emerges from Brussels, opinions in the Commission have already been set and it may be difficult to budge them.[16] It is argued that there needs to be more information-sharing on what is in the pipeline. The attention of those who make such criticisms should be drawn to the emphasis already placed by both Committees (and in the Lords, the sub-committees, as explained below) to 'upstream scrutiny'. The Committees undertake scrutiny of the Commission's annual work programme, and increasingly both Committees are engaged in examining strategic decisions and recommendations of the European Council (*e.g.,* the recent Hague Programme[17]), action plans, green and white papers, and staff working documents. This would become increasingly important were proposals of the kind which were originally made in the Constitutional Treaty ever to be adopted – national parliaments would want to signal[18] at the earliest opportunity that the principle of

[16] D. Jones, *UK Parliamentary Scrutiny of European Union Legislation* (Foreign Policy Centre, London, 2005).

[17] Editor's note: the Hague programme is a programme for closer cooperation in justice and home affairs at European Union level from 2005 to 2010.

[18] Even if they could not formally flourish the 'yellow card'. See in this regard the discussion in the text below following n. 51.

subsidiarity might have been breached. It should also be recalled that both Houses have representatives based in the United Kingdom National Parliament Office in Brussels. They are a key part of the Committees' eyes and ears. There is nevertheless a case for saying that engagement between Parliament and interested parties (such as industry, consumers *etc.*) could be improved – although those interested parties must bear some responsibility for communicating their concerns promptly to Parliament.

In its recent report, the Modernisation Committee of the House of Commons has accepted that there is a case for establishing a system for examining legislative proposals before the Commission has produced its first formal document. The Committee has recommended that the Government give an undertaking to alert the Commons' European Scrutiny Committee by letter at an early stage of consultation exercises on important proposals in which it is involved. The Scrutiny Committee could then decide whether to ask for an explanatory memorandum on the proposal from the Government, or to supplement the information supplied by the Government with information from interested parties. The Scrutiny Committee might then decide to take evidence and produce a report on the proposal itself, to recommend a standing committee debate, or to draw the attention of the relevant departmental select committee to the proposal.[19]

(b) The Scrutiny Reserve Resolution

The linchpin of the system is the Scrutiny Reserve Resolution. One of these has been adopted in respect of each House.[20] They provide that no Minister of the Crown shall give agreement to any proposal either for European Community legislation, or for one of the specific instruments under Title V or Title VI of the Treaty on European Union which is still subject to scrutiny. By 'still subject to scrutiny' is meant a proposal on which the Scrutiny Committee has not completed its scrutiny, or which is awaiting consideration by the house in that it has been recommended for debate and the debate has not yet taken place. The Resolution makes an exception of any proposal

---

[19] See Second Report of the Select Committee on Modernisation of the House of Commons, *Scrutiny of European Business*, (2004–05, HC 465), at paras. 48 and 49. Originally established in 1979, departmental select committees have the task of examining the expenditure, administration and policy of the Government department they cover. For example, the Trade and Industry Select Committee concerns itself with activities of the Department of Trade and Industry.

[20] Resolution of the House of Commons of 17 November, 1998, modifying the resolution of 24 October, 1990, which replaced a 1980 Resolution, which in turn replaced successive ministerial undertakings to similar effect. Resolution of the House of Lords of 6 December 1999. This latter resolution is reproduced in the annex to this chapter.

which is 'confidential, routine or trivial, or is substantially the same as a proposal on which scrutiny has been completed'. The Minister may also give agreement to a proposal still subject to scrutiny 'if he decides that for special reasons agreement should be given'. But in that event he is required to explain his reasons to the committee or the house at the first opportunity.

It has been said that there are signs that ministers are increasingly reluctant to override the scrutiny reserve.[21] Certainly there is much more transparency about the process of overriding scrutiny. The Government (via the Cabinet Office) now provides the Scrutiny Committees with statistical information about how many times scrutiny has been overridden. This information is published in the Committees' annual reports. In 2004, the scrutiny reserve resolution was overridden on 38 occasions, sixteen times in the first six months of the year and 22 in the second. Overriding scrutiny is a matter to which both Committees pay careful attention. The Commons Scrutiny Committee has given notice that they will normally call a minister before it when the Committee believe that the scrutiny reserve resolution has been overridden without good cause, and has done so on a number of occasions.[22]

7. Scrutiny in the House of Commons

(a) The European Scrutiny Committee

The scrutiny system in the House of Commons has two main components; (a) the weekly meeting and report of the European Scrutiny Committee; and (b) debates either in one of three European Standing Committees, or on the floor of the House. The European Scrutiny Committee examines every year approximately 1,000 documents (a number of which have to be looked at several times) and aims to produce rapidly a short report on all significant documents; it reports on approximately 500 each year. It aims to draw the main elements and the contentious features of each such document to the attention of the House and recommends whether or not it should be debated and, if so, whether on the floor of the House or by a Standing Committee. Each year, the Committee recommends about fifty documents for debate. Only a handful of such debates take place on the floor of the House. The remainder take place in the Standing Committee.

---

[21] Jones, above, n. 16, at 5.

[22] House of Commons European Scrutiny Committee, *The Work of the Committee in 2004* (Sixth Report, 2004–05), at para. 14.

(b) The Weekly Report

The Committee usually meets on Wednesdays when the House is sitting. A brief on every document on the agenda for the meeting will have been prepared by the Committee's staff and circulated to members before the meeting. In the case of documents that appear to raise questions of legal or political importance, the staff also circulate draft reports for the consideration of the Committee. These reports are drafted by four clerk advisers (usually retired civil servants who are familiar with the working of the European Union and with the subject matter of the legislation). The clerk advisers are the engine-room of the European Scrutiny Committee. Documents are put on the Committee's agenda as soon as possible after the Explanatory Memorandum has been received. The Committee may arrive at any one of four conclusions in relation to each document.

First, it may decide that the document is not legally or politically important, and thus that there is no need to report substantively on it to the house or for the Committee or the House to give it any further consideration. About half of the documents are disposed of in this way. Secondly, it may conclude that the document is of political or legal importance and so merits a substantive report for the information of the House, but there is no need for it to be debated. Thirdly, it may decide that the document is legally or politically important, but the decision whether there should be a debate should be deferred until later. For example, if, in the case of a proposal for legislation, the Government has gone out to consultation, the Committee may wish to see the response before deciding whether a debate would be appropriate. If the Explanatory Memorandum is, in important respects, unclear or incomplete, the Committee may wish to seek further information from the Minister before recommending a debate. The fourth possible conclusion the Committee may arrive at is that the document is legally or politically important and should be recommended for debate either in a European Standing Committee or on the floor of the house. When the Committee recommends a debate, it has been the practice to help to focus the debate by listing the main issues in the Committee's report.

When considering documents, the Committee meets privately. The Modernisation Committee has recently recommended that the Scrutiny Committee should have the option to conduct this part of its business in public.[23]

---

[23] Select Committee on Modernisation of the House of Commons, *Scrutiny of European Business*, (Second Report, 2004–05, HC 465) at para. 54.

(c) European Standing Committees

The idea of European Standing Committees was an innovative one. These Committees were introduced in 1990 to provide a more effective forum for debate than the late-night debates on the floor of the House, which had previously been the practice. There are three such Committees, each specialising in particular areas of Union activity.[24] Each Committee has thirteen permanent members. Any other member of the house may attend and participate in the proceedings, but he or she may not vote. The proceedings, which are public, last for up to two and a half hours. The first hour is set aside for questions to the responsible minister attending the debate. For the rest of the time, the Committee debates the document on the basis of a draft resolution (to which amendments may be tabled) moved by the minister. The question time followed by debate format provides an effective means of requiring ministers to explain and defend the Government's policy in relation to Community proposals.

The Modernisation Committee of the House of Commons has recently recommended that the number of European Standing Committees be increased from three to five, that the Committees be designated by names, which indicate clearly their functional ambit, rather than letters, and that the core membership of each Committee be reduced from thirteen to nine. Each European Standing Committee would be given a permanent chairman.[25]

8. Scrutiny in the House of Lords – The Select Committee on the European Union and its Sub-Committees

From the outset, the work of the House of Lords Select Committee on the European Union has been characterised by two aspects: the width of its terms of reference (which do not inhibit the Committee from examining in detail

[24] Standing Committee A deals with matters within the responsibility of the following Departments: Environment, Food and Rural Affairs; Transport; the Office of the Deputy Prime Minister; the Forestry Commission; and the analogous responsibilities of the Scotland, Wales, and Northern Ireland Offices. Standing Committee B deals with matters within the responsibility of the following Departments: Her Majesty's Treasury; Work and Pensions; the Foreign and Commonwealth Office; International Development; the Home Office; the Department for Constitutional Affairs (excluding those responsibilities of the Scotland and Wales Offices which fall to Standing Committee A); together with any matters not otherwise allocated to a European Standing Committee. Finally, Standing Committee C deals with matters within the responsibility of the following Departments: Trade & Industry; Education and Skills; Culture, Media and Sport; and Health.

[25] Select Committee on Modernisation of the House of Commons, above, n. 23.

the merits of proposals or restrict its activities to examination of deposited European Union documents) and its ability to appoint sub-committees.

The Committee normally has about twenty members.[26] Its chairman[27] is appointed as a salaried officer of the House, the Principal Deputy Chairman of Committees. The Committee has a clerk and a legal adviser.[28] It meets regularly (at least fortnightly) when Parliament is in session. Much of the work of the select committee – in particular its detailed enquiries into current legislative proposals or other topical matters – is effected by its sub-committees. There are seven such sub-committees, each having particular sectoral responsibilities, *viz.*, the Economic and Financial Affairs, and International Trade Sub-Committee (Sub-Committee A), the Internal Market Sub-Committee (Sub-Committee B), the Foreign Affairs, Defence and Development Policy Sub-Committee (Sub-Committee C), the Agriculture and Environment Sub-Committee (Sub-Committee D), the Law and Institutions Sub-Committee (Sub-Committee E), the Home Affairs Sub-Committee (Sub-Committee F) and the Social Policy and Consumer Affairs Sub-Committee (Sub-Committee G).

Each of the sub-committees is made up of (usually) two or three members of the Select Committee and other peers who are co-opted. Sub-committees normally meet weekly. Each sub-committee is chaired by a member of the select committee and has its own clerk. It is possible, though extremely rare, for additional sub-committees to be set up *ad hoc*.[29]

9. The Process and 'Spectrum' of Scrutiny in the Lords

(a) The Sift

The Select Committee has delegated to the chairman the task of conducting a first sift of all the documents formally deposited for scrutiny.[30] The chairman examines each document and its explanatory memorandum and

[26] Appointed by the House, on a proposal from the Committee of Selection.

[27] At the time of the writing of this chapter, Lord Grenfell.

[28] Second Counsel to the Chairman of Committees. The legal adviser, who is aided by the legal assistant, provides legal advice to the select committee and each of its sub-committees, especially Sub-Committee E (Law and Institutions).

[29] The last time was in 1994 when an *ad hoc* committee was appointed to examine the possible agenda for the 1996 Inter-Governmental Conference, leading to the report *1996 Inter-Governmental Conference* (Twenty-First Report, 1994–95, HL 105).

[30] The process of deposit of documents and submission of explanatory memoranda is described above. See text after n. 15 above.

decides whether it should (a) be referred to one or more of the sub-committees, or (b) retained for examination by the Select Committee itself. (The latter course is relatively rare but is important for dealing with matters affecting all the sub-committees, such as the Commission's annual work programme). or cleared from scrutiny. The clerks and the legal adviser aid the chairman in this process.

No criteria for determining which documents should be cleared from scrutiny at the time of sifting (and which should not) have been defined either by the Select Committee, the chairman, or the clerk to the Select Committee. In broad terms, the political, practical, or legal implications of the document are examined. Some of the factors which, in the light of experience, the legal adviser has considered to be relevant in advising the chairman whether to sift a document to a sub-committee for further examination are[31]:

(a) the nature of the document (*e.g.*, a green or white paper, draft legislative proposal or routine report);
(b) the scope of application of the proposal (including both its geographic scope and the degree of interest it holds for the United Kingdom);
(c) the policy implications of the document (which are usually identified and assessed by the Government), including any acknowledged problems of which the Committee should be aware and/or might have a view;
(d) the existence of legal problems (such as *vires*, subsidiarity, competence and implementation issues);
(e) whether the document gives rise to comitology issues (*i.e.*, if it involves the creation and application of Commission implementing powers)[32];
(f) the broad political or public impact of the document (to which the 'tabloid test' is applied, *viz.*, a document will be sifted for further examination if not doing so might lead to the reaction 'surely you could not have let that pass without examination!');
(g) existing media coverage of the issues raised in the document;
(h) the reactions of the European Parliament or other national parliaments;
(i) advice which is given by a reputable non-governmental organisation or other interested party;

[31] This list is based on that set out in Appendix 3 (Scrutiny of European Union Legislation – the sift process) to the Select Committee's Annual Report 2003 (Forty-Fourth Report, Session 2002–03, HL 191).

[32] The importance of the Committee not neglecting comitology questions was referred to in its report, *Review of Scrutiny of European Legislation* (First Report, 2002–03, HL Paper 15) at paras 89 and 90.

(j) the previous involvement of either the Select Committee itself or one of its sub-committees, whether in relation to a document sifted earlier or an earlier report (whether this was a general report or one of a more focused nature);

(k) the completeness of the documentation or explanatory memorandum (in particular the absence of a regulatory impact assessment where the measure could have substantial implications for producers, suppliers, users, consumers or taxpayers); and

(l) the particular interests or expertise of members of the sub-committee.

In practice, the sift is undertaken once a week when the House is in session. The results, in particular the identity of those documents cleared by the chairman from scrutiny, are circulated to sub-committee chairmen. About a third of all documents submitted for scrutiny are sifted to a sub-committee. Just over a half of those sifted for further examination are formal legislative proposals.

(b) Detailed Inquiries

On receipt of a document, a sub-committee has three basic options, namely, to conduct a detailed inquiry, to engage in correspondence with the relevant minister, or simply to note the document. The choice made will depend largely on the degree of importance of the document, the information already available, and the amount of time available.

A sub-committee may, at one end of the spectrum, undertake a detailed inquiry into the proposal. This will entail the sub-committee taking written and oral evidence from the relevant Government department, European Union institutions (which will usually include the Commission), other experts and interested parties. A specialist adviser may be appointed to assist the sub-committee in a particular enquiry.[33] The outcome is a report on the matter from the Select Committee to the House. Reports conclude with a recommendation whether the report should be 'for debate' or 'for information'. Reports are published both by the Stationery Office and on the House's homepage on the internet.[34] Copies of the report are sent to the responsible minister who responds on behalf of the Government within two months.[35]

[33] This is extremely rare in the case of Sub-Committee E but is standard practice for the other sub-committees.

[34] See www.parliament.uk.

[35] Formerly it was the practice to publish Government responses in 'Correspondence with Ministers' reports, described in the text below, at n. 37. They are now published in a separate 'Government Responses' report. See for an example, the Twenty-Sixth Report, 2003–04.

Analysis of Sifts in the House of Lords Select Committee on the European Union

	2002-3 Session (19 November 2002– 18 November 2003)	2003–4 Session (2 December 2003 – 23 November 2004)	2004–5 Session (30 November 2004 – 9 April 2005)
Number of sifts undertaken	40	38	16
Documents/explanatory memoranda considered	1079	1072	347
Number sifted for examination	372	314	115
Documents sifted to the select committee itself	2	5	5
Documents sifted to Sub-Committee A (Economic and Financial Affairs, and International Trade)	47	46	9
Documents sifted to Sub-Committee B (Internal Market)	68	54	11
Documents sifted to Sub-Committee C (Foreign Affairs, Defence and Development Policy)	43	45	28
Documents sifted to Sub-Committee D (Agriculture and the Environment)	64	41	10
Documents sifted to Sub-Committee E (Law and Institutions)	76	37	21
Documents sifted to Sub-Committee F (Home Affairs)	72	45	18
Documents sifted to Sub-Committee G (Social Policy and Consumer Affairs)	-	41	13
Number of Supplementary Explanatory Memoranda* also considered during this period.	36	23	12

* Supplementary Explanatory Memoranda are a means of providing the Scrutiny Committees with additional information about a document under scrutiny. They are considered in the sift procedure but have been excluded from the figures given for documents considered and sifted because they relate to documents which have already been subject to the sift procedure.

The Select Committee may itself conduct inquiries. It did so recently, for example, in relation to the application of the principle of subsidiarity under the Constitutional Treaty.[36] The Select Committee also publishes reports of its regular meetings with the Government's Minister for Europe (covering current issues and developments), representatives of the Presidency (concerning the latter's six-month programme), and the Commission (regarding its Annual Work Programme).

(c) Ministerial Correspondence

In practice only a very few proposals are subject to such detailed examination. On average, each sub-committee will conduct three inquiries either each year or in each parliamentary session. What of the rest? The sub-committee may, having looked at a particular proposal, decide to write to the minister seeking further information on it or recording its views on the matter. Sometimes that letter may be written with the benefit of written evidence volunteered or solicited from interested parties. All such and other significant correspondence from the select committee and its sub-committees to the Government is reproduced in twice (sometimes thrice) yearly reports entitled "Correspondence with Ministers".[37] In the interim, copies of letters may be posted on the relevant sub-committee's website.

At the other end of the spectrum, the sub-committee may simply note the document and clear it from scrutiny. Even in this case, the committee may write to the minister asking to be kept informed of developments and reserving the right to conduct a detailed inquiry at a later stage.

10. The Purpose of National Parliamentary Scrutiny of European Union Legislation

Before offering an assessment of the impact of the work of the European Union Select Committee, it is helpful to recall what the Committee itself considers to be the purpose of national parliamentary scrutiny of European Union legislation. In its 2002 Report reviewing the scrutiny process, the Committee emphasised the constitutional importance and purpose of the scrutiny of European Union legislation which, once adopted, may not be

[36] *Strengthening national parliamentary scrutiny of the EU* – the *Constitution's subsidiarity early warning mechanism.* (Fourteenth Report, Session 2004–05, HL Paper 101).

[37] This relatively unknown series of reports contains a mass of varied information about the work of the committees. For a recent example, see *Correspondence with Ministers* (Fourth Report, 2005–06, HL Paper 16).

reversed by national parliaments, even if the measure in question has to be given effect to by means of domestic primary or secondary legislation. The committee said

> "we accordingly stress that national parliamentary scrutiny of European Union legislation has a clear constitutional purpose. Scrutiny at an early stage is therefore essential and must be effective as possible. To that end, scrutiny should include:
>
> - The accumulation, presentation and summary of relevant material, including information, statistics, explanation and analysis.
> - The provision of information to the House and the public as a contribution to transparency.
> - Drawing the attention of the House, the Government, European institutions and the public to significant matters contained within that information and in particular making recommendations – "focusing the debate".
> - Contributing to the law-making process by detailed analysis of draft texts, by exposing difficulties and proposing amendments.
> - An examination of the Government and its role in agreeing European legislation and, as part of that process, compelling the Government not only to think through what it is doing or has done but sometimes to account for it.
> - An examination of the Commission and the policies it formulates".[38]

11. The Impact of the Scrutiny Process in the United Kingdom

It is difficult to assess what effect parliamentary scrutiny has in practice. Perhaps only ministers and civil servants can give a meaningful answer to this question. But from the perspective of a former civil servant now working for Parliament, three (personal) comments may be helpful. First, the discipline of ministers having to submit explanatory memoranda and to respond in writing and sometimes in person to questions raised by the Scrutiny Committees should not be dismissed. There can be little doubt that it is an important means of keeping the Government of the day accountable to Parliament. Though, as mentioned, there have been a substantial number of occasions when the scrutiny reserve has been overridden by the Government, it remains a real check on ministers. They have to explain their actions in public.

[38] *Review of Scrutiny of European Legislation* (First Report, 2002–03, HL Paper 15), at para. 13.

Secondly, parliamentary scrutiny can contribute substantially to the transparency and openness of the European Union's legislative process. Perhaps the best examples of this can be seen in the scrutiny of Third Pillar measures. The House of Lords work on the European Police Office (Europol) is a good instance of this. The Select Committee has issued a number of reports concerning Europol.[39] The first report, *Europol* (published in 1995), examined the Europol Convention (*i.e.*, the legal basis of Europol) in draft form. The later reports considered some of the detailed rules and regulations made under the Convention (those on the Confidentiality Regulations and the Joint Supervisory Body), proceeding further with the issues identified in the first report (especially the need to monitor the exchange of personal data and to protect individual rights) and, significantly, placing in the public domain thc details of how rules are made under the Convention. A later report (published in 2003) assessed Europol's role in fighting crime and made a number of recommendations relating to its remit and practices.[40] More recently, Europol was one of a number of bodies whose work was assessed by the Committee in its report *After Madrid: the European Union's response to terrorism*.[41]

Thirdly, the work of the Scrutiny Committees can have a direct impact on the progress or content of legislation. It is frequently said that Commission officials read House of Lords Reports assiduously. Whether or not that is true, there have been instances where the Select Committee's recommendations have led to change in the measure being negotiated. An example can be seen in the 1999 Comitology Decision.[42] At the outset of its inquiry into the (then) draft decision, the Committee asked to be supplied with a complete list of comitology committees. According to the Community institutions, this could not be done. But the fact that the Select Committee required it and that the Government then produced a list showed that it was not impossible. The Select Committee's recommendation that there should be a published list of comitology committees was put into the final text of the Decision.[43] It must be said, however, that the number of cases where Committee reports lead directly to changes in proposals is hard to measure.

---

[39] *EUROPOL* (Tenth Report, 1994–95, HL 51), *EUROPOL: Confidentiality Regulations* (First Report. 1997–98. HL 9), *EUROPOL: Joint Supervisory Body* (Thirteenth Report, 1997–98, HL 71), *EUROPOL: Third Country Rules* (Twenty-Ninth Report, 1997–98, HL 135).

[40] *Europol's Role in Fighting Crime* (Fifth Report, 2002–03, HL 43).

[41] Fifth Report, 2004–05, HL 53.

[42] Council Decision 1999/468 of 28 June 1999 laying down the procedures for the exercise of implementing powers conferred on the Commission, [1999] OJ L184/23.

[43] See *Delegation of Powers to the Commission: Reforming Comitology* (Third Report, 1998–99, HL 23)

12. The Protocol on the Role of National Parliaments in the European Union

The Protocol on the Role of National Parliaments in the European Union (annexed to the founding treaties and the Treaty on European Union at the time of coming into force of the Amsterdam Treaty) marked a significant step in political terms in the relationship between national parliaments and the European Union. Subject to the general comment that the Protocol has not, at least in the United Kingdom, had a very noticeable effect in practice (there having been little, if any, change in the behaviour of the Community institutions or successive Presidencies, or national governments), some observations on the nature and scope of the Protocol and of its purported successor, Protocol No. 1 to the Constitutional Treaty, may be helpful. The Protocol itself deals with two matters: information for national parliaments of member states and the Conference of European Affairs Committees (COSAC).[44] The first is particularly relevant in the present context.

Paragraph 1 of the Protocol requires "all Commission documents (green and white papers and communications)" to be "promptly forwarded to national parliaments of the Member States". This provision underlines the experience of the Select Committee that it is important for national parliaments to become involved at the earliest stage in the development of a proposal. In practice, informed intervention at this stage has a greater chance of influencing the shape and content of proposals. Basic issues and interests can be identified and policy formulated without the burden of a detailed text to which at least one party, the Commission or (where it retains the right of initiative) a member state, is already committed. The experience of the Select Committee is that national parliaments can play a useful role at this stage of proceedings.

[44] COSAC is made up of representatives of committees of national parliaments dealing with European affairs (six coming from each national parliament) as well as representatives from the European Parliament. Representatives from the national parliaments of the candidate countries participate as observers. COSAC meets twice a year, meetings normally taking place in the capital of the country holding the European Union presidency. (See Rules of Procedure [2004] OJ C270 1.) COSAC is formally recognised in the Protocol on the Role of National Parliaments in the European Union (annexed to the founding treaties and the Treaty on European Union at the time of coming into force of the Amsterdam Treaty). Under that Protocol, COSAC may "make any contribution it deems appropriate for the attention of the institutions of the European Union, in particular on the basis of draft legal texts which the representatives of governments of the Member States may decide to forward to it, in view of the nature of their subject matter". Similar words appeared in Art. 10 of Protocol No. 1 to the Constitutional Treaty. That Article also refers to the role of COSAC in promoting the exchange of information and best practice between national parliaments and the European Parliament. See generally in relation to COSAC the chapter in this book by Morten Knudsen and Yves Carl.

Protocol No. 1 on the Role of National Parliaments in the European Union,[45] which was annexed to the Constitutional Treaty, would have made the following changes. First, the newer Protocol expressly referred to national parliaments being supplied with the Commission's "annual legislative programme as well as any other instrument of legislative planning or policy". This was a significant addition, although (as will be explained in more detail below) it would not have affected the working patterns of the United Kingdom Scrutiny Committees, which already regularly consider such documents. Secondly, the agendas and outcomes of meetings of the Council of Ministers would have had to be forwarded to national parliaments at the same time as they are sent to member states' governments. There seems to be no legal reason why this should not be done even now as a matter of good administration, irrespective of the position as regards ratification of the Constitutional Treaty (or any successor treaty). Finally, the newer Protocol provided that where the European Council intended to make use of the simplified procedure (*passarelle*)[46] for amending voting or legislative procedures laid down in the Constitutional Treaty, national parliaments had to be informed of the initiative at least six months before any European decision was adopted. This was intended to enable national parliaments to exercise their veto on such a step under Article IV-444 (3) of the Constitutional Treaty.

Paragraph 2 of the current Protocol requires "Commission proposals for legislation", as defined by the Council in accordance with Article 207(3) of the EC Treaty, to be "made available in good time so that the government of each Member State may ensure that its own national parliament receives them as appropriate". This makes clear that it is the responsibility of national governments to transmit documents to parliaments. The experience in the United Kingdom has, from time to time, been one of delays in obtaining documents. Protocol No. 1 on the Role of National Parliaments in the European Union which was annexed to the Constitutional Treaty provided that Commission consultation documents (green and white papers and communications) would have had to be 'forwarded directly' to national parliaments upon publication. Documents would not come only from national governments. The newer Protocol envisaged direct (electronic) communication between the Commission and national parliaments. Again there seems to be no legal bar to this being put into effect immediately, as a matter of good administration.

---

[45] This is examined in detail in the text below.

[46] See Art. IV-444 of the Constitutional Treaty.

Paragraph 3 of the existing Protocol agreed at Amsterdam provides that, pursuant to Article 251 or 252 of the EC Treaty, a

> "six-week period shall elapse between a legislative proposal or a proposal for a measure to be adopted under Title VI of the Treaty on European Union being made available in all languages to the European Parliament and the Council by the Commission and the date when it is placed on a Council agenda for decision either for the adoption of an act or for adoption of a common position".

This is made 'subject to exceptions on grounds of urgency, the reasons for which shall be stated in the act or common position'. The newer Protocol would have retained this six-week rule.

Paragraphs 1 and 3, taken together, are consistent with the ongoing nature of United Kingdom parliamentary scrutiny described above. But the definition of "European Union documents" adopted by both Houses of Parliament[47] extends beyond the matters mentioned in paragraphs 1 and 3 of the Amsterdam Protocol. These provisions do not limit the extent of national parliamentary scrutiny. Rather, the Protocol imposes a minimum obligation on the relevant Community institutions. There has seemed to be no reason to change domestic requirements such as those in the United Kingdom, although the Protocol may help to focus Government departments on the scrutiny timetable. Six weeks may sound a long period but from the Select Committee's perspective there may still be time pressures, particularly if the views of interested parties are to be sought. Under the Protocol annexed to the Constitutional Treaty, a six-week delay would have remained the rule.[48] As will be explained in the text below, the six-week time period would have taken on an added importance under the related Protocol on subsidiarity.

The wording of paragraph 3 of the current Protocol might suggest that national parliaments need only to be given the opportunity of seeing the proposal in its original form. In practice it is rare for a proposal to be adopted without some amendment.[49] The prerogative of national parliaments, recognised by the Protocol, to consider and comment upon

[47] See further in this regard the text above.
[48] Editor's note: see now the introduction to this book in relation to the most recent pre-publication developments concerning the Constitutional Treaty.
[49] Emergency measures, such as those imposing trade and other sanctions, are the exception which come most immediately to mind.

proposals is not limited to original proposals emerging from the Commission. Paragraph 3, it is suggested, has to be construed with regard to its purpose. It is well-settled in Community law that where the European Parliament is given the right to be consulted, it has the right to be re-consulted in certain circumstances – for example, where the (amended) text to be adopted "differs in essence" from the text on which the Parliament was first consulted.[50] It is at least arguable that for consultation under the Protocol to be meaningful the same should apply in the case of consultation of national parliaments. Moreover it would be odd if the European Parliament alone was to be re-consulted where a proposal is substantially amended. The existing position was not sought to be changed or clarified under Protocol No. 1 on the Role of National Parliaments in the European Union which was annexed to the Constitutional Treaty. It is noteworthy, however, that Protocol No. 2 on the Application of the Principles of Subsidiarity and Proportionality annexed to the Constitutional Treaty expressly contemplated amended proposals being remitted for consideration by national parliaments. The precise extent of the involvement of national parliaments where measures are amended during negotiations in the Council and Parliament (always assuming that these provisions – or, as now seems more likely, equivalent such ones – ever come into force) remains to be seen.[51]

13. The Protocol on Subsidiarity

The essence of the principle of subsidiarity is that the Union should only act if the objectives of the proposed action cannot be sufficiently achieved by Member States and can, by reason of the scale or effects of the proposed action, be better achieved by the Union. This was set out in Article I-11(3) of the Constitutional Treaty, and was not new. What was new, however, were the procedures set out in Protocol No. 2 on the Application of the Principles of Subsidiarity and Proportionality, annexed to the Constitutional Treaty. The Protocol would have provided national parliaments with two ways of raising objections on the grounds of subsidiarity: (a) an early warning mechanism or so-called 'yellow card' procedure and (b) a challenge before the Court of Justice.

[50] See Case C-392/95 *Parliament v Council* [1997] ECR I-3213, at para. 15.

[51] This is a matter upon which the Select Committee has sought clarification from the Government: see *Strengthening National Parliamentary Scrutiny of the EU* – the *Constitution's Subsidiarity Early Warning Mechanism* (Fourteenth Report, Session 2004–05, HL Paper 101) at para. 141.

(a) The Early Warning Mechanism

The early warning mechanism provided for by the Constitutional Treaty a means by which national parliaments could register objections against proposed European legislation[52] where they identified a possible breach of the subsidiarity principle. Where a third[53] of national parliaments (or chambers thereof – each parliament was to have two votes, one for each chamber in bicameral parliaments) raised objections (by way of a reasoned opinion) then the Commission or other initiator was to have been obliged to reconsider its proposal. National parliaments would have had six weeks from receipt of a draft legislative act in which to take a view and, if necessary, submit objections.[54]

National parliaments were to have been entitled to have the case for action at Union level fully explained and justified. Article 5 of the Protocol set out what was required of the Commission or other initiator of Union action[55]: *viz.,* (a) a detailed statement making it possible to appraise compliance with the principle of subsidiarity, which, it was provided, should include an assessment of the proposal's financial impact and, in the case of a European framework law, of its implications for the rules to be put in place by member states; and (b) the reasons for concluding that a Union objective could be better achieved at Union level. This was required to be substantiated by qualitative and, wherever possible, quantitative indicators.

Had these provisions come into force, national parliaments ought to have ensured that they were satisfied that the proposal was supported by such information. It was clear from Article 5 of the Protocol that compliance with the principle of subsidiarity should not have been a matter which the Commission could comply with simply by drafting a suitably-worded assertion in a recital to the proposal in question. A statement that a measure has 'international/cross-border implications' does not necessarily mean that the subsidiarity test is met. The Protocol reaffirmed that application of the principle had to be properly substantiated in each case. If a national

[52] The procedure was restricted to 'draft European legislative acts', which term presumably referred to European laws and framework laws as defined in Arts I-33 and I-34 of the Constitutional Treaty.
[53] The threshold was reduced to one quarter in the case of in the case of a draft European legislative act submitted on the basis of Art III–264 of the Constitutional Treaty on the area of freedom, security and justice.
[54] Editor's note: see now in this regard the introduction to this book concerning the most recent pre-publication developments relating to the Constitutional Treaty.
[55] The measures subject to the early warning mechanism were not restricted to draft legislative acts prepared by the Commission but also included those initiated by the Court of Justice, the European Central Bank, the European Investment Bank, a group of member states, or the European Parliament.

parliament believed that the Commission (or other initiator of a legislative act) had failed to provide such a statement and substantiated reasons, it should set out its reasons for reaching that conclusion.

It is to be noted that although the title of Protocol No. 2 referred to 'the Principles of Subsidiarity and Proportionality', the Protocol only provided for national parliaments raising objections on the grounds of subsidiarity. The issue of national parliaments also considering a legislative proposal's compatibility with the principle of proportionality had been discussed in the Convention[56] but the Protocol limited national parliaments' remit to subsidiarity. This might have caused problems. The difficulty is that in application, the two principles, subsidiarity and proportionality, are frequently closely related and intermixed. The definition of subsidiarity in the Constitutional Treaty and the Protocol envisaged an assessment of the appropriateness of European Union action by reference to its scale, extent, and effects. The intensity of Community legislation might therefore have raised both subsidiarity and proportionality questions. While it may in practice be difficult to separate the two concepts, national parliaments would, nonetheless, have needed to be careful in framing any objections in terms of subsidiarity.

Any such early warning mechanism procedure would be novel. Various practical considerations arise, and national parliaments had at the time of writing of this chapter already begun a detailed examination of how they might best give effect to such an early warning mechanism. Investigations and discussions have taken place both within and among national parliaments. COSAC has played a key role here. Already a trial exercise has been undertaken.[57] Improved information-sharing and increased cooperation, though not necessarily coordination of action, seem likely to be one immediate outcome.

---

[56] That national parliaments should not be able to raise proportionality objections at the same time and in the same way as subsidiarity appears to have been a conscious choice on the part of the Convention and of the intergovernmental conference that adopted the Constitutional Treaty. The absence of a specific Working Group on proportionality did not mean that the issue of extending national parliaments' remit to include proportionality was not raised and discussed in the Convention. (See Summary Report of the plenary session (Brussels, 3 and 4 October, 2002. Doc CONV 331/02)).

[57] COSAC agreed at its meeting in the Hague on 23 November, 2004 to conduct a pilot project on the Third Railway Package in order to assess how the subsidiarity early-warning mechanism might work in practice. National delegations exchanged information on their experience of the pilot project at the COSAC meeting in Luxembourg on 17–18 May, 2005.

COSAC may also provide the forum for taking forward improved and more co-ordinated scrutiny of subsidiarity issues. The essential elements could, it is submitted, be put into effect under the Amsterdam Protocol on the Role of National Parliaments in the European Union.[58] Parliaments could, as many already do, examine proposals purposefully to see whether they comply with the principle of subsidiarity. Even without Treaty change, the effect of one third of the chambers of national parliaments delivering negative opinions on grounds of subsidiarity would almost certainly oblige the Commission to reconsider its proposal. COSAC, at its meeting during the United Kingdom Presidency in the second half of 2005, was invited to agree a 'contribution'[59] that would indicate the support of the various national European Scrutiny Committees represented in COSAC for a commitment by them to ensuring compliance with the principle of subsidiarity, working together under the currently applicable rules.

(b) Challenges before the Court

Article 8 of the Constitutional Treaty's Protocol No. 2 on the Application of the Principles of Subsidiarity and Proportionality provided that the Court of Justice was to have jurisdiction to hear challenges on the grounds of subsidiarity brought by the member states on behalf of their parliaments. Perhaps the most important question for national parliaments is the extent of the rights they would have to pursue, in the Court, any perceived infringement of the principle of subsidiarity. Early texts produced by the Convention appeared to give national parliaments no powers in this respect which they did not already enjoy.[60] Would the Constitutional Treaty have strengthened the position of national parliaments before the Court?

Article 8 was unclear on this point, perhaps deliberately so. The Article identified two ways in which actions on grounds of infringement of the principle of subsidiarity might be brought. First, they could be brought by member states. Secondly, they could be "notified [by member states] in accordance with their legal order on behalf of their national Parliament or a

---

[58] See regarding this Protocol, the section of text above which follows n. 43.

[59] The name given to an opinion adopted by COSAC and addressed to the institutions of the European Union pursuant to the Amsterdam Protocol on the Role of National Parliaments. (See Rule 10 of COSAC Rules of Procedure, [2004] OJ C270/1.) A list of the contributions and conclusions adopted at meetings of COSAC is to be found online at http://www.cosac.eu/en/documents/contributions/

[60] See *The Future of Europe: National Parliaments and Subsidiarity – the Proposed Protocols* (Eleventh Report, 2002–03, HL Paper 70) at paras 59–60.

chamber of it". In the first case, the action had to be "brought in accordance with the rules laid down in Article III-365 of the Constitution", the general provision governing the Court's jurisdiction and the grounds for judicial review of the legality of European laws. The wording of Article 8 of the Protocol seemed to suggest that Article III-365 would not apply to the second type of action. But, it is submitted, the requirement that actions initiated by national parliaments be notified "in accordance with their [Member States] legal order" could not have meant that the Court's jurisdiction and procedures in such cases were a matter to be determined individually by the member states. It would be most surprising if it had been the intention of Article 8 to confer any different or exceptional jurisdiction on the Court in the circumstances. Article III-365 would, it seems, have applied, though what procedurally would have been involved where an action was 'notified' by a Member State on behalf of a national parliament was unclear.

If – as appeared to be the case – where a national parliament sought to challenge the validity of a European law on subsidiarity grounds, the action was to be brought by the member state under Article III-365, a number of questions arose. Would governments be obliged to act? If so, how far would this obligation be a matter of Union law? Would national parliaments derive any rights by virtue of the Constitutional Treaty? Or would the position of national parliaments be wholly dependent on national laws and constitutions? It might be argued that the effect of Article 8 of the Protocol, coupled with the obligations placed by the Constitutional Treaty on national parliaments to ensure compliance with the principle of subsidiarity (Article I-11(3)) would be that a national parliament (and each chamber of a national parliament) will have a right, as a matter of Union law, to have proceedings brought before the Court on grounds of infringement of the principle of subsidiarity. On the other hand, the reference to actions being notified by member states "in accordance with their legal order on behalf of their national Parliament or a chamber of it" could have been construed as merely requiring the executive to act where the national legal order would require it to do so, and thus the Constitutional Treaty not be regarded as interfering in the internal constitutional relationship between the parliament and the executive within a member state.

The answers to these questions would determine the extent to which Article 8 – or any equivalent provision in a successor treaty – would be merely declaratory of the current position[61] or would create new rights and duties the execution of

[61] It should be noted that it is open even now for a national parliament to request the government of the member state concerned to commence proceedings on the grounds that the principle of subsidiarity has been violated.

which would potentially have a direct impact on the effectiveness of the Protocol (or any successor provisions) as a means of national parliamentary control over the exercise of Union legislative power on subsidiarity grounds. The Select Committee drew attention to these issues in its Constitutional Treaty's report on the subsidiarity Protocol[62] and, at the time of writing of this chapter, a response from the Government, the next step in the debate, was awaited.

14. Reform of the Scrutiny Process

As mentioned in the text above, the process of scrutiny in the United Kingdom has recently come under criticism, notably because of the lack of awareness both on the part of MPs and, more generally, of the public about legislative proposals emanating from Brussels. The good work of the two Scrutiny Committees has been acknowledged but there remains, it is strongly argued (both by the Government and bodies such as the Confederation of British Industry), a failure on the part of MPs to engage with and in the European legislative process. One solution promoted in the last Parliament was the creation of a Joint Grand Committee for Europe (described above).[63] It was envisaged that the committee would meet about four times a year, two of which would be devoted to considering the Foreign Secretary's regular six-monthly white papers on Europe. Members of the European Parliament would be allowed to attend. Commissioners and Commission officials might also participate in meetings of the new Committee but, the report makes clear, would not be subject to scrutiny by the Joint Committee. Their role would be to share information, to inform the debate, and to foster dialogue between the Commission and Parliament. What seems clear is that the new Joint Committee would not take over or displace the regular detailed scrutiny work undertaken by the two Scrutiny Committees. The Director General of the Confederation of British Industry commented that:

> "clearly such an infrequently-meeting committee could not launch an inquiry, or examine an issue in any detail, and thus would not contribute significantly to the scrutiny process".[64]

Such criticisms themselves deserve careful scrutiny. To take one issue as an example, it is true that the Joint Committee might well have to be selective.

---

[62] See Chapter 5 of the Select Committee's Report, *Strengthening National Parliamentary Scrutiny of the EU – the Constitution's Subsidiarity Early Warning Mechanism.* (Fourteenth Report, Session 2004–05, HL Paper 101).

[63] Select Committee on Modernisation of the House of Commons Second Report, *Scrutiny of European Business*, (2004–05, HC 465).

[64] Jones, above, n. 16, at 5.

On the other hand, the possibility can not be ruled out that a well-prepared meeting could examine a minister or Commissioner on a particular proposal (*e.g.*, the controversial draft Services Directive) in some detail. How the existence of such a Grand Committee might strengthen parliamentary awareness and scrutiny of European legislation and policies would have to be seen. Whether, and how best, such a Committee might complement and supplement the detailed work of the Scrutiny Committees needs further consideration. We must await developments in the present Parliament.

ANNEX

House of Lords Scrutiny Reserve Resolution

Monday 6th December 1999

(1) No Minister of the Crown should give agreement in the Council to any proposal for European Community legislation or for a common strategy, joint action or common position under Title V or a common position, framework decision, decision or convention under Title VI of the Treaty on European Union–

  (a) which is still subject to scrutiny (that is, on which the European Union Committee has not completed its scrutiny)

  (b) on which the European Union Committee has made a report to the House for debate, but on which the debate has not yet taken place

(2) In this Resolution, any reference to agreement to a proposal includes –

  (a) agreement to a programme, plan or recommendation for European Community legislation;

  (b) political agreement;

  (c) in the case of a proposal on which the Council acts in accordance with the procedure referred to in Article 251 of the Treaty establishing the European Community (co-decision), agreement to a common position, to an act in the form of a common position incorporating amendments proposed by the European Parliament, and to a joint text; and

  (d) in the case of a proposal on which the Council acts in accordance with the procedure referred to in Article 252 of the Treaty establishing the European Community (co-operation), agreement to a common position.

(3) The Minister concerned may, however, give agreement to a proposal which is still subject to scrutiny or which is awaiting debate in the House –

  (a) if he considers that it is confidential, routine or trivial or is substantially the same as a proposal on which scrutiny has been completed;

(b) if the European Union Committee has indicated that agreement need not be withheld pending completion of scrutiny or the holding of the debate.

(4) The Minister concerned may also give agreement to a proposal which is still subject to scrutiny or awaiting debate in the House if he decides that for special reasons agreement should be given; but he should explain his reasons -

(a) in every such case, to the European Union Committee at the first opportunity after reaching his decision; and

(b) in the case of a proposal awaiting debate in the House, to the House at the opening of the debate on the Committee's Report.

(5) In relation to any proposal which requires adoption by unanimity, abstention shall, for the purposes of paragraph (4), be treated as giving agreement.

14.
Too Little, Too Late? Comparing the Engagement of Nordic Parliaments in European Union Matters

Tapio Raunio and Matti Wiberg[1]

1. Introduction

National parliaments are normally described as the political institutions which lose most in the process of European integration. Apart from the centralisation of policy-making powers in the direction of the European Union, and the increasing use of qualified majority voting in the Council, the fact of European Union membership naturally also sets significant policy constraints on the member states and their parliaments. In particular, both the requirements of the Single Market and the criteria for entry into and continued membership of Economic and Monetary Union have narrowed the policy options available to national governments. Nevertheless, the domestic legislatures of the member states are, at least potentially, important fora for the formulation, scrutiny, and implementation of European Union legislation. Perhaps more significantly, national legislatures legitimise European integration by providing a means by which public opinion can be incorporated into the governance of the European Union, a function highlighted recently in the debates on the democratic deficit in the Union.

The empirical evidence clearly shows, however, that national parliaments have not made full use of the possibilities open to them to engage in European Union matters, be it through scrutiny of supranational legislation or through debating European affairs in plenary session.[2] It is merely being realistic to assert that

---

[1] Professors of Political Science, Department of Political Science, University of Turku.

[2] For more detailed information on national scrutiny procedures in European Union matters, see T. Bergman, "The European Union as the next step of delegation and accountability" (2000) 37 *European Journal of Political Research* 415; T. Bergman, "National parliaments and EU Affairs Committees: notes on empirical variation and competing explanations" (1997) 4 *Journal of European Public Policy* 373; D. Judge, "The Failure of National Parliaments" (1995) 18 *West European Politics* 79; F. Laursen and S. Pappas (eds.), *The Changing Role of Parliaments in the*

national parliaments get involved in European Union affairs too little and too late. Most European Union business is entirely government-driven, with little prospect of any radical change in this state of affairs in the near future.

Existing research also shows that there is a lot of variation between national parliaments in terms of the degree of their involvement in European matters. Comparative studies suggest that this variation is primarily explained by two factors: the role of the parliament in the political system of the member state, and public and party opinion on European integration. The key variable has been argued to be the executive-legislature relationship, with the parliament controlling the government to the same extent in European matters as it does in the context of domestic legislation. Similarly the contentiousness of the European dimension is important, with those countries in which integration issues produce divisions within parties and among the public adopting tighter scrutiny mechanisms.[3]

Thus it comes as no surprise that according to these studies the Nordic parliaments have adopted tighter scrutiny mechanisms than the legislatures of central and southern European member states.[4] In the first place, data produced

European Union (EIPA, Maastricht, 1995); P. Norton (ed.), *National Parliaments and the European Union* (Frank Cass, London, 1996); E. Smith (ed.), *National Parliaments as Cornerstones of European Integration*. (Kluwer Law International, London, 1996); T. Raunio and S. Hix, "Backbenchers Learn to Fight Back: European Integration and Parliamentary Government" (2000) 23 *West European Politics* 142; T. Raunio, "Always One Step Behind? National Legislatures and the European Union" (1999) 34 *Government and Opposition* 180; and see in particular A. Maurer and W. Wessels (eds.), *National Parliaments on their Ways to Europe: Losers or Latecomers* (Nomos, Baden-Baden, 2001).

[3] Bergman, above, n. 2 (both references); J. Fitzmaurice, "National parliaments and European policy-making: The case of Denmark" (1976) 76 *Parliamentary Affairs* 281; Judge, above, n. 2, R. Pahre, "Endogenous Domestic Institutions in Two-Level Games and Parliamentary Oversight of the European Union" (1997) 41 *Journal of Conflict Resolution* 147; T. Raunio and M. Wiberg, "Does Support Lead to Ignorance? National Parliaments and the Legitimacy of EU Governance" (2000) 35 *Acta Politica* 146; O. Rozenberg, "The Involvement of National Parliaments in European Union Affairs. An empirical test of two variables" (Paper delivered at European Consortium for Political Research, Joint Sessions of Workshops, March 2002, Turin, available at the time of writing at www.essex.ac.uk/ecpr/events/jointsessions/paperarchive/turin/ws16/Rozenberg.pdf); T. Raunio, "Holding Governments Accountable in European Affairs: Explaining Cross-National Variation" (2005) 11 *Journal of Legislative Studies* 319.

[4] The most comprehensive study of the role of national parliaments (conducted prior to the 2004 enlargement) concluded that the Danish *Folketinget* exercises the tightest control over the government, followed by the parliaments of Finland, Austria, and Sweden. Germany and the Netherlands come next, followed by the French and British legislatures. The parliaments of Belgium, Greece, Ireland, Italy, Luxembourg, Portugal, Spain are largely powerless in relation to their governments in European matters (see Maurer and Wessels, above, n. 2, at 462.) The information

in surveys – such as Eurobarometers – has shown that support for integration among Nordic voters (measured both as support for their countries' membership of the Union and as approval of initiatives for the deepening of integration) is constantly below the European Union average. Moreover, political parties in the Nordic countries are divided over integration. Secondly, comparative studies normally rank the Nordic parliaments as among the most powerful in Europe.[5] Not surprisingly, Nordic governments have repeatedly emphasised the importance of national parliaments in the European Union political system, with relatively lukewarm support existing for increasing the powers of the European Parliament. Therefore both preconditions for tight control of government are in place. It should, however, be emphasised here that subjecting the government to relatively tight scrutiny in European Union affairs does not mean that the Nordic legislatures are able to effectively control their respective governments on European issues. It only means that they do this more effectively than their counterparts in other European Union member countries.

This chapter examines the powers and involvement in the European Union decision-making system of four Nordic legislatures (namely, those of Denmark, Finland, Norway, and Sweden). We have three main goals: first, to examine the institutional rules and practices adopted by the four legislatures to control their governments in European matters; secondly, to evaluate the effectiveness of these procedures, and thirdly, to explain the variation between the four cases. In the next section we analyse the effectiveness of parliamentary scrutiny procedures in the Danish, Finnish, and Swedish parliaments. Norway is also included in our study. While not a member of the European Union, its inclusion is warranted by virtue of its membership of the European Economic Area, the result of which is that European Union decisions have significant consequences for the country, with the Norwegian parliament facing broadly similar challenges to those of the three Nordic states which are members of the Union. We compare the four case studies, and end the chapter with a critical discussion on the ability of national legislatures to wield influence in the European Union's political system.

---

received by the Danish, Finnish, and Swedish parliaments is among the most extensive of European Union national parliaments (Maurer and Wessels, above, n. 2, at 439), with governments producing explanatory statements and other relevant complementary material in addition to explaining the national position.

[5] See P. Norton (ed.), *Parliaments and Governments in Western Europe* (Frank Cass, London, 1998); H. Döring, "Time as a Scarce Resource: Government Control of the Agenda" in H. Döring (ed.), *Parliaments and Majority Rule in Western Europe*. (Campus and St. Martin's Press, Frankfurt and New York, 1995) at 223–246.

2. The Nordic Legislatures

In this section we describe the procedures established by the parliaments of the four Nordic countries, focusing in particular on the European affairs committees in the four legislatures and the differences and similarities between these committees.[6]

(a) Denmark

When Denmark began negotiations to join the then European Economic Community in 1961, the *Folketing* decided to set up a special committee, the *Markedsforhandlingsudvalg* (Market Negotiations Committee), to guarantee a dialogue between members of parliament and the government. The committee suspended its operations in the wake of de Gaulle's veto of enlargement in 1963. However, now renamed the *Markedsudvalg* (Market Relations Committee), it resumed its normal functions in the early 1970s after membership negotiations were relaunched. When Denmark became a member of the EEC in 1973, the *Markedsudvalg* became a permanent committee. On 4 October 1994, after the EEC had become the European Community and the European Union had been launched, the Committee changed its name from the Market Committee to the *Europaudvalg* (European Affairs Committee). Like other standing committees, the *Europaudvalg* has seventeen members chosen proportionally from among

[6] The analysis in this section is primarily based on the following case studies: as regards Denmark, F. Laursen, "The Danish Folketing and its European Affairs Committee: Strong Players in the National Policy Cycle" in Maurer and Wessels, above, n. 2, at 99–115; and E. Damgaard and A. Nørgaard, "The European Union and Danish Parliamentary Democracy" (2000) 6 *Journal of Legislative Studies* 33); as regards Finland, T. Raunio, "The Parliament of Finland: A Model Case for Effective Scrutiny?" in Maurer and Wessels, above, n. 2, at 173–198; as regards Sweden, H. Hegeland, "The Parliament of Sweden: A Successful Adapter in the European Arena" in Maurer and Wessels, above, n. 2, at 377–394; and H. Hegeland and I. Mattson, "Another Link in the Chain: The Effects of EU Membership on Delegation and Accountability in Sweden" (2000) 6 *Journal of Legislative Studies* 81; and as regards Norway, H. Narud and K. Strøm, "Adaptation without EU Membership: Norway and the European Economic Area" (2000) 6 *Journal of Legislative Studies* 125). For further and more detailed information on the involvement of the Nordic legislatures in their countries' European Union policies, see T. Bergman and E. Damgaard (eds.), *Delegation and Accountability in European Integration: The Nordic Parliamentary Democracies and the European Union* (Frank Cass, London, 2000) (also published as a special issue of the *Journal of Legislative Studies* 6.1, Spring, 2000) and M. Wiberg (ed.), *Trying to Make Democracy Work: The Nordic Parliaments and the European Union* (Gidlunds, Stockholm, 1997), and the comparative analysis in T. Raunio and M. Wiberg, "Parliaments' Adaptation to the European Union" in P. Esaiasson and K. Heidar (eds.), *Beyond Westminster and Congress: The Nordic Experience* (Ohio State University Press, Columbus, 2000), at 344–364.

the parties. Normally it convenes on Fridays, each session lasting from two to five hours. Its meetings are not open to the public, but most of the material processed by the Committee is accessible to the public and is routinely forwarded to the press, together with information about the positions of political parties. The government must seek a mandate from the *Europaudvalg* on matters falling under the First Pillar. On second pillar issues, the government must keep both the *Europaudvalg* and the Foreign Affairs Committee informed. On matters falling under the Third Pillar, both the *Europaudvalg* and the Legal Affairs Committee are consulted.

The Committee has extensive access to European Union documents. In May 1994, the *Europaudvalg* decided to extend its scrutiny of European Union proposals to the very start of the legislative process. This means that the foreign ministry must send 'basic notes' about Commission proposals for European Union legislation, and other important documents (such as green and white papers), to the committee as soon as they have been translated into Danish. Specialised committees must be sent material falling under their respective spheres of competence. Information on the effects of forthcoming European Union legislation on Denmark is required to be included as well. In its May 1994 report, the *Europaudvalg* made it clear that the specialised standing committees must be given a greater role in the handling of European Union issues. However, the input of specialised committees has so far been relatively limited. When an issue appears on the Council's agenda, the Committee must be sent 'topical notes' about it at least one week before the relevant Committee meeting. Normally, however, these notes are little more than brief summaries produced by the Government. Moreover, neither basic nor topical notes contain information about the Government's stance, which is only revealed to the Committee orally before the Council meeting. Before European Council summits, the Prime Minister must inform the *Europaudvalg* of issues likely to be on the agenda of the meeting. If the Government expects important decisions to be made, it must obtain a mandate from the Committee.

The *Europaudvalg* is famous for its ability to impose a mandate on Danish ministers. The mandate is not legally binding, but in practice the Government is bound by the Committee's instructions. This practice dates from 1973, when the Minister for Agriculture, Ib Frederiksen, failed to bring home the expected 'bacon', whereupon the Opposition threatened a 'no confidence' vote.[7] The Cabinet remained in office by agreeing from then on

[7] Mr Frederiksen had given his consent to a compromise over Danish export bacon in the Council which is thought to have cost the Danes 400–500 million kroner. The Social Democratic minority government only survived the vote with support from the Opposition.

to be bound by the instructions of the Committee. To a great extent this informal norm has been followed. The so-called 'negative majority' rule applies: the Government's position is approved provided there is no parliamentary majority against it. It is important to note that the traditional 'one man, one vote' rule is not employed. One MP from each parliamentary party casts the votes for his or her party. These votes are then weighted according to the number of seats each party holds in the *Folketing*. After each Council meeting, the government sends a written report to the Committee. These reports have been made public since 1993. The Government or the *Europaudvalg* can also decide that a minister must appear before the committee to explain the proceedings of the Council meeting.

(b) Finland

In the *Eduskunta* (the Finnish parliament), adaptation to European Union membership began during the European Economic Area phase, which preceded membership of the Union. Instead of establishing a completely new committee, the *Eduskunta* decided to charge a previously existing body, the Grand Committee (*Suuri valiokunta*), with the main responsibility for European Union matters. The composition of the Grand Committee (25 members) reflects the parties' share of seats in the *Eduskunta*. In addition, the member of parliament representing the autonomous Åland Islands is entitled to participate in the meetings. The Grand Committee convenes behind closed doors on Wednesdays and Fridays, with meetings normally lasting between two and two and a half hours. The Grand Committee deals with First and Third Pillar issues. The Foreign Affairs Committee handles matters falling under the Second Pillar. The documents considered by the Grand Committee, together with the minutes of the meetings, are normally available to the public after the meetings.

Insofar as concerns any matter that falls within the remit of parliament, the *Eduskunta* must be informed without delay of any proposal for a Council decision, as well as of the tentative position of the government. This usually involves legislative proposals by the Commission. According to the Constitution, however, the Grand Committee has the right to require information – and to be informed by the government – on any issue relating to the European Union. Normally, the *Eduskunta* receives information about forthcoming European Union legislative proposals well before the Commission officially publishes them. Prior to Council meetings, members of the committee are provided with the agenda of the meetings together with memoranda prepared by the ministries detailing Finland's position on the issues. These memoranda include the appropriate document references, a historical summary, a list of outstanding questions, and the

Government's proposed course of action. The Prime Minister is obliged to inform the Grand Committee of questions arising in the European Council. He or she is also required to furnish information afterwards on the deliberations of the European Council to the plenary session or the committee. The *Eduskunta* does not issue binding mandates to Finnish representatives. Exact voting instructions are seldom given, with the Grand Committee normally discussing the acceptability of various outcomes and thereby establishing the negotiating range of the Cabinet. Following Council meetings, the Committee is always supplied with a report of the meeting and its decisions. Ministers must be prepared to appear before the Committee, and to explain in detail any deviations from the given policy guidelines.

The standing committees were assigned an influential role from the very beginning. When a European Union legislative proposal arrives in parliament, it is simultaneously forwarded to the Grand Committee and to one or several specialised committees. The latter prepare an opinion, and it is rare for the Grand Committee to deviate from it. When several specialised committees have stated a position, the Grand Committee summarises and mediates the result. The majority of European Union legislative proposals (in addition to other European matters) are processed by more than one standing committee. This early and proactive involvement on the part of specialised standing committees enables the whole *Eduskunta* to scrutinise more effectively the position of the government.

(c) Sweden

The Swedish Parliament (the *Riksdag*) followed Sweden's membership negotiations by means of a European Union delegation consisting of eighteen members of parliament. It was important, in the view of the Constitutional Committee, that the *Riksdag* have an influential and proactive role in preparing European Union policy. The Advisory Committee on European Affairs, the *EU-nämnden*, was seen as providing the answer. The *EU-nämnden* is not a standing committee. However, it operates much as a normal committee. It comprises seventeen MPs, chosen proportionally from among the *Riksdag* parties, and meets on Fridays, convening behind closed doors, with meetings usually lasting approximately two-and-a-half hours. The *EU-nämnden* is charged with all European Union questions, including Common Foreign and Security Policy matters.

The Government has a duty to inform parliament of developments in the Union and of Commission legislative proposals. The Government must also submit statements on its position and on the effects of proposed

European Union legislation on Sweden. Before each Council meeting, members of the Committee are required to be sent memoranda on the questions appearing on the agenda. The Government is not permitted to adopt positions contrary to the wishes of the *EU-nämnden*. Decisions are taken according to the negative majority rule. The deliberations of the Committee, in the form of a shorthand verbatim record, normally become public two weeks after the meeting. The *EU-nämnden* has been relatively easy on ministers, and has refrained from criticising them in the manner of its counterpart in Denmark. Following Council meetings, the Government is required to produce a report stating Sweden's final position. These reports leave much room for improvement. The role of standing committees in the *Riksdag* has so far remained limited. Each standing committee has the right to receive information from the Government on issues falling within its competence. However, while the standing committees are sent the relevant documents, they very rarely bother to issue any opinions on the basis of that information. Most of the information between standing committees and the *EU-nämnden* is exchanged within party groups.

(d) Norway

While Norway has remained outside the European Union, its membership of the European Economic Area has meant taking on many of the rights and duties entailed by European Union membership. Insofar as concerns First Pillar issues, the European Economic Area Agreement has no application to agriculture, fisheries, taxation, commercial policy, tariffs, and the field of Economic and Monetary Union. Nor are European Economic Area countries bound by the Second and Third Pillars of the Union. Nevertheless, by virtue of the European Economic Area Agreement, Norway has adopted almost all European Union legislation on the four freedoms, on competition and on state aid. European integration therefore sets significant policy constraints on Norway, and unlike European Union member states, it is largely excluded from the decision-making process leading to the adoption of supranational legislation.

In the Norwegian parliament (the *Storting*), European issues have traditionally been the domain of the Foreign Affairs Committee (established in 1922). Prior to the 1994 referendum, there were plans to form a special European Affairs Committee in the event that Norway joined the Union. In May 1994, a special European Economic Area Consultative Committee was established. The Consultative Committee consists of the members of the Foreign Affairs Committee, supplemented by the six Norwegian representatives to the European Economic Area Joint Parliamentary

Committee,[8] thus making it virtually an extended version of the Foreign Affairs Committee. In the 1993–1997 *Storting*, the Consultative Committee had seventeen members. The committee meets behind closed doors and the minutes of its meetings become public one year after the meetings. As its name implies, the Consultative Committee is a purely consultative body. It does not vote or take formal decisions, nor does it submit written reports to the *Storting*.[9] Normally it meets just once a month, on the Tuesday preceding the monthly meetings of the EEA Joint Committee. It is informed of the Government's negotiating position, and the representatives of the various parties indicate whether or not they accept this position. The foreign minister usually represents the government. There is no reporting back after meetings in Brussels. Specialised standing committees play a very limited role. Thus the Foreign Affairs Committee is the main, and largely the only forum for processing European Union and European Economic Area issues. This situation reflects the fact that European issues are still perceived in the *Storting* – and indeed in Norway at large – mainly as foreign policy questions.

2. Comparing the Nordic Parliaments

The institutional choices adopted by the Danish, Finnish, and Swedish legislatures are substantially similar and conform to the general model prevailing across the other European Union member states. This is not surprising, since both Finnish and Swedish members of parliament studied the operation of the Danish European Affairs Committee closely when designing their own European Committees. Reflecting their classification as 'working parliaments',[10] the preparation of European Union matters in the Nordic legislatures is essentially based on the committee system, with the plenary session playing a less active role. The goal of 'speaking with one voice' in the European Union institutions is reflected in the rather consensual nature of forming national positions, with Opposition parties and interest groups being closely involved in the handling of European Union matters.[11] Table 1 presents basic information on the five European Affairs Committees.

---

[8] The European Economic Area Joint Parliamentary Committee, bringing together representatives from the national parliaments of European Economic Area countries and the European Parliament, supervises the implementation and overall development of the European Economic Area Agreement. It convenes twice a year.

[9] Constitutionally the position of the *Storting* under the European Economic Area agreement is very strong as decisions are based on unanimity and ratification by national legislatures. However, the *Storting* has so far refrained from using its veto power.

[10] D. Arter, *Scandinavian Politics Today* (Manchester University Press, Manchester, 1999), at 211–223.

[11] Bergman and Damgaard, above, n. 6.

Table 1

Member State Parliament	European Affairs Committee	Date Created	MPs (%)	Frequency of Meetings	Mandating Power
Denmark *Folketinget*	*Europaudvalget*	1972	9.5	Weekly	Strong
Finland *Eduskunta*	*Suuri valiokunta*	1995	12.5	Weekly	Moderate
Sweden *Riksdagen*	*EU-nämnden*	1994	4.9	Weekly	Moderate
Norway *Stortinget*	Foreign Affairs Committee / EEA Consultative Committee	1994 (EEA Consultative Committee)	12.3	Monthly	Weak

Despite the overall similarity between the Nordic countries, however, there are considerable variations between them as well. The main differences concern the involvement of specialised standing committees and the mandating of the government by the European Affairs Committee. Comparative analysis shows that only the *Eduskunta* makes efficient use of the cumulative expertise of the specialised standing committees. In Finland, committee deliberation is required by the Constitution, and this regular involvement of the committees enables all members of parliament to participate in the processing of European Union legislation. In both Denmark and Sweden, the standing committees do receive the relevant information and are encouraged to formulate views on European Union matters, but there is still much variation in how active the various committees are. Both parliaments recognise the need to get standing committees more actively involved in European questions. Another strength of the Finnish system is the fact that the *Eduskunta* gets involved in the processing of European Union matters earlier in the game than most other national parliaments, sometimes even before the Commission publishes its legislative proposals. The Danish and Swedish legislatures enter the game later, and this probably reduces their ability to influence the positions of their governments.

As regards the ability to issue instructions to the government, the Danish *Folketing* is without a doubt the strongest of the Nordic European Affairs Committees. The Danish mandating system reflects both the tradition of minority cabinets and the Euroscepticism that prevails among Danish parties. However, since 1995, Sweden has also been governed by minority governments and there the position of the *EU-nämnden* is substantially weaker. Finland has since the beginning of its European Union membership in 1995 been governed by oversized majority coalitions, including a broad rainbow coalition between 1995 and 2003, bringing together five parties that control around seventy per cent of parliamentary seats, but still the *Eduskunta* and the Grand Committee have subjected the government to relatively tight scrutiny in European matters. This suggests that the main explanatory factor is not perhaps so much the share of seats controlled by the government, but the level of party cohesion on integration. In the Nordic parliaments, practically all political parties are, to a varying degree and depending on the issue, divided over the development of integration, and therefore the Government will normally not merely be criticised by the Opposition, but in addition has to be prepared for criticism coming from individual legislators and from cross-party coalitions of MPs.

3. Critical Discussion

The Nordic legislatures arguably subject their respective governments to relatively tight scrutiny in European matters. Nevertheless, this is in itself no cause for great celebration, as national parliaments – both in the Nordic region and elsewhere in the European Union – face severe difficulties in trying to influence European Union politics. Without in any way wanting to underestimate the efforts made by Nordic MPs to engage in European matters, we shall discuss in this concluding section the main practical difficulties national parliaments face when trying to influence European Union politics.

As outlined in the introductory section, we believe that the existing literature on the role of national parliaments in European governance is far too optimistic about the potential for domestic legislatures to influence what the European Union does – or even how the national government acts at the European level. There seems to be a perceptive fallacy here: the fact that most national parliaments have improved their scrutiny processes since the early 1990s does not mean that they are truly able to control their governments in European Union issues. Let us approach this issue from the perspective of control instruments – that is, by asking what possibilities there are for parliamentarians to control the government and how effectively these instruments can be used in European Union matters.

(a) Instruments Available to Individual Members of Parliament

In the context of national politics, individual representatives have a variety of tools at their disposal for controlling the government, the most important of which are private members' bills and parliamentary questions. Regarding private members' bills, no such options are available in European issues. A member of parliament can obviously – either informally or through a parliamentary question – ask the government (or a member of the European Parliament) to undertake certain action at European Union level, but the Commission has no duty to respond to such requests. MPs can naturally ask parliamentary questions on European matters, but this hardly amounts to effective *ex ante* control.

(b) Parliamentary Groups *vis-à-vis* the Government

Parliamentary democracy as a form of government requires a viable opposition that is able to challenge the government genuinely, and to present alternative policy packages to the electorate. However, in most European Union countries, parties are internally divided over integration, and hence have an electoral incentive not to have public debates about European integration. As a result of these divisions, it is fairly infrequent for European Union issues to be raised on the floor of national parliaments, with scrutiny primarily taking place instead in the European affairs committees of the various legislatures. The same applies to the parliamentary groups of the governing parties: given the central role of national governments in the European Union's political system, it is typically the Government (perhaps together with the central party office) which formulates a party's overall policy on integration. Members of parliament may thus be able to exert control over individual pieces of European Union legislation (although even here they normally enter the game much too late to have much impact on the final outcome), but challenging the Government on the overall direction of national European Union policy would be unwise, as it might have a negative impact on the party's electoral fortunes (and might even result in the worst case in the calling of early elections).[12]

(c) National Parliament (and the Government) *vis-à-vis* the European Union

National parliaments could also be classified as strong if they were influential in setting the agenda of the European Union. It would be an exaggeration to claim that any of the national parliaments examined in this chapter would be strong in this sense. Despite some attempts to establish proactive consultation mechanisms (*e.g.*, hearings with civil servants in Finland), national parliaments always get involved in the processing of

[12] Moreover, it could be argued that civil servants have a much larger impact on the government's European Union policy than any governing party as such – at least in formulating national positions on individual pieces of European Union legislation. In line with developments across the Union, in the Nordic countries integration has strengthened the role of civil servants who have become more important at all stages in decision-making. (See Bergman and Damgaard, above, n. 6).

European Union legislation rather late, almost always after the Commission has already published its proposal. At that stage, it is basically too late to prevent the proposal from becoming European Union law, at least when the Council is making its decision by qualified majority vote. This means that national parliaments are reactive bodies, not policy formulating ones. There simply is no constitutionally guaranteed mechanism for introducing an item to the political or legislative agenda of the European Union.

The foregoing discussion has been intended to illustrate considerable difficulties national parliaments face in an integrative Europe. In sum, all four Nordic legislatures have their work cut out for them – the European Union's institutions are physically and politically too remote. To be sure, the Nordic parliaments do enjoy some success in attempting to exert a modicum of influence over how their ministers conduct themselves in the Council, and the Danish parliament especially can exercise control over ministers. Nonetheless, it is the governments of the day which more or less dictate the agendas of the parliaments, and the parliaments do not use their potential to control the governments. European integration affairs are no exception to this general rule – and scholars should stop pretending that they are.

15.
Ensuring Democratic Control over National Government in European Affairs – the Slovenian Experience

Danica Fink-Hafner[1]

1. Introduction

Slovenia is regarded as a unique case among recently-acceded European Union member states because of the relatively important role which has been given to its parliament in managing European Union affairs. While negotiations on accession to the European Union were marked by a relatively high level of transparency and a high level of involvement on the part of the Slovenian parliament, full European Union membership has brought about some important shifts in the executive-parliament relationship. Despite the fact that a legal basis exists for the conferring of a relatively influential role on the National Assembly (or rather, in the main, on the Assembly's working bodies), the experience of, at the time of writing, over a year of Slovenian membership of the European Union has been that of a shift towards a more executive-directed system – Slovenia's own contribution to the European Union's democratic deficit.

2. National Parliaments and the Enlarged European Union[2]

The enlargement and deepening of the European Union has made the impact of European integration on domestic politics and public policies increasingly visible. The experience of both old and new European Union members has been that Europeanisation first challenges the executive to adapt itself institutionally. This challenge, however, expands to other sectors of national

---

[1] Professor of Political Science and Head of the Centre for Political Science Research, Faculty of Social Sciences, University of Ljubljana.

[2] This paper is based in part on the research results of the European project *Organising for Enlargement: A Challenge for Member States and Candidate Countries* (HPSE-CT-2001-00083), the European Union's Fifth Framework Programme (as to which see www.oeue.net).

political systems and becomes an increasingly significant factor in bringing about change in national political systems.[3] Two key findings in existing literature regarding how nations adapt to managing European Union affairs have been, first, that executives adapt in stages, and, secondly, that domestic responses to European Union engagement have remained diverse.[4] Although recently there has been a greater general concern for building European public administration capacities, Page has expressed doubts as to whether the impact of the European Union, and of Europeanisation generally, is sufficiently powerful to bring about homogeneity in administrative systems in European Union member states or homogeneity in how domestic politico-administrative structures and practices are adjusted to exigencies of participating in a European system of decision-making.[5] A very similar phenomenon seems to be identifiable if one looks at how national parliaments have adapted themselves and how they function within the framework of processes of Europeanisation. While there are some signs of convergence in the process of adaptation by national parliaments, there are also indications of continuing variations in their responses.

In contrast with early research on how national parliaments had adapted – which quite often focused on the organisational adaptation of national parliaments – more recent research has focused on relations between

---

[3] See S. Hix, and K.H. Goetz, "Introduction: European Integration and National Political Systems" in H. Goetz and S. Hix (eds.), *Europeanised Politics? European Integration and National Political Systems* (Frank Cass, London, 2001).

[4] See, *e.g.* C. Spanou, "European Integration in Administrative Terms: A Framework for Analysis and the Greek Case" (1998) *Journal of European Public Policy* 467; H.R. Harmsen, "The Europeanization of National Administrations: A Comparative Study of France and the Netherlands" (1999) 1 *Governance*, 81; H. Kassim, "Conclusion. The National Co-ordination of EU Policy: Confronting the Challenge" in H. Kassim, G. Peters and V. Wright (eds.), *The National Co-ordination of EU Policy. The Domestic Leve*l (Oxford University Press, Oxford, 2000); C. Knill, *The Europeanisation of National Administrations* (Cambridge University Press, Cambridge, 2001); S. Bulmer and M. Burch, "Organizing for Europe: Whitehall, the British State and European Union" (1998) 4 *Public Administration* 601; S. Bulmer and M. Burch "The 'Europeanization' of Central Government: The UK and Germany in Historical Institutionalist Perspective" in G. Schneider and M. Aspinwall (eds.), *The Rules of Integration. Institutionalist Approaches to the Study of Europe* (Manchester University Press, Manchester, 2001); J. Olsen, "Towards a European Administrative Space?" (2002) *Arena Working Papers*, WP 02/26 (available at www.arena.uio.no/publications/wp02_26.htm); B. Laffan, *Organizing for a Changing Europe: Irish Central Government and the European Union* (2001, Policy Institute, Trinity College, Dublin); B. Laffan, *Managing Europe from Home. The Europeanisation of the Irish Core Executive* (2003, OEUE PHASE I Occasional Paper 1.1 – 09.03) (available at www.oeue.net/papers/ireland-theeuropeanisationofth.pdf).

[5] C. Page, "Europeanization and the Persistence of Administrative Systems" in J. Hayward and A. Menon (eds.), *Governing Europe* (Oxford University Press, Oxford, 2003).

executive and legislative power in European public policy-making. National parliaments have adapted organisationally in both member states and candidate states.[6] But even up to and beyond the time of the 2004 enlargement of the European Union, variations in the role of national parliaments in the management of Union affairs at national level (across member states both old and new) have been a key characteristic of this process of adaptation.[7] National models of some new and old member states have more in common than have the models of new member states, it may be noted.[8]

National parliaments are quite often seen as latecomers and losers in the process of European integration, or even its 'victims'.[9] Important variations in mandates and the real influence of national parliaments on European decision-making should not, however, be forgotten. In broad terms, if national political systems are classified according to the role which is given to the national parliament in managing European Union affairs (including its

---

[6] See *e.g.*, P. Norton (ed.), *National Parliaments and the European Union* (1995) 1 *Journal of Legislative Studies* (Special Issue); P. Norton (ed.), *National Parliaments and The European Union* (Frank Cass, London and Portland, 1996); A. Ágh, *Anticipatory and Adaptive Europeanization in Hungary* (Hungarian Centre for Democracy Studies, Budapest, 2003); D. Zajc, "The Role of a National Parliament in a Complex Supranational Decision Making Process" in *EU Accession and National Parliaments* (Central European Political Science Association, Budapest, 2004); D. Zajc, *Vloga nacionalnega parlamenta v EU – primer Državnega zbora RS, part 2.*, (Centre for Political Science Research, Faculty of Social Sciences, Ljubljana, 2005); and A.C. Jungar and S.A. Oberg, "Are National Parliaments Lagging Behind? The Influence of the Swedish and Finnish Parliaments over Domestic EU Policies" in *EU Accession and National Parliaments* (Central European Political Science Association, Budapest, 2004). Note that the statement in the text above holds good not only for those former candidate states which subsequently became members in the 2004 enlargement but also to Bulgaria and Romania which were to accede to the Union in 2007 as well as the other states which had gained candidate status by the time of writing of this chapter.

[7] See, *e.g., Second Biannual Report: Developments in European Union Procedures and Practices Relevant to Parliamentary Scrutiny*, prepared by the COSAC Secretariat and presented to the XXXII Conference of Community and European Affairs Committees of Parliaments of the European Union (22–23 November 2004, The Hague, Netherlands) and *Third Biannual Report: Developments in European Union Procedures and Practices Relevant to Parliamentary Scrutiny*, prepared by the COSAC Secretariat and presented to the XXXII Conference of Community and European Affairs Committees of the Parliaments of the European Union, 17–18 May 2005, Luxembourg.

[8] See, *e.g.,* B. Laffan, "Managing Europe from Home. The Europeanisation of the Irish Core Executive", above, n. 3; D. Fink-Hafner, "Europeanization of the Core Executive in the Transition from Circumstances of EU Accession to Full EU Membership", paper presented at the European Union Studies Association Ninth Biennial International Conference, 31 March–2 April, 2005, Austin, Texas (available at http://aei.pitt.edu/archive/00003041/).

[9] See P. Norton (ed.), *National Parliaments and The European Union* (1996), above, n. 6; A. Maurer and W. Wessels (eds.), *National Parliaments on their Ways to Europe: Losers or Latecomers?* (Nomos, Baden-Baden, 2001). See also the chapter in this book by Tapio Raunio.

relations with the national executive), three models can be identified: (a) national political systems with very weak parliaments; (b) national political systems with a relatively important role for parliaments but without strict parliamentary mandates to the executive; and (c) a national political system in which the parliament can give mandatory guidelines to the executive as to how it should behave (a model which, so far, only the Danish system corresponds to).

In the group of ten states which joined the European Union in the 2004 enlargement, Slovenia provided an exception to the pattern of a relatively weak role being accorded to national parliaments in managing European Union affairs during the period of membership negotiations (which may be described as a 'policy-taking stage'[10]). It is argued in this chapter (on the basis of a preliminary view of recent developments in policy-making since Slovenia became a full member of the European Union) that a significant reduction in parliament's role in managing European Union matters can be identified as having taken place during the first year of Slovenia's membership of the European Union.

On the one hand, this can be attributed to Slovenia's "imported EU democratic deficit".[11] On the other hand, specific national circumstances, *viz.*, the fact that 2004 was an election year, and the consequent gradual slowdown in the functioning of the old government and old parliament as well as the gradual start of the functioning of the new parliament and new government – created good grounds for parliament to lose the role accorded to it in the pre-accession period.[12] Despite these political circumstances (and the possibility that improvement will take place in the level of collaboration between the executive and legislative branches of government in managing European Union matters on the expiry of a time-lag), it seems unlikely that the National Assembly will be involved in European Union policy-making in the future to the same extent to which it was during the phase of 'policy-taking' from the European Union. The argument for this lies not only in

[10] See Fink-Hafner, above, n. 8. The concept of 'a policy-taking stage' refers to the pre-accession stage of joining the European Union, when accession countries must integrate the *acquis* as it stands into their national law, without having the opportunity to alter it. (In other words, they have simply to 'take' it). As full members, they can participate in European Union policy-making.

[11] H. Grabbe, "How Does Europeanization Affect CEE Governance? Conditionality, Diffusion and Diversity" (2001) 6 *Journal of European Public Policy* 1013.

[12] Slovenia's first elections to the European Parliament were held on 13 June 2004, followed by national parliamentary elections on 3 October 2004. The new government was approved by Parliament on 3 December 2004.

recent practice but also in the legal rules defining the relationship between the two branches of power when it comes to European Union policy-making.

3. The Slovenian Parliament's Role in Managing European Union Matters before Accession

One of Slovenia's distinctive features so far has been its commitment to the principle of full transparency in integration with the European Union.[13] A parliamentary constitutional spirit remained a crucial ingredient in what was otherwise a pragmatic institutional adaptation to Europeanisation. The publication of all negotiating positions, a significant role being accorded to parliament and the participation of civil society characterised Slovenia's negotiating style.

The National Assembly's role in the discussion and approval of negotiating positions (with these positions only becoming final and official when the Assembly adopted them) meant that there was transparency not merely as regards decisions involving the exercise of legislative power but also as regards the level of parliamentary control over the executive. In fact, the process of Europeanisation also provided the functioning of Slovenia's political system with completely new strengths – namely, excellence not only in the degree of circulation of information between the executive and the National Assembly's working bodies, but also in the general standard of the relationship between the two branches of power regarding the issue of European Union accession.

Although relations – and particularly the flow of information – between the National Assembly and the executive have otherwise frequently been described as unsatisfactory, this was not the case insofar as managing European Union matters was concerned. The Slovenian parliament played a very important role in European matters, probably unique for a parliament in a candidate country in that European Union integration is normally seen as a political task for the elites (both in government and opposition). The Slovenian government recognised relatively quickly the importance of involving the National Assembly in European affairs. Since the National Assembly had to approve the negotiating positions, it was in the government's interest for the National Assembly to be informed as well as was possible about all relevant European Union matters.

[13] By the word 'integration' here is meant not merely the actual entry into the European Union, but also the whole gradual process which is already underway during the accession stage, and includes, among other things, the accession negotiations and the integration of European Union law into national law.

The procedure for adopting a national negotiating position in Slovenia was relatively complicated. It involved not only actors at state level but also actors from civil society. Interest groups were consulted in an organised way, even in the early stages of preparations of negotiating positions,[14] while the publishing of the proposed negotiating positions on the internet and the presentation of these positions by governmental representatives to all interested actors opened up additional space for civil society. In addition to the direct flow of information from the executive to parliament, relevant information was made available to the National Assembly *via* the internet. In addition, the National Assembly's research department supplied MPs with an increasing variety of studies including those with European content.[15]

The preparation of a negotiating position started in the relevant working group within the executive. The working group first prepared a draft negotiating position based on the results of multilateral and bilateral screenings[16] and the current situation in an individual negotiating

---

[14] Thus although the Europeanisation process can be seen as elite-led (involving cooperation between parties in government and opposition parties), it also involved civil society in Slovenia, and Slovenia's corporatist tradition was visible even in the negotiating structures: besides the presence of experts and representatives of employers and employees in 31 working groups, there was a practical role for civil society in preparing negotiating positions. Economic interest groups in particular were in a position to influence the process of the creation of negotiating positions from within structures in the executive framework (especially in working bodies of the Negotiation Team of the Republic of Slovenia for Accession to the European Union) as well as via other channels (in particular, parliament, and also, to some extent, the mass media). In addition, representatives of European Union institutions often called for the opinions of civil society (*i.e.,* interest groups) in relation to specific issues of European Union integration. (See further D. Fink-Hafner, *The 'Europeanisation' of Slovenian Interest Groups*, paper presented at the annual conference of the British Association for Slavonic and East European Studies, 7–9 April 2001, Fitzwilliam College, Cambridge University). In cases where interest groups were not happy with the final outcome of the European Union-Slovenian negotiations, some of them even used institutional veto-points in the Slovenian political system in order at least to postpone the implementation of the relevant outcome. (See here, *e.g.,* D. Fink-Hafner and D. Lajh, "Lessons from Managing Conflict Situations in the EU Accession Negotiations: The Case of Slovenia" (2004) 5 *Central European Political Science Review* 52).

[15] D. Fink-Hafner and D. Lajh, *Managing Europe from Home: The Europeanization of the Slovenian Core Executive* (Faculty of Social Sciences, Ljubljana, 2003) at 136. See also D. Fink-Hafner and D. Lajh, *Proces evropeizacije in prilagajanje političnih ustanov na nacionalni ravni* (Faculty of Social Sciences, Ljubljana, 2005) at 91.

[16] 'Screening' entailed the explanation by the Commission to applicant countries of what the body of European Union law known as the *acquis* meant and the exploration of problems which might arise in future negotiations in implementing that law in those countries. In 'multilateral screening', the Commission met with all the applicants at the same time. The process of 'bilateral screening', in contrast, was used to determine the status of implementation of European Union legislation in a specific country.

chapter.[17] Already in this initial phase of preparation, external experts and institutions were invited to take part in preparing the draft negotiating position by providing their opinions and positions on a particular substantive area. Because the main responsibility for preparing a negotiating position remained with the relevant ministries, the minister responsible for an individual policy area confirmed the draft negotiating position. After that confirmation, pressure groups also became involved in shaping the negotiating position by submitting their opinions and proposals.

On the proposal of the relevant minister, the draft negotiating position was then submitted to the Negotiation Team of the Republic of Slovenia for Accession to the European Union. Representatives of the relevant working group and the Negotiation Team then prepared the proposed negotiating position together on the basis of several working meetings and other forms of cooperation (including informal methods). Usually this took about five meetings and several discussions, depending on the chapter's complexity. The head of the Negotiation Team, a member of the Negotiation Team responsible for the given chapter, and the editing group of the Department for Negotiations within the Government Office for European Affairs participated in editing the negotiating position. External experts from individual fields were again invited to cooperate in this phase. If the drafting of a proposed negotiating position required coordination between ministers, the Prime Minister mediated and convened a 'European Meeting' of the Government for all ministers concerned. At this point, the Mission of the Republic of Slovenia to the European Union would make another important contribution to the negotiating position by providing substantive and editorial comments on the negotiating position.

The proposed negotiating position was then discussed by two Government committees: the Committee on Economic Affairs and the Committee on State Administration and Public Affairs. After being adopted by the Government, the negotiating positions were presented to non-governmental organisations and trade union representatives. After this, the Government submitted the negotiating position to the National Assembly where it was discussed by the relevant working bodies and eventually approved by the

[17] The *acquis* was divided into 31 chapters which Slovenia (like other accession countries) had to adopt and implement by the time of accession to the European Union. Examples of individual chapters were those relating to free movement of goods, freedom of movement of persons, company law, competition policy, agriculture, transport, taxation, social policy and employment, energy, industrial policy, the environment, justice and home affairs and consumer and health protection.

Committee on Foreign Policy. The final verification only followed the translation of the negotiating position into English, as prepared by the Department for Negotiations or the Translation Unit of the Government Office for European Affairs. Thereafter, the negotiating positions were physically packed and prepared for their 'journey' to Brussels. The Negotiation Team and the Government Office for European Affairs then submitted the English version of the negotiating positions to the Council *via* the Slovenian Mission in Brussels.

Despite this relatively complicated procedure, the Slovenian management of European Union business during membership negotiations was commonly viewed not only as extremely transparent but also as a relatively effective one.[18]

4. Adaptation to Full Membership of the European Union: Development of the Legal Basis for Parliamentary Involvement

(a) Partial Change of the Constitutionally-Defined Political System

In adapting to its involvement in day-to-day participation in common European policy-making, Slovenia seems to be sticking to its gradualist mode of adaptation. The first step in the legal adaptation of the Slovenian constitutional system was the amendment of the 1992 Constitution of the Republic of Slovenia. The new Article 3a[19] allows Slovenia to transfer the exercise of part of its sovereign rights to international organisations, provided (a) that these international organisations are based on respect for human rights and fundamental freedoms, democracy, and the principles of

[18] For more on interviewees' perceptions, see D. Fink-Hafner and D. Lajh, *Managing Europe from Home: The Europeanization of the Slovenian Core Executive*, above, n. 15.

[19] The Constitutional Act Amending Chap. I and Arts 47 and 68 of the 1991 Constitution of the Republic of Slovenia (UZ3a, 47, 68) was adopted on 27 February 2003, a little over one year before Slovenian entry to the European Union. Pursuant both to Art. 90 of the Slovenian Constitution and the Law on the Referendum and Popular Initiative, a consultative referendum on European Union membership was held in Slovenia on 25 March 2003. (See further regarding four types of referendum in the Slovenian legal system, D. Fink-Hafner, "Slovenia, Political Data Yearbook" (1998) 34 *European Journal of Political Research* (No. 7/8) 1129). The number of ballots cast was 970,422 (60.29% of the electorate) with 964,771 (99.41%) of these being valid. Of the ballots validly cast, 864,542 (89.61%) were 'yes' votes and 100,229 (10.39%) 'no' votes.

the rule of law; and (b) that the international treaty by which this transfer is effected is ratified by the National Assembly by a two-thirds majority vote of all deputies.[20]

The same article states that in procedures for the adoption of legal acts and decisions in such international organisations, the Government is to promptly inform the National Assembly both of proposals for such acts and decisions, and of its own activities. The National Assembly *may* adopt positions thereon, which the Government is required take into consideration in its activities. Article 3a also provides that the relationship between the National Assembly and the Government in this regard is to be regulated in detail by a law adopted by a two-thirds majority vote of deputies present in the National Assembly.

Slovenia has tried to combine its own national traditions and initial national experiences in managing European Union matters with learning from others. Slovenians were particularly interested in the models of Scandinavian countries, due to the deliberate emphasis placed in these systems on the role of national parliaments. A careful comparative investigation of the Danish, Swedish, and Finnish models led to the final development of the Slovenian model for managing European Union matters as a full European Union membership – a system which is in fact very close to the Finnish one.

(b) Partial Formal Redefinition of Relations between the Legislature and the Executive

The Law on Collaboration between the National Assembly and Government in European Union Matters[21] was adopted on 25 March 2004. It defines the government as an actor which represents and asserts positions on behalf of the Republic of Slovenia in European Union institutions. The Government is independent and responsible for carrying out its functions within the framework of the Constitution, the Law on the Executive, and the Law on Collaboration between the National Assembly and Government in European Union Matters. One of the Government's duties is to inform the parliament

[20] Article 3a also provides that under the same conditions Slovenia may also enter into a defensive alliance with states which are based on respect for the above-mentioned values.

[21] The Law on Collaboration between the National Assembly and the Government on European Union Matters (*Zakon o sodelovanju med državnim zborom in vlado v zadevah evrpske unije – ZSDZVZEU*), 25 March 2004, National Assembly of the Republic of Slovenia (*Državni zbor Republike Slovenije*), Number: 007-01/03-11/3.

about European Union matters, especially those which would (insofar as concerns their content) be the subject of parliamentary competence (in line with the Slovenian Constitution and the law).

According to Article 4, the National Assembly participates in formulating the Republic of Slovenia's positions especially on the European Union matters which would be the subject of parliamentary competence, although it may also discuss other European Union matters either on the basis of a Government proposal or on its own initiative.

The Government is obliged to provide all sorts of important information to the National Assembly in respect of every European Union matter the National Assembly discusses: the decision-making procedure in the European Union; the key objectives and solutions in a proposed legal act; the timetable for the decision to be made at European Union level; the proposed negotiating position of the Republic of Slovenia, including an assessment of the impact and consequences of the European Union proposal for the Republic of Slovenia (in terms of the need to amend Slovenian law; the consequences for the budget; the impact on the economy; the impact on the public administration; and the impact on the environment).[22]

Some provisions of the law provide particular support for procedural efficiency in managing European Union affairs, the provision of a Slovenian input into European Union decision-making and the assertion of Slovenian interests. Of these, there is a requirement that the National Assembly respects the deadlines given by European Union institutions when it discusses draft positions prepared by the government. In the event the National Assembly does not intervene (*i.e.*, does not discuss the matter or express an intention to do so), the government's position automatically becomes the official Slovenian position.

The executive branch has a relatively high level of autonomy when participating in European Union decision-making. Even when the National Assembly adopts an official position, the Government is still not always obliged to follow it. The Government may decide differently during negotiations at the European Union level whenever it believes that the assertion of Slovenian interests or their full assertion is not feasible or would

[22] The Government is allowed to change the content of such assessments as well as the content of a proposed negotiating position.

not benefit the country. However, it is still obliged to inform the National Assembly about this promptly and to clarify the circumstances and arguments surrounding any such decision.

(c) Impact of the Change in the Parliamentary Statutory Rules 2002 and 2004 – the Ever More Formally-Defined Role of Parliamentary Working Bodies[23]

The National Assembly's management of European Union matters has been impacted upon by two processes of institutional adaptation. The first has been the adaptation of the parliamentary decision-making procedure with the objective of rationalising policy-making processes by giving more powers and autonomy to legislative working bodies. This adaptation was effected by the amendment of the Slovenian National Assembly's Statutory Rules in 2002, a step which in turn was primarily linked to the fulfilment of Slovenia's obligations in the pre-accession period. More specifically, the European Commission had criticised some serious delays in the implementing of the National Programme for Adoption of the *acquis communautaire* and had encouraged Slovenia, among other things, to recast its slow legislative procedure.[24] The second process of institutional adaptation was effected in 2004 and involved the adoption of formal rules defining the procedure and competences of working bodies and the legislative body as a whole in deciding on European Union matters.

When the Slovenian National Assembly's Statutory Rules were amended in 2002 they redefined the administrative procedure, identified in detail the responsibilities of the authorities when submitting draft laws, enhanced the role of parliament's working bodies, rationalised its work in plenary sessions, and boosted the role of the Collegium of the National

---

[23] In the Slovenian Parliament, the term parliamentary working bodies covers two organisational forms: (a) committees (established according to policy fields covered by an individual ministry or several policy fields covered by two or more ministries); and (b) commissions (established for the purpose of investigating common questions – such as the Commission for the Rules of Procedure, and the Commission for Mandates and Elections – or to investigate certain affairs, *e.g.*, the Commission for Supervision of the Security and Intelligence Services, and the Commission for Budgetary and Other Public Finance Control).

[24] For more, see D. Fink-Hafner and D. Lajh, *Managing Europe from Home: The Europeanization of the Slovenian Core Executive,* above, n. 15, at 131–132.

Assembly's Speaker (who took on decision-making competences regarding certain issues). Especially important insofar as concerns the domestic management of European Union affairs was that these new Statutory Rules (at least in the view of most parliamentary experts) significantly empowered parliamentary working bodies.[25] The new Rules replaced the consultative status of working bodies in all three stages of the legislative process with a decision-making role in the first two stages (subject to some exceptions). The amendments to the Statutory Rules which were adopted in May 2004[26] continued the policy of empowering the working bodies, but defined the structure of the key working bodies (*viz.*, the Committee on European Affairs and the Committee on Foreign Policy)[27] and the rules of procedure applicable in the management of European Union affairs in more detail.

Preliminary research has shown that the adoption of the 2002 Statutory Rules, which formally empowered parliament's working bodies, has not brought about significant changes in interest groups' influence on policy-making processes.[28] Still, it is probably now much more difficult for interest groups to influence decision-making on European Union matters anyway *via* the parliamentary route because of practical time-pressures (which have led to the sending of invitations for parliamentary working bodies' meetings as well as of the relevant documentation on European Union matters at relatively short notice).[29]

---

[25] According to the new 2002 Rules, the first stage of the legislative process is complete when parliamentary materials are distributed both to members of parliament and to working bodies. (The only exception to this is if MPs demand, within a certain period, a plenary session). In the second stage, working bodies, under the 2002 Rules, issue opinions on proposed bills. After a discussion, the working bodies can propose that parliament continue a legislative process or that it stop it. If the working bodies propose that parliament stop a legislative process, then MPs are merely entitled to vote on the proposal at a plenary session – they are not permitted to discuss it.

[26] See the new Arts 154a to 154m of the Statutory Rules.

[27] Among the most interesting such reforms were the requirement that both working bodies were to be structured proportionally by reference to the number of members of parliament from each party list elected to the Parliament; the requirement that each parliamentary group was to have at least one seat in each of the two working bodies; the rule that each of these two bodies was to have one chairperson and two vice-chairpersons; and the additional requirement that at least one of these three positions was to be filled by an MP from an opposition parliamentary group.

[28] D. Fink-Hafner and A. Krašovec, "Is Consultation Everything? The Influence of Interest Groups on Parliamentary Working Bodies in Slovenia" (2005) 41 *Czech Sociological Review* 401.

[29] According to the Statutory Rules (as amended in 2004), para. 154e, for example, stipulates that "representatives of an expert community, of civil society, of the economy and associations whose work is linked to the content of the discussed matters" may be invited to attend regarding specific

5. Initial Experiences with the 'Full-Membership' Model: A Shift to a More Executive-Directed System

Research carried out prior to the 2004 enlargement of the European Union on the adaptations made by national political systems to accommodate European-level policy-making revealed a shift to more executive-directed systems.[30] It seems that the member states which joined the European Union in 2004 are also following this pattern: in Slovenia's first year of full European Union membership, a shift in the same direction was seen both in the new formal rules on relations between the executive and parliament in dealing with European Union issues and – to an even greater extent – in general political practice.

(a) Formal Changes

A comparison between the formal rules governing relations between the executive and parliament in dealing with European Union issues in the pre-accession period, on the one hand, and in the circumstances of full Slovenian European Union membership, on the other show a tendency to maintain both (a) the relatively important role accorded to parliament in managing European Union affairs, and (b) transparency in the Slovenian management of European Union business (especially compared to some European Union member countries with less important parliamentary competences in these policy areas). Nevertheless, the empowerment of the executive and partial decrease in public transparency of the whole process of managing European affairs at home is impossible to overlook. (See Table 1.)

---

items on the working body agenda and may present their opinions to the Committee of European Affairs' meetings. Slovenian Members of the European Parliament may also participate in the working body's discussion, but not in decision-making. The meetings of this parliamentary working body are supposed to be called at least seven days in advance, but in urgent cases, shorter notice is acceptable. Especially in the latter cases, it is very difficult for specialised bodies and the upper chamber of the Slovenian parliament, the National Council, to react quickly enough to be able to provide the Committee of European Affairs with their special input. Specialised parliamentary working bodies and the National Council are expected to inform the Committee of European Affairs of their proposed amendments to a Slovenian negotiating position two days before the Committee of European Affairs meets. It is for the Committee of European Affairs to decide whether or not to accept these proposed amendments. Where the Committee of European Affairs is not informed of such proposed amendments, this is regarded as equivalent to there not being any.

[30] T. Raunio and S. Hix, "Backbenchers Learn to Fight Back: European Integration and Parliamentary Government" in K.H. Goetz and S. Hix (eds.), *Europeanised Politics? European Integration and National Political Systems* (Frank Cass, London, 2001).

Table 1: Similarities and dissimilarities in the formal rules on the management of European Union matters in Slovenia during the time of accession negotiations and in the circumstances of full membership of the European Union

	During accession negotiations	**During the period of membership**
Representation of Slovenian interests *vis-à-vis* the European Union	Executive	Executive
Preparation of negotiating positions	Executive	Executive
Participation of the National Assembly in taking national policy positions	All positions had to be approved by parliament	Selected positions only (consisting of the narrow type of issues defined by the law and those issues autonomously selected by parliament from a broader set of issues).[31]
Discussion and decisions on the treaties which form the basis of the European Union	Parliament	Parliament
Transparency of parliamentary plenary sessions and parliamentary working bodies	Open to the public	Working bodies' sessions are closed to the public. General information is published after the sessions; there is publication of more detailed information on positions only where they are not secret.
Information on European Union matters available on the internet	Yes – mainly linked to the activities of the Ministry of European Affairs	Yes – in the process of creation (this being a legal obligation on the executive). Additionally, a special information base is being developed within the framework of the parliament's information system.

[31] Pursuant to Art. 4 of the Law on Collaboration between the Executive and Legislative Branches in Managing European Union Matters, the National Assembly should participate in formulating negotiating positions on any European Union proposals which should (depending on their content, and on the Slovenian Constitution and Slovenian law) fall within the competence of Parliament. However, the National Assembly can also discuss other European Union matters when required by the government or when the National Assembly decides to do so.

As is shown in Table 1, the biggest changes have been seen in the narrowing of the scope of the European issues parliament is to be involved in (notwithstanding the amended formal rule that the National Assembly can interfere in any specific policy issues it selects) and in a major increase in the level of secrecy in managing European Union issues.

(b) Shifts in Practice

The first year of Slovenia's full European Union membership was an unusual political year, as elections to the European Parliament – the first for Slovenia – were held on 13 June 2004, and national parliamentary elections were held on 3 October 2004.[32] A new government, representing the first radical ideological shift since 1992, was formed on 3 December of that year. To some extent, these circumstances explain the decline in the level of information on European Union matters provided by the government to the National Assembly.[33] As will be outlined later in this section, the national parliament has been able to rely only on its own initiative and knowledge and on the culture of the pre-accession period.[34] A preliminary examination of what is happening in practice shows that the National Assembly has tended simply to approve the government's proposals, and that the ability of parliament to control the government in its participation in decision-making processes at European Union level has declined. A comparison of the process of adaptation of Slovenian domestic management of European Union issues to the circumstances of full EU membership over two successive periods (see Table 2) reveals that during the first year of full European Union membership the formally-defined relationship between the executive and parliament was implemented only partially, gradually, and after a time lag.

---

[32] For more on the changes in Slovenia's party system and its governments between 1990 and 2004, see D. Fink-Hafner, "Slovenia: Between Bipolarity and Broad Coalition-Building" in S. Jungerstam-Mulders (ed.), *Post-Communist EU Member States – Parties and Party Systems* (Ashgate, Houndsmill, 2006).

[33] It should also be noted, however, that because of the European Parliament elections and the summer holiday period between May and October, 2004, there was a period during which there was a lack of European Union legislative initiatives.

[34] By 'the culture of the pre-accession period' is meant in this context, the formal and informal knowledge acquired the members of parliament and the patterns of behaviour internalised by them.

Table 2: A comparison of the provisions of the 2004 Law and practical relations between the executive and Parliament since 1 May, 2004[35]

Provisions of the March 2004 law	The practice from May to October 2004	The practice from November, 2004 to March, 2005
Government to send documentation on individual European Union matters to parliament together with the proposed negotiating position.	A lack of such Government documentation,[36] but Government proposals of Slovenian negotiating positions were made available on the internet 'European Union portal'.	Gradual development of practice of Government sending documentation on individual European Union matters to Parliament together with proposed negotiating position.
Internet 'European Union portal' to be made available.	A main EU portal was made available with key documents being provided in English from EU level concerning individual European matters to be dealt with, rarely accompanied by Slovenian government documents and accessible by the government and the National Assembly only.	A European Union portal with main European Union documents, a growing number of additional Slovenian government and parliament documents; accessible only by the government and the National Assembly.[37]
Parliament to select European Union matters to be discussed by it before finally formulating the Slovenian negotiating	This was the predominant practice.	A new practice is in the process of development after the change of government of December 2004 position.
Autonomous European Union document database to be provided in the National Assembly.	A database was in the process of creation.	An electronic database – accessible by the National Assembly only – is still in the process of creation.

35 The sources of information for this table were T. Krašovec, "Sodelovanje med Državnim zborom Republike Slovenije in vlado po vključitvi v Evropsko unijo – prve izkušnje" (Paper presented at the Slovenian Political Science Association annual meeting, Portorož, 26–28 May 2005); interviews in May 2005 conducted in the research section of the National Assembly as well as with members of parliament; and (publicly available) invitations to meetings of the Committee on European Affairs (accessible at the time of writing at *http://www.dz-rs.si*).

36 Krašovec (cited in the foregoing footnote) reports that the Committee on European Affairs did not receive any Commission legislative proposal for discussion from the Slovenian government during this period. The Committee did, however, discuss 28 separate agenda items at eight meetings (mostly at its own initiative), primarily discussing issues related to the activities of Slovenian Government representatives in European Union institutions (especially the Council) and key documents such as those providing information on the Stability and Growth Pact and information on the 2007–2013 Financial Perspective.

37 The European Union portal was scheduled to be available to the broader public by the end of 2005.

The data available[38] also shows that in this first year the national parliament's substantive input into the day-to-day management of European Union affairs was far less than had been formally provided for, and indeed, had been expected (see Table 3). According to Zajc, among the causes of this situation has been the lack of cultural capacity (*i.e.*, both routines and specific knowledge) within the National Assembly.[39]

However, there have been some clear examples of the distinct role and power of the legislative branch being asserted. Uniquely, the National Assembly appeared to be the only decision-making body in Slovenia involved in defining the country's approach to its forthcoming assumption of the European Union Presidency in 2008.[40] This was because at that time it was the only institution which possessed the legitimacy and the legal basis necessary to take this decision. The position had been proposed by the old government which no longer had full competence, while the new government (after the national elections in October, 2004) had still not been formed. The National Assembly thus took its decision on the basis of the proposal by the Committee on European Union Affairs of 17 November 2004.

New technologies even enabled the National Assembly to be an active participant at the intergovernmental conference from 17 to 18 June 2004 in Brussels. Krašovec reports that the National Assembly was an active participant in the ongoing formulation of Slovenian positions during that conference while being in constant communication with Slovenian representatives in Brussels *via* an audio conference link.[41] More exactly, it was the Parliamentary Committee on Foreign Affairs which was constantly informed about the process of negotiation and was even directly actively involved in it.

---

[38] See, *e.g.,* Krašovec, above, n. 35. In addition the content and timing of invitations to parliamentary working bodies' sessions (published on the National Assembly home page) indicated both that meetings were being held at very short notice and that relevant materials were being given at a very late stage to MPs.

[39] D. Zajc, *Vloga nacionalnega parlamenta v EU – primer Državnega zbora RS, part 2* (Faculty of Social Sciences, Centre for Political Science Research, Ljubljana, 2004).

[40] Krašovec, above, n. 35, at 5–6.

[41] Krašovec, above, n. 35.

Table 3: Provisions of the 2004 law and the practice in the National Assembly since 1 May, 2004

Provisions of the March 2004 law	The practice from May to October 2004	The practice from November 2004 to March 2005
Discussion of European Union matters to take place in Committee on European Union Affairs.[42]	Eight sessions held, dealing with 28 European Union matters, mostly selected on the Committee's own initiative. No government initiatives.[43]	Sixteen sessions held (half of them extraordinary, and three held together with the Committee on Foreign Policy).[44]
Discussion of European Union matters related to foreign and security policies to take place in the Committee on Foreign Policy.	At seven (out of 16) sessions, European Union matters were discussed; approval of governmental positions before each meeting of the Council.[45]	Seven out of 15 sessions linked with common European Union foreign and security policy (three out of seven sessions together with Committee on European Union Affairs).[46]
Opinions formulated by other parliamentary working bodies to be sent to the above mentioned bodies for final formulation of he parliamentary position.	Data not available.	Opinions of the Committees on Agriculture, Forestry and Food, the Committee on the Economy and the Committee on Internal Affairs and Justice sent to the Committee on European Union Affairs.[47]
Annual discussion to be held in Parliament on the situation in the European Union, on the status of Slovenia in the Union, and defining political strategies for Slovenia's future functioning in European Union institutions.	Not held.	On 29 March 2005, the National Assembly adopted a Declaration on Strategies for Slovenia's Activities in European Union Institutions in 2005.

[42] The Committee on European Affairs has eighteen members, including one president and two vice-presidents (20% per cent of all MPs), while Raunio and Hix (above, n. 30) reported that in 1998 the average size of a European Union committee in the fifteen member states was 7.4% of all representatives.

[43] Krašovec, above, n. 30. Note that under the National Assembly Statutory Rules, initiatives by the President of the Assembly are also a possibility in addition to those by the government and by the Committee itself,.

[44] *Ibid.*. Note that extraordinary sessions are called in urgent cases where it is not possible to put matters on the agenda of regular sessions in time.

[45] *Ibid.*.

[46] *Ibid.*.

[47] *Ibid.*.

The change of government after the national parliamentary elections of October 2004 seems to led to some discontinuity, however. Some Opposition critics have publicly expressed the view that the mode of governance in the management of European issues changed for the worse under the new government, judged by the standards of democracy and of cooperation between Government and Opposition.[48]

6. A Temporary or a Long-term Shift towards Less Democratic Governance?

For the purposes of Slovenian participation in European Union policy-making, a practical relationship does seem to have been established in Slovenia between the executive and parliament, based, for the most part, on the initiative of the National Assembly's working bodies. No serious conflicts between the two branches of government were visible during most of the first year of full European Union membership. This was probably largely due to the informal agreement that during the first year of full European Union membership, neither the executive nor parliament would 'complicate' European Union decision-making.[49] Still, some recent vigorous clashes between government and opposition MPs on particular issues (*e.g.*, in negotiations on the European Union's financial perspective for the period 2007–2013,[50] on the Slovenian regional structure,[51] and on the problem of Slovenia's insufficient absorption capacity for European Union funding during the first year of full European Union membership) have shown the public that the politics of management of European Union affairs have changed.

Among the more general indications of problems in the relationship between the executive and parliament in the process of formulating and representing

48 See in this regard the views expressed, *e.g.*, by Milan Cvikl, the former Minister for European affairs, who is currently an MP of the Liberal Democracy of Slovenia Party, Chair of the Commission for Budgetary and Other Public Finance Control and a member of the Committee on European Affairs, in his contribution to the seventh talks organised by the President of the Republic of Slovenia on the Future of Slovenia, on 25 May 2005 (information available at time of writing at http://www.up-rs.si and http://www.prihodnost-slovenije.si).

49 Interview with head of the Committee on European Affairs in a broadcast *Dosje: Leto v EU*, transmitted by TV Slovenija I on 26 April 2005.

50 Liberal Democracy of Slovenia (the party of the former Prime Minister) criticised the government heavily for taking an unfavourable negotiating position on the Luxembourg Presidency's proposal. Similar criticisms by the Chair of the Commission for Budgetary and Other Public Finance Control were also published in a public letter to the Prime Minister dated 26 May 2005.

51 This is an important 'European' issue since it is related to opportunities for obtaining access to European Union funds.

Slovenian positions on European Union matters can be listed the following.[52] First, there is deep dissatisfaction on the part of members of parliament – especially opposition MPs – with the executive's attitude to the National Assembly in the management of European affairs. Since the giving of a relatively large degree of autonomy to the Government in the management of European Union matters from 1 May 2004 onwards, it has not so far manifested any particular interest in the development of a dynamic relationship with parliament. There has been a lack of initiative on the part of the executive in searching for parliamentary positions on specific European Union matters. MPs have been especially unhappy over instances of negotiating positions being sent to Brussels on behalf of the executive before they were sent to parliament, of ministers travelling to Brussels without proper documentation, and even of ministers not travelling to Brussels at all to present the Slovenian positions.[53]

Secondly, the criticism has also been openly expressed that the government does not act sufficiently in line with the law governing collaboration between the two branches of power.[54] Expression has been given to the general view that Slovenia is contributing to the European Union's democratic deficit, with a gap now existing between the level of democracy which formerly existed in the pre-accession period and the level of democracy which has existed during the period of full European Union membership. Some interest groups have also expressed their concern about the exclusion of civil society actors from the management of European Union affairs (in particular because of the lack of responsiveness of political players both to interest group proposals, and to interest group warnings about specific European Union policy proposals).

Thirdly, Parliament has not played its role proactively enough. For the most part, it has approved positions which have been prepared by the executive.

---

[52] This enumeration is based on the analysis by Krašovec (above, n. 35), as well as on information published on the National Assembly's home page, and the web pages of parliamentary political party groupings and of the President of the Republic of Slovenia, in addition to information published in the mass media, interviews in the National Assembly in May, 2005 and interviews in broadcast on TV Slovenia I, above, n. 49.

[53] In the public letter to the Prime Minister of 26 May 2005, above, n. 50, the Minister of Foreign Affairs was explicitly criticised for not having attended key negotiating meetings of European and foreign ministers where the next Financial Perspective was discussed. In the mass media, the Minister of Agriculture was also criticised for not travelling to Agriculture and Fisheries Council meetings.

[54] The Law on Collaboration between the National Assembly and Government in European Union Matters, above, n. 21.

There have not been many alterations of such positions by the National Assembly so far. Among the few which were publicly visible (and at the same time highly politicised) was the issue of the regionalisation of Slovenia. Reasons for this general lack of a proactive role probably include the very tight time pressures involved.[55]

Fourthly, in contrast to the pre-accession period, conflicts between the Government and the Opposition have emerged in the European Union policy area. Recourse has even been had to obstruction on the part of the Opposition.[56]

At the moment it is impossible to answer fully the question of whether these problems, which involve issues of institutional learning, of the capacity of institutions to make cultural adjustments, and of the redistribution of power and influence among national players are just temporary or are a long-term and unavoidable 'importing of the democratic deficit'.[57] Slovenia now seems to find itself confronted with the following options (which are not mutually exclusive): either (a) to fatalistically join the club of which most parliaments in the European Union are already members — that of parliaments unable to supervise efficiently their governments in the European Union policy area[58]; (b) to enforce to the maximum extent its own legal norms supporting parliament's important role in managing European Union affairs; or (c) to join the transformative European tendency to search for new institutional and political cultural ways in which to enhance the role of national parliaments and democratise European Union policy-making.

The National Assembly still makes inefficient use of several mechanisms and methods of actively and efficiently involving itself in European policy-making – including that of scrutiny of the national executive. Desirable

[55] It is obvious from the many published invitations to meetings of the Committee on European Affairs that they are issued just a day or a few days before a meeting. Furthermore, it is not uncommon for invitations to indicate that the materials for a specific meeting will be delivered to MPs later.

[56] Unhappy with the manner in which discussion was being conducted in the Committee on European Affairs at its twelfth meeting, held on 20 May 2005, the Liberal Democracy of Slovenia's members of parliament walked out. The main reason for their taking this action (according to information available, at the time of writing, at www.lds.si/article.cp2?uid=4258&linked=6) was that without explanation and contrary to the Statutory Rules, the Chair of the Committee (a member of parliament from one of the ruling parties) had refused to allow the Liberal Democracy's MEP to participate in the discussion at the meeting.

[57] Grabbe, above, n. 11.

[58] See in this regard the chapter in this book by Tapio Raunio.

changes include more intensive activity on the part of parliamentary working bodies, a more systematic building-up of cultural capacity on the part of members of parliament, and of the National Assembly itself to deal with European issues, parliament's learning about good practices (both foreign and home-grown) and the more efficient use of new technologies. It remains to be seen if the Slovenian parliament will really be a 'victim' of the European integration process and how the changes which have come about in the national parliament's practical role (especially in its relations with the executive) will affect the level of success enjoyed by Slovenia in European Union policy-making.

16. Parliamentary Scrutiny over European Union Decision-Making in the Netherlands

Ronald Holzhacker[1]

1. Introduction

The European Union is transforming the function and power of the Dutch parliament as an institution, and the way in which its principal actors – the governing and opposition parliamentary party groups – interact with each other and the Government. Commentators for years have bemoaned the democratic deficit that exists in the European Union. Pointing a finger at the supranational institutions of the Union, critics complain about the excessive number of decisions made by civil servants in the bureaucratic labyrinth of Brussels, the lack of accountability of the European Commission to elected officials, and the ineffectiveness of the European Parliament in overseeing and legitimising decisions. Many observers argue that the European Union and the member states face a democratic deficit which is eroding the tradition of parliamentary democracy in Europe and undermining a sense of legitimacy in the political system.

Yet an increasing number of the most important and far-reaching decisions are made within the intergovernmental institutions of the European Union: the European Council and the Council of Ministers. It is in these institutions that the prime ministers (or heads of state) and other cabinet ministers gather to stake out their positions and negotiate with their counterparts from other member states. The process of decision-making in the member states preceding these meetings may be subject to scrutiny by the national parliaments. Here is where the Dutch parliament has begun to act to redress the democratic deficit within the national decision-making process over European Union issues. This chapter seeks to address the questions: how does parliamentary scrutiny over European Union decision-making function

[1] Assistant Professor of Political Science, University of Twente, the Netherlands.

in the Netherlands, and how has this new role for parliament changed both parliament/executive relations in the country and the interaction of parties in parliament?

2. Europeanisation

A new wave of empirical research has focused on how the European Union has impacted on the member states and on the underlying causal mechanisms for the process of Europeanisation.[2] The European Union impacts on member states directly by imposing a European policy on them to which they have to adapt, principally through the issuance of directives which must be transformed into national law. Another direct consequence has been the establishment of administrative infrastructures in member states, in national capitals, and in offices in Brussels, to deal with European affairs. But consequences that are by definition indirect have been left relatively under-explored – for instance, those on processes of democratic input such as social cleavages, parties, and patterns of democratic legitimation in the member states.[3]

The institutional structures of national parliaments designed to perform parliamentary scrutiny, and the interaction between governing and opposition political parties within these institutions, are central to the system of democratic representation and legitimacy in the member states. In the research that exists on parliamentary-executive relations regarding European Union matters, empirical analysis of the main strategic actors within parliament – the political parties – is often lacking. Political parties are the premier mass-elite linkage institutions in parliamentary democracies, connecting the object of voter choice in periodic elections to the decision-making processes of government and ultimately to public policies.

The emergence of multi-level governance in the European Union[4] has influenced the national parliaments of the member states in two fundamental

[2] See M. Green Cowles, J. Caporaso and T. Risse (eds.), *Transforming Europe: Europeanization and Domestic Change* (Cornell University Press, Ithaca, New York, 2001); K. Featherstone and C. Radaelli (eds.), *The Politics of Europeanization* (Oxford University Press, Oxford and New York, 2003); S. Hix and K. Goetz, "Introduction: European Integration and National Political Systems" (2000) 23 *West European Politics* (Special Issue) 1, at 15, R. Holzhacker and Markus Haverland (eds.), *European Research Reloaded: Cooperation and Integration among Europeanized States* (Kluwer, 2006).

[3] Hix and Goetz, above, n. 2.

[4] See L. Hooghe and G. Marks, *Multi-Level Governance and European Integration* (Rowman & Littlefield, London, 2001).

ways. First, increasing proportions of sovereign decision-making in important policy areas are being transferred to European Union level, decreasing the independent decision-making capability of the nation-state. Secondly, to the extent that the authority that has been transferred to the European Union resides in the European Council or the Council of Ministers, there has been a transfer of decision-making authority from the parliamentary level to the member states' executives. The power to reach decisions in policy areas that have traditionally been vested in national parliaments now rests in part either in the supranational decision-making institutions of the European Union or in national governments when they vote in the intergovernmental decision-making institutions of the European Union.

3. Parliamentary Scrutiny

Parliamentary scrutiny is the exercise of power by the legislative branch to control, influence, or monitor government decision-making. Dahl defines the term 'influence' as:

> "a relation among actors such that the wants, desires, preferences or intentions of one or more actors affect the actions, or predisposition to act, of one or more other actors".[5]

This influence may be either 'manifest', in which parliament explicitly acts to achieve a given outcome, or 'implicit', in which parliament is successful in achieving a given outcome without taking any overt action because a government may act in anticipation of reactions from parliament.[6]

Parliaments and party groups have a variety of ways in which they attempt to control and monitor governmental decision-making on European Union issues. Parliamentary scrutiny of government decision-making over European Union issues may occur publicly within the formal institutions of parliament, such as committee deliberations, parliamentary questioning and debate in plenary session. Or this scrutiny may take in a place in a process out of thc public cyc and within party groups, in forms such as consultation with Government ministers or officials and deliberations within a party group.

---

[5] R. Dahl, *Democracy and its Critics* (Yale University Press, New Haven, 1989), at 32.
[6] *Ibid.*

What are the likely goals of parliamentary party groups when scrutinising the executive? Governing party groups are likely concerned with the stability and maintenance of their government during a parliamentary period and the party's re-election at the end of the period. Opposition party groups also have an incentive to scrutinise their government's decision-making. These party groups may be successful at pushing government policy closer to their own preferences, or they may destabilise the Government and bring about early elections, or they may make points with the electorate that could be beneficial to the party during the next election. Indeed, a Government's perceived degree of accountability rests to a great extent on the ability of competing parties publicly to criticise governmental decisions during a parliamentary term and during the election campaign.

Representativity and legitimacy of Government decision-making emerges in the first instance from parliament – the body directly elected by the people in periodic, competitive elections. It is not sufficient that a parliament installs a government at the beginning of the parliamentary term or holds the ultimate power to dissolve government. Representation and legitimacy demands an ongoing, continual role for parliament. Traditional concepts of legislative-executive relations emphasise two formal powers of parliament: first, those of installing a government after an election and the exercise of the power of dissolution, and secondly, law-making powers. But parliamentary oversight and scrutiny over government decision-making is becoming an increasingly important power on the part of parliaments and the object of a growing volume of research.[7]

One of the reasons why national parliamentary scrutiny is so important for the purposes of increasing the legitimacy and participation in the process of European decision-making is that it is the primary institutional source for

[7] T. Bergman, "National parliaments and EU Affairs Committees: notes on empirical variation and competing explanations" (1997) 4 *Journal of European Public Policy* 373; P. Esaiasson and K. Heidar, *Beyond Westminster and Congress: The Nordic Experience* (Ohio State University Press, Columbus, 2000); J. Fitzmaurice, "National Parliamentary Control of EU Policy in the Three New Member States" (1996) 19 *West European Politics* 88; R. Holzhacker, "National Parliamentary Scrutiny over EU issues: Comparing the Goals and Methods of Governing and Opposition Parties" (2002) *European Union Politics* 3; D. Judge, "The Failure of National Parliaments" (1995) 18 *West European Politics* 79; R. Katz and B. Wessels, *The European Parliament, National Parliaments, and European Integration* (Oxford University Press, Oxford, 1999); P. Norton (ed.), *National Parliaments and the European Union* (Frank Cass, London, 1996); T. Raunio, "Always One Step Behind? National Legislatures and the European Union" (1999) 34 *Government and Opposition* 1; A. Maurer and W. Wessels (eds.), *National Parliaments on their Ways to Europe: Losers or Latecomers?* (Nomos, Baden-Baden, 2001).

receiving input from Opposition parties. In the Council of Ministers, only governments – elected from governing parties – are represented and participate in setting European policy. Yet traditional democratic structures normally allow some opportunity for Opposition parties to discuss and debate laws and policies set by the Government. It is important that the voice of Opposition parties is heard at the national level, because their voice is non-existent or weak within the European Union institutions themselves.

Involvement by parliament in the decision-making processes of national governments contributes to the democratisation of the entire multi-level governance system of the European Union. It means that a part of the decision-making process moves from the civil servants in the ministries and closed cabinet meetings to a wider circle of representatives of both governing and Opposition party groups. Opening the decision-making process may at a minimum bring with it involvement of members of parliament with a specialised interest in a particular topic, a smattering of interest groups, and the stakeholders interested in an issue, but at other times it may bring entire party groups, a wide range of competing interest groups, and media attention to carry the debate to the wider public for discussion and consideration. These processes reduce the democratic deficit in the European Union and the member states, improve representation, and increase a sense of democratic legitimacy among the European electorates in the evolving system of governance.

4. Parliamentary–Executive Relations

It is important to place parliamentary scrutiny over European Union issues into the broader context of relations between parliament and the executive. The interactions between MPs and Government ministers (in the sense either of cooperation or confrontation between them) are commonly analysed under the rubric of 'executive-legislative' or – using a term more appropriate for parliamentary democracies – 'parliamentary-executive relations'. Traditionally, whereas Government and parliament are viewed as two different constitutional bodies (a perspective referred to as 'dualism'), governing party groups and the government have been seen as essentially one entity (a perspective referred to as 'monism'). But increasingly scholars have begun to develop a richer view of the variations in interactions between parliament and Government.[8] Indeed, a whole range of interactions between

8 For example, N. Polsby, "Legislatures" in F. Greenstein and N. Polsby (eds.), *Handbook of Political Science, Vol. 5: Governmental Institutions and Processes* (Addison Wesley, Reading, 1975) at 257–319; W. Steffani, "The Bundestag at the Intersection of Four Systems" in N. Orstein (ed.), *The Role of the Legislature in Western Democracies,* (American Enterprise Institute, Washington, DC, 1981) at 50–66.

individual MPs and governing and Opposition party groups, and between parliament and Government ministers is possible.

King has created a typology of executive-legislative relations,[9] which others have applied to specific countries.[10] Here, a modified form of King's typology[11] is presented, setting out three basic types of parliament-Government relations, *viz.,* a non-party mode, an inter-party mode, and a cross-party mode.

A non-party mode of parliament-Government relations is where members of 'the' Government interact with (again, in the sense either of cooperating with or confronting) members of 'the' parliament. This mode conforms to the two-body image, and relations between the two are viewed in terms of the fulfilment of their constitutional roles.

An inter-party mode is where ministers and MPs from one party interact with ministers and MPs from another party group. Here, parliament is seen as the arena in which ideological competition between political parties occurs. Within this mode, three sub-modes can be distinguished: (a) an *intra-coalition mode*, which is where, in cases of multi-party government, ministers and MPs from one governing party interact with ministers and MPs from another governing party group; (b) an *opposition mode*, which is where ministers and MPs belonging to the governing party groups interact with MPs of Opposition parliamentary parties; and (c) a *'floating coalition' mode*, which is where MPs belonging to a governing party interact with MPs from one or more Opposition party groups in order to influence or amend a government proposal.

A cross-party mode is where ministers and MPs interact on the basis of cross-party interests. Here, parliament is seen as a marketplace in which sectoral interests, which supersede party boundaries, are traded.

---

[9] A. King, "Modes of Executive-Legislative Relations: Great Britain, France and West Germany" (1976) 1 *Legislative Studies Quarterly* 11.
[10] As regards Germany, see T. Saalfeld, "The West German Bundestag after 40 years: The Role of Parliament in a Party Democracy" (1990) 13 *West European Politics* 68. As regards the Netherlands, see R. Andeweg, "Executive-Legislative Relations in the Netherlands: Consecutive and Coexisting Patterns" (1992) 17 *Legislative Studies Quarterly* 161. In relation to Austria, see W. Mueller, "Changing Executive-Legislative Relations in Austria (1945–1992)" (1993) 18 *Legislative Studies Quarterly* 467.
[11] The modification was proposed by Andeweg and Nijzink. See R. Andeweg and L. Nijzink, "Beyond the Two-Body Image: Relations Between Ministers and MPs" in H. Doering (ed.), *Parliaments and Majority Rule in Western Europe* (St. Martin's Press, Frankfurt-am-Main, 1995).

When engaged in parliamentary scrutiny, the goals of party groups vary according to the mode of parliament-Government relations. There are times when parliament-Government relations involving parliamentary scrutiny over European Union matters may function in a non-party mode. Parliaments act as a whole at times to press their right for timely information concerning decision-making over European Union matters. In these cases, parliament acts as an institution in a non-party mode to define and defend what it perceives are its rightful constitutional powers within the democratic system of government.

There may also be examples of parliamentary scrutiny regarding European Union matters taking on the character of the cross-party mode. Here, MPs from various party groups unite to press a Government minister to consider sectoral or geographical interests of the MPs. However, although such cross-party activity may be successful at influencing Government, it usually occurs through channels other than the exercise of the formal powers of parliament. The formal exercise of parliamentary power across party lines poses a severe threat to the cohesiveness of party groups and to the stability of governments in parliamentary systems.

Most of the interactions between parliament and Government occur in the inter-party mode. Inter-party issues are those in which the goals of governing and Opposition party groups *vis-à-vis* the Government diverge along party lines. Here, distinctions may be drawn between the various party groups' goals in engaging in parliamentary scrutiny on a given issue, whether to protect and defend the Government (intra-coalition mode), oppose the Government (opposition mode), or persuade and bargain with other party groups to modify a Government proposal ('floating coalition' mode).

5. Scrutiny in the Dutch *Tweede Kamer*

The European Affairs Committee of the *Tweede Kamer*[12] in the Netherlands meets as a whole two or three times a month in an open meeting, which is normally held only for the purposes of questioning the Prime Minister, the Minister for Finance, or the Minister for Foreign Affairs (or the State Secretary for Foreign Affairs). In the Committee, the agendas of upcoming meetings of the European Council, the General Affairs Council, and the Justice and Home Affairs Council are discussed. The other configurations of the Council of Ministers, such as economic affairs, transport, finance, or

[12] The *Tweede Kamer* is the lower house of the Dutch parliament.

social affairs, are discussed with the relevant minister in a joint committee format. Meetings are held both before the Council meetings to discuss the agenda and also afterwards to judge the outcome of the negotiations. Formally, these meetings are listed on the parliamentary agenda as a joint meeting of the European Affairs Committee and a given specialised policy committee. Typically, however, the meeting is attended by a single member of parliament – the party spokesperson on the issue area – from each of the major parties. In practical terms, the meeting may be considered a form of joint subcommittee between the European Affairs Committee and the policy committee.

Overlapping membership on the European Affairs Committee is a way of bringing a diverse expertise to the Committee, and bringing knowledge and experience which the members may have acquired through service on other parliamentary committees. This broadens and strengthens the Committee and allows it to understand the implications of policy in one area and prepared by one ministry, with other policy areas perhaps prepared by other ministries. This institutional feature clearly strengthens the power of parliament *vis-à-vis* the Government. It is especially important to Opposition parties because such parties typically have fewer members than the governing parties and the Opposition parties cannot rely on Government expertise to inform them of the policy and political implications of European Union proposals.

The extent to which other committees in parliament also discuss European Union matters and upcoming business on the Council of Ministers agenda is another way in which parliamentary power *vis-à-vis* the executive is strengthened. It allows a specialised committee to consider matters arising for the Government at European Union level, in terms of the committee's own institutional expertise of the policy area. The involvement of other committees proceeds even further than a system of overlapping membership, but allows the specialised committee in its full institutional competency to analyse European Union matters, increasing parliamentary power as a result. Because the voice of Opposition parties is often heard more in committee than in plenary sessions of parliament, institutional arrangements which bring European Union decision-making to the specialised committees strengthen the power of Opposition parties.

At times the specialised committees in the Netherlands will pick up issues that become particularly salient for a committee or a political party by virtue of interest group activity or through media attention. This has been most apparent in the Environmental Committee, but also increasingly in the Justice Committee because of the increasing saliency of decision-making in this area. Furthermore, the Commerce Committee will address European Union issues at times, although the great bulk of the measures aimed at creating the single market have now been adopted. Finally, there are times when the Foreign Relations Committee will assert itself, refusing to allow the European Affairs Committee to completely dominate scrutiny of decision-making concerning the European Union. In particular, it discusses developments in the European Union's Second Pillar (*i.e.,* the Common Foreign and Security Policy), and also engages in discussions during periods when treaty changes are being discussed.

6. Goals and Methods of Parties when Scrutinising the Government over European Union Matters

We now turn from these institutional features of scrutiny to consider the strategies of parties which act within the relevant institutions.[13] In the Netherlands, with a coalition government typically consisting of two relatively equal parties and one smaller one, the Government needs to consult frequently with parliament to make sure that it maintains these broad coalitions. There have been times when portions of the parties within the governing coalition have threatened to defect temporarily and to side with an Opposition party to bring a policy proposal closer to their own party's view, a phenomenon which was seen, for example, at the time of the very politically diverse coalition which held power in the Netherlands from 1994 to 2002, the so-called 'Purple Coalition', combining labour (PvdA) and conservative liberal (VVD) parties, with a smaller social liberal party (D66).

The power of the Dutch Opposition parties to set the agenda at times stems not only from formal rights of the Opposition parties enshrine in parliamentary procedural rules, but also from their occasional ability to get

[13] The research presented here focused on the strategies, *i.e.,* the goals and methods which party groups use in their attempt to oversee the government. The idea of the research was that of analysing the interactions between governing coalition parties and opposition parties, the *Fracties* of the Dutch *Tweede Kamer*, and the differing coalition dynamics that occasionally emerge when scrutinising the government's European Union activities. The prime source of information for this examination comes from in-depth personal interviews with members of the parliament (MPs) serving on the European Affairs Committee in February 2000. Additional interviews were carried out with MPs serving on one of two specialised policy committees, the Economic and the Environmental Committees, which may also deal with European Union issues at times. If an MP was unavailable, an interview with a senior policy adviser to the MP or party group was conducted. Please note that interviews were conducted by the author and quotations from oral interviews have been edited to standard English usage. Persons interviewed have been identified by their party and position, but not by name, in order to preserve confidentiality and to encourage more frank responses.

one of the governing parties to temporarily defect and amend the Government proposal in a way that brings it closer to their own preferences. A governing party will not do this if the coalition agreement between the parties has spoken on this matter, but many European Union issues are not envisioned at the start of a Government's term and are thus not part of the written coalition agreement. Thus, at times a proposal of the Government, which emerged from a compromise from the politically mixed bag coalition referred to above, would be modified by either the Green-Left Alliance opposition party encouraging the governing PvdA to temporarily defect from the coalition, and bring policy more to the left. Similarly, at times the Christian Democratic Appeal (CDA) was successful at getting the VVD to defect on issues and bring policy more to the right. This occurred a number of times during the lifetime of the government under consideration here, with the Green-Left Alliance party bringing environmental policy closer to its preferences, and the CDA bringing agriculture policy closer to its preferences. Normally, the temporarily defecting governing parties tried to accomplish this without voting against a formal proposal of the government, so these actions were discussed during preliminary discussions between government and parliament, or perhaps in a resolution to the government, which is less binding than passing a law.

This was a development which also occurred in relation to domestic issues. As Andeweg and Irwin have observed,

> "the characteristic lines of conflict are now between parties, rather than between the institutions of parliament and government, pitting ministers and MPs of one party against (ministers and) MPs of another party. Of these lines of conflict, the one between ministers plus MPs of the governing parties on the one hand, and opposition MPs on the other hand, is most visible, but also rather sterile in terms of policy outcome. By definition, the opposition is a minority, and therefore powerless except for the rare occasion when a wedge can driven between the governing parties. Conflicts between the governing parties, both in government and Parliament, are much more interesting, as the outcome is less predictable and directly affects government policy".[14]

(a) Governing Parties

The goal of the governing parties in the Netherlands appeared to consist mainly of protecting their interest in the compromise which went into

[14] R. Andeweg and G. Irwin, *Dutch Government and Politics* (Macmillan, London, 1993) at 147.

making up the governing coalition, rather than to protect the government as a whole. For example, the governing parties in the *Tweede Kamer* did not normally attempt to find a common position on issues on the agenda of the Council of Ministers. On issues where there was some political controversy, a party spokesperson for a given issue area might have to reach agreement within their own *fractie,* but this was not normally done with the other parties in the coalition. For example, a VVD MP serving on the Economics Committee said

> "I sometimes discuss issues beforehand in my *fractie* when there is a political problem and I am not sure that my colleagues have the same opinion .... Dualism makes it possible that the VVD [in parliament] may say that we do not agree with the minister of economic affairs, who is a member of the VVD. Most of the time we do agree, but sometimes we do not".

Even though the governing parties felt free to scrutinise ministers from their own party in public, they took special care to ensure that government ministers from other governing parties toed the line. For example, a PvdA MP serving on the European Affairs Committee said

> "it is not our primary objective to bring down a minister who is a member of our own party, but that does not mean we wouldn't ever rebuke him. But the tendency is to be more critical towards the ministers of the other coalition partners than towards our own ministers. This is done to preserve the party interest ... the greatest tensions and contradictions exist between the biggest coalition partners, especially between the PvDA and the VVD. This struggle is partly fought in parliament and partly fought in the Government".

If a governing party in the coalition is unhappy with a Government compromise, the party may try to find partners in the Opposition who support their position in order to bring about a change in government policy. For example, when asked whether D66 occasionally worked with the Green Left or other Opposition parties to move a Government proposal closer to their own point of view, a D66 MP responded

> "sometimes you choose your allies – of course, foremost within the Government fractions – depending on the subject. On the left side [with the PvDA] or you look for support on the right, with the CDA. You always try to influence Government policy, which is the role of the parliamentary fraction."

When such matters were discussed openly in a plenary session of parliament, there were limits to how far this behaviour was acceptable. The D66 MP said the party felt free to speak in the plenum in a variety of situations:

> "[to express] a critical judgement of the government's position, including the prime minister's in a [European] Council meeting, to make a judgment on what Europe has achieved, when there is bad publicity about the Commission or Council, when there is a feeling that the Council has missed chances, or has not properly addressed pressing issues. I feel free to address the Government [*i.e.*, in a critical manner]. Of course I am bound by some coalition discipline. I can not go too far".

On what kinds of issues does the parliament have the most say? A member of one of the governing parties, a VVD MP serving on the European Affairs Committee, said

> "it depends on the political sensitivity of the subject. Thus, on some issues we hardly care. But if you talk about an [intergovernmental conference], about changing institutions in Brussels, or about very sensitive political issues like BSE ... then parliament takes a position which makes the Government really aware that they can not go out to Brussels and negotiate something without listening to parliament."

(b) Opposition Parties

The Dutch opposition parties expressed frustration about their lack of information on European matters. A CDA policy adviser on European issues said

> "they [*i.e.*, the parties in government] have much more access to information, far earlier in the process; a lot of times we are completely surprised by what they know. We try to have our ways of knowing things".

Opposition parties attempt to use alternative sources of information regarding European Union issues because they cannot depend on the Government so much. This information may come from interest groups in Brussels or from members of their party in the European Parliament. (Thus, asked about his sources of information, a policy adviser to the Green Left party responded that he talked to people from the environmental movement and to a spokesperson for the Greens in the European Parliament.)

The Opposition parties also complained that debate and scrutiny were very splintered and diffuse. With so many points of view, the minister might be required to listen; yet they doubted that this had much impact. The policy adviser to the Green Left pointed out that, at committee meetings

> "you can speak for maybe ten minutes and make two or three points. But then the PvdA has three other points, the CDA has three other points, and the VVD ... anyway. You end up with ten priorities from the different factions. When the minister has to answer, he just runs through them in the last ten minutes of the meeting. There is no time to ask a second question, or to interrupt, or to really have a debate. There are just certain answers, and then the meeting is over".

In order to overcome this problem, the policy adviser's strategy was to build up a coalition:

> "[I] try to contact my colleagues in the PvdA, for example, then maybe we adopt the same priorities in meetings. Because at these meetings, on those issues, we do not compete for voters, because they do not see it anyway. We try to work together if possible".

When ministers returns from a Council meeting in Brussels, they report back to one of the configurations of the European Affairs Committee and a policy committee on the course of the negotiations and the final outcome. The CDA policy adviser observed

> "it will come as no surprise that the opposition does this more often than the *fracties* of the Government. We try to be critical and follow developments closely. A lot of the subjects are not just dealt with during one Council meeting. There is a margin of influence which the parliament can have; if the Government parties agree with us, then this will be a reason for the Government to change their policy a bit. But we can also go to the extreme of requesting a plenary debate".

When asked about an example of Opposition parties being able to influence policy developments in this way, the CDA policy adviser pointed out that his party works closely with others on European social policy and on justice and home affairs, adding that 'we have the opportunity to get our views across in certain policy fields'. There were also examples of this 'floating coalition' behaviour occurring more publicly in plenary sessions of parliament. But how often did it get to the point of successfully passing a resolution in the plenum? The CDA policy adviser's reply to this question was that this occurred only exceptionally, perhaps once or twice a year.

7. Discussion

The Dutch *Tweede Kamer* has established a European Affairs Committee that draws on the expertise and knowledge of its specialised policy committees. However, the institutional structure of the Dutch European Affairs Committee fails to ensure a unified parliamentary voice on European issues because it rarely meets as a single committee. The Dutch Committee fractures the power of a unified group by frequently formally meeting instead in a joint meeting with the relevant policy committee. In practice, this meeting does not consist of everyone serving on the two committees, but of a representative from each party who serves on both committees. This means that there are very specialised members of the Dutch parliament (usually one member from each of the larger party groups) who deal with European issues in a specific policy area (for example, economics or agriculture). These people, however, have less opportunity to gain an overview of all European Union issues confronting the Government. This diminishes the power of the parliament to present a unified voice on European issues to the Government.

The relationship between the governing and Opposition party groups in the Netherlands is important here. The governing coalition in existence during this research (and which continued until the 2002 parliamentary elections) consisted of the Labour Party (PvdA), the Liberal Party (VVD) and the Democrats '66 (D66). The parties in opposition were the Christian Democratic Appeal (CDA), a party with a long tradition of being in the Government coalition, as well as the Green Left (GL), the Socialist Party (SP), and a grouping of small Christian parties. Rather unusually for a parliamentary democracy, different coalitions emerged occasionally (although rarely) to offer resolutions in an attempt to influence Government policy.

In terms of the three basic types of parliament-Government relations, to use King's typology, the Dutch parliament most often behaves as an inter-party arena. Parliamentary party group discipline is strong, so normally the interaction within the parliament can be analysed in terms of the interaction occurring between the party groups, not among individual MPs. However, the behaviour of the Dutch party groups is unusual in that some activity is seen outside the traditional sub-modes of inter-party bargaining, the intra-coalition and opposition modes.

A limited amount of activity in the Dutch parliament under study here consists of interactions between different combinations of governing and opposition party groups, which are able temporarily to coalesce to pass an amendment to a bill proposed by the Government or to pass a resolution on a particular issue. This is possible without apparently threatening the stability of the coalition in Government. Normally, this does not happen when the coalition parties have already reached agreement and compromise on an issue and this appears in the coalition agreement (*regeerakkoord*) entered into by the parties after the election. But on issues not dealt with in this agreement, including many European issues, some of the governing parties feel free at times to form temporary alliances with Opposition parties in order to modify the Government's proposal. This happened on one occasion over environmental issues, when Opposition parties on the left successfully moved Government policy closer to their own position. In August 2001, Opposition parties on the right successfully influenced the Government to move a piece of agricultural legislation closer to their own position. This must be considered a separate mode of inter-party behaviour in King's typology, labelled here a 'floating coalition' mode.

Members reported that the biggest clashes between the party groups in parliament occurred not between the governing party groups and those in Opposition, but between the VVD and PvdA. This meant that the Government might be considering proposing a policy based upon support from the ministers representing the different governing party groups, but the policy was at times subsequently influenced by a different coalition of party groups. The left in the Dutch parliament had exactly half the votes (MPs from the SP, GL, PvdA and D66), so that a coalition of party groups on the left could at times influence Government policy or pass a resolution not supported by the Government. This of course created tensions within the governing coalition, because in such cases the PvdA in parliament was supporting a position contradicting that agreed to with the VVD by the ministers in government.

Once again, this kind of unfaithfulness would not have been tolerated in situations where the coalition agreement between the PvdA, VVD and D66 explicitly mentioned the issue. A breach in the voting behaviour of the party groups on these issues would certainly have been grounds for the Government to lose the confidence and support of parliament for its continued existence. But measures seen as not explicitly discussed in the coalition agreement were open to new coalitions temporarily forming to support an amendment or parliamentary resolution. European Union issues were often not regulated in the coalition agreement, because it was difficult to foresee these issues before the agreement was signed at the start of the legislative period.

The Dutch governing parties placed emphasis on protecting their own party's interests within the coalition. With three parties in the Government under study here, and with no party being clearly dominant in parliament, each party in the coalition scrutinised a proposal to see if their own party's interest or viewpoint was being sufficiently protected in the compromise that was reached in the cabinet. Because of the occasional unfaithfulness of the party groups in the governing coalition, a 'floating coalition' could emerge in which opposition party groups might be temporarily successful in attracting support for their point of view from one of the governing party groups. They might then be able to pass an amendment or resolution to push government policy towards the party's preferences. They pursued this goal by publicly or privately persuading other party groups to modify the government's proposal.

8. Contrasts with Scrutiny over Domestic Issues

In what ways is scrutiny over European Union decision-making in the country different from the traditional role of the Dutch parliament in the purely domestic arena? There are three principal differences.

The first is that whereas the Dutch parliament's discretionary power is at its greatest when it is enacting national laws, the room to deviate from a government proposal is severely constrained when parliament is transposing European Community directives. Here the transformation into national law must take place within the rather narrow constraints of the directive passed by the Council of Ministers.

The second difference is that in the decision-making process concerning European Union issues, the parliament's power is at the maximum level when scrutinising a minister's position prior to a vote in the Council of Ministers, *i.e.,* prior to the adoption of a directive which must later be transformed into national law. But here, the parliament does not have ultimate law-making powers. Instead, the parliament only has the right to advise the government on its views (an important exception to this is under the Third Pillar in the area of justice and home affairs, in which parliament has the right to give the government a strict mandate).

Finally, the interaction between the various governing parties in the coalition, and with opposition parties, may at times differ from that pertaining to the national situation. This is the case for two reasons. First, whereas the *regeerakkoord* has grown in importance and is used to attempt to set out the agreed position between the governing parties in the coalition, European Union issues are not generally predicted in advance and settled in the agreement. Secondly, because the parliamentary power concerned is that of advising the government, instead of the power to pass binding law, governing parties feel at times they have more leeway to try to alter the compromise taken between the parties in the cabinet.

9. Conclusion

The need for democratic input and parliamentary scrutiny over European Union decision-making has created new opportunities for competition and cooperation among governing and opposition parties in the Netherlands. Using King's typology of executive-legislative relations, this chapter has examined party behaviour during this process of oversight. Although the parliamentary party groups may at times interact in a 'non-party mode' to strengthen their institutional power *vis-à-vis* the government or to make sure government ministries provide the parliament with timely information, most interaction conforms to the 'inter-party mode'. This means that party interactions during parliamentary scrutiny in relation to European Union matters have become increasingly similar to those where domestic political issues are concerned. Thus, private discussions within a party group may precede a process of intra-coalition bargaining. This is followed by interactions with opposition parties in the formal institutional structures of parliament. But we have also seen in this research that occasionally (but rarely) the parties will demonstrate a 'floating-coalition mode' and opposition parties will be able to successfully work with part of the governing coalition to encourage the government to modify a proposal before parliament.

Overall, the process of parliamentary scrutiny in the Netherlands regarding European Union matters is no longer exclusively about finding a national consensus *vis-à-vis* the outside world, but increasingly mirrors the rough and tumble of normal, domestic politics.

17.

Ensuring Democratic Control Over National Government in European Affairs: the French Model

David Siritzky[1]

Were reforms of the kind which were envisaged in the Constitutional Treaty ever to enter into force, it would (in line with the earlier Laeken Declaration) give an active role to national parliaments in the European Union. The involvement of parliaments in the European Union is a means by which the Union's democratic legitimacy can be strengthened, with the most prominent change proposed in the Constitutional Treaty having been the new early warning mechanism, which would have allowed national parliaments to deliver a reasoned opinion if they considered that the principle of subsidiarity had not been complied with. Parliaments would also have been allowed to bring actions before the Court of Justice on the grounds of that the principle of subsidiarity had been infringed, and to oppose the use of the simplified revision procedure of the Constitutional Treaty.

It was these features of the Constitutional Treaty which required a revision of the French Constitution, which was enacted on 1 March 2005. A significant revision of Article 88-4 of the Constitution, which sets out the Parliament's current scrutiny powers over European Union affairs, was also adopted on this occasion.

The purpose of this chapter is to explain how the system of parliamentary scrutiny has worked in France, since the creation in 1979 of the European Delegations of the National Assembly and of the Senate. This parliamentary monitoring has gradually expanded over time in order to compensate for the increasing powers of European Union institutions and to preserve the Government's accountability.

[1] The views expressed in this paper are those of the author writing in his personal capacity, and not those of the *Assemblée Nationale.*

1. The French Parliament and European Union Decision-Making

The approval of the French Parliament is needed for all European Union treaties, other than those submitted to referendum. With the rise of the Convention method for the drafting of European Union treaties, the Parliament's role in their drafting will be reinforced. Daily parliamentary control over European Union legislation, however, is exercised by the European Delegations via the procedure of Article 88-4 of the French Constitution.

(a) The French Parliament and Treaties Relating to the European Union

(i) Approval of European Union Treaties

According to Article 53 of the French Constitution,

> "peace treaties, commercial treaties, treaties or agreements relating to international organisation, those that commit the finances of the State, those that modify provisions which are matters for statute, those relating to the status of persons, and those that involve the cession, exchange or addition of territory, may be ratified or approved only by virtue of an Act of Parliament".

Hence, all of what might be called the European Union Treaties have been submitted to the French Parliament. In accordance with this Article, the French Parliament approved the Treaty of Paris in 1951, the Treaties of Rome in 1957, the Single European Act in 1986, the Treaty of Amsterdam in 1999 and the Treaty of Nice in 2001. It also gave its approval to the ratification of the Treaty Amending Certain Budgetary Provisions of 1970, the Council Decision and Act concerning the election of the representatives of the European Parliament by direct universal suffrage of 1976,[1a] and the various accession treaties. However, the National Assembly refused to approve the Treaty Establishing the European Defence Community in 1954, thereby burying that particular project.

When approving a treaty, Parliament can neither amend it, nor add a reservation or declaration to it. Pursuant to Article 11 of the Constitution, the President of the Republic can also decide to submit to referendum any

[1a] See Council Decision 76/787 [1976] OJ L2781.

treaty that, although not contrary to the Constitution, would affect the functioning of the institutions. The President chose to use this prerogative in 1972 for the Accession Treaty of Denmark, Great Britain and Ireland, and in 1992 for the Maastricht Treaty. The same provision was used again for the Treaty Establishing a Constitution for Europe on 29 May 2005. Accession treaties subsequent to these, other than those already entered into with Bulgaria and Romania and, in future, Croatia, are required to be submitted to referendum, under the new Article 88-5[2] introduced into the Constitution in March 2005.

(ii) The Convention Method

The Convention on the Future of Europe – modelled on the Convention which drew up the Charter of Fundamental Rights in 2000 – gave national parliaments the opportunity to play a much more active role in the drafting of the Constitutional Treaty. Involving parliamentarians helped create a direct link between the Convention and European citizens. The 56 national parliamentarians formed a less cohesive group than the sixteen MEPs in the Convention, but their contribution during its final phase was decisive. If provisions similar to those which were included in the Constitutional Treaty ever enter into force, the convention method will become the normal procedure for amending the Treaty,[3] thus increasing the role of national parliaments.

(b) The French Parliament and Community Legislation

Community legislation is not subject to a ratification requirement, unlike the constitutive treaties, and is essentially negotiated by the Government. Therefore, traditional means of parliamentary scrutiny are not adequate insofar as such legislation is concerned. The extension of the European Union's competences, in successive treaties, has impinged upon the competences *ratione materiae* of the French parliament. This has resulted in a strengthening of the executive branch of government to the detriment of the legislature.

(i) The Delegations for the European Union

These changes led to the creation, in each of the parliament's chambers, of a Delegation for the European Communities by an Act of 6 July 1979. The

[2] Article 88-5 would have become Article 88-7 if the Constitutional Treaty had entered into force.

[3] Under Art. IV-443 of the Constitutional Treaty.

creation of these was the consequence of the establishment in 1979 of direct universal suffrage for the election of the members of the European Parliament, a step which broke the tie between the Strasbourg Assembly and national MPs (from whose ranks Members of the European Parliament had previously been drawn).

These two Delegations have statutory status only, unlike the six Standing Committees, the existence of which is provided for by the Constitution. But their institutional role has been gradually expanded.

The Josselin Act of 10 May 1990 doubled the number of their members from eighteen to 36. It also granted them new instruments by which they could keep themselves informed, by authorising them to hear members of Government and representatives of the Community institutions. This is an important means of obtaining information and of exercising control. Thus, for instance, in a six month period in early 2005, the European Delegation of the National Assembly heard, the French Ministers for Finance, for Foreign Affairs, for European Affairs and for Justice, as well as the President of the European Parliament and the European Commissioners for Justice and Home Affairs and for Transport Policy. In addition to the foregoing, the Josselin Act made it mandatory for the Government to transmit to the Delegations "any necessary documents drawn up by the European Communities institutions". (The subsequent Pandraud Act of 1994 was to go further, by extending this obligation to Second and Third Pillar documents).

In 1992, Article 88-4 was inserted into the French Constitution by a constitutional amendment, which was effected prior to the ratification of the Maastricht Treaty. This article requires the Government to "lay before the National Assembly and the Senate any drafts of, or any proposal for, instruments of the European Communities containing provisions which are matters for statute, as soon as they have been transmitted to the Council of the European Union". Article 88-4 also gives the French Parliament the right to pass resolutions on the drafts or proposals thus transmitted.

The Pandraud Act of 10 June 1994 makes it mandatory for the Government to transmit to the Delegations "any necessary documents drawn up by the various European Union institutions". This Act also changed the name of the Delegations for the European Communities into Delegations for the European Union.

Article 88-4 was altered in 1999 by the constitutional amendment which was effected prior to the ratification of the Amsterdam Treaty. This amendment extended the scope of Article 88-4 to the Second and Third Pillars of the European Union.[4] It also added an 'optional clause' to the 'mandatory clause'. This optional clause offers the Government the possibility of submitting to the chambers European texts, which although not legislative in nature,[5] are of such political significance that it is felt that they should be transmitted to Parliament.

The composition of the Delegations is such as to ensure the proportional representation of political groupings, as well as the balanced representation of the Standing Committees. The latter point means that all members of the Delegations are simultaneously members of one of the six Standing Committees of the chambers. This brings diverse expertise to the Delegations and facilitates their work, which intersects multiple policy areas.

The Delegation bureau is made up of the chairman,[6] four deputy chairmen and two secretaries. The chairmen are elected for the life of the legislature in the National Assembly and for three years in the Senate. They set the agenda of meetings and convene the Delegations.

(ii) The Functioning of Article 88-4 of the French Constitution

Under the Josselin and Pandraud Acts, the Delegation receives between 1,000 and 2,000 European documents (comprising draft regulations, draft directives, decisions, white papers, green papers, communications, *etc.*) each year. On average, some 250 of these documents are transmitted under Art. 88-4, as they contain provisions which are matters for statute under French law or because the Government decides to use the 'optional clause'. The Commission annual work programmes and green and white papers are systematically transmitted to the Parliament by virtue of the optional clause.

It is the *Conseil d'État*[7] which decides if a draft European Community or European Union act includes provisions, which are matters for statute according to Article 34 of the French Constitution.

---

[4] Which relate, as is well known, to the Common Foreign and Security Policy and to police and judicial cooperation in criminal matters.

[5] Article 34 of the French Constitution states which matters – such as civil rights, criminal law or taxation – are of a legislative nature.

[6] At the time of writing of this chapter, Pierre Lequiller was the chairman of the Delegation of the National Assembly for the European Union and Hubert Haenel was the chairman of the Delegation of the Senate for the European Union.

[7] *I.e.,* the Council of State, the highest administrative court in the French legal system.

Political Composition of the National Assembly's Delegation for the European Union as of May 2005.

	Number of members who are also members of Cultural Affairs Standing Committee (Total: 7)	**Number of members who are also members of Economic Affairs Standing Committee** (Total: 6)	**Number of members who are also members of Foreign Affairs Standing Committee** (Total: 11)	**Number of members who are also members of Defence Standing Committee** (Total: 3)	**Number of members who are also members of Finance Standing Committee** (Total: 2)	**Number of members who are also members of Acts Standing Committee** (Total: 7)
Union pour un mouvement populaire (UMP) (Number of members of Delegation: 24)	4	4	8	3	2	3
Socialiste (SOC) (Number of members of 9) Delegation:	3	1	2			3
Union pour la démocratie française (UDF) (Number of members of Delegation: 2)		1				1
Communiste et Républicain (Number of members of Delegation: 1)			1			

Number of documents received according to the Josselin and Pandraud Acts and in application of Article 88-4 of the Constitution (as of January 2005)

	1992	1993	1994	1995	1996	1997	1998	1999	2000	2001	2002	2003	2004	Total
(Documents received under the Josselin and Pandraud Laws)	568	994	1038	1060	2818	1592	2215	2096	1776	1652	1425	1431	1253	**19 920**
(Documents received under Article 88-4)	40	143	171	206	201	231	206	197	274	295	285	317	331	**2 897**
Documents received under the 'optional clause'.[8]								6	18	17	11	22	19	**93**

[8] *I.e.,* Documents transmitted to parliament by the government under Article 88-4 of the Constitution in the absence of any obligation on the government to do so because the documents are not of a legislative nature according to Article 34.

Each text transmitted to parliament according to Article 88-4 of the Constitution is systematically examined by the Delegations for the European Union. They can decide:

(a) to approve the text (possibly by adopting conclusions or a draft resolution to explain their position in detail);

(b) to defer taking a decision if they take the view that they lack adequate information to assess the scope of the text. They may in such instances decide to appoint an 'information *rapporteur*' to conduct an in-depth examination of the issues raised by the document. This *rapporteur* will take written and oral evidence from the relevant government departments, European Union institutions, academics and other experts, interested parties, non-governmental organisations, *etc.*; or

(c) to oppose the adoption of the text (possibly by adopting conclusions or a draft resolution).

Conclusions are adopted by the Delegations for the European Union and express only their position. In contrast to conclusions, resolutions express the position of the National Assembly or the Senate as a whole. Hence, a draft resolution is automatically sent for examination to one of the National Assembly's or the Senate's six Standing Committees competent on the matter. The Standing Committee in question can then appoint its own *rapporteur*. It hands down an opinion on the Delegation's draft resolution, which it can adopt, amend or reject. It must give its opinion within a period of one month following the referral.

Within eight days following the distribution of the Standing Committee's report, the draft resolution can be included on the National Assembly's agenda to be debated in plenary session, upon request by the chairperson of a political group, a Committee chairperson, the chairperson of the Delegation or the Government. If no request is made, the resolution adopted by the Committee is considered final, published in the *Journal Officiel* and transmitted to the Government. The Senate and the National Assembly can not adopt a common resolution.

Each member of parliament also has the right to propose a draft resolution, which must be examined by the responsible committee if the Government or the chairperson of a political group expressly requests it to be examined.

Since the entry into force of the Amsterdam Treaty in 1999, the Protocol on the role of national parliaments in the European Union provides for a period of six weeks between the time when the Commission forwards a draft legislative act to the Council and to the European Parliament and the date when this proposal is placed on the Council's agenda for adoption. In addition, the French Government made a commitment to wait a period of one month before adopting a position in Brussels during Council negotiations. This 'parliamentary scrutiny reserve' was introduced by the 'Balladur circular' of 19 July 1994 and was taken up by the 'Jospin circular' of 13 December 1999. The effect of this is that the Government has undertaken to oppose, for a period of one month, the placing of any draft act on the agenda of the European Council of ministers if the French Parliament has not completed scrutiny. An emergency procedure allows the Government to ask the chairmen of the Delegations to directly approve or reject a draft European text, without convening the Delegation, if the Community schedule requires the urgent adoption of a text. This procedure remains an exceptional one – at the time of writing, it had been used on only 277 occasions since 1994.

The scrutiny thereby exercised is a political process rather than a legal one, as France does not recognise the practice of the 'negotiating mandate' which is used in a broad manner by Scandinavian states, and by which a government is bound by the position of its parliament. Resolutions have a political impact, but they are not legally binding on the Government, which usually take them into account during the negotiations. Usually, a parliamentary resolution strengthens the Government's position, by enabling it to lean on the resolution to defend its position, especially on issues of national interest such as public services or the Common Agricultural Policy. Sometimes they re-orientate the Government's position, when Parliament adopts a stance that, without being opposed to that of the Government, can prove more daring (which it did *e.g.*, on the issue of the European Public Prosecutor).

Since 1993, 141 resolutions have been adopted by the National Assembly, of which only 45 have been adopted in public sessions (including 33 during the first four years of Article 88-4, from 1993 to 1996). Statistics reveal that the majority of resolutions were adopted during the first years of the implementation of Article 88-4: 70 between 1993 and 1996, 47 between 1997 and 2000 and only 24 since 1 January 2001. This significant decrease does not mean, however, that there has been a drop in the intensity of parliamentary scrutiny of European affairs. It is due to the cumbersome nature of the procedure for adopting resolutions, which constitutes a deterrent to the use of this instrument.

The French Parliament can not take a position on a text which is transmitted according to the Josselin or Pandraud Acts but which does not fall under Article 88-4.

Number of resolutions adopted by the National Assembly (as of January, 2005)

	1993	**1994**	**1995**	**1996**	**1997**	**1998**	**1999**	**2000**	**2001**	**2002**	**2003**	**2004**	**TOTAL**
Number of proposals for resolutions by Delegation rapporteur:	16	21	20	20	11	15	14	11	7	4	13	5	157
Total number of proposals for resolutions:	24	31	27	37	13	18	17	11	7	6	15	6	212
Number of resolutions adopted by the National Assembly:													
– in commission	5	8	11	13	12	10	7	11	5	4	8	2	**96**
– in public session	6	15	7	5	0	2	5	0	1	0	1	3	**45**
– in total	11	23	18	18	12	12	12	11	6	4	9	5	**141**

It may be noted before proceeding to an evaluation of the scrutiny practice, that the National Assembly and the Senate each have a Permanent Office to the European Union. These offices are housed on the premises of the European Parliament and of the French Permanent Representation to the European Union in Brussels. They are a highly valuable source of information for the Delegations and promote the development of inter-parliamentary relations.

(iii) Evaluation of Scrutiny Practice

The main objective of parliamentary scrutiny is making the Executive accountable in respect of European Union affairs. The extent to which this objective is fulfilled is difficult to assess, however, as there is no single performance indicator on the basis of which to judge this matter. According to the European Convention's Working Group on National Parliaments, the key factors that have an impact on the effectiveness of scrutiny are (a) the timeliness, scope and quality of information, covering all activities of the Union; (b) the existence of the possibility for a national parliament to formulate its position with regard to a proposal for a European Union legislative measure or action; (c) regular contacts and hearing with Ministers before and after Council meetings and European Council meetings; (d) the active involvement of sectoral or standing committees in the scrutiny process; (e) regular contacts between national parliamentarians and Members of the European Parliament; and (f) the availability of supporting staff, including the existence of a representative office in Brussels.[9]

According to these factors, the efficiency of the French parliamentary scrutiny over European Union affairs seems high. As regards (a), the European Delegations receive almost all European Union documents, including Second and Third Pillar documents in addition to work programmes, green and white papers, reports and communications and successive drafts of a legislative proposal. Insofar as concerns (b), they can formulate a position on the most important proposals, which are transmitted under Article 88-4 of the Constitution. As for (c), regular meetings are held with ministers before and after Council meetings, as well as European Council meetings. As regards (d), the Delegations have a representative office in Brussels and have significant resources. Some twenty-two staff members (including seven senior counsel and five administrators) work for the European Delegation of the National Assembly and ten (including three senior counsel and four administrators) for the European Delegation of the Senate.

[9] *Final Report of Working Group IV on the Role of National Parliaments*, CONV 353/02, 22 October 2002, p. 4–5.

However, on a negative note, the involvement of Sectoral Committees remains quite low and contacts between national parliamentarians and MEPs are scarce, even though MEPs are regularly invited to the European Delegations meetings.

Moreover, the parliament does not always make full use of its power to scrutinise the action of the Government. The majority of MPs belong to the ruling party and have no political interest in putting the Government in a difficult position on European Union affairs. Only Opposition parties would have an interest in doing so. In practice, however, they seldom challenge the Government on these issues. Their electoral incentive to do so is limited, due to the absence of any media coverage, and hence of any politicisation on most of the matters tackled by the European Delegations. The treatment of such sensitive issues as asylum and immigration, or of such controversial texts as directives on the liberalisation of services or the organisation of working time could gradually lead to greater political awareness. This would in turn reinforce the control exerted on the Government.

2. The French Parliament and the Implementation of European Union Law

The French parliament has a key role in implementing European Union Law, especially directives, once they are adopted. In view of France's poor record concerning the transposition of directives, the French parliament has undertaken a number of initiatives to reduce the number of directives which are not transposed on time.

(a) Implementing Directives: the Poor Record of France

The European Council which met in Stockholm in March 2001 took steps to speed up the implementation of Single Market directives in each member state by agreeing as an interim target that the implementation deficit of each member state should not exceed 1.5 per cent. The Council also set a 'zero tolerance' target for directives whose implementation was over two years late.

The Commission's Single Market Scoreboard ranks the performance of member states in terms of the number of directives not transposed by the due date and also shows the number of infringement cases against states arising from those directives. This 'name and shame' strategy helps governments of defaulting states to focus on improving their scores.

According to the Commission's Single Market Scoreboard of January 2005, France's transposition deficit was at this time more than double the 1.5 percent target, at 3.2 percent. With five directives whose implementation was over two years late, France also ranked last of the 'old' fifteen EU member states in terms of compliance with the 'zero tolerance' target in this regard. This backlog explains why at the time of writing France had recently been ranked second, behind Italy, for the number of infringement proceedings which had been instituted against it.[10]

(b) Spurring Action to Reduce the Backlog

The Government has resorted twice to ordinances under Article 38 of the French Constitution (which gives it the ability to legislate by the means of ordinances), in 2001 and 2004, in order to transpose directives. In 2004, the number of directives transposed through this procedure was limited (24 directives, compared to 48 directives and eleven regulations in 2001) and there was preliminary consultation between the Government and the Parliament. However, such resort to ordinances is not considered a satisfactory procedure, because it limits parliamentary debate.

For this reason the Delegation of the National Assembly for the European Union took the initiative of publishing an annual report listing the directives not transposed on time. This report lists directives the transposition period for which has expired and analyses the causes for the delay. This is a strong incentive for French Departments and Ministers to speed up transposition.

The Government also recently decided that a monthly transposition meeting would be held in the National Assembly and the Senate.

3. Strengthening the French Parliament's Scrutiny of European Union Affairs

A treaty which contains provisions of the kind which were to be found in the Constitutional Treaty will give a new role to national parliaments in the Union's legislative process. It is proposed to focus on the changes that would affect the French Parliament's scrutiny over European Union affairs, as well as on the amendment of the French Constitution of 1 March 2005, which was needed for the purposes of permitting ratification of the Constitutional Treaty.

[10] These figures dated from 31 October 2004.

(a) The French Constitution and the Implementation of the Constitutional Treaty

(i) The Protocol on the Role of National Parliaments

The Constitutional Treaty provided for an adapted form of the existing Protocol on the role of national parliaments in the European Union (which was annexed at Amsterdam to the Treaty on European Union and the Treaty Establishing the European Community). The newer Protocol was to increase the information transmitted to national parliaments, by adding the annual legislative programme as well as any other instrument of legislative planning or policy to the documents sent to MPs. However, this addition would not have affected the French Parliament, which already examines such documents in any case. The agendas and minutes of the Council of Ministers were also to be forwarded to national parliaments.

The revised Protocol required the Commission to forward directly all its draft European legislative acts and other documents to national parliaments upon publication. This was a minor change, which represented little progress. In the age of the internet, access to these texts, which are public, no longer poses difficulties.

(ii) The Protocol on the Application of the Principles of Subsidiarity and Proportionality

The Constitutional Treaty also adapted the Protocol on the application of the principles of subsidiarity and proportionality (which, again, had originally been annexed at Amsterdam to the Treaty on European Union and the Treaty Establishing the European Community.

The first innovation was the creation of the 'early warning' mechanism – a system of *a priori* political scrutiny (also referred to as the 'yellow card' mechanism). This procedure was to allow each chamber of all member states' parliaments to review any draft European legislative act and to submit, within six weeks, a reasoned opinion if it considered that the principle of subsidiarity had not been complied with. If such reasoned opinions asserting non-compliance with the principle of subsidiarity represented at least one third of the votes allocated to the national parliaments,[11] then the draft had to be reviewed. Following this review, the

[11] Each national parliament was allocated two votes, shared out on the basis of the national parliamentary system. In the case of a bicameral parliamentary system, each of the two chambers was to have one vote. The one third threshold was reduced to one quarter in the case of draft European legislative acts concerning judicial co-operation in criminal matters and police co-operation.

institution or the member states from which the draft European legislative act originated could decide to withdraw, maintain or amend the proposal and had to give reasons for this decision.

The second innovation was the right of national parliaments to bring an action before the Court of Justice, *via* their member states, on the grounds of infringement of the principle of subsidiarity by a legislative act.[12] This was thus an *ex post facto* jurisdictional scrutiny device.

The French Constitutional Council (*conseil constitutionnel*) ruled, in its decision of 19 November 2004, that these provisions required an amendment to the French Constitution,[13] as the French Parliament is not allowed to vote in situations which are not specifically provided for in the Constitution. The Constitution was thus amended on 1 March 2005[14] with the introduction of Article 88-5, the wording of which is as follows: [15]

> "Art. 88-5. – The National Assembly or the Senate may express a reasoned opinion on the compliance of a draft European legislative act with the principle of subsidiarity. The President of the Assembly concerned should send the reasoned opinion to the Presidents of the European Parliament, the Council and the Commission of the European Union. The government shall be informed thereof.
>
> Each Assembly may, in the same conditions, bring an action before the Court of Justice of the European Union against a European legislative act for infringement of the principle of subsidiarity. This action shall be transmitted to the Court of Justice by the government.

[12] Hence Article 8 of the Protocol on the Application of the Principles of Subsidiarity and Proportionality, which provided that

> "the Court of Justice of the European Union shall have jurisdiction in actions on grounds of infringement of the principle of subsidiarity by a European legislative act, brought in accordance with the rules laid down in Article III-365 of the Constitution by Member States, or notified by them in accordance with their legal order on behalf of their national Parliament or a chamber of it."

[13] Decision n° 2004-505 DC, available on the Constitutional Council web site: http://www.conseil-constitutionnel.fr/decision/2004/2004505/2004505dc.htm.

[14] On this revision, see National Assembly's Law Committee report n° 2033, 24 January 2005 ; National Assembly's European Delegation report n° 2024, 12 January 2005; Senate's Law Committee report n° 180, 9 February 2005.

[15] Note however that Article 88-5 was expressly stipulated to enter into force only if all the member states ratified the Constitutional Treaty. Editor's note: see for the latest developments in this regard prior to publication, the introduction to this book.

> In the manner laid down by the rules of procedure of each assembly, resolutions may be adopted to this end, even if Parliament is not in session".[16]

This new Article 88-5 explicitly recognised the individual right of each chamber, separately, to adopt reasoned opinions. Reasoned opinions would take the legal form of resolutions. The procedure for adopting reasoned opinions was to be specified by each House's regulations. It would not necessarily be identical in the National Assembly and the Senate.

In the National Assembly, the European Delegation published a report on the application of the principle of subsidiarity in November, 2004, which contained several proposals.[17] The Delegation would be given a central role. Subsidiarity *rapporteurs* of the Delegation would be entrusted with the task of identifying proposals which might violate the principle of subsidiarity. They would submit a draft reasoned opinion if they felt that a legislative act failed to comply with the subsidiarity principle. The Delegation would then adopt or reject the draft reasoned opinion. As regards what would happen after this first stage, three options were considered and reflected upon in the 2004 paper. At the time of writing it had not yet been decided yet which one of these options would be implemented. The first of the three options was that the Delegation's position would need to be endorsed by the Standing Committee concerned. (No examination in plenary session would be possible, because of the need to comply with the six week examination period specified by the Protocol). The second option was that the Standing Committee could confirm or quash the Delegation's position. However, in the event of a divergent position between the Delegation and the Standing Committee, examination in plenary would take place by right within a time period to be specified, only upon the request of a political group chairman. This option offered the opportunity for a debate in plenary, but hardly seemed compatible with the six-week deadline. The third option being considered was that no examination by a Standing Committee would be required and that the Delegation's position would be the National Assembly's final position. However, examinations in plenary would take place by right within a period of time to be specified, upon the request of the Government, a committee chairman or a group chairman.

Regarding the right to bring actions before the Court of Justice, it is worthy of note that under the new Article 88-5 of the Constitution, the French

[16] Author's translation.

[17] J. Lambert and D. Quentin, *Information Report no. 1919 on the application of the principle of subsidiarity*, 16 November 2004.

Government would be obliged to act if a chamber requested it to do so. However, this provision was to enter into force only if the Constitutional Treaty itself ever did so.[18]

(iii) The Right of Veto of National Parliaments under Article IV-444 of the Constitutional Treaty

Article IV-444 of the Constitutional Treaty provided for a so-called 'simplified revision procedure' regarding voting rules under the Treaty. This simplified procedure included provision for the extension by the European Council of qualified majority voting in the Council of Ministers to any area in which it was formerly required to act by unanimity.[19] Under Article IV-444, each national parliament was given a veto on the use of the simplified revision procedure. They were to have six months to exercise this right.

The French Constitutional Council decided that this provision also required an amendment of the 1958 Constitution.[20] Article 88-6 was therefore inserted into the French Constitution by the amendment of 1 March 2005. It reads as follows:

> "the Parliament may oppose a change of the rules on adoption of European Union acts according to the simplified revision procedure of the Treaty establishing a Constitution for Europe, by a resolution passed by the National Assembly and the Senate in identical terms".

The requirement that the resolution be passed by the National Assembly and the Senate in identical terms meant that there would have to be a procedure for the two chambers to reach agreement. During the debate leading up to the amendment of 1 March 2005, several deputies suggested that in the event of a disagreement between the two chambers, the National Assembly should make the final decision (as is the case for domestic statutes under Article 45 of the Constitution). However, this amendment to the constitutional bill was rejected. Indeed, the official government position on this matter, as well as the Senate's position was the contrary one that both Houses should have equal powers on this matter, as they do for the amendment of the French Constitution by virtue of Article 89.

---

[18] Editor's note: see concerning the latest developments regarding the Constitutional Treaty, the introduction to this book.

[19] Provision for extension of qualified majority voting in this manner is sometimes referred to as a "passerelle" procedure.

[20] Decision n° 2004-505 DC, *op. cit.*

(b) Towards a Strengthening of Art. 88-4 and of the European Delegations?

(i) The revision of Article 88-4 of the French Constitution

The Constitutional Treaty did not require a revision of Article 88-4. However, the subsidiarity early warning mechanism[21] might have created difficulty, because its scope is not the same as Article 88-4. The scope of the Constitutional Treaty's "European legislative acts" was not the same as that of Article 88-4 (which, it will be recalled, relates to draft measures at European Community or European Union level that are matters requiring legislation by statute under Article 34 of the Constitution of France).

If Article 88-4 had remained unchanged, there would have been cases where parliament would have been able to adopt a reasoned opinion on the basis of Article 88-5 (the early warning mechanism), but without the possibility of passing a resolution on the grounds of Article 88-4. This is why an amendment to the constitutional bill suggested by several deputies was adopted. This amendment provided that Article 88-4 would extend to all European legislative acts, in addition to the acts currently covered. This was a welcome simplification and a significant improvement.

The scope of Article 88-4

Scope of the current Article 88-4	Scope of Article 88-4 from the entering into force of the Constitutional Treaty
Any drafts of or proposals for instruments of the European Communities or the European Union containing provisions which are matters for statute under Article 34 of the French Constitution	- Any European legislative acts (including acts that do not contain provisions which are matters for statutes under Article 34 of the French Constitution) - Any other drafts of or proposals for instruments of the European Union containing provisions which are matters for statute (including non legislative European acts, such as regulations, if they fall under Article 34 of the French Constitution)
The Government may also lay before them other drafts of or proposals for instruments or any document issuing from a European Union institution (optional clause)	Unchanged

[21] Discussed in the text above.

Several MPs, including Edouard Balladur (the former Prime Minister of France and at this time chairperson of the Foreign Affairs Committee of the National Assembly), proposed another amendment to Article 88-4. They suggested that the Government should be obliged to transmit to parliament, under Article 88-4, any European act if the President of the National Assembly or the Senate, the chairperson of a Standing Committee or sixty deputies or senators, requested it. This would have made the "optional clause" of Article 88-4 mandatory for the Government in such cases.[22] This proposed amendment stemmed from the fact that the French Parliament was not able to pass a resolution on the recommendation of the European Commission of 6 October 2004 on Turkey's progress towards accession, because the Government refused to transmit it to the Parliament in application of the optional clause of Article 88-4. This amendment was rejected. However, the Government committed itself to transmit, as a general rule subject to limited exceptions, all documents requested by members of parliament. This commitment should be formalised in a forthcoming circular.

(ii) Towards a Strengthening of the European Delegations?

The European Delegations are called 'Delegations' because the number of Standing Committees is limited to six by Article 43 of the French Constitution. France is the only Member State, where the authority tasked with monitoring and scrutinising European Affairs is not called a 'Committee' or 'Commission'. This is the reason why several MPs proposed either to increase the number of Standing Committees to seven, thus enabling the creation of a seventh – European Affairs – Standing Committee, or to insert mention of a European Affairs Committee into Article 88-5 of the French Constitution. However, these amendments were rejected.

The impact of parliamentary scrutiny on the actual content of European Union legislation is difficult to assess as in most instances the majority in each of the two Houses will adopt a position similar to that of the Government. Nonetheless, the system makes a worthwhile contribution to the transparency and legitimacy of the European Union's legislative process and to bridging the gap between citizens and European Union institutions.

It may be added that the strengthening of European inter-parliamentary co-operation, especially through the Conference of Community and European

[22] See National Assembly's Foreign Affairs Committee report n° 2023, 11 January 2005.

Affairs Committees of Parliaments of the European Union (COSAC)[23] has been an important means of improving the parliamentary scrutiny of the European Union. Looking to the future, the creation of a COSAC permanent secretariat (which occurred in 2004), as well as the introduction of the possibility of COSAC adopting contributions by a three-quarters majority instead of unanimity, should enhance this body's efficiency. In addition, the launch of the new IPEX (interparliamentary EU information exchange) website is also expected to help to increase links between national Parliaments and to create a real network between them.[24]

Annex

Article 34 of the French Constitution of 1958

"Statutes shall be passed by Parliament.

Statutes shall determine the rules concerning:

- civic rights and the fundamental guarantees granted to citizens for the exercise of their public liberties; the obligations imposed for the purposes of national defence upon citizens in respect of their persons and their property;
- nationality, the status and legal capacity of persons, matrimonial regimes, inheritance and gifts;
- the determination of serious crimes and other major offences and the penalties applicable to them; criminal procedure; amnesty; the establishment of new classes of courts and tribunals and the regulations governing the members of the judiciary;
- the base, rates and methods of collection of taxes of all types; the issue of currency.

Statutes shall likewise determine the rules concerning:

- the electoral systems of parliamentary assemblies and local assemblies;
- the creation of categories of public establishments;
- the fundamental guarantees granted to civil and military personnel employed by the State;
- the nationalisation of enterprises and transfers of ownership in enterprises from the public to the private sector.

[23] COSAC was created in 1989 on the initiative of the then president of the National Assembly, Mr Laurent Fabius. See further the chapter on COSAC in this volume by Morten Knudsen and Yves Carl.
[24] The internet address of IPEX is http://www.ecprd.org/ipex/index.asp.

Statutes shall determine the fundamental principles of:

- the general organisation of national defence;
- the self-government of territorial units, their powers and their resources;
- education;
- the regime governing ownership, rights *in rem* and civil and commercial obligations;
- labour law, trade-union law and social security.

Finance Acts shall determine the resources and obligations of the State in the manner and with the reservations specified in an institutional Act.

Social Security Finance Acts shall determine the general conditions for the financial balance of social security and, in the light of their revenue forecasts, shall determine expenditure targets in the manner and with the reservations specified in an institutional Act.

Programme Acts shall determine the objectives of the economic and social action of the State.
The provisions of this article may be enlarged upon and complemented by an institutional Act."

Article 88-4 of the French Constitution of 1958 (current version)

"The Government shall lay before the National Assembly and the Senate any drafts of or proposals for instruments of the European Communities or the European Union containing provisions which are matters for statute as soon as they have been transmitted to the Council of the European Union. It may also lay before them other drafts of or proposals for instruments or any document issuing from a European Union institution.

In the manner laid down by the rules of procedure of each assembly, resolutions may be passed, even if Parliament is not in session, on the drafts, proposals or documents referred to in the preceding paragraph."

Article 88-4 of the French Constitution of 1958 (stipulated to apply from the time of the entering into force of the Constitutional Treaty)

"The Government shall lay before the National Assembly and the Senate any European legislative acts as well as any other drafts of or proposals for instruments of the European Union containing provisions which are matters for statute as soon as they have been transmitted to the Council of the

European Union. It may also lay before them other drafts of or proposals for instruments or any document issuing from a European Union institution.

In the manner laid down by the rules of procedure of each assembly, resolutions may be passed, even if parliament is not in session, on the drafts, proposals or documents referred to in the preceding paragraph."

18.
COSAC – its Role to Date and its Potential in the Future

Morten Knudsen and Yves Carl[1]

1. Introduction

1989 – the year in which the Conference of Community and European Affairs Committees of Parliaments of the European Union (or COSAC[2]) was established – was a turbulent one for Europe. It was in this year that a peaceful revolution swept over Communist Central and Eastern Europe, leading to the collapse of the Soviet Union and the reunification of Germany. On 9 November, 1989, the Berlin wall was demolished by crowds of East and West Germans. The new geopolitical situation led the governments in Paris and Berlin to take the view that there was a need for further European integration. The then French President, François Mitterrand and German Chancellor, Helmut Kohl therefore promoted the idea that an intergovernmental conference should be convened to meet these new challenges and discuss how the European Communities could develop into a political union alongside an economic and monetary union. Talks on the future of this Europe began at an intergovernmental conference in December, 1990. It was in the shadow of these dramatic events that the first meetings of COSAC took place, with its first conference being held in Paris in the French National Assembly on 16 and 17 November 1989.

The development in the role of COSAC since this time has to a large extent mirrored the development of European integration and the role and functions

[1] Morten Knudsen is principal advisor on European Union affairs in the Danish Parliament. Prior to taking up this position, he worked for over two years on secondment as the permanent member of the COSAC secretariat. Yves Carl is the permanent representative of the Luxembourg Chamber of Deputies to the European institutions and a former member of the COSAC Secretariat.. The contents of this chapter reflect the personal views of the authors and should not be taken to represent the official position either of COSAC or of the national parliaments of Denmark or Luxembourg.
[2] The acronym COSAC derives from the French name of this body, 'la conférence des organes spécialisés dans les affaires communautaires'.

of the national parliaments within the European Union. Four – at the time of writing, shortly to be five – intergovernmental conferences have already been convened together with two Conventions during the short lifetime of COSAC. Of these, three – shortly to be four – of the intergovernmental conferences and one of the Conventions have reflected on the role of national parliaments.

However, the most appropriate way in which COSAC itself ought to develop has never been clear. Several schools of thought have existed. One main objective of COSAC has always been to reinforce the involvement of national parliaments in European matters and thereby to increase the accountability and democratic legitimacy of the European Union. A key question in this context has always been whether COSAC should become a player in the decision-making process at European level or whether COSAC should rather serve to enhance European Union scrutiny within member states by facilitating an exchange of information and best practices between the parliaments at European level.

Over the years, some national parliaments promoted the idea of creating a European Senate to reduce the democratic deficit, but today such notions have been definitively abandoned by the parliaments: the debate in the European Convention which produced the first draft of the Constitutional Treaty showed that there was only very limited support for such ideas. At this point, COSAC seems to be in the process of establishing itself as a platform for exchange of information and best practices for scrutiny of European Union issues in national parliaments. However new issues are beginning to appear on the horizon.

It is difficult to predict how the role of COSAC will evolve in the coming years. But the increased involvement of sectoral committees in the scrutiny of European matters in some national parliaments is challenging the traditional monopoly of European affairs committees – and that of COSAC. In addition, a broader range of inter-parliamentary activities, aimed at involving sectoral committees in European matters, is emerging in the European Union: some such activities are orchestrated by national parliaments, and some by the European Parliament. Some are organised on an *ad hoc* basis, and others are intended to become more regular events. An appropriate key discussion point for COSAC is whether or how sectoral committees should be involved in the process of inter-parliamentary cooperation.

The challenge for COSAC will be to adapt to a situation in which more players are involved in the scrutiny of European Union matters – a European inter-parliamentary cooperation in which sectoral committees play a more prominent role.

The purpose of this chapter is to give account of COSAC's role to date and its future potential. As such, it is divided into two parts. The first part provides a detailed historical description of the creation and development of COSAC in the context of the intensive acceleration of European integration that took place in the years from COSAC's establishment in 1989 up to COSAC's meeting in Luxembourg in May, 2005. In the second part, the question of the future role of COSAC is addressed, although the answer to this question was rendered at least temporarily less certain by the double rejection of the Constitutional Treaty in France and the Netherlands, given that certain changes to the functions and role of COSAC were foreseen in this Treaty. The task of trying to predict the future of COSAC has thus become more hazardous. Because of this, it is proposed to focus on two of the main challenges which COSAC currently faces: first, how does COSAC fit into the wider picture of inter-parliamentary activities in the European Union, as new actors (*i.e.,* sectoral committees) move into the field of parliamentary scrutiny of European matters? And secondly, what could COSAC's role be in monitoring the application of the principle of subsidiarity?

2. COSAC: Historical Development[3]

(a) Creation of COSAC

The paternity of COSAC is commonly and correctly attributed to Laurent Fabius, the then Speaker of the French National Assembly, who took the initiative to propose the establishment of an inter-parliamentary body composed of members of national parliaments specialised in European affairs in 1989. But important inspiration had already come from a conference organised by the Belgian House of Representatives in Brussels in May 1987 which had brought together some seventy delegates both from committees of the national parliaments which specialised in European affairs and from the European Parliament. During this meeting, many participants had expressed the hope that the experiment would be followed up by regular meetings, if possible organised on a half-yearly basis by the country which held the presidency of the Council. The European Parliament had also provided important impetus for the creation of COSAC by promoting a similar initiative in a resolution which it had adopted in February 1989, in which it called for regular joint meetings to be held between representatives

[3] This part of the chapter is based on documents made available by the Belgian parliament, the French parliament, and the COSAC archives.

of European affairs committees of national parliaments and the European Parliament's standing committees.[4]

A number of reasons lay behind these initiatives. One important reason was a feeling of loss of contact with Community policies in many national parliaments in the wake of the introduction of direct elections to the European Parliament in 1979. Up until 1979, members of the European Parliament had been appointed from and by national parliaments.

The aspiration of national parliaments to increase their role in the European decision-making process was formally endorsed by the speakers of the parliaments of the then twelve member states at a meeting of the Conference of the Speakers of the Parliaments of the Member States of the EEC and of the European Parliament in Madrid in May, 1989. In accordance with an initiative tabled by Mr Fabius, the speakers proposed a number of initiatives to strengthen the role of national parliaments in the Community in European affairs.[5] One of these was to create a special forum where European affairs committees of the parliaments could discuss topics of common interest on a regular basis. The speakers proposed that this conference should meet on a regular basis in order to debate topics of common interest decided in advance,[6] and that the conference should in principle be organised biannually by the parliament of the member state holding the presidency of the Community's Council of Ministers.

---

[4] The European Parliament resolution (based on a report by Hans-Joachim Seeler MEP (A2-348/88, 6 January 1989) was adopted on 16 February, 1989. (See [1989] OJ C69/149 (20 March 1989)). This initiative probably stemmed more from a desire on the part of the European Parliament to control the process than from any wish by it to see regular meetings between European affairs committees of national parliaments. As was stated in a note from the European Parliament's Secretary General, Mr Vinci and the Director General of its Directorate General for Research, Mr Palmer, to the President of Parliament, Lord Plum, "it would not be in the European Parliament's interest to allow such meetings to develop outwith its control". (Note reference number FP/ms, Luxembourg, 14 September, 1988, Directorate General for Research (Division for Relations with National Parliaments)).

[5] See L. Fabius, *Les Parlements Européens dans la perspective de l'Europe de 1993. Le traitement des affairs communautaires et la collaboration entre les chambres* (Report presented at the Conference of the Speakers of the Parliaments of the Member States of the EEC and of the European Parliament, held in Madrid on 20 May 1989).

[6] Conference of the Speakers of the Parliaments of the Member States of the EEC and of the European Parliament, Madrid, 20 May 1989.

The First Conference

The first meeting of this inter-parliamentary conference (which was not called COSAC from the beginning but rather was provisionally styled the Interparliamentary Conference of Bodies Specialised in European Affairs) was convened by the French National Assembly on 16 and 17 November 1989 and involved the participation of ten of the then twelve member states of the Community (the representatives of two countries being absent because of recent elections).[7] The agenda of the meeting focused on an issue which is still of concern today – namely, how to increase parliamentary scrutiny of European Union affairs. The main question was how the involvement of national parliaments in European Union affairs could be reinforced either through a strengthening of parliamentary scrutiny at the national level or by enhanced inter-parliamentary cooperation between parliaments.

The first meeting revealed fundamental differences of opinion on how democratic legitimacy could best be attained in the European Union. In particular the idea of creating a European Senate composed of representatives of national parliaments – an idea which had been launched by the Speaker of the French Senate, Mr Poher in an article in *Le Figaro* – provoked a very lively debate.[8] However, most parliaments favoured achieving democratic legitimacy either by increasing the role of national parliaments at the national level, or by strengthening the role of the European Parliament.

The French Presidency of the Conference had prepared an ambitious set of draft conclusions, but the divergent views of the parliaments permitted only a less elaborate set of conclusions in which the parliaments confined themselves to agreeing to improve the reciprocal provision of information by means of the systematic exchange of texts adopted by them concerning European affairs.

(b) Establishment Phase

The question of how to remedy the democratic deficit in the European Union stayed on the agenda of the next COSAC conferences, influenced by the

[7] The two countries which did not send representatives were Spain and Greece. Some parliaments, such as the Luxembourg Chamber of Deputies, the Belgian Senate, and the Italian Chamber of Deputies did not yet have bodies which specialised in European affairs. The Belgian Senate and the Italian Chamber were therefore represented by their foreign affairs committees, while Luxembourg was represented by the President of the Chamber.

[8] See *Le Figaro*, 15 November 1989.

debate on the future of the European Communities which was effectively launched with the European Council's decision in April 1990 to convene an intergovernmental conference with the aim of examining how the then European Economic Community could develop into a political, economic, and monetary union.[9]

Members of national parliaments agreed at these conferences that there was a need to strengthen the democratic legitimacy of the Community, but were unable to agree how this problem could be resolved. Some felt it necessary to strengthen the role of the European Parliament, while others favoured a stronger role for national parliaments in scrutinising European affairs at the national level. The idea of a European Senate was reiterated by some delegations, but no serious attempts were made to formulate concrete proposals concerning its composition or powers.

Two issues in particular preoccupied COSAC in relation to this debate at the first meetings, which we will address in more detail: the organisation of the so-called 'Assizes', which were to bring together national and European parliamentarians for a debate on the future development of the Community and the adoption of COSAC's first rules of procedure.

(i) The Assizes

The Assizes were held in the Italian Chamber of Deputies in Rome from 27–30 November 1990 on the eve of the beginning of the intergovernmental conference that would ultimately lead to the Treaty on European Union. It was comprised of 173 national parliamentarians and 85 members of the European Parliament.

The idea of organising the Assizes had been proposed by the French President, François Mitterrand in a speech on 25 October 1989 before the European Parliament, and had later been supported by two resolutions of the European Parliament, which had seen this as an opportunity to gain support for its Spinelli Report proposals, which had provided a blueprint for a Treaty Establishing a European Union.[10] At its meeting in Cork in May 1990, COSAC had welcomed the principle of organising the Assizes in order to discuss possible treaty changes but had wanted to exercise influence on their organisation. Hence delegations had considered it necessary that a restricted

---

[9] See the Presidency Conclusions of the special meeting of the European Council in Dublin, 28 April 1990.

[10] The Spinelli Report was adopted by the European Parliament on 14 February 1984.

meeting of the chairpersons of European affairs committees and of the European Parliament be held with a view to preparing the conference. This meeting had subsequently taken place in the Belgian parliament on 26 June and a number of organisational issues had been addressed. However, the formal decision to convene the Assizes and settle the organisation of the event had been taken by the speakers of the parliaments at a meeting on 20 September 1990. Apart from settling issues such as the composition, working method, and presidency of the Assizes, the speakers had also ensured a link to COSAC by establishing a drafting committee composed of the chairmen of European affairs committees in addition to five MEPs charged with the task of drafting the final declaration of the Assizes.[11]

At the end of the Assizes a final declaration was adopted endorsing a number of proposals for treaty reform (mostly proposals which emanated from the European Parliament). But despite this apparently successful outcome to the Assizes, many parliaments refused to repeat the experiment. For some parliaments, the Assizes had failed to agree on the kind of parliamentary participation in the Community which they had hoped for. Others felt that the European Parliament had hijacked the conference for its own purposes.

(ii) The First Rules of COSAC

Another key issue for COSAC in the first years of its existence was the question of its organisation and composition. Both the first and second conferences (in Paris and Cork, respectively) decided on some points concerning its organisation. However, a genuine set of rules of procedure was not endorsed until the fourth conference, which took place in Luxembourg from 6–7 May 1991.[12] It was on this occasion that the name 'COSAC' was agreed upon.

---

[11] At its conference of 1–2 October, 1990 in Rome (just eight weeks before the Assizes) COSAC attempted to influence the agenda of the Assizes by recommending that the debate be divided into four general topics: (i) the new goals of the Community; (ii) the strengthening of democratic legitimacy; (iii) the allocation of competences; and (iv) relations with other countries and institutions of Europe. It was agreed that the chairpersons of the European affairs committees in addition to five Members of the European Parliament (*i.e.,* a body identical with the drafting committee established by the Speakers) should finalise the preparations of the Assizes. However, at a meeting on 12 November, the triple presidency of the Assizes (*i.e.,* the two Italian chambers and the European Parliament) refused to accept COSAC's proposal for the agenda, which they felt would effectively alter the decision which had been reached by the speakers in Rome on 20 September.

[12] The formal adoption of COSAC's first rules of procedure had to wait until the fifth COSAC meeting in The Hague from 11–12 November 1991, because the question about the procedure for revising the rules of procedure could not be resolved at the fourth COSAC meeting in Luxembourg.

The new rules were agreed only after exhausting negotiations, in which the composition and voting methods of COSAC became points of contention. The European Parliament feared that the adoption of a set of rules of procedure would be a first step towards the creation of a second parliamentary chamber which would call into question the European Parliament's prerogatives. At the insistence of the European Parliament, therefore, the draft rules presented by the Luxembourg Presidency were significantly amended. The position of the European Parliament was non-negotiable on two points in particular. First, it wanted to be involved together with the presidential troika in the preparation of the agendas of COSAC.[13] Secondly, it wanted all decisions to be taken by consensus. Both of these points were conceded to the European Parliament.

A further matter which gave rise to serious difficulties was reaching agreement on the procedure for revising COSAC's rules of procedure. For the European Parliament, the requirement of unanimity in this regard was a *conditio sine qua non* of its participation in the Conference, and the idea of allowing the rules of procedure to be amended by the two thirds majority proposed by the Luxembourg Presidency was firmly rejected. Delegations eventually agreed to endorse the European Parliament's demand for unanimity.

The European Parliament was also dissatisfied with the number of seats it had been allocated (*i.e.*, six – the same number as all other parliaments), partly from its fear that COSAC could become the framework for future Assizes, and the European Parliament had accounted for a full third of the seats at the Rome Assizes. However the other delegations were not willing to compromise on this point. The number of participants per member state was eventually fixed at six, with the composition of each delegation being left to the individual parliaments themselves.

(c) The Entry into Force of the Treaty of Maastricht

(i) National Parliaments in the Treaty

The Treaty on European Union (or the Treaty of Maastricht, as it is also known) which was signed by heads of state or government on 7 February

[13] The so-called Presidential troika of COSAC is composed of representatives of the parliament of the member state holding the presidency of the Council, representatives of the parliament of the member state which held the preceding presidency, representatives of the parliament of the member state which will hold the next presidency, and representatives of the European Parliament. Each parliamentary delegation consists of two members.

1992, and which established at least the beginnings of a political union alongside an economic and monetary union, included a small victory for national parliaments. Two Declarations attached to the Treaty for the first time mentioned the role of national parliaments.

The first – Declaration No. 13 on the Role of National Parliaments in the European Union – was aimed at strengthening the scrutiny of European Union matters at national level. The declaration expressed the intergovernmental conference's view that it was important to encourage "greater involvement of national Parliaments in the activities of the European Union" and called for an increased exchange of information between national parliaments and the European Parliament. Governments were asked to "ensure, inter alia, that national Parliaments receive Commission proposals for legislation in good time for information or possible examination". The other Declaration – Declaration No. 14 on the Conference of the Parliaments – invited national parliaments and the European Parliament to meet as necessary as a Conference of the Parliaments or "Assizes" and declared that this body would be consulted on the main features of the European Union. It was even foreseen that the Presidents of the European Council and of the Commission would report to each session of these Assizes on the state of the Union.

Despite this breakthrough, delegates of many parliaments in COSAC expressed disappointment with the outcome of the intergovernmental conference and proposed the adoption of a resolution calling upon governments to convene a new intergovernmental conference to address the democratic deficit properly. According to critics, the Maastricht Treaty had not taken sufficiently into account the recommendations of the Rome Assizes. But no agreement could be reached on any such initiatives. This was first and foremost because of divergences in views between parliaments on the future development of the Community at a very sensitive time (*i.e.* just before Denmark's referendum on the Maastricht Treaty). However, it also clearly demonstrated one of the limitations of COSAC's decision-making: its consensus-based approach.

The call in Declaration No. 13 on governments to ensure that national parliaments receive Commission proposals for legislation in good time was generally welcomed by COSAC, even if some would have preferred to see legally binding provisions obliging governments to forward these proposals. Most delegations, however, had major doubts about the creation of the Conference of the Parliaments (Assizes) as had been suggested in Declaration 14. The unfortunate experience of the 1990 Assizes had not been forgotten by national parliaments.

(ii) Ratification Crisis

The question of the democratic deficit suddenly became highly topical when a majority of Danish voters rejected the Maastricht Treaty in a referendum on 2 June 1992. And when only a very small majority voted 'yes' in a popular vote on the same topic in France the following September, a sense of shock was created in the Community.

The European Council's response to the crisis was to promote the concepts of subsidiarity, openness and democracy. However, COSAC was paralysed and kept a rather low profile throughout the ratification crisis, which lasted until Denmark finally endorsed the treaty following the positive result of a second referendum in May 1993. There was simply no consensus among national parliaments about how to proceed. No joint communiqués were adopted by COSAC during the crisis. At the COSAC meeting held in London in November 1992, the United Kingdom Presidency drew up some conclusions in the name of the COSAC chairpersons, which supported the declaration adopted by the European Council in Birmingham confirming the need for more democracy, subsidiarity and openness. This was not saying very much. The Copenhagen COSAC, which took place in May 1993, shortly before the second Danish referendum on the Maastricht Treaty, examined the role and working methods of COSAC, but no conclusions could be reached on how matters could be improved.[14]

(d) Treaty status for COSAC

It did not take COSAC long to regain the initiative after the conclusion of the ratification process which allowed the Treaty of Maastricht to come into force on 1 November 1993. Already, at the COSAC meeting in Athens in May 1994, discussions began again about how the role of national parliaments and COSAC could be strengthened. In particular the prospects of a new debate on the future of the European Union in the run-up to yet another intergovernmental conference (which was envisaged by the Maastricht treaty for 1996) influenced the agenda of COSAC. The role of national parliaments returned as a top priority for COSAC, and for the first time serious discussions about giving COSAC treaty status were initiated. The idea of enshrining COSAC in the treaties was conceived in this context. Deliberations in COSAC revealed two schools of thought. One group of

[14] Discussions took place on the basis of a paper which had been prepared by the Dutch Parliament and which suggested that the main purpose of COSAC was that of exchanging information between the parliaments on an informal basis rather than that of being a decision-making body.

delegations wanted to create a mechanism for a collective representation by national parliaments – which they believed was possible without establishing a new second chamber. Other delegations, however, opposed this suggestion, because they preferred arrangements that strengthened the national scrutiny procedures. At the Paris COSAC in February, 1995, the French National Assembly and the Senate once again launched the idea of giving national parliaments a collective role at European level – either in the form of some kind of European Senate or as a 'High Consultative Council' monitoring the principle of subsidiarity.[15] Both ideas were rejected at the COSAC meeting. However, this was not to be the last word on this matter.

(i) Reflection Groups

Member state governments had decided at the Corfu European Council in June 1995 to establish a so-called 'Reflection Group' under the chairmanship of the Spanish state secretary of foreign affairs, Carlos Westendorp, to prepare the agenda of the intergovernmental conference. National parliaments were not invited to participate.[16] Notwithstanding this lack of representation, the question of an enhanced role for national parliaments in the European Union was considered very seriously by the Reflection Group. When it published its progress report in September 1995, the Reflection Group suggested two broad areas for reflection regarding the future role of national parliaments. First, it advocated (i) the exploration of formulas for associating national parliaments with the Community institutions, in addition to (ii) the study of the possibility of inserting Declarations 13 and 14 into the Treaty as legally binding instruments, and (iii) the examination in more detail of ways of simplifying the task of each national parliament of supervising Union decisions. Secondly, it advocated the study of a proposal to create a High Consultative Council composed of delegations from national parliaments, in order to monitor the principle of subsidiarity.

Three months later, however, in December 1995, when the Reflection Group published its final report,[17] it had become generally positive about the idea of giving treaty force to some elements of Declaration 13, but the notion of

[15] The two chambers of the French parliament were not in agreement on the details, however. It was the Senate which proposed the creation of a second chamber, whereas the National Assembly suggested the establishment of an inter-parliamentary council dealing with the application of the subsidiarity principle.

[16] The European Parliament, however, had two representatives in the Reflection Group: Elmar Brok (PPE) and Elisabeth Guigou (PSE).

[17] Both reports of the Westendorp reflection group referred to in the text above are to be found, at the time of writing, at http://europa.eu.int/en/agenda/igc-home/eu-doc/reflect/.

establishing a High Consultative Council or any kind of second chamber was firmly rejected by it. Instead the Group stated ambiguously that COSAC was 'a favourable formula' for the improvement of relations between national parliaments and the European Parliament. At the same time, however, the Group expressed doubts about the wisdom of giving COSAC treaty status.

This view was not shared by a special parliamentary reflection group, which had been created to compensate for the lack of representation in the Westendorp Group.[18] Most importantly, this body called for the insertion into the Treaty of a role for national parliaments and for COSAC, and suggested that a body like COSAC should be empowered to monitor the compliance of draft European Union legislation with the principle of subsidiarity. Finally, the European institutions should be obliged to transmit legislative proposals directly to national parliaments.

The Turin European Council of March 1996, which initiated the intergovernmental conference, finally settled the question of whether the conference should address the issue of collective representation of national parliaments at European level, by declaring that the intergovernmental conference should 'examine how and to what extent national parliaments could, also collectively, better contribute to the Union's tasks'.

(ii) COSAC

The full COSAC proved itself to be not quite as bold as the parliamentary reflection group. The largely French-driven proposal to incorporate COSAC in a Treaty article was rejected by many delegations, because they feared this would be a first step towards the creation of a second chamber. However, most delegations accepted the need to improve the functioning of COSAC. It was therefore decided to mandate the COSAC presidential troika to prepare a report on an improved functioning of COSAC to be presented at the Dublin COSAC on 15–16 October 1996.

As so often before, however, there was no consensus among national parliaments about COSAC's functions and future role. At the Dublin

[18] The parliamentary reflection group was established on the initiative of the Speaker of the Belgian Chamber of Representatives, Charles-Ferdinand Nothomb, and was backed by the French National Assembly. The group was established by the Conference of Speakers at a meeting on 19 April in Paris, was chaired by the Vice-President of the French *National Assembly*, Ms Nicole Catala, and met for the first time in Paris on 29 June 1995. Its next meetings were held in Brussels on 23 September, Luxembourg on 26 October, and Athens on 4 December 1995.

COSAC, delegations could not agree on the proposal that COSAC should be mentioned in the Treaty. However, it was accepted that COSAC should be able to pursue certain specific issues, *e.g.*, subsidiarity, Second and Third Pillar items, and questions relating to the fundamental rights of European Union citizens, with a view to arriving at some ideas as to how progress could be made in respect of these issues. This was made subject to the condition that the conclusions which COSAC arrived at should not be binding for national parliaments.

A note which the Irish European Union Presidency submitted to the intergovernmental conference on 15 October[19] – the first day of the Dublin COSAC meeting – showed a certain similarity with the conclusions of the Dublin COSAC meeting, but the inspiration which it drew from the parliamentary reflection group was even clearer. The note fully endorsed the proposals that COSAC should be given treaty status and be empowered to express its views on the compliance of legislative proposals with the subsidiarity principle or on legislative proposals within the area of justice and home affairs which might have direct bearing on the freedoms of individuals.

(e) The Amsterdam Protocol on the Role of National Parliaments

Agreement was reached by the heads of state and government on the Treaty of Amsterdam in the early hours of 18 June 1997. The agreement on this Treaty constituted a breakthrough for COSAC. A special Protocol on the Role of National Parliaments in the European Union contained the first acknowledgment of COSAC in a document of treaty status.[20] The Protocol provided for the possibility of COSAC examining draft European Union legislation and making any contribution it deemed appropriate for the attention of the institutions of the European Union – notably in relation to the application of the principle of subsidiarity, the area of freedom, security, and justice, and questions regarding fundamental rights. However, the Protocol provided that such contributions would in no way bind national parliaments or prejudge their positions. It should also be borne in mind that because COSAC's own rules of procedure provided for it proceeding only when unanimity existed, the new powers could only be used if all parliaments were willing to do so.

---

[19] CONF 3948/96, 15 October 1996.

[20] This Protocol was annexed by the High Contracting Parties at Amsterdam – in other words, by the member states – to the Treaty on European Union and the Treaties establishing the European Communities.

Notwithstanding the agreement by the member states on the Protocol and the strengthened role which this gave to COSAC, the controversy concerning the most appropriate role for COSAC – and the underlying differences concerning the possibility of giving national parliaments a role at European level – did not come to an end. Instead the Protocol revived the old divisions between parliaments about the role of national parliaments in the European Union. Discussions in COSAC on how to implement the Protocol went on for almost two years without any agreement being reached.

Eventually a working group set up by the Berlin COSAC in Spring 1999 managed to broker a deal which was endorsed by all delegations, except on two particular points.[21] Germany, supported by Austria and Luxembourg, wanted to add German as a working language for COSAC along with English and French. Denmark and Portugal insisted that the European Parliament should not participate in votes on contributions which were addressed to the European Union institutions. Proposals for setting up a secretariat and introducing majority decisions were rejected at this stage as clearly lacking sufficient support among delegations.

At the full COSAC meeting in Helsinki in October, 1999, the question, in particular, of the European Parliament's participation led to a heated debate. Spain, France, the Netherlands, Portugal, Denmark, and Italy insisted on making it absolutely clear in the rules of procedure that the European Parliament should not participate in votes on contributions addressed to the European Union institutions. On the other side, the European Parliament's delegation led by Vice-President David Martin, insisted on maintaining a principle of equality in COSAC between the European Parliament and national parliaments. Mr Martin said he had no mandate to accept the demand concerning COSAC's rules of procedure by the parliaments, but was willing to issue a unilateral declaration stating that the European Parliament would abstain from voting on any contribution which was addressed to it.

Despite the differences of opinions, the Helsinki COSAC adopted the new rules of procedure without any changes to the rules themselves being made which would have accommodated the views of those parliaments which felt that the European Parliament should not participate in votes on contributions addressed to the European Union institutions – but

[21] The working group was composed of representatives from all parliaments except those of Greece and Spain and also the European Parliament, which did not participate.

nonetheless with the declaration from the European Parliament having made it clear that it would refrain from participating in votes on contributions addressed to itself. It was agreed that the position of the European Parliament within COSAC should be studied further during the Portuguese Presidency of the Council which followed, in order to make changes to the rules of procedure on this question. The COSAC meeting in Lisbon in May 2000 did not, however, pursue the question any further. Instead, a more general debate was held about the relations between the members of the national parliaments and the European Parliament. No one suggested any further rule changes in relation to the question of the European Parliament's role in COSAC.

(f) En Route to the Future of Europe

With the agreement on the implementation of the Amsterdam Protocol, COSAC was in principle ready to become a player in the legislative process of the European Union. However, many parliaments remained reluctant to take up this new role, and with unanimity still prevailing in the decision-making process of COSAC, it became clear that the putting into effect of the new powers to examine European Union draft legislation would have to wait.

Instead COSAC meetings in the period 2000 to 2001 were dominated by a new round of discussions on the future of Europe. Despite noteworthy progress by the Amsterdam Treaty in a number of fields such as the extension of the use of qualified majority voting in the Council and the increased use of co-decision (favouring the role of the European Parliament in the legislative process), a small number of key institutional issues were left unresolved. The European Union therefore had to embark on another intergovernmental conference, which was convened in early February 2000, under the Portuguese Presidency, and concluded in Nice during the French Presidency in December 2000.

Many parliaments felt that the rules of the Amsterdam Protocol had failed to address their concerns adequately. But whereas there was no consensus on the reopening of the provisions concerning the role of COSAC, the idea of adjustments to the part of the Protocol which concerned the transmission of European Union documents to national parliaments was supported by all parliaments. The meeting of COSAC in Versailles in October 2000 therefore called on the Nice intergovernmental conference to modify the Protocol so as to ensure that a minimum delay of fifteen days (or one week in urgent cases) should be observed between the conclusion of any discussion of a legislative proposal in COREPER and the final decision on it in the Council.

However, this proposal was not taken up in the Nice Treaty.[22] In fact, the intergovernmental conference did not address the question of the role of national parliaments at all.

(i) The Role of National Parliaments Back on the Agenda

The question of the role of national parliaments was, however, effectively put back on the European Union agenda with the decision at the Nice intergovernmental conference to launch a wider and more in-depth debate on the future of Europe. This was first and foremost because in a Declaration agreed upon by the member states at Nice – Declaration No. 23 on the Future of the Union – four themes were identified which were to be addressed in another series of reforms at an intergovernmental conference in 2004: the division of competences between the European Union on the one hand, and member states on the other; the status of the Charter of Fundamental Rights of the European Union; the simplification of the treaties; and finally (and most interestingly, for COSAC), "the role of national parliaments in the European architecture".[23] Secondly, however, it was because the outcome of the Nice intergovernmental conference provoked a debate as to how the European Union could most appropriately prepare the 2004 intergovernmental conference. The then President of the Council, the Swedish Prime Minister, Göran Persson, called upon COSAC to contribute to these future discussions at the Stockholm COSAC meeting in May 2001. Support for the idea of organising a special European Convention composed of national parliamentarians along with MEPs, government representatives, and representatives from the Commission, was at this time becoming more and more widespread. Yet securing the focused support of COSAC was far from a foregone conclusion.[24] Finally, at the last COSAC before the Laeken European Council (which agreed to organise the Convention), COSAC decided to concentrate its efforts on giving full support to the idea of a

---

[22] A similar proposal was taken up by the Constitutional Treaty a few years later. Art. 4 of the Protocol on the role of national parliaments in the European Union annexed to the Constitutional Treaty stipulated that "save in urgent cases for which due reasons have been given, a ten-day period shall elapse between the placing of a draft European legislative act on the provisional agenda for the Council and the adoption of a position". This extended the required delay between a draft European legislative act being made available and its adoption from six weeks to six weeks plus ten days, as Art. 3 of the existing Amsterdam Protocol requires only a six-week period to elapse between a legislative proposal being made available and the date when it is placed on a Council agenda for decision (subject to exceptions on grounds of urgency).

[23] See paras 5 and 7 of Declaration No 23.

[24] Thus the Stockholm COSAC agreed merely to suggest two simultaneous ways in which the relevant discussions could be contributed to: (a) *via* COSAC; and (b) by convening a 'Convention'.

Convention. At a subsequent meeting of COSAC, the Convention on the Future of Europe was invited by COSAC to present "a coherent draft proposal to the 2004 intergovernmental conference contributing solutions to the problems it was confronted with". This slightly ambiguous wording, however, concealed a split between those delegations who wanted the convention to prepare a single proposal for a new Treaty and those who preferred the conclusions of the Convention to include different alternatives.

(g) COSAC in Reform Mode

The decision by the European Council at Laeken in December 2001 to convene a European Convention involving national parliaments directly in the preparations of a treaty reform triggered much debate both in national parliaments and within COSAC on how to reinforce the role of national parliaments in European Union matters and, not least, on how to reform COSAC itself.

COSAC was engaged in this discussion from the beginning and followed the proceedings of the Convention closely and actively throughout the period. The COSAC meeting in Stockholm in May 2001 agreed to keep the question of the future of the European Union on COSAC's agenda for as long as the Convention worked, and keep the Convention informed of any contributions by COSAC. However, in reality the parliaments were split on the question of what role COSAC should play in this debate. Whereas some parliaments insisted that COSAC needed to develop specific proposals for reform for the Convention (and for the subsequent intergovernmental conference), other parliaments found such discussions in COSAC superfluous or even counterproductive. The latter believed that the appropriate place for the involvement of national parliaments was in the Convention and not in COSAC. Recommendations from COSAC risked creating confusion about the positions of the national parliaments and the European Parliament.

(i) Reform of COSAC

It had already been generally acknowledged for some time that COSAC lacked continuity and the capacity to plan and organise a work schedule for a longer time span than the six months of a Presidency. COSAC had no existence in between its biannual conferences in various European Union cities. In addition, the fact that some parliaments were beginning to involve sectoral committees in scrutinising European affairs raised the question whether COSAC should remain a conference exclusively for European affairs committees.

A reform initiative was launched in October 2002 by the Danish COSAC Presidency. A window of opportunity had been opened five months earlier when the 26th COSAC meeting in Madrid called upon the COSAC troika to prepare "a detailed proposal for a more effective COSAC, focusing its activities more on the role of national parliaments".[25] The bulk of the negotiations took place in a working group composed of the chairpersons of the European affairs committees of the then fifteen European Union member states.[26] After seven months of difficult negotiations, a reform package was finally endorsed in the first half of 2003.

Most importantly, it was agreed that COSAC's activities should focus more on the work of national parliaments. The aim that COSAC should first and foremost function as a platform for the exchange of information and best practices was strengthened and the intention clearly expressed in COSAC's Rules of Procedure with the provision that

> "the principal business on every agenda shall be derived from COSAC's role as a body for exchanging information and, in particular on the practical aspects of parliamentary scrutiny".[27]

Almost symbolically, COSAC also managed to adopt a set of minimum standards for national parliamentary scrutiny on European Union affairs, after having inserted a number of safety clauses assuring delegations that the minimum standards were merely guidelines and not legally binding.[28] However, where this reorientation of its activities was relatively easily approved in COSAC, agreement on a number of other points, which aimed at making COSAC more effective as a player at European level, proved much more difficult to attain.

Following extremely intensive discussions, COSAC managed to agree on a model for the introduction of majority decisions. COSAC should still seek to adopt contributions with consensus, but in case this was not possible, contributions could be adopted by a majority of three quarters of the votes cast – constituting at least fifty per cent of the votes.[29]

---

[25] Resolution adopted by the 26th COSAC meeting in Madrid on 12–14 May 2002.

[26] Preparations took place in the working group that met in Copenhagen on 17–18 November and 15–16 December 2002.

[27] See para. 7.1 a of the Rules of Procedure of COSAC.

[28] These Copenhagen Parliamentary Guidelines or 'Guidelines for relations between governments and Parliaments on Community issues' were published as 'instructive minimum standards' at [2003] OJ C154/1 (2 July, 2003). At the time of writing they are available at www.cosac.eu/en/documents/basic/rules/doc/.

[29] Para. 10.5 of COSAC's Rules of Procedure provides for contributions to be adopted with a qualified majority of at least three quarters of the votes cast – if a consensus cannot be achieved.

Another very sensitive issue was the establishment of a secretariat for COSAC. Following a heated debate, a very delicate compromise was struck between those parliaments which wanted a lightweight secretariat composed of a small permanent staff and those who did not want a secretariat, but were willing to accept secretarial support based on rotating staff seconded from the parliaments represented in the presidential troika of COSAC. The agreement was that the secretariat should be comprised of one permanent member and four members seconded from the three national parliaments on the troika and the European Parliament.[30]

(ii) The Convention

The Convention on the Future of Europe, which had been asked by the European Council to address the question of national parliaments' role in the European Union architecture, also reflected on the possibility of reforming COSAC.[31] After sixteen months of negotiations, the Convention finally agreed on a draft Constitutional Treaty in June 2003. The draft Treaty contained a number of proposals for enhanced involvement of national parliaments in European affairs.

The most innovative proposal was the subsidiarity early-warning mechanism, the so-called 'yellow card', allowing national parliaments to invite the European Commission to review a draft legislative act if at least one third of the national parliaments within six weeks submitted a reasoned opinion that stated that a proposal did not comply with the subsidiarity principle.[32] But the Convention failed to address the question of how national parliaments could best exchange information among themselves within this mechanism.

---

[30] The Athens COSAC meeting in May 2003 agreed a short set of guidelines for the establishment of the secretariat, which were to be implemented in detail by the Rome COSAC meeting. The final decision to set up the secretariat was taken in Rome in October 2003.

[31] This debate took place primarily in Working Group IV of the Convention, which was chaired by the United Kingdom MP Gisela Stuart. Many chairpersons of national European affairs committees participated on behalf of their parliaments. Because these chairpersons also participated in COSAC, there was a certain spillover effect. In other words, many of the same points and themes were raised in both fora.

[32] Note that Art. 3 of Protocol No. 1 of the Constitutional Treaty on the Role of National Parliaments in the European Union provided for the forwarding by the President of the Council of national parliaments' reasoned opinions to the governments of a group of member states, to the Court of Justice, to the European Central Bank, or to the European Investment Bank in cases where the draft European legislative act originates with any of these.

The Convention further proposed a refocused COSAC whose functions were to be extended into two new areas. First, it was decided that, in future, COSAC should promote the exchange of information and best practices between member states' parliaments and the European Parliament, including their respective special committees.[33] The idea of increasingly focusing COSAC's activities on the exchange of information and best practices was merely a confirmation of an already existing practice, but the proposal to include sectoral committees in COSAC was a highly controversial one, because only a small number of parliaments involved their sectoral committee in the scrutiny of European affairs. Secondly, the Convention suggested that COSAC should play a role in organising inter-parliamentary conferences on specific topics, in particular to debate matters of common foreign and security policy and of common security and defence policy. The Convention at the same time encouraged national parliaments and the European Parliament to establish regular inter-parliamentary cooperation through mutual agreement.

(h) Implementation of the Reforms

The Dublin COSAC in May 2004 was the first meeting to take place after COSAC's own reforms, and would show whether COSAC could work effectively as a platform for exchange of information and best practices between national parliaments on the procedures for the scrutiny of European affairs. The perfect opportunity to test this point was provided by the (then still-unsigned) Constitutional Treaty in which a special role for national parliaments in monitoring the subsidiarity principle was proposed. An urgent need for the exchange information would be created by the planned subsidiarity check which national parliaments would be called upon to set up. The new subsidiarity early-warning mechanism was breaking completely new ground in most national parliaments. Only a very few national parliaments had effective scrutiny systems in place for monitoring the compliance of European Union draft legislation with the subsidiarity principle. And only a few parliaments had any clear idea of how they wanted to organise their national subsidiarity check. There was a real need for an exchange of information and best practices.

The 32nd COSAC held in The Hague in November, 2004 therefore decided to facilitate this debate and to allow national parliaments to reflect further on

33 This was a point which was of relevance primarily to the sectoral committees of national parliaments, as the European Parliament already participates in COSAC with members of its sectoral committees (in addition to its two vice-presidents and the chairman of its Constitutional Committee) because, unlike national parliaments, it does not have a European affairs committee.

this by conducting a pilot project in all parliaments testing the subsidiarity early-warning mechanism in order to assess how the subsidiarity review mechanism might work in practice. It was decided to examine the legislative proposals contained in the Commission's Third Railway Package as the subject for this initiative. The exercise was commenced on 1 March 2005 and was completed by national parliaments six weeks later on 12 April. Parliaments reported at the COSAC meeting held in Luxembourg in May 2005 on their experience and on any difficulties they had encountered.

Apart from being a perfect occasion for testing the mechanics of the subsidiarity early-warning system in the member states and for exchanging information between the parliaments, the experiment also provided a good opportunity for testing the subsidiarity principle itself, and not least the Commission's compliance with the existing Protocol on the subsidiarity principle. The Luxembourg COSAC thus adopted a contribution addressed to the European Union institutions criticising the Commission for providing insufficient justification for its proposals as regards their compliance with the subsidiarity principle. COSAC called on the Commission to produce more in-depth arguments in future and declared that further work should be done to clarify the distinction between the principles of subsidiarity and proportionality.

The pilot project clearly demonstrated that its reforms had not just made COSAC a better instrument for promoting exchange of information and best practices, but also that they had strengthened COSAC's capacity to prepare a debate on a specific piece of draft European Union legislation and to act effectively as a European player.

3. COSAC's Role in the Future

(a) COSAC Today: A Platform for the Exchange of Information and Best Practices

From the beginning, conceptions of what COSAC's role should be have divided opinions both in member state parliaments and in the European Parliament. Two different possibilities have dominated thinking in COSAC: that of COSAC as a player in the decision-making process at European level, and that of COSAC as a platform for the exchange of information and best practices between parliaments.

Today the different views of what the role of COSAC should be still exist, but the gap has narrowed. Developments over the last five years have oriented COSAC more in the direction of becoming a platform for the exchange of information and best practices between parliaments – in other words, a forum for enhancing national scrutiny of European affairs. The establishment of a secretariat has strengthened COSAC further in this regard by providing it with greater capacity to prepare meetings, documents, and debates. In particular, the decision to ask the secretariat to draw up a biannual report on European Union procedures and practices has facilitated discussions and the exchange of information and best practices at COSAC meetings. Recent practice in COSAC since the conclusions of its internal reform processes confirm this reorientation. All COSAC meetings since 2004 have placed scrutiny of European Union matters at national level to the fore of debates within COSAC. The Constitutional Treaty has also focused attention on COSAC's reorientation towards this role.

Its reforms have also strengthened COSAC as a possible player in the decision-making process at European level, however. It is first and foremost the possibility of COSAC's use of qualified majority voting for the adoption of contributions to the European Union institutions, which has constituted the breakthrough in this regard. But the institutionalisation of the meeting of COSAC chairpersons[34] as a regular biannual event as well as the establishment of the secretariat have also been significant, as they have strengthened the continuity of COSAC.

(b) COSAC's Potential

Despite the many efforts to reform COSAC over the last five years, the need for further reforms may have to be confronted in the near future.

Recent developments in the scrutiny procedures in member state parliaments and in the wider inter-parliamentary co-operation in the European Union have raised important questions for COSAC to address. First and foremost, the fact that an increasing number of national parliaments are involving their sectoral committees in the scrutiny of European Union matters poses the question of whether sectoral committees should also be invited to participate in COSAC.[35] Secondly, an even greater number of parliaments are scrutinising European Union legislation for its

[34] The COSAC chairpersons consist of the chairpersons of national European affairs committees (two of whom are sent from each member state so as to ensure representation from both parliamentary chambers in those member states of the European Union which have bicameral systems) in addition to two representatives of the European Parliament.

[35] COSAC's Third Biannual Report of May 2005 reports on the involvement of sectoral committees in the scrutiny of European Union matters in the national parliaments

compliance with the principle of subsidiarity in the context of their general scrutiny at the national level.[36] This raises the question as to how national parliaments can best monitor the subsidiarity principle. Is there a need for an improved exchange of information or coordination between the parliaments on this matter?

Both points were addressed in two Protocols to the Constitutional Treaty concerning, respectively, the role of national parliaments and the application of the subsidiarity principle. The Protocols first and foremost confirmed the current practice of COSAC as a platform for exchange of information and best practices, but they also support (a) the involvement of sectoral committees in COSAC and the possibility of organising inter-parliamentary conferences in areas outside the traditional area of European affairs committees such as foreign and security policy and defence; and (b) enabling national parliaments to monitor the subsidiarity principle *via* a subsidiarity early-warning mechanism.

In addition to the foregoing issues, there is the question of how COSAC should fit into wider inter-parliamentary co-operation in the European Union in the future, when more players are moving into the field? In July 2004, the Conference of Speakers of the Parliaments of the European Union decided to create an Inter-parliamentary European Union Information Exchange (IPEX) to provide a platform for the electronic exchange of European Union-related information between the parliaments of the European Union – including information related to national parliaments' subsidiarity checks.[37] The intention was that the IPEX system would store and organise all Commission proposals and other relevant documents – in addition to information uploaded onto it by national parliaments concerning their scrutiny of

[36] According the Fourth Biannual Report of COSAC (published in October, 2005) 18 national parliaments or parliamentary chambers (in 14 member states) scrutinised European Union legislation for compliance with the principles of subsidiarity and proportionality.

[37] The Inter-Parliamentary European Union Information Exchange was originally the name of a working group which was set up in Stockholm in March 2001 by the secretaries general of the national parliaments of the member states and of the European Parliament, under the chairmanship of Anders Forsberg, the secretary-general of the Swedish Parliament. The secretaries general have not formed a separate organisation, but rather act in the context of the Conference of Speakers of the Parliaments of the European Union, and in this particular case acted on the basis of a mandate provided by the latter Conference.

The technical development of the IPEX website was carried out by the services of the European Parliament. See further n. 44 below and the associated text.

European Union documents.[38] IPEX covers the exchange of European Union information which is relevant both to European affairs committees and to sectoral committees. The question obviously arises of how COSAC and IPEX will relate to one another in the future so as to avoid duplication of work. It should be noted, however, that IPEX is not a new inter-parliamentary body but a tool, which may be used by national parliaments, the European Parliament, and COSAC to exchange information concerning European Union affairs.[39]

(i) Sectoral Committees in COSAC

In most national parliaments, European affairs committees are at the heart of the scrutiny procedure. However, in an increasing number of parliaments, sectoral committees also participate in the scrutiny process, typically by providing specialist advice to European affairs committees in the early stages of European Union decision-making. This raises the question of whether there is a need for sectoral committees to meet at European level in order to exchange information and best practices. Some sectoral committees already meet from time to time. This includes in particular foreign affairs committees, committees on justice and home affairs, environmental committees, and development committees. But these meetings are generally held on an *ad hoc* basis. It is at the discretion of the national parliament from the country holding the Council presidency to decide whether and which sectoral committees should meet throughout its presidency. To an increasing extent, the European Parliament invites members of sectoral committees to participate in meetings of its standing committees. The issue therefore presents itself as to whether there is a need for COSAC to be open to sectoral committees (as seemed to be envisaged in Protocol No. 1 to the Constitutional Treaty on the Role of National Parliaments in the European

[38] The Conference of Speakers (which is composed of the speakers of the member state parliaments and of the European Parliament) also adopted a set of guidelines for inter-parliamentary cooperation in July, 2004, which are known as the Hague Guidelines. This was a response to the effective call in Protocol No. 1 annexed to the Constitutional Treaty on the Role of National Parliaments in the European Union for an agreement between the European Parliament and national parliaments, with its provision that "the European Parliament and national Parliaments shall together determine the organisation and promotion of effective and regular interparliamentary cooperation within the Union". At the time of writing, the Hague Guidelines are available at www.cosac.eu/en/documents/basic/interparliamentary/.

[39] According to the Hague guidelines, COSAC "handles the cooperation between EU Affairs Committees".

Union[40]) or whether these are already sufficiently catered for by existing inter-parliamentary arrangements.

The idea of opening COSAC to sectoral committees has already been considered by COSAC during the reform process in 2002 and 2003, but, at that time, the idea was rejected by the parliaments.[41] However, if the main purpose of COSAC is to provide a platform for exchange of information and best practices on the scrutiny of European Union issues, there seems to be a role for those sectoral committees that take part in the scrutiny process at the national level. All stakeholders in the scrutiny of European affairs should participate in order to ensure that enough is known about best practices in COSAC. The invitation of sectoral committees to participate in COSAC should not be seen as an attempt by COSAC to monopolise inter-parliamentary co-operation on European affairs.

The Constitutional Treaty suggested that there was a special case for COSAC in organising inter-parliamentary conferences in the area of the common foreign and security policy and defence. However, in most parliaments, this is an area which is covered by foreign and security affairs committees and defence committees, and in which European affairs committees are not involved. Regular meetings already take place between foreign affairs committees of national parliaments, and the question poses itself of how meaningful a discussion COSAC could have on these matters without the participation of members of the competent committees. If national parliaments really wish to proceed with involvement in this policy area, then it seems that COSAC will have to give up its character of a meeting exclusively for European affairs committees and allow members of sectoral committees to participate in its meetings.

(ii) Monitoring the Principle of Subsidiarity?

With the agreement on the Amsterdam Protocol on the Role of National Parliaments in the European Union, which entered into force in 1999, the member states of the European Union agreed that COSAC should be empowered to examine specific draft legislative acts of the European Union

---

[40] Hence the provision in Art. 10 of the Protocol that a 'conference of Parliamentary Committees for Union Affairs may…organise interparliamentary conferences on specific topics, in particular to debate matters of common foreign and security policy, including common security and defence policy…'

[41] All that was accepted was a short paragraph in the preamble of the revised rules of procedure stating that sectoral parliamentary committees may "apply the rules" if convened by the parliament holding the presidency.

with a view to ensuring their compliance with the principle of subsidiarity.[42] This possibility was never taken up by national parliaments, however, due to, *inter alia*, disagreements about the question of whether national parliaments (via COSAC) should become players in the decision-making process at European level. Some parliaments feared that this could give rise to an unwanted new institution.

When the Convention on the Future of Europe drafted the subsidiarity early-warning mechanism (a mechanism retained in the final version of the Constitutional Treaty), it had learned this lesson. It therefore granted the right to apply the mechanism to each individual national parliament and not to a collective representation of national parliaments. The mechanism empowered national parliaments to demand that the European Commission should review a draft legislative act if votes representing at least one third of the national parliaments submitted a reasoned opinion within six weeks stating that a proposal did not comply with the subsidiarity principle.[43] This setting of a threshold number of votes by parliaments in order to trigger the mechanism obviously creates incentives for national parliament to cooperate. The key question of how such cooperation should be coordinated was left open by the Convention, however.

The Conference of Speakers of the Parliaments of the European Union was quick to respond to this challenge. As has already been noted in the text above,[43a] in July, 2004, it reached agreement that the IPEX system should provide a platform for the electronic exchange of European Union-related information between national parliaments and the European Parliament, and the system was launched in connection with the Conference of Speakers held in Copenhagen in June 2006. IPEX ensures that national parliaments have direct access to Commission proposals and other relevant documents – including information from other national parliaments with regard to, among other things, issues raised on subsidiarity grounds.[44] COSAC, however, will still have a significant role. It is the only forum where contacts on

[42] Note in this regard the provision of Art. 6 of the Protocol that "COSAC may address to the European Parliament, the Council and the Commission any contribution which it deems appropriate on the legislative activities of the Union, notably in relation to the application of the principle of subsidiarity...".

[43] See also in this regard, above, n. 32.

[43a] See text at n. 37, above.

[44] A special subscription service notifies users automatically by e-mail as soon as new information is uploaded into the system. IPEX has the potential to becoming a valuable and significant contribution to the more effective exchange of electronic information between national parliaments regarding specific subsidiarity-related issues.

subsidiarity issues can take place between the competent committees of national parliaments at political level. Its function should be to facilitate an exchange of information and best practices regarding how to deal with the control of the principle of subsidiarity in the national context. In addition COSAC can discuss common problems and occasionally approve common recommendations for improved compliance with the subsidiarity principle by the European institutions. A first example of how this could be done was provided, as has already been noted in the text above,[44a] by the Luxembourg COSAC in May 2005, when the third railway package was examined as a pilot project to test the subsidiarity early-warning mechanism in the Constitutional Treaty. COSAC is the ideal forum for this, because it is comprised of the main actors in most national parliaments when it comes to monitoring subsidiarity, *i.e.,* the European affairs committees. But, as has already been indicated,[44b] it would be an even more useful forum if national parliaments would open COSAC up to the participation of sectoral committees, which have a major role in the scrutiny of European Union matters in some of the national parliaments.

(iii) Bridging the Gap

The double rejection of the Constitutional Treaty by the French and Dutch voters in May and June 2005 brought the European Union reform process to a halt and created uncertainty about the future role of national parliaments and COSAC. But while waiting for the period of reflection to come to an end and more clarity about the fate of the Constitutional Treaty to evolve, COSAC decided to provide impetus to the process at its meeting in London on 9–11 October 2005. Here Parliaments endorsed ways to explore how the role of national parliaments could be strengthened with regard to monitoring the principle of subsidiarity on the basis of existing provisions. COSAC decided to conduct a subsidiarity and proportionality check on forthcoming European Union legislative proposals on the basis of the powers provided for in the Amsterdam Protocol. It was agreed to conduct a real-time examination of two proposals in the framework of COSAC: one concerning the questions of jurisdiction and the applicable law in matrimonial matters, and the other concerning the liberalisation of postal services.[45] A significant number of

---

[44a] See text above on p. 475.

[44b] See text above on p. 479.

[45] See Proposal presented by the Commission for a Council Regulation amending Regulation (EC) No 2201/2003 as regards jurisdiction and introducing rules concerning applicable law in matrimonial matters (COM(2006) 399 final, 17 July 2006); and Proposal presented by the Commission for a Directive of the European Parliament and of the Council amending Directive 97/67/EC concerning the full accomplishment of the internal market of Community postal services (COM(2006) 594 final, 18 October 2006).

parliaments took part in the two subsidiarity checks. The process thus constituted a valuable breakthrough for those parliaments who wanted COSAC to act as a kind of clearing house at European level responsible for coordinating the exchange of information between parliaments where these were monitoring the principle of subsidiarity. In practice, an overwhelming number of national parliaments welcomed the subsidiarity checks, which they found, gave important added value to the scrutiny of European Union affairs in national parliaments.[46] A similar approach was adopted by the Heads of State or Government of the European Union member states at the meeting of the Brussels European Council of 15–16 June 2006. The conclusions of that summit "encouraged national parliaments to strengthen cooperation within the framework of COSAC when monitoring subsidiarity".

The Berlin COSAC on 13–15 May 2007 recommended that subsidiarity checks in the future should become a regular activity within the framework of COSAC. It was agreed to organise (at least) two subsidiarity and proportionality checks per year. A procedure was fixed for the selection of future proposals and it was suggested that if a significant number of delegations in COSAC raised serious concerns about a specific proposal, COSAC could be called upon on the basis of an initiative of the Presidency to deliberate on whether further action should be taken regarding the proposal. Finally the Berlin COSAC suggested that the effectiveness of future subsidiarity checks could be enhanced if conducted on the basis of commonly agreed criteria.

Yet it still remains to be seen how the recommendations of the Berlin COSAC will be implemented in practice. The COSAC subsidiarity checks launched by the COSAC at its meetings in London and Berlin represent a valuable contribution to finding a response to the key question that the Constitutional Treaty left open regarding the establishment of effective monitoring of the subsidiarity principle – specifically that of how national parliaments can ensure that there is an effective exchange of relevant information between the competent committees in national parliaments. A solution must be found which facilitates both the bulk of the parliaments which use their European affairs committees as the principal committees in

[46] Further information on the views of national parliaments concerning the above-mentioned subsidiarity checks can be found in COSAC, *Seventh biannual report: Developments in European Union Procedures and Practices Relevant to Parliamentary Scrutiny* (May 2007), available at http://www.cosac.eu/en/documents/biannual/

monitoring the subsidiarity principle, and that small group of parliaments (such as the Italian Chamber of Deputies) where the sectoral committees are the main committees when it comes to the scrutiny of European Union affairs. Connecting the Speakers Conference and IPEX with COSAC, something proposed by the London COSAC – and by the Speakers Conference at its recent meeting in Bratislava in May 2007 – seems a good point of departure

Whether or not the forthcoming intergovernmental conference will succeed in concluding its work on a new treaty by the end of 2007, the Constitutional Treaty already seems to have triggered considerable momentum with regard to inter-parliamentary co-operation. First and foremost, the creation of the subsidiarity early-warning system seems to have convinced national parliaments that they have a role to play in monitoring the subsidiarity principle. A number of parliaments have already strengthened their national scrutiny of the subsidiarity principle as a result of the provisions of the Constitutional Treaty. And both the Conference of Speakers of the Parliaments of the European Union and COSAC have launched initiatives which may, in a complementary manner, enhance the exchange of information between parliaments – an exchange which is needed in order to make the monitoring of the subsidiarity principle effective.

Index